Reading and All That Jazz

Reading and All That Jazz

Tuning Up Your Reading, Thinking, and Study Skills

FOURTH EDITION

Peter Mather

Retired from Glendale Community College
Glendale, Arizona

Rita McCarthy

Glendale Community College
Glendale, Arizona

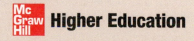 **Higher Education**

Boston   Burr Ridge, IL   Dubuque, IA   New York   San Francisco   St. Louis
Bangkok   Bogotá   Caracas   Kuala Lumpur   Lisbon   London   Madrid   Mexico City
Milan   Montreal   New Delhi   Santiago   Seoul   Singapore   Sydney   Taipei   Toronto

Higher Education

Published by McGraw-Hill, an imprint of The McGraw-Hill Companies, Inc., 1221 Avenue of the Americas, New York, NY 10020. Copyright © 2010, 2007, 2003, 1999. All rights reserved. No part of this publication may be reproduced or distributed in any form or by any means, or stored in a database or retrieval system, without the prior written consent of The McGraw-Hill Companies, Inc., including, but not limited to, in any network or other electronic storage or transmission, or broadcast for distance learning.

This book is printed on acid-free paper.

3 4 5 6 7 8 9 0 BAN/BAN 0 9

Student Edition
ISBN: 978-0-07-338576-1
MHID: 0-07-338576-X

Instructor's Edition
ISBN: 978-0-07-730488-1
MHID: 0-07-730488-8

Editor in Chief: *Michael Ryan*
Editorial Director: *Beth Mejia*
Director of Development: *Dawn Groundwater*
Sponsoring Editor: *John Kindler*
Development Editor: *Gillian Cook*
Editorial Coordinator: *Jesse Hassenger*
Marketing Manager: *Allison Jones*
Media Project Manager: *Thomas Brierly*
Project Manager: *Meghan Durko*
Designer: *Cassandra Chu*
Photo Research Coordinator: *Kim Adams, Roaring Lion Image Research LLC*
Production Supervisor: *Louis Swaim*
Permissions Coordinator: *Marty Moga*
Composition: *10/13 Palatino by Aptara®, Inc.*
Printing: *45# New Era Matte Plus Recycled by RR Donnelley*

Cover: © Digital Vision/Getty Images; © Royalty-Free/Corbis

Credits: The credits section for this book begins on page C-1 and is considered an extension of the copyright page.

Library of Congress Cataloging-in-Publication Data
McCarthy, Rita.
    Reading and all that jazz : tuning up your reading, thinking, and study skills /
Rita McCarthy and Peter Mather.— 4th ed.
        p.   cm.
    ISBN-13: 978-0-07-338576-1
    ISBN-10: 0-07-338576-X
    1. Reading (Higher education)—United States.   2. English language-Rhetoric.
    3. Critical thinking—Study and teaching (Higher)—United States.   4. Study
    skills—United States.   I. Mather, Peter.   II. Title.
LB2395.3.M28 2010
428.4071'1—dc22   2009001528

The Internet addresses listed in the text were accurate at the time of publication. The inclusion of a Web site does not indicate an endorsement by the authors or McGraw-Hill, and McGraw-Hill does not guarantee the accuracy of the information presented at these sites.

www.mhhe.com

Peter dedicates this book to his late parents,
Carl and Dorothy; and his brother and sister-in-law,
John and Peggy.

Rita dedicates this book to her parents,
Adolph and Bertha; her sons, Ryan and Steve;
her daughter-in-law, Bonnie;
her grandchildren, Zachary and Kate;
and especially her husband, Greg.

About the Authors

Peter Mather—earned his BA in government from the University of Redlands; his first MA, in African studies, from the University of California, Los Angeles; his second MA, in reading, from California State University, Los Angeles; and his EdD in curriculum and instruction from the University of Southern California. Before recently retiring from Glendale Community College, he taught at the secondary, adult-education, and community-college levels for over 30 years. While at Glendale Community College, he taught both developmental reading and critical and evaluative reading. He also taught American government and was the college director of the America Reads/Counts Program. In addition to being coauthor of *The Art of Critical Reading,* now in its second edition, and *Racing Ahead with Reading,* he has published articles in the *Journal of Reading.*

Rita Romero McCarthy—earned a BA in sociology and history from the University of California, Berkeley, and an MA in education from Arizona State University. She has taught at the elementary, secondary, adult-education, and community-college levels. For the past 20 years, she has taught ESL, developmental reading, and critical and evaluative reading at Glendale Community College. Ms. McCarthy has published articles in professional journals and other media on the use of bibliotherapy. She has also published reading lists for beginning and remedial readers and is a reading specialist. In addition to this textbook, she is coauthor of *The Art of Critical Reading* and *Racing Ahead with Reading.*

Brief Contents

Contents

Preface to the Instructor

In 1999, we published the first edition of *Reading and All That Jazz*. We have been extremely gratified by *Jazz*'s success. Teachers and students alike have complimented us on the outstanding reading selections and engaging exercises. With this fourth edition of *Jazz*, in response to suggestions from reviewers, we set out to include more textbook selections and add more cultural diversity through questions and exercises. To that end, the majority of the new selections in the fourth edition are from popular textbooks on issues of interest and concern to students. We hope that students find them useful and thought-provoking. Additionally, we have placed further emphasis on jazz and the theme of music in general.

We initially selected the theme of jazz to emphasize a positive, exciting, personally involved approach to reading and learning. Because jazz, like reading, includes a great deal of improvisation, we wanted teachers to feel free to improvise in their use of this book so that it will become an effective learning tool for classes of varying skill levels and areas of interest. Just as jazz musicians bring their individual backgrounds to the music they play, we wanted our students to feel free to draw from their individual backgrounds when they read and interpret various types of written material. Jazz, an American art form, drew on many cultures throughout its history. We wanted our textbook to emphasize the influence of various peoples and cultures. The selections enable the students to clarify their own values and experience events through the eyes of others. New selections were chosen with these criteria in mind. We also made an effort to have all of the new selections classroom-tested. After all, our own students are our best critics!

Organization of the Text

This book is organized along two dimensions. First, the successive parts of the book focus on different skills that an effective learner and reader must master. Second, the book begins with a narrow perspective, focusing on the student as learner, and then moves to increasingly broader perspectives, focusing in turn on interpersonal, social, national, and then international issues.

Part 1 is designed to capture students' attention and interest by helping them discover more about themselves as learners. The goals in Part 1 are to develop the skills likely to lead to a successful college experience and to help students recognize the individual strengths and weaknesses they bring to the learning process. The mood of the selections is "upbeat" in the sense of being positive and encouraging. The Introduction in Part 1 is meant to be completed in the first week of class. The pretest and the short written assignments that follow the selections are designed so that the instructor can use them for quickly assessing the skills of individual students and classes as a whole. The theme of Part 1 is the student as learner.

- New: "Louis Armstrong, Ambassador of Jazz" by Studs Terkel
- New: "What a Wonderful World" (Louis Armstrong song)
- New: "Optimism and Success" by Martin Seligman
- New: "An Update on the Daniel Huffman Story"
- New: "Internet Etiquette" (multimedia literacy textbook)

Part 2 is directed at developing the basic skills needed to make reading easier and more productive. The focus is on the process and structure of reading. Skills emphasized include identifying the topic, main idea, and supporting details; determining the author's purpose and transition words and patterns of organization. Themes touched on in Part 2 include communication, anger, and work.

- New: Exercises on topics, main ideas, and details, using material on cultural diversity and nonverbal communication
- New: "Communication at Work" (psychology textbook)
- New: Inclusion of the "Listing" pattern of organization
- New: "Identity Theft" (criminal justice textbook)

Part 3 emphasizes reading as an interpretive process. The goal of Part 3 is to enable students to become proficient at "reading between the lines." Topics introduced in Part 3 include inference, figurative language, and author's tone.

- New: An introduction to clichés
- New: "The Black Widow"

Part 4 focuses on modes of writing. Part 4 first introduces students to the primary modes of narrative, descriptive, expository, and persuasive writing. This chapter features the theme of relationships. Part 4 also familiarizes students with the various modes of organization, such as cause and effect, categories, and chronological order. This part extensive chapter on modes of organization features the topic of happiness.

- New: "Sibling Relationships and Birth Order" (child development textbook)
- New: "The Sound of Silence" (Paul Simon song)
- New: "The Big Win: Life after the Lottery" (sociology textbook)
- New: "Media Literacy" (mass culture textbook)

Part 5 concentrates on developing critical reading and thinking skills. Topics discussed include fact and opinion, bias, propaganda techniques, and evaluation of the evidence. The theme of Part 5 concerns such social issues as DNA fingerprinting, the prevalence of violence on television and in video games, and the medical use of marijuana.

In Chapter 10, "Fact and Opinion"

- New: "The Nature of Public Opinion" (government textbook)
- New: "Waiting on the World to Change" (John Mayer song)
- New: "What's in Your Toothpaste?" by David Bodanis

In Chapter 13, "Evaluating the Evidence"

- New: "Medical Marijuana—Background Information" (health textbook)
- New: A visual map on the status of medical marijuana

Part 6 is devoted to improving classroom skills, including skimming and scanning, outlining, and mapping. Part 6 has two themes: the environment and jazz. Chapter 15 has been completely revised with a new textbook selection and comprehension checkups and exercises.

In Chapter 14, "Scanning and Skimming"

- New: "Scanning the TV Guide"

In Chapter 15, "Organizing Textbook Information"

- New, "Jazz in America" from *The World of Music* (music appreciation textbook)

The Appendices focus on the specific skills of using dictionaries and interpreting visual aids, such as charts and graphs. The visual aids section can be used as a separate unit or in conjunction with specific reading selections. Sections on taking subjective tests, sample assignment sheets, and student summaries are also included.

- New: "Identity Theft" visual aids

Additional New Features

- New cartoons, full-color photographs, and visual aids
- More in-depth questions for "In Your Own Words" and "Written Assignments"
- Updated "Internet Activity" sections

Popular Recurring Features

- **A vocabulary unit on homonyms,** which includes practice exercises and a crossword puzzle.
- **Seven independent vocabulary units emphasizing Latin and Greek word parts.** Each unit includes practice exercises and a crossword puzzle.
- **Thorough coverage of each chapter topic.** Each chapter contains a sequential series of exercises ranging from the relatively easy to the quite difficult. Exercises are designed so that the instructor can have the students work either individually or in groups. Exercises appear in many different formats to maintain student interest.
- **A wealth of quality material to choose from.** The textbook is designed to enable the instructor to select the material that best fits each class.
- **A standardized format for presenting the reading selections.** A section titled "Tuning In to Reading" contains questions designed to actively engage the student with the subject of the upcoming selection. A "Bio-sketch" provides information about each author's background. "Notes on Vocabulary" offers a discussion of unusual words that appear in the selection.
- **A standardized format for "Comprehension Checkup" sections.** Objective questions, written in the style of those found on the TASP or CLAST, come first, followed by "Vocabulary in Context" questions designed to test knowledge of vocabulary used in the selection. This is followed by a series of open-ended questions for critical thinking titled "In Your Own Words." A section titled "Written Assignment" that calls for more in-depth writing on the students' part is next, and finally "Internet Activity" asks students to research, on the Internet, interesting or unusual topics covered in the selection.
- **Quotations in the margins** for student journal writing, discussion, and extra credit.

Teaching and Learning Aids

- *PowerPoint Slides.* The instructional content of each chapter is summarized for overhead projection on PowerPoint slides.
- *Multiple-Choice Quiz.* A multiple-choice quiz on the instructional content is provided for each chapter of the text.
- *Comprehension Exercises.* Comprehension exercises are provided for all the substantive reading selections.

- *Merriam-Webster's Notebook Dictionary.* A compact word resource conveniently designed for three-ring binders, *Merriam-Webster's Notebook Dictionary* includes 40,000 entries for widely used words with concise, easy-to-understand definitions and pronunciations.

- *The Merriam-Webster Dictionary.* This handy paperback dictionary contains over 75,000 definitions, yet is small enough to carry around in a backpack, so it's always there when it's needed.

- *Random House Webster's College Dictionary.* This authoritative dictionary includes over 160,000 entries and 207,000 definitions. The most commonly used definitions are always listed first, so students can find what they need quickly.

- *Merriam-Webster's Collegiate Dictionary & Thesaurus* **CD-ROM.** This up-to-the-minute electronic dictionary and thesaurus offers 225,000 definitions, 340,000 synonyms and related words, and 1,300 illustrations.

- *Merriam-Webster's Notebook Thesaurus.* Conveniently designed for three-ring binders, this thesaurus provides concise, clear guidance for over 157,000 word choices.

- *Merriam-Webster Thesaurus.* This compact thesaurus offers over 157,000 word choices, and includes concise definitions and examples to help students choose the correct word for the context.

Novel Ideas

These Random House and HarperCollins paperbacks are available at a low cost when packaged with the text: *The Monkey Wrench Gang* (Abbey); *Things Fall Apart* (Achebe); *The Lone Ranger and Tonto* (Alexie); *Integrity* (Carter); *The House on Mango Street* (Cisneros); *Heart of Darkness* (Conrad); *Pilgrim at Tinker Creek* (Dillard); *Love Medicine* (Erdrich); *Their Eyes Were Watching God* (Hurston); *Boys of Summer* (Kahn); *Woman Warrior* (Kingston); *One Hundred Years of Solitude* (García Márquez); *Clear Springs* (Mason); *All the Pretty Horses* (McCarthy); *House Made of Dawn* (Momaday); *Joy Luck Club* (Tan); and *Essays of E. B. White* (White).

Acknowledgments

No textbook can be created without the assistance of many people. First, we relied on the thoughtful reactions and suggestions of our colleagues across the country, who reviewed this project at various stages:

Jesus Adame, El Paso Community College

Edith Alderson, Joliet Junior College

Ellen Bagby, Midlands Technical College

Charlotte Brown, Norfolk State University

Helen Carr, San Antonio College

Diane Cole, Pensacola Junior College

Gertrude Coleman, Middlesex County College

Barbara Culhane, Nassau Community College

Vicci Fox, Pima Community College

Dennis Gabriel, Cuyahoga Community College West

Robert Gibson, Truman College

Amy Girone, Arizona Western College

Suzanne Gripenstraw, Butte College

Kevin Hayes, Essex Community College

James R. Henson, Northeast State Community College

Glenda Jackson, Gaston College

Lorna Keebaugh, Taft College

Sandi Komarow, Montgomery College

Jeanne Mauzy, Valencia Community College West

Margaret McClain, Arkansas State University

Sherry Mosher, University of Akron

Debbie Naquin, Northern Virginia Community College

Elizabeth Nelson, Tidewater Community College Thomas Moss Campus

Cynthia Ortega, Phoenix College

Aida Pavese, Suffolk Community College

Bethany Plett, Seattle University

Peggy Porter, Houston Community College System Northwest

Elizabeth Ragsdale, Darton College

Keflyn Reed, Bishop State College

Karen Reilly, Ivy Tech Community College, Fort Wayne

Mitye Jo Richey, Community College of Allegheny County

Alan Rosati, Oakton Community College

Deirdre Rowley, Imperial Valley College

Joanne Russell, Wright State University

Victoria Sarkisian, Marist College

Lisa Schuemer, College of DuPage

Carole Shaw, Northeast State Technical Community College

Margaret Sims, Midlands Technical College

Sharon Smallwood, St. Petersburg Junior College

Katie Smith, Riverside Community College

Anne G. Solomon, South Plains College

Diane Starke, El Paso Community College

Peggy Strickland, Gainesville College

Marjorie Susman, Miami-Dade Community College

Shirey VanHook, Ozarks Technical Community College

Carole Widsor, Santa Fe Community College

Barbara Wilan, Northern Virginia Community College

Anne Willekens, Antelope Valley College

Andrea Williams, Purdue University

Nancy Wood, University of Arkansas

We owe a special thanks to the honest and valuable criticism from our colleagues in the Maricopa Community College District. In particular, we would like to thank Frederica Johnson, Cindy Ortega, Mary Jane Onnen, Ruth Callahan, Viva Henley, Richard Heary, and Rodd Scott. Others who helped us with the third edition of this book include Linda Smith, Reinhold Kiermayr, Cindy Gilbert, Marilyn Brophy, Nancy Edwards, Lucy Ehlers, and Tom Mather.

We'd also like to thank all of those at McGraw-Hill who have helped us in the production of the fourth edition of *Reading and All That Jazz*. We owe a special debt of gratitude to our first editor, Sarah Touborg, who shepherded our first unwieldy manuscript into something close to its present form. We are especially grateful to John Kindler, our senior sponsoring editor, and Gillian Cook, senior development editor, for always being willing to discuss our ideas and give us positive (or negative) feedback. They have all been a pleasure to work with. In addition, we are grateful to Allison Jones, marketing manager; Marty Moga, permissions editor; and Jesse Hassenger, editorial coordinator for English. We have been especially fortunate in having Sherree D'Amico as our local McGraw-Hill sales representative: Whatever book we deemed necessary, Sherree magically obtained it. We owe special thanks to our production editors, David Staloch and Meghan Durko.

We also wish to thank our students, who, in addition to reading the selections and completing the exercises, made many helpful suggestions.

Peter Mather
Rita McCarthy

Preface to the Student

"Reading furnishes the mind only with materials of knowledge;
it is thinking that makes what we read ours."—John Locke

Our goal in this book is not only to improve your reading and study skills but also to encourage you to be excited about reading. With this in mind, we have chosen jazz as a theme that loosely holds the reading selections in this textbook together. The words *jazz* or *jazzy* indicate a certain upbeat, positive style that we hope reflects your own excitement about learning and reading. Just as jazz draws on many cultures, so, too, does this textbook, with readings from the United States and around the world. As jazz brings together a wide array of exciting instruments, musicians, and styles to move, amuse, and inspire, so, too, will the reading selections that follow engage and excite you. We hope you'll find the same kind of satisfaction in the pages of this book that listeners find in jazz.

Not only is the book organized loosely around the theme of jazz, it is also organized to move from the individual student to the broader world around us. At the beginning of the text, we start with readings that emphasize the individual. Then, as the book moves forward, the topics of readings gradually broaden into interpersonal and social issues, before concluding with community and global issues. The reading selections in each chapter are set to look like they did in their original sources. Magazine articles are designed to look like magazine articles, newspaper articles like news stories you'd find in your daily paper, and so forth. We hope that this will not only make the text more interesting to look at but will also make for a smooth shift from the reading selections in this book to the texts you'll be challenged by in your other college courses and in the reading you'll do after you graduate from college.

Before most of the reading selections, you will find a section titled "Tuning In to Reading." The purpose of these sections is to help you prepare to read the upcoming reading selection by presenting you with information about the topic you'll encounter. In other ways, too, we try to make connections between the reading selections and your own personal experiences. For example, we include background information and a photograph of the author before most readings; we also include quotations from the famous and not-so-famous in the margins. Before each reading you will find a section called "Notes on Vocabulary" that will introduce unusual words and phrases found in the selection.

After each selection, you will find a variety of questions and activities to test your knowledge of the material covered. Some are objective questions like those you'll see on standardized reading tests or in tests in your other college courses. Practicing with these types of questions will not only test your comprehension of what you've read here but will also give you useful practice at taking quizzes and tests. You'll also find open-ended questions for discussion and writing. While it's important to master the factual information you find in a selection, it is also crucial that you learn to be a critical thinker and careful writer. Discussing issues or writing about them in your journal or for your teacher and classmates can help you develop these central skills. Because familiarity with the Internet is also important to college success, you will find Internet activities throughout this text.

Like a jazz musician, students arrive in class with various styles and talents, each an individual but each also sharing the desire to develop his or her skills. We hope that by the end of this class, you will find reading as exciting an activity as listening to music and that, as with listening to music, you'll make reading a daily part of your life.

Walkthrough: A Guided Tour

Contents

Welcome! The following pages illustrate how this book works. Spending a few minutes getting to know the features and organization of the text will help you get the most out of *Reading and All That Jazz.*

The text begins with a **table of contents** to give you an overview of what you will find in the book.

Chapter titles

Main topics

Longer reading selections

Each chapter begins with a **preview,** which lists the goals for the chapter. The first part of each chapter offers an **explanation** of the chapter's topics and provides **examples** and **exercises** to help you master the material.

The **goals** let you know what you will learn in the chapter.

Exercises encourage mastery of the material.

Short examples help you achieve the chapter's goals.

---

3 Determining an Author's Purpose

CHAPTER PREVIEW
In this chapter, you will

• Learn the difference between a general and a specific purpose.
• Learn how to determine whether the author's purpose is to entertain, inform, or persuade.
• Learn how to summarize short articles.

Entertain, Inform, or Persuade?

Most writers create a story, essay, article, or poem with at least one **general purpose** in mind. Because most writers do not directly state their general purpose, readers must use indirect clues to determine it. We can identify the general purpose by asking "Why did the author write this?" or "What did the author want to accomplish?" Usually, this purpose will fall into one of three broad categories: to entertain, to inform, or to persuade.

An author whose purpose is to **entertain** will tell a story or describe someone or something in an interesting way. A piece of writing meant to entertain will often make an appeal to readers' imagination or sense of humor. If the writing is humorous, the author might say things in an exaggerated fashion or use understatement. Witty, unusual, dramatic, or exciting stories usually have entertainment as their purpose. A romance, suspense, or mystery novel is usually meant to entertain. Writing meant to entertain may be either fiction or nonfiction. The following is an example of a paragraph whose purpose is to entertain:

Highlight or underline several words that define each boldfaced term.

> I assume you are on the Internet. If you are not, then pardon my French, but *vous êtes un big loser.* Today EVERYBODY is on the Internet, including the primitive Mud People of the Amazon rain forest. In the old days, when the Mud People needed food, they had to manually throw spears at wild boars, whereas today they simply get on the Internet, go to www.spearaboar.com and click their mouse a few times (the Mud People use actual mice). Within three business days, a large box (containing a live boar) is delivered to them by a UPS driver, whom they eat.

From Dave Barry, *Dave Barry Is Not Taking This Sitting Down.* New York: Crown Publishers, 2000, p. 107.

An author whose purpose is to **inform** will explain something to readers or provide them with knowledge they did not possess before. Ordinarily, the material will be presented in an objective, unemotional fashion. Authors who write textbooks presenting factual material usually have this purpose in mind. Encyclopedias, research

136

Each chapter also includes a number of longer **reading selections**. These reading selections start with an introductory section that aims to spark your interest and provide background information.

A **quotation** from the reading engages your interest.

Tuning In to Reading provides background information.

The **Bio-sketch** provides information about the author's life and writing experience.

The **Notes on Vocabulary** help you understand the more difficult words in the reading selection.

The reading selections are designed to look like **magazine articles, news stories,** and **excerpts from books**. This will help you as you make the transition from reading for school to reading for yourself.

Many of the reading selections include **illustrations** that reinforce topics and provide context.

First boxed example:

READING

"Tom Broderick in so many ways embodies the best qualities of his generation. . . . He didn't blame the world for his condition."

TUNING IN TO READING

Tom Brokaw wrote the book *The Greatest Generation* to "pay tribute to those men and women who have given us the lives we have today." These individuals from the World War II era are now in their seventies and eighties and are, according to the Department of Veterans' Affairs, dying at the rate of about 32,000 a month. Brokaw dedicated himself to memorializing their stories of sacrifice, honor, and courage before it was too late.

BIO-SKETCH

Tom Brokaw anchored the *NBC Nightly News* for 21 years and is now retired from that position. He has received many journalism awards, including the Peabody Award for a report called "To Be an American," and seven Emmy Awards. He considers the publication of *The Greatest Generation,* from which this article is taken, to be one of his greatest achievements.

NOTES ON VOCABULARY

abundant   plentiful; more than enough. The word comes from the Latin word *abundo,* meaning "to overflow." In Latin, *ab* means "from" and *unda* means "to billow, wave, or surge." The word *abundant* refers to a profusion of things "as plentiful as the waves of the sea."

cocky   conceited; arrogant. The word refers to a rooster's proud strut around the barnyard and his early morning cry of "cock-a-doodle-doo" as he surveys his domain.

appalled   caused to feel shock or horror. The word *appalled* is derived from the Latin words *ad,* meaning "to," and *palleo,* meaning "to be pale."

braille   a system of printing and writing for the blind that relies on raised dots that represent numbers and letters that can be identified by touch. This type of writing was developed in a primitive form by the French military. It consisted of a series of raised marks on cardboard that could be passed in darkness and decoded by sentries on duty without resorting to illumination. Later, the inventor, Louis Braille, refined the system that bears his name.

Thomas Broderick
Tom Brokaw

IN WORLD WAR II, MORE THAN 292,000 Americans were killed in battle, and more than 1.7 million returned home physically affected in some way, from minor afflictions to blindness or missing limbs or paralysis, battle-scarred and exhausted, but oh so happy and relieved to be home. They had survived an extraordinary ordeal, but now they were eager to reclaim their ordinary lives of work, family, church,

---

Second boxed example:

READING

"The more horrifying the world becomes, the more art becomes abstract."
— Pablo Picasso

"The Germans bombed the town of Guernica. . . . Guernica was devastated and its civilian population massacred."

TUNING IN TO READING

To learn more about one of the greatest achievements of 20th-century art, read the following selection from an art history textbook.

BIO-SKETCH

Although Pablo Picasso (1881–1973) was born in Spain, he spent most of his adult life in France. His early works revealed his strong compassion for those who were poor and suffering. He once said, "Painting is stronger than me, it makes me do what it wants." One of Picasso's finest paintings, *Guernica,* is a passionate expression of social protest, which Picasso painted during the Spanish Civil War (1937). It is hard to view *Guernica* (pictured below) without vicariously experiencing the agony and destruction of war. Picasso was a dominant figure in Western art in the 20th century and is credited with helping to bring back storytelling to art.

NOTES ON VOCABULARY

fury   from Latin *furia* meaning "violent passion, rage, or madness." In classical mythology, the three Furies were winged female monsters with snakes for hair. Their goal was to pursue and punish those who had committed evil deeds.

procrastinate   to put off doing something unpleasant or burdensome until a future time. The word *procrastinate* can be broken down into parts, *pro* meaning "toward" and *cras* meaning "tomorrow." So when you *procrastinate,* you are pushing something toward tomorrow.

Guernica © 2003 Estate of Pablo Picasso/Artists Rights Society (ARS), New York/© Giraudon/Art Resource, NY.

Guernica
Rita Gilbert

[*Guernica*] was created by an artist whose sympathies lay with those not in power, an artist who took up his brush with a sense of fury at the "ins" who caused devastation. From his fury came one of the great masterpieces of 20th-century art. The artist was Picasso, and the painting is called *Guernica.*

A reading selection from a **magazine**

READING *continued*

BIO-SKETCH

Dr. Mary Pipher is a clinical psychologist, part-time instructor at the University of Nebraska, nationwide lecturer, and best-selling author. Her book *Reviving Ophelia*, published in 1994, explored the stresses placed on teenage girls by modern society. In 1999, Pipher published *Another Country*, a book about elderly people in America. She observes that "to grow old in the U.S. is to inhabit a foreign country, isolated, disconnected, and misunderstood." In her 1996 book *The Shelter of Each Other*, from which this excerpt is taken, Pipher turns her attention to the stresses placed on the family as a whole. In Pipher's view, the family is so burdened with problems that it can no longer protect family members from the "enemy within," which she defines as inappropriate stimulation from a variety of sources, with TV being at the top of her list.

According to the A. C. Nielsen Company, the average American watches 3 hours and 46 minutes of television each day (more than 52 days of nonstop television watching per year). By age 65, the average American will have spent nearly 9 years glued to the tube.

NOTES ON VOCABULARY

Romeo and Juliet a tragedy by William Shakespeare about two ill-fated lovers whose romance ends in death because of the feud between their two families.

persona a character in a fictional work; the public role or personality a person assumes. In Latin, the word for "mask" was *persona*. In ancient Rome, actors wore masks that covered the entire face. Each Roman god was represented by a particular mask so that the audience always knew what god an actor was portraying.

nuance a slight difference or distinction. The term was borrowed from French and originally referred to a slightly different shade of color.

decry to denounce or disparage openly.

rule of thumb a practical method or principle that is based on the wisdom of experience. The expression dates from the 1600s and originally referred to making rough estimates of measurements by using one's thumb.

Tonga Islands a group of islands in the southwest Pacific Ocean slightly east of Fiji. They are also known as the Friendly Islands.

TV

Mary Pipher

I N A COLLEGE CLASS I ASKED, "What would it be like to grow up in a world without media?" A student from the Tonga Islands answered, "I never saw television or heard rock and roll until I came to the United States in high school." She paused and looked around the room. "I had a happy childhood. I felt safe all the time. I didn't know I was poor. Or that parents hurt their children or that children hated their parents. I thought I was pretty."

2 Television has probably been the most powerful medium in shaping the new community. The electronic community gives us our mutual friends, our significant events and our daily chats. The "produced" relationships of television families become our models for intimacy. We know media stars better than we know our neighbors. Most

---

A reading selection from a **popular book**

The Roots of Happiness: An Empirical Analysis

Wayne Weiten and Margaret A. Lloyd

What exactly makes a person happy? This question has been the subject of much speculation. Commonsense theories about the roots of happiness abound. For example, you have no doubt heard that money cannot buy happiness. But do you believe it? A television commercial says, "If you've got your health, you've got just about everything." Is health indeed the key? What if you're healthy but poor, unemployed, and lonely? We often hear about the joys of parenthood, the joys of youth, and the joys of the simple, rural life. Are these the factors that promote happiness?

2 In recent years, social scientists have begun putting these and other theories to empirical test. Quite a number of survey studies have been conducted to explore the determinants of happiness. The findings of these studies are quite interesting. As you will see, many commonsense notions about happiness appear to be inaccurate.

3 The first of these is the apparently widespread assumption that most people are relatively unhappy. Writers, social scientists, and the general public seem to believe that people around the world are predominantly dissatisfied, yet surveys consistently find that the vast majority of respondents characterize themselves as fairly happy. When people are asked to rate their happiness, only a small minority place themselves below the neutral point on the various scales used. The overall picture seems rosier than anticipated.

What Isn't Very Important?

Money.

4 There is a positive correlation between income and feelings of happiness, but the association is surprisingly weak. Admittedly, being very poor can make people unhappy, but once people ascend above the poverty level, there is little relation between income and happiness. On the average, very wealthy people are only slightly happier than those in the middle classes. The problem with money is that in this era of voracious consumption, most people find a way to spend all their money and come out short, no matter how much they make. Complaints about not having enough money are routine even among affluent people who earn six-figure incomes.

Age.

5 Age and happiness are consistently found to be unrelated. Age accounts for less than 1 percent of the variation in people's happiness. The key factors influencing people's thoughts about their own well-being may shift some as people grow older—work becomes less important, health more so—but people's average level of happiness tends to remain remarkably stable over the life span.

Gender.

6 Women are treated for depressive disorders about twice as often as men, so one might expect that women are less happy on the average. However, like age, gender accounts for less than 1 percent of the variation in people's happiness.

Parenthood.

7 Children can be a tremendous source of joy and fulfillment, but they also can be a tremendous source of headaches and hassles. Compared to childless couples, parents worry more and experience more marital problems. Apparently the good and bad aspects of parenthood balance each other out, because the evidence indicates that people who have children are neither more nor less happy than people without children.

A reading selection from a **textbook**

READING

"A group of psychology researchers have made the breakthrough discovery that—prepare to be astounded—males and females are different."

TUNING IN TO READING

A popular advice book by John Gray is titled *Men Are from Mars, Women Are from Venus*. Do you think men and women are so different that they might as well be from different planets? Think about your own personal experiences with this issue before reading the following article.

BIO-SKETCH

Dave Barry, the Pulitzer Prize–winning columnist, is also the author of numerous best-selling books including *Dave Barry's Complete Guide to Guys*, from which this excerpt is taken. The *New York Times* calls Barry the funniest man in America. His life was featured in the hit TV show *Dave's World*. He lives in Miami with his wife, a sportswriter for the *Miami Herald*, and his two children, who, according to Barry, do not think he is funny.

NOTES ON VOCABULARY

Hindenburg an airship (dirigible) named after the president of Germany, Paul von Hindenburg. The airship was inflated with highly flammable hydrogen gas. On May 6, 1937, the Hindenburg caught fire. The flames quickly engulfed the ship, and of the 97 people on board, 35 were killed.

Smurfs little blue cartoon characters created by the artist Peyo. The Smurfs became a worldwide success after a television show featuring them premiered in 1981. Smurf plush toys, figurines, video games, and CDs are still popular with children and collectors.

subatomic particles smaller than an atom.

syndrome a pattern of behavior that tends to occur under certain circumstances; a number of symptoms that occur together to make up a particular condition.

Neither Man nor Rat Can Properly Fold Laundry

BY DAVE BARRY

Are you a male or a female? To find out, take this scientific quiz:

2 Your department is on a tight deadline for developing a big sales proposal, but you've hit a snag on a key point. You want to go one way; a co-worker named Bob strongly disagrees. To break the deadlock, you:

3 Present your position, listen to the other side, then fashion a workable compromise.

4 Punch Bob.

5 Your favorite team is about to win the championship, but at the last second the victory is stolen away by a terrible referee's call. You:

6 Remind yourself that it's just a game, and that there are far more important things in your life.

7 Punch Bob again.

8 HOW TO SCORE: If you answered "b" to both questions, then you are a male. I base this statement on a recent article in *The New York Times* about the way

---

A reading selection from a **newspaper**

After the longer reading selections, you will find a **Comprehension Checkup**, with a variety of exercises to test your understanding and provide practice for other college tests.

Objective questions test your understanding and provide practice for standardized tests.

Vocabulary in Context exercises help you expand your vocabulary.

In Your Own Words and **Written Assignments** give you a chance to express your own thoughts.

Internet Activity sections send you to the World Wide Web to find out more.

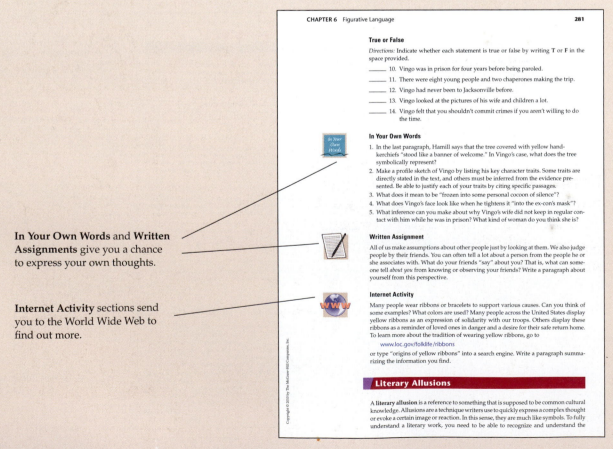

The embedded page images show:

490   PART 5 Reading Critically

COMPREHENSION CHECKUP

Multiple Choice

Directions: For each item, write the letter corresponding to the best answer on the line provided.

_____ 1. The first paragraph of the narrative serves to
a. express Orwell's feelings about capital punishment.
b. introduce the reader to the person being executed.
c. introduce the reader to the setting of the story.
d. describe the hanging process in detail.

_____ 2. From the story, you could infer that Orwell
a. would support the continued use of capital punishment.
b. viewed the death penalty process as ironic.
c. saw no problems in executing a man.
d. had been opposed to the death penalty before he went to Burma.

_____ 3. Orwell serves as the narrator of the story. Which role does the narrator play?
a. the person responsible for hanging the prisoner
b. a fellow prisoner due to be executed later
c. the superintendent of the prison
d. an observer to the hanging process

_____ 4. The organizational pattern used in paragraph 17 is
a. cause and effect.
b. comparison-contrast.
c. chronological order.
d. definition and example.

True or False

Directions: Indicate whether each statement is true or false by writing **T** or **F** in the space provided.

_____ 5. The prisoner was accused of committing murder in a fit of rage.

_____ 6. A British official was responsible for serving as the executioner.

_____ 7. On the way to the gallows, they were interrupted by a large, friendly dog.

_____ 8. After the hanging, everyone felt a great deal of grief and began to wail and cry.

_____ 9. The men, both British and local, later drank together quite amicably.

_____ 10. It was possible to see the prisoner's face when he was executed.

Vocabulary in Context

Directions: Use the context clues to determine the meaning of the italicized words, and then write a definition for that word in the space provided.

1. a *sodden* morning of the rains (1)   _____

2. a *puny* wisp of a man (2)   _____

3. a bugle call, *desolately* thin in the wet air (3)   _____

4. Everyone stood *aghast* (6)   _____

5. it danced and *gamboled* (8)   _____

CHAPTER 6 Figurative Language   **281**

True or False

Directions: Indicate whether each statement is true or false by writing **T** or **F** in the space provided.

_____ 10. Vingo was in prison for four years before being paroled.

_____ 11. There were eight young people and two chaperones making the trip.

_____ 12. Vingo had never been to Jacksonville before.

_____ 13. Vingo looked at the pictures of his wife and children a lot.

_____ 14. Vingo felt that you shouldn't commit crimes if you aren't willing to do the time.

In Your Own Words

1. In the last paragraph, Hamill says that the tree covered with yellow handkerchiefs "stood like a banner of welcome." In Vingo's case, what does the tree symbolically represent?

2. Make a profile sketch of Vingo by listing his key character traits. Some traits are directly stated in the text, and others must be inferred from the evidence presented. Be able to justify each of your traits by citing specific passages.

3. What does it mean to be "frozen into some personal cocoon of silence"?

4. What does Vingo's face look like when he tightens it "into the ex-con's mask"?

5. What inference can you make about why Vingo's wife did not keep in regular contact with him while he was in prison? What kind of woman do you think she is?

Written Assignment

All of us make assumptions about other people just by looking at them. We also judge people by their friends. You can often tell a lot about a person from the people he or she associates with. What do your friends "say" about you? That is, what can someone tell *about you* from knowing or observing your friends? Write a paragraph about yourself from this perspective.

Internet Activity

Many people wear ribbons or bracelets to support various causes. Can you think of some examples? What colors are used? Many people across the United States display yellow ribbons as an expression of solidarity with our troops. Others display these ribbons as a reminder of loved ones in danger and a desire for their safe return home. To learn more about the tradition of wearing yellow ribbons, go to

www.loc.gov/folklife/ribbons

or type "origins of yellow ribbons" into a search engine. Write a paragraph summarizing the information you find.

Literary Allusions

A **literary allusion** is a reference to something that is supposed to be common cultural knowledge. Allusions are a technique writers use to quickly express a complex thought or evoke a certain image or reaction. In this sense, they are much like symbols. To fully understand a literary work, you need to be able to recognize and understand the

Because much of your college work requires you to read and study college textbooks, this book provides **shorter textbook selections** throughout. It also provides a **longer textbook selection** in Chapter 15 on which you can practice your study skills.

The **notes in the margin** and the **underlining** demonstrate how to take notes on college reading.

NEW ORLEANS AND CHICAGO JAZZ

Differences	Similarities
1. No recordings of New Orleans jazz were made in New Orleans.	1. Both have high energy and rhythmic vitality.
2. Chicago jazz was largely developed by transplanted New Orleans musicians.	2. Both styles have clarinet, trumpet or cornet, and trombone as solo instruments.
	3. Both styles use head arrangements.
	4. _____
	5. _____

Jazz in America

Introduction

Jazz—divergent styles, ever changing

Although Jazz is a relatively recent, twentieth-century American phenomenon, jazz artists and styles are recognized worldwide. Jazz includes widely divergent styles ranging from entertainment music to art music. It is ever changing and defies simple definition.

Jazz began in early part of 20th century

2   Jazz began in the early part of the twentieth century in the bars and night-clubs of poor urban neighborhoods, particularly in New Orleans. These bars and clubs were the places where musicians who aspired to a career playing jazz were able to find employment. The jazz they played emerged from combining the songs, dances, and musical instincts and preferences of people of African and European (particularly French and Spanish) heritage.

International in scope

3   Jazz has come a long way over the past hundred years. Today it is international in scope—performed and listened to nearly everywhere—and it has a strong following, especially in continental Europe, Scandinavia, Japan, Africa, South America, and Canada. It is heard not only in bars and nightclubs but also in the finest hotels, on college campuses, in concert halls, and even in churches. Jazz has become an accepted part of the music curriculum in schools and colleges. Courses are devoted to the study of jazz, and music students in many schools can pursue degrees in jazz. Students can play in jazz ensembles for academic credit in American colleges and universities, and most high schools have stage bands. The International Association of Jazz Educators was organized to further the study and performance of jazz in our educational system.

Accepted in music curriculums

Women have been influential in jazz

4   Many women, such as Mary Lou Williams, Shirley Horn, Hazel Scott, Marian McPartland, and Toshiko Akiyoshi, have achieved distinction as jazz musicians, not to mention the large number of distinguished women jazz singers, such as Billie Holiday, Ella Fitzgerald, and Sarah Vaughn. In addition, many women have been influential as composers or arrangers, as leaders of jazz groups, or as writers and teachers.

What Is Jazz?

5   Jazz began in the early days of radio and recordings, and these media brought it to the attention of the public. Recordings, especially, brought the music of jazz musicians to their colleagues; they became an invaluable way to share, learn, grow, and influence other musicians and, indeed, the future course of jazz.

Photographs, interesting facts, and trivia questions enhance your study of vocabulary words.

Throughout the book, you will also find **vocabulary units**. Each unit includes a list of words with traditional definitions supplemented with items to reinforce what you've learned.

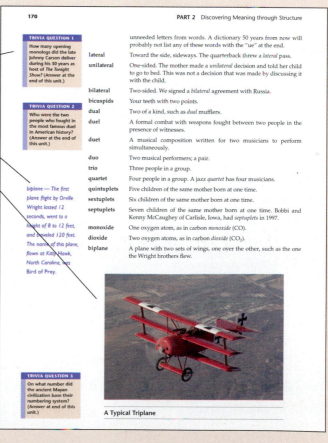

TRIVIA QUESTION 1
How many opening monologs did the late Johnny Carson deliver during his 30 years as host of *The Tonight Show*? (Answer at the end of this unit.)

TRIVIA QUESTION 2
Who were the two people who fought in the most famous duel in American history? (Answer at the end of this unit.)

biplane — The first plane flight by Orville Wright lasted 12 seconds, went to a height of 8 to 12 feet, and traveled 120 feet. The name of this plane, flown at Kitty Hawk, North Carolina, was Bird of Prey.

TRIVIA QUESTION 3
On what number did the ancient Mayan civilization base their numbering system? (Answer at end of this unit.)

unneeded letters from words. A dictionary 50 years from now will probably not list any of these words with the "ue" at the end.

lateral	Toward the side, sideways. The quarterback threw a *lateral* pass.
unilateral	One-sided. The mother made a *unilateral* decision and told her child to go to bed. This was not a decision that was made by discussing it with the child.
bilateral	Two-sided. We signed a *bilateral* agreement with Russia.
bicuspids	Your teeth with two points.
dual	Two of a kind, such as *dual* mufflers.
duel	A formal combat with weapons fought between two people in the presence of witnesses.
duet	A musical composition written for two musicians to perform simultaneously.
duo	Two musical performers; a pair.
trio	Three people in a group.
quartet	Four people in a group. A jazz *quartet* has four musicians.
quintuplets	Five children of the same mother born at one time.
sextuplets	Six children of the same mother born at one time.
septuplets	Seven children of the same mother born at one time. Bobbi and Kenny McCaughey of Carlisle, Iowa, had *septuplets* in 1997.
monoxide	One oxygen atom, as in carbon *monoxide* (CO).
dioxide	Two oxygen atoms, as in carbon *dioxide* (CO_2).
biplane	A plane with two sets of wings, one over the other, such as the one the Wright brothers flew.

A Typical Triplane

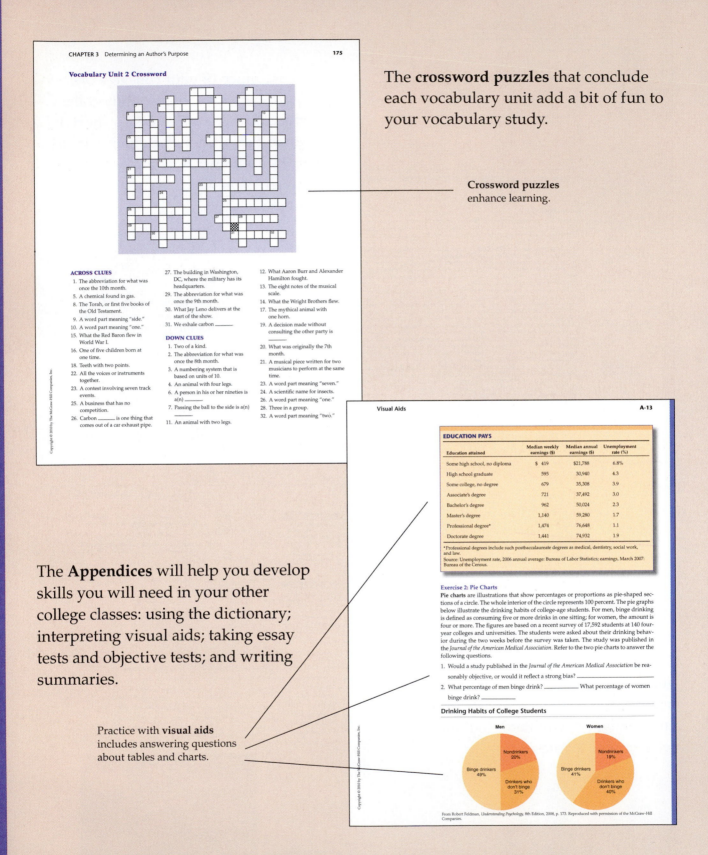

The **crossword puzzles** that conclude each vocabulary unit add a bit of fun to your vocabulary study.

Crossword puzzles enhance learning.

The **Appendices** will help you develop skills you will need in your other college classes: using the dictionary; interpreting visual aids; taking essay tests and objective tests; and writing summaries.

Practice with **visual aids** includes answering questions about tables and charts.

We hope that your experience with the fourth edition of *Reading and All That Jazz* will be entirely successful.

Reading and All That Jazz

Getting a Handle on College

Louis Armstrong

In jazz, the essential quality is the right to be an individual.

—**Ornette Coleman**

It is as if jazz were saying to us that not only is far greater individuality possible to man than he has so far allowed himself, but that such individuality, far from being a threat to a cooperative social structure, can actually enhance society.

—**Martin Williams,** from *Jazz Is* by Nat Hentoff

CHAPTERS IN PART 1

Because musicians bring their individual backgrounds and talents to the music they play, each musician has a distinctive style of playing. A musician's style of playing is what works best for the musician and produces the kind of music the musician enjoys. So, too, with learning: Each of you brings your individual backgrounds and talents to learning. These backgrounds and talents determine your learning style, which is the method of learning that works best for you. No two of you will have the same learning style. The objective of Part 1 of this book is to help you discover your individual learning style so that you can do better, in school and in life.

Your First Week in Class

CHAPTER PREVIEW

In this chapter, you will

- Learn how to keep track of your assignments.
- Examine your motivations for attending college.
- Learn techniques for discovering the meanings of words.

"There are no secrets to success. It is the result of preparation, hard work, and learning from failure."

— Colin Powell

Some of you just recently graduated from high school. Others have been out in the "real world" and now realize the importance of a college education. Each of you decides what is important in your life, and you have decided that going to college is important. Besides investing your time, you are also investing money, and so you want to get as much benefit as you can out of college. In high school, perhaps many of you did well in your classes without trying very hard. This won't happen in college because college is more demanding. Whether you succeed in college is up to you. It is your responsibility to attend class, study, and turn in your work on time. No one else can do it for you.

Reading and studying will be an important part of your college career. You can't expect to do well in college without having good reading and studying skills. In this book, we will provide you with techniques for improving these skills. Using these techniques will make the time you spend in college more enjoyable and productive.

Assignment Sheets

Success in college requires an organized and disciplined approach. So, one of the first things you need to think about is how to organize yourself as a serious student. Perhaps the easiest way to improve your college performance is to take charge of your assignments. Many of your assignments will be listed in the class syllabi, while other assignments will be announced in class. In some classes, late assignments will receive less credit, and in others, they will not be accepted at all—no excuses!

The best way to keep a record of your classroom assignments is by using assignment sheets. Developing the habit of carefully recording your assignments is crucial not only in this class but in your other classes as well. On the next page are samples of three different types of assignment sheets. The first sample shows a weekly format, the second a monthly format, and the third a "continuous log" format. You can find a copy of each type of assignment sheet in the Appendices. Whichever format you prefer, be sure to make additional copies of it for future use.

Weekly Assignment Sheet

ASSIGNMENTS
MONDAY
TUESDAY
WEDNESDAY
THURSDAY
FRIDAY
OTHER ASSIGNMENTS, TESTS, ETC.

Monthly Assignment Sheet

MONTH						
SUNDAY	MONDAY	TUESDAY	WEDNESDAY	THURSDAY	FRIDAY	SATURDAY

Continuous Log Assignment Sheet

ASSIGNMENT SHEET			
Subject(s)			
Date	Assignments	Due	Finished

Are You Ready for College?

College is not for everyone. Only 60 percent of those who begin a four-year degree program will receive their diplomas. Half of the students who begin taking classes at a community college will drop out by the end of the first year. Notice how many cars there are in the parking lot now. As the days and weeks pass, you will see more empty parking spaces as students drop out for one reason or another. You are the one who decides whether you are going to be a survivor. *Decide to be a survivor!*

Below is a quiz for assessing how difficult it may be for you to stay in college. This quiz is just for you and is *not* to be turned in. Place a check mark beside each statement that applies to you.

Motivational Quiz

_____ 1. I have not yet really decided what my career objective is. Or it is difficult for me to visualize what I will be doing in five years.

_____ 2. High school was easy for me and I never really had to study hard to get good grades. Or I never really studied in high school and got average or below-average grades.

_____ 3. My main reason for being here is athletics.

_____ 4. I have small children at home I must take care of.

_____ 5. I need to stay in school so that I can remain on my parents' health insurance.

_____ 6. My parents want me to go to college, and I want to please them.

_____ 7. I am working 30 to 40 hours a week and taking 12 to 15 units. (Consider unpaid activities such as athletics as part of these 30 to 40 hours.)

_____ 8. I am living with two or more roommates and plan to do most of my studying at home or in my dorm room.

_____ 9. I am at this college mostly because my boyfriend or girlfriend goes here.

_____ 10. I need to work part-time to pay for my car, clothes, stereo, etc.

_____ 11. This is the first time I have been away from home on my own.

_____ 12. I plan to get married soon. Or I am going through a divorce.

Now take a look at the number of statements you checked. The more you checked, the greater your chances of not making it. If you checked a lot, this does not mean that you will drop out. But it does mean that you need to do some thinking about your priorities and goals. Your chances of not making it are greater if you are here for the wrong reasons or if you have too many other commitments.

Your First Assignment

Now you can write down your first assignment for this class. This assignment will be due the next class session. Below you will find a crossword puzzle that will introduce you to the material covered in this book. Read the clues, use the table of contents and index to find the answers in the book, and record the answers in the puzzle. Bring your completed puzzle the next time class meets.

Introduction

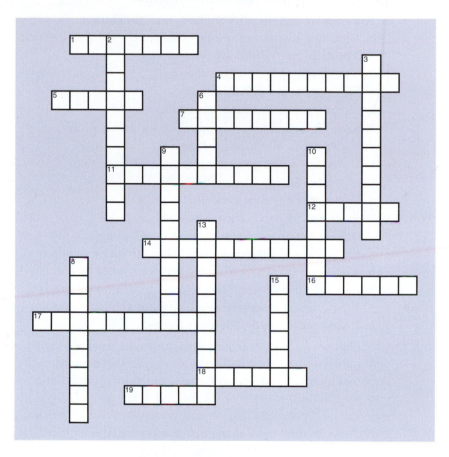

ACROSS CLUES

1. _____ are one type of figure of speech. They use words such as *like* and *as*.

4. "Notes on _____" will introduce you to new words. (Preface to the Student)

5. A word part meaning "four." (Vocabulary Unit 2 in Chapter 3)

7. One type of pattern of organization in Chapter 4 is the comparison-_____ pattern.

11. Chapter 5 contains information about _____(s).

12. You will learn how to improve your reading and _____ skills. (Preface to the Student)

14. One type of learning style discussed in Chapter 1.

16. The author of "Ode to the Present" is Pablo _____.

17. Both authors of this textbook attended colleges in _____.

18. The author of "A Hanging" is George _____.

19. A Robert Frost poem in Chapter 6 is titled "The Road Not _____."

DOWN CLUES

2. The publisher of this book is _____. (Don't use a hyphen.)

3. Chapter 12 discusses _____ techniques.

6. "It is thinking that makes reading ours" is a quote by John _____. (Preface to the Student)

8. In the table of contents under Chapter 15, _____ is listed as one way to organize textbook material.

9. The first type of context clue discussed in "Vocabulary: Words in Context" in Chapter 1.

10. The "Q" in SQ3R stands for _____.

13. In the table of contents "TV" by Mary Pipher is listed as Reading _____.

15. The author of "Louis Armstrong, Ambassador of Jazz" is Studs _____.

Optimism and Success

According to Martin Seligman, a University of Pennsylvania psychologist, how people respond to setbacks—optimistically or pessimistically—is a good indicator of how well they will succeed in school, sports, and certain kinds of work. To test his theory, Seligman devised a questionnaire to screen insurance agents at the Metropolitan Life Insurance Company. Job applicants were asked to imagine a hypothetical event and then choose the response (a or b) that more closely resembled their own. Some samples from his questionnaire follow:

1. You gain weight over the holidays and can't lose it.
   a. Diets don't work in the long run.
   b. The diet I tried didn't work.

2. You lose your temper with a friend.
   a. He or she is always nagging me.
   b. He or she was in a hostile mood.

3. You are penalized for returning your income-tax forms late.
   a. I always put off doing my taxes.
   b. I was lazy about getting my taxes done this year.

4. You've been feeling run-down.
   a. I never get a chance to relax.
   b. I was exceptionally busy this week.

5. A friend says something that hurts your feelings.
   a. She always blurts things out without thinking of others.
   b. My friend was in a bad mood and took it out on me.

6. You forgot your spouse's (boyfriend's/girlfriend's) birthday.
   a. I'm not good at remembering birthdays.
   b. I was preoccupied with other things.

Seligman found that insurance agents who answered with more Bs than As were better able to overcome bad sales days, recovered more easily from rejection, and were less likely to quit. In short, they were more optimistic. People with an optimistic view of life tend to treat obstacles and setbacks as temporary (and therefore surmountable). Pessimists take them personally; what others see as fleeting, localized impediments, they view as pervasive and permanent.

Optimism does have a downside, though. Unrealistic optimism can make people believe they are invulnerable and keep them from taking sensible steps to avoid danger. The recipe for well-being includes enough optimism to sustain hope, a dash of pessimism to prevent complacency, and enough realism to understand the difference between those things we can control and those we can't.

From *Learned Optimism* by Martin E. P. Seligman, pp. 33, 35, 37, 39. Copyright © 1990, 1998, 2006 by Martin E. P. Seligman. Used by permission of Alfred A. Knopf, a division of Random House, Inc. and Arthur Pine Associates.

Is Fred Bassett in the cartoon below an optimist or a pessimist?

FRED BASSETT: Solo Syndication/Daily Mail

People who are successful in higher education and other pursuits in life are often optimistic.

Pessimists may be overwhelmed by their problems, whereas optimists are challenged by them, according to Alan McGinnis, author of *The Power of Optimism.* "Optimists think of themselves as problem-solvers, as trouble-shooters," he says. This does not mean they see anything through rose-colored glasses. Rather, they have several qualities that help them have a positive attitude while still remaining realistic and tough-minded.

Optimists . . .

1. Look for partial solutions.
2. Believe they have control over their future.
3. Interrupt their negative trains of thought.
4. Heighten their powers of appreciation.
5. Are cheerful even when they can't be happy.
6. Like to swap good news.
7. Accept what cannot be changed.

The following selection features the well-known musician Louis Armstrong. Armstrong accepted the many adversities in his life as challenges. He is an example of a person who sees a glass as half-full rather than as half-empty.

READING

"He loved the music as much as life itself."

TUNING IN TO READING

Louis Armstrong was a master technician of the trumpet who produced such classics as "Ain't Misbehavin'," "Basin Street Blues," and "Muskrat Ramble." Over the long years of his career, he became well known for his distinctive singing style, which some said sounded like "a wheelbarrow crunching its way up a gravel driveway." Nicknamed "Satchmo," Armstrong made over 2,000 recordings, starred in movies, and traveled the world as a "jazz" goodwill ambassador. At age 64, he had his greatest commercial success, the hit recording "Hello, Dolly!" The song that is most associated with Louis Armstrong is "What a Wonderful World," which was first released in 1968.

BIO-SKETCH

Studs Terkel, best known for his interviews and oral histories, has written 16 books, including *Working* and *Hard Times.* His goal in most of his books was to record the stories of ordinary people. In 2007, at the age of 95, he published his memoir titled *Touch and Go.* Born Louis Terkel in 1912 to working-class parents, he changed his first name to "Studs" in honor of the character Studs Lonigan in the James T. Farrell novels. A graduate of the University of Chicago, Terkel was a well-known disc jockey and jazz columnist.

NOTES ON VOCABULARY

Joe Oliver   Joe "King" Oliver (1885–1938) was a noted jazz cornet player, bandleader, and composer. Armstrong called Oliver "Papa Joe" and considered him to be his inspiration. In his autobiography, Armstrong said, "If it had not been for Joe Oliver, jazz would not be what it is today."

READING *continued*

breadwinner   a member of a family who provides most of its financial support.

cabaret   a restaurant or nightclub providing short programs of live entertainment.

reveille   the sounding of a bugle or trumpet early in the morning to awaken and summon people in a camp.

taps   a bugle or trumpet call used to signal "lights out."

repertoire   the collection of songs, musical selections, or other works that an artist is prepared to perform.

Louis Armstrong, Ambassador of Jazz

Studs Terkel

A THIRTEEN-YEAR-OLD BOY FIRED A .38 revolver high in the air. *Bang! Bang! Bang!*

2   His three young pals, with whom he had been singing and dancing in the streets for pennies, howled gleefully.

3   "'Atta boy, Dipper! Listen to that noise! Oooweee!"

4   Louis Armstrong—the boy they called "Dipper," short for "Dippermouth"—was celebrating New Year's Eve in New Orleans. It was 1913.

5   He had seen grown men greet the new year in this fashion. It was the custom to fire a gun straight up, aiming at the sky. No harm was intended. It was just plain fun. Louis didn't know it was against the law.

6   Suddenly his buddies shouted a warning: "Cheese it, Dipper! A cop! Run, boy, run!"

7   It was too late.

8   As the boy was led to the police station, he sobbed and pleaded, "Please, please, please, Mister. Lemme go home to my mama. I won't do it again. I promise!"

9   It was no use. He was sent to the Colored Waifs' Home for Boys.

10   Louis was terribly lonely during those early days at the home. The other boys were not the least bit friendly at first. He missed his mother—Mayann. Her red beans and rice were so delicious; he had none here. He missed his younger sister, Beatrice, whom they called Mama Lucy. But most of all, he missed freedom.

11   He used to roam through all those New Orleans streets at will. He used to dance lightheartedly behind those brass bands that played at picnics, funerals, and carnivals. He missed the exciting music that poured out of the open doors of the rough-and-tumble cabarets. He missed the slow blues, the fast stomps, and the stirring, syncopated marches. He loved this music as much as life itself.

12 But he did find a happiness at the home. It was in listening to the rehearsals of the Waifs' Home Band. If only Mr. Peter Davis, the music teacher, would invite him to join! If only he would teach him how to blow that golden cornet! Louis felt if he could just get his hands on that horn, he might one day learn its secrets and blow it like the great men of New Orleans: Bunk Johnson, Freddie Keppard, and his idol, the one and only Joe Oliver, "Papa Joe."

13 One day, as the boy sat in the rear of the hall wistfully listening to the young musicians, Peter Davis ambled up beside him.

14 "Armstrong, is that all you do? Spy at our rehearsals?"

15 The boy looked up, frightened. The man smiled. "How would you like to play in our band?"

16 Louis was so overwhelmed he couldn't speak.

17 The man repeated the question.

18 Finally the lad stammered, "Sure, Mr. Davis. I sure would." And so Louis Armstrong became a member of the Waifs' Home Band.

19 Instead of a cornet, he was handed the lowly tambourine. Oh, well, he didn't mind. He was part of a *band!* That's all that mattered. In no time he was promoted to the drums. Peter Davis sensed the boy's vigor and joy, his natural feeling for the beat.

20 Quite suddenly the day he had been patiently awaiting came. The boy who regularly blew the bugle was called for by his parents and taken home. Who would now blow reveille and taps and mess call? Louis crossed his fingers. Peter Davis knew this. Immediately he made a decision. Shoving the departed boy's bugle into Louis's hands, he said, "The job is yours. Practice."

21 The first thing Louis did was to polish that horn from a dirty green to shiny gold. After all, it was *his* instrument now. It was a matter of personal pride. A horn should look as good as it sounds.

22 When the others saw the shining bugle, they cheered and stomped. "Hooray for Dipper! He's our man!"

23 As they awoke each morning to the sound of the bugle, it was a mellow awakening. As they were called to bed each night by the horn at young Armstrong's lips, they felt oh, so good! He blew those notes so easily, so naturally.

24 Mr. Davis felt good, too. "Louis, you're ripe for the cornet."

25 The boy jumped for joy. "That's the horn Joe Oliver blows! That's my dream comin' true, Mr. Davis!"

26 "Now look, boy," admonished the man, "it's not gravy. I'll be able to teach you a few tunes like 'Home, Sweet Home,' but the rest is up to you. You'll have to practice, practice, and practice!"

27 "Oh, I'll do that, Mr. Davis. Don't you worry about that," the elated boy replied.

28 "Tone—that's the important thing," murmured the man. "With tone, you can play anything, ragtime or classical."

29 "Yes sir. I'll remember that."

30 "And you got to work hard, awful hard."

31 Louis nodded solemnly.

32 Peter Davis grinned. "If you do that, I've a hunch you'll be leader of this band long before your ma or your pa calls for you."

33   It was a sure-fire prophecy.

34   The Waifs' Home Band often played at picnics and social clubs. Because the boys loved to march, they were usually requested to parade up and down the streets of the city. And there was Louis Armstrong, up front, the leader of the band, blowing the cornet high and clear. He was so proud, dressed in a fancy uniform of cream-colored long pants, turned up at the ankles, and a snazzy blue gabardine coat. On days when the band marched down his old neighborhood, through the rough and tough streets of his birth, Back o' Town, he was most excited.

35   The crowds, jamming the sidewalks, recognized him. Gamblers, dancing girls, bartenders, and bouncers—they tossed all kinds of money at him. Enough coins to fill several hats. These he presented to the home. "Let's buy new uniforms for the band," he suggested. "Little Louis" was the pride and joy of the old neighborhood.

36   "Lookit that child blowin' 'at horn! 'At's Mayann's boy!"

37   "Oooweee! Listen to that kid's tone!"

38   "Dipper, play that thing!"

39   "Man, oh man, he's a baby Joe Oliver!"

40   He was a mature fourteen-year-old when he was released from the home and returned to his family. Louis Armstrong was ready to play the horn anywhere, anytime.

41   Life outside the home was a hard lot. Sure, jobs were plentiful for jazz musicians in New Orleans in 1914, but the pay wasn't good. Louis was a growing boy with a hearty appetite. His mother and sister had to eat, too. Luckily Mayann was a magnificent cook. She could make the finest of meals for as little as fifteen cents. Creole gumbo, cabbage and rice, and, of course, red beans and rice were among her special concoctions. Still poverty plagued the three Armstrongs.

42   His parents had been separated a long time. Though his father worked mighty hard in a turpentine factory, he contributed nothing to Mayann and the two children. It was hardly his fault. He barely earned enough to support his second family, with whom he was living. Thus a fourteen-year-old boy became the breadwinner. Louis held down two jobs.

43   During the day, from seven to five, he worked on a coal cart, hauled by a mule.

44   "Stone coal! Stone coal!" shouted the boy. "Five cents a bucket!"

45   He enjoyed this job. A lot of his customers were cabaret owners and night-lifers. On occasions when he made late evening deliveries, he was able to hear the music that came from the honky-tonks.

46   Often, with bucket in hand, he'd suddenly pause in the doorway.

47   "What're you doin' there, boy? Git a move on!" a woman with a hard, painted face barked at him. "Set down that bucket an' git!"

48   "I'm listenin', ma'am, just listenin'," the boy replied simply. "Mm! Mm! Just listen to Papa Joe! He's the King!" His hero, Joe Oliver, was playing cornet next door, with Kid Ory's Band at Pete Lala's Cafe. The boy waited till the end of the number. Then he'd continue with his chores, happily muttering, "Ump! Listen to 'im play that 'Panama.' What a punch! Nobody can shout a tune like Papa Joe!"

49   At night Louis put on his long pants and blew the cornet, himself, at Ponce's. It was one of the toughest places in town. Though there were frequent fights and squabbles, they all liked the young cornetist. "Our Little Louis, he's the best!" they shouted. "Play us a

"People never improve unless they look to some standard or example higher and better than themselves."

—Tyron Edwards

bit of blues, Dipper," murmured the women as they straggled in during the early hours of the morning. Sometimes the tips they shoved at him added up to more than his pay.

50   In the midst of life, Louis began to play everywhere, playing just as he felt. He was singing, too. "Sing it the way you play it," he said. "If you can't sing it, you can't play it."

51   Just as he was feeling his way toward a new style of playing, so he was reaching out toward a new style of singing. His voice was becoming as important as his horn. It was developing into a guttural baritone of great charm: one of intense feeling, deeply warm and joyous. He was beginning to use his voice as he used his horn, improvising, letting the spirit move him as it would. He wasn't worried about the words of a song; it was the *feeling* that counted. Though Louis was unaware of it at that time, it was a new style of singing that hundreds of others were to imitate many years later.

52   The folks of the neighborhood sensed the warmth and freedom of genius here and cheered him on—with shouts, applause, and lusty humor.

53   "Keep 'at up, little ol' boy. You'll be the shoutin'est horn blower in the whole wide worl'!" boomed "Slippers," the tough bouncer at Matranga's. It was at this place that Louis was leading his own band, at the age of seventeen. There was Black Benny, too. He was the number-one bass drummer of the city's street bands; also, he was the strongest man of the district. Whenever he attended crowded picnics, where Louis's comet would drive the folks wild, he'd handcuff the boy to himself with a handkerchief. "That's so's you don't git lost, kid. You're too good; somebody's li'ble to snatch you."

54   The man who taught Louis the most was Joe Oliver. They had met shortly after Louis left the Waifs' Home. Through these years he was the boy's closest friend. Patiently he revealed to him the mysteries of the cornet.

55   "Play that lead, son, you gotta play that lead. An' don't you ever forget it. Melody, don't you ever forget melody."

56   Young Armstrong never forgot the day this big, scar-eyed man gently shoved a battered cornet at him. "From me to you, Little Louis. It's been mighty good to me. You take it from here."

57   The boy was deeply moved. It was a well-used horn, but it was much better than his own.

58   "Why you doin' 'all this for me, Papa Joe?"

59   Oliver squinted at Louis and murmured softly: " 'Cause you're like a son to me— 'at's why. I never had a boy of my own. You might as well be it. I'll call you stepson, you call me stepfather. Yes, sir, that's it."

60   In 1918, Papa Joe was called to Chicago: It was a city crying for jazz. Thousands of Blacks had been moving up from the Deep South into Chicago. As the audience moved up north, there was a need for the music. Two jobs were offered to Oliver. He accepted both.

61   At the railroad depot, a whole crowd of musicians had come down to bid Oliver good-bye. It was a sad farewell. The big question was, who would take Papa Joe's chair as the lead cornet man with Kid Ory's Band? As the train pulled out, Ory called out to Louis, "Little Louis, you're elected. Run home, wash up, get your horn. You got yourself a steady job, startin' tonight. Oh—one more thing. Better start wearin' your long pants *all* the time. You're a *man,* now!"

62   The boy's heart was beating wildly. "Me settin' in Papa Joe's chair! Oh, I'll blow my heart out!"

63   There was no doubt about it. Young Armstrong was an immediate success. He remembered all that Oliver had taught him and played exactly as he had heard his idol play. He even wrapped a bath towel around his open collar, the way he had so often seen Papa Joe do. "So's I can blow free an' easy."

64   The modest boy was unaware that he was already surpassing his teacher. His tone was clearer and bigger; his drive was more exciting; his feeling was deeper. The signs were obvious to other musicians and to patrons that Louis Armstrong was lifting the art of the cornet, and of jazz itself, to lofty heights.

65   Kid Ory's Band was the most popular one in New Orleans. They played just about everywhere, for fancy parties as well as for rough-and-tumble get-togethers. Louis was the most sought-after jazzman. He had no days off. When the Ory group was resting, he'd be playing at some dance or funeral. Often he blew second cornet with the Papa Celestin's Tuxedo Brass Band. In later years he recalled, "I thought I was in heaven, playing with that band. They had funeral marches that would touch your heart they were so beautiful."

66   One day he was approached by a red-headed band leader. It was Fate Marable, the riverboat king. Excellent jazz was being played on the excursion boats that glided up and down the Mississippi. Easily the best of these boat bands was Marable's, of the steamer *Sydney.* His repertoire was far more varied than that of any New Orleans band. His men could *read* music.

67   "Come on, Louis," urged Fate. "Join us and see what the rest of the country looks like." Armstrong, eager for new adventures and new learning, readily accepted.

68   With Marable's band he unraveled the mystery of reading music. He discovered for the first time the meaning of those little marks on the lined sheets of paper, those curlicues and bars. Up to now, Louis had to listen to others play a song before he could tackle it. Now he was able to take off on his own.

69   Others were learning from Louis too, something even more important. People in Memphis, St. Louis, Davenport, all along the river wherever Armstrong was heard, were learning something: What is written on paper is not all there is to jazz music. A man must *feel* it, deep down inside. The curlicues and bars are only the beginning. The man, the musician, must take off from there. He must feel free. From Louis Armstrong they were learning the true meaning of jazz.

70   In 1922, a telegram was waiting for him. It was from Chicago. WILL YOU JOIN ME AT LINCOLN GARDENS? SALARY $30 A WEEK. SIGNED, JOE OLIVER.

71   A dream realized! At last he would be playing side by side with Papa Joe. As Louis sat in that day coach, heading for Chicago, he felt a pang of regret at leaving his beloved city and so many of his old friends. And yet his heart was pounding excitedly. He knew a fresh chapter in his life was just beginning.

72   It was a new chapter in the story of jazz, too.

✔ **PRETEST**

Multiple Choice

Directions: For each item, write the letter corresponding to the best answer.

A 1. The first instrument that Armstrong played was the
   a. tambourine.
   b. drums.
   c. bugle.
   d. cornet.

C 2. The best title for this selection would be
   a. "A Hard-Luck Life."
   b. "Move over Papa Joe."
   c. "Louis Armstrong, the early years."
   d. "Play It with Feeling."

b 3. Which of the following can you infer from this selection?
   a. Joe Oliver was jealous of his young disciple, Louis Armstrong.
   b. Armstrong's genius was recognized early in his career.
   c. The ability to read music was a largely wasted skill.
   d. Armstrong was not very influential in the history of jazz.

U 4. Even in his early years, Armstrong was noted for all of the following *except* for which?
   a. an innovative style of singing and playing
   b. making joyous music
   c. an improvisational style
   d. a poor work ethic

U 5. Armstrong developed his musical skills in all of the following ways *except* for which?
   a. learning to play the cornet at the Colored Waifs' Home for Boys
   b. learning to read music while working for Fate Marable
   c. practicing the violin for hours at a time
   d. "studying" under Joe Oliver

True or False

Directions: Indicate whether each statement is true or false by writing **T** or **F** in the space provided.

T 6. Armstrong was sent to a boys' home for waifs.

F 7. Under the instruction of Peter Davis, Armstrong learned how to play the clarinet.

F 8. Joe Oliver inspired and taught Louis Armstrong.

F 9. Joe Oliver moved west to California in search of a better life.

T 10. After Oliver left New Orleans, Armstrong took his chair in Kid Ory's Band.

T 11. Armstrong received an opportunity to join Joe Oliver in Chicago.

F 12. After playing with Oliver in Chicago, Armstrong played in Fate Marable's band, which performed on a Mississippi riverboat.

Vocabulary in Context

Directions: Without consulting a dictionary, write a definition in the blank provided for each of the following phrases.

1. in this fashion (paragraph 11.5) _Starting a trinten_
2. ripe for the cornet (paragraph 12.24) _Your ready to do this_
3. jumped for joy (paragraph 13.25) _Our raygeist for happhes_
4. it's not gravy (paragraph 14.26) _Frs not cosy_
5. a hunch (paragraph 15.32) _has a Idea_
6. sure-fire (paragraph 16.33) _Ir was good_
7. most sought-after (paragraph 17.65) _alwasy busy_
8. tackle it (paragraph 18.68) _Ger ir donc_

Understanding the Words in the Selection

Directions: In the blanks below, write the word from the list that best completes the sentence. Use each word only once.

admonished	glided	lofty	overwhelmed
amble	guttural	lowly	patrons
elated	idols	modest	surpassing

1. When the young child approached, the cat made a low _gatturn_ sound, which indicated that it did not want to be petted.

2. Because she was trying to work full-time, take care of her family, and attend college, Susan often felt _overwheld_ by her responsibilities.

3. Juan was _admonished_ to discover that his hard work had paid off with a full-ride scholarship to any college of his choice.

4. The young mother _____ her children to stay away from busy intersections.

5. After graduating with honors from college, she was expecting never to have to work at _____ jobs again.

6. No matter how famous he became, he remained a _____, unassuming person who never put on airs.

7. She didn't like to run or jog, instead preferring to _____ along at a relaxed pace.

8. Picasso was such a gifted artist that he was soon _Surpassing_ all of his teachers.

9. His _____ goal was to be president of the corporation.

10. Many young people revere sports stars as _____.

11. There are many _patrons_ of the arts who raise vast amounts of money for museums around the country.

12. The skaters _____ across the ice.

In Your Own Words

1. By all accounts, Louis Armstrong faced many hardships before becoming a successful musician. What character traits do you think helped him overcome adversity? What character traits helped him become successful?

2. Across the United States, many communities have banned celebratory gunfire. In fact, in many places it is now a felony to fire a gun in the air. And yet every year there are headlines like the following:

   "Stray bullet strikes, kills local girl."

   "Stray shot strikes girl; 11-year-old was waiting for fireworks."

   "Stray bullet hits infant; 5-month-old was in crib."

   What can be done to educate the public about the hazards of firing guns in the air?

3. What do you think Louis Armstrong meant by the following quotes?

   "You blows who you is."

   "If ya ain't got it in ya, ya can't blow it out."

Written Assignment

1. Write a few paragraphs explaining what the following quotes reveal about Armstrong's personal philosophy of life.

   "The memory of things gone is important to a jazz musician. Things like old folks singing in the moonlight in the back yard on a hot night or something said long ago. What we play is life."

   "My whole life, my whole soul, my whole spirit is to blow that horn."

2. Following are the lyrics from a song that was a favorite of Louis Armstrong. What do the lyrics reveal about his personal philosophy of life? What character traits is he demonstrating? Write a few paragraphs giving your opinion.

   "What a Wonderful World" by George Weiss and Bob Thiele

   I see trees of green, red roses too
   I see them bloom for me and you
   And I think to myself, what a wonderful world

   I see skies of blue and clouds of white
   The bright blessed day, the dark sacred night
   And I think to myself, what a wonderful world

   The colors of the rainbow, so pretty in the sky
   Are also on the faces of people going by
   I see friends shakin' hands, sayin' "How do you do?"
   They're really saying "I love you"

   I hear babies cryin', I watch them grow
   They'll learn much more than I'll ever know
   And I think to myself, what a wonderful world
   Yes, I think to myself, what a wonderful world

   Oh yeah!

Internet Activity

To learn more about Louis Armstrong, consult one of the following Web sites. Then write a short paragraph discussing your findings.

This is the official site of the Louis Armstrong house and archives:

www.satchmo.net

This is the Sony Records Armstrong site. The site provides biographical information as well as samples of his recordings.

www.louis-armstrong.net

This is the Rock and Roll Hall of Fame Web site. Armstrong was inducted into the Hall of Fame in 1990.

www.rockhall.com/inductee/louis-armstrong

A Short Poem

Pablo Neruda (1904–1973), widely regarded as the greatest Latin American poet of the 20th century, received the Nobel Prize for Literature in 1971. Neruda, whose real name is Ricardo Eliezer Neftali Reyes y Basoalto, was born in Parral, Chile, the son of a railroad worker. He began to write poetry as a young teenager and later studied to be a teacher. At one point in his life, he was forced into exile because of his political beliefs. The movie *Il Postino* is based on this period of his life. In addition to being a poet, he served as a Chilean diplomat in various foreign countries, including Burma, Ceylon, Argentina, Mexico, and France. The following is the last stanza from one of Neruda's poems, which was translated from Spanish by Professor Maria Jacketti and appears in *Neruda's Garden: An Anthology of Odes.*

"We are what we believe we are."

—Benjamin Cardoza

"Ode to the Present" by Pablo Neruda

You	Tú
are	eres tu presente,
your present,	tu manzana:
your own apple.	tómala
Pick it from	de tu árbol,
your tree.	levántala
Raise it	en tu mano,
in your hand.	brilla
It's gleaming,	como una estrella,
rich with stars.	tócala,
Claim it.	híncale el diente y ándate
Take a luxurious bite out	silbando en el camino.
of the present,	
and whistle along the road	
of your destiny.	

Pablo Neruda, "Oda al presente," from the work *Nuevas odas Elementales* © Fundación Pablo Neruda, 2008. English translation ("Ode to the Present") from *Neruda's Garden: An Anthology of Odes,* trans. Maria Jacketti. Pittsburgh, PA: The Latin American Review Press, 1995, p. 105. Reprinted by permission of Agencia Carmen Balcells.

Try to explain the meaning of the poem in your own words.

_____

_____

_____

_____

_____

Internet Activity

Type in Pablo Neruda's name in a search engine such as Google, MSN, or Yahoo!; find a Web site about Neruda; and write down five things you learned about him.

VOCABULARY | **Introduction**

One purpose of this book is to help you improve your reading and writing skills by expanding your vocabulary. Vocabulary and reading are like the chicken and the egg—which comes first? Your reading is made easier if you know more words; and the more reading you do, the more words you will learn. Is there an effortless way to learn more words and become a better reader? The answer is no. But there are some techniques that can help. Some of the techniques we will be working with are the following:

Context: When you come across an unfamiliar word in your reading, the first step you should take toward finding its meaning is to look for context clues. The context of a word is what surrounds it, which includes the sentence it appears in, other nearby sentences, and even the whole article. Try placing your finger over the unfamiliar word, and see if you can supply another word that gives the sentence meaning, or at least enough meaning for your purposes. Remember that if you are reading a light novel for enjoyment, the exact meaning of a word may not be as important as when you are reading your psychology textbook.

Let's try a sentence with a word you may not know. See if you can figure out the meaning of the word from the context of the sentence.

Imagine Sue's *chagrin* when she realized that all of the other women at the office party were wearing long dresses and she was wearing shorts.

You could go to the dictionary to look up the definition of *chagrin,* but you can probably guess from context clues that *chagrin* in this sentence means "embarrassment."

We use context clues all the time when we read cartoons. The following cartoon uses the word *comatose.* What do you think the word means?

Luann

LUANN: © GEC Inc./Dist. by United Feature Syndicate, Inc.

Structure: Word structure gives you a way to discover the meaning of a word by breaking it down into its parts. Knowing the meaning of a word's parts should help you decipher the word's meaning. Let's try an example:

Synchronized diving is a new Olympic sport that requires tremendous precision.

The word *synchronized* has in it the word parts *syn* and *chron*. *Syn* means "same" and *chron(o)* means "time." So, *synchronized* divers must leave the diving board at the same time, mirror each other's movements, and then enter the water in unison.

The eight vocabulary units inserted throughout the book will give you practice in using over 75 word parts. A complete list of these word parts is located at the end of Chapter 14.

"The first book of the nation is the dictionary of its language."

— Contanitin, Conte Volney

Dictionary: Often when people come across a word they don't know, their first thought is to look it up in the dictionary. But this should be your last way of determining the meaning of a word. It's best to try first to use context clues and word structure. If these methods don't give you an accurate enough definition, then go to the dictionary.

Before you grab the dictionary, it helps to know a little bit about the meaning of the word you are looking up. This is because the dictionary, which is a vast resource with much information (sometimes too much), may give several meanings, and you have to be able to select the appropriate one. For example, suppose in your reading you come across the following sentence and don't know what the word *annual* means:

The man decided to buy *annual* plants for his front yard.

You look up *annual* in your dictionary and find two definitions. The first definition may be "something happening once every year," and the second may be "a plant that lasts for one season or year." You can see that the second definition is the one that fits this sentence. If the man buys annual plants, let's hope that he doesn't expect them to bloom again.

We have placed the dictionary section in the Appendices. Your instructor may decide to have you work through that section as a class, or you can complete the exercises on your own. If nothing else, you should read the first part of that section before you purchase a dictionary.

Combination: In trying to determine the meaning of an unfamiliar word, you can use all of these techniques in combination. Take the following example:

Jay Leno is a *contemporary* of many of your instructors.

You may be thinking that *contemporary* means "modern or recent," but that meaning doesn't make sense in this context. *Con* means "with" and *temp* means "time or moderate." Now you are getting closer to the meaning in this sentence. The word *contemporary* as used here means "with time." Now go to the dictionary. You will find the definition "modern," but you will also find the definition "same time period or age group." So, Jay Leno is approximately the same age as many of your teachers.

Homonyms: As part of our vocabulary study, we also will be covering homonyms. Although homonyms are not a technique for discovering the meanings of unfamiliar words, we have included them because misuse of homonyms is a common mistake. *Homo* means "same" and *nym* means "name," so homonyms are words with the same "name," or pronunciation, but different spellings or meanings.

Look at the following sentence:

Your grandfather *passed* away.

A common mistake when writing such a sentence is to use the word *past* instead of *passed*. Because "passing away" is an action, it is a verb, and you need to use the word *passed*. In the section on homonyms, you will learn how to use many homonyms correctly.

Naming and Identity

What's in a Name?

What's in a name? Quite a bit, perhaps. Puff Daddy or P. Diddy is a more intriguing name for a pop star than Sean Combs. Madonna is more exotic than Madonna Ciccone. Bill Clinton is closer to the people than William Jefferson Clinton.

Our names and nicknames can also reflect our attitudes toward ourselves. Although we may have one legal given name, the variations or nicknames we select say something about our self-concepts. For example, are you a Bob, Bobby, or Robert? An Elizabeth, Betty, or Liz? Names have an influence on our perceptions.

According to Eric Berne, the names our parents give us and the way in which they refer to us often reflect their expectations about who we are to become:

> Charles and Frederick were kings and emperors. A boy who is steadfastly called Charles or Frederick by his mother, and insists that his associates call him that, lives a different life style from one who is commonly called Chuck or Fred.[1]

Names are not interchangeable. No child named Oliphant will tell you that his life would have been the same if he were called Michael. *When Harry Met Gertrude* could never be the title of a romantic movie; *Romeo and Sue Ann* doesn't sound like a Shakespearean tragedy. And Tragedy, well, as a name that would be a tragic mistake—one that psychologist and name expert Cleveland Evans, PhD, of Nebraska's Bellevue University, says some less-than-thoughtful parents actually make. "Obviously, names tell you more about the parents than about the kids," he says. "They reveal their values and goals for their children."[2]

How Important Is a Name?

Experts in child psychology say that while names may have powerful connotations, in the great scheme of things, they are not what determines an individual's personality, popularity, or future success. "There are other factors that are much more important," says Antonius Cillessen, PhD, assistant professor of psychology at the University of Connecticut and an expert in social development in middle childhood and early adolescence. "Names are sort of in the category of athletic ability and physical attractiveness. Most of us think those are of primary importance in determining a child's acceptance or happiness, but in truth factors such as ability to show concern for others and social behavior are far more significant."[3]

In the next couple of weeks, most of your instructors will be trying hard to learn the names of their students. They do this not only for convenience but also out of politeness—they know your name is important to your sense of identity. Think about how annoyed you become when your name is forgotten or mispronounced by someone who should know better. Many of you were given your name by a close relative who chose it because it had some personal significance. Perhaps it was the relative's name, or the name of a movie star or athlete the relative admired. Some people are even named after special places or the day of the week on which they were born.

"A human being's name is a principal component in his person, perhaps a piece of his soul."

—Sigmund Freud

[1]Spencer Rathus and Jeffrey Nevid, *Psychology and the Challenges of Life*, 8th Edition. New York: John Wiley & Sons, 2002, p. 81.

[2]Rathus and Nevid, p. 82.

[3]Rathus and Nevid, p. 83.

A long time ago, people were given names that had very specific meanings. For example, the name Peter, the first name of one of your authors, originally meant a "rock." The name Rita, the first name of your other author, meant a "pearl of great value." In the Middle Ages, many last names had meanings related to occupations. If someone was called Baker, that person probably made bread. If a person's last name was Smith, that person was probably a blacksmith. The name Mather, which is Peter's last name, means mower or reaper of hay. Although this may not sound too important, hay was used not only as feed for animals but also as bedding.

READING

"They call me Ted where I work and they've called me that for over a decade now and it still bothers me."

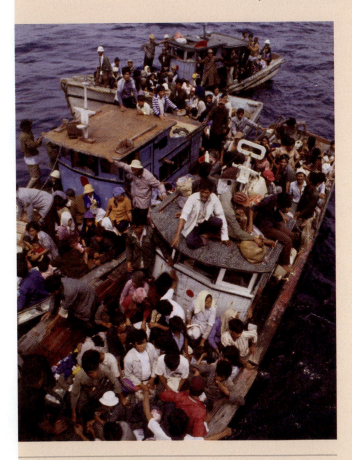

After the fall of South Vietnam to the North in 1975, thousands of Vietnamese fled the country, many—like the character Thieu in "Crickets"—in overcrowded, flimsy boats like these.

TUNING IN TO READING

Robert Olen Butler's short story "Crickets," which is excerpted below, explores how names may play a role in the process of becoming part of a new culture. People new to this country might choose to "Americanize" their names to avoid difficulties in pronunciation or to blend better into the dominant culture. Thus *Katya* might become *Kathy,* and *Jorge* might become *George.*

In "Crickets," the Vietnamese father, Thieu, recognizes that his son Bill, who was born in the United States, is now very different from him. Do you and your parents have different backgrounds? How has your background made you different from your parents? Read the following profile of the author before beginning the short story.

BIO-SKETCH

Robert Olen Butler won the 1993 Pulitzer Prize for Fiction for the collection of stories titled *A Good Scent from a Strange Mountain.* The short story "Crickets," which appears in that collection, is written from the perspective of an immigrant from Vietnam and describes the difficulties of adjusting to American society. Butler gained knowledge of the Vietnamese culture when he served during the Vietnam War as both a U.S. Army intelligence officer and an interpreter. Many of his novels are based on his Vietnam experiences. Butler feels that fiction about Vietnam "has not dealt adequately with the Vietnamese people; it has not found their humanity." He says this is because most novels about the Vietnamese are written from the viewpoint of the American soldier facing an enemy in a time of war. Butler currently lives in Lake Charles, Louisiana, where he is a professor of English and creative writing at McNeese State University. Butler has published 13 books, including *Mr. Spaceman, Tabloid Dreams,* and *Had a Good Time.*

READING *continued*

NOTES ON VOCABULARY

bowler   a low-crowned, hard felt hat. *Bowler* is the common British name for what Americans call a "derby." Some say that the bowler was so named because of its resemblance to a bowling ball.

bayou   a small, marshy stream or inlet. The word *bayou* is the Louisiana French version of *bayuk,* used by the Choctaw Indians, the original inhabitants of the region.

bluff   to fool or attempt to fool someone by acting very sure of oneself. The word is derived from the late-17th-century Dutch word *bluffen* or *bluf,* which meant "to brag." In the mid-19th century, the term was used in the United States to refer to *bluffing* in the game of poker. In poker, it is common to *bluff,* or pretend that one has better cards than one's opponents. If someone *calls your bluff* in poker, it means he or she is forcing you to reveal your cards.

muster   gather, summon, assemble, often for military service. The word is derived from the Latin word *monstrare,* meaning "to show." The antonym is *muster out,* which means "leaving the service or being discharged." In addition, people use the term *to pass muster,* meaning "to meet a required standard." In the military, troops are required to assemble and *pass muster* (inspection).

Crickets

Robert Olen Butler

In the margin:

In 1682, the French explorer Sieur de La Salle explored what became known as the Louisiana Territory. He named it after the king of France at the time, Louis XIV. Later, in 1803, France sold the Louisiana Territory to the United States for $15 million. This purchase by President Thomas Jefferson doubled the size of the United States.

They call me Ted where I work and they've called me that for over a decade now and it still bothers me, though I'm not very happy about my real name being the same as the former President of the former Republic of Vietnam. Thieu is not an uncommon name in my homeland and my mother had nothing more in mind than a long-dead uncle when she gave it to me. But in Lake Charles, Louisiana, I am Ted. I guess the other Mr. Thieu has enough of my former country's former gold bullion tucked away so that in London, where he probably wears a bowler and carries a rolled umbrella, nobody's calling him anything but Mr. Thieu.

2   I hear myself sometimes and I sound pretty bitter, I guess. But I don't let that out at the refinery, where I'm the best chemical engineer they've got and they even admit it once in a while. They're good-hearted people, really. I've done enough fighting in my life. I was 18 when Saigon fell and I was only recently mustered into the Army, and when my unit dissolved and everybody ran, I stripped off my uniform and put on my civilian clothes again and I threw rocks at the North's tanks when they rolled through the streets. Very few of my people did likewise. I stayed in the mouths of alleys so I could run and then return and throw more rocks, but because what I did seemed so isolated and so pathetic a gesture, the gunners in the tanks didn't even take notice. But I didn't care about their scorn. At least my right arm had said no to them.

3 And then there were Thai pirates in the South China Sea and idiots running the refugee centers and more idiots running the agencies in the United States to find a place for me and my new bride, who braved with me the midnight escape by boat and the terrible sea and all the rest. We ended up here in the flat bayou land of Louisiana, where there are rice paddies and where the water and the land are in the most delicate balance with each other, very much like the Mekong Delta, where I grew up. These people who work around me are good people and maybe they call me Ted because they want to think of me as one of them, though sometimes it bothers me that these men are so much bigger than me. I am the size of a woman in this country and these American men are all massive and they speak so slowly, even to one another, even though English is their native language. I've heard New Yorkers on television, and I speak as fast as they do.

4 My son is beginning to speak like the others here in Louisiana. He is 10, the product of the first night my wife and I spent in Lake Charles, in a cheap motel with the sky outside red from refineries. He is proud to have been born in America, and when he leaves us in the morning to walk to the Catholic school, he says, "Have a good day, y'all." Sometimes I say good-bye to him in Vietnamese and he wrinkles his nose at me and says, "Aw Pop," like I'd just cracked a corny joke. He doesn't speak Vietnamese at all and my wife says not to worry about that. He's an American.

5 But I do worry about that, though I understand why I should be content. I even understood 10 years ago, so much so that I agreed with my wife and gave my son an American name. Bill. Bill and his father Ted. But this past summer I found my son hanging around the house bored in the middle of vacation and I was suddenly his father Thieu with a wonderful idea for him. It was an idea that had come to me in the first week of every February we'd been in Lake Charles, because that's when the crickets always begin to crow here. This place is rich in crickets, which always makes me think of my own childhood in Vietnam. But I never said anything to my son until last summer.

6 I came to him after watching him slouch around the yard one Sunday pulling the Spanish moss off the lowest branches of our big oak tree and then throwing rocks against the stop sign on our corner. "Do you want to do something fun?" I said to him.

7 "Sure, Pop," he said, though there was a certain suspicion in his voice, like he didn't trust me on the subject of fun. He threw all the rocks at once that were left in his hand and the stop sign shivered at their impact.

8 I said, "If you keep that up, they will arrest me for the destruction of city property and then they will deport us all."

9 My son laughed at this. I, of course, knew that he would know I was bluffing. I didn't want to be too hard on him for the boyish impulses that I myself had found to be so satisfying when I was young, especially since I was about to share something of my own childhood with him.

10 "So what've you got, Pop?" my son asked me.

11 "Fighting crickets," I said.

12 "What?"

13 Now, my son was like any of his fellow 10-year-olds, devoted to superheroes and the mighty clash of good and evil in all of its high-tech forms in the Saturday-morning cartoons. Just to make sure he was in the right frame of mind, I explained it to him with

one word, "Cricketmen," and I thought this was a pretty good ploy. He cocked his head in interest at this and I took him to the side porch and sat him down and I explained.

14   I told him how, when I was a boy, my friends and I would prowl the undergrowth and capture crickets and keep them in matchboxes. We would feed them leaves and bits of watermelon and bean sprouts, and we'd train them to fight by keeping them in a constant state of agitation by blowing on them and gently flicking the ends of their antennas with a sliver of wood. So each of us would have a stable of fighting crickets, and there were two kinds.

15   At this point my son was squirming a little bit and his eyes were shifting away into the yard and I knew that my Cricketman trick had run its course. I fought back the urge to challenge his set of interests. Why should the stiff and foolish fights of his cartoon characters absorb him and the real clash—real life and death—that went on in the natural world bore him? But I realized that I hadn't cut to the chase yet, as they say on the TV. "They fight to the death," I said with as much gravity as I could put into my voice, like I was James Earl Jones.

16   The announcement won me a glance and a brief lift of his eyebrows. This gave me a little scrabble of panic, because I still hadn't told him about the two types of crickets and I suddenly knew that was a real important part for me. I tried not to despair at his understanding and I put my hands on his shoulders and turned him around to face me. "Listen," I said. "You need to understand this if you are to have fighting crickets." There are two types, and all of us had some of each. One type we called the charcoal crickets. These were very large and strong, but they were slow and they could become confused. The other type was small and brown and we called them fire crickets. They weren't as strong, but they were very smart and quick."

17   "So who would win?" my son said.

18   "Sometimes one and sometimes the other. The fights were very long and full of hard struggle. We'd have a little tunnel made of paper and we'd slip a sliver of wood under the cowling of our cricket's head to make him mad and we'd twirl him by his antenna, and then we'd each put our cricket into the tunnel at opposite ends. Inside, they'd approach each other and begin to fight and then we'd lift the paper tunnel and watch."

19   "Sounds neat," my son said, though his enthusiasm was at best moderate, and I knew I had to act quickly.

20   So we got a shoe box and we started looking for crickets. It's better at night, but I knew for sure his interest wouldn't last that long. Our house is up on blocks because of the high water table in town and we crawled along the edge, pulling back the bigger tufts of grass and turning over rocks. It was one of the rocks that gave us our first crickets, and my son saw them and cried in my ear, "There, there," but he waited for me to grab them. I cupped first one and then the other and dropped them into the shoe box and I felt a vague disappointment, not so much because it was clear that my boy did not want to touch the insects, but that they were both the big black ones, the charcoal crickets. We crawled on and we found another one in the grass and another sitting in the muddy shadow of the house behind the hose faucet, and then we caught two more under an azalea bush.

21   "Isn't that enough?" my son demanded. "How many do we need?"

22   I sat with my back against the house and put the shoe box in my lap and my boy sat beside me, his head stretching this way so he could look into the box. There was no more vagueness to my feeling. I was actually weak with disappointment because all six of these were charcoal crickets, big and inert and just looking around like they didn't even know anything was wrong.

23   "Oh, no," my son said with real force, and for a second I thought he had read my mind and shared my feeling, but I looked at him and he was pointing at the toes of his white sneakers. "My Reeboks are ruined!" he cried, and on the toe of each sneaker was a smudge of grass.

"Don't limit a child to your own learning, for he was born in another time."

—Rabbinical saying

24   I glanced back into the box and the crickets had not moved, and I looked at my son and he was still staring at his sneakers. "Listen," I said, "this was a big mistake. You can go on and do something else."

25   He jumped up at once. "Do you think Mom can clean these?" he said.

26   "Sure," I said. "Sure."

27   He was gone at once and the side door slammed and I put the box on the grass. But I didn't go in. I got back on my hands and knees and I circled the entire house and then I turned over every stone in the yard and dug around all the trees. I found probably two dozen more crickets, but they were all the same. In Louisiana there are rice paddies and some of the bayous look like the Delta, but many of the birds are different, and why shouldn't the insects be different too? This is another country, after all. It was just funny about the fire crickets. All of us kids rooted for them, even if we were fighting with one of our own charcoal crickets. A fire cricket was a very precious and admirable thing.

28   The next morning my son stood before me as I finished my breakfast, and once he had my attention, he looked down at his feet, drawing my eyes down as well. "See?" he said. "Mom got them clean."

29   Then he was out the door, and I called after him, "See you later, Bill."

 COMPREHENSION CHECKUP

Multiple Choice

Directions: For each item, write the letter corresponding to the best answer.

_____ 1. What reason does Thieu give for feeling bothered in his new homeland?
    a. He is smaller than most American men.
    b. His coworkers call him by his Vietnamese name.
    c. He is a chemical engineer.
    d. None of the above.

_____ 2. Which of the following would be true about Thieu?
    a. He likes his Vietnamese name, Thieu, because it is the same name as the former president of the Republic of Vietnam.
    b. He has no problem with his American name, Ted.
    c. His name was given to him by his mother.
    d. He had an easy time getting to the United States from Vietnam.

_____ 3. In paragraph 2, Thieu's "isolated and pathetic" gesture
   a. was ignored by the men in the tanks because he could do no real harm to them.
   b. resulted in his arrest by the authorities.
   c. was meant as an act of defiance.
   d. both a and c.

___A___ 4. What actions on the part of his son concern Thieu?
   a. His son does not speak Vietnamese.
   b. His son is disturbed by things like grass stains on his shoes.
   c. His son is too interested in cartoon characters.
   d. All of the above.

___b___ 5. The charcoal crickets were
   a. hard to find in the Louisiana soil.
   b. bigger than the fire crickets.
   c. small but very smart.
   d. the crickets that the Vietnamese children always rooted for.

True or False

Directions: Indicate whether each statement is true or false by writing **T** or **F** in the space provided.

___T___ 6. Bill was born in Vietnam and then moved to the United States as a young child.

___T___ 7. Bill feels more Vietnamese than American.

___T___ 8. Thieu uses the term "Cricketmen" as a hook to spark his son's interest in finding the crickets.

___F___ 9. Bill displays little interest in trying to locate the fire crickets.

___T___ 10. As a boy growing up in Vietnam, Thieu trained crickets to fight.

Vocabulary

Directions: Using a dictionary, define the following words. Then use each of the words in a sentence. You may change or add endings. The paragraph number in parentheses tells you where the word is located in the story.

1. pathetic (paragraph 2) _Miserably_

2. massive (paragraph 3) _Large and heavy or solid_

3. slouch (paragraph 6) _Stand, move, or sit in a lazy, drooping way_

4. devoted (paragraph 13) _Very Loving or Loyal_

5. agitation (paragraph 14) _a state of anxiety or nervous excitement_

In Your Own Words

1. Why are the two types of crickets of such importance to Thieu? What do the two types of crickets represent in terms of human beings?

2. What is the significance of the son's concern for his soiled Reeboks?

3. What is the father acknowledging when he excuses his son from searching for more crickets?

4. What does the father hope to gain by continuing the search alone?

5. How do we know that the father has come to terms with his son's allegiance to another culture?

Written Assignment

Directions: Choose one of the following activities to complete.

1. Do you ever wish that you had a different name? Choose a new name for yourself, and explain in a paragraph the reasons behind your choice. For instance, you might choose the name Dawn because that is your favorite part of the day.

2. When George W. Bush was running for president, it was reported that he had a habit of giving nicknames to those individuals he had close contact with on a daily basis. What are your feelings about nicknames? Do you like or dislike them? Did you have any nicknames while you were growing up? Did they affect you in any way? If you could choose your own nickname, what would it be, and why? Write a paragraph on this issue.

3. In your culture, how do you address people to show respect? How do you address people who are older than you? People in positions of authority? When do you address people with their first name only? Their last name? Using personal examples as illustrations, write a paragraph in which you discuss these issues.

4. If you are already familiar with the Internet, you can use it to explore the meaning of your name and then write a paragraph describing your findings. Go to a search engine and type in "names and meanings." There are a variety of Web sites devoted to the meanings of names. One of the more complete Web sites related to names is www.behindthename.com. See if you can locate your name and its meaning. Did the people who named you take the meaning of your name into account when they gave it to you? If not, what were their reasons for giving you your name?

"Names" Group Exercise

1. Gather in groups of four. Each group has four sheets of paper that have columns for males and females. One sheet is for your grandparents' generation (over 60); another is for your parents' generation (between 40 and 60); another is for young adults (between 20 and 40); and the last one is for children. Each person in the group should list the names of family members in the appropriate columns. When each of you has contributed to each sheet, study the lists to find patterns for how people are named. For instance:

   Do the names reflect ethnic, cultural, or religious heritage?

   Do the names have unusual spellings?

   Do the female names tend to be more creative than the male names?

   Have the names changed over the generations? If so, how?

   Do you see any reasons for the popularity of particular names?

   Are names repeated from one generation to another? If so, why?

2. Almost all English and Continental surnames (last names) fall into four basic categories: place names, patronyms, occupational names, and personal descriptions. Place names derive from names of actual places or descriptions of places close to where an ancestor lived. Patronyms are derived from the name of a father or other ancestor. Patronyms are often created by adding a suffix or prefix indicating descent, as in Johnson (son of John) or McDonald (son of Donald). Occupational

names derive from the occupations of an ancestor. Personal description names derive from physical attributes of ancestors such as height. For example, John Long probably had a tall ancestor.

Example

Place names	Winston Churchill (church on a hill)
Patronyms	David Robinson, Ronald McDonald
Occupational names	Anne Archer, Karen Carpenter
Personal descriptions	Henry Wadsworth Longfellow, Martin Short

Go through this list of well-known individuals, and state into which category each surname fits.

Faith Hill	Clint Eastwood
Justin Timberlake	Alan Greenspan
Jesse Jackson	Martin Luther King Jr.
Paul Newman	Chris Rock
Harry Truman	Vanna White
Tiger Woods	George W. Bush
Bill Gates	David Letterman
Conan O' Brian	Holly Hunter
Neil Armstrong	John McCain
Pamela Anderson	Will Smith
Larry Bird	John Goodman

Can you think of any other examples?

3. For some people today, names matter, especially when applied to sports teams and mascots. Of particular sensitivity are names and symbols that seem to mock or demean Native Americans, such as the team name Savages and tomahawk-wielding mascots.

In 2005 the National Collegiate Athletic Association (NCAA) adopted a new policy to prohibit the display of abusive racial or ethnic names, mascots, or imagery at any of the 88 NCAA championships. Some 18 colleges and university teams felt the impact of the policy, ranging from the Florida State Seminoles to the Southeast Oklahoma University Savages.

Designed to promote cultural respect, the policy soon ran into trouble. Some people objected that the ruling prohibited even positive team names like Warriors and Chieftains just because they referred to Native Americans. At the same time, similar names that referred to other groups, such as Trojans and Aztecs, were tolerated. As one editorial writer put it, that sends "a message that Native Americans are sensitive in a way that other groups are not."[1] Others argued that the policy did not go far enough in ridding sports of insulting references.

This controversy is likely to linger in political and legal circles for years and to spark endless debate. For some, Native American names and mascots represent a way of honoring a group; for others, that same use represents racism. What is your opinion or this issue?[2]

---

[1]From the *Boston Globe*, June 5, 2005.
[2]From Judy Pearson, *Human Communication*, 3rd Edition. New York: McGraw-Hill, 2008, p. 32.

Internet Activity

Do you want to find out how popular your first name is? Visit www.babynamewizard.com/voyager and click on "NameVoyager." Has your name become more or less fashionable over time? What year was your name the most popular? Write a short paragraph discussing your results.

Chapter Summary and Review

In this chapter, you were given an introduction to college. You learned how to keep track of your assignments, analyzed your motivations for attending college, and learned how to unlock the meaning of words. Based on the material in the Introduction, answer the following questions.

Short Answer

Directions: Answer the questions briefly, in a few sentences or paragraphs.

1. Which type of assignment sheet works best for you? Explain what you like about it. If you want to use another method of keeping track of your assignments, describe the method you are going to use.

2. What are some ways for improving your vocabulary?

Vocabulary in Context

Directions: Choose one of the following words to complete the sentences below. Use each word only once.

dictionary	homonyms	structure

3. Understanding word _____ helps you unlock the meanings of words.

4. A good way to confirm the meaning of a word is to use your _____.

5. _____ are pronounced the same but have different meanings and are usually spelled differently.

1

How We Learn

Finding Out about Ourselves

CHAPTER PREVIEW
In this chapter, you will

- Discover your preferred learning style.

- Learn techniques for using context to discover the meanings of new words.

- Assess your stress level and learn ways of dealing with stress.

- Develop a study schedule compatible with your learning style.

- Become familiar with homonyms and other confusing words.

- Practice using SQ3R.

- Become familiar with evaluating Internet sites.

Auditory, Visual, or Kinesthetic

What Is Your Learning Style?

In this chapter you are going to discover a little bit more about yourself. Are you the kind of person who works best at night or during the day? Are you a visual learner or an auditory one? What kinds of things are most likely to cause stress in your life? We will be trying to answer these and many other questions in the pages that follow.

Each of us is an individual with particular strengths and weaknesses. If you want to do better in school, you must learn how to use your strengths and minimize your weaknesses. Research is beginning to demonstrate that most of us have a learning style that will work best for us.

Your learning style is partially dependent on whether you are a visual, auditory, or kinesthetic learner. The following test will help you determine your learning style. Keep in mind that there are no right or wrong answers.

Adult Learning Styles Inventory

Directions: Read each question and place a check mark on the appropriate line. If the question doesn't directly apply to you, think of a similar situation that might apply to you.

	Often	Sometimes	Seldom
1. I need to see a map or written directions to drive to someone's house.	_____	_____	_____
2. I remember material from a lecture without studying, or I have to tape the lecture and play the tape.	_____	_____	_____
3. I feel comfortable touching others, shaking hands, etc.	_____	_____	_____
4. I would rather learn a new recipe from a TV show than from a recipe book.	_____	_____	_____
5. When I watch sports on TV, I pay more attention to the play than to the explanation of the play by the announcers.	_____	_____	_____
6. I enjoy sewing, cooking, gardening, or working with tools.	_____	_____	_____
7. I remember a news event best by reading about it in a newspaper or magazine.	_____	_____	_____
8. I am good at making and interpreting graphs and charts.	_____	_____	_____
9. In order to learn material, I write notes over and over again.	_____	_____	_____
10. Without writing them down, I remember oral directions for assignments well.	_____	_____	_____
11. I smoke, chew gum, or play with coins or keys in my pockets.	_____	_____	_____
12. In order to learn material, I read notes out loud to myself.	_____	_____	_____
13. When taking a trip, I would rather drive than be responsible for giving directions or reading a map.	_____	_____	_____
14. When I encounter a new word while I am reading, I usually sound it out.	_____	_____	_____
15. When I am trying to learn something, I form pictures in my mind.	_____	_____	_____

	Often	Sometimes	Seldom
16. When I am studying for a test, I can visualize my notes on the page.	___	___	___
17. I frequently tap my pencil or my pen.	___	___	___
18. When oral introductions are made at a party, I am likely to remember the names of people I have not met before.	___	___	___

Score your test below. For each question, give yourself 5 points if you answered "often," 3 points if you answered "sometimes," and 1 point if you answered "seldom." For example, if you answered "often" to question 1, you would place a 5 on the line next to that question. When you have finished, add up the points for each column.

Visual	Auditory	Kinesthetic
1. ___	2. ___	3. ___
5. ___	4. ___	6. ___
7. ___	10. ___	9. ___
8. ___	12. ___	11. ___
15. ___	14. ___	13. ___
16. ___	18. ___	17. ___
Totals ___	___	___

Now look at the differences between the totals for each learning style. A small difference—say, less than 4 points—doesn't mean much, but larger differences do. The larger the difference, the more dominant your learning style. For example, if your total for visual learning far exceeds the other two totals, this would be a good indication that you are basically a visual learner.

As you work through this book, you will be introduced to various study techniques. One study technique is placing notes in the margins of the text. Look at the sample margin notes for visual learners and then fill in the blanks for the other two types of learners.

Eye Smart

Visual Learner

Definition: learns best by seeing

Application: highlights key points, and recopies notes

What does it mean to be a visual learner? A **visual learner** is one who learns best by seeing. Visual learners like to use textbooks, course outlines, maps, diagrams, and charts. Their goal is to be able to visualize the subject they are trying to learn. Visual learners prefer teachers who use a whiteboard, an overhead projector, or PowerPoint slides over ones who primarily talk. Visual learners often have a superior ability to visualize pages of print. They learn material well by highlighting key points and by copying and recopying their notes. Most people are visual learners.

Ear Smart

Auditory Learner

Definition: _____

_____

What does it mean to be an auditory learner? An **auditory learner** is one who learns best through hearing. Auditory learners have a superior ability to hear and remember sounds in their mind. Auditory learners like to listen, and they prefer teachers who lecture and encourage discussion. They learn material well by talking to themselves and

Application: _____
_____
_____
_____

_____

Kinesthetic Learner
Definition: _____
_____

Application: _____
_____
_____
_____

repeating words and phrases out loud. If you are an auditory learner, you might learn best by reading your textbook out loud or by studying with a friend and talking through the key points. Auditory learners might do very well in class group activities. Many people are auditory learners.

Action Smart

What does it mean to be a kinesthetic learner? **Kinesthetic learners,** who are the smallest group, learn best by doing and performing. They are hands-on, or tactile, learners. They have a superior ability to remember their actions. Kinesthetic learners like to be in movement while learning. Their special talent is in associating ideas and concepts with motion. When learning material, they may prefer to gesture or walk around. These students need to take frequent short study breaks. It is a good idea for kinesthetic learners to take notes and underline key points as they read. Kinesthetic learners might benefit from taking part in classroom skits and role-playing activities.

Keep in mind, though, that even if one of your scores was way above the other two, all that the test results show is a *tendency* on your part. For example, if you have a high score for auditory learning, this just means that you tend to be an auditory learner, but you are still likely to have a significant ability to learn in visual and kinesthetic ways. Most of us learn best by using some combination of all three learning styles. Suppose, for example, you want to learn how to ski. You might attend a lecture where someone discusses how to ski (auditory). Or you might watch a video in which someone demonstrates skiing techniques (visual). Or you might strap on a pair of skis and go down the beginner slope (kinesthetic). But the person who involves all three learning styles by doing all three things might learn to ski faster. The trick is to find the combination that works best for you.

VOCABULARY / Words in Context

One technique for discovering the meaning of unfamiliar words is the use of context clues. By paying attention to what an author is saying, we may discover the meanings of words without having to look them up in the dictionary. As you will see, often our own background or experiences also will help us determine the meanings of unfamiliar words. Here are some common techniques for using context to determine the meaning of new words.

Definition: Sometimes a writer simply provides us with a definition of a word somewhere within the sentence, especially if the word is one that we are unlikely to be familiar with:

> A *thesaurus,* or dictionary that lists synonyms, antonyms, and other related words, can help you express your ideas more clearly and effectively.

You can see that the author defines a *thesaurus* as a special type of dictionary.

Synonym: A synonym, which is another word with a similar meaning, may be used elsewhere in the sentence.

> Four types of objects *revolve* around the sun; however, the planets are the largest objects that circle our fiery star.

If you did not know the meaning of *revolve,* you could determine its meaning from the word *circle.* To circle and to revolve mean approximately the same thing.

Antonym: Sometimes you can determine the meaning of a word by finding an antonym, a word with an opposite meaning, somewhere in the sentence.

> Gustavo was a very skillful soccer player, but Pedro was *inept*.

You can see that the writer is making a contrast, and that skillful is the opposite of *inept*.

Examples: Sometimes examples illustrate the meaning of a word.

> In a *brazen* act of defiance, Marco lit his cigarette while standing in front of a "No Smoking" sign and then refused to put it out when asked to do so.

This example suggests to you that a *brazen* act is one that is bold and shameless.

Explanation: Sometimes a writer simply gives an explanation of what a word means.

> In your communications class, you will probably have to give an *impromptu* speech. For this type of speech, you will be given a topic and only a few minutes to prepare your talk.

The writer is telling you that an *impromptu* speech is one that is given with very little preparation.

Experience: This way of discovering the meaning of a word draws on your personal experience.

> Have your efforts to complete a paper for a class ever been *thwarted* because your computer broke down?

Perhaps you have experienced this or a similar situation, and you remember that your efforts were "hindered" or "frustrated" at least for the time being.

Knowledge of Subject: In this technique, you have just enough familiarity with the subject the writer is discussing to enable you to figure out the meaning of the unknown word.

> Although many Americans often diet, many have difficulty maintaining a *svelte* shape for more than a few months.

You know that people often diet to make themselves "slim" or "slender."

Combination: Can you use a number of these techniques at the same time to detect the meaning of a word? You bet!

> The man at the party was a real *extrovert*. He acted like a clown and had everyone laughing the whole evening.

Here you probably used explanation, experience, and familiarity with the subject to determine that an *extrovert* is a very outgoing person.

Now work with a partner on the following exercises. Remember, no peeking at your dictionary.

Context Clue Practice 1

Directions: On the first line, write your own definition for the italicized word. Then on the second line note the technique you used to arrive at the definition. The first item is done for you.

1. Everyone in the family was *elated* to discover that Howard had the winning million-dollar lottery ticket in his pocket.

   Definition: __jubilant; overjoyed__

   Technique(s) used: __knowledge of subject, explanation, maybe experience__

2. Believing the 12-year-old offender to be *contrite,* the judge decided to give him another chance before putting him in juvenile detention.

Definition: _to Punish him_

Technique(s) used: _____

3. Should football games be canceled because of *inclement* weather?

Definition: _to be canceled_

Technique(s) used: _____

4. Should sexually *explicit* scenes be deleted from movies when they are shown on television?

Definition: _have sexually intercouse_

Technique(s) used: _graph_

5. Carol was extremely relieved to discover that her tumor was *benign* rather than malignant and so she would require no further treatment.

Definition: _not Sever_

Technique(s) used: _____

6. Her house was so *immaculate* that you could literally eat off the floor.

Definition: _very clean_

Technique(s) used: _____

7. Many boys in high school *aspire* to be professional athletes, but very few are actually good enough to make it to the professional ranks.

Definition: _want to be_

Technique(s) used: _____

8. The FBI conducted *covert,* or secret, operations to find out information about the drug-smuggling ring.

Definition: _Something un Puili_

Technique(s) used: _____

9. Many students are not *affluent* enough to attend college without working part-time or receiving some type of financial assistance.

Definition: _At very not Surro_

Technique(s) used: _____

Context Clue Practice 2

Directions: Use the context clues in the second sentence to define the italicized word in the first. Circle the clue word (or words) in the second sentence that provided the clue(s).

1. "Yes, this computer is *obsolete,*" said Matt. "But out of date or not, it's too expensive to replace."

2. "I can't accept any *remuneration* for taking care of your dog while you were in the hospital," said Carrie. "Nonsense dear," said Mrs. Watson, "you should get paid for doing a good deed."

3. It would be *presumptuous* to accuse him of the crime. Taking him in for questioning without solid evidence would simply be too bold.

4. Mountain climbing is full of *hazards.* However, the adventure is worth all of the risks.

5. He considered it an *indignity* for his parents to ignore his college graduation. He couldn't envision a worse insult.

6. Martha complained that she was getting tired of *goading* her son to do his homework. At his age, he should be able to finish it without her urging.

7. Some people *feign* injuries after their car is rear-ended. They don't stop pretending until they have received a cash settlement.

8. Todd, the pilot of our small airplane, seemed very *apprehensive* about taking off during the storm. His anxious behavior was upsetting the passengers.

9. I was certain he was *despondent* because he hadn't smiled all week. Perhaps he had good reason to be so depressed.

10. The teacher was *cognizant* of the difficulties involved in learning a new language. Her awareness was based on the fact that she too had once emigrated from her homeland.

11. In the United States, many families celebrate Thanksgiving with a *sumptuous* meal. However, after the lavish feast, many Americans begin dieting in earnest.

Context Clue Practice 3

Directions: Use the context clues in each sentence to help determine the missing word. Briefly describe the clue or clues that helped you.

1. If you believe that you control your own destiny, you have an internal locus of control; however, if you believe that your fate is determined by chance or outside forces, you have an ___external___ locus of control.

   Clue: ___either___

2. Successful students are naturally ___smart___ because they have a hopeful attitude and believe that effort, good study habits, and self-discipline will make their grades go up. "They can because they think they can."

   Clue: ___t___

3. Students exhibit what is called self-serving bias. When they get an exam grade back, if they did well they tend to accept personal credit. They consider the exam to be a valid indication of their abilities. However, if they did very poorly, they are much more likely to ___discredit___ the teacher or the exam.

   Clue: _____

4. Interestingly enough, teachers do the same thing. They are likely to take credit for whatever success is associated with their students and blame the student for any ___failure___. "Teachers, it seems, are likely to think, 'With my help, Maria graduated with honors. Despite all my help, Melinda flunked out.'"

   Clue: _____

5. College students need to be especially careful about those with whom they associate. Researchers have verified that students learn more from their friends and other students than they do from their ___teachers___ or from books. Out-of-class relationships are clearly the major influence in a student's life.

   Clue: _____

From David G. Myers, *Social Psychology,* 8th Edition, p. 59. Copyright © 2005 by The McGraw-Hill Companies, Inc. Reprinted with permission.

Day versus Night People

Are You More of a Morning Lark or a Night Owl?

You probably already have some idea whether you are more alert in the morning, afternoon, or evening. The following test is intended to determine whether you are a morning person or a night person. Answer the questions and then add up your points to determine your score.

	Points Possible	Points Earned

1. I feel best if I get up around

5–6:30 A.M.	5	
6:30–7:30 A.M.	4	
7:30–9:30 A.M.	3	
9:30–11 A.M.	2	
11–noon	1	_____

2. If I had to describe how easy it is for me to get up in the morning, I would say

it is not easy at all!	1	
it is not very easy.	2	
it is fairly easy.	3	
it is very easy.	4	_____

3. The way I feel for the first half-hour after I wake up is

very tired.	1	
fairly tired.	2	
fairly refreshed.	3	
very refreshed.	4	_____

4. If I could choose the best time to take a difficult test, it would be

8–10 A.M.	4	
10 A.M.–1 P.M.	3	
1–5 P.M.	2	
7–9 P.M.	1	_____

5. If my job would require that I work from 4 to 6 A.M. one day, I would choose to

not go to bed until after I worked.	1	
take a nap before and sleep after.	2	
sleep before work and nap after.	3	
get all the sleep I need before work.	4	_____

6. If someone asked me to jog with them at 7 A.M. one morning, I would perform

well.	4	
reasonably well.	3	
not very well.	2	
not well at all.	1	_____

	Points Possible	Points Earned

7. If I have to wake up at a specific time each morning, I

don't depend on my alarm at all.	4	
depend on my alarm slightly.	3	
depend on my alarm quite a lot.	2	
depend on my alarm desperately.	1	_____

8. I am usually tired and wanting to go to bed by

8–9 P.M.	5	
9–10:30 P.M.	4	
10:30 P.M.–12:30 A.M.	3	
12:30–2 A.M.	2	
2–3 A.M.	1	_____

Total Number of Points Earned _____

An average score would be 17. The higher the score, the more of a morning or day person you are; the lower the score, the more of an evening person you are.

From Gary Funk and Jan Bradley, *Thrills, Spills, and Study Skills.* Dubuque, IA: Kendall/Hunt, 1992, pp. 65–66.

In another section, we will show you how to use this information in making a study schedule. If at all possible, you should plan the activities that require the most concentration when you are the most alert. For example, if math is a difficult subject for you and you are a morning person, plan to take that class in the morning and do your homework while you are still fresh.

READING

"By understanding our body clocks, we can improve our health and continue to foster our survival."

TUNING IN TO READING

Before we see how your circadian cycle might affect how you set up your class and study schedule, read the following article from *Reader's Digest.* The article describes our circadian, or daily, cycles, and how these cycles affect us.

BIO-SKETCH

Lowell Ponte currently hosts a national talk radio show on the Genesis Communication Network and writes for FrontPageMag.com. He was formerly the roving science and technology editor for *Reader's Digest.* He has written essays for the *New York Times,* the *Los Angeles Times,* and the *Wall Street Journal* and has been a correspondent in 32 countries.

NOTES ON VOCABULARY

circadian rhythm   A person's *circadian rhythm*, popularly known as one's "body clock," is a biological rhythm that governs our routine of working, eating, and sleeping through a 24-hour period. *Circadian* is derived from the Latin words *circa*, meaning "about," and *dies*, meaning "day."

READING *continued*

dexterity   skill in using the body or hands; cleverness. The word *dexterity* is derived from the Latin word *dexter,* meaning "right." The origin suggests a bias in favor of right-handed people. In the 15th century, you were not considered "skillful" unless you were right-handed.

endurance   ability to bear pain, hardship, or adversity. *Endurance* is derived from the French word *endurer,* meaning "harden" or "make hard." The meaning has changed little over time. Today we talk about *enduring* pain and about *endurance* training for long-distance runners.

THE TWO MOST DANGEROUS HOURS OF YOUR DAY   BY LOWELL PONTE

You awaken after a good night's sleep and start to climb out of bed. Take care! You are beginning the most dangerous time of your day.

2   For the next two hours or so, you are two to three times more likely to suffer a heart attack or a stroke than you are in the late evening, the safest cardiovascular time of your day. According to a study headed by Merrill Mitler of Scripps Clinic and Research Foundation in La Jolla, California, 6 A.M. to 10 A.M. is the average peak time for many other major causes of death: ischemic heart disease, cancer, bronchitis, emphysema and asthma.

3   Until recently doctors were taught that the human body lives in homeostasis, changing little during the day. The science of chronobiology—the study of how time affects life—is sparking a medical revolution by revealing how much our bodies change through circadian (daily) rhythms.

4   "These natural biological rhythms are as vital as our heartbeat," says Lawrence E. Scheving of the University of Arkansas for Medical Sciences in Little Rock. "By learning their secrets, we are discovering new ways to prevent and cure illness. There isn't a function in your body that doesn't have its own rhythm. The absence of rhythm is death."

5   While you sleep, your blood pressure falls, your temperature drops more than a degree from its daily afternoon high, and some blood pools in your body's extremities. Come morning, the body has to "jump start" itself from its sleeping to waking stages with a surge of excitation chemicals called catecholamines. Heart rate increases and blood vessels constrict, raising blood pressure and reducing blood flow to the heart muscle; this might cause ischemia, or angina, as well as sudden death from myocardial infarction. If hardened plaques of cholesterol coat arteries, fragments may break loose, causing the clots that lead to heart attacks.

6   Also, your blood swims with cell granules called platelets that are most likely to stick together during these morning hours. When a leap from bed and a surge of catecholamines combine to "get your blood moving," your blood is near its daily peak in thickness and tendency to clot. Packing kids off to school and rushing to get ready for work add emotional tension to the physical stress.

7   This circadian cardiovascular risk comes not from your bedside clock but from your interior biological clock. "Whatever hour you get up," says Dr. James Muller, chief of cardiology for New England Deaconess Hospital in Boston, "your peak risk of myocardial infarction will come within two to three hours after awakening."

8   The master timekeepers in our bodies help synchronize us with such outside cycles as day and night. Like orchestra conductors, they coordinate hundreds of functions inside us. Our body dances through the day to complex inner rhythms

of rising and falling tides of hormones, immune cells, electrolytes and amino acids.

9   The long-held belief that some of us are "larks," or morning people, and others are "owls," or evening people, has now been confirmed. Measurements of circadian rhythms in morning people show heart rates peaking between 1 and 2 P.M., while evening people peak between 5 and 6:30 P.M. Larks produce more of the stimulating hormone adrenaline during the morning hours, followed by decreasing levels of performance through the day. Owls start the day more slowly, produce more nearly level amounts of adrenaline, and improve performance through the day and into early evening.

10   Most people enjoy a peak in short-term memory and mental quickness in the late-morning hours until shortly after noon. Then a measurable dip in energy and efficiency begins around 1 P.M. In some Mediterranean cultures, shops close during the afternoon for a period of siesta.

11   In the afternoon, exercise endurance, reaction time and manual dexterity are at their highest. Some research indicates that from then until early evening, athletes put in their best performances. From 6:30 P.M. until 8:30 P.M. is the sharpest time of day for long-term memory, an optimal time to study.

12   Our daily rhythms can bring a dark side to the early evening, however. These hours include a second daily peak in heart attacks, although smaller than the morning's. Around 7 P.M., alcohol takes longer to be cleared by your liver, and hence can be more intoxicating and performance-impairing than at other times of day—except 11 P.M., which brings a second peak of high ethanol susceptibility.

13   Students often cram during late-night and early-morning hours. Research, however, shows this is the time of the circadian cycle when long-term memory, comprehension and learning are at their worst.

14   Sensitivity to pain has generally increased throughout the day; it reaches its peak late at night. But by early morning the body may have almost doubled its night-time levels of beta endorphins, which help relieve pain. Researchers theorize that this is what increases the body's pain tolerance during the hours after awakening.

15   For most of us, sleep is a time of life's renewal. Within the first 90 minutes or so of sleep, we reach our daily peak of growth hormone, which may help regenerate our bodies. And among pregnant women, the hours between midnight and 4 A.M. most commonly mark the start of labor. "Early morning labor and birth may be part of our genetic inheritance and may have had some survival value for the species," speculates chronobiologist Michael Smolensky of the University of Texas Health Science Center in Houston.

16   By understanding our body clocks, we can improve our health and continue to foster our survival. Without grasping, for instance, that our natural temperature rises one to two degrees from morning until evening, we could misjudge thermometer readings. A temperature of 99 degrees might signal perfect health at 5 P.M. but augur illness at 7 A.M.

17   The effects of drugs are also subject to our rhythms. For instance, many doctors are learning to give powerful cancer drugs with the patient's biological clocks in mind. A given chemotherapy drug may be highly toxic to the kidneys at one time of day, for example, and far less harmful at another. "For every one of more than 20 anti-cancer drugs, there is an optimal time of day," says Dr. William Hrushesky of the Stratton Veterans Administration Medical Center in Albany, New York.

18   Some prescription drugs can reduce morning heart-attack risk, as can aspirin. One major study found that taking an aspirin *every other day* reduced overall incidence of heart attack in men by almost 45 percent and morning risk by more than 59 percent. You should, of course, consult your doctor about the use of aspirin.

19   Aside from using medicine, there are ways to make your mornings less stressful and, perhaps, less risky. Set the alarm clock a bit earlier to give yourself time to stretch arms and legs slowly while still lying down, the way your dog or cat does. This gets the pooled blood in your extremities moving.

Move slowly. Don't subject yourself to the thermal shock of a very hot or cold shower, which could boost blood pressure. Then eat breakfast. Dr. Renata Cifkova at Memorial University of Newfoundland at St. John's says, "Skipping breakfast apparently increases platelet activity and might contribute to heart attacks and stroke during morning hours."

20   To avoid the "Monday morning blues," don't change your schedule on weekends. Your body's clock naturally runs on a cycle of about 25 hours. During the week, your body uses mechanical clocks, mealtimes, and

work schedules and other cues to reset itself to 24 hours each day. On weekends it is tempting to let the clock "free run" forward by staying up late Friday and Saturday, then sleeping late Saturday and Sunday. This action will leave you "jet-lagged," an unnecessary stress.

21   By turning the cycles of your biological clock in your favor, you may reduce your daily danger and increase your days of life.

"The Two Most Dangerous Hours of Your Day" by Lowell Ponte, *Reader's Digest,* March 1992. Copyright © 1992 by The Reader's Digest Assn., Inc. Reprinted with permission.

✔ COMPREHENSION CHECKUP

Multiple Choice

Directions: For each item, write the letter corresponding to the best answer.

 1. Your circadian rhythm is
   a. a daily cycle.
   b. a 1-hour cycle.
   c. a 1-month cycle.
   d. none of the above.

 2. Which of the following statements is true based on paragraph 9?
   a. Owls are awake at night.
   b. Larks are more lively during the morning.
   c. Some people are morning people and some are evening people.
   d. All of the above.

 3. When do you think you would be least likely to suffer a heart attack or stroke?
   a. just after you wake up
   b. early evening
   c. late evening
   d. 2 hours after you wake up

 4. Which of the following statements is true based on the information in the article?
   a. Orchestra conductors can help coordinate the functions of our body.
   b. Babies are most likely to be born in the early morning hours.
   c. It's best to sleep in on Saturday and Sunday mornings to readjust to the 25-hour cycle.
   d. None of the above.

 5. The human body
   a. changes little during the day.
   b. lives in homeostasis.
   c. changes a lot through daily rhythms.
   d. has no rhythm.

True or False

Directions: Indicate whether each statement is true or false by writing **T** or **F** in the space provided.

_F__ 6. Cramming for exams late at night is unlikely to benefit most students.

_F__ 7. Most people show a decline in energy around 1 P.M.

_F__ 8. For most people, alcohol is more intoxicating in the morning.

_T__ 9. If you need to have surgery, you should plan on having it in the early evening when you are least sensitive to pain.

_T__ 10. Your body temperature increases as you go through the day.

_T__ 11. If someone *speculates* about something, he or she is sure to know the answer.

_F__ 12. If you're *sensitive* to pain, be sure to tell the dentist to avoid the use of all anesthetics.

Vocabulary in Context

Directions: In a previous section you were introduced to finding the meaning of new words by using context clues. In the following exercise, try to discover the meaning of each of the italicized words by using a technique called *scanning*. Scanning involves quickly searching reading material to locate a specific piece of information. In this exercise, we have indicated the specific paragraph in which the vocabulary word is located. Quickly scan the paragraph for the context clues that will give you the answer.

1. In paragraph 2, the word *cardiovascular* refers to what specific organ of the body? _Time of your day_

2. In paragraph 3, what is a synonym, or word that has a similar meaning, for *circadian*? _daily_

3. After scanning paragraph 3, what do you think *chronobiology* means? ____
   the study of how time affects life

4. According to the context of paragraph 3, what does *homeostasis* mean? ____
   Changing during the day

5. In paragraph 6, what is the synonym for *platelets*? _Cells_

6. In paragraph 9, if something is *stimulating* to you, does it depress or energize you? _hormons_

7. In paragraph 10, is a *peak* a high point or a low point? _high_

8. In paragraph 10, what is a *siesta*? _____

9. In paragraph 11, define *optimal*. _____

10. In paragraph 15, what do you think the prefix *re-* means? As another example, one might need to *renew* a library book. _____

11. In paragraph 16, if we *misjudge*, are we judging badly or well? _____

12. In paragraph 16, what is the synonym for *augur*? _____

13. Use the context of paragraph 17 to define the word *toxic*. _____

14. According to the context of paragraph 17, if you are *anti* something, are you for it or against it? _____

15. After scanning paragraph 19, name some parts of your body that would be considered *extremities*. _____

In Your Own Words

The *Zits* cartoon that follows illustrates what happens when teenagers are sleepy at the start of the school day.

As the cartoon suggests, teenagers appear to have a different circadian cycle. New research suggests that they are "wired" to stay up later at night and to sleep longer in the morning. Many prominent educators are saying that the traditional high school day is out of sync with teenagers' body clocks. These educators feel that the school day should not begin before 9 or 10 A.M. What is your opinion on this issue?

Zits

© ZITS Partnership. King Features Syndicate.

Internet Activity

Some of you have taken long plane flights and then experienced the tiredness known as "jet lag." Did you know that jet lag can also affect athletic performance? Read the article "Jet-Lag, Circadian Rhythms and Athletic Performance" by Dan Graetzer at

www.sportsguidemag.com/archive/December/TrainFit-jet-lag.asp

Then write down three effects of jet lag mentioned in the article and three recommendations for controlling and limiting jet lag. (If the URL above does not work, go to a search engine such as Google or Yahoo! and type in "jet lag in *Sports Guide* magazine.")

Left-Brain and Right-Brain Orientation

Which One Are You?

Over the past 20 years, psychologists have been studying how the two hemispheres of the brain operate. Research shows that the two sides of the brain think in quite different ways. In general, the left half is more analytical, logical, and likely to break down thoughts into parts. The right half is more likely to focus on the whole picture,

Frank and Ernest

FRANK & ERNEST: © Thaves/Dist. by Newspaper Enterprise Association, Inc.

to think in analogies, and to interpret things imaginatively. We use both halves of the brain together, but one side may be dominant. Being right-brain oriented or left-brain oriented has little to do with whether you are right-handed or left-handed.

Take the following test to see which half of your brain is dominant.

Which Side of Your Brain Is Dominant?

Directions: Check the statements that apply to you.

_____ 1. When reading or watching TV, I prefer a true story to one that is fictional.

_____ 2. I like to read or write poetry.

_____ 3. I prefer to take tests that have no right or wrong answers rather than tests having objective and definite answers.

_____ 4. I find myself solving a problem more by looking at the individual parts than by looking at the big picture.

_____ 5. I usually do several tasks at once rather than one task at a time.

_____ 6. I would prefer a job with a set salary over one such as sales where my income might vary considerably.

_____ 7. I usually follow new directions step by step rather than improvising or taking steps out of order.

_____ 8. When planning a vacation, I usually like to just go, without doing much planning in advance.

_____ 9. The papers in my notebook are usually neat and orderly and not simply thrown in every which way.

_____ 10. When listening to someone else's problems, I usually become emotional instead of trying to come up with logical solutions.

To Score Your Test

To score your test, circle the number for each statement that you checked.

Right-brain hemisphere	2	3	⑤	8	10
Left-brain hemisphere	①	④	6	⑦	⑨

Now compare the results. Which hemisphere has the most circled numbers? The bigger the difference between the two scores, the greater your right-brain dominance or left-brain dominance. If you circled about the same number for both hemispheres, neither one of your hemispheres is dominant.

What does all this mean? One hemispheric orientation is not better than the other, but the thinking processes are different. People who are more left-brain oriented tend to be more organized, be more analytical, and use more logic. So, it is not surprising that engineers, accountants, scientists, and auto mechanics are more likely to have a dominant left hemisphere.

Those with a dominant right hemisphere, on the other hand, tend to focus on the whole more than individual parts, be imaginative, jump to conclusions, and be emotional. Poets, artists, musicians, and inventors are more likely to have a dominant right hemisphere.

We will apply this information later on when we discuss study techniques. Students with a dominant left hemisphere will probably do better organizing material by outlining, while those with a dominant right hemisphere might find mapping easier. Those who are left-brain oriented will probably find study schedules easier to stick to than those who are right-brain oriented.

Left-brain-oriented students will probably find it easier to do well in classes that require analysis and linear thinking than will students who are right-brain oriented. Examples of such classes are algebra, science, accounting, logic, computers, and engineering. Those who are more right-brain oriented might do better in classes such as art, social science, music, English, history, and geometry.

"Intuition becomes increasingly valuable in the new information society precisely because there is so much data."

—John Naisbitt

Multiple Intelligences

What Are Your Strengths?

Merriam Webster's Collegiate Dictionary defines intelligence as "the ability to learn or understand" and "the ability to cope with a new situation." We have discovered in the previous sections that we are all unique individuals who learn in different ways. Some psychologists believe that intelligence can also be expressed in a variety of ways. Many of you may remember taking the Stanford-Binet IQ test. After completing the test, you were assigned a score and then evaluated based on that score. If your mental age, as measured by the test, and your age in years were the same, you had an IQ of 100. This meant that you were considered "average." The higher the score above 100, the more intelligent you were considered to be, while a score of 80 meant that you were below average.

Critics argue that one problem with this test is that it is based on the principle that our intelligence is one-dimensional. Howard Gardner, a Harvard professor, has proposed the idea that there are eight different types of intelligence. His theory is based on biological research showing different parts of the brain to be the sites of different abilities. He says that "the concept of 'smart' and 'stupid' doesn't make sense. . . . You can be smart in one thing and stupid in something else." As you read a description of each different type of intelligence, try to determine your own strengths and weaknesses.

In the beginning of this chapter, you learned how to put key information in the margin of the text. Another study technique is to highlight important words and phrases. Highlight (or underline) the definition for each of the following types of intelligences. Follow the example given below for verbal/linguistic intelligence.

"The art of writing is the art of discovering what you believe."

—David Hare

"A word after a word after a word is power."

—Margaret Atwood

Word Smart—Verbal/Linguistic Intelligence

This intelligence <u>relates to language skills</u>. It includes the <u>ability to express yourself verbally</u>, to <u>appreciate complex meanings</u>, and to <u>detect subtle differences in</u> the <u>meanings of words</u>. It is considered to be a key intelligence for success in college.

People with this type of intelligence are likely to be good writers and good spellers. For recreation, they often like to do crossword puzzles or play word games like Scrabble. They have good memories for names and dates. They are often good at telling stories or giving speeches.

Logic Smart—Logical/Mathematical Intelligence

This intelligence involves the ability to reason, solve abstract problems, and understand complex relationships. Intelligence in this area is also a good predictor of academic success.

People with this type of intelligence are logical, orderly thinkers. It is easy for them to comprehend factual material. In school, they often ask a lot of questions. They like working with equations in subjects such as math and chemistry. They are often proficient with the computer. For recreation, they like games such as Clue, Battleship, chess, or computer games.

Picture Smart—Visual/Spatial Intelligence

This is the ability to think in three dimensions and to re-create experiences visually. Painters, sculptors, and architects are all able to manipulate a form in space.

People who have this type of intelligence like to visualize each step in their mind when they are given a set of directions. They are the "finders." Many can readily retrieve missing objects in the home by tapping a visual memory of where the objects were last seen. In order to process complex information, they like to draw pictures, graphs, or charts. They learn more in class when information is given by means of videos, movies, or PowerPoint slides. For recreation, they often like to do puzzles or mazes.

Music Smart—Musical/Rhythmic Intelligence

This is the ability to hear pitch, tone, and rhythm.

People with this type of intelligence may sing or hum throughout the day. They enjoy dancing and can keep time with the music. They often need to listen to music when they study. It is very easy for them to remember the words and melodies of songs.

Body Smart—Bodily/Kinesthetic Intelligence

This intelligence places the emphasis on control of the body and the skillful handling of objects. The mind clearly coordinates the movements of the body. Athletes, pianists, and dancers might excel in this area.

People with this type of intelligence are often Mr. or Ms. Fix-it. They enjoy repairing things, they use many gestures when they speak, and they are good at competitive sports. For recreation, they prefer physical activities such as bicycling, rollerblading, skateboarding, and swimming.

People Smart—Interpersonal Intelligence

This is the ability to interact well with people. People who excel in this area are especially skillful in detecting the moods and intentions of others. Politicians might display this type of intelligence.

People with this type of intelligence are often found in leadership positions. They tend to be empathic individuals who communicate well with others. They often make good mediators and are called upon to help settle other people's problems and conflicts.

Self Smart—Intrapersonal Intelligence

This is the ability to understand one's own feelings and to use the insight gained to guide actions.

"You're wise, but you lack tree smarts."

People with this type of intelligence set reasonable goals for themselves and take steps to accomplish those goals. They often study by themselves, and they need time to be alone with their thoughts.

Environment Smart— Naturalistic Intelligence

This is the ability to appreciate and respect the environment and nature.

People with this type of intelligence probably enjoy being outdoors and participating in hiking, camping, and gardening. They tend to notice and value diversity among plants and animals. They like studying such subjects as astronomy, zoology, and geology. Farmers or oceanographers might display this type of intelligence.

Is there a relationship between these intelligences and the learning styles we have been studying? Probably, but our knowledge of how the brain functions is still in the early stages. One problem, of course, is that although we are all human beings, we are all distinctly different, making it difficult for scientists to generalize.

Another problem concerns the controversy over how much of our intelligence is fixed at birth and how much is determined by our environment. More than likely our intelligence is a combination of both of these factors, but the nature-versus-nurture debate is far from resolved. In the meantime, many educators and psychologists are not only attempting to define intelligence more broadly but also devising new methods to teach thinking skills once thought to be fixed for life.

Internet Activity

In this chapter, you have been trying to improve your understanding of yourself by taking various assessment tests. Go to one of the following Web sites and take one of the tests. Try to take a test that is different from one that you have already taken. What can you conclude about yourself after taking the test?

www.intelligencetest.com

www.iqtest.com

www.queendom.com

READING

"Well, then, suppose my auto repairman devised questions for an intelligence test."

TUNING IN TO READING

You are now going to read an essay by Isaac Asimov (1920–1992). This essay, written 10 years before Gardner began his research on multiple intelligences, demonstrates how we can be "smart" in many different ways. As you read the essay, try to determine which of Gardner's eight intelligences Asimov likely possessed. Which intelligences did the mechanic in the essay display? What intelligences did Asimov and the mechanic have in common?

READING *continued*

BIO-SKETCH

According to David N. Samuelson, in *Twentieth Century Science-Fiction Writers,* Asimov is "the world's most prolific science writer" who wrote "some of the best-known science fiction ever written." In addition to science fiction, Asimov, a former professor of biochemistry, wrote many essays explaining scientific principles to the general public. The following essay, "What Is Intelligence, Anyway?" is a sample of his autobiographical writings. In these essays, Asimov recounts many incidents from his own life, both painful and pleasurable. He never forgot his early origins and often invited readers "to wonder, with him, at the rise to prominence of a bright Jewish boy brought to this country from Russia at the age of three and raised in a collection of Brooklyn candy stores." In his lengthy career, he received numerous honors and awards, including having his short story "Nightfall" chosen by the Science Fiction Writers of America as the best science fiction story of all time.

NOTES ON VOCABULARY

private   (in the Army) the lowest rank in the army. Comes from the Latin *privare,* meaning "to separate or deprive." A *private* is separated from those of higher rank and is deprived of the privileges of higher rank.

oracle   a person of great knowledge, or a wise statement or authoritative prediction. *Oracle* was originally the shrine where ancient Greeks and Romans consulted their gods and asked their advice. The *oracle* of Delphi was the most famous.

moron   fool. From the Greek word *moros,* meaning "foolish."

What Is Intelligence, Anyway?

Isaac Asimov

WHAT IS INTELLIGENCE, ANYWAY? When I was in the Army, I received a kind of aptitude test that all soldiers took and, against a normal of 100, scored 160. No one at the base had ever seen a figure like that, and for two hours they made a big fuss over me. (It didn't mean anything. The next day I was still a buck private with KP—kitchen police—as my highest duty.)

2   All my life I've been registering scores like that, so that I have the complacent feeling that I'm highly intelligent, and I expect other people to think so, too. Actually, though, don't such scores simply mean that I am very good at answering the type of academic questions that are considered worthy of answers by the people who make up the intelligence tests—people with intellectual bents similar to mine?

3   For instance, I had an auto repairman once, who, on these intelligence tests, could not possibly have scored more than 80, by my estimate. I always took it for granted that I was far more intelligent than he was. Yet, when anything went wrong with my car I hastened to him with it, watched him anxiously as he explored its vitals, and listened to his pronouncements as though they were divine oracles—and he always fixed my car.

4   Well, then, suppose my auto repairman devised questions for an intelligence test. Or suppose a carpenter did, or a farmer, or, indeed, almost anyone but an academician. By every one of those tests, I'd prove myself a moron. And I'd *be* a moron, too. In a world where I could not use my academic training and my verbal talents but had to do something intricate or hard, working with my hands, I would do poorly. My intelligence, then, is not absolute but is a function of the society I live in and of the fact that a small subsection of that society has managed to foist itself on the rest as an arbiter of such matters.

5   Consider my auto repairman, again. He had a habit of telling me jokes whenever he saw me. One time he raised his head from under the automobile hood to say: "Doc, a deaf-and-mute guy went into a hardware store to ask for some nails. He put two fingers together on the counter and made hammering motions with the other hand. The clerk brought him a hammer. He shook his head and pointed to the two fingers he was hammering, the clerk brought him nails. He picked out the sizes he wanted, and left. Well, doc, the next guy who came in was a blind man. He wanted scissors. How do you suppose he asked for them?"

6   Indulgently, I lifted my right hand and made scissoring motions with my first two fingers. Whereupon my auto repairman laughed raucously and said, "Why you dumb jerk, he used his *voice* and asked for them." Then he said, smugly, "I've been trying that on all my customers today." "Did you catch many?" I asked. "Quite a few," he said, "but I knew for sure I'd catch *you*." "Why is that?" I asked. "Because you're so god-damned educated, doc, I *knew* you couldn't be very smart."

7   And I have an uneasy feeling he had something there.

Isaac Asimov, "What Is Intelligence, Anyway?" Copyright © by Isaac Asimov. Reprinted by permission of the Estate of Isaac Asimov.

✔ COMPREHENSION CHECKUP

Multiple Choice

Directions: For each item, write the letter corresponding to the best answer.

_____ 1. While serving in the Army, Asimov was
   a. rewarded for receiving such a high score on the aptitude test.
   b. belittled and made to feel inferior.
   c. fussed over momentarily.

_____ 2. The people who write the tests are emphasizing the kinds of questions
   a. they do poorly on.
   b. they do well on.
   c. they are indifferent to.

_____ 3. The auto repairman mentioned in the essay on a traditional aptitude test most probably would score
   a. superior.
   b. average.
   c. below average.

_____ 4. When Asimov says that he listened to the auto repairman's pronouncements "as though they were divine oracles," he means he listened
   a. closely.
   b. with distrust.
   c. angrily.

_____ 5. If a carpenter devised an aptitude test, Asimov would most probably score
   a. superior.
   b. average.
   c. below average.

_____ 6. When Asimov _indulgently_ lifted his hand to make scissoring motions, he
was indicating he
   a. felt uncertain of the correct answer.
   b. was confident he was correct.
   c. knew he was wrong.

_____ 7. When the auto repairman succeeded in fooling Asimov, he felt _smug_. In
this context, the word _smug_ most probably means
   a. frustrated.
   b. self-satisfied.
   c. silly.

_____ 8. Does the auto repairman have respect for Asimov's type of intelligence?
   a. most probably
   b. not likely
   c. absolutely

Vocabulary in Context

Directions: In the blanks below, write the word from the list that best completes the
sentence. Use each word only once.

aptitude	arbiter	complacent	foist	fuss
hastened	indulgent	intricate	mute	raucous

1. Tara's kids weren't turning out very well because she was far too _____ in
disciplining them, letting them do whatever they felt like.

2. Sam's _____ test indicates that he would probably do well to consider law
enforcement as a possible career choice.

3. Eddie Murphy's trademark _____ laugh has been displayed in the _Shrek_
movies.

4. The coffin cover of the ancient Egyptian King Tut features a(n) _____ design
of gold inlaid with enamel and semiprecious stones.

5. Realizing she had forgotten to turn off the oven, Tina _____ home before her
turkey dinner was ruined.

6. Darryl was feeling smug and _____ over how well he did on the last test,
and so he quit working hard.

7. Whenever Cathy, the cartoon character by Cathy Guisewhite, goes home to visit
her mother at the holidays, a real _____ is made over her.

8. The two sides can't agree on a deal, so Robyn has agreed to serve as a(n)
_____ in the dispute.

9. Mark gets really angry every time some of his coworkers try to _____ some of their work on him.

10. Tony pushes the _____ button whenever there is a loud, annoying commercial on TV.

In Your Own Words

1. What does the auto repairman mean when he says, "Because you're so goddamned educated, doc, I *knew* you couldn't be very smart"?

2. Do you think it is a good idea for people to be made aware of their score on an IQ test?

3. What does the word *intelligence* mean to you?

Written Assignment

In the book *The Learning Gap* by Harold W. Stevenson and James W. Stigler, the authors compare the Asian and American models of education. The authors believe that the American system places too much emphasis on innate abilities as measured by traditional IQ tests. In contrast, the Asian educational system is less enthusiastic about intelligence testing and instead stresses effort. While differences among people are clearly recognized, the Asian system focuses on how hard people are willing to work to develop their particular abilities. "Lack of achievement, therefore, is attributed to insufficient effort rather than lack of ability or to personal or environmental obstacles." The authors provide examples of this philosophy in proverbs such as this one from China: "The slow bird must start out early." Write a few paragraphs giving your opinion of the two different approaches to intelligence. Which approach do you think is better? Why?

Stress Inventory

How Much Stress Is There in Your Life?

Although there is no exact correlation between how well students do in college and the stress in their lives, students need to pay attention to personal stress. To be successful in college, you must be able to give full attention to your studies. This means that you must come to terms with all facets of your life, including whatever is causing you stress. If the stress in your life is controlling you, you need to do something about it. You may be able to solve the problem yourself, or you might want to consider seeking professional help. Most college campuses have a counseling center to help students deal with too much stress and other emotional problems. When we have physical problems, most of us are willing to consult a doctor. On the other hand, many of us have difficulty seeking help for other personal problems. But if you need help and help is available, why not take advantage of it?

The following test is meant to be confidential and is for your use only.

Stressful Events in Your Life

Directions: The events listed below commonly occur in the lives of college students. Check the space provided for the events that have occurred in your life during the last

12 months. When you have finished checking off all of the appropriate events, total the point values in parentheses for each checked item.

(100)	_____	Death of a close family member
(80)	_____	Jail term
(63)	_____	Final year or first year in college
(60)	_____	Pregnancy (yours or caused by you)
(53)	_____	Severe personal illness or injury
(50)	_____	Marriage
(45)	_____	Any interpersonal problems
(40)	_____	Financial difficulties
(40)	_____	Death of a close friend
(40)	_____	Arguments with your roommate (more than every other day)
(40)	_____	Major disagreements with your family
(30)	_____	Major change in personal habits
(30)	_____	Change in living environment
(30)	_____	Beginning or ending a job
(25)	_____	Problems with your boss or professor
(25)	_____	Outstanding personal achievement
(25)	_____	Failure in some course
(20)	_____	Final exams
(20)	_____	Increased or decreased dating
(20)	_____	Change in working conditions
(20)	_____	Change in your major
(18)	_____	Change in your sleeping habits
(15)	_____	Several-day vacation
(15)	_____	Change in eating habits
(15)	_____	Family reunion
(15)	_____	Change in recreational activities
(15)	_____	Minor illness or injury
(11)	_____	Minor violations of the law
	_____	**Total Life Events Score**

Now add up your points. If you scored between 150 and 199 points, you may be experiencing a "mild life crisis." A score between 200 and 300 may indicate a "moderate life crisis," and a score over 300 may indicate a "major life crisis." Studies have shown that the higher your score, the more likely you are to become ill.

From John W. Santrock, *Psychology*, 7th Edition, Figure 15.6 (p. 607). Copyright © 2003 by The McGraw-Hill Companies, Inc. Reprinted with permission.

Context Clue Practice Using Textbook Material:
Why Students Get the Blues

Directions: Use the context clues to determine the meaning of the italicized word, and write a definition for that word in the space provided.

1. During the school year, up to 78 percent of all college students suffer some symptoms of depression. At any given time, from 16 to 30 percent of the student population is depressed. Why should so many students be "blue"? Various factors contribute to depressive feelings. Here are some of the most *prevalent:*

   prevalent: _____

2. Stresses from the increased difficulty of college work and pressures to make a career choice often leave students feeling that they are missing out on fun or that all their hard work is *for naught*.

   for naught: _____

3. *Isolation* and loneliness are common when a student leaves his or her support group behind. In the past, family, a circle of high school friends, and often a boyfriend or girlfriend could be counted on for support or encouragement.

   isolation: _____

4. Problems with studying and grades frequently trigger depression. Many students enter college with high *aspirations* and little experience with failure. At the same time, many lack *rudimentary* skills necessary for academic success.

   aspirations: _____

   rudimentary: _____

5. Another common cause of college depression is the breakup of an *intimate* relationship with a boyfriend or girlfriend.

   intimate: _____

6. Students who find it difficult to live up to their idealized images of themselves are especially *prone* to depression.

   prone: _____

7. Stressful events frequently *trigger* depression. An added danger is that depressed students are more likely to abuse alcohol, which is a depressant.

   trigger: _____

From Dennis Coon, *Introduction to Psychology*, 8th Edition, p. 465. © 1998 Wadsworth, a part of Cengage Learning, Inc. Reproduced by permission. www.cengage.com/permissions.

Internet Activity

Vitality is a monthly magazine devoted to health and wellness issues. If you are already Internet "savvy," go to its Web site, www.vitality.com, and click on "Vitality on Demand." Then type in #543 for an article titled "Self-Care: Reducing Your Stress Now." You also can type in "stress" to find other articles on stress. Write a paragraph about what you learned about stress.

READING

> *"[Daniel] learned the dangers of becoming a kidney transplant donor."*

TUNING IN TO READING

The next article you will read describes a unique teenager who has encountered many stresses in his young life. Faced with the prospect of losing his beloved grandmother, he makes a very unselfish decision to give one of his kidneys to her. What decision would you make if you were to find yourself facing the same circumstances?

BIO-SKETCH

For over 20 years, Rick Reilly has been a writer for the weekly magazine *Sports Illustrated*. During that time he has been named National Sportswriter of the Year eight times. The excerpt that follows is from a collection of his favorite stories.

NOTES ON VOCABULARY

scrimmage line   the imaginary line between opposing teams where the ball is put into play. In football, the ball is placed on the *scrimmage line* and the two teams face each other across it. The word *scrimmage* comes from *skirmish*, which is a brief fight or encounter between two groups.

fullback, halfback, quarterback   backfield positions on the offensive side in football. In the 1890s, when football was played quite a bit differently than it is today, the *quarterback* played a quarter of the way back directly behind the linemen at the line of scrimmage; behind him on either side and halfway back were two halfbacks; and then behind them in the middle and all the way back was the *fullback*.

dicier   comes from *dicey*, meaning "chancy." Derived from British slang, the word *dicey* was first made popular by RAF (Royal Air Force) pilots during World War II, who spoke of their missions, and the chances of their safe return, as *dicey*.

valiant   brave, heroic. The word is derived from the Latin word *valere*, meaning "to be strong or worthy."

hierarchy   any system of persons or things ranked one above another. The word *hierarchy* is derived from the Greek word *hieros*, meaning "holy." Originally a *hierarchy* was a government by priests.

title implies what?
mark words you don't know

An Easy Choice

Rick Reilly

WHEN DANIEL HUFFMAN QUIT FOOTBALL, he did exactly what his mom told him not to do and started messing around with needles, and folks in tiny Rossville, Illinois, shook his hand. How else was he supposed to save his grandmother's life?

2   Still if there was one kid in town you hated to see quit the high school team, it was Daniel. "That kid *lived* for football," said his grandfather Daniel Allison. Young Daniel

would count the days from the end of school to the start of summer two-a-day practices. He was the screamer on the team, the human pep rally. O.K., so maybe he wasn't going straight to Florida State, but at 6′2″ and 275 pounds, Daniel was where a lot of enemy tailbacks ended up. "He would just engulf them like some huge amoeba," recalls his former coach, Dave McDonald. "And then he'd yell some more."

3   This is Daniel's senior year at Rossville High. He is an honor-roll student (A-plus average), a member of the school chorus, the class vice president, a writer of poetry, a part-time cleanup boy at a discount store and a onetime shot-putter on the track team, but none of those things have made him as proud as being a co-captain, starting defensive tackle and occasional offensive tackle on the football team. In a town such as Rossville (pop. 1,400), a hiccup of a place 118 miles south of Chicago, your senior year of football is precious, and Daniel had planned to make this season a doozy.

4   Though he played primarily on defense, he had the soul of an offensive lineman. He had no designs on stardom. Of the team's star running back, Zeb Stephenson, Daniel once said, "It will be my privilege to block for him."

5   Daniel is very big on making other folks' paths a little easier. When diabetes left his grandmother Shirlee Allison legally blind for a while, 14-year-old Daniel and his 13-year-old sister, Kristina, did the dishes and folded the laundry. Daniel became Shirlee's eyes, helping her walk, reading the mail to her. When Shirlee's husband had his quintuple bypass two years ago, Daniel got his grandmother through it. "Sometimes we raised them," Shirlee says of her grandchildren, "and sometimes they raised us."

6   Daniel is just as attentive to his friends. "He'll do anything for us," says Lisa Masengale, a high school classmate. "He writes me poetry when I'm down. He can always make me laugh."

7   Hard to figure where he got all the spare sunshine. Daniel's mother, Alice, left the family when he was four. His father, Barry, remarried, and an evil stepmother/ungrateful stepkids thing broke out. Daniel and Kristina were miserable, but Barry wasn't one to interfere. "He's kind of a partier," Daniel says. So the summer after Daniel finished seventh grade, he and Kristina moved to Florida to live with Alice. That didn't work out either, so after a year everyone agreed that the kids would be best off living with their grandparents, the Allisons.

8   "My grandparents kinda saved me," says Daniel. "There's a whole lot of drugs and stuff around here. I probably would've ended up all messed up." Kristina eventually moved back to Florida, which left Daniel and Shirlee as the oddest couple in town. Sure, they shared a love of books and a certain hardheadedness, but he was a 17-year-old growing uncontrollably, and she was a 60-year-old disappearing before the town's eyes. After a time, her diabetes-ravaged kidneys were producing almost no urine. All that poison the kidneys were supposed to filter out was circulating through her.

9   As last spring grew warmer, Shirlee's trips to the hospital in nearby Danville for dialysis got more frequent, and her condition worsened. Her muscles were atrophying, her heart was enlarged, and her blood pressure was dangerously low. "We all figured there was no hope for her," says her neighbor Madge Douglas.

10   But then Daniel had this crazy idea. He was sitting at a Burger King with Shirlee after another brutal day of watching her on the dialysis machine ("the metal and

plastic vampire," he called it in his diary). He had been thinking about how much he missed her. Where was Gran, the kidder? Gran, the one you couldn't get to shut up? Who was this 101-pound ghost? Who was this clothes hanger of a woman, all bone where he used to plant his good-night kiss? "Mrs. Allison," the doctor had told her, "many people can live on dialysis, but you aren't one of them."

11   Well, that made the situation sticky. She refused to take a kidney from a relative. She was on the waiting list for a cadaver kidney. That was good enough for her. "I'm not imposing on anybody," she said. Daniel was so scared that he couldn't watch her undergo treatment anymore. He started picking up medical handbooks about dialysis. He talked to Shirlee's doctors. He learned the dangers of becoming a kidney transplant donor. He knew that if he gave Shirlee one of his kidneys, he would have to give up contact sports forever—one hard hit from behind, and he could end up on life support. On the other hand, he learned that eight people die each day in the U.S. while waiting for an organ. The wait for a cadaver kidney can be two years. At the rate Shirlee was shrinking, that would be a year and a half too much.

"To know just what has to be done, then to do it, comprises the whole philosophy of practical life."

—Sir William Osler

12   And so, somewhere between the Whopper and the onion rings, Daniel made up his mind. "Gran," he said, "I can't take it anymore. I want you to take my kidney."

13   "No, no, no," she said. "You're too young. What if something happens?"

14   "Gran, I don't care what happens to me. I'm doin' this!"

15   "Absolutely not," she said. "Besides, when I think about you giving up football, it makes me sick to my stomach."

16   Daniel got good and mad. He yelled, "Gran, you always told me, 'Stand up for what you believe in.' Well, I'm standin' up! You're taking my kidney!"

17   You do not hear that every day at Burger King. Every head in the joint turned. "Well," Shirley whispered, sliding back in her chair, "we'll see if we match."

18   Getting around Daniel's mother was even dicier. Alice was foursquare against the donation. When Daniel decided to go ahead with the operation anyway, Alice took action. She wrote a letter to the University of Illinois Medical Center, where Daniel and his grandmother wanted the transplant to take place, and asked how the surgeons could take organs from minors. The center, which had not known Daniel's age, declined to allow the operation.

19   Daniel was dogged. If he waited until his 18th birthday—December 24—Shirlee might be too weak to survive the operation. "He was ready to go to court on this," says Jeff Miller, transplant coordinator for Dr. Frederick K. Merkel, who performs surgery at the Illinois Medical Center and Chicago's Rush Presbyterian Hospital and accepts living-relative transplant donors as young as 16. The operation was on, at Rush.

20   The night before the July 9 surgery, Daniel was scared for both Shirlee and himself. "Gran," he said, "I gotta ask you one thing: Is this worth risking your life for?"

21   "Oh, honey," she said, laying her withered hand on his huge one. "I have no life without this."

22   When she woke up in the intensive care unit, she already had her color back. "My stars!" she said to a nurse. "Now that I've got this 17-year-old kidney in me, I hope I

don't feel like going out and tackling somebody!" Across the hall, though, Daniel was hurting. After a kidney transplant the donor gets months of tests—the constant blood work, the working knowledge of the hierarchy of hospital needles. Shirlee's scar is small and on her pelvis. Daniel's is 18 inches long and wraps from his navel nearly to his spine. It was Daniel who was in pain long after the surgery, not Shirlee. Who said it's more blessed to give than to receive?

23   But a lot of wonderful things also started happening. Daniel had quit the football team, but the football team refused to quit him. The players insisted that he wear his football jersey each Friday. He went to every practice when he wasn't working at the discount store. He rode on the senior players' float at homecoming and made the speech at the pep rally before the game. And on Friday nights you could hear his voice all over the field: "C'mon, everybody! *Clap!*" Funny, how somebody who wasn't even playing could be the toughest kid on the team.

24   Daniel is almost completely recovered. In fact, the doctors say his remaining kidney will soon be twice the size it used to be. They still haven't figured out how to measure his heart.

25   Daniel wants to be a writer, and he's applying for college scholarships like crazy. As for Shirlee, her weight is up to 128, she rarely uses her cane, and her vision has improved. She has even gone to some of Rossville's football games—something she couldn't do before the surgery. You should have seen her there, bursting with pride. "The boy loved his grandma more than football," she marveled, wiping a tear from the corner of her eye. "Whaddya think a that?"

26   Folks in town seem to think a lot of it. Folks out of town too. Governor Jim Edgar wrote Daniel to say how proud he was of him, and the story of Daniel's donation was on national as well as local TV programs.

27   The Rossville football team didn't do too well, finishing the season last Friday at 3−6. "We sure could have used Daniel to put a body on somebody," said lineman Chad Smith. With 24 seconds left in Rossville's final game, a 28−3 win over Palestine High, Rossville's Shaun York asked to leave the game and be replaced by Daniel—who with the coach's permission, had put on shoulder pads, a helmet and a borrowed pair of cleats. Daniel lined up 20 yards behind the line of scrimmage, and as his quarterback took the snap and downed the ball, Daniel raised his hands in a V for victory. "It was," he says, "the single best memory of my life."

28   Now Daniel hopes for a victory for his friend Lisa. When she was sick for two weeks last month, doctors discovered that she had a badly infected kidney. Now Lisa, too, is learning all about needles and even transplants. Luckily, she's got a 17-year-old Mayo Clinic encyclopedia to talk to on the phone, to keep her calm—and make her laugh. "He's getting me through it," she says.

29   Shirlee Allison knows how well Daniel can do that sort of thing. After she went home from the hospital, she ran a two inch-by-one-inch ad in the Danville paper expressing her love for her grandson. She says, "Every morning I wake up, I get on my knees and thank two people: God and Daniel."

have been waiting for a transplant. Do you see any problems with the selling of organs in India by poor people?

Written Assignment

Directions: Read the following information from *Human Biology* by Sylvia S. Mader. Then write a paragraph answering one of the questions that follows.

Transplantation of the kidney, heart, liver, pancreas, lung, and other organs is now possible due to two major breakthroughs. First, solutions have been developed that preserve donor organs for several hours. This made it possible for one young boy to undergo surgery for 16 hours, during which time he received five different organs. Second, rejection of transplanted organs is now prevented by immunosuppressive drugs; therefore, organs can be donated by unrelated individuals, living or dead. After death, it is possible to give the "gift of life" to someone else—over 25 organs and tissues from one cadaver can be used for transplants. The survival rate after a transplant operation is good. So many heart recipients are now alive and healthy that they have formed basketball and softball teams, demonstrating the normalcy of their lives after surgery.

One problem persists, however, and that is the limited availability of organs for transplantation. At any one time, at least 27,000 people in the United States are waiting for a donated organ. Keen competition for organs can lead to various bioethical inequities and dilemmas such as the following:

1. When the governor of Pennsylvania received a heart and lungs within a relatively short period of time, it appeared that his social status might have played a role. Do you think it's ethical to put a famous person at the top of the list for an organ transplant? Why or why not?

2. If a father gives a kidney to a child, he has to undergo a major surgical operation that leaves him vulnerable to possible serious consequences in the future. Is it ethical to ask a parent to donate an organ to his or her child? Why or why not?

3. If organs are taken from those who have just died, who guarantees that the individual was indeed dead? Is it ethical to remove organs from a newborn who is brain dead but whose organs are still functioning? Why or why not?

4. When xenotransplants (transplants for humans from other animals) are available, should they be for sale? Why or why not? Does this make the wealthy more likely to receive a transplant than those who cannot pay? Finally, is it right to genetically alter animals to serve as a source of organs for humans?

From Sylvia S. Mader, *Human Biology*, 8th Edition, p. 177. Copyright © 2004 by The McGraw-Hill Companies, Inc. Reprinted with permission.

Internet Activity

In the United States, organ donations and transplant surgeries are becoming more common. Although kidneys are often taken from living donors, most organs used as transplants are removed immediately after death. The demand for donated organs is far greater than the supply. To find out more about transplants, visit one of the Web sites listed below. The first site is sponsored by the National Foundation for Transplants, and the second site has been created by a group of government health agencies. Working with a partner, print out a page from either site and write a short paragraph emphasizing something you learned about transplants.

www.transplants.org

www.organdonor.gov

What follows is a very sad postscript to the Daniel Huffman story.

"Daniel Huffman, 25, who gave up football to aid ailing grandmother, is found with a gunshot wound to head."

Organ Donor with FSU Connection Dies

ASSOCIATED PRESS

ROSSVILLE, Ill.—Daniel Huffman gave up football eight years ago when he donated a kidney to his grandmother so she could live. Now his grandmother has lost her hero.

2 The 25-year-old, a former Florida State employee, was found dead with a gunshot wound to the head Monday at his home in central Illinois. Authorities said there was no sign of foul play.

3 "He was always so happy, so fun," Huffman's grandmother, Shirlee Allison, told the *Chicago Tribune* for today's editions. "He put a lot of joy into everyone's life. He was always doing things for you, making you feel so special."

4 Huffman, a defensive tackle on Rossville's high school football team, decided to put away his football gear in 1996 for his grandmother, whose diabetes left her seriously ill and in need of a kidney transplant.

5 His grandmother could have waited for a transplant, but Huffman, then 17, did some research and pressed doctors to allow him to be her donor.

6 He loved football, but the sacrifice meant he could no longer play contact sports. Huffman had the surgery before his senior year, and word spread about the boy from Rossville, a small town about 130 miles southwest of Chicago.

7 Florida State gave Huffman a scholarship though he couldn't play football and he later spent three years as an FSU athletic trainer, then worked in the sports information office.

8 *Sports Illustrated* did a story on him and he was honored with a Disney Wide World of Sports Spirit Award. A television movie was made about his donation: *Gift of Love: The Daniel Huffman Story,* which starred Elden Henson as Daniel and Debbie Reynolds as his grandmother.

9 But Huffman didn't think of his donation as an act of heroism. "If you love someone and you can help them, any way you can, you're going to do it," he told the Associated Press in 1999.

10 Huffman moved back to Illinois in 2000 after his grandfather died to help care for his grandmother.

11 He worked in various security jobs, and every weekend he would visit Allison, take her shopping and do her laundry. Friends say he recently talked of completing his college degree and dreamed of someday teaching college English.

12 His best friend, Shaun York, discovered Huffman's body in the garage.

13 "There is no answer," he said. "No one knows why."

Short Answer

Directions: Answer the questions briefly.

1. Does this new information change your opinion about the wisdom of allowing minors to donate organs?
2. Should Daniel have had a psychiatrist or health-care provider monitoring his progress throughout his college years?

Study Schedules

How do you create a study schedule that makes you more efficient?

Where to Study

"Dost thou love life? Then do not squander time; for that's the stuff life is made of."

—Benjamin Franklin

The last part of the puzzle we will work with, before writing up your study schedule, is looking at *where* you should study. It is important to separate your studying from the other phases of your life. There should be a time to study and a time to be with your children, spouse, or friends, and the two should be separate. You may want to study at your boyfriend's or girlfriend's apartment, but you may be studying something else other than your course work.

Mary Kaye Perrin, at the College of St. Theresa, asks students in her classes to complete the following Study Area Analysis handout. Completing this survey helps students recognize the best places to study. You will notice that you may be able to study in one place better than another depending on the time of day. Now take the following test, and later we will talk some more about how to choose a good place to study. This is not going to be turned in, but is only meant to help you.

Finding a Place to Study

Directions: List two or three places where you frequently study.

Place A _____

Place B _____

Place C _____

After reading each statement below, circle the answer (T or F) that applies to each of these places. It's easiest to do all of the questions for Place A first, all of the questions for Place B second, and then, if you have a third place, all of the questions for Place C.

	Place A	Place B	Place C
1. Other people often interrupt me.	T F	T F	T F
2. The environment reminds me of things not related to studying.	T F	T F	T F
3. I can often hear the radio or TV.	T F	T F	T F
4. I can often hear the phone ringing.	T F	T F	T F
5. I take too many breaks.	T F	T F	T F
6. I seem to be especially bothered by distractions.	T F	T F	T F

7. My breaks tend to be too long.	T	F	T F	T F	
8. I tend to start conversations.	T	F	T F	T F	
9. Temperature conditions are ideal.	T	F	T F	T F	
10. Chair, table, lighting arrangements are not conducive to studying.	T	F	T F	T F	

From David B. Ellis, *Becoming a Master Student: Course Manual*, 7th Edition, p. 248. © 1994 Wadsworth, a part of Cengage Learning, Inc. Reproduced by permission. www.cengage.com/permissions.

What does this survey tell you about where you should study? Is that place best because of when you study there or because of the location? You will need to think about the answer to this question when you fill out your study schedule.

When to Study

Now let's begin to put some of this information you have learned about yourself to practical use. Would you like to be prepared for a test two nights before the test is given? Would you like to have that paper written a day early? If so, follow along. The purpose of this section is to show you how to organize yourself so that you can take charge of your life and do better in school. After all, you don't want to find yourself in a predicament such as Jeremy's in the Zits comic strip below.

You will find a practice form on page 64. Another copy is located in the Appendices for future use.

Completing a Weekly Study Plan

Step 1: First, fill in your class schedule. For example, if your math class is MWF from 9 to 10, write in Math in the three blocks for those days and time. You have no control over these items; you have to go to class.

Step 2: Now fill in your work schedule. We hope it is fairly regular, because if it is not, keeping a regular study schedule from week to week will be difficult. Write in "work" in the appropriate blocks. If your schedule changes from week to week, try to approximate it. If some weeks you work more than in others, go by your busier weeks.

Step 3: Fill in time for school activities such as sports events, clubs, and student council.

Zits

© ZITS Partnership. King Features Syndicate.

Step 4: Fill in time for other regularly scheduled activities, such as church, laundry, meetings, and grocery shopping. If it's something you do almost every week, put it in. If you do something only about once a month, leave it out.

Step 5: Fill in time commitments to your family, spouse, friends, and so forth. Remember that those people also will need your attention. This includes such things as putting your children to bed and spending time at your boyfriend's house. As mentioned previously, begin to separate your academic life from your family and social life. Don't try to study and cook dinner simultaneously. Don't try to study at your girlfriend's house. Plan time for studying and time for your personal life—but not at the same time. The two don't mix. You and your children will be happier. You and your significant other will be happier. You will be able to do higher-quality schoolwork in a shorter period of time.

Step 6: Fill in other times when you are not likely to be studying—for example, Friday and Saturday nights, the time of your favorite TV show, or times when you exercise. Remember, exercise is also important for your health and well-being.

Step 7: At the bottom of the schedule sheet you are working on, list the classes you are taking. For each of your classes, estimate the total number of hours you think you will need to study in that class each week to achieve an A or B. This number may vary from class to class. For example, you may need only 4 hours per week for psychology but 8 hours per week for math and 10 hours per week for biology. Remember that one of the differences between high school and college is that college requires more work outside the classroom. Generally, you need to plan for about 2 hours outside of class for every hour in class. You need to include in your estimate time for studying the textbook, reviewing your notes, writing your papers, and studying for tests. If unsure, for example, whether to put down 6 or 7 hours for your English class, put down the larger number.

Step 8: Now decide which class is the most difficult and will take the most concentration. Think back to the test you took on your circadian cycle. Also think about the test on study areas you just took. If math is your most difficult subject, then find a time when you can concentrate on it the most. Unless you are a real night owl, always wide awake at 11:00 P.M., don't try to study just before you go to bed. Also recall whether you are an auditory, visual, or kinesthetic learner, and take this into account. For example, if you are a visual learner who is taking a class in psychology that involves mostly lectures, plan time the night before each lecture to read and study the textbook. That way you are emphasizing a strength rather than a weakness.

   If you can plan a regular time every day for each subject, you will be better off because you will have put order into your life. Two-hour blocks of time work fairly well for many people, but you need to decide what your own attention span is. Don't try to study one subject for more than 2 hours because you will probably lose your concentration. If your attention span is a problem, try 1-hour blocks at first.

Step 9: You now have a guide for your daily and weekly routine. You have to go to class on a regular basis, so why not study on a regular basis? What should you be doing during your scheduled study time? You can read the chapter before going to class, review your notes from each day's class, review the previous chapter, begin to review and study for the test the following week, or work on that paper you have to write that is due next Friday.

WEEKLY STUDY SCHEDULE

	Monday	Tuesday	Wednesday	Thursday	Friday	Saturday	Sunday
6:00–7:00							
7:00–8:00							
8:00–9:00							
9:00–10:00							
10:00–11:00							
11:00–12:00							
12:00–1:00							
1:00–2:00							
2:00–3:00							
3:00–4:00							
4:00–5:00							
5:00–6:00							
6:00–7:00							
7:00–8:00							
8:00–9:00							
9:00–10:00							
10:00–11:00							
11:00–12:00							
12:00–1:00							

This schedule does not have to be inflexible. It can be changed as your life changes. But if you have a regular study schedule that you use from week to week, you will finish your studying more quickly and do a better job of it. Don't be caught trying to cram for a test the night before or beginning to write your paper for English at 10:00 P.M. on Tuesday night when it is due at 10:00 A.M. on Wednesday morning. It won't work, or at least it won't work very well!

SQ3R

A Classic Way to Study

SQ3R (**S**urvey, **Q**uestion, **R**ead, **R**ecite, **R**eview) is a system for reading and studying textbook material that was developed by Dr. Francis P. Robinson more than 50 years ago. Most "new" study techniques are variations of this old classic.

Step 1: Survey

You survey a reading selection by looking it over before actually beginning to closely read it. When you complete your survey, you should have a general understanding of what the selection is about. Following are some suggestions for surveying:

1. Read the title or subtitle and any information given about the author.
2. Read the first paragraph or the introduction.
3. Scan the headings or subheadings.
4. Notice any boldfaced or italicized words.
5. Read the first sentence of each paragraph.
6. Notice the charts, diagrams, pictures, or other graphical material.
7. Read the last paragraph, the conclusion, or the summary.
8. Read any questions at the end of the selection.
9. Think about what *you* already know about the topic.

Step 2: Question

After completing your survey, you should have some questions in mind about the material. If you can't think of any questions, try turning a subheading into a question. For a section with the title "SQ3R," you might ask, "What is SQ3R?" or, "Why is it a classic technique of studying?" If the material you are reading doesn't have subheadings, try turning the first sentence of every paragraph into a question. It is much easier to keep yourself actively involved in the material if you are reading to answer specific *how, why,* or *what* questions. Your attention is less likely to wander if you actually write down the questions, and their answers, on a separate sheet of paper, or even in the textbook. You might want to try conducting an imaginary conversation with the author—talk to the author, ask her or him for answers, and keep a continuous conversation going.

Step 3: Read

Now carefully read the entire selection from beginning to end. Look for main ideas and the answers to your questions. You may also want to mark key points by underlining, highlighting, or jotting notes in the margins. Remember, most textbook material will need to be read more than once. The first reading will give you only a limited understanding of the material. If the material is particularly long, divide it into sections, read a section at a time, and perhaps take a short break between sections.

Read
SQ3R
be able
to explain
terms

Step 4: Recite

To do this step, you must put the information you have learned into your own words, and then say it either to yourself or out loud. While it might seem odd at first, talking out loud can be a very effective technique for remembering material because it involves hearing and speaking at the same time. You might pretend someone has asked you a question about the material and then respond (out loud or to yourself) by giving the answer. Or you might pretend that you are the teacher giving a lecture on the material. Be sure you can recite the answers to *who, what, where, when, why,* and *how* questions. When you organize the material mentally and put it into your own words, you are demonstrating your understanding of the material.

Step 5: Review

In this last step, look over your questions, notes, and highlighted material. Practice giving the answers to the questions you originally posed. By now you should be able to define special terms and give relevant examples. You might want to do your review with a classmate by explaining the material to that person or by taking turns quizzing each other on the material. Review frequently so the material will stay with you.

Practice your SQ3R techniques with the following reading selection. Read the first paragraph, the first sentence of subsequent paragraphs, the subheadings, the information in boldface type, and the graphical material. Then read the questions at the end. What do you already know about this topic? Before you start reading the selection, highlight (or underline) the definitions for all of the key terms. Use the margins for any notes you wish to make.

READING

"Thou shalt always use a computer in ways that ensure consideration and respect for your fellow humans."

TUNING IN TO READING

Communication is the most popular Internet activity, and its impact cannot be over-estimated. At a personal level, friends and family can stay in contact with one another even when separated by thousands of miles. At a business level, electronic communication has become a standard, and many times the preferred, way to stay in touch with suppliers, employees, and customers. The three most popular types of Internet communication are electronic mail (e-mail), instant messaging, and discussion groups.

In the selection that follows, you will learn techniques for communicating more effectively via *e-mail,* which is a store-and-forward method for communicating. Specifically, you will learn some "rules of the road" (Internet etiquette) for communicating effectively on the information superhighway.

BIO-SKETCH

Fred T. Hofstetter, a professor in the School of Education at the University of Delaware, teaches courses in multimedia literacy. Currently, he is involved in developing a Web-based teaching and learning environment called Serf.

NOTES ON VOCABULARY

esoteric   private or secret; belonging to a select few. The word *esoteric* derives from a Greek word meaning "inner." It was originally used to describe the secret doctrines that Pythagoras, a Greek philosopher and mathematician, taught to a select group of his disciples.

READING *continued*

acronym a word formed from the initial letters or groups of letters of the words in a name or phrase, as in AIDS from "acquired immune deficiency syndrome."

jargon special words or expressions used by a profession or group that may be difficult for others to understand. The word, derived from Old French, originally meant "twittering or chattering."

newsgroup an electronic Internet site where people can read and post messages relevant to a particular topic.

listserv a mailing list service that enables users to send messages to people on a particular mailing list.

worm A program that replicates itself over a computer network and usually performs malicious actions, such as using up the computer's resources and possibly shutting down the system.

Excerpt from *Internet Literacy*

Fred T. Hofstetter

Internet Etiquette (Netiquette)

Netiquette is a term coined by combining the words *Internet etiquette* into a single name. **Netiquette** is the observance of certain rules and conventions that have evolved in order to keep the Internet from becoming a free-for-all in which tons of unwanted messages and junk mail would clog your inbox and make the information superhighway an unfriendly place to be. This excerpt presents the rules for commercial and educational use of the Internet, suggests a way for you to become a good citizen of the Net (network citizens are called *Netizens*), and defines everyday terms and jargon used on the Net.

Netiquette Guidelines

2   The most commonly known Netiquette rules are as follows:

- Use business language and write professionally in all work-related messages.
- Remember that your message may be printed or forwarded to other people.
- Proofread and correct errors in your message before sending it.
- Do not use all capital letters because this connotes shouting.
- Keep in mind that your reader does not have the benefit of hearing your tone of voice and [seeing] facial clues.
- Remember that the time, date, and reply address are added automatically to your e-mail message; therefore, you do not need to type this information.
- Always include an appropriate subject line [in your] e-mail message.
- Respond promptly to e-mail.

3   Whenever you use the Internet, you should observe the ethics principles [listed here as] the Ten Commandments of Computer Use. These principles were developed by the Computer Ethics Institute in Washington, DC.

> ***The Ten Commandments of Computer Ethics***
> 1. Thou shalt not use a computer to harm other people.
> 2. Thou shalt not interfere with other people's computer work.
> 3. Thou shalt not snoop around in other people's computer files.
> 4. Thou shalt not use a computer to steal.
> 5. Thou shalt not use a computer to bear false witness.
> 6. Thou shalt not copy or use proprietary software for which you have not paid.
> 7. Thou shalt not use other people's computer resources without authorization or proper compensation.
> 8. Thou shalt not appropriate other people's intellectual output.
> 9. Thou shalt think about the social consequences of the program you are writing or the system you are designing.
> 10. Thou shalt always use a computer in ways that ensure consideration and respect for your fellow humans.
>
> Copyright 1991 Computer Ethics Institute. Author: Dr. Ramon C. Barquin, 1707 L. Street, NW, Suite 1030, Washington, DC 20036, Ramon C. Barquin, President, Computer Ethics Institute.

Spam

4   On the Internet, the term **spam** refers to unwanted messages posted to newsgroups or sent to a list of users through e-mail. The term can be used either as a verb or as a noun. To *spam* means to send unwanted messages to a list of users on the Internet. Likewise, unwanted messages that you receive are called *spam*.

5   Perhaps the most obnoxious form of spam is unwanted commercial advertising. The Coalition Against Unsolicited Commercial Email (CAUCE) has done the math, and the outlook is daunting. As CAUCE chairman Scott Hazen Mueller explains, "There are 24 million small businesses in the United States, according to the Small Business Administration. If just one percent of those businesses sent you just one e-mail advertisement a year, that's 657 e-mail advertisements in your inbox each day."

6   To prevent this from happening, Congress has enacted the CAN-SPAM Act, which took effect January 1, 2004. This legislation requires that e-mailed advertising contain a working Unsubscribe link. Furthermore, the CAN-SPAM Act makes it illegal to falsify the From and Subject lines of an e-mail message. For violations, spammers can be jailed for up to five years and fined up to a million dollars. In practice, however, few spammers have been convicted, while the amount of spam has mounted to consume as much as 75 to 80 percent of the typical user's e-mail. As a result, ISPs are looking to technological instead of legislative means of reducing the amount of spam on the Internet. The strategy is to create e-mail authentication technology that would make it harder for spammers to falsify the origin of their messages.

7   There are other forms of spam besides unwanted commercial advertising. A lot of chain letters, for example, are circulating on the Internet. Chain letters are spam; do not send or forward them. If you get one, you may be tempted to send a message to the originator stating that chain letters are an unethical use of the Internet, and that the sender should be ashamed of so littering the information superhighway. Be aware, however, that responding to spam lets the spammer know that your e-mail address is valid, thereby increasing the likelihood that you may receive more spam.

Hoaxes

8   Some pretty incredible hoaxes have been propagated across the Internet. The hoaxes are designed to prey upon people's fears, desires, and sensitivities to keep the hoax spreading to other uses over the Net. An example is the

Netscape-AOL giveaway hoax. It was sent all over the Internet via e-mail by the following chain letter:

> Netscape and AOL have recently merged to form the largest internet company in the world. In an effort to remain at pace with this giant, Microsoft has introduced a new e-mail tracking system as a way to keep Internet Explorer as the most popular browser on the market. This e-mail is a beta test of the new software, and Microsoft has generously offered to compensate those who participate in the testing process. For each person you send this e-mail to, you will be given $5. For every person they give it to, you will be given an additional $3. For every person they send it to, you will receive $1. Microsoft will tally all the e-mails produced under your name over a two-week period and then e-mail you with more instructions. This beta test is only for Microsoft Windows users because the e-mail tracking device that contacts Microsoft is embedded into the code of Windows 95 and 98.
>
> I know you guys hate forwards. But I started this a month ago because I was very short on cash. A week ago I got an e-mail from Microsoft asking me for my address. I gave it to them, and yesterday I got a check in the mail for $800. It really works. I wanted you to get a piece of the action. You won't regret it.

9   Sometimes you may not be sure whether a message is a hoax or not. The major hoaxes are catalogued at the U.S. Department of Energy's Computer Incident Advisory Capability (CIAC) Web site, where you can look to see whether the hoax is a recognized one. For many of the hoaxes, the CIAC will recommend what actions you can take to discourage the spreading of the hoax. At the CIAC site, you will also find links to Web pages warning you about the major chain letters and viruses that you need to watch out for on the Internet.

Viruses

10   Some of the more harmful chain letters and hoaxes have transmitted viruses across the Internet. While it is not possible for your computer to catch a virus from an e-mail address directly, the mail message may contain attachments that can give your computer a virus if you open them. One of the most harmful such e-mail viruses was the Love Bug virus. It spread as an attachment to an e-mail virus entitled "I Love you" and asked you to open the attachment, which was named LOVE-LETTER-FOR-YOU.TXT.VBS. When you opened the attachment, the virus caused computers using the Microsoft Outlook and Outlook Express e-mail programs to send copies of the message to all of the users in your computer's address book. The messages appear to come from the person who owns the computer, serving as further enticement to open the attachment, since it appeared to come from someone you knew. In addition to spreading itself to your friends, the message also deleted certain kinds of files from your computer and replaced them with more copies of the virus.

11   The best way to guard against catching a virus through e-mail is never to open an attachment to an e-mail message, especially if the attachment has an executable filename extension such as *.exe, .vbs,* or *.class.* Before you open any e-mail attachment, make very sure that . . . the message actually came from the person listed as the source. If you have any doubts, check the antivirus Web pages to see if the message you received is part of a nationally recognized virus attack.

12   A message may appear to come from a trusted acquaintance, when in fact it came from a worm. Recently, some viruses spread via e-mail that did not require the recipient to open the attachment. In addition, there are malicious virus programs that mimic the e-mail addresses of people from your address book. As a result, it is very important to keep current antivirus protection software on your computer.

Lurking

13   To **lurk** means to participate in a conversation on the Internet without responding to any of the messages. You receive and read the messages, but you do not say anything in return. Thus, you are lurking!

14   It is not unethical to lurk. To the contrary, it is often a good idea to lurk at first. For example, suppose you join a listserv that has been going on for a while. Instead of jumping right in and writing something that may make you seem really out of touch with what is going on, it is smarter to lurk for a while, so you can pick up the gist of the conversation before joining in.

15   The same guideline applies to newsgroups. Before you begin writing messages in a newsgroup, spend some time looking around at what has been written previously in that newsgroup. When you write something, you want it to sound as though you know what is going on. It is inconsiderate to write messages that waste the time of other users on the Net.

16   Ditto for chat rooms. When you enter a chat room in which other people are talking, spend some time listening to get the gist of the conversation before you chime in.

Flames

17   On the Internet, a **flame** is a message written in anger. The term "flame" can be used as either a verb or a noun. To *flame* someone is to send them an angry message. Angry messages that people send you are known as *flames*.

18   You need to be careful, especially if you have a temper. Form the habit of thinking carefully about what you write, and proofread several times before you send the message. Make sure the message truly conveys the emotions you want to communicate. If you are extremely mad, and send a hastily written flame, you may regret it later on. When you cool off a few minutes later, you may wish you could tone down the message a little, but it will be too late. The message has already been sent, and unfortunate damage may be done to your relationship with the receiving party.

Firefighters

19   Sometimes flaming can get out of hand, especially when it occurs in a newsgroup or a listserv with a lot of users. People start sending hotter messages, and things can get ugly. Someone has to step in and write a message intended to restore peace. Because that puts an end to the flames, such peacemakers on the Internet are known as **firefighters.**

SHOUTING

20   Messages written on the Internet are normally written in lowercase letters, with capital letters appearing only at the start of the first word of each sentence, and on proper nouns, such as the term *Internet*. WHEN YOU WRITE IN ALL CAPS, ON THE OTHER HAND, YOU ARE SHOUTING! **Shouting** means to add emphasis to something by writing in all capital letters. Shouting is almost always regarded as in poor taste, however, so do it sparingly, if at all.

21   If you hit the Caps Lock key by mistake, everything you enter will be written in all caps. Do not turn on the Caps Lock option unless you really want to shout.

22   An alternative to writing in all caps is to add emphasis to a word or phrase by surrounding it with asterisks, such as: It is *rude* to shout on the Internet.

Smileys and Emoticons

23   One of the problems inherent in text messages is that you cannot see the body language or facial expression of the person sending the message. Not knowing for sure whether something is said in jest can lead people to make false assumptions about the intent of a message. You need to be careful, because a miscommunication can cause serious problems.

24   To give the person reading your message a clue about your emotions, emoticons were devised. **Emoticons** are combinations of a few characters that conjure a facial expression when turned sideways. The most common form of emoticon is the smiley, which conveys a happy facial expression. Turn your book clockwise, and you will see that the characters :) convey a happy face. The smiley often has a nose :-) and sometimes winks at you ;-).

25   Emoticons are not always happy. For example, :(is a frown, and :-(is a frown with a nose. Someone really sad may be crying:~~ (and someone obnoxious may stick out their tongue :-P at you. You can even convey drooling :-P~~ with an emoticon.

Three-Letter Acronyms (TLAs)

26   To shorten the amount of keyboarding required to write a message, some people use three-letter acronyms, which are appropriately known as TLAs. A **three-letter acronym (TLA)** is a way of shortening a three-word phrase such as "in my opinion" by simply typing the first letter of each word, such as *imo*. Cell phone users use TLAs to reduce the amount of keypresses required to TXT a message to another phone. Some of the more common three-letter acronyms are

brb	be right back	**j/k**	just kidding
bbl	be back later	**oic**	oh, I see
btw	by the way	**ott**	over the top (excessive, uncalled for)
imo	in my opinion	**thx**	thanks
lol	laughing out loud		

27   There are also two-letter acronyms, such as

np	no problem	**wb**	welcome back
re	hi again, as in "re hi"	**b4**	before

28   Some of these are more intuitive than others! There are also acronyms with more than three letters, including

bbiaf	be back in a flash	**nhoh**	never heard of him/her
hhoj	ha ha, only joking	**rotfl**	rolling on the floor laughing
imho	in my humble opinion	**ttfn**	ta ta for now
morf	male or female		

From Fred T. Hofstetter, *Internet Literacy*, 4th Edition, pp. 84–91. Copyright © 2006 by The McGraw-Hill Companies, Inc. Reprinted with permission.

 **COMPREHENSION CHECKUP**

Short Answer

Directions: Answer the questions briefly.

1. What is the selection about? _____

2. List three TLAs that you commonly use.

_____

_____

_____

Multiple Choice

Directions: For each item, write the letter corresponding to the best answer.

_____ 1. Which of the following statements is true according to the information in
the selection?
   a. Hoaxes work by misleading and deceiving.
   b. Many are fooled by the hoaxes they find on the Internet.
   c. There isn't any way to determine the truthfulness of Internet hoaxes.
   d. Both a and b.

_____ 2. Which of the following is the most popular Internet activity?
   a. communication
   b. shopping
   c. searching
   d. entertainment

_____ 3. Unwanted and unsolicited e-mails are called
   a. spam.
   b. junk.
   c. flame.
   d. lurk.

_____ 4. According to the author, all of the following should be done before
sending an e-mail message *except*
   a. proofreading and correcting errors.
   b. writing in lowercase letters, using capitals only at the beginning of a
      sentence and for proper nouns.
   c. typing in the time, date, and reply address.
   d. including an appropriate subject line.

_____ 5. The author considers all of the following to be principles for computer
use *except*
   a. Respect other people's privacy by not reading their e-mail.
   b. The best ethical guideline is to do only what you can get away with.
   c. Stealing material from others is prohibited.
   d. Be sure to pay for what you use.

True or False

Directions: Indicate whether each statement is true or false by writing **T** or **F** in the
space provided.

_____ 1. Many spammers have been convicted and jailed.

_____ 2. A typical computer user's e-mail consists of 50 percent spam.

_____ 3. According to the author, chain letters are not considered to be spam.

_____ 4. The author of the selection advises the reader not to send or forward
chain letters.

_____ 5. If you respond to spam, you have let the spammer know that your e-mail address is a valid one.

_____ 6. A computer can't catch a virus from an e-mail directly.

_____ 7. The author recommends that antivirus protection be kept current.

_____ 8. According to the author, it is unethical and immoral to lurk.

_____ 9. Peacemakers on the Internet are referred to as firefighters.

_____ 10. In an attempt to control spam, antispam laws have been enacted.

Vocabulary Matching

Directions: Match the vocabulary words in Column A with the definitions in Column B. Place the correct letter in the space provided.

Column A	Column B
_____ 1. emoticon	a. to send an e-mail message intended to insult or provoke
_____ 2. e-mail	b. on the Internet, typing a message IN ALL CAPITAL LETTERS to add emphasis
_____ 3. flame	c. Internet etiquette, which is the observance of certain rules and conventions
_____ 4. shouting	d. to send unwanted messages to a list of users on the Internet
_____ 5. smiley	e. a character combination that, when turned sideways, conjures a facial expression
_____ 6. spam	f. a malicious or unwanted code that installs itself on your computer without your knowledge by hiding inside other programs
_____ 7. firefighter	g. to participate in a conversation on the Internet without responding to any of the messages
_____ 8. Netiquette	h. a peacemaker who works to quell flames on the Internet
_____ 9. virus	i. electronic mail
_____ 10. lurk	j. an emoticon that conveys a happy facial expression

Vocabulary in Context

Directions: In the blanks below, write the word or phrase from the list that best completes the sentence.

compensate	daunting	deleted	enticement	free-for-all
gist	merged	prey	sensitized	tally

1. Sue gave Marie the _____ of her conversation with Mark.

2. After the president announced his resignation, the press conference deteriorated into a _____.

3. The western diamondback rattlesnake's _____ is primarily small rodents, rabbits, and birds.

4. After the two airlines _____, passengers experienced higher fares and fewer flights.

5. I was advised by my boss to _____ all of my out-of-pocket expenses and submit them for reimbursement.

6. I inadvertently _____ some important information from my computer.

7. As an _____ for finishing my degree, my mother promised me a trip to Hawaii.

8. When her car broke down in the desert, she faced the _____ task of hiking 10 miles to get help.

9. Nothing can _____ for the loss of a child.

10. Some people need to be _____ to the effect their words have on others.

In Your Own Words

1. Patricia T. O'Conner, author of *Woe Is I*, suggests that while it's one thing to be creative with grammar, spelling, and punctuation with friends, it's quite another to use "goofy English" when writing instant messages or e-mails to teachers and people in the business community. She suggests that the audience you're writing to should influence how you write the message. What do you think?

2. Many of you post messages to blogs, bulletin boards, discussion groups, and other public forums, which are often read by complete strangers. Do you agree or disagree with the statement "You are what you write"? If you are unfamiliar with the person you're writing to, how careful should you be about what you say?

3. Your e-mail address is seen by everyone you send e-mail to. In a personal e-mail account, you often choose your own address, which says something about you in a way similar to a vanity plate on a car. How important do you think it is to avoid having an e-mail address that is too cute or too personal? Do you think people should get into the habit of using different e-mail addresses for different purposes?

4. A student turned in a term paper and, when he got it back, was surprised to see points deducted because he wrote, "In some situations, sympathy can be 2 much." Do you think shorthand expressions should be acceptable in formal papers?

5. Why has text messaging become so popular? When are you likely to use text messaging?

Written Assignment

1. The principal problem with online communication is that nonverbal communication is difficult. When you can't see or hear the other person, how can you tell what he or she is really thinking or feeling? How do you convey your feelings online to others? What clues do you rely on in determining what others are really saying to you? What kinds of problems could a nonnative speaker encounter?

2. How do you think emoticons in e-mail messages can help prevent miscommunication? How might an emoticon create a misunderstanding? Why do you think some people actively dislike the use of emoticons in written communication? When you see an emoticon in an e-mail message, what is your initial reaction?

3. Write a few short paragraphs giving your opinion of the following tips provided by *Computing Essentials*. Which tip is most valuable to you?

Tips

Are you tired of sorting through an inbox full of spam? Americans receive over 200 billion spam e-mails every year. Here are a few simple tips to help ensure that your inbox is spam-free:

1. **Choose a complex address.** sally_smith@hotmail.com is much more likely to get spam than 4it3scoq2@hotmail.com. Consider using a more complicated, and less personal, user name.

2. **Keep a low profile.** Many spammers collect e-mail addresses from personal Web sites, chat rooms, and message boards. Use caution when handing out your address and be sure to read the privacy policy of a site before you hand over your address.

3. **Don't ever respond to spam.** Once you respond to spam, either in interest or to opt out of a list, you have confirmed the address is valid. Valid addresses are worth more to spammers, who then sell the addresses to others.

4. **Use e-mail filter options.** Most e-mail programs have a filter option that screens in-coming e-mail based on a set of preferences you choose. You can set up your inbox to accept only mail from certain addresses or to block mail from others.

5. **Use spam blockers.** There are plenty of programs available to help protect your inbox. For example, MailWasher provides an effective and free program available at www.mailwasher.com.

From Timothy J. O'Leary and Linda I. O'Leary, *Computing Essentials 2008,* Complete Edition, 19th Edition, p. 35. Copyright © 2008 by The McGraw-Hill Companies, Inc. Reprinted with permission.

Internet Activity

Check out one of the following Web sites devoted to the topic of netiquette.

1. Take the short netiquette quiz and summarize your results:

   www.albion.com

2. This site is presented by the Boston Public Library. Of the tips listed, which do you think are most valuable to children? Write a short paragraph giving your opinion.

   www.bpl.org/kids/netiquette

3. This site provides good links to the Library of Congress's Guide on Copyright Basics and Citation. What information is the most relevant in terms of writing research papers?

   www.studygs.net/netiquette.htm

4. Review the sections on the netiquette of replying to e-mails and the netiquette of confidentiality. What information is most important to you in regard to your own correspondence?

   www.livinginternet.com

Chapter Summary and Review

In Chapter 1, you learned about various learning styles and how to develop a study schedule that suits your learning style. You also learned about the theory of multiple intelligences. In addition, you learned more about how to determine the meanings of words from context. Furthermore, you learned about SQ3R and how to apply it to a reading selection. Finally, you learned some rules for effective Internet communication.

Short Answer

Directions: Answer the questions briefly, in a sentence or two.

1. What are your personal learning styles? How can you use them to do better in college?

2. What are four techniques for discovering the meanings of words from context clues?

3. Are you more of a day or night person? How will this knowledge help you prepare for your classes?

4. Which multiple intelligences are your strengths? Your weaknesses?

Vocabulary in Context

Directions: Choose one of the following words to complete the sentences below. Use each word only once.

antonyms	circadian	death	kinesthetic
left-brain	married	paragraphs	survey

5. Accountants and computer engineers are probably _____ oriented.

6. If you are a(n) _____ learner, you may want to take notes, highlight your textbook, or get up and walk around the room.

7. You can easily throw off your _____ cycle when you get on a plane and fly to a different time zone.

8. Two of the biggest stressors for people are a(n) _____ in the family and getting _____.

9. A good way to _____ a chapter in one of your textbooks is to read the first and last _____ and look at the headings and subheadings.

10. _____ for homeostasis are *change* and *variation*.

VOCABULARY   Unit 1 Homonyms and Other Confusing Words

As you learned in the Introduction, homonyms are words that sound the same but may have different spellings or meanings. There are other words that could be added to our list of homonyms below, but these are the ones students most commonly have trouble with. Mastering these words will help you make a good impression in written assignments, so we have included homonyms in Chapter 1. *Affect* and *effect* are discussed in a separate box because they are especially difficult.

accept	a verb meaning "to receive, take, or hold." Did you *accept* the money given to you by your rich uncle?
except	a preposition meaning "without." Everyone *except* you was invited to the party.

U.S. Capitol

capital—The highest capital city, before being taken over by China, was Lhasa, Tibet. Its elevation is 12,087 feet above sea level.

know—"All men by nature desire to know."
    —Aristotle

expect a verb meaning "to look forward to an event." *Expect* is not technically a homonym, but students sometimes confuse it with *except*. I *expect* to get an A in English, but if I don't do well on the final I might end up with a B.

capitol a noun meaning "the physical building where laws are made." From now on, you should use this word for the actual building. The *capitol* building in Washington, DC, has two branches, the Senate and the House of Representatives.

capital a noun or adjective meaning "most important or most serious," including the *capital* city, money, *capital* letters, *capital* punishment, and the top of a column of a building. What is the *capital* city of your state?

Think about This Sentence: Your state *capitol* building is located in the *capital* city of your state.

know a verb meaning "to understand." Did you *know* all the important information for the test?

no adverb, sometimes an adjective, used to express something negative. Did you stay up all night studying for the test? *No,* you went to bed.

knew a verb, past tense of the verb *know*. I *knew* the material for the test.

new adjective meaning "present, modern"; an antonym of *old*. Did you spend your money on a *new* car?

past a noun meaning "former time." In the *past* you did not study as much as you should have.

an adjective meaning "former." One of our *past* presidents was Thomas Jefferson.

an adverb meaning "beyond something." Did you walk *past* the library on the way to the student union?

passed the past tense of the verb *pass*. The quarterback *passed* the ball to the tight end, who ran for a touchdown. The student *passed* the test with an A. My father *passed* away. Each of these sentences uses the word *passed* as a verb expressing action.

Think about This Sentence: Most of our *past* presidents have *passed* away.

principal a noun meaning "head of a school, or other person who is the main person."

a noun meaning "sum of money." When you buy a house, you will pay on *principal* and interest.

an adjective meaning "main" or "chief." Was the *principal* cause of the Civil War the desire to abolish slavery or the need to keep our country unified?

principle a noun meaning "fundamental moral beliefs." Cheating people out of their money should go against the *principles* your parents taught you.

a noun meaning "fundamental theory," as in physics. A fundamental *principle* in physics is that the atoms or molecules in gases are more widely spaced than in solids or liquids.

Think about This Sentence: Your *principal* beliefs are the *principles* you live by.

quiet	an adjective meaning "silent." Are you a *quiet* person?
quite	an adverb meaning "very" or "extremely." The line of cars trying to get into the parking lot of the football stadium was *quite* long.
quit	a verb meaning "to discontinue" or "give up." This word is not really a homonym, but is often confused with *quiet* and *quite.* The student *quit* her job at McDonald's so that she could devote more time to her studies.
their	an adjective indicating possession; the possessive form of "they." *Their* car was stolen from the parking lot.
there	an adverb indicating direction, meaning "in that position." Notice how the word *here* appears in the word *there.* The computer lab is located over *there.*
	a pronoun used to begin a sentence or phrase. *There* are a few students absent from class today.
they're	a contraction for "they are." *They're* going to the party after the game.
to	a preposition indicating direction, and meaning "toward." Are you going *to* your house after you finish class?
	part of a verb indicating an infinitive statement. Unless you are independently wealthy, you will need *to* work for a living. You may want *to* study in the library.

Think about This Sentence: You are going *to* work because you need *to* work for a living. The first *to* is a preposition indicating direction; the second *to* is part of the verb "to work."

too	an adverb meaning "also" or "excessively." He, *too,* was allowed to leave class early. She drank *too* much at the party.
two	the number 2. The baseball team scored *two* runs in the fifth inning.
threw	the past tense of the verb *throw.* The shortstop *threw* out the runner at first base.
through	a preposition indicating direction. The drunk driver drove *through* the red light.
	a preposition meaning "finished." When the student was *through* with the test, he took it to the instructor at the front of the class.
	Finish the sentence: The boy *threw* the ball *through* the _____.

weather—Don't talk on the phone or take a shower during a thunderstorm. The electrical current of lightning can travel through phone lines and water pipes.

weather	a noun meaning "temperature, climate." The *weather* was so hot that you just had to stay inside with the air conditioner running.
whether	a conjunction similar to "if." Some people believe it really doesn't make much difference *whether* we have a Republican or Democratic president.
were	a past tense of the verb *be.* We *were* in the mountains when the fire broke out.
we're	a contraction for *we are.* *We're* going to go to the store.

Affect versus Effect

Now for the difference between *affect* and *effect*. We won't insist on perfection in your use of these words, but you can get better. The key to working with these words is knowing the difference between a noun and a verb. Remember that a verb indicates *action* or *state of being*. A noun is a person, place, or thing; remember that things can be intangible (for example, feelings, causes, and hopes).

action   The team *won* the game last night.

affect   a verb meaning "influence." This word will *almost always* be used as a verb. If one thing *affects* something else, it influences it. If you are using one of these words as a verb, you will use *affect* 95 percent of the time. Weather *affects* our personalities and how we feel. (The weather is influencing your personality.)

In psychology, *affect* can be used as a noun meaning "emotional response." After her mother died, Maria became depressed and had a flat *affect*.

state of being   The team *is* excellent because its players *are* quick and play good defense.

effect   Ninety-nine percent of the time this word will be a noun. *Effect* as a noun usually means "the result of an action." What will be the *effect* on you if Congress cuts back the financial aid program?

Using *effect* as a verb is very tricky, but on the positive side you will probably need to use it this way very rarely. As a verb, *effect* means "to cause or bring about." Congress may *effect* a change in the income tax laws.

wear   a verb meaning "to have on the body" or "to diminish." What are you going to *wear* to the party on Saturday? You are going to *wear* out the carpet walking back and forth so much.

where   an adverb, conjunction, or noun indicating location. *Where* did I leave my books?

Now write your own sentences using *affect* and *effect*. (You may find it helpful to refer to the sample sentences above.)

_____

_____

_____

Homonym Exercise 1

Directions: For each exercise, complete the following sentences using the correct homonym.

1. Did she ___accept___ the marriage proposal?
   accept/except

2. In the United States, the issue of ___capital___ punishment is controversial.
   capitol/capital

3. I don't ___know___ what to do to help you study for that quiz.
   know/no

4. That room definitely needs ___new___ paint.
   knew/new

5. In the ___past___, I was not available to work on Tuesdays.
   past/passed

6. My ___principles___ include not speaking harshly of anyone.
   principals/principles

7. I want you to __*quite*__ making that very annoying noise.
   quit/quite

8. While I am the talkative one in the family, my husband is the __*quite*__ one.
   quiet/quite

9. The noise was __*quit*__ loud and as a result gave me a headache.
   quite/quit

10. Write a sentence of your own using *capital* correctly.

_____

Homonym Exercise 2

1. People don't realize they are __*affectd*__ by advertising.
   affected/effected

2. What possible __*effects*__ does drinking alcohol have on teenagers?
   affects/effects

3. Special __*effect*__ in the movie *Star Wars* look tame by today's standards.
   affects/effects

4. The teacher told me my absences __*affected*__ my grade in her class.
   affected/effected

5. The __*weather*__ forecast today shows a chance of showers in the north.
   weather/whether

6. It doesn't matter __*whether*__ I exercise or not; I still can't lose weight.
   weather/whether

7. It's not possible to __*know*__ all of the material for the quiz.
   know/no

8. I don't know __*where*__ to turn in my finished essay.
   were/where

9. They __*were*__ not able to attend the luncheon held in their honor.
   were/where

10. The babysitter wants to give the children __*their*__ lunch at noon.
    their/there

11. __*there*__ are too many people enrolled in the nine o'clock English class.
    their/there

12. Jan said that she wanted to come to the party __*too*__.
    to/too/two

13. I am not able __*to*__ visit him in the hospital today.
    to/too/two

14. Her resignation from the position was __*accepted*__ by her supervisor.
    accepted/excepted

15. The hostess __*accepted*__ my apologies when I declined the invitation.
    accepted/excepted

Vocabulary Unit 1 Crossword

ACROSS CLUES

2. _____ on their way to class.
4. We have all done things in the _____ that we later regretted.
7. All students need _____ study several times each week for each class.
9. Did you drive your car _____ the exit on the freeway?
10. _____ is a good program on TV tonight.
11. Will you _____ your friend's invitation to the party?
13. Will you go _____ your graduation ceremony?
14. The student was _____ upset when he was withdrawn from class.
15. Many students _____ college before they graduate.
16. Do you _____ who won the game last night?
17. One of the _____ ingredients in soda is sugar.
19. Why were you over _____ when you should have been over here?

20. _____ house was broken into several times last summer.
24. You must walk _____ the hallway to get to the classroom.
25. Did you _____ your job?
26. _____, I do not want any more ice cream.
27. Everyone _____ you received an A on the test.
28. _____ you at home last night studying?
29. The elderly person _____ away.
30. One _____ of life is to do unto others as you would want them to do unto you.

DOWN CLUES

1. We went to Wal-Mart to buy _____ clothes.
2. There are _____ wheels on a typical bike.
3. All of the student's grades were As _____ for the B on the final.
5. Studying hard should positively _____ your grade.

6. The basketball player _____ the ball out-of-bounds, by accident.
8. What is the _____ city of your state?
12. Using drugs will have a negative _____ on a person.
13. _____ little sleep will probably make you drowsy and cranky.
14. Was the room _____ while students were taking the test, or was it too noisy?
16. The student _____ all the important information for the test.
17. Religious books lay down basic _____s of life.
18. Where is the _____ building located?
21. When will you be _____ with your work and able to go home?
22. _____ is the closest McDonald's?
23. The first letter of a sentence should be a(n) _____ letter.

Discovering Meaning through Structure

Written music is like a route map, or a set of instructions for a journey. It is a diagram which shows a musician how a piece of music should be played.

—**Caroline Grimshaw**, from *Music Connections*

"[Musical] notation can be used as a point of reference, but the notation does not indicate music. It indicates a direction."

—**Cecil Taylor**, from *Jazz Is* by Nat Hentoff

CHAPTERS IN PART 2

Ray Charles

A musician composing a piece of music has a purpose or direction in mind—to communicate a certain mood or feeling. This mood or feeling could be called the main idea of the piece. The composer will organize the piece around the main idea by finding instruments, notes, and chords that support the main idea and bring it to life. All of these elements will fit together in a smooth way to form the structure of the piece, which is what gives it meaning.

A writer works in a similar way. A writer constructing a paragraph has a purpose or direction in mind, which is to communicate a main idea. The writer organizes the paragraph around the main idea by stating the main idea and then presenting details that support it. How the supporting details relate to one another and to the main idea forms the structure of the paragraph. It is the structure of the paragraph that gives it meaning. In Part 2, we will discuss the different ways that paragraphs can be organized or structured.

2

Topics, Main Ideas, and Details

CHAPTER PREVIEW

In this chapter, you will

- Learn how to distinguish between general ideas and specific details.

- Learn how to identify the topic of a paragraph.

- Learn how to locate the stated main idea of a paragraph.

- Learn how to diagram a paragraph by identifying its main idea sentence and key details.

- Become familiar with paraphrasing.

- Learn how to formulate implied main ideas.

Description of Topics, Main Ideas, and Details

Write your own definition for each boldfaced term. Use your own words.

topic or subject:

_____

_____

main idea:

_____

_____

details:

_____

_____

Most paragraphs are about a particular **topic** or **subject.** The topic is usually a single word or phrase and is often the noun that is mentioned most frequently in a paragraph. We can identify the topic by asking ourselves "What is this all about?" or "Who is this all about?"

Paragraphs are supposed to be organized around a **main idea,** with all sentences supporting this main idea, or key point. The main idea can be identified by asking "What key point does the author want me to know about the topic?"

The main idea may be directly stated in a paragraph, usually, but not always, in the first or last sentence, or it can be implied. When trying to find a main idea that is directly stated, it helps to remember that you are looking for a general statement, not a specific one. When main ideas are implied, you, the reader, are responsible for coming up with a general statement that unites the author's key details. This general statement should be no more than one sentence long.

While all paragraphs have a topic, not all paragraphs have main ideas. Some background or descriptive paragraphs, which are meant to set the tone or mood of a piece of writing, may not have any main idea at all.

Details are supporting sentences that reinforce the main idea. While the main idea is a general statement, supporting details provide specific information such as facts, examples, or reasons that explain or elaborate on the main idea. Details answer the question words about the topic: *who, what, where, when, why,* and *how.*

84

Baby Blues

© Baby Blues Partnership. King Features Syndicate

As an illustration of the difference between main ideas and details, study the *Baby Blues* cartoon. In it, Darryl provides Wanda with the main idea of the phone conversation but is unable to provide her with any of the supporting details.

major supporting details:

_____

_____

minor supporting details:

_____

_____

Those supporting sentences that directly reinforce the main idea are called **major supporting details,** and those sentences that serve only to reinforce the major supporting details are called **minor supporting details.** To gain an understanding of how main ideas and major and minor supporting details work in a paragraph, read the following paragraph on posture as body language and study the outline.

Posture often indicates feelings of tension or relaxation. We take relaxed postures in non-threatening situations and tighten up in threatening situations. Based on this observation, we can tell a good deal about how others feel simply by watching how tense or loose they seem to be. For example, watching tenseness is a way of detecting status differences. The lower-status person is generally the more rigid, tense-appearing one, whereas the higher status person is more relaxed. This is the kind of situation that often happens when an employee sits ramrod straight while the boss leans back in her chair. The same principle applies to social situations, where it's often possible to tell who's uncomfortable by looking at pictures. Often you'll see someone laughing and talking as if he were perfectly at home, but his posture almost shouts nervousness. Some people never relax, and their posture shows it.

From Ronald B. Adler, Russell F. Proctor II, and Neil Towne, *Looking Out, Looking In,* 11th Edition, p. 229. © 2005 Wadsworth, a part of Cengage Learning, Inc. Reproduced by permission. www.cengage.com/permissions

In the outline, MI refers to the main idea, MSD to major supporting details, and msd to minor supporting details.

I. Posture often indicates feelings of tension or relaxation. (MI)
    A. Person displays relaxed posture when not threatened. (MSD)
    B. Person displays tense posture when feeling threatened. (MSD)
    C. Tension or relaxation in posture may indicate status. (MSD)
       1. Tense-appearing person has low status. (msd)
       2. Relaxed-appearing person has high status. (msd)
    D. Posture indicates who's comfortable in a social setting. (MSD)

In the following example, the general topic is sensitivity to nonverbal communication. The format is fairly typical of information presented in college textbooks. The main idea is given in the first sentence of the paragraph. The sentences following the main idea are all meant to serve as examples illustrating it. The last sentence concludes the paragraph and reinforces the main idea.

> <u>Cultural diversity in the workplace has created a need for greater sensitivity among managers and employees regarding people's use of nonverbal communication.</u> For example, white Americans define eye contact in the course of a conversation as showing respect. But many Latinos do not, and many Americans of Asian ancestry deem eye contact with an employer to be exceedingly disrespectful behavior. Potential conflicts may arise when white supervisors consider Hispanic or Asian employees furtive or rude for casting their eyes about the room. <u>Multicultural training programs seek to teach employers and employees to look beyond their culture-bound notions about what constitutes "proper" and "improper"</u> behavior.

From Michael Hughes and Carolyn J. Kroehler, *Sociology: The Core*, 7th Edition, p. 79. Copyright © 2005 by The McGraw-Hill Companies, Inc. Reprinted with permission.

You may have experienced difficulty finding the main ideas in these two sample paragraphs. But don't be discouraged. This chapter will give you the skills you need to readily find main ideas and supporting details.

Distinguishing between General and Specific

In order to be able to recognize a main idea, you must be able to determine the difference between something that is general and something that is specific. Remember, a main idea is a general statement that is supported by specific details. In the first example below, a car is something that is general because there are more specific kinds of cars. A sedan would be one specific kind of car, and a convertible would be another. In the second example, tree is the broad category. An ash tree is a specific kind of tree, as is an elm tree.

Car	Tree
sedan	ash
convertible	elm

Exercise 1: Writing General and Specific Terms

Directions: Give two specific terms for each general category.

Example:

Professional baseball teams

Los Angeles Dodgers

New York Yankees

1. Wild animals

   Bear

   Lion

2. Countries

   US

   South Africa

3. Weekly magazines

   Times Union

   _____

4. Universities

   UNF

   UF

5. College courses

   Anome

   Religion

6. U.S. presidents

   Andrew Jackson

   Teddy Roosevelt

Directions: Give a general term that covers the specific items.

Example:

Jazz musicians

Louis Armstrong

Wynton Marsalis

Miles Davis

1. _____   2. Famos Puinter   3. Movies

   Aleve   Picasso   *Mission: Impossible III*

   Bayer   Van Gogh   *War of the Worlds*

   Excedrin   Monet   *Jerry McGuire*

Exercise 2: Writing Specific Sentences

Directions: A general or main idea sentence is given to you. Working in a group, try to come up with two sentences that support the main idea. Your sentences should provide specific details by giving reasons or examples.

Example: Many people do not use antibiotics properly.

   a. They stop taking the antibiotic when they start feeling better.

   b. They pass them around to their friends like candy.

1. Children today don't treat their parents with much respect.

   a. They don't care about what thir parents think

   b. They really don't care or know what respect is

2. Young boys are more interested in active, aggressive play than little girls.

   a. Boys play more aggressive because of volint games

   b. Girls play Less aggressive because they mature faster

3. In the last 10 years, a new kind of father has emerged.

   a. Fathers now are spending more time with thire kids.

   b. Fathers now are working less hours hours

4. For a student in the United States, school is just like a job.

   a. Students have to be in school full time

   b. Students have to Go through school so they can make thire parents proud

5. Holding a part-time job can benefit students.

   They Leail to be more

   a. They learn respoindly and they learn how the working world works

   b. They learn they can to mange thire money,

6. People are more isolated from their neighbors today than they were 50 years ago.

   a. They no longer comualti with one another.

   b. They no longer ~~stay in conitita~~ no longer trust caurr because the way the world is.

7. The traditional family (husband as breadwinner, wife as homemaker) has all but disappeared.

a. Today _No one is family orardaded_

b. Today _People just dont care about fainly_

Exercise 3: Identifying Topics of Paragraphs

Now apply what you have learned about general and specific to help you identify the topic of a paragraph. A good topic is comprehensive because it covers all of the ideas mentioned in the paragraph. Sometimes it helps to think of the topic as a title for the paragraph.

Directions: For each paragraph, determine the best topic and put a **T** on the line. Put a **G** on the line of the topic that is too general or broad and an **S** on the line of the topic that is too specific.

1.   There is no doubt that advertisers have zeroed in on the child audience. The last few years have seen the growth of kid-specific media: Nikelodeon, websites, kid-oriented magazines, movie tie-ins, and even hamburger wrappers. From 1993 to 1999, advertising in these media increased more than 50 percent, to $1.5 billion per year. Part of the reason behind this increase is the fact that kids have become important factors in family buying decisions. First, they have more money to spend. The under-14 set gets allowances, earns money, and receives gifts to the tune of about $20 billion per year. In addition, kids probably influence another $200 billion worth of shopping decisions. Second, the increase in single-parent families and dual-career families means that kids are now making some of the purchasing decisions that were once left to Mom and Dad. It is not surprising, then, to find that companies are intensifying their efforts to reach this market segment.

From Joseph R. Dominick, *The Dynamics of Mass Communication,* 8th Edition, p. 379. Copyright © 2005 by The McGraw-Hill Companies, Inc. Reprinted with permission.

Example:

_____ a. Audiences (This is too broad—it covers all types of audiences, not just child audiences.)

_____ b. A 50 percent increase in child advertising (This provides one specific detail from the paragraph.)

_____ c. Advertisers target child audiences (This covers all the ideas in the paragraph.)

2.   Which sex is healthier: women or men? We know that women have a higher life expectancy than men and lower death rates throughout life. Women's greater longevity has been attributed to genetic protection given by the second X chromosome (which men do not have). However, factors such as men's greater propensity for risk taking and their preference for meat and potatoes rather than fruits and vegetables, also may play a part. Despite their longer life, women are more likely than men to report being in fair or poor health, go to doctors or seek outpatient or emergency room care more often, are more likely to seek treatment for minor illnesses, and report more unexplained symptoms. Men are *less* likely to seek professional help for health problems, but they have longer hospital stays, and their health problems are more likely to be chronic and life-threatening. Women's greater tendency to seek medical care does not necessarily mean that

they are in worse health than men, nor that they are imagining ailments or are preoccupied with illness. They may simply be more health conscious. Men may feel that illness is not "masculine," and seeking help means a loss of control. Research suggests that a man is least likely to seek help when he perceives a health problem as a threat to his self-esteem or if he believes his male peers would look down on him. It may well be that the better care women take of themselves helps them live longer than men.

From Diane E. Papalia, Sally Wendkos Olds, and Ruth Duskin Feldman, *Human Development*, 10th Edition, pp. 482–83. Copyright © 2007 by The McGraw-Hill Companies, Inc. Reprinted with permission.

_____G_____ a. Men and women

_____T_____ b. Which sex is healthier?

_____S_____ c. Men and longer hospital stays

3.   Engineers and inventors often appropriate their best ideas directly from the natural world. Perhaps the best example of this is the development of Velcro fasteners. Today, Velcro has hundreds of uses in diapers, running shoes, space suits, even in sealing the chambers of artificial hearts. But it all started in 1948, when George de Mestral, a Swiss hiker, observed the manner in which cockleburs clung to clothing and thought that a fastener could be designed using the pattern. Cockleburs have up to several hundred curved prickles that function in seed dispersal. These tiny prickles tenaciously hook onto clothing or the fur of animals and are thus transported to new areas. De Mestral envisioned a fastener with thousands of tiny hooks, mimicking the cocklebur prickles on one side, and on the other side thousands of tiny eyes for the hooks to lock onto. It took 10 years to perfect the original concept of the "locking tape" that has become Velcro, and is so common in modern life.

From Estelle Levetin and Karen McMahon, *Plants and Society*, 5th Edition, p. 6. Copyright © 2008 by The McGraw-Hill Companies, Inc. Reprinted with permission.

_____G_____ a. Velcro use in diapers and shoes

_____G_____ b. Inventions

_____S_____ c. The development of Velcro

4.   Women absorb and metabolize alcohol differently than men do. A woman cannot metabolize much alcohol in the cells that line her stomach. Women also have less body water in which to dilute the alcohol than do men. So, when a man and a woman of similar size drink equal amounts of alcohol, a larger proportion of the alcohol reaches and remains in the woman's bloodstream. Overall, women develop alcohol-related ailments such as cirrhosis of the liver more rapidly than men do with the same alcohol consumption habits.

From Gordon Wardlaw, *Contemporary Nutrition*, 6th Edition. New York: McGraw-Hill, 2007, p. 221.

_____G_____ a. Alcohol

_____S_____ b. The development of cirrhosis of the liver in women

_____T_____ c. Gender differences in alcohol effects

5.   Ethnocentrism is the belief that our own group or culture—whatever it may be—is superior to all other groups or cultures. If you were born and raised in the United States, you may find it strange that most people in India regard the cow

as a sacred animal and forgo using it as a source of food. On the other hand, if you were born and raised in India, you might well be shocked at the use of cows in the United States for food, clothing, and other consumer goods. If you are a Christian, you most likely think of Sunday as the "normal" day of worship. But if you are Jewish, you probably regard Saturday as the "correct" Sabbath. And if you are Muslim, you doubtless see both Saturday and Sunday as unusual times for worship. For you, Friday is the "right" day.

From Stephen E. Lucas, *The Art of Public Speaking,* 9th Edition, p. 25. Copyright © 2007 by The McGraw-Hill Companies, Inc. Reprinted with permission.

___AS___ a. The meaning of ethnocentrism

___St___ b. Cows as a sacred animal in Indian culture

___G___ c. Feeling superior to others

6. In a culture like ours that values time highly, waiting can be an indicator of status. "Important" people (whose time is supposedly more valuable than that of others) may be seen by appointment only, while it is acceptable to intrude without notice on lesser beings. To see how this rule operates, consider how natural it is for a boss to drop into a subordinate's office unannounced, while the employee would never intrude into the boss's office without an appointment. A related rule is that low-status people must never make high-status people wait. It would be a serious mistake to show up late for a job interview, whereas the interviewer might keep you cooling your heels in the lobby. Important people are often whisked to the head of a restaurant or airport line, while presumably less exalted people are forced to wait their turn.

From Ronald B. Adler, Russell F. Proctor II, and Neil Towne, *Looking Out, Looking In (with CD-ROM and InfoTrac),* 11th Edition, p. 242. © 2005 Wadsworth, a part of Cengage Learning, Inc. Reproduced by permission. www.cengage.com/permissions

___G___ a. Waiting

___I___ b. Waiting as an indicator of status

___S___ c. Important people found at the head of the line

Exercise 4: Locating Main Ideas

Directions: The main idea sentences are missing from the following paragraphs on nonverbal communication. Locate the main idea sentence for each paragraph in the Main Ideas box on page 93 and write it on the designated line.

Main idea: _____

_____

1. Chinese tradition associates red with good fortune, but Korean Buddhists use red to announce death. In the United States, red is associated with a stop sign or a warning light but also symbolizes love, as in Valentine's Day. Black is the color of joy in Japan, but it is the color of death in the United States. White is the color of funerals and mourning in eastern countries, but in the United States it is the color of brides. Green is perceived to be a very lucky color in western countries like Britain, Ireland, and the United States. During the uncertain, tension-filled times following 9/11, green became a favored color. Green is perceived as being safe and serene, and it makes people feel better. Even the

Department of Homeland Security put green at the bottom of the terrorist alert code, meaning we're safe. In Japan, green is associated with youth and energy.

From Kitty O. Locker and Donna S. Kienzler, *Business and Administrative Communication*, 8th Edition, p. 443. Copyright © 2008 by The McGraw-Hill Companies, Inc. Reprinted with permission.

Main idea: _____

_____

2.   The intense aroma of spicy curry or barbecue may strike you differently if you are European American than if you are Arab American. At first you may find these new odors unpleasant. But as you get to know the culture and the people, you become accustomed to the new smells and may even find them inviting. People in the United States are especially concerned with body smells, spending a great deal of money to prevent bad breath and natural body odors. In the U.S., we equate such smells with the lack of personal hygiene. Most other cultures, however, find body smell natural and are bewildered by our attempt to disguise such odors with deodorant, mouthwash, and toothpaste.

From Bethami A. Dobkin and Roger C. Pace, *Communication in a Changing World*, 2006 Edition, p. 169. Copyright © 2006 by The McGraw-Hill Companies, Inc. Reprinted with permission.

Main idea: _____

3.   Our clothes, jewelry, cars, houses, and other objects or possessions all say something about us and are sometimes important expressions of our personalities, values, and interests. A large house, expensive car, and designer clothes all convey the nonverbal message of privilege and wealth. Military uniforms convey very precise ranks and status. Similarly, high school letter jackets convey specific ranks or awards, with a series of bars, letters, or patches. At commencement, students graduating with honors sometimes wear robes or chords, and those with PhDs wear special hoods. Objects or possessions can also communicate inclusion in or identification with a group. Students often wear caps or sports jerseys from their favorite team or school. License plates can communicate a person's home state while bumper stickers reveal a person's favorite music group, political party, religious preference, or social cause.

From Bethami A. Dobkin and Roger C. Pace, *Communication in a Changing World*, 2006 Edition, p. 171. Copyright © 2006 by The McGraw-Hill Companies, Inc. Reprinted with permission.

Main idea: _____

4.   The handshake is the most common greeting in the United States, but in Japan people bow with hands at their waists. The depth of the bow is a sign of social status, gender, or age. The Thai, Laotians, and Khmer make a slight bow at the waist while placing their hands, palms together, under the chin. The Finnish, New Zealander, Bedouin, Polynesian, and Inuit touch noses. The tip of the nose is brought into contact with the tip of another person's nose or with another part of his or her head. Hawaiians raise their arms and wiggle the hand gently. The thumb and little finger are extended with the other fingers curled. North Africans place their index fingers side by side.

From Bethami A. Dobkin and Roger C. Pace, *Communication in a Changing World*, 2006 Edition, p. 164. Copyright © 2006 by The McGraw-Hill Companies, Inc. Reprinted with permission.

Main idea: _____

_____

5.   Some Muslim women wear a veil to express their strongly held convictions about gender differences and the importance of distinguishing men from

women. Others wear a veil, which can cover just the head or the entire body, as a sign of disapproval of an immodest Western culture or to protect themselves from the unwanted sexual advances of men. However, the primary reason for wearing a veil is that it is believed to be commanded in the Koran and is thus a symbol of devotion to Islam.

From Mary Kay DeGenova, *Intimate Relationships, Marriages, & Families,* 7th Edition. New York: McGraw-Hill, 2008, p. 252.

Main idea: _____

_____

6.   Some years ago, during the Olympic games in Mexico, some African-American athletes raised clenched fists to protest racial discrimination and symbolize Black power. It is all too common for professional athletes to make obscene gestures at officials, members of the opposing team, or fans. Even more to the point, one college basketball player, Toni Smith, elected to symbolize her displeasure with U.S. foreign policy by turning her back on the U.S. flag and looking down at the floor during the playing of the national anthem before games. Others in Smith's presence signaled their support for U.S. policy and expressed their patriotism by choosing to use different nonverbal cues. Some carried flags onto the court to counter Smith's actions. Others wore American flag lapel pins. Still others indicated their support for or opposition to Smith's behavior with their cheers or boos.

From Terry Kwal Gamble and Michael Gamble, *Communication Works,* 9th Edition, p. 137. Copyright © 2008 by The McGraw-Hill Companies, Inc. Reprinted with permission.

Main idea: _____

7.   Typically, we respond more positively to those we perceive to be well dressed than we do to those whose attire we find questionable or unacceptable. The National Basketball Association (NBA) has long had a dress code for coaches, requiring them to wear a jacket and tie during games. Now the commissioner of the NBA, David Stern, is requiring players and all other personnel to wear a jacket and tie when traveling to or from a game, home and away. The thinking is that these clothes will improve the players' image. Among the items players are prohibited from wearing are T-shirts, chains or pendants, sunglasses when indoors, headphones, and jerseys and baseball caps.

From Terry Kwal Gamble and Michael Gamble, *Communication Works,* 9th Edition, p. 150. Copyright © 2008 by The McGraw-Hill Companies, Inc. Reprinted with permission.

Main idea: _____

8.   In an effort to enhance the relationships between the external environment and the inner self, the Chinese, and now others, use feng shui (pronounced "fung SHWAY"), the ancient Chinese art of placement, to add harmony and balance to living spaces. Feng shui introduces the five elements in nature into design: earth, fire, water, wood, and metal. For example, it uses green plants to bring the outdoors inside, and red candles and fabrics to increase energy. The goal is to arrange space, furniture, walls, colors, and objects to promote blessings and to harness the life force (chi).

From Terry Kwal Gamble and Michael Gamble, *Communication Works,* 9th Edition, p. 163. Copyright © 2008 by The McGraw-Hill Companies, Inc. Reprinted with permission.

Main idea: _____

_____

9.   The numerous signs indicating city, country, state, and national borders are examples of our strong need to communicate the boundaries of our territory. In

our personal lives, we communicate boundaries by building fences around homes or putting names on office doors. National and state parks always post signs indicating their boundaries. Landscaping not only beautifies one's yard but also communicates, "This is my land." Gangs "tag" territory with graffiti or other recognizable symbols. Even universities construct elaborate entrances to identify the boundaries of campus and to restrict access from unwanted visitors. Territorial markers also extend to personal space. For example, you might place your coat or books on the chair or seat next to you at the library or on a bus. Finally, territorial markers personalize and distinguish space. For instance, many office workers mark their computer monitors with pictures, stickers, or drawings. Similarly, many university students mark their apartment or dorm room with pictures, posters, or other personal items.

From Bethami A. Dobkin and Roger C. Pace, *Communication in a Changing World,* 2006 Edition, p. 166. Copyright © 2006 by The McGraw-Hill Companies, Inc. Reprinted with permission.

Main idea: _____

10.   The voice can be used to produce a wide range of nonverbal behaviors such as sounds that are not words, laughter, pauses, silence, breathing patterns, and voice qualities. Laughter is an almost universal sign of happiness and good feelings. Pauses during a conversation can convey a variety of meanings, including confusion, concentration, thoughtful reflection, anger, nervousness, or suspense. The way you breathe often reflects your emotional state. Breathing quickly and loudly might signal arousal, physical exertion, or anxiety, whereas breathing slowly might communicate that one is relaxed or tired.

From Bethami A. Dobkin and Roger C. Pace, *Communication in a Changing World,* 2006 Edition, p. 167. Copyright © 2006 by The McGraw-Hill Companies, Inc. Reprinted with permission.

Main Ideas

A. Objects and possessions can be forms of nonverbal communication.
B. Culture affects the treatment of space.
C. Reasons for wearing a veil (hijab) when out in public vary among Muslim women.
D. The voice itself can be used to communicate nonverbally.
E. How people dress affects how others respond to them.
F. Sometimes people deliberately use nonverbal cues to send specific messages.
G. Humans mark and defend their territory by communicating with objects or signs.
H. Culture plays a big role in determining what smells people consider pleasant and what smells they find repugnant.
I. Countries around the world have different gestures for friendly greetings.
J. Colors can have varying meanings in different cultures.

Exercise 5: Locating Topics and Main Ideas

Directions: Now locate the topic of each paragraph and the main idea sentence. The main idea can be identified by asking, "What key point does the author want me to know about the topic?"

1.   Physical motions and gestures provide signals. The "preening behavior" that accompanies courtship is a good illustration. Women frequently stroke their hair,

check their makeup, rearrange their clothes, or push the hair away from the face. Men may adjust their hair, tug at their tie, straighten their clothes, or pull up their socks. These are signals that say, "I'm interested in you. Notice me. I'm an attractive person."

Topic: _____Signals_____

Main idea: _____Difference in Men+Women's signals_____

2.   Students who sit in the front rows of a classroom tend to be the most interested, those in the rear are more prone to mischievous activities, and students on the aisles are primarily concerned with quick departures. As you can see, the way we employ social and personal space also contains messages.

Topic: _____Space_____

Main idea: _____where students sit contains_____
_____messages._____

3.   Through physical contact such as touch, we convey our feelings to one another. However, touch can also constitute an invasion of privacy, and it can become a symbol of power when people want to make power differences visible. For example, a high-status person might take the liberty of patting a low-status person on the back or shoulder, something that is deemed inappropriate for the subordinate.

Topic: _____touch (physical contacts)_____

Main idea: _____physical contacts convey feelings._____

_____

From James W. Vander Zanden, *Sociology: The Core,* 4th Edition. New York: McGraw-Hill, 1996, pp. 74–75.

4.   Gestures that mean approval in the United States may have different meanings in other countries. The "thumbs up" sign, which means "good work" or "go ahead" in the United States and most of western Europe, is a vulgar insult in Greece. The circle formed with the thumb and first finger that means OK in the United States is obscene in southern Italy and can mean you're worth nothing in France and Belgium. And in Japan the circle gesture is associated with money.

From Kitty O. Locker and Donna S. Kienzler, *Business and Administrative Communication,* 8th Edition, p. 441. Copyright © 2008 by The McGraw-Hill Companies, Inc. Reprinted with permission.

Topic: _____Gestures._____

Main idea: _____Gestures have different meanings_____
_____in different countries._____

5.   Even the gestures for such basic messages as "yes" and "no," "hello" and "good-bye" are culturally based. In the United States people nod their heads up and down to signal "yes" and shake them back and forth to signal "no." In Thailand the same actions have exactly the opposite meaning! To take another example, the North American "good-bye" wave is interpreted in many parts of Europe and South America as the motion for "no," while the Italian and Greek gestures for "good-bye" is the same as the U.S. signal for "come here."

From Stephen E. Lucas, *The Art of Public Speaking,* 9th Edition, p. 24. Copyright © 2007 by The McGraw-Hill Companies, Inc. Reprinted with permission.

Topic: _gestures (basic messages)_

Main idea: _sometimes some gestures mean opposite. depends on countries._

Kiss on the cheek: How many are appropriate? Zero to one in Britain, two on most of the Continent, three in Belgium and French-speaking Switzerland— and in Paris, four.

The V sign: What Churchill meant was "victory"— but the same signal with the knuckles turned out is England's and Australia's equivalent of the American middle finger.

Tapping the nose: In England, Scotland, and strangely, Sardinia, this means, "You and I are in on the secret." But if a Welshperson does it, he means, "You're really nosy."

Twisting the nose: The French gesture of putting one's fist around the top of the nose and twisting it signifies that a person is drunk, but it is not a gesture used in other cultures.

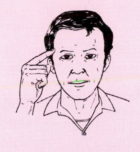

Tapping the temple: Do this almost anywhere in Europe if you want to say someone or something is crazy—except in Holland, where the gesture means, "How clever!"

Thumbs up: This gesture was employed by Roman emperors to spare the lives of gladiators in the Colosseum. It is now favored by American and Western European airline pilots, truck drivers, and others to mean "All right." But in Sardinia and northern Greece, it is an insulting gesture paralleling the middle-finger gesture of American society.

Thumb-and-index circle: America's "OK" sign means just that in much of Europe—though not in Germany, where it is an obscene anatomical reference.

The chin rub: That's what people in France, French-speaking Switzerland, and Belgium do when they're bored. Don't try it elsewhere: no one will get it.

The wave: Careful with this friendly greeting while in Greece. It could be misinterpreted as "Go to hell." When Greeks wave goodbye, they show the backs of their hands.

Symbolic Gestures: Barriers to Cross-Cultural Communication

From Michael Hughes and Carolyn J. Kroehler, *Sociology: The Core*, 7th Edition, Figure 3.1 (p. 80). Copyright © 2005 by The McGraw-Hill Companies, Inc. Reprinted with permission.

Paragraph Diagrams

In previous exercises, we saw that the main idea in a paragraph is frequently located at either the beginning or end of the paragraph. However, the main idea also may appear in other locations within a paragraph, such as in the middle, or at both the beginning and the end. Wherever the main idea is located, it must be supported by details. Most authors provide examples, illustrations, major points, reasons, or facts and statistics to develop their main idea. While a main idea can be either directly stated somewhere in the paragraph or implied, supporting details are always directly stated. The ability to recognize supporting details is of crucial importance in the reading process. Locating supporting details will tell you whether you have correctly identified the main idea.

For those of you who are visual learners, diagrams showing the development of a paragraph and the position of the main idea and supporting details might be helpful. The topic of each of the following paragraphs is the healing power of laughter.

From *Mind/Body Health* by Brent Q. Hafen, Keith J. Karren, Kathryn J. Frandsen, and N. Lee Smith, paragraph 1, p. 541, paragraph 2, p. 545. Copyright © 1996 by Allyn & Bacon. Reprinted by permission of Pearson Education, Inc.

Directions: After reading the explanation for each type of paragraph, write several key supporting details on the line provided.

Main Idea Sentence

Details

1.   Laughter as medicine is probably as old as humankind. One of the earliest written accounts recognizing the healing power of humor is found in the Bible, in which King Solomon remarked that a "merry heart doeth good like medicine" (Proverbs 17:22). Sixteenth-century educator Richard Mulcater prescribed laughter for those afflicted with head colds and melancholy; a favorite "cure" was being tickled in the armpits. The famous seventeenth-century physician Thomas Sydenham said that "the arrival of a good clown exercises more beneficial influence upon the health of a town than twenty donkeys laden with drugs."

"He deserves paradise who makes his companions laugh."

—The Koran

In paragraph 1, the main idea is stated in the first sentence. The supporting details are a series of examples illustrating the main idea. A diagram of this type of paragraph would be a triangle with the point aiming downward. The main idea is represented by the horizontal line at the top.

Supporting detail: *favorite cure was being tickled*

Supporting detail: *in the arm pits*
the arrival of a good clown exercises

Details

Main Idea Sentence

2.   Some researchers have found that a humorous outlook on life can have far-reaching benefits such as enhancing self-esteem and promoting creativity. Others suggest that humor improves negotiating and decision-making skills. Still others have found that a healthy sense of humor helps maintain a balanced outlook, improves performance, and bestows a feeling of power. At the very least, humor helps to relieve stress and improves coping abilities. As you can see, a sense of humor has tremendous psychological benefits.

In paragraph 2, the author gives examples at the beginning and uses the main point to draw a conclusion. A diagram for this type of paragraph places the main idea at the bottom of the triangle.

Supporting detail: _enhancing self-esteem and promoting_

Supporting detail: _improves negotiating and decision making skill._

Details

Main Idea
Sentence

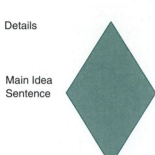

Details

3.   Laughter requires <u>no special training</u>. It requires <u>no special equipment</u>. You don't have to do it at the gym or on the track or on a Nautilus machine. <u>Laughter is one of the best exercises around</u>. It improves your digestion, stimulates <u>your central nervous system</u>, improves and tones the cardiovascular system, thereby providing what some experts have called "a total inner body workout."

In paragraph 3, the author begins with reasons explaining why laughter is one of the best exercises, states the main idea, and then concludes with additional reasons. Because the main idea is in the middle, the diagram resembles a diamond.

Supporting detail: _Laughter requires no special traing._

Supporting detail: _It improves your digestion, stimulates_

Main Idea
Sentence

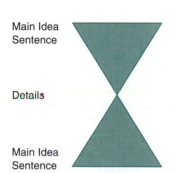

Details

Main Idea
Sentence

4.   <u>A sense of humor can give us a sense of power</u>. Anatoly Sharansky, the Russian human rights advocate, was confined for nine years in Soviet prisons. The Soviet police constantly threatened Sharansky with the *rastrel* (firing squad). Sharansky started to win the war against <u>fear with humor</u>. He started joking about the firing squad and talking about it on a daily basis. "You make jokes fifteen to twenty times," Sharansky remembers, "and the word becomes like any other word." <u>Humor can turn any situation around and give us a feeling of power over our circumstances.</u>

In paragraph 4, the author begins with the main idea, provides a detailed illustration of it, and concludes with a restatement of the main idea. A diagram of this type of paragraph would have an hour-glass shape.

Supporting detail: _threatened Sharanky with the rastrel_

Supporting detail: _fear with humor_

5.   In a study by University of Maryland psychologist Alice Isen, she split volunteers into two groups. One either watched a math film or did a monotonous exercise; the other group watched a clip of funny television "bloopers" or received candy.

In paragraph 5, the main idea is not stated in any specific sentence. Instead, all of the sentences are working together to create a word picture in your mind of an experiment in progress. Because no one sentence is clearly the main idea, a diagram of this paragraph might resemble a square or a rectangle.

It takes 17 muscles to smile, 43 muscles to frown.

For additional practice, identify the main idea in the paragraphs below. Then draw a diagram of the paragraph and list the supporting details.

6.   ᴹᴵ Humor has been used across the span of cultures to <u>make people feel better</u>. A number of American Indian tribes—the Zunis, Crees, Pueblos, and Hopis among them—had <u>ceremonial clowns</u> whose sole purpose was to

SD

provide humor for their tribesmen. According to accounts, they were called in "to entertain and heal the sick with hilarity, frightening away the demons of ill health."

Diagram: _____

Main idea: _Huum hus Been used across the spain of._

Supporting detail: _Entertain And uBal the silck_ _____

7. A sense of humor can actually promote good health by strengthening the immune system. Researchers subjected volunteers to a set of "hassles," situations known to invoke stress. The researchers found that people with a low sense of humor reacted strongly to the hassles causing a significant drop in their ability to withstand disease. Those who rated high on the humor scale demonstrated a strengthened immune function, even when subjected to hassles and stressors. It appears that people who tend to have a humorous outlook have greater immunity against a variety of diseases as well as increased ability to fight off infection.

Diagram: _____

Main idea: _A sense of humor can actually_

Supporting details: _It appears that People who tend to have a humorous outlook_

8. There are strong gender differences in laughter. Research shows that while both sexes laugh a lot, females laugh more. In male–female conversations, females laugh 126 percent more than their male counterparts. But across cultures, from early childhood on, men seem to be the main instigators of humor. Think back to your high school class clown—most likely he was a male. And so women tend to do the most laughing while males tend to do the most laugh-getting. The gender pattern of everyday laughter also suggests why there are more male than female comedians.

Diagram: _____

Main idea: _____

Supporting details: _____

9. Humor can be used inappropriately and actually cause distress. Anyone who has seen the hurt and puzzled expression on another's face in response to an ironic remark, or remembers how she or he may have felt as an object of a joke, has witnessed humor's power to cause distress. Because humor's effects are not always predictable, experts recommend that humor be used carefully when helping someone else with stress so as not to make the situation worse. However, once consideration is given to the potential negative effects of humor and they are judged to be minimal, don't hesitate to use this approach when you think it would be helpful.

From Jerrold S. Greenberg, *Comprehensive Stress Management*, 8th Edition, paragraph 9, p. 121. Copyright © 2004 by The McGraw-Hill Companies, Inc. Reprinted with permission.

Diagram: _____

Main idea: _____

Supporting detail: _____

10.   Pain reduction is one of laughter's promising benefits. Rosemary Cogan, a professor of psychology at Texas Tech University, found that subjects who laughed at a Lily Tomlin video or underwent a relaxation procedure tolerated more discomfort than other subjects. James Rotton, a professor at Florida International University, reported that orthopedic surgery patients who watched comedy videos requested fewer aspirin and tranquilizers than the group that viewed dramas. It appears that humor may help alleviate intense pain.

From Robert Provine, "The Science of Laughter," *Psychology Today*, November/December 2000.

Diagram: _____

Main idea: _____

Supporting details: _____

_____

_____

Exercise 6: Locating the Main Idea

Directions: The main idea sentence appears at different locations in the following paragraphs. Write the letter of the main idea sentence on the line. Then draw a diagram of the paragraph and list the supporting details.

1.   (a) American males may feel uncomfortable when Middle Eastern heads of state greet the U.S. president with a kiss on the cheek. (b) A German student, accustomed to speaking rarely to "Herr Professor," considers it strange that at American colleges most faculty office doors are open and students stop by freely. (c) An Iranian student on her first visit to an American McDonald's restaurant fumbles around in her paper bag looking for the eating utensils until she sees the other customers eating their French fries with, of all things, their hands. (d) In many areas of the globe, your best manners and my best manners may be exceedingly offensive to people of different nationalities and may cause us to make a serious breach of etiquette. (e) Foreigners visiting Japan often struggle to master the rules of the social game—when to take their shoes off, how to pour the tea, when to give and open gifts, how to act toward someone higher or lower in the social hierarchy.

Main idea sentence: __D__   Diagram: _____

Supporting details: __A,B,C,e_____

_____

2.   (a) Cultures also vary in their norms for personal expressiveness and time. (b) To someone from a relatively formal northern European culture, a person whose roots are in an expressive Mediterranean culture may seem "warm, charming, inefficient, and time-wasting." (c) To the Mediterranean person, the northern European may seem "efficient, cold, and over concerned with time." (d) Latin American business executives who arrive late for a dinner engagement may be mystified by how obsessed their American counterparts are with punctuality.

Main idea sentence: __A__   Diagram: _____

Supporting details: __B,C,d_____

3.   (a) Adults maintain more distance from each other than children. (b) Men keep more distance from one another than do women. (c) Cultures near the equator prefer less space and more touching and hugging. (d) Thus the British and Scandinavians prefer more distance than the French and Arabs; North Americans prefer more space than Latin Americans. (e) As you can see, individuals and groups differ in their need for personal space.

Main idea sentence: _____e_____   Diagram: _____

Supporting detail: _Adults maintain more distance from each other than children._

Information is from David G. Myers, *Social Psychology*, 9th Edition, pp. 158–59. Copyright © 2008 by The McGraw-Hill Companies, Inc. Reprinted with permission.

4.   (a) Once in Mexico I raised my hand to a certain height to indicate how tall a child was. (b) My hosts began to laugh. (c) It turned out that Mexicans have a more complicated system of hand gestures to indicate height: one for people, a second for animals, and a third for plants. (d) What had amused them was that I had ignorantly used the plant gesture to indicate the child's height.

Main idea sentence: _____C_____   Diagram: _____

Supporting detail: _I had ignorantly used the plant gesture to indicate the child's height._

5.   (a) To get along in another culture, then, it is important to learn the gestures of that culture. (b) If you don't, you will not only fail to achieve the simplicity of communication that gestures allow but you will also miss much of what is happening, run the risk of appearing foolish, and possibly offend people. (c) In some cultures, for example, you would provoke deep offense if you were to offer food or a gift with your left hand, because the left hand is reserved for dirty tasks, such as wiping after going to the bathroom.

Main idea sentence: _____a_____   Diagram: _____

Supporting details: _____

From James M. Henslin, *Essentials of Sociology: A Down-to-Earth Approach*, 7th Edition, p. 41. © 2007 Pearson Education, Inc. Reproduced by permission of Pearson Education, Inc.

6.   (a) When Big Boy opened a restaurant in Bangkok, it quickly became popular with European and American tourists, but the local Thais refused to eat there. (b) Instead they placed gifts of rice and incense at the feet of the Big Boy statue (a chubby boy holding a hamburger) because it reminded them of Buddha. (c) In Japan, customers were forced to tiptoe around a logo painted on the floor at the entrance to an Athlete's Foot store because in Japan, it is considered taboo to step on a crest. (d) And, in Brazil, a donut shop failed because consumers felt the hole meant they were being cheated or shortchanged. (e) As these examples illustrate, many businesspeople engaged in international trade underestimate the importance of social and cultural differences.

Main idea sentence: _____e   a_____   Diagram: _____

Supporting details: _____C_____

From O. C. Ferrell, Geoffrey Hirt, and Linda Ferrell, *Business: A Changing World*, 5th Edition. New York: McGraw-Hill, 2006, paragraph 6, p. 83.

7.   (a) Coor's slogan "Turn it loose" was translated into Spanish where it was read as "Suffer from diarrhea." (b) Colgate introduced Cue toothpaste in France, only to discover that Cue is a French pornographic magazine. (c) Translated into Chinese, Pepsi's "Come alive with the Pepsi generation" became "Pepsi brings

back your ancestors from the grave." (d) Clairol introduced the <u>Mist Stick</u> curling iron in Germany where "mist" is German slang for manure. (e) These examples underscore that firms that want to market a product globally and reach consumers of varying cultures need to become thoroughly acquainted with the language, customs, prejudices, and tastes of the intended market.

Main idea sentence: _____ *e* _____   Diagram: _____ △ _____

Supporting details: _____ *d* _____

8.   (a) Even numbers have different meanings in different countries. (b) <u>Marketers should avoid using the number four when addressing Chinese, Korean,</u> <u>and Japanese consumers.</u> (c) Although advertising that says "four times the savings" would probably appeal to American consumers, it would not appeal to an Asian audience because four is the number for death in Asian numerology.

Main idea sentence: _____ *a* _____   Diagram: _____ ▽ _____

Supporting details: _____ *b* _____

9.   (a) Westerners consider direct eye contact important, but many cultures see it as a personal affront, conveying a lack of respect. (b) In Japan, for example, when shaking hands, bowing, and especially when talking, it is important to glance only occasionally into the other person's face. (c) <u>One's gaze should</u> <u>instead focus on fingertips, desk tops, and carpets.</u> (d) In the words of one American electronics representative, "Always keep your shoes shined in Tokyo. (e) You can bet a lot of Japanese you meet will have their eyes on them."

From David H. Olson and John DeFrain, *Marriage and Families*, 5th Edition. New York: McGraw-Hill, 2006, p. 104.

Main idea sentence: _____ *a* _____   Diagram: _____ ▽ _____

Supporting details: _____ *c* _____

10.   (a) In <u>New York City, the party invitation may say 9:00 P.M., but nobody</u> <u>would think</u> of showing up before 9:30 P.M. (b) In Salt Lake City, guests are expected to show up on time, or perhaps even a bit early. (c) Consider your own experience. (d) In school, some instructors begin and end class punctually, while others are more casual. (e) With some people you feel comfortable talking for hours in person or on the phone, while with others time seems to be precious and not "wasted." (f) As you can see, even within a culture, rules of time vary.

From Ronald B. Adler, Russell F. Proctor II, and Neil Towne, *Looking Out, Looking In,* 11th Edition, p. 242. © 2005 Wadsworth, a part of Cengage Learning, Inc. Reproduced by permission. www.cengage.com/permissions.

Main idea sentence: _____ *f* _____   Diagram: _____ ◇ _____

Supporting details: _____ *A* _____

Internet Activity

To discover more about nonverbal communication, visit the following Web site sponsored by the University of California at Santa Cruz:

http://noverbal.ucsc.edu/

You can test your skill at "reading" samples of nonverbal communication in the areas of gestures and personal space. Write a short paragraph explaining what you learned.

Exercise 7: Locating Topics, Main Ideas, and Details

Directions: In the following passages from Kitty Locker's *Business and Administrative Communication,* locate the topic of each paragraph and the main idea sentence, and write them on the designated lines. One supporting detail has been omitted from each paragraph. Look at the supporting details list at the end of the exercise, match each one to its correct paragraph, and then enter the paragraph number on the line.

1.   In the United States smiling varies from region to region. Thirty years ago, Ray Birdwhistell found that "middle-class individuals" from Ohio, Indiana, and Illinois smiled more than did people from Massachusetts, New Hampshire, and Maine, who in turn smiled more than did western New Yorkers. People from cities in southern and border states—Atlanta, Louisville, Memphis, and Nashville—smiled most of all. Students from other countries who come to U.S. universities may be disconcerted by the American tendency to smile at strangers—until they realize that the smiles don't "mean" anything.

Topic: _____smiling_____

Main idea: _____

2.   Repeated studies have shown that older people are healthier both mentally and physically if they are touched. It is well-documented that babies need to be touched to grow and thrive. Touch, while necessary for optimum health, can communicate many messages. A person who dislikes touch may seem unfriendly to someone who's used to touching. A toucher may seem overly familiar to someone who dislikes touch. Studies in the United States have shown that touch is interpreted as power: more powerful people touch less powerful people.

Topic: _____touch + power_____

Main idea: _____

_____

3.   People who don't know each other well may feel more comfortable with each other if a piece of furniture separates them. For example, a group may work better sitting around a table than just sitting in a circle. Lecterns and desks can be used as barricades to protect oneself from other people. One professor normally walked among his students as he lectured. But if anyone asked a question he was uncomfortable with, he retreated behind the lectern before answering it. Spatial arrangements mean different things within a culture and between cultures. In the United States, the size, placement, and privacy of one's office connotes status. Large corner offices have the highest status. An individual office with a door that closes connotes more status than a desk in a common area. Japanese firms, however, see private offices as "inappropriate and inefficient," reports Robert Christopher. Only the very highest executives and directors have private offices in the traditional Japanese company, and even they will also have desks in the common area.

Topic: _____Spatial arrangements_____

Main idea: _____

_____

4.   People in many cultures want to establish a personal relationship before they decide whether to do business with each other. For example, to do business in Mexico, you need to develop a personal relationship. Tell me about you as a person. That's very important. Then I tell you about me, and we do this sometimes

not just one time, but several times. Then I will trust you and I will value your qualities. Then I will like to work with you.

Topic: _Personal relationship_

Main idea: _____

_____

A   5.   Many North Americans measure time in five-minute blocks. Someone who's five minutes late to an appointment or a job interview feels compelled to apologize. If the executive or interviewer is running half an hour late, the caller expects to be told about the likely delay upon arriving. Some people won't be able to wait that long and will need to reschedule their appointments. But in other cultures, 15 minutes or half an hour may be the smallest block of time. To someone who mentally measures time in 15-minute blocks, being 45 minutes late is no worse than being 15 minutes late to someone who is conscious of smaller units. Different cultures also have different lead times. In some countries, you need to schedule important meetings at least two weeks in advance. In other countries, not only are people not booked up so far in advance, but a date two weeks into the future may be forgotten. Various cultures mentally measure time differently.

Topic: _time_

Main idea: _____

D   6.   Symbols (clothing, colors, and age) carry nonverbal meanings that vary from culture to culture. In North America, certain styles and colors of clothing are considered more "professional" and more "credible." In Japan, clothing denotes not only status but also occupational group. Students wear uniforms. Workers wear different clothes when they are on strike than they do when they are working. In the United States, youth is valued. Some men as well as some women color their hair and even have face-lifts to look as youthful as possible. In Japan, younger people defer to older people. Americans attempting to negotiate in Japan are usually taken more seriously if at least one member of the team is noticeably gray-haired.

Topic: _Symbols_

Main idea: _____

_____

H   7.   Height connotes status in many parts of the world. Executive offices are usually on the top floors; the underlings work below. Even being tall can help a person succeed. Studies have shown that employers are more willing to hire men over 6 feet tall than shorter men with the same credentials. In one study, every extra inch of height brought in an extra $1,300 a year.

Topic: _height_

Main idea: _____

E   8.   Differences in eye contact can lead to miscommunication in the multicultural workplace. For example, North American whites see eye contact as a sign of honesty. But in many cultures, dropped eyes are a sign of appropriate deference to a superior. Puerto Rican children are taught not to meet the eyes of adults, and in Korea, prolonged eye contact is considered rude. The lower-ranking person is expected to look down first. Arab men in laboratory experiments looked at each other more than did two American men or two Englishmen. Eye contact is so important that Arabs dislike talking to someone wearing dark glasses or while walking side by side. It is considered impolite not to face someone directly. In Muslim countries, women and men are not supposed to make eye contact.

Topic: _eye contact_

Main idea: _____

_____

From Kitty O. Locker and Donna S. Kienzler, *Business and Administrative Communication*, 8th Edition, pp. 440–43. Copyright © 2008 by The McGraw-Hill Companies, Inc. Reprinted with permission.

Supporting Details

5 __A__ In Arab countries, appointments are scheduled only three or four days in advance.

3 __B__ In North America, a person sitting at the head of a table is generally assumed to be the group's leader.

4 __C__ North Americans who believe that "time is money" are often frustrated in negotiations with people who place more emphasis on personal relationships.

0 __D__ Company badges indicate rank within the organization.

8 __E__ Superiors may feel that subordinates are being disrespectful when they look down, but the subordinate is being fully respectful—according to the norms of his or her culture.

2 __F__ When the toucher had higher status than the recipient, both men and women liked being touched.

1 __G__ Some scholars speculate that northerners may distrust the sincerity of southerners who smile a lot (like former President Jimmy Carter).

7 __H__ Studies of real-world executives and graduates have shown that taller men make more money.

REVIEW TEST 1: *Topics, Main Ideas, and Details*

Directions: Each of the following groups contains a series of related statements: One of the statements gives a topic, another gives a main idea, and the rest give supporting details. Identify the role of each statement in the space provided using the following abbreviations: **T** for Topic, **MI** for Main Idea, and **SD** for Supporting Detail.

Group 1

SD a. A four-leaf clover means good luck.

SD b. Red roses convey passionate love.

T c. The symbolic meaning of plants.

MI d. Even today, several plants have symbolic meanings.

SD e. An olive branch indicates peace.

Group 2

SD a. Red indicates passion.

SD b. White indicates sympathy.

_I_ c. The meaning of floral colors.

_MI_ d. Floral colors also can communicate feelings.

_SD_ e. The color orange signifies friendship.

Group 3

_SD_ a. In the 1870s, an ardent suitor might have sent his beloved a bouquet
          of flowers that expressed a complete message.

_MI_ b. The symbolism of flowers reached its peak during the Victorian era,
          when almost every flower and plant had a special meaning.

_SD_ c. A bouquet of forget-me-nots conveyed the sentiment "remember me."

_SD_ d. A bouquet of jonquils, white roses, and ferns indicated that a suitor
          desired a return of affection, was worthy of his intended's love, and
          was fascinated by her.

_I_ e. The "language" of flowers.

Group 4

_SD_ a. In 1875, in Switzerland, Daniel Peter and Henri Nestle created milk
          chocolate by adding condensed milk to chocolate liquor.

_SD_ b. In the 1890s, the first candy bar was created by adding nuts, fruits,
          caramels, and other ingredients to the chocolate liquor.

_I_ c. For the love of chocolate.

_MI_ d. There have been many changes in chocolate candy since it was created
          in 1847.

_SD_ e. Milton Hershey modified the Peter process by adding whole milk.

Group 5

_I_ a. Food of the gods.

_SD_ b. According to Aztec mythology, the god Quetzalcoatl gave cacao beans
          to the Aztec people.

_SD_ c. The beans were later offered as gifts to the gods.

_MI_ d. The cacao tree, the source of chocolate, has long been cultivated by
          native peoples of Central and South America for religious purposes.

_SD_ e. The beans also were used to make a beverage consumed by priests on
          ceremonial occasions.

Group 6

_MI_ a. Originally chocolate candy bars were promoted as health foods.

_I_ b. A high energy treat.

_SD_ c. In World War I, candy bars were given to the soldiers as a source of
          quick energy.

_SD_ d. In the 1920s, many candy bars claimed to aid the digestion and had
          names like Vegetable Sandwich.

From Estelle Levetin and Karen McMahon, _Plants and Society,_ 5th Edition, pp. 128, 272. Copyright
© 2008 by The McGraw-Hill Companies, Inc. Reprinted with permission.

REVIEW TEST 2: *Topics, Main Ideas, and Details*

Directions: The following group contains a series of related statements: One of the statements gives a topic, another gives a main idea, and four give supporting details. Identify the role of each statement in the space provided using the following abbreviations: **T** for Topic, **MI** for Main Idea, and **SD** for Supporting Detail.

Group 1

_SD_ a. Between 9 and 12 months of age, for example, Maika pointed to things to show that she wanted an object, nodded her head to mean *yes*, and shook her head to mean *no*.

_MI_ b. Babies develop a rich repertoire of nonverbal gestures before saying their first words.

_SD_ c. At 13 months, she was using representational gestures such as holding up her arms to show that she wanted to be picked up, or holding an empty cup to her mouth to show that she wanted a drink.

_T_ d. Symbolic gestures of babies.

From Diane E. Papalia, Sally Wendkos Olds, and Ruth Duskin Feldman, *Human Development*, 10th Edition, p. 179. Copyright © 2007 by The McGraw-Hill Companies, Inc. Reprinted with permission.

Group 2

_T_ a. Demonstration of affection.

_SD_ b. For example, middle-class Brazilians teach their male and female children to kiss every adult relative they ever see.

_SD_ c. While females continue kissing throughout their lives, Brazilian men greet each other with a hearty handshake and a traditional male hug.

_MI_ d. Brazilians do not fear demonstrations of physical contact and affection.

From Conrad Phillip Kottak, Anthropology: *The Exploration of Human Diversity*, 12th Edition, p. 285. Copyright © 2008 by The McGraw-Hill Companies, Inc. Reprinted with permission.

Group 3

_SD_ a. In a suit brought by New Jersey importer, John Nix, tomatoes were legally declared vegetables in 1893 by the U.S. Supreme Court.

_SD_ b. The Spanish conquistadors introduced the tomato to Europe, where it was first known as the "Apple of Peru."

_T_ c. What is a fruit?

_SD_ d. Later it was known as *pomo doro*, golden apple in Italy, and *pomme d'amour*, love apple (it was believed by many to be an aphrodisiac) in France.

_MI_ e. Tomatoes, one of the most common, popular, and v[...]
bles," is technically a fruit.

_SD_ f. Justice Horace Gray said that although tomatoes are [...]
the fruits of the vine, they are usually served at dinn[...]
fruits, generally as dessert.

From Estelle Levetin and Karen McMahon, *Plants and Society*, 5th Edition, p. 93. Copyright © 2008 by
The McGraw-Hill Companies, Inc. Reprinted with permission.

REVIEW TEST 3: *Topics, Main Ideas, and Details*

Directions: The main idea sentence appears at different locations in the following
paragraphs. Write the letter of the main idea sentence on the line. Then draw a diagram of the paragraph and list the supporting details by letter.

1.   (a) Americans eat oysters but not snails. (b) The French eat snails but not
locusts. (c) The Zulus eat locusts but not fish. (d) The Jews eat fish but not
pork. (e) The Hindus eat pork but not beef. (f) The Russians eat beef but not
snakes. (g) The Chinese eat snakes but not people. (h) The Jalé of New Guinea
find people delicious. (i) The diversity of our customs and expressive behavior
suggests that much of our behavior is socially programmed, not hardwired.

From David G. Myers, *Social Psychology*, 9th Edition, p. 157. Copyright © 2008 by The
McGraw-Hill Companies, Inc. Reprinted with permission.

Main idea sentence: ___ _I_ ___   Diagram: ___ △ ___

Supporting details: ___ _A b c d e f g h_ ___

2.   (a) Most North Americans value "fairness." (b) "You're not playing fair" is
a sharp criticism calling for changed behavior. (c) In some countries, however,
people expect certain groups to receive preferential treatment. (d) Most North
Americans accept competition and believe that it produces better performance. (e) The Japanese, however, believe that competition leads to dishar-
mony. (f) U.S. business people believe that success is based on individual
achievement and is open to anyone who excels. (g) However, in England and
in France, success is more obviously linked to social class. (h) Many people in
the United States value individualism, but other countries may value the
group. (i) In traditional classrooms, U.S. students are expected to complete assignments alone; if they get much help from anyone else, they're "cheating."
(j) In Japan, in contrast, groups routinely work together to solve problems.
(k) It appears that values and beliefs, often unconscious, affect our response to
people and situations.

From Kitty O. Locker and Donna S. Kienzler, *Business and Administrative Communication*, 8th Edition,
pp. 437–38. Copyright © 2008 by The McGraw-Hill Companies, Inc. Reprinted with permission.

Main idea sentence: ___ _ek_ ___   Diagram: ___ ∇ ___

Supporting details: ___ _k_ ___

3.   (a) The world's cultures have strikingly different notions about displays of affection and about matters of personal space. (b) "Don't touch me." (c) "Take your hands off me." (d) Such statements are not uncommon in North America, but they are virtually never heard in Brazil. (e) Brazilians like to be touched more than North Americans do. (f) When North Americans talk, walk, and dance, they maintain a certain distance from others—their personal space. (g) Brazilians, who maintain less physical distance, interpret this as a sign of coldness. (h) When conversing with a North American, the Brazilian moves in as the North American retreats. (i) Cocktail parties in international meeting places such as the United Nations can resemble an elaborate insect mating ritual as diplomats from different cultures advance, withdraw, and sidestep. (j) How people show affection and respect personal space varies greatly from culture to culture.

From Conrad Phillip Kottak, *Anthropology: The Exploration of Human Diversity*, 13th Edition, p. 34. Copyright © 2009 by The McGraw-Hill Companies, Inc. Reprinted with permission.

Main idea sentence: _____   Diagram: _____

Supporting details: _____

Paraphrasing

In this section, you will learn how to **paraphrase.** When you paraphrase something, you express the author's meaning in your own words. Often you will substitute synonyms for some words, but you may leave key words the same. The ability to paraphrase is important when you are trying to formulate an implied main idea.

Example: "The man who most vividly realizes a difficulty is the man most likely to overcome it." (Joseph Farrell)

Paraphrase: The man who clearly recognizes a problem is the one likely to solve it.

Exercise 8: Paraphrasing Quotations

Directions: Working in a group, paraphrase the following quotations. When you finish, check to make sure the meaning of both statements is the same.

1. Every man is the architect of his own fortune. (Anonymous)
   A man has control of his life.

2. A life lived in fear is a life half-lived. (Spanish proverb)
   If you live in fear you won't fulfill anything

3. "The crisis of yesterday is the joke of tomorrow." (H. G. Wells)
   What happen six month ago dosn't matter today

4. "I am a great believer in luck, and I find the harder I work, the more I have of it." (Thomas Jefferson)
   work hard and opperntuned will
   Persont it self

5. "Once you have been stung by a wasp, it is easier to tolerate a mosquito, and you can be downright friendly with a fly." (Ellen Marek)

When you Get thru the hard ships of Life you can deal with the little things in Life.

6. "Victory finds a hundred fathers, but defeat is an orphan." (Count Galeazzo Ciano)

_____

_____

7. "The things which hurt, instruct." (Benjamin Franklin)

_____

8. "Courage is resistance to fear, mastery of fear—not absence of fear." (Mark Twain)

Courage overpowers fear

_____

A good way to begin learning how to paraphrase is to paraphrase nursery rhymes.

Exercise 9: Paraphrasing Rhymes

Directions: Working with a partner, paraphrase each of these nursery rhymes using your *own* words. Leave the key names, such as Humpty Dumpty, the same.

Example: There was an old woman who lived in a shoe,
　　　　　She had so many children she didn't know what to do;
　　　　　She gave them some broth without any bread;
　　　　　She whipped them all soundly and put them to bed.

An elderly woman, who was residing in a shoe, felt so overwhelmed by her large family that she fed all the children clear soup, spanked them, and sent them to bed.

1. Jack Sprat could eat no fat,
   His wife could eat no lean,
   And so betwixt them both, you see,
   They licked the platter clean.

2. Humpty Dumpty sat on a wall,
   Humpty Dumpty had a great fall.
   All the king's horses, and all the king's men,
   Couldn't put Humpty together again.

3. Tom, Tom, the piper's son,
   Stole a pig and away did run!
   The pig was eat, and Tom was beat,
   And Tom went howling down the street.

4. Three wise men of Gotham
   Went to sea in a bowl;
   If the bowl had been stronger
   My song had been longer.

5. Little Polly Flanders
   Sat among the cinders,
   Warming her pretty little toes;
   Her mother came and caught her,
   And whipped her little daughter
   For spoiling her nice new clothes.

6. Jack and Jill
   Went up the hill,
   To fetch a pail of water;
   Jack fell down,
   And broke his crown,
   And Jill came tumbling after.

Exercise 10: Paraphrasing a Poem

Directions: Read the poem by Tran Thi Nga carefully, noting the key words and main ideas. Try to explain the meaning of the poem in your own words, and then write a paraphrase of it.

Grandmother's Fable

Once upon a time there lived a farming family.
The mother died, leaving three sons
to live with their father.
When the father became ill
and thought he was going to die, he called his children to his bedside
and handed each of them
a large bunch of chopsticks tied together.

He said, "Whoever can break this,
I will reward."
Not one was able to.

The father then handed each of them
only one set.
This they broke easily.

The father said, "If you remain united,
no one can harm you,
but if you separate, then you will be hurt.
This is the advice I leave with you.
The heritage I have for you
is in the rice fields."

After the father's death,
the three brothers stayed together
even after they married.
They did not find any golden treasures

buried in the rice fields.
They plowed and planted
and the ground gave successful harvests.
They realized working together
and working hard were life's riches.

Nga emigrated to the United States in 1975.

Tran Thi Nga, "Grandmother's Fable" from *Shallow Graves: Two Women and Vietnam* by Wendy Wilder Larsen and Tran Thi Nga. Reprinted by permission of Leona P. Schecter Literary Agency on behalf of the author.

Grandmothers Fable, when you are alone you are easily pushed over but when you stand together you are strong.

Exercise 11: Paraphrasing a Fable

Directions: First, read the fable by Aesop below. Then answer the following questions. Finally, rewrite the fable in your own words.

A lion used to prowl about a field in which four oxen lived. Many a time he tried to attack them. But, whenever he came near, they turned their tails to one another, so that whichever way he approached them, he was met by the horns of one of them. At last, however, they fell to quarreling among themselves, and each went off to the pasture alone in a separate corner of the field. Then the lion attacked them one by one and soon put an end to all four.

1. How would you express the moral of this fable?
2. How is this fable similar to the previous fable?
3. In what ways are the advice of Tran Thi Nga and that of Aesop the same?

be on your game
Stay strong together

Implied Main Ideas

Not all main ideas are directly stated. Sometimes you have to look closely at the details the author has provided in order to determine the main idea. Read the following paragraph from *The Art of Public Speaking* by Stephen Lucas and try to identify the implied main idea.

It had been a long day at the office, and the going-home traffic was bumper to bumper. By the time Jason Whitehawk pulled his late-model car into the driveway at home, he was exhausted. As he trudged into the house, he routinely asked his wife, "How did things go with you at work today?"

"Oh, pretty well," she replied, "except for the attack by space aliens in the morning and the outbreak of bubonic plague in the afternoon."

Jason nodded his head as he made his way toward the sofa. "That's nice," he said. "At least someone had a good day. Mine was awful."

From Stephen E. Lucas, *The Art of Public Speaking,* 7th Edition, p. 56. Copyright © 2001 by The McGraw-Hill Companies, Inc. Reprinted with permission.

The topic of this paragraph is listening. The implied main idea is that sometimes without really listening, people give the appearance of being interested in what someone is saying.

In the next example, the topic could be parenting or child-rearing patterns. In order to formulate the main idea, we must mention the three categories of parents.

"Train a child in a way he should go, and when he is old, he will never depart from it."

—Proverbs 12:4

> Authoritarian parents are rigid and punitive and value unquestioning obedience from their children. They have strict standards and discourage expressions of disagreement. Permissive parents give their children lax or inconsistent direction and, although warm, require little of them. Authoritative parents are firm, setting limits for their children. As the children get older, these parents try to reason with and explain things to them. They also set clear goals and encourage their children's independence.

From Robert S. Feldman, *Understanding Psychology,* 8th Edition, pp. 419–20. Copyright © 2008 by The McGraw-Hill Companies, Inc. Reprinted with permission.

From the details presented, we can conclude that each parent's child-rearing style is likely to have a different effect. Our implied main idea should be stated something like this:

Main idea: Three different parenting styles—authoritarian, permissive, and authoritative—shape children in different ways.

Determining an implied main idea is simply reducing all of the key information contained in the paragraph to one sentence.

It is sometimes helpful to first identify the topic and then ask *who, what, where, when, why,* and *how* about the topic.

Read the following paragraph and try to determine the main idea.

> In general, young males tend to be more aggressive than girls. They play more loudly; they roughhouse more and are more apt to try to dominate other children and challenge their parents. Boys argue and fight more often and are more apt to use force or threats of force to get their way, while girls try to solve conflicts by persuasion rather than confrontation. Girls are more likely to cooperate with their parents and they tend to set up rules to avoid clashes. Girls are more likely to be empathic, that is, to identify with other people's feelings.

From Diane E. Papalia and Sally Wendkos Olds, *Human Development,* 6th Edition, p. 246. Copyright © 1995 by The McGraw-Hill Companies, Inc. Reprinted with permission.

Who: boys and girls

What: display different personality characteristics

Where: in social settings

When: during interactions with others

Why: boys are more aggressive; girls are more cooperative and empathic

How: boys dominate, fight, threaten; girls persuade, cooperate, set up rules

The topic of this paragraph appears to be personality differences between boys and girls. If we look at all the key details, our main idea will look something like this:

Main idea: Young boys are more likely to display an aggressive personality, and young girls are more likely to display an empathic, cooperative personality.

The next paragraph provides an explanation for male behavior in interpersonal relationships.

Boys' play illustrates why men tend to be on the lookout for signs they are being put down or told what to do. The chief commodity that is bartered in the boys' hierarchical world is status, and the way to achieve and maintain status is to give orders and get others to follow them. A boy in a low-status position finds himself being pushed around. So boys monitor their relations for subtle shifts in status by keeping track of who's giving orders and who's taking them.

From Deborah Tannen, *You Just Don't Understand*. New York: Morrow, 1990, pp. 236–37.

Who: boys/men

What: try to achieve and keep status

Where: in settings with others

When: in relationships

Why: to avoid being pushed around

How: by monitoring who's giving and taking orders

When we put together these key details, we arrive at a main idea that looks something like this:

Main idea: Boys and men are very concerned with status, with high status going to the person who gives orders and low status going to the person who must take orders.

Now look closely at these examples illustrating the differences in the ways men and women communicate.

Two male friends share lunch at a restaurant. In the next hour they talk about sports, cars, sports cars, the *Sports Illustrated* swimsuit edition, sports, cars, and golf. (Did I mention sports and cars?) Janis, who was at a nearby

Baby Blues

© Baby Blues Partnership. King Features Syndicate.

table, overheard the entire conversation. Here's her summary of what the men said to each other: "Absolutely nothing!"

The topic or title of the paragraph could be male-to-male conversation. The main idea is implied because no one sentence is broad enough to include all the key details.

Main idea: In their casual conversations, men like to talk about such things as sports and cars.

In the next example, there is no sentence that unites the key details of both male and female friendships.

In North American culture, most male friendships are activity-based. Men tend to do things together—a pattern that provides companionship without closeness. In general, men live their friendships "side by side." On the other hand, the friendships of women are more often based on shared feelings and confidences. If two female friends spent an afternoon together and did not reveal problems, private thoughts, and feelings to one another, they would assume that something was wrong. For women, friendship is a matter of talking about shared concerns and intimate matters. Women tend to live their friendships "face to face."

Main idea: While male friendships are primarily based on shared activities with little emotional closeness, women base their friendships on shared confidences and intimacy.

In the next few paragraphs, the topic and part of the main idea are already provided for you.

1.   Nearly 50 percent of the women surveyed said they called friends at least once a week just to talk, whereas less than half as many men did so. In fact, forty percent of the men surveyed reported that they never called another man just to chat.

Topic: chatting

Main idea: In contrast to men, women ___call friends just to talk___

2.   Women ask more questions in mixed-sex conversations than do men—nearly three times as many, according to one study. Other research has revealed that in mixed-gender conversations, men interrupt women far more than the other way around.

Topic: mixed-gender conversations

Main idea: In mixed-gender conversations, women ___ask more___ ___questions___

In the following examples, write the topic and the main idea on your own.

3. Women are more likely than men to use *tag questions*. A tag question is a short phrase that turns a statement into a question. For example, "That was a hard test, wasn't it?" instead of simply saying, "That was a hard test." One interpretation of this is that women's tendency to use tag questions reflects uncertainty. A tag question is seen as weakening the statement being made. Another interpretation, however, is that the tag question encourages the other person to express an opinion. This view says that rather than reflecting uncertainty, a woman's use of tag questions might reflect greater sensitivity and warmth.

From Curtis O. Byer, et al., *Dimensions of Human Sexuality*, 6th Edition, pp. 27–28. Copyright © 2002 by The McGraw-Hill Companies, Inc. Reprinted with permission.

Topic: ___tag - questions___

Main idea: ___Women tend to use tag questions that reflect sensitivity + warmth___

4. Conversational differences between men and women begin early in childhood. Deborah Tannen summarizes a variety of studies showing that boys use talk to assert control over one another, while girls' conversations are aimed at maintaining harmony. Transcripts of conversations between preschoolers aged 2 to 5 showed that girls are far more cooperative than boys. They preceded their proposals for action by saying "let's," as in "Let's go find some," or "Let's turn back." By contrast, boys gave orders like "Lie down," or "Gimme your arm."

From Ronald B. Adler, Russell F. Proctor II, and Neil Towne, *Looking Out, Looking In*, 11th Edition, p. 216. © 2005 Wadsworth, a part of Cengage Learning, Inc. Reproduced by permission. www.cengage.com/permissions.

Topic: ___conversational differences___

Main idea: ___Girls' conversations are aimed at maintaining harmony where boys' use talk to assert control over one another___

5. According to communication researchers, women converse in e-mail messages in a manner similar to the way they speak. Their language in the electronic medium is lavish, intimate, and intended to connect with people and build rapport. Men's e-mail messages also reflect the way they speak. Their style is brief, precise, and functional.

From Joyce Cohen, "He-Mails, She-Mails." From *The New York Times*, May 17, 2001. © 2001 The New York Times. All rights reserved. Used by permission and protected by the Copyright Laws of the United States. The printing, copying, redistribution, or retransmission of the Material without express written permission is prohibited. www.nytimes.com

Topic: ___e-mail manner___

Main idea: ___Women's language is lavish + intended to connect w/ people while men's style is brief, precise, + functional___

6. When it comes to public e-mail, researchers have noted that in online groups, men tend to make strong assertions, disagree with others, and use profanity, insults, and sarcasm. In contrast, women tend to ask questions, offer suggestions, and use polite expressions. They are supportive and agreeable, peppering their messages with more emoticons, such as "smiley faces," and representations of laughter like "haha," "heehee," and "lol," for

"laughing out loud." Men come online to give information or give an answer, while women encourage others to engage.

Topic: _____e-mail_____

Main idea: ___Men come online to give info while women encourage others to engage___

Exercise 12: Writing General or Main Idea Sentences

Directions: Two specific detail sentences are given to you. Working in a group, try to write a main idea sentence that will cover both of the details.

Example: Dying today has become more lonely and impersonal.

   a. Today people are more likely to die in a hospital hooked up to a machine.

   b. At the time of death, people are often surrounded by strangers, such as hospital personnel, instead of loved ones.

1. _____

   a. Research shows that a 15-minute nap can improve concentration.

   b. Truck drivers who pull over to the side of the road whenever they feel sleepy are less likely to have an accident on long-haul trips. *for 15 min can,*

2. ___Truck drivers that pull over improve concentration___

   a. Air bags have been responsible for the deaths of 31 young children.

   b. Air bags deploy with a 200-pound force, sometimes injuring children and small adults in minor fender-bender accidents.

3. ___People lie to avoid punishment or to be in a "position"___

   a. A local minister was caught telling a lie to a member of his church.

   b. Kids as young as two years of age routinely lie to avoid punishment.

4. ___Americans eat too much junk food, exercise very little + watch TV too much___

   a. Americans exercise very little and watch too much TV.

   b. Americans eat far too many foods classified by nutritionists as "junk."

5. ___People that have pet recover faster from being hurt___

   a. Pet owners enjoy better health and have fewer visits to the doctor.

   b. Pet owners recover more quickly from surgery. *are more hurt and do not have macs*

6. ___Boy that go through a divorce___

   a. After a divorce, boys are more likely to be low achievers in school.

   b. After a divorce, many boys suffer from a poor self-image.

7. ___Toothpaste has very harmful ingredients___

   a. Toothpaste contains unappetizing ingredients like chalk, detergent, seaweed, and formaldehyde.

   b. Toothpaste can actually create cavities.

[handwritten: College athletes spends loads of time on their sport]

8. *[handwritten: and receives no compensation]*

   a. College athletes spend enormous amounts of time and energy on their sport.

   b. Although individual athletic departments generate large sums from team sports, the individual student-athlete receives no compensation.

Exercise 13: Aunt Caroline—Identifying the Implied Main Idea

Directions: Aunt Caroline is a fictional advice columnist who tries to help people solve personal problems. Read each paragraph below and then write the main idea. Because the main idea is not stated directly in just one sentence, you must identify the key details and unite them to form the main idea. The first one is done for you as an example.

Dear Aunt Caroline,

   Do you think my boyfriend really loves me? He gives me a present every Saturday. However, he always asks me to return the one he gave me the week before.

Main idea: My boyfriend gives me gifts but asks me to return the old ones.

1.   Last Saturday, my boyfriend was really furious with me for using up half a bottle of perfume in a week. I told him that I had spilled some on my floor. He took the perfume from me anyway.

   Main idea: *[handwritten: My boyfriend gives me gifts but asks me to return the old ones.]*

2.   Yesterday, on my way to work, I eavesdropped on the conversation of the woman sitting behind me on the subway. She told her friend that her boyfriend had given her a half-empty bottle of perfume last Sunday. She told her friend that her boyfriend gives her a new gift every Sunday.

   Main idea: *[handwritten: Yesterday on my way to work]*

3.   I became very curious. So, before I could stop myself, I turned around and asked her if he makes her return the gifts to him the next week. She indignantly replied, "Of course not!"

   Main idea: *[handwritten: I become very curious.]*

4.   Then I asked her if he had given her a half-eaten box of candy the week before, and she replied, "How on earth did you know?" I didn't tell her, but I'm positive my boyfriend is giving my used gifts to her.

   Main idea: *[handwritten: I didn't tell her, but I'm positive my boyfriend is giving my used gifts to her]*

5.   What do you think, Aunt Caroline? Who does a man usually love more, the woman he gives a fresh gift to, but takes it away from, or the woman he lets keep the used gift? And how can I get my boyfriend to love only me?

                 Half-loved Helen

   Main idea: *[handwritten: Who does a man usually love more]*

Adapted from *Finding the Main Idea, Reading Comprehension, Level A, Activity Workbook.* Baltimore, MD: American Guidance Service, Inc., 1982, p. 15.

Written Assignment

What advice would you give "Half-loved Helen"? Write a short paragraph providing Helen with an answer to her dilemma.

Exercise 14: Urban Legends—Identifying the Implied Main Idea

Most of you are familiar with urban legends, those bizarre stories that are just too good to be true. Maybe you've heard the one about the man who unsuspectingly eats a fried rat at a local fast food restaurant. Or the one about the mice in Coca-Cola bottles. Or how about the one about the babysitter who receives a threatening phone call that turns out to be coming from inside the house where she's sitting. All of these stories have one thing in common: They happened to a friend of a friend's next-door neighbor's brother-in-law. Although these tales are widely believed, easily spread by word of mouth, and ever present on talk radio and the Internet, most require you to suspend all logic and just go along. And most of us are willing to suspend disbelief because the world is, after all, a scary place. The tales, many with a strong cautionary note, exploit our fears that danger lurks everywhere—even in our own homes. Like folktales, urban legends often impart real lessons by serving as warnings. The tales that follow were adapted from material by University of Utah folklorist Jan Harold Brunvand, the nation's leading expert on urban legends.

Directions: After reading each urban legend, write the lesson or moral. Then write the implied main idea.

1. Old vs. Young

   An older woman drives her Mercedes into a crowded parking lot. After searching in vain for a parking space she spies another car getting ready to leave, so she pulls up nearby and waits. But just as the other car pulls out a shiny blue sports car zips into the space. The young driver smiles as he gets out and shouts, "You've got to be young and fast!" The woman thinks about this a moment, then rams the sports car. She backs up and rams it again and again. The young man comes running in horror. "What are you doing?" he shouts. The woman smiles and says, "You've got to be old and rich." Then she drives away.

   From *The Mexican Pet: More "New" Urban Legends and Some Old Favorites* by Jan Harold Brunvand, p. 67. Copyright © 1986 by Jan Harold Brunvand. Used by permission of W. W. Norton & Company, Inc. This selection may not be reproduced, stored in a retrieval system, or transmitted in any form or by any means without the prior written permission of the publisher.

   Example:

   Moral: <u>It's always wise to be considerate of others.</u>

   Implied main idea: <u>When a young man steals the parking spot of a wealthy</u>
   <u>older woman, she retaliates by damaging his car.</u>

2. The Killer in the Back Seat

   Phoenix (UPI)—As the woman walked to her car in a parking lot, she noticed a man following her. She jumped in her car and tore off, only to notice to her dismay that the man was following her in his car. The woman drove through downtown Phoenix trying to elude him, passing stores, houses, and bars. When that failed, she drove across town to the home of her brother-in-law, a policeman. Horn honking, she pulled up and her brother-in-law came running out. She explained that a man was following her and "There he is, right there!" The policeman ran up to the man's car and demanded to know what he was doing.

"Take it easy. All I wanted to do was tell her about the guy in her back seat," the man said. And, indeed, there was a man huddled in the woman's back seat.

From *The Mexican Pet: More "New" Urban Legends and Some Old Favorites* by Jan Harold Brunvand, p. 58. Copyright © 1986 by Jan Harold Brunvand. Used by permission of W. W. Norton & Company, Inc. This selection may not be reproduced, stored in a retrieval system, or transmitted in any form or by any means without the prior written permission of the publisher.

Moral: Always be alert,

Implied main idea: woman running from danger

3. The Solid Cement Cadillac

It seems that a man was delivering a load of wet cement to an address near his own neighborhood when he decided to detour slightly and say hello to his wife. When he came in sight of his home, he saw a shiny new Cadillac in the driveway, and he parked the ready-mix truck and walked around the house to investigate. He heard voices coming from the kitchen, and when he looked in through the window there was his wife talking to a strange, well-dressed man. Without checking any further, and without alerting the couple inside, the truck driver lowered a window of the Cadillac, and emptied the entire load of cement inside it, filling the car completely. But when he got off work that evening and returned home, his tearful wife informed him that the new (now solid-cement car) was her birthday present to him, and that the stranger was the local Cadillac dealer who had just delivered the car and was arranging the papers on it with her.

From *The Vanishing Hitchhiker: American Urban Legends and Their Meanings* by Jan Harold Brunvand, p. 126. Copyright © 1981 by Jan Harold Brunvand. Used by permission of W. W. Norton & Company, Inc. This selection may not be reproduced, stored in a retrieval system, or transmitted in any form or by any means without the prior written permission of the publisher.

Moral: look feather in a sitation before making

Implied main idea: The husbems pours lemen in to his cadillac

of IMpuls destion.

4. The Fatal Can

A couple of men walking along a stream bank to do some fishing see a little boy sitting there with his fishing line in the water and a can of bait on the ground next to him. One of them asks the lad how the fish are biting, and he replies, "Well, the fish aren't biting so well, but the worms sure are." The men chuckle about this odd answer as they continue along their way, but coming back later in the day they notice the boy slumped down in the same place he had been sitting before. He is unconscious, and they see that his hands and forearms are full of bite marks. Checking the bait can, they discover that he has been using baby rattlesnakes for bait, thinking them to be worms. They rush him to the hospital in their car but arrive there too late to save his life.

From *The Mexican Pet: More "New" Urban Legends and Some Old Favorites* by Jan Harold Brunvand, p. 28. Copyright © 1986 by Jan Harold Brunvand. Used by permission of W. W. Norton & Company, Inc. This selection may not be reproduced, stored in a retrieval system, or transmitted in any form or by any means without the prior written permission of the publisher.

Moral: Pay antion to kids

Implied main idea: boy using baby rattle snakes for bait.

5. The Bump in the Rug

    A carpet layer could not find his pack of cigarettes. He had just finished laying a customer's carpet when he reached for his pack of Winstons. They were gone. He then noticed a small mound under the carpet in the middle of the room. He concluded that his pack must have slipped out of his pocket. Rather than rip up his day's work, the carpet layer hammers the lump flat and walks out to his van. To his amazement, there on the dash, are his cigarettes. Confused, he re-enters the house only to have the lady of the house ask if he had seen her precious pet parakeet that minutes ago crawled out of its cage.

Moral: *don't Be Lazy on the Job*

Implied main idea: *The man beats the Lump thinking it was his cigarettes*

6. The Hook

    A couple was dating and they went out to a place by a lake and parked. They had their radio on and heard a flash warning about a dangerous man with a hook on his arm who had escaped from prison. They sat there for a while, but the girl started getting scared. She looked over and locked her door. Then he locked his door too. Finally, he said, "This is really ridiculous getting upset about it." And she said, "Well, you know, I'm kinda scared about this thing." So they sat there for a while, and she said, "Listen, let's go back into town." and he said, "No, let's not worry about it, don't worry about it." And she said, "Listen, I'm getting kinda scared. I don't like it here anymore. Let's go into town." And so he says, "OK." So he takes her back into town, and when they drive up to her house, he gets out and he goes over to her side of the car, and on the door was a hook.

Moral: *When something seems dangers get out*

Implied main idea: *Man wanted to stay women wanting to go they left, they found a hook on the door*

7. The Baby on the Roof

    A young couple with their baby were driving through the desert of Utah. They stopped briefly at a rest area to switch drivers so that each one could take a turn at driving and neither one would get overtired. The husband, who was driving, stayed in his seat while the wife got out on the right, placed the baby, who was asleep in her car seat, on the roof, and walked around the car to slip behind the wheel. The husband, then, just slid over and pulled the right-hand door shut, and away they went. The baby stayed on the roof. After a few miles a state police cruiser flagged them down, and the baby was rescued, still sleeping peacefully in her little plastic seat.

Moral: _irresponsible parents_

Implied main idea: _for parnts to pay more attion to kids_

8. The Jogger's Wallet

A jogger had been running along at his customary pace early one morning in Central Park. He was surrounded by streams of others out getting their prework exercise, when suddenly another jogger passed by him on the path and bumped him rather hard. Checking quickly, the jogger discovered that his wallet was missing from his pocket, and he thought, "This can't happen to me; I'm not going to let it happen." So he upped his speed a bit, caught up to the other jogger, and confronted him. "Give me that wallet," he snarled, trying to sound as menacing as possible, and hoping for the best. The other jogger quickly handed it over, and our hero turned back toward his apartment for a shower and a quick change of clothes. But when he got home, there was his own wallet on the dresser, and the one he had in his pocket belonged to someone else.

From *The Choking Doberman and Other "New" Urban Legends* by Jan Harold Brunvand, pp. 188–189. Copyright © 1984 by Jan Harold Brunvand. Used by permission of W. W. Norton & Company, Inc. This selection may not be reproduced, stored in a retrieval system, or transmitted in any form or by any means without the prior written permission of the publisher.

Moral: _don't react to quickly or avoid_

Implied main idea: _Jogger misplace his wallet and asumed that it was stolen_

Internet Activity

Not too long ago, an alarming e-mail message showed up on computers on selected college campuses:

Students beware!!!! My neighbor's son's best friend went to a fraternity party and was offered a cup of red punch. He thought it had alcohol in it so he drank it slowly. After a couple of sips he began to feel woozy, and he passed out. When he woke up, he found he was sitting in a hotel room bathtub full of ice. A cellular phone was next to the tub. On the mirror there was a message scrawled in lipstick, "Do not move. Call 911 immediately or you will die." He called 911 and was instructed by the operator to reach behind him and see if there was a tube coming out of his lower back. He found the tube and answered yes. The 911 operator told him to lie still and that paramedics were on the way. When the paramedics arrived, they examined him and said that both of his kidneys had been removed, probably to be sold for medical use.

From Joseph R. Dominick, *The Dynamics of Mass Communication*, 6th Edition. New York: McGraw-Hill, 1999, p. 324.

Pretty scary, huh? Except for one thing: It never happened. Thanks to the Internet, a whole new lineup of urban legends has been circulated to millions of computer owners, most of them complete with postscripts that proclaim, "This really happened" or "This is no joke."

Find an interesting urban legend and print it. Explain why you find it interesting. Then list the topic, main idea, and a few supporting details. Finally, note the lesson or moral. A good Web site for finding urban legends is

urbanlegends.about.com

Exercise 15: Gender and Communication— Identifying the Implied Main Idea

Directions: Each of the following paragraphs from Curtis Byer's *Dimensions of Human Sexuality* deals with the topic of men's and women's communication patterns. Write the implied main idea for each paragraph.

1.   Comparing the sexes, Deborah Tannen states that men's conversations are negotiations in which they try to achieve and maintain the upper hand if they can, while protecting themselves from others' attempts to put them down and push them around. Tannen says that women's conversations, on the other hand, are negotiations for closeness in which people try to seek and give confirmation and support, and to reach consensus. Women try to protect themselves from others' attempts to push them away. Life is seen as a struggle to preserve intimacy and avoid isolation.

   Implied main idea: In women's conversation, they negotiate for closeness where men's negotiate to achieve + maintain the upper hand

2.   Women tend to speak and hear a language of connection and intimacy. In contrast, men tend to speak and hear a language of status and independence. As a result, the stage is set for misunderstandings and misinterpretations. Not seeing style differences for what they are, people draw faulty conclusions about each other, such as "You don't listen," "You are putting me down," or "You don't care about me."

   Implied main idea: Men and women tend to speak and hear for different reasons

3.   Most studies have shown that, while talking, men touch women slightly more often than women touch men. Whether touching relates to power and dominance issues, sexual interest, or expression of warmth, solidarity, or caring is not always clear. One study found that women reported less positive attitudes toward other-sex touch than did men. This study also reported that men initiated touch more in casual relationships but that women initiated touch more in married relationships.

   Implied main idea: Men touch women more often than women touch men while conversation

4.   One nonverbal communication difference between the sexes is in the area of smiling. For example, women tend to smile more than men. We can only speculate on why this is, but smiling appears to be a part of the stereotypical female role. People tend to expect women to smile. A woman's smile does not necessarily reflect happiness or friendliness and can even be associated with fear or other negative feelings. Another nonverbal communication difference is that women tend to prefer to stand or sit closer to other people while men tend to prefer a greater distance.

   Implied main idea: Women and men have difference rxn while communicate w/ others

5.   One last point involves gender bias rather than gender-based communication differences. As women in many organizations have long suspected, research has

shown that women's ideas can be devalued in a mixed-gender decision-making group. An idea introduced by a man has a higher probability of acceptance and use than if it were introduced by a woman. Female-introduced ideas are likely to be evaluated more stringently. If women in mixed-gender groups want their ideas to be taken seriously, they must learn to speak with authority.

Implied main idea: there's a higher probability of acceptance when the idea was introduced by men than women.

From Curtis O. Byer, et al., *Dimensions of Human Sexuality,* 6th Edition, pp. 27–28. Copyright © 2002 by The McGraw-Hill Companies, Inc. Reprinted with permission.

Determining Your Gender Communication Quotient

How much do you know about how men and women communicate with one another? The items in this questionnaire are based on research conducted in classrooms, private homes, businesses, offices, hospitals—places where people commonly work and socialize. The answers appear at the end.

True or False

Directions: Indicate whether each statement is true or false by writing **T** or **F** in the space provided.

_____ 1. Men talk more than women.

_____ 2. Men are more likely to interrupt women than they are to interrupt other men.

_____ 3. During conversations, women spend more time gazing at their partners than men do.

_____ 4. Nonverbal messages carry more weight than verbal messages.

_____ 5. Female managers communicate with more emotional openness and drama than male managers.

_____ 6. Men not only control the content of conversations, they also work harder at keeping conversations going.

_____ 7. Women are more likely to touch others than men are.

_____ 8. In classroom communications, male students receive more reprimands and criticism than female students.

_____ 9. Women are more likely than men to disclose information on intimate personal concerns.

_____ 10. Female speakers are more animated in their conversational style than are male speakers.

_____ 11. Women use less personal space than men.

_____ 12. When a male speaks, he is listened to more carefully than a female speaker, even when she makes the identical presentation.

_____ 13. In general, women speak in a more tentative style than do men.

_____ 14. Women are more likely to answer questions that are not addressed to them.

_____ 15. Female managers are seen by both male and female subordinates as better communicators than male managers.

_____ 16. Teachers give more verbal praise to female students than to male students.

_____ 17. In general, men smile more often than women.

_____ 18. When people hear generic words such as "mankind" and "he" they respond inclusively, indicating that the terms apply to both sexes.

From "How Wide Is Your Communication Gender Gap?" by Hazel Rozema, Associate Professor, Communication Department, University of Illinois at Springfield, and John Gray, Emeritus Professor, University of Arkansas at Little Rock. Reprinted with permission of Hazel Rozema, Ph.D.

The topic of many of the previous exercises has been communication, both verbal and nonverbal. Some of the exercises noted the differences between male and female styles of communication. After reading the following selection by humorist Dave Barry, list the key communication differences.

True answers: 1–4, 8–13, 15

False answers: 5–7, 14, 16–18

READING

"A group of psychology researchers have made the breakthrough discovery that—prepare to be astounded—males and females are different."

TUNING IN TO READING

A popular advice book by John Gray is titled *Men Are from Mars, Women Are from Venus.* Do you think men and women are so different that they might as well be from different planets? Think about your own personal experiences with this issue before reading the following article.

BIO-SKETCH

Dave Barry, the Pulitzer Prize–winning columnist, is also the author of numerous best-selling books including *Dave Barry's Complete Guide to Guys,* from which this excerpt is taken. The *New York Times* calls Barry the funniest man in America. His life was featured in the hit TV show *Dave's World.* He lives in Miami with his wife, a sportswriter for the *Miami Herald,* and his two children, who, according to Barry, do not think he is funny.

NOTES ON VOCABULARY

Hindenburg   an airship (dirgible) named after the president of Germany, Paul von Hindenburg. The airship was inflated with highly flammable hydrogen gas. On May 6, 1937, the Hindenburg caught fire. The flames quickly engulfed the ship, and of the 97 people on board, 35 were killed.

Smurfs   little blue cartoon characters created by the artist Peyo. The Smurfs became a worldwide success after a television show featuring them premiered in 1981. Smurf plush toys, figurines, video games, and CDs are still popular with children and collectors.

subatomic   particles smaller than an atom.

syndrome   a pattern of behavior that tends to occur under certain circumstances; a number of symptoms that occur together to make up a particular condition.

Neither Man nor Rat Can Properly Fold Laundry
BY DAVE BARRY

1   Are you a male or a female? To find out, take this scientific quiz:

2   Your department is on a tight deadline for developing a big sales proposal, but you've hit a snag on a key point. You want to go one way; a co-worker named Bob strongly disagrees. To break the deadlock, you:

3   Present your position, listen to the other side, then fashion a workable compromise.

4   Punch Bob.

5   Your favorite team is about to win the championship, but at the last second the victory is stolen away by a terrible referee's call. You:

6   Remind yourself that it's just a game, and that there are far more important things in your life.

7   Punch Bob again.

8   HOW TO SCORE: If you answered "b" to both questions, then you are a male. I base this statement on a recent article in *The New York Times* about the way

animals, including humans, respond to stress. According to the article, a group of psychology researchers have made the breakthrough discovery that—prepare to be astounded—males and females are different.

9   The researchers discovered this by studying both humans and rats, which are very similar to humans except that they are not stupid enough to purchase lottery tickets. The studies show that when males are under stress, they respond by either fighting or running away (the so-called "fight or flight" syndrome), whereas females respond by nurturing others and making friends (the so-called "tend and befriend" syndrome).

10   This finding is big news in the psychology community, which apparently is located on a distant planet. Here on Earth, we have been aware for some time that males and females respond differently to stress. We know that if two males bump into each other, they will respond like this:

11   FIRST MALE: Hey, watch it!

12   SECOND MALE: No, YOU watch it!

13   FIRST MALE: Oh yeah? (They deliberately bump into each other again.)

14   Two females, in the identical situation, will respond like this:

15   FIRST FEMALE: I'm sorry!

16   SECOND FEMALE: No, it's my fault!

17   FIRST FEMALE: Say, those are cute shoes! (They go shopping.)

18   If the psychology community needs further proof of the difference between genders, I invite it to attend the party held in my neighborhood each Halloween. This party is attended by several hundred small children, who are experiencing stress because their bloodstreams—as a result of the so-called "trick or treat" syndrome—contain roughly the same sugar content as Cuba. Here's how the various genders respond:

19   —The females, 97 percent of whom are dressed as either a ballerina or a princess, sit in little social groups and exchange candy.

20   —The males, 97 percent of whom are dressed as either Batman or a Power Ranger, run around making martial-arts noises and bouncing violently off each other like crazed subatomic particles.

21   Here are some other gender-based syndromes that the psychology community might want to look into:

22   —The "laundry refolding" syndrome: This has been widely noted by both me and a friend of mine named Jeff. What happens is, the male will attempt to fold a piece of laundry, and when he's done, the female, with a look of disapproval, will immediately pick it up and re-fold it so that it's much neater and smaller. "My wife can make an entire bed sheet virtually disappear," reports Jeff.

23   —The "inflatable-pool-toy" syndrome: From the dawn of human civilization, the task of inflating the inflatable pool toy has always fallen to the male. It is often the female who comes home with an inflatable pool toy the size of the Hindenburg, causing the youngsters to become very excited. But it is inevitably the male who spends two hours blowing the toy up, after which he keels over with skin the color of a Smurf, while the kids, who have been helping out by whining impatiently, leap joyfully onto the toy, puncturing it immediately.

24   I think psychology researchers should find out if these syndromes exist in other species. They could put some rats into a cage with tiny pool toys and miniature pieces of laundry, then watch to see what happens. My guess is that there would be fighting. Among the male researchers, I mean. It's a shame, this male tendency toward aggression, which has caused so many horrible problems, such as war and ice hockey. It frankly makes me ashamed of my gender.

25   I'm going to punch Bob.

✔ COMPREHENSION CHECKUP

Write the main idea of the article below.

Main idea: to show how man and women deal with stress

Why do you think Dave Barry wrote this article?

to inform the way men and we

Multiple Choice

Directions: For each item, write the letter corresponding to the best answer.

_C_ 1. From this article, you could conclude that
   a. women do a poor job of folding the laundry.
   b. girls like to be Super Heroes for Halloween.
   c. many men would rather fight than compromise.
   d. men and women react similarly to stress.

_C_ 2. What is the meaning of the phrase *hit a snag* as used in paragraph 1?
   a. encounter a problem or obstacle
   b. run into an unexpected difficulty
   c. both a and b
   d. none of the above

_C_ 3. The topic of this article is
   a. the "inflatable pool toy" syndrome.
   b. aggression.
   c. gender differences in response to stress.
   d. the problems with excessive sugar consumption.

_A_ 4. The article is meant to be
   a. amusing.
   b. shocking.
   c. serious.
   d. grim.

_B_ 5. From this article, you could assume that the author
   a. thinks buying lottery tickets is a good idea.
   b. disapproves of buying lottery tickets.
   c. thinks buying lottery tickets is fun.
   d. thinks rats should learn to purchase lottery tickets.

_d_ 6. The author would agree that
   a. males and females are different.
   b. scientists spend too much time investigating the obvious.
   c. males are likely to respond more aggressively to stress than females.
   d. all of the above.

_B_ 7. The author ends the article with
   a. examples of the male tendency to nurture.
   b. examples of the male tendency to settle disagreements by fighting.
   c. praise of male aggressiveness.
   d. examples of female cooperation.

_A_   8. According to the author, after two males bump into each other, they
- a. deliberately bump each other again.
- b. settle their differences with fists.
- c. apologize profusely.
- d. go watch a hockey game together.

_C_   9. An antonym for the word *befriend* as used in paragraph 9 is
- a. assist.
- b. support.
- c. antagonize.
- d. counsel.

_C_   10. An antonym for the word *dawn* as used in paragraph 23 is
- a. daybreak.
- b. daydream.
- c. sunset.
- d. midnight.

True or False

Directions: Indicate whether each statement is true or false by writing **T** or **F** in the space provided.

_T_   11. According to the author, flight is the same as running away.

_F_   12. The author's quiz to determine if someone is male or female is well-respected by the scientific community.

_T_   13. The author is exaggerating the amount of sugar consumption by young children at the neighborhood Halloween party.

_F_   14. The young boys at the Halloween party behave in a docile fashion.

_F_   15. The "laundry refolding" syndrome has been researched by the scientific community.

_T_   16. The author is exaggerating when he asserts that only men blow up inflatable pool toys.

Vocabulary in Context

Directions: Look at the italicized words in the following sentences. Do these sentences make sense (**S**) or are they nonsense (**N**)?

_S_   1. In a major medical *breakthrough,* doctors at Johns Hopkins discovered a new treatment for early stage lung cancer.

_N_   2. *Puncturing* a balloon will cause it to inflate rapidly.

_S_   3. The vice president's vote broke a Senate *deadlock* so that the bill could pass.

_S_   4. The teacher was *astounded* that so many of her past students attended her retirement party.

_N_   5. Marla did such a good job *nurturing* her plants that all of them died.

_S_   6. A new day *dawned* with the invention of the printing press.

_N_   7. All was smooth sailing once the merger hit a *snag.*

_S_   8. Miriam's grade for the research paper dropped because she turned it in past the *deadline.*

_S_   9. They *compromised* by agreeing to take turns driving the car to work.

_S_   10. Marco has to stay in bed for long periods of time because of chronic fatigue *syndrome.*

In Your Own Words

1. Although Barry is humorously overstating his case, do you think his position has any validity? Are men and women really as different as he portrays them to be? Base your answers on your own personal experiences.

2. In previous exercises, we saw studies asserting that in social groups boys tend to talk to attempt to exert control over others, while girls tend to talk to create harmony and generate empathy. Can you think of examples from your own life that either support or counter these claims?

Written Assignment

Dave Barry includes many examples of pretend syndromes such as the "trick or treat" syndrome, the "laundry refolding" syndrome, and the "inflatable pool toy" syndrome. However, "fight or flight" and "tend and befriend" are actual syndromes. Do some research on both of these and write a few paragraphs discussing your findings.

Internet Activity

Most of Dave Barry's articles were originally written for the *Miami Herald* and then syndicated (sold) to other newspapers around the country. Go to the Web site for the *Miami Herald*, www.miami.com/herald/, find an article by Dave Barry, print it, and write the main idea.

You might want to check out Dave Barry's Official Web site at www.davebarry.com.

Barry also has a blog (short for *weblog*), an online journal that he updates regularly. You can check out his blog at http://blogs.herald.com/dave_barrys_blog/.

More Practice with Main Ideas and Context Clues

READING

"Getting a job, keeping it, and excelling in your work all depend on knowing how to communicate clearly with others."

TUNING IN TO READING

The workplace today is often rife with stress. Many employees work long hours and have long commutes. They don't feel their jobs are secure and as a result worry about downsizing, layoffs, budget cuts, pay freezes, and outsourcing. Burnout is commonplace. All too frequently we hear about workers losing their tempers, screaming, cursing, and even assaulting their fellow employees. This type of behavior is known as "desk rage." The people most likely to experience it are those who have the least power. Most psychologists agree that desk rage is a serious and growing phenomenon in the workplace. Have you ever seen it? Or, more to the point, have you ever been a recipient of it? In addition to desk rage, many employees have to contend with rudeness, gossip, depression, and irritability in the workplace. The following reading selection discusses specific ways to help improve communication in the workplace

BIO-SKETCH

Dennis Coon was a professor of psychology at Santa Barbara City College for over 22 years. He has since retired and is living in Tucson, Arizona, where he continues to write and edit college textbooks.

NOTES ON VOCABULARY

bottom line   the crucial factor; the main point. The term was originally used in accounting to refer to the earnings figures that appear on the last line of a statement.

goes belly-up   fails; goes bankrupt. The term originally referred to the way a dead fish looks in the water.

ASAP   as soon as possible.

circle the wagons   to take defensive action; prepare for an attack. In the American West, groups of people traveled in wagon caravans for safety. The circling of the wagons was a defensive action used to provide the best defense against attackers. The defenders could keep their women and children, livestock, and valuables within the ring of wagons. Today, the term *circle the wagons* is used in a business or political sense. It means that when a group in a corporation, a government, or a political faction is under attack (sometimes when it has done something wrong), its members must stick together and defend the group as a whole.

bean counter   a person whose job it is to keep statistics; an accountant.

ANNOTATION EXERCISE

Directions: For this selection, you will be asked to underline or highlight the directly stated main ideas for some of the paragraphs. For other paragraphs, which do not contain directly stated main ideas, you will be asked to formulate the implied main idea. Some examples are provided for you. Do the rest on your own.

Communication at Work—Getting the Message Across

Dennis Coon

Survey Question: *What Can Be Done to Improve Communication at Work?*

1   "The bottom line is we've got to round-file this puppy ASAP before it goes belly-up. Stan says we're talking mouth-breather here. Copy Monica, Steve, and the bean-counters with your input and let's circle the wagons in the A.M."

2   "I was just, like, totally embarrassed. I mean, like abso-double-lutely totally incinerated, you know? I mean, to the max. I'm all, I'm just totally sorry, Mr. Thomson. And he's all, If this is the way you do business, I'm not interested."

Underline the directly stated main idea of paragraph 4.

3   The people just quoted probably intended to express their ideas clearly. As you can see, however, their efforts are less than a model of clarity.

4   Effective communication is crucial in many work settings. When communication is muddled, important messages may get lost. Feelings can be crushed. Trust may be damaged. Poor decisions are made. Almost always, group effectiveness is impaired.

Effective Communication

Underline the directly stated main idea of paragraph 6.

5   Getting a job, keeping it, and excelling in your work all depend on knowing how to communicate clearly with others. To improve your communication skills, or to keep them sharp, remember the following points.

6   • **State your ideas clearly and decisively.** News reporters learn to be precise about the "who, what, when, where, how, and why" of events. At work, the same list is a good

Example: (paragraph 7)
<u>Avoid overusing ambiguous words and phrases because others might mistake your true meaning.</u>

Write the implied main idea of paragraph 8. Try combining the first and last sentences.

_____

_____

_____

_____

Underline the directly stated main idea of paragraph 10.

_____

_____

Write the implied main idea of paragraph 11. Try combining two sentences in the middle of the paragraph.

_____

_____

_____

_____

_____

Underline the directly stated main idea of paragraph 15.

_____

guide when you are making a request, giving instructions, or answering a question. Rather than saying, "I need someone to give me a hand sometime with some stuff," it would be better to say, "Blake, would you please meet me in the storeroom in 5 minutes? I need help lifting a box." Notice that the second request answers all of these questions: Who? Blake. What? Could you help me? How? By lifting a box. When? In 5 minutes. Where? In the storeroom. Why? It takes two people.

7   As you speak, avoid overuse of ambiguous words and phrases ("wiggle words") such as *I guess, I think, kinda, sort of, around, some, about, you know,* and *like.* Here's an example: "Basically, I sort of feel like we should kinda pause. I mean, and, let's see, maybe reconsider, you know, rethink some of this stuff." It would be better to say: "I believe we should revise our plans immediately." Ambiguous messages leave others in doubt as to your true thoughts and wishes.

8   Also, try not to overuse intensifiers (*very, really, absolutely, extra, super, awesome, ultimate, completely,* and so on). Super extra frequent use of such awesome words really causes them to completely lose their ultimate effectiveness.

9 • **Eschew the meretricious utilization of polysyllabic locutions. (Don't overuse big words.)** Overuse of obscure vocabulary is often a sign of insecurity. Big words may make you sound important, but they can also blur your message. Which of the following two statements is clearer—"Pulchritude possesses solely cutaneous profundity" or "Beauty is only skin deep"?

10   Trendy, overused "buzz words" or phrases should also be avoided. Often they are just a way of *sounding like* you are saying something: "Personally, I feel we've got to be more synergistically proactive and start networking in a pro-grammatic fashion if we want to avoid being negatively impacted by future megatrends in the client-purveyor interface." Translation: I don't have any worthwhile thoughts on the topic."

11 • **Avoid excessive use of jargon or slang.** Most professions have their own special-ized terminology. Here's an example of some printer's jargon: "TR the last two lines but STET the leading." (Reverse the order of the last two lines but don't change the spacing between them.) Jargon can provide a quick, shorthand way of expressing ideas. However, jargon and technical lingo should be avoided unless you are sure the others are familiar with it. Otherwise, people may misunder-stand you or feel left out. Using slang can have the same effect as jargon. Slang that excludes people from a conversation makes them feel belittled. (The quota-tions at the beginning of this section [are] full of slang.)

12 **Avoid loaded words.** Words that have strong emotional meanings (loaded words) can have unintended effects on listeners. For example, the observation "What a stupid-looking tie" implies that anyone who likes the tie is stupid. In the same way, saying "I think the supervisor's new schedule is a *dumb* idea" brands anyone who agrees with the schedule as foolish. Good decision-making and problem-solving require an atmosphere in which people feel that their ideas are respected, even when they disagree.

13 • **Use people's names.** Work relationships go more smoothly when you learn names and use them. An impersonal request such as "Hey you, could you make five copies of this for me?" is not likely to promote future cooperation. Of course, whether you use a first or last name will depend on how formal your relationship to a person is. In any case, learning names is well worth the effort.

14 • **Be polite and respectful.** Being polite is important, but don't be artificially servile or stilted. Overuse of expressions such as *sir, madam, with your permission, if you would be ever so kind,* and so on can actually be insulting. True politeness puts oth-ers at ease. Phony politeness makes people feel they are being made fun of, or ma-nipulated, or that you are faking it to win approval.

15   Being polite can be difficult when tempers flare. If you have a dispute with someone at work, remember to be self-assertive, rather than aggressive. Self-assertion is a direct, honest expression of feelings and desires. In contrast to

assertive behavior, aggression doesn't take into account the feelings or rights of others. It's an attempt to get one's own way no matter what. Assertion techniques emphasize firmness, not attack. Remember, you have the right to refuse, to request, and to right a wrong. Self-assertion involves standing up for these rights by speaking out in your own behalf.

16   Be aware that your behavior sends messages, too. Actions can parallel, amplify, contradict, or undermine what you are saying. For example, being late for a meeting tells others that they are not very important to you. Likewise, your manner of dress, personal grooming—even the way you decorate your personal work space—all send messages. Think about the message you want to send and be sensitive to non-verbal channels of information.

17   The art of effective communication is well worth cultivating. The points made here are basic, but they can go a long way toward ensuring your success at work—like, totally, abso-double-lutely, you know what I mean?

From Dennis Coon, *Psychology*, 10th Edition, pp. 652–54. © 2006 Wadsworth, a part of Cengage Learning, Inc. Reproduced by permission. www.cengage.com/permissions

 COMPREHENSION CHECKUP

Short Answer

Direction: Answer the questions briefly.

1. What is the topic of this selection? _____ communication _____

2. What is the selection's main idea? _comm_ _____

   _____

3. List three details supporting the author's main idea. _____

Multiple Choice

Directions: For each item, write the letter corresponding to the best answer.

___d___ 1. Harry tells a group of employees that they must shift their paradigm so they can become more synergistically proactive. Harry has violated which principle(s) of effective communication?
   a. Be polite and respectful.
   b. Use people's names.
   c. Avoid loaded words.
   d. Don't overuse big words.

___b___ 2. Which of the following is true according to the selection?
   a. It's a good idea to be candid and call your coworkers' ideas "dumb" or "stupid" when you don't agree with them.
   b. Most professions have their own jargon.
   c. It's a good idea to use slang to show that you know what you're talking about.
   d. Choose big words to demonstrate your feeling of confidence.

___c___ 3. From the selection, you could conclude that ineffective communication in the workplace could result in all of the following *except*
   a. messages being lost.
   b. trust being damaged.
   c. workplaces being made more fun.
   d. group effectiveness being reduced.

_____ 4. According to the selection, all of the following are true *except* for which?

 a. Actions send messages too.

 b. Actions can undermine what you're saying.

 c. Actions have little effect on what you're saying.

 d. Actions can amplify what you're saying.

_____ 5. According to information presented in the selection

 a. it's a good idea to use intensifiers to make your feelings known.

 b. your speech should be full of trendy words to demonstrate that you are "with it."

 c. you should try to avoid the use of wiggle words.

 d. the use of ambiguous messages is a good idea so that people are kept uninformed.

True or False

Directions: Indicate whether each statement is true or false by writing **T** or **F** in the space provided.

_____ 6. The author recommends paying attention to nonverbal forms of communication.

_____ 7. If you are habitually late to group meetings, you are telling your fellow employees that they are important to you.

_____ 8. How you decorate your cubicle can send a message to your fellow employees.

_____ 9. In the workplace, being self-assertive and being aggressive are the same thing.

_____ 10. In the workplace, it makes little sense to learn your coworkers' names.

Vocabulary in Context 1

Directions: Use the context clues from the paragraph indicated to determine the meaning of the italicized words. (Remember, no looking in the dictionary.)

1. Paragraph 3: *clarity*

 Definition: _____

2. Paragraph 4: *crucial*

 Definition: _____

3. Paragraph 4: *muddled*

 Definition: _____

4. Paragraph 8: *overuse*

 Definition: _____

5. Paragraph 11: *excludes*

 Definition: _____

6. Paragraph 13: *promote*

 Definition: _____

7. Paragraph 15: *dispute*

 Definition: _____

8. Paragraph 16: *sensitive*

 Definition: _____

9. Paragraph 17: *cultivating*

   Definition: _____

10. Paragraph 17: *basic*

   Definition: _____

Vocabulary in Context 2

Directions: Choose one of the following words to complete each of the sentences below. Use each word only once. Be sure to pay close attention to the context clues provided.

ambiguous	belittles	impair	revise	stilted
amplify	contradicted	obscure	servile	undermined

1. The earthquake _undermine_ the main support to the bridge.

2. His stiff and _stilted_ speech made him appear arrogant.

3. Marla _belittles_ her son's attempts to swim by calling him names. If she keeps it up, he soon won't want to be in the water.

4. A microphone will _amplify_ her voice.

5. The doctor worried that frequent ear infections would _impair_ the young child's ability to hear.

6. We had a great deal of trouble locating the student union because we were given unclear, _ambiguous_ directions.

7. Instructors need to periodically _revise_ their classroom material to keep it relevant.

8. I said my dress was blue, but my friend _contradicted_ me when she said that it was black.

9. He did not want to be employed in a _servile_ position; instead, he wanted to be in charge.

10. Although the assignment was to research someone famous or well-known, the teacher allowed Martha to give her report on an _obscure_ inventor.

In Your Own Words

1. If you have a clash with a coworker, what do you think is the best way to handle it? What steps do you take to smooth ruffled feelings?

2. How common do you think desk rage is? Do you know anyone who has personally experienced it? What was the outcome? Do you think workplace outbursts are rising? If so, why?

3. Have you ever worked in an office where someone has damaged the office equipment? Why did the incident occur? Could it have been prevented?

4. Many incidents of desk rage occur among people who work in cubicles. Why do you think it is difficult to work in a cubicle? How can people make the experience of working in a cubicle better?

5. How common are yelling and verbal abuse in your workplace? Do you think anger is contagious? Do you think many people bring their problems from home to work with them? Do you think long commutes add to the tension at work?

6. Do you ever fear for your physical safety at work?

Written Assignment

1. Write a short paragraph explaining the meaning of the first paragraph of this selection in your own words.

2. Write a short essay discussing the six suggestions for effective communication and explain how these suggestions could improve communication within an organization.

Internet Activity

Do a search using the following key words: "office manners" or "office etiquette." Write a paragraph summarizing the most useful information you learn.

Chapter Summary and Review

In Chapter 2, you learned about the structure of paragraphs and how to identify topics, main ideas, and details. You also learned how to paraphrase directly stated main ideas and short paragraphs and how to formulate implied main ideas. Based on the material in Chapter 2, answer the following questions.

Short Answer

Directions: In a few words or a sentence, define each of the following terms.

1. Topic _A matter dealt with in a text, discourse, or conversation_
2. Main idea _The main points of a specific ___ ___ at the_
3. Major supporting details _are statements that support the main idea_
4. Minor supporting details _details help fill out the major details and make them clear_

Paragraph Diagramming

Directions: Insert the shape from pages 96–97 that best depicts the paragraph development described.

5. No sentence clearly expresses the main idea. _____
6. The main idea is expressed in both the first and last sentences. _X____
7. The main idea is expressed in the last sentence. _△____

Vocabulary in Context

Directions: Choose one of the following words to complete the sentences below. Use each word only once.

   ~~implied~~   last   ~~paraphrasing~~   specific

8. When you put a sentence or paragraph into your own words, you are _Paraphrasing_.

9. Sometimes paragraphs have a main idea that is not explicitly stated in any one sentence. Such a main idea is _Implied_.

10. Main ideas are supported by _specific_ details.

11. The main idea is usually found in the first or _last_ sentence.

Determining an Author's Purpose

CHAPTER PREVIEW

In this chapter, you will

- Learn the difference between a general and a specific purpose.
- Learn how to determine whether the author's purpose is to entertain, inform, or persuade.
- Learn how to summarize short articles.

Entertain, Inform, or Persuade?

Most writers create a story, essay, article, or poem with at least one **general purpose** in mind. Because most writers do not directly state their general purpose, readers must use indirect clues to determine it. We can identify the general purpose by asking "Why did the author write this?" or "What did the author want to accomplish?" Usually, this purpose will fall into one of three broad categories: to entertain, to inform, or to persuade.

Highlight or underline several words that define each boldfaced term.

An author whose purpose is to **entertain** will tell a story or describe someone or something in an interesting way. A piece of writing meant to entertain will often make an appeal to readers' imagination or sense of humor. If the writing is humorous, the author might say things in an exaggerated fashion or use understatement. Witty, unusual, dramatic, or exciting stories usually have entertainment as their purpose. A romance, suspense, or mystery novel is usually meant to entertain. Writing meant to entertain may be either fiction or nonfiction. The following is an example of a paragraph whose purpose is to entertain:

> I assume you are on the Internet. If you are not, then pardon my French, but *vous êtes un big loser.* Today EVERYBODY is on the Internet, including the primitive Mud People of the Amazon rain forest. In the old days, when the Mud People needed food, they had to manually throw spears at wild boars, whereas today they simply get on the Internet, go to www.spearaboar.com and click their mouse a few times (the Mud People use actual mice). Within three business days, a large box (containing a live boar) is delivered to them by a UPS driver, whom they eat.

From Dave Barry, *Dave Barry Is Not Taking This Sitting Down.* New York: Crown Publishers, 2000, p. 107.

An author whose purpose is to **inform** will explain something to readers or provide them with knowledge they did not possess before. Ordinarily, the material will be presented in an objective, unemotional fashion. Authors who write textbooks presenting factual material usually have this purpose in mind. Encyclopedias, research studies, and articles in newspapers are usually meant to inform. The following is an example of a paragraph whose purpose is to inform:

> In the United States, the most "wired" nation in the world, only 65 percent of Americans have Internet access at home. In many developing countries almost no one has Internet access. According to a recent report by the United Nations, 88 percent of all Internet users live in industrialized countries. One of the major barriers to Internet use in developing countries is the cost. In 1999 it cost $10.50 an hour to use the Internet in the African nation of Chad, where the average annual income was $187. The Web is also largely limited to people who read English, since 80 percent of the world's websites are in English. Another barrier in many countries is that there is no way to log on. Consider that in the industrialized nations there are about 50 phone lines for every 100 people, while developing nations average 1.4 phone lines per 100 people. According to the United Nations, half the world's population has yet to make a phone call, much less log on to the Internet.

From Ralph E. Hanson, *Mass Communication,* 1st Edition. New York: McGraw-Hill, 2005, p. 286.

Finally, the author's purpose may be to **persuade.** Persuasion goes beyond merely entertaining or providing information. This kind of writing tries to change readers' opinions by appealing to their emotions or intellect. If the author is making an emotional argument, vivid descriptive passages may be used to manipulate readers' feelings. If the author is making an appeal to intelligence, a rational or logical argument may be used. Political literature is a common example of writing meant to persuade. While articles in newspapers are usually meant to inform, newspaper editorials ordinarily have persuasion as their purpose. The following is an example of a paragraph whose purpose is to persuade:

Pop-Ups and Spam: The Evil Twins of Internet Advertising

> Suppose you are doing online research when all of a sudden an ad appears: Order DVDs by mail! You close that one but another pops up: Find low fares! Get rid of that and there is another: Lower your mortgage rates! Click to close it and there is another. And another. Pretty soon you are doing the cyber equivalent of swatting flies as you try to get rid of those intrusive pop-up and pop-under ads. Pop-up ads are bad enough, but they pale in comparison to spam. The Internet is literally stuffed full of junk e-mail for low-cost prescription drugs, debt consolidation plans, schemes that will make you a millionaire in only six months, and various treatments to enlarge certain body parts. What, if anything, can you do about it? The ultimate solution might be a legal one. It's time for Congress to pass legislation to create a national Do-Not-Spam list that resembles the Do-Not-Call list that limited telemarketers.

From Joseph R. Dominick, *The Dynamics of Mass Communication,* 8th Edition, p. 309. Copyright © 2005 by The McGraw-Hill Companies, Inc. Reprinted with permission.

To determine whether the author's general purpose is to entertain, inform, or persuade, look for clues in the title, in headings and subheadings, and in the introduction or conclusion. Also, pay attention to the source of the article.

Authors also take into account their **audience**—those they are writing for—when they choose their general purpose. Writers of fiction usually want to entertain readers by creating interesting characters and stories. If an author writes an article for a wellness magazine, the general purpose probably will be to provide information promoting good health. If an author writes a letter to solicit campaign contributions for a political candidate, the general purpose will be to persuade, because the author is trying to convince people to give money.

In addition to a general purpose, authors also usually have a **specific purpose,** which gives more information about the article than the general purpose. Take the previous "wellness" example. The general purpose is to "inform." The specific purpose might be "to inform people about foods that protect against cancer."

Sometimes an author may have more than one purpose in mind. For instance, an author might want to both entertain and persuade. Or the author might write an entertaining article that also provides information about something important. When an author has more than one purpose in mind, usually one of the author's purposes will be primary. To determine the author's primary purpose, first identify the main idea and the key details that support the idea. Then note the source of the article or passage. Often the publication that the article or passage appears in will help you identify the author's primary purpose. Finally, note the author's choice of words. Is the vocabulary neutral and unbiased? Is it meant to influence your judgment in some way? These steps should help you identify the author's primary purpose.

Read the paragraph below and identify the writer's topic, main idea, and general and specific purposes.

> One of the reasons that occupational stress has been receiving so much attention lately is that businesses are genuinely beginning to care about employee welfare. You don't buy that? Well, how about this? Work stress is costing businesses billions of dollars. Sounds more plausible doesn't it? It is estimated by the International Labor Organization that stress on the job costs businesses over $200 billion per year. These costs include salaries for sick days, costs of hospitalization and outpatient care, and costs related to decreased productivity. Other stress-related factors are catching the eyes of business leaders. For example, health benefit costs to employers have increased dramatically. Employees trained over a long period of time, at great cost, may break down when stressed on the job. They may make poor decisions, miss days of work, begin abusing alcohol and other drugs, or die and have to be replaced by other workers who need training. All of this is costly. These effects of occupational stress have caused companies to give high priority to stress management programs.

From Jerrold S. Greenberg, *Comprehensive Stress Management*, 8th Edition, pp. 275–76. Copyright © 2004 by The McGraw-Hill Companies, Inc. Reprinted with permission.

Topic: occupational stress

Main idea: businesses giving high priority to stress management programs because of the high costs of employee occupational stress

General purpose: to inform

Specific purpose: informing readers about why businesses are paying attention to employee stress

The following exercises will give you some practice in determining an author's general purpose.

Exercise 1: Determining the General Purpose

Directions: Label each sentence according to its general purpose: to inform (**I**), to entertain (**E**), or to persuade (**P**).

_____ 1.   I have been thinking a lot about food lately. This is because I am not getting any. My wife, you see, recently put me on a diet. It is an interesting diet of her own devising that essentially allows me to eat anything I want so long as it contains no fat, cholesterol, sodium, calories, and isn't tasty. In order to keep me from starving altogether, she went to the grocery store and bought everything that had "bran" in its title. I am not sure, but I believe I had bran cutlets for dinner last night. I am very depressed.

From Bill Bryson, *I'm a Stranger Here Myself*, New York: Broadway Books, 1999, p. 223.

___P___ 2.   Most sharks are harmless—at least to humans. Actually we threaten the survival of sharks more than they threaten us. They reproduce slowly, and their numbers are already being depleted by overfishing in many areas. This attitude toward sharks may be shortsighted, because they play an important role in marine communities. Some people catch shark only for the shark's fins or jaws. Others practice shark hunting for sport, leaving the meat to waste. A magnificent predator, the shark may soon be exterminated by humans, the fiercest predator of them all.

From Peter Castro and Michael E. Huber, "Sharks," *Marine Biology*, 6th Edition. New York: McGraw-Hill, 2007, p. 159.

___I___ 3.   The idea of a family consisting of a wage-earning husband and a wife who stays at home has largely given way to the dual-income household. Among married people between the ages of 25 and 34, 92 percent of the men and 75 percent of the women are in the labor force. Why has there been such a rise in the number of dual-income couples? A major factor is economic need. In 2003, the median income for households with both partners employed was 99 percent more than in households in which only one person was working outside the home. Of course, because of such work-related costs as child care, not all of a family's second wage is genuine additional income.

From Richard T. Schaefer, *Sociology*, 10th Edition, p. 306. Copyright © 2007 by The McGraw-Hill Companies, Inc. Reprinted with permission.

Exercise 2: Determining the Primary Purpose and Main Ideas

Directions: Read each of the following paragraphs to determine if the author's primary purpose is to entertain, persuade, or inform. Indicate the clues that enabled you to make your decision. In the space provided, write the directly stated or implied main idea.

1.   Most crimes are committed in large urban areas rather than in small cities, suburbs, or rural areas. National Crime Victimization Survey data tell us the safest place to be is at home, although we are likely to be victimized when we are in familiar territory. In 2004, only one-quarter of violent crimes took place near or at the victim's home. Almost three-quarters of violent crimes occurred within five miles of home. Common locations for violent crimes are streets other than those near the victim's home (15 percent), at school (14 percent), or at a commercial establishment (8 percent).

From Freda Adler, et al., *Criminology*, 6th Edition. New York: McGraw-Hill, 2007, p. 44.

Purpose: ___Inform___   Clues: _____

Main idea: _Most crimes are committed in big urban area_

2.   You know how when you buy your pants, there's a piece of paper in one of the pockets that says "inspected by #47." Who ARE these people anyway? Has

anyone out there met one of these inspectors? What do they inspect? I mean seriously, if someone bends over and their pants rip, should we say, "Oh no! Who inspected that? Number 63? Whew. That was close. Mine were done by number 34." If there was a problem, what are you supposed to do? Call up the manufacturer and say, "Hello. I hate to be the one to break it to you, but you know number 63? She just isn't going to cut it anymore."

From Tom Mather, *The Cheeseburger Philosophy*, 1996, p. 15.

Purpose: _Eentertain_   Clues: _inspected_ _____

Main idea: _pants inspect_ _____

3.   Child labor laws prohibit a 13-year-old from punching a cash register for 40 hours a week, but that same child can labor for 40 hours or more inside a gym or an ice skating rink without drawing the slightest glance from the government. The U.S. government requires the licensing of plumbers. It demands that even the tiniest coffee shop adhere to a fastidious health code. It scrutinizes the advertising claims on packages of low-fat snack food. But it never asks a coach, who holds the lives of his young pupils in his hands, to pass a minimum safety and skills test. Coaches in this country need no license to coach children, even in a high-injury sport like elite gymnastics.

From Joan Ryan, *Little Girls in Pretty Boxes*, New York: Warner Books, 1995, pp. 11–12.

Purpose: _Pursuad inform_   Clues: _ise skating_ _____

Main idea: _child labor laws coachs not having license_

4.   Alcohol abuse by college students usually takes the form of a drinking pattern called *binge drinking*. Binge drinking is defined as the consumption of five drinks in a row. One large study of more than 17,000 students on 89 campuses found that 49.7 percent of students binged. The strongest predictors for binging were living in a fraternity or sorority, adopting a party-centered lifestyle, and engaging in other risky behavior. The study also suggested that many college students began binge drinking in high school.

From Wayne A. Payne, Dale B. Hahn, and Ellen B. Lucas, *Understanding Your Health*, 10th Edition, p. 242. Copyright © 2009 by The McGraw-Hill Companies, Inc. Reprinted with permission.

Purpose: _inform_ _____ Clues: _____

Main idea: _Alcohol abuse_ _____

5.   Tina was found dead last week—her neck broken by the jaws of a steel trap. I didn't know Tina. But John and Rachel Williamson knew her, and so did their children, Tyrone and Vanessa. Tina had been a beloved member of their family for 10 years. She was a Samoyed—a handsome, intelligent dog, pure white with soft, dark eyes. When she died she was only 200 yards from her back door. Tina had gone out to play that morning as usual, but this time she found something *un*usual—an odd-shaped box with delicious-smelling food inside. She put her head inside the box to get at the food. When she did, the trap closed and Tina was killed. Unless we crack down on illegal trapping within town property, this tragedy will be repeated. The next time it might be *your* family dog. Or your pet cat. Or your child.

Purpose: _purso_ _____   Clues: _watch your kids_ ___

Main idea: _____

_____

6.   To keep an adequate supply of pennies in circulation, the U.S. Mint creates approximately 12 billion new pennies each year. The cost of manufacturing these new pennies is .66 of a cent apiece, which adds up to approximately $80 million a year. According to Treasury officials, when you add on storage and handling expenses, it costs the U.S. government more than a penny to transact a penny's worth of business.

Purpose: _inform_____   Clues: _____

_____

Main idea: _____

7.   As we wait for the plane to climb to the jump altitude of 12,000 feet, my mind races with a frenzied jumble of thoughts: "Okay, this is the moment you've been waiting for. It's going to be great. Am I really going to jump out of an airplane from 12,000 feet? What if something goes wrong? Can I still back out? Come on now, don't worry. It'll be fine." My palms are sweating and my heart is pounding so hard I think it may burst. "Get ready," yells the instructor. As I jump into the blue, I wonder, "What am I doing here?" The blast of air resistance blows me backward like a leaf at the mercy of the autumn wind. In about ten seconds my body levels out and accelerates to a speed of 120 miles an hour. The air supports my body like an invisible flying carpet. Any fears or doubts I had are gone in the exhilaration of free flight. Every nerve in my body is alive with sensation; yet I am overcome by a peaceful feeling and the sense that I am one with the sky.

From Stephen E. Lucas, *The Art of Public Speaking,* 9th Edition, pp. 389, 458. Copyright © 2007 by The McGraw-Hill Companies, Inc. Reprinted with permission.

Purpose: _Entertain_____   Clues: _____

Main idea: _free flying_____

The articles presented in the next section all deal, directly or indirectly, with the world of work. Read each article noting the purpose and then answer the questions.

Author's Purpose: To Entertain

The following short story by William Saroyan has entertainment as its purpose.

READING

"(My grandmother) said to me: 'You must learn to do some good work, the making of some item useful to man.'"

TUNING IN TO READING

Have your grandparents ever given you advice about how to conduct your life? Was it advice that you agreed or disagreed with?

BIO-SKETCH

William Saroyan (1908–1981) was an American writer of Armenian descent. Throughout his long and prolific career, he drew upon his heritage to provide him with inspiration for his short stories, novels, and plays. He is best known for the short story

Photographed by
Paul Kalinian 1976.

READING *continued*

collection *The Daring Young Man on the Flying Trapeze;* the play *The Time of Your Life,* which won the Pulitzer Prize; and the novel *The Human Comedy.* In many of his stories, Saroyan invents a family life much different from his own. At the age of 3, he lost his father and was placed in an orphanage by his mother. At the age of 8, he began selling newspapers and working at a variety of odd jobs. He learned to read at the age of 9 and shortly afterward began to write. Eventually, at the age of 15, he left school altogether. Over the years, he has said, it was his writing that kept him sane.

NOTES ON VOCABULARY

humble   to lower in condition, rank, or position. *Humble* is derived from the Latin word *humilis,* which in turn comes from *humus,* meaning "soil." The literal meaning of *humble* is "not far above the ground" or "low."

dungeon   a dark underground cell, vault, or prison.

The Shepherd's Daughter

William Saroyan

IT IS THE OPINION OF MY GRANDMOTHER, God bless her, that all men should labour, and at the table, a moment ago, she said to me: You must learn to do some good work, the making of some item useful to man, something out of clay, or out of wood, or metal, or cloth. It is not proper for a young man to be ignorant of an honourable craft. Is there anything you can make? Can you make a simple table, a chair, a plain dish, a rug, a coffee pot? Is there anything you can do?

2   And my grandmother looked at me with anger.

3   I know, she said, you are supposed to be a writer, and I suppose you are. You certainly smoke enough cigarettes to be anything, and the whole house is full of the smoke, but you must learn to make solid things, things that can be used, that can be seen and touched.

Ancient Persia was located in the Middle East where Iran is today.

4   There was a king of the Persians, said my grandmother, and he had a son, and this son fell in love with a shepherd's daughter. He went to his father and he said, My Lord, I love a shepherd's daughter, and I would have her for my wife. And the king said, I am king and you are my son, and when I die you shall be king, how can it be that you would marry the daughter of a shepherd? And the son said, My Lord, I do not know but I know that I love this girl and would have her for my queen.

5   The king saw that his son's love for the girl was from God, and he said, I will send a message to her. And he called a messenger to him and he said, Go to the shepherd's daughter and say that my son loves her and would have her for his wife. And the messenger went to the girl and he said, The king's son loves you and would have you for his wife. And the girl said, What labour does he do? And the messenger said, Why he is the son of the king; he does no labour. And the girl said, He must learn to do some

labour. And the messenger returned to the king and spoke the words of the shepherd's daughter.

6   The king said to his son, The shepherd's daughter wishes you to learn some craft. Would you still have her for your wife? And the son said, Yes, I will learn to weave straw rugs. And the boy was taught to weave rugs of straw, in patterns and in colours and with ornamental designs, and at the end of three days he was making very fine straw rugs, and the messenger returned to the shepherd's daughter, and he said, These rugs of straw are the work of the king's son.

7   And the girl went with the messenger to the king's palace, and she became the wife of the king's son.

8   One day, said my grandmother, the king's son was walking through the streets of Baghdad, and he came upon an eating place which was so clean and cool that he entered it and sat at the table.

9   This place, said my grandmother, was a place of thieves and murderers, and they took the king's son and placed him in a large dungeon where many great men of the city were being held, and the thieves and murderers were killing the fattest of the men and feeding them to the leanest of them, and making sport of it. The king's son was of the leanest of the men, and it was not known that he was the son of the king of the Persians, so his life was spared, and he said to the thieves and murderers, I am a weaver of straw rugs and these rugs have great value. And they brought him straw and asked him to weave and in three days he weaved three rugs, and he said, Carry these to the palace of the king of the Persians, and for each rug he will give you a hundred gold pieces of money. And the rugs were carried to the palace of the king, and when the king saw the rugs he saw that they were the work of his son and he took the rugs to the shepherd's daughter and he said, These rugs were brought to the palace and they are the work of my son who is lost. And the shepherd's daughter took each rug and looked at it closely and in the design of each rug she saw in the written language of the Persians a message from her husband, and she related this message to the king.

10   And the king, said my grandmother, sent many soldiers to the place of the thieves and murderers, and the soldiers rescued all the captives and killed all the thieves and murderers, and the king's son was returned safely to the palace of his father, and to the company of his wife, the little shepherd's daughter. And when the boy went into the palace and saw again his wife, he humbled himself before her and he embraced her feet, and he said, My love, it is because of you that I am alive, and the king was greatly pleased with the shepherd's daughter.

11   Now, said my grandmother, do you see why every man should learn an honourable craft?

12   I see very clearly, I said, and as soon as I earn enough money to buy a saw and a hammer and a piece of lumber I shall do my best to make a simple chair or a shelf for books.

William Saroyan, "The Shepherd's Daughter," from *The Daring Young Man on the Flying Trapeze.* © 1934 by William Saroyan. Reprinted by permission of the Trustees of Leland Stanford Junior University.

COMPREHENSION CHECKUP

Multiple Choice

Directions: For each item, write the letter corresponding to the best answer.

_____ 1. At first the king of the Persians
   a. was pleased by his son's selection of a bride.
   b. was puzzled by his son's selection of a bride.
   c. ignored his son's selection of a bride.
   d. was angered by his son's selection of a bride.

_____ 2. The messenger was of the opinion that
   a. a king's son must do the bidding of a shepherd's daughter.
   b. a king's son is above doing tasks of manual labor.
   c. the shepherd's daughter should not be made queen.
   d. the king's son should not marry someone of a lowly station.

_____ 3. The grandson is going to please his grandmother
   a. by giving up his smoking habit.
   b. by learning to weave straw rugs.
   c. by abandoning his desire to be a writer.
   d. by earning enough money by writing to enable him to build something.

_____ 4. The king's son was initially spared by the thieves and murderers because
   a. he was lean.
   b. it was considered unwise to kill the son of a king.
   c. he was overweight.
   d. he was a well-known weaver.

True or False

Directions: Indicate whether each statement is true or false by writing **T** or **F** in the space provided.

___T___ 5. The grandmother has the most respect for someone who can create something useful.

___F___ 6. The grandmother saved the life of the king's son.

___T___ 7. Before the shepherd's daughter agreed to marry the king's son, she required that he learn a craft.

___F___ 8. The grandmother approves of her grandson's chosen profession.

___T___ 9. The king's son was grateful to the shepherd's daughter for helping rescue him.

Vocabulary in Context

Directions: Look through the given paragraph and find a word that matches the definition.

1. lacking in knowledge or training (1)   _____

2. worthy of respect (1)   _____

3. decorative (6)   _____

4. without much flesh or fat (9)   _____

5. not subjected to harm or death (9)   _____

6. hugged (10)   _____

In Your Own Words

1. What is the main idea of the story?

2. According to the grandmother, what kind of work is admirable? Would the grandmother think that the practice of law is honorable? Include the supporting details from the story that helped you answer this question.

3. What character in the fable has the same attitude toward work as the grandmother?

4. What is the significance of the ending of the fable?

5. What is meant by the last sentence of the story? How will the grandson earn the money for the materials to build a chair or bookshelf?

6. How much respect is given to the advice of elders in your family?

Choose one to write a

Written Assignment

Benjamin Franklin said, "He that hath a trade hath an estate." Compare Franklin's view with that of the grandmother and the shepherd's daughter.

Internet Activity

Directions: Complete one of the following:

1. The ancient Persian Empire was located in western Asia. At the height of its power, it encompassed much of what today is known as the Middle East, extending east to India and west to the Aegean Sea. Its great cities were Babylon and Persepolis, and its great leaders were Cyrus the Great, Darius the Great, and Xerxes. The Persian Empire lasted for more than 200 years. It was conquered about 330 B.C. by Alexander the Great. Until 1935, Persia was the official name of Iran. Use the Internet to find additional information about the Persian Empire.

2. Louis Armstrong, Elvis Presley, Madonna, and other well-known U.S. personalities have had U.S. postage stamps printed in their honor. However, William Saroyan is probably the only person to have a stamp printed in both the United States and the Soviet Union at the same time. Although Saroyan was born in the United States, his parents emigrated from Armenia. Today, Armenia is an independent country, but in 1991, when the postage stamps were issued, Armenia was still a part of the Soviet Union. Go to the Web sites listed below to find out more about William Saroyan. The first site will show you pictures of the two stamps. The second site will provide you with information about the William Saroyan Collection at Stanford University. Briefly summarize what you learn about Saroyan. If there is a problem with either of these sites, use your favorite search engine and type in Saroyan's full name.

   www.cilicia.com/armo22_william_saroyan.html

   www-sul.stanford.edu/depts/hasrg/ablit/amerlit/saroyan.html

Author's Purpose: To Inform

Read the following article, "From a Melted Candy Bar to Microwaves," by Ira Flatow. Flatow's purpose is to present information about the discovery of the microwave.

READING

*"Next time you make a bag of Orville Redenbacher's,
you'll be repeating an experiment that heralded the
dawning of the age of microwave cooking."*

TUNING IN TO READING

Do you own a microwave? If you have one in your home, do you use it for more than reheating coffee or leftovers? By 1997, 90 percent of all American households had a microwave. If you were forced to eliminate one of your appliances, which one could you most easily do without, and why?

Practice your SQ3R techniques with this reading selection. Survey the material by reading the first two paragraphs, the last two paragraphs, and the bio-sketch.

BIO-SKETCH

Ira Flatow, National Public Radio's science correspondent, is the host of *Talk of the Nation*'s "Science Friday." In his book *They All Laughed,* "he demonstrates that truth is stranger than fiction." Each of the stories, including this one about the invention of the microwave, is really a story about inquisitive people who won't take no for an answer. While doing research about inventors, Flatow discovered that most of them are hearty souls, unafraid of appearing ridiculous by asking silly questions. He calls this the "quack like a duck" discovery method. If something looks like a duck, walks like a duck, but doesn't quack like a duck, these bold inventors want to know why. In this excerpt, Perry Spencer, noticing the melted candy bar in a lab coat he'd been wearing all day long, should have assumed his own body temperature had been the culprit. Because that answer didn't make "quack noises," Spencer went on to invent the microwave oven.

NOTES ON VOCABULARY

nuke   slang for cooking food in a microwave oven.

cynical   disbelieving; sarcastic, sneering. In ancient Greece, a *Cynic* was a member of a school of philosophers who believed that being virtuous was the highest good. Because *cynics* had contempt for worldly needs and pleasures, they were extremely critical of the rest of society. Today the word refers to anyone who questions the motives or actions of other people.

maven   an expert, a really knowledgeable person. The word *maven* comes from Yiddish.

Microwave oven

From a Melted Candy Bar
to Microwaves

Ira Flatow

NEXT TIME YOU NUKE A BAG of Orville Redenbacher's, you'll be repeating an experiment that heralded the dawning of the age of microwave cooking.

2   Almost 50 years ago, 1946 to be exact, one of the great minds in the history of electronics accidentally invented microwave popcorn.

3   Shortly after World War II, Percy L. Spencer, electronic genius and war hero, was touring one of his laboratories at the Raytheon Company. Spencer stopped in front of a magnetron, the power tube that drives a radar set. Suddenly he noticed that a candy bar in his pocket had begun to melt.

4   Most of us would have written off the gooey mess to body heat. But not Spencer. Spencer never took anything for granted. During his 39 years with Raytheon, he patented 120 inventions. When England was battered by German bombs in the 1940 Battle of Britain, Spencer turned his creative mind toward developing a better version of the British invention radar. His improved magnetron allowed radar tube production to be increased from 17 per week to 2,600 per day. His achievements earned him the Distinguished Service Medal, the U.S. Navy's highest honor for civilians.

5   So when this inquisitive, self-educated, and highly decorated engineer who never finished grammar school came face to face with a good mystery, he didn't merely wipe the melted chocolate off his hands and shrug off the incident. He took the logical next step. He sent out for popcorn. Holding the bag of unpopped kernels next to the magnetron, Spencer watched as the kernels exploded.

6   The next morning Spencer brought in a tea kettle. He wanted to see what microwaves would do to raw eggs. After cutting a hole in the side of the kettle, Spencer placed an uncooked egg into the pot. Next he placed a magnetron beside the kettle and turned on the machine.

7   An unfortunate (cynical?) engineer poked his nose into the pot and was greeted by an explosion of yolk and white. The egg had been blown up by the steam pressure from within. Spencer had created the first documented microwave mess—an experiment to be inadvertently repeated by countless thousands of microwave cooks. He had also shown that microwaves had the ability to cook foods quickly.

8   Legend has it that this demonstration was reproduced before unsuspecting members of Raytheon's board of directors who had trouble visualizing exactly what microwaves could do to food. The ensuing egg shower convinced the board of directors to invest in the "high frequency dielectric heating apparatus" patented in 1953.

9   That demo and the fact that the military no longer needed 10,000 magnetron tubes per week for radar sets helped shape the future of microwaves. What better way

to recover lost sales than to put in every American home a radar set disguised as a microwave oven?

10   But first the device needed a better name. Raytheon's marketing mavens felt few people would demand a high-frequency dielectric heating apparatus for their kitchens even if they could pronounce it. A contest followed to rename the apparatus. Seeing as how the oven owed its roots to radar, the winning entry suggested "Radar Range." The words were later merged to Radarange. But no words could hide the woeful inadequacies of this first-generation oven.

11   Weighing 750 pounds and standing five and a half feet [tall], the Radarange required water—and plumbing—to keep its hefty innards cool. Hardly the compact unit that fits under today's kitchen cabinets. The early 1953 design—with its three-thousand-dollar price tag—was strictly for restaurants, railroads (the Japanese railroad system bought 2,500), and ocean liners. These customers would be Raytheon's prime market for two decades.

12   The microwave oven was no pleasure to cook with, either. Culinary experts noticed that meat refused to brown. French fries stayed white and limp. Who could eat this ugly-looking food? Chefs were driven to distraction. As chronicled in *The Wall Street Journal,* "the Irish cook of Charles Adams, Raytheon's chairman, who turned his kitchen into a proving ground, called the oven 'black magic' and quit."

13   It would take decades before the consumer oven was perfected. The Tappan Company took an interest in the project and helped Raytheon engineers shrink the size of the magnetron. A smaller power unit meant the hideous plumbing could be done away with and air cooling fans could take over.

14   Then someone had the brilliant idea that perhaps the magnetron should not be pointed directly at the food but rather out of sight. That's it. Put the food in a box, put the microwave source at the back, and lead the microwaves into the box via a pipe. Now we could truly call it an oven.

15   And that's what happened. In 1955 Tappan introduced the first consumer microwave oven. Did you have one? Hardly anyone did. It was still too big and costly. Then came 1964 and a breakthrough. From Japan, the country that had a reputation for making "transistorized" (read: small) products out of everything, came an improved electron tube. Smaller than the old magnetron, it put Raytheon on track to placing a microwave oven under everyone's kitchen cabinet.

16   Needing a consumer-oriented vehicle to sell its new ovens, Raytheon bought up Amana Refrigeration, Inc., in 1965 and put out its first affordable ($495), compact, and practical microwave oven in 1967.

17   The specter of little microwaves leaking out of the oven scared a lot of people. Their worst fears were realized in 1968 when a test of microwave ovens at Walter Reed Hospital found microwaves did indeed leak out. Federal standards set in 1971 solved that problem.

18   Today more homes have microwave ovens than dishwashers. And we owe it all to an inquisitive man with a melted candy bar in his pocket and egg on his face.

COMPREHENSION CHECKUP

Multiple Choice

Directions: For each item, write the letter corresponding to the best answer.

___a___ 1. The original Radarange achieved little acceptance in which of the following situations?
   a. restaurants
   b. ocean liners
   c. railroads
   d. small kitchens

___c___ 2. The original Radarange had all of the following qualities *except* for which?
   a. cooked food to perfection
   b. had large size and weight
   c. required water for cooling
   d. was very expensive

___d___ 3. All of the following led to our modern microwave oven *except* for which?
   a. Japan reduced the size of the electron tube.
   b. Air cooling fans were introduced.
   c. The microwave source was placed at the back.
   d. Microwave-safe dishes were invented.

___c___ 4. The author's primary purpose is to
   a. inform us of hazards involved in the use of microwaves.
   b. persuade people to buy microwaves.
   c. explain how a microwave oven works.
   d. explain the events leading to the creation of the modern microwave.

True or False

Directions: Indicate whether each statement is true or false by writing **T** or **F** in the space provided.

___T___ 5. The magnetron caused the candy bar in Spencer's pocket to melt.

___F___ 6. Spencer performed additional experiments with the magnetron using unpopped kernels and raw eggs.

___F___ 7. The microwave oven was perfected quickly.

___T___ 8. Spencer was chosen to select an appropriate name for his new invention.

___F___ 9. Chefs were eager to work with the new oven.

___T___ 10. Initially, microwaves leaked out of the ovens.

___F___ 11. Homes are more likely to have a dishwasher than a microwave oven.

Vocabulary in Context

Directions: Look through the given paragraph and find a word that matches the definition.

1. announced (1)   _____

2. pessimistic (7)   _____

3. unintentionally (7)   _____

4. resulting (8)   _____

5. experts (10)   _____

6. pitiful (10)   _____

7. kitchen (12)   _____

8. object of fear (17)   _____

In Your Own Words

1. What does the author admire about Spencer? What is the author's main idea?
2. How was the timing of Spencer's discovery beneficial to the military?
3. What were the drawbacks of the original microwave oven?
4. Although Spencer lacked formal education, he was a highly successful engineer. In the world today, how likely is it that a person without formal education could achieve success in a technical field?
5. What does context tell us about the meaning of the word *inquisitive* in the last sentence of the reading? In paragraph 5?

Internet Activity

To read a biography of Ira Flatow, or to visit "Science Friday," check out the following Web site:

www.npr.org/programs/scifri/

Author's Purpose: To Persuade

The following article, "Students Who Push Burgers," was first published in *The Christian Science Monitor.* The author, Walter S. Minot, worries that too many students are working too many hours a week while also trying to be full-time students. He would like to see college students give a higher priority to their studies and work fewer hours. Although this article was written in 1988, the information presented is still relevant today. In fact, the actual percentage of working students has increased slightly.

READING

"The world seems to have accepted the part-time job as a normal feature of adolescence. . . . But such employment is a cause of educational decline."

TUNING IN TO READING

Do you think students should have jobs? Are there good reasons and bad reasons for students to hold down jobs? Do your fellow students work too much at their jobs and not put enough effort into their studies?

BIO-SKETCH

Walter Minot, professor emeritus at Gannon University, taught rhetoric and writing for 36 years before retiring.

NOTES ON VOCABULARY

scapegoat   a person, group, or thing made to take the blame for the crime or mistake of others. Under the law of Moses, the high priest of the ancient Jews would bring two goats to the altar on the Day of Atonement. The high priest then cast lots to see which goat would be sacrificed to the Lord and which would be the *scapegoat.* After the priest had confessed the sins of his people over the head of the *scapegoat*, it was taken to the wilderness and allowed to escape, carrying with it all the sins of the people. The other goat was then given in sacrifice. Definition of *scapegoat* from William Morris and Mary Morris, *Morris Dictionary of Word and Phrase Origins.* Copyright © 1987 by William Morris and Mary Morris. Reprinted by permission of HarperCollins Publishers.

tripe   slang for nonsense, or anything offensive; part of the stomach of cattle, goats, and deer when used for food.

Minot argues that students today often work to support a luxurious lifestyle. Do you agree?

Students Who Push Burgers

BY WALTER MINOT

A COLLEGE FRESHMAN SQUIRMS anxiously on a chair in my office, his eyes avoiding mine, those of his English professor, as he explains that he hasn't finished his paper, which was due two days ago. "I just haven't had the time," he says.

2 "Are you carrying a heavy course load?"

3 "Fifteen hours," he says—a normal load.

4 "Are you working a lot?"

5 "No, sir, not much. About 30 hours a week."

6 "That's a lot. Do you have to work that much?"

7 "Yeah, I have to pay for my car."

8 "Do you really need a car?"

9 "Yeah, I need it to get to work."

10 This student isn't unusual. Indeed, he probably typifies today's college and high school students. Yet in all the lengthy analyses of what's wrong with American education, I have not heard employment by students being blamed.

11 I have heard drugs blamed and television—that universal scapegoat. I have heard elaborate theories about the decline of the family, of religion, and of authority, as well as other sociological theories. But nobody blames student employment. The world seems to have accepted the part-time job as a normal feature of adolescence. A parochial school in my town even had a day to honor students who held regular jobs, and parents often endorse this employment by claiming that it teaches kids the value of the dollar.

12 But such employment is a major cause of educational decline. To argue my case, I will rely on memories of my own high school days and contrast them with what I see today. Though I do have some statistical evidence, my argument depends on what anyone over 40 can test through memory and direct observation.

13 When I was in high school in the 1950s, students seldom held jobs. Some of us baby-sat, shoveled snow, mowed lawns, and delivered papers, and some of us got jobs in department stores around Christmas. But most of us had no regular source of income other than the generosity of our parents.

14 The only kids who worked regularly were poor. They worked to help their families. If I remember correctly, only about five people in my class of 170 held jobs. That was in a working-class town in New England. As for the rest of us, our parents believed that going to school and helping around the house were our work.

15 In contrast, in 1986 my daughter was one of the few students among juniors and seniors who didn't work. According to Bureau of Labor statistics, more than 40 percent of high school students were working in 1980, but sociologists Ellen Greenberger and Laurence Steinberg in "When Teenagers Work" came up with estimates of more than 70 percent working in 1986, though I suspect that the figure may be even higher now.

16 My daughter, however, did not work; her parents wouldn't let her. Interestingly, some of the students in her class implied that she had an unfair advantage over them in the classroom. They were probably right, for while she was home studying, they were pushing burgers, waiting on tables, or selling dresses 20 hours a week. Working students have little time for homework.

17 I attended a public high school, while she attended a Roman Catholic preparatory school whose students are mainly middle class. By the standards of my day, her classmates did not "have to" work. Yet many of them were working 20 to 30 hours a week. Why?

18 They worked so that they could spend $60 to $100 a week on designer jeans, rock concerts, stereo and video systems, and, of course, cars. They were living lives of luxury, buying items on which their parents refused to throw hard-earned money away. Though the parents would not buy such tripe for their kids, the parents somehow convinced themselves that the kids were learning the value of money. Yet, according to Ms. Greenberger and Mr. Steinberg, only about a quarter of these students saved money for college or other long-term goals.

19 How students spend their money is their business, not mine. But as a teacher, I have witnessed the effects of their employment. I know that students who work all evening aren't

ready for studying when they get home from work. Moreover, because they work so hard and have ready cash, they feel that they deserve to have fun—instead of spending all their free time studying.

20 Thus, by the time they get to college, most students look upon studies as a spare-time activity. A survey at Pennsylvania State University showed that most freshmen believed they could maintain a B average by studying about 20 hours a week. (I can remember when college guidebooks advised two to three hours of studying for every hour in class—30 to 45 hours a week.)

21 Clearly individual students will pay the price for lack of adequate time studying, but the problem goes beyond the individual. It extends to schools and colleges that are finding it difficult to demand quantity or quality of work from students.

22 Perhaps the reason American education has declined so markedly is because America has raised a generation of part-time students. And perhaps our economy will continue to decline as full-time students from Japan and Europe continue to outperform our part-time students.

"Students Who Push Burgers" by Walter S. Minot as appeared in *The Christian Science Monitor*, Nov. 22, 1988. Copyright © 1988 Walter S. Minot. Reprinted by permission of the author.

COMPREHENSION CHECKUP

Multiple Choice

Directions: For each item, write the letter corresponding to the best answer.

___b___ 1. The college freshman who spoke to Professor Minot
   a. has to work so much so that he can pay for his food and rent.
   b. takes a lighter course load than other college students.
   c. has completed his English paper on time.
   d. is fairly typical of today's college students, according to the author.

___b___ 2. The main idea expressed in this article is that
   a. drugs and television are directly responsible for the decline in American education.
   b. the decline in religious values has led to a corresponding decline in American education.
   c. student employment in the United States is a major cause of educational decline.
   d. parochial schools, unlike public schools, are still able to provide a quality education.

___d___ 3. Which of the following statements is true according to the author?
   a. Students in the 1950s rarely worked.
   b. The majority of students save their wages from part-time jobs for long-term goals.
   c. A parochial school honored students who had regular employment.
   d. Both a and c.

___d___ 4. From Minot's article, we can conclude that many parents
   a. no longer believe that going to school and helping out at home should be a student's only work.
   b. are reluctant to spend their money on frivolous items such as designer jeans.

       c. are convinced that students learn the value of money by working at a
         part-time job.

       d. all of the above.

_____ 5. The author's primary purpose is to

       a. describe the educational system of the 1950s.

       b. argue that student employment contributes to educational decline.

       c. describe one student's academic dilemma.

       d. applaud the attitude of today's parents toward part-time student
         employment.

True or False

Directions: Indicate whether each statement is true or false by writing **T** or **F** in the space provided.

_____ 6. A Penn State survey indicates that college freshman believe they can maintain an A average with only 20 hours of studying per week.

_____ 7. Minot believes that there is a correlation between student employment and a college's ability to maintain high academic standards.

_____ 8. Although Minot is opposed to student employment, he did allow his daughter to work while she was in high school.

_____ 9. According to the statistics given in the article, teenage employment has continued to rise over the years.

_____ 10. Minot has personally observed how student employment harms academic achievement.

Vocabulary in Context

Directions: Indicate whether the word in italics is used correctly or incorrectly by writing **C** or **I** in the space provided.

_____ 1. It's an act of *generosity* to refuse to help others.

_____ 2. After golfer Tiger Woods *endorsed* the product, sales immediately rose.

_____ 3. The student became bored by the lecture and began to *squirm* about in his seat.

_____ 4. A person who strives for perfection is likely to be satisfied with an *adequate* performance.

_____ 5. Alejandro was walking down the sidewalk when he *witnessed* a car accident on the nearby street.

_____ 6. Tenssy made *elaborate* plans for her formal wedding ceremony that was to have over five hundred guests.

_____ 7. A person in the stage of *adolescence* is very close to retirement age.

_____ 8. Shawn *typifies* college student-athletes who work long hours at both their studies and their sports.

In Your Own Words

In Your Own Words

1. Do you think parents today still support the notion that a student's only "job" should be going to school and getting good grades? Why or why not?

2. In grade school, most students are in class until three or four in the afternoon. Most high school students are dismissed much earlier than this. Do you think high schools should require students to spend more time at school?

3. What do parents hope a student will learn from work experience? What do you think students learn from work experience? Would it be better for students with free time to do volunteer work or internships instead of working for a salary?

4. It is well known that students in the United States spend less time in school than do students in any other modern industrial country. What are the global implications of being a nation of part-time students?

5. Many high school and college teachers comment that they no longer require the same amount of work from their students. For example, where once two research papers were required for English 101, now only one is required. What are some possible effects of these reduced standards?

6. Many teachers report that the number of students trying to do their homework in class has increased over the years. The main idea from paragraph 16 supports the observation of these teachers. Write the main idea below.

_____

Written Assignment

Minot's main idea is that student employment is a major cause of educational decline in this country. Do you agree with Minot's viewpoint? Why or why not?

What's Your Opinion?

How much homework do you think is appropriate for children of various ages?

YOU BE THE JUDGE: HOMEWORK SHOULD BE

A Major Part of a Student's Life Because . . .

There is too much material to be mastered only during school time. Given demands on students to learn more and to increase their test scores, much study and learning needs to take place at home. After all, students are in school for just five hours of a 24-hour day.

It brings parents into the learning process. School cannot accomplish its goals alone. Students achieve much more when academics are reinforced at home. By providing guidance and monitoring homework, parents demonstrate their support of learning, becoming true partners with teachers. Closing the school-home gap fosters competent and attentive students.

Many students do not use their time wisely. The average student comes home from school, talks on the phone with friends, "hangs out" at the mall, watches television for hours, and then plays a computer game or two before going to bed. Homework at least gives students something meaningful to do with their time.

Limited and Brief Because . . .

Too much stress is placed on students as it is. Schools have been taken over by this growing obsession with tests. The last thing we need to do is extend this angst to home life. Besides, homework is mostly busywork, unrelated to real learning.

It favors some students and penalizes others. Some children have highly educated parents, home computers, and the resources needed to produce quality homework. Other students have poor and uneducated parents, who may not speak English and who may be working two or more jobs. All too often homework is simply a measure of family resources.

Many students do not have the luxury of extra time. Many students go directly from school to their part-time job. Their families may need the money. Other students must care for younger siblings at home while parents are at work. Increasing homework would place an enormous burden on their families.

From Myra Sadker and David Sadker, *Teachers, Schools, and Society*, 8th Edition, p. 204. Copyright © 2008 by The McGraw-Hill Companies, Inc. Reprinted with permission.

Writing Summaries

In your reading and English classes, you will be called upon to write summaries. **Summarizing** simply means restating the main ideas of a reading in your own words. Because many supporting details are omitted, a summary is much shorter than the original on which it is based. When you write summaries, you need to present the main ideas in order of importance in an objective fashion. Keep in mind that you are reporting the author's viewpoints and not your own. When writing a summary, you never write something like "I feel" or "I think" or "it seems to me." Instead, you always write only the author's opinions. In a summary, it is always the *author* who feels, thinks, or believes.

It takes practice to learn how to write a good summary. However, since we have now learned how to identify directly stated main ideas and how to state implied ones, we are ready to begin learning how to write a summary of a short article. You just read an article by Walter S. Minot titled "Students Who Push Burgers." This is a relatively easy article to summarize because the author presents his main ideas in a logical sequence. Try to locate the directly stated main ideas. Because not all of the main ideas are stated directly, you will have to come up with several implied main ideas.

In order to identity the key supporting details, try to answer as many of the question words (*who, what, where, when, why,* and *how*) about the topic as possible.

Exercise 3: Summarizing an Article

Directions:

1. Provide answers to *who, what, where, when, why,* and *how.* (Not all of these question words will apply to every article.)

    Who: _____

    What: _____

    Where: _____

    When: _____

    Why: _____

    How: _____

2. List four to five main ideas from the article, paraphrasing each main idea. The overall main idea of the article is: Student employment is a major cause of the decline in American education.

    1st main idea: _____

    _____

    2nd main idea: _____

    _____

    3rd main idea: _____

    _____

    4th main idea: _____

    _____

    5th main idea: _____

    _____

3. Write at least a half-page summary of the article. Be sure to include the information from numbers 1 and 2 in your summary. Your completed summary should contain no trivia (useless information) and should not be redundant (give information more than once). Remember to present the information in an organized way. After writing your summary, compare your version to the student sample in the Appendices.

Exercise 4: Determining an Author's Purpose

Directions: Label each paragraph according to its general purpose: to inform (**I**), to entertain (**E**), or to persuade (**P**).

_I___ 1.　　Since earliest times the fragrances of certain plants, owing to their essential oils, have been valued as a source of perfumes. It is difficult to pinpoint when people first began using plant fragrances to scent their bodies, but by 5,000 years ago the Egyptians were skilled perfumers, producing fragrant oils that were used by both men and women to anoint their hair and bodies. Fragrances were also used as incense to fumigate homes and temples in the belief that these aromas could ward off evil and disease. In fact, our very word *perfume* comes from the Latin *per* meaning through and *fumus* meaning smoke, possibly referring to an early use of perfumes as incense.

From Estelle Levetin and Karen McMahon, "Alluring Scents," *Plants and Society*, 5th Edition, p. 84. Copyright © 2008 by The McGraw-Hill Companies, Inc. Reprinted with permission.

_P___ 2.　　The images are vivid and appalling. Emaciated children with haunting eyes and distended stomachs, and too weak to cry, stare at us from news photos and television screens. Throughout the world, the problems of poverty and undernutrition are widespread and growing. The majority of undernourished people live in Asia. However, the largest increases in numbers of chronically hungry people occur in eastern Africa, particularly in Ethiopia, Sudan, Rwanda, Burundi, Sierra Leone, Kenya, Somalia, Eritrea, and Tanzania. Their eyes haunt us. If undernutrition is to be eradicated, the world's nations must examine the problem and assume responsibility. Life is not necessarily fair, but the aim of civilization should be to make it more so. The world has both enough food and the technical expertise to end hunger. What is lacking is the political will and cooperation to do so. It is time for leaders of rich and poor nations alike to come to an agreement on the best possible means to serve all of the world's citizens.

From Gordon Wardlaw, "Undernutrition throughout the World," *Contemporary Nutrition*, 6th Edition. New York: McGraw-Hill, 2007, pp. 558, 582.

_E___ 3.　　Are you lost in Cyberspace? You went away for three days and returned to find 1,892 messages in your mailbox. You just came out of the computer room and your dog is barking at you as if you were a stranger. You just missed your daughter's soccer game, your son's piano recital, or your best friend's wedding because you were traveling the information superhighway. Your family thinks you moved out a year ago.

From Nancy E. Willard, "Get a Life," *The Cyber Ethics Reader*, p. 65. Copyright © 1997 by The McGraw-Hill Companies, Inc. Reprinted with permission.

_E___ 4.　　U.S. society strongly supports marriage, and about nine out of ten people at some point "tie the knot." But many of today's marriages unravel. By 2003, almost four in ten marriages were ending in divorce. Ours is the highest divorce rate in the world. At greatest risk of divorce are young couples—especially those who marry after a brief courtship, have little money, and have yet to mature emotionally. The chance of divorce also rises if a couple marries after an unexpected pregnancy or if one or both partners have substance abuse problems. People whose parents divorced also have a higher divorce rate themselves. Finally, people who are not religious are more likely to divorce than those who have strong religious beliefs.

From John J. Macionis, *Society,* 8th Edition. Upper Saddle River, NJ: Pearson/Prentice-Hall, 2006, p. 358.

_____ 5.   How would you describe the behavior of Bruce Damon, who held up the Mutual Federal Savings Bank near Brockton, Massachusetts? Using a gun, Damon demanded $40 million. When the teller explained that the bank kept only $40,000 on the premises, he said, "Okay, $40,000." Now get this: He demanded not cash, but a check! You can imagine the ending. He was arrested a short time later when he tried to deposit the check into his account in another bank. Way to go, Bruce! Not very smart!

From Hamilton Gregory, "Incompetent Criminals," *Public Speaking for College and Career,* 7th Edition, p. 427. Copyright © 2005 by The McGraw-Hill Companies, Inc. Reprinted with permission.

_____ 6.   Something must be done about high school dropouts. A student who drops out of high school not only hurts himself or herself, but the decision to leave high school before graduation also has harmful consequences for society. Dropping out of high school does not guarantee poverty, but dropouts do have to scramble harder to start a career—if they ever have one. Society suffers when many young people do not finish school. Dropouts are more likely to end up on welfare, to be unemployed, and to become involved with drugs, crime, and delinquency. In addition, the loss of taxable income burdens the public treasury. Fortunately, with a strong commitment by government, educators, and parents, it is possible to prevent dropping out. We can help millions of young people to have a brighter future. Doing nothing is a national tragedy.

From Diane E. Papalia, Sally Wendkos Olds, and Ruth Duskin Feldman, "Dropping Out of High School," *Human Development,* 10th Edition, p. 429. Copyright © 2007 by The McGraw-Hill Companies, Inc. Reprinted with permission.

More Practice in Determining the Author's Purpose

READING

*"There've been nights when I've been so tired, I've been
ready to quit on papers. But then I look in on Olivia
sleeping, and turn right around and go back to my paper.
I can't imagine a life without her."*

TUNING IN TO READING

The following story is about Wil Smith, a recent graduate of Bowdoin College in Maine. While attending college, Wil had full custody of his four-year-old daughter Olivia. He juggled his Bowdoin classes with parenting, playing basketball, and serving in the

READING *continued*

Naval Reserve. Mel Allen, senior editor at *Yankee Magazine,* met Wil Smith last fall and wrote a letter to Olivia about Wil. As you read this story, notice the obstacles that Wil managed to overcome. Are any of you trying to raise a child by yourself? What kinds of difficulties do you experience?

BIO-SKETCH

Mel Allen has been senior features editor for *Yankee Magazine* since 1979. A former Peace Corps volunteer in Colombia, Mel became a fourth-grade teacher in Maine before publishing his first magazine story in 1977. As the father of two sons, he was especially moved by Wil's devotion to his daughter. "Wil's story is one of the most inspirational I have ever covered," Mel says.

NOTES ON VOCABULARY

pickup   a game in which whoever shows up can play. In *pickup* games, there are no established teams.

conference   an athletic *conference* is a group of schools or colleges that compete against each other on a regular basis. The team with the best record wins the *conference* championship. It comes from the Latin words *con,* meaning "together," and *ferre,* meaning "to carry or bring."

anonymous   not named or identified. Derived from the Greek words *an,* meaning "without," and *onymos,* meaning "name."

custody   the legal right to provide a home for and to care for a child. *Custody* is often established by court ruling.

asthma   a condition of the lungs in which many of the air passages are obstructed. *Asthma* is a chronic condition. *Asthma* attacks may be caused by exposure to allergens, a change in weather, or physical exertion. *Asthma* is the Greek word for "panting." A person with *asthma* is literally panting for breath.

reserves   units in the armed forces whose members are in civilian life; these units can be called up for active duty when needed.

Olivia

A LETTER TO OLIVIA   BY MEL ALLEN

Dear Olivia,

I am writing this letter to you on November 27, 1999, your father's 31st birthday. I want to tell you the story about your father, Wil Smith, and about your years together at Bowdoin College. One day you will probably ask him about these years, when he was a single dad, with a young daughter, struggling to stay in school, to compete in a tough Division III basketball program, and to provide a home for both of you. Everyone who knows your father says how modest he is, so I suspect he will leave out a lot of the details.

2   You are a bouncy, pretty little four-year-old girl, with braided pigtails and happy brown eyes. During the games you roam through the stands as the free-spirited, and totally trusting child that you are; it must seem as if the whole world knows your name. Wil says that he plays with his head on a swivel, always looking to find you during breaks in the action.

3   You live together in a two-bedroom apartment a few blocks from campus. Both of you eat in the student cafeteria. Most nights you are in bed by nine, and while you sleep Wil studies until 2, then wakes up at 6:30 to get you ready for your day.

4   Assistant basketball coach Charlie Gordon is Maine-born, used to waking at daybreak. He says on road trips he'll be up at 6, only to find Wil dressed and studying in the hotel lobby. "He never complains," says coach Gordon. "He just does what has to be done." We have good kids on the team, but they complain they're tired, or overworked. They have no idea what it means to be Wil Smith."

5   Olivia, when you are older you will remember little of these days, but when you are 12 or 14, or 16, I hope your father gives you this story, so you'll understand why Craig McEwen, the Dean for Student Academic Affairs, calls Wil "the most remarkable and unique student I have known in 20 years at Bowdoin."

6   Wil calls you "my complex joy." He says, "I know people look at it as a disadvantage having Olivia." Wil says, "I see it as an advantage. If it was just me, with the academic background I had coming to Bowdoin, I'd never have made it. There've been nights when I've been so tired, I've been ready to quit on papers. But then I look in on Olivia sleeping, and I turn right around and go back to my paper. To tell you the truth, I can't imagine a life without her."

7   You have always come first, but he is also co-captain of the men's basketball team, a four-year starter on a nationally ranked team at 31—an age when other men are playing weekly pickup games at the YMCA. You will have only a vague memory of seeing your dad play, and even then he was what we call past his prime. As Wil puts it, "I've lost a few steps." None of his teammates or coaches or opponents has seen him at his prime. When he was younger he was a shooter and a scorer; now he takes pride in stopping the other team's scorers. Last year he led Bowdoin in assists and steals, and he made the conference All-Defensive team. I watched him practice. If a teammate is not playing hard enough he'll hear about it from Wil. Coach Gilbride says, "Next year without Wil, we'll really have to coach again."

8   Over half of the Bowdoin students arrive from lives of privilege and private schools. Your father came from the Navy, a decade after graduating from a public urban high school in Florida. "I remember going to school when a successful day for a teacher was just getting home," he says. "When parents were just concerned with getting food on the table." His first year at college he had to work twice as hard just to keep up with the others. He feels angry about the disparity between his high school preparation and that of his Bowdoin classmates. "All the friends I grew up with," he says, "never had the opportunities that Bowdoin students have had."

9   College administrators say Wil is the first single father to attend Bowdoin. He is a black student and athlete at a college and in a state with few people of color, and he

has made it his business to make life better for others who will come after him. "I try to educate people about the people I come from," he says.

10 Wil's story begins in Jacksonville, Florida. When you see your father, when you remember his caring, you are also seeing a woman you never knew, your grandmother Mildred.

11 "My mother was the most incredible person I ever met," Wil says. "I was the last of ten children she raised, pretty much on her own. She worked every day, and still found time to coach boys' and girls' baseball and basketball. When people say it's incredible what I'm doing," Wil says, "I say 'This isn't extraordinary. This is what I'm supposed to do.' My mother always put us first. A lot of what I do today is because I just want her to be proud of me."

12 Everyone in northwest Jacksonville knew the Smith boys, because they were athletes. At five-foot-ten, Wil was the smallest of all the Smith boys, but he was fast and tough, and nobody worked harder. He wanted to play on his mother's teams, but she said no, she wanted her children exposed to the best competition. She sent her sons to play for coaches who knew the sport better than she did. Wil played sports year-round. Wil was an all-star in football, basketball, and baseball.

13 Mildred never missed a game. She learned how to drive at age 50, just so she could get to the games. When she died of cancer on November 27, 1983, Wil's 15th birthday, she took a lot of Wil's passion for sports with her. "My mother was my biggest fan," Wil says. "When she passed away, it was like, 'Why am I still playing?' A lot of my joy in sports came from my mother's presence."

14 Wil struggled to cope. "I'd never dealt with loss," he says. He still played, and his talent carried him to all-conference honors in three sports. But he was drifting. "I never reached the heights everyone thought I would," Wil says. When colleges sent recruiting letters, he didn't bother to respond.

15 Reluctantly Wil attended Florida A&M in Tallahassee for a year. He played one season of winter baseball, but his heart wasn't in it. He left school. It was now 1987.

16 "I was hanging out at a store with my friends," Wil says, "and I'll never forget this. ESPN came on. It was a baseball highlight. One guy said, 'Wil, man, you don't belong here. You're different. I expected to see you up there, playing ball on TV.' I always remember that. I witnessed pretty heavy stuff. But there's no way to get away from good roots. It's so hard to enjoy being bad if you have good roots."

17 In May 1989, three years after graduating from high school, Wil enlisted in the Navy. He was trained to be an aviation electronics technician, specializing in land-based anti-submarine aircraft. In June 1991, while stationed in Italy his orders sent him to the Naval Air Station in Brunswick, Maine. "I was happy," he says. "I thought it was Brunswick, Georgia, near my family in Jacksonville. I'd never heard of Brunswick, Maine." In Maine people still glance with curiosity at a black man walking down the street. "Kids at Bowdoin see a police car and think, 'I'm safe,'" says Wil. "When I came to Maine and I'd see a police car, I'd think, 'trouble.'"

18 One night he was driving back to the Navy base with his nephews in the car. He had brought two nephews from Jacksonville to live with him so they could attend Brunswick High School, a school that he knew would give them a better chance to succeed in college. Three squad cars of base policemen pulled him over. "They were looking for a black man driving a blue Thunderbird who had committed a crime," Wil remembers. "It didn't matter that my Thunderbird was white. I showed four different forms of I.D. Still they refused to believe me. They were trying to make me say I was someone else."

19 Each day at the base when Wil finished work he'd head to the gym for pickup basketball, but he wanted to do more with his time. "I'm best as a human being when I have others besides myself to focus on," he says. He saw an ad in the local newspaper for a volunteer football coach at Brunswick Middle School. Wil was the only applicant, and he got the job.

20   "I was 22 years old and I had sixty white kids on my team," Wil says. "Most of these kids had never been in contact with a black man. I had no problem with the kids, but it wasn't an easy adjustment for the parents seeing a young black man coaching their kids. They asked for a meeting with me. They said I was too intense, they didn't think their kids were ready for it. I told them that every day after practice I'd ask the kids, 'Anybody hurt? Anybody not having fun?' The kids always said they were fine. I told the parents, 'I'd like you to be on my side, but as long as your kids are with me, they're mine for three hours a day.'" By the end of the season, some of those same parents would phone Wil and tell him their kids were slipping in their work, would he come talk with them. Soon Wil became a community fixture, coaching basketball as well as football. His teams played hard, and they won. During the summer of 1995, while coaching at a basketball camp, Wil's ability and character caught the eye of Tim Gilbride, Bowdoin's men's basketball coach. Coach Gilbride asked Wil if he had considered college. Would he like to apply to Bowdoin?

21   Wil was at a professional and personal crossroads. He had served seven years in the Navy. He was due to re-enlist. But the Navy meant six months overseas every year, and by that summer he was your father. You'd been born in May. He had met your mother in Portland after returning from overseas duty. Their relationship broke up. You lived then with your mother, but Wil came for you every Thursday, and kept you until Monday.

22   Wil applied to Bowdoin then left for a six-month overseas assignment to Sicily. It was there that he decided he would go to college and not leave you again for that length of time. His last day of active duty was April 25, 1996, a date that stands out for him because that is also the day your mother gave him full custody of you, then 11 months old.

23   Though Wil had been accepted to Bowdoin, he did not know the questions to ask, questions that so many parents of college students take for granted. He did not know how to apply for student aid or room and board. He started school in September 1996. You were 14 months old, and he had no choice but to bring you to class with him. The professors learned that when you were sick, Wil would not be able to come. The money he had saved from the Navy went faster than he could have imagined. Some days he did not eat for two or three days, just so he had enough food to feed you. "Coach didn't know," Wil says, "but I lost seventeen pounds. I couldn't sleep. I got an F in a course that required you to read about twenty books. I didn't have money for books, and I didn't know about books being on reserve in the library. I said to myself, 'I can't make it. This is just too hard.'" What he told his advisor was simply, "Things are hard for me right now." The advisor called Betty Trout-Kelly, who oversees Bowdoin's multicultural programs and affirmative action.

24   On a Sunday afternoon late in his first semester Betty Trout-Kelly sat Wil down in her car. "I told him, 'I know you feel you shouldn't need this support system,'" she says, "'but if you don't take the help we can offer, it will be your fault. And if you don't accept it, you won't make it.'"

25   For the first time, Wil told her about his struggles. Later, after meeting with school officials, Trout-Kelly notified Wil that an anonymous donor would give him nearly $25,000 for Olivia's day care and after-school care. Wil would be able to move to campus housing and eat regularly with his daughter at the school. "Thank you," Wil told her. "I'll prove myself worthy."

26   Olivia, in four years your father has become as well-known off-campus as he is on it. He says, "I feel like I have an obligation to every young person I come in contact with." He is a sociology major, and he puts what he learns in the classroom to work. He is the community advisor for civil rights teams at Brunswick and Mount Ararat high schools. He travels around the state of Maine giving talks to educators about the problems and challenges of diversity. During the summer he is a counselor at Seeds of Peace International Camp in Otisfield, Maine, where Israeli and Palestinian kids live together.

27   None of this has come easily. Olivia, you have asthma, and when you're sick, he

still has trouble trusting anybody else with your care. Last season you had a fever at the same time the team had a weekend road trip. It took all of Coach Gilbride's skills of persuasion, and his saying that his wife had raised three kids, and would care for you, before Wil agreed to go.

28 During spring semester of his junior year, Wil was called to active duty—he's still a member of the Navy reserves— during the Balkan conflict. Just before he left, he received the Bowdoin Athletic Department's Leadership Award. Before leaving, he scrambled to get you to your aunt in Florida, finished work for two courses, and took incompletes in the rest. He came back before summer, picked you up, finished some papers, and got ready for his final year as a student-athlete.

29 Wil is torn about what to do in the future. Whatever he decides will be in large part because of you, Olivia, because you are more important to him than anything in the world. I talked to Wil on the phone tonight, as I am writing you this letter, and he said he had forgotten to tell me a story about you.

30 "When she was two," he said, "I was walking her to school. It was cold, and I was holding her hand. My mind was in turmoil. I had midterms; my car had broken down; we had no money. Olivia was talking about leaves and trees. I didn't even realize she had let go of my hand. I had taken another ten steps without her when I suddenly turned. She said, 'Dad, talk to me.' She was saying in her own way, 'Look, none of this other stuff matters.' She put life in perspective for me. All she cared about is that we were there. She was glad the car had broken down. That meant we could walk to school together."

Postscript:

31 On May 27, 2000, more than 400 students graduated from Bowdoin College. At the ceremony on the campus quadrangle, when Bowdoin president Robert H. Edwards read off the names "Wil and Olivia Smith," the crowd cheered and gave a standing ovation.

32 Wil, now 33, works as Bowdoin's coordinator of Multicultural Student Programs.

33 Olivia, five years old, is in kindergarten. She accompanies Wil when he does volunteer work. "She is right there along for the ride," Wil says. "I can't imagine a life without her."

"I've learned that simple walks with my father around the block when I was a child did wonders for me as an adult."

—Andy Rooney

"A Letter to Olivia" by Mel Allen. Copyright © 2000 Bowdoin Magazine. Reprinted by permission.

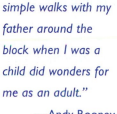

✔ COMPREHENSION CHECKUP

Short Answer

Directions: Answer each question briefly, in one or two sentences.

1. Write the main idea: _____

   _____

2. Write two major details that support the main idea.

   a. _____

   b. _____

3. What is the author's purpose? _____

   _____

4. Give two reasons to support your choice.

   a. _____

   b. _____

Multiple Choice

Directions: For each item, write the letter corresponding to the best answer.

1. Olivia was born while Wil was
   a. attending Florida A&M.
   b. in the Navy.
   c. in the Naval Reserves.
   d. attending Bowdoin College.

2. This letter was written
   a. to inform readers about Wil's athletic talent.
   b. to inform Olivia and the readers of Wil's exemplary character.
   c. to persuade small schools to welcome cultural diversity.
   d. to persuade students to take their academic studies seriously.

3. The example of Mrs. Gilbride babysitting Olivia was used to illustrate
   a. Wil's protectiveness and devotion to Olivia.
   b. Wil's age and declining athletic ability.
   c. the difficulties involved in being co-captain of the football team.
   d. Wil's lack of perspective in academic matters.

4. Which of the following statements is true according to the author?
   a. Wil's mother served as a role model for her son.
   b. Wil lost his mother on his 15th birthday.
   c. Much of Wil's love of sports was temporarily lost after his mother's death.
   d. All of the above.

5. The writer of this article probably feels that
   a. Wil has been a positive role model for those he has come in contact with.
   b. Wil has succeeded at Bowdoin despite poor academic preparation in his early years.
   c. Wil was wrong to always put the welfare of his daughter Olivia first.
   d. Both a and b.

6. The author suggests that
   a. Bowdoin had many minority students.
   b. if Wil had to do it over again, he would not have assumed full custody of Olivia.
   c. the administration at Bowdoin College had little interest in helping Wil succeed.
   d. at times Wil suffered as a result of racial stereotypes.

7. The example of the ESPN baseball highlight was used to illustrate
   a. how Wil Smith used his special skills to succeed in professional sports.
   b. that Wil Smith felt his mom had provided him with a poor foundation for life.
   c. that Wil had not fulfilled his potential at that point in his life.
   d. that Wil disliked hanging out with old friends.

8. All of the following are accurate according to the story *except* for which?
   a. At times while raising Olivia, Wil had to do without sufficient food and sleep.
   b. Olivia suffered from asthma.
   c. Wil was viewed unfavorably by the dean for Student Academic Affairs.
   d. Wil maintains that he couldn't have been successful without Olivia.

9. All of the following are accurate according to the story *except* for which?
   a. On road trips, Wil was often up earlier than the assistant coach of his team.

b. In his late twenties and early thirties, Wil proved himself to be an offensive star.

c. At Bowdoin, the majority of students are from well-to-do backgrounds.

d. Wil's mother learned to drive at age 50 in order to see her son play sports.

___C___ 10. It still makes Wil angry that

a. he failed to make the conference all-defensive team.

b. he was unable to motivate his teammates.

c. there was such disparity between his educational preparation and that of his classmates.

d. his nephews were unable to attend high school in Brunswick, Maine.

True or False

Directions: Indicate whether each statement is true or false by writing **T** or **F** in the space provided.

_____ 11. Wil's mother never missed one of his games.

___F___ 12. Wil's mother frequently coached her son's teams.

___F___ 13. Wil was the first single father at Bowdoin College.

___F___ 14. A donor gave $50,000 so that Olivia could attend day care.

___T___ 15. At 22, Wil was a community fixture in Brunswick, coaching both basketball and football.

Sequencing

Directions: Number the sentences to put the events they describe in the correct order.

Year	Order of Event	
_____	___9___	Wil begins to attend Bowdoin College.
_____	___3___	Wil joins the Navy.
_____	___1___	Wil's mother died.
_____	___2___	Wil attends Florida A&M.
_____	___4___	Wil goes to the Naval Air Station in Brunswick, Maine.
_____	___8___	Wil celebrates his 31st birthday.
_____	___5___	Olivia is born.
_____	___7___	Wil graduates from college.
_____	___6___	Wil gains full custody of Olivia.

Vocabulary in Context

Directions: In the paragraph indicated in parentheses find a word that matches the definition given, and write it in the space provided.

1. having a moderate or humble estimate of oneself (1) _____

2. to turn freely around; to revolve (2) _____

3. indefinite or indistinct (7) _____

4. to face and deal with problems and responsibilities (14) _____

5. pursuing a particular line of study or work (17) _____

6. having or showing great seriousness (20) _____

7. a point at which a vital decision must be made (21) _____

8. loud and long applause by a crowd to show approval (31) _____

In Your Own Words

1. According to the article, what roadblocks did Smith encounter in his quest to get an education?

2. Why do you think the author goes into such descriptive detail of Wil Smith and his daily life with Olivia? What stereotypes of single fathers are being discredited by this article? (*Example:* Single fathers put their own needs first.)

3. After Wil asked for help, Bowdoin College provided services to enable him to succeed as both student and parent. What kind of services should school systems provide to meet the needs of students who have family obligations?

4. Racial profiling occurs when police officers make use of racial characteristics to decide whether to stop or arrest a person. Does this article describe an incident involving racial profiling? Should police officers be allowed to engage in racial profiling?

Written Assignment

New research reveals that children who have contact with involved, loving fathers are much less likely to suffer from low self-esteem, do poorly in school, become involved with drugs, or have behavioral disorders. What can be done to encourage single fathers to have more involvement with their children? Write a paragraph giving some concrete suggestions of your own on ways to accomplish this.

Internet Activity

Several Web sites offer useful information on parenting. The first two sites listed below are sponsored by physician groups, while the other sites are commercial. Find an article of interest to you, and describe the author's general and specific purposes.

> www.aap.org (American Academy of Pediatrics)
>
> www.kidshealth.org (Nemours Foundation)
>
> parenting.ivillage.com (Scroll down.)
>
> www.parentandchildonline.com (*Scholastic Magazine*)

REVIEW TEST: *Topics, Main Ideas, Details, and Purpose*

Multiple Choice

Directions: Read each passage. Then for each item, write the letter corresponding to the best answer.

A.   If our business enterprises are to be as flexible and innovative at all levels as they need to be, our youngsters must be prepared to work with and through other people. While there will always be a need for a certain number of solo practitioners, the more usual requirement will be that combinations of individual skills are greater than their sums. Most of the important work will be done by groups, rather than by individual experts. . . . Young people must be taught how to work constructively together. Instead of emphasizing individual achievement and competition, the emphasis in the classroom should be on group performance. Students need to learn how to seek and accept criticism from their peers, to solicit help, and to give credit to others, where appropriate. They must also learn to negotiate—to articulate their own needs, to discern what others need and see things from others' perspectives, and to discover mutually beneficial outcomes.

From Robert Reich, "Dick and Jane Meet the New Economy" in *The Resurgent Liberal*. New York: Vintage Books, a division of Random House, 1989, p. 102.

_____ 1. The main idea expressed in this passage is that
   a. most of the work in the future will be done by individuals working alone.
   b. there are advantages and disadvantages to working collectively.
   c. many students are capable of learning to work together productively.
   d. young people need to be taught how to work together productively so that our business enterprises can successfully meet new challenges.

_____ 2. The author's primary purpose is to
   a. convince us of the necessity of emphasizing group activities in our educational systems.
   b. explain the dynamics of a business enterprise.
   c. entertain us with an interesting anecdote concerning the world of business.
   d. inform us of problems students are likely to face in the near future.

_____ 3. The examples of seeking and accepting criticism, soliciting help, and giving appropriate credit were used to illustrate
   a. skills students need to develop in order to work individually.
   b. skills students need to develop in order to work cooperatively.
   c. requirements of a top-notch school system.
   d. the complexity of a business organization.

_____ 4. The best title for the paragraph would be
   a. "Group Dynamics in Action."
   b. "Cooperative Learning."
   c. "The Solo Practitioner."
   d. "Group Learning and Business."

B.   In the same way that doctors, janitors, lawyers, and industrial workers develop unique ways of looking at and responding to their work environment, so too do police officers. Police officers are often viewed as suspicious and authoritative. Police work is potentially dangerous, so officers need to be constantly aware of what is happening around them. They are frequently warned about what happens to officers who are too trusting. They learn about the many officers who have died in the line of duty because they did not exercise proper caution. On the street, they need to stay alert for signals that crimes may be in progress: an unfamiliar noise, someone "checking into" an alleyway, a secret exchange of goods. The working environment also demands that officers gain immediate control of potentially dangerous situations. They are routinely called on to demonstrate authority. Uniforms, badges, nightsticks, and guns signify authority—but officers soon learn that this authority is often challenged by a hostile public.

From Freda Adler, Gerhard O. W. Mueller, and William S. Laufer, *Criminal Justice*, 5th Edition, p. 192. Copyright © 2009 by The McGraw-Hill Companies, Inc. Reprinted with permission.

_____ 5. The best title for this paragraph would be
   a. "Jobs."
   b. "The Outlook of Police Officers."
   c. "The World of Work."
   d. "Becoming a Police Officer."

_____ 6. All of the following were given as reasons for the effect of police work on an officer's outlook *except* for which?
   a. a belief that courts are too lenient on criminals

b. a realization of what happens to officers when they are too trusting

c. the need to constantly monitor a situation

d. the need to assert authority

Written Assignment

Directions: Choose one of the following:

1. What kind of work gives you the most satisfaction? What kind of work do you find least rewarding? Write a paragraph discussing your answers.

2. Write a paragraph describing your job history. Explain why you liked or disliked your previous jobs. What did each of your previous jobs teach you about what you want to do as a future career?

3. Write a paragraph describing the difference between a "good" boss and a "bad" boss.

4. What kind of work do you want to do? Interview some people already active in the career of your choice. How do these people feel about their work? Write a paragraph discussing your findings.

Chapter Summary and Review

In this chapter, you learned how to determine whether the author's purpose is to entertain, inform, or persuade. You also learned how to summarize. Based on the material in Chapter 3, answer the following questions.

Short Answer

Directions: Answer the questions briefly.

1. What do you do when you summarize?

2. What question words should you keep in mind when writing a summary?

Vocabulary in Context

Directions: Choose one of the following words to complete the sentences below. Use each word only once.

audience	entertain	details
persuasive	purpose	textbooks

3. An author needs to take into account the intended _____, the people who will be reading the work.

4. An author who is telling a story or making an appeal to your imagination is probably trying to _____ you.

5. What you read in your _____ is probably informative writing.

6. Political advertisements that you receive in the mail before elections are good examples of _____ writing.

7. A good summary of an article will include the main ideas and significant supporting _____.

8. To determine an author's _____, you should ask yourself why the author wrote the article.

VOCABULARY   **Unit 2**

Introduction

The Greeks and Romans came up with a system for creating words by putting together smaller word parts. They used three types of word parts: prefixes, suffixes, and roots. *Pre* means "before," and so it makes sense that a prefix comes before the main part of a word. *Suf* means "after," and so a suffix comes at the end of a word. A root word is the main part of a word and usually comes in the middle. Many English words are composed of at least one root, and many have one or more prefixes and suffixes.

Part of the Greek and Roman system was a set of prefixes that represented numbers. There are many words in English derived from specific numbers. One way to help you remember many of these number prefixes is to think of the months of the year. For example, October has the prefix *oct,* meaning "eight." That might help you remember what *oct* means, except for one big problem—October is not the 8th month, but the 10th. How can this be? The answer is that our calendar evolved from the original Roman calendar, which began in March instead of January and had only 10 months. The months of Januarius and Februarius were added later, around 700 B.C. You can see that making March the first month makes October the eighth month.

Vocabulary Units 2 and 3 will draw on your knowledge of the numbering system. Make sure that you remember that the calendar began in March.

Now we are going to learn some number prefixes.

uni—one	**tetra—four**	**oct—eight**
mono—one	**quint—five**	**nov—nine**
bi—two	**pent—five**	**dec—ten**
duo—two	**sex—six**	**lat—side**
di—two	**hex—six**	**ped—foot**
tri—three	**sept—seven**	**pod—foot**
quad—four	**hept—seven**	

biped — One biped, the frigate bird, can fly 260 miles an hour.

biped   *Ped* means "foot" as in *pedal* and *pedestrian,* so a *biped* is an animal with two feet, such as a bird.

tripod   Sometimes there are slight variations in the spellings of word parts. *Pod* also means "foot," so a *tripod* has three feet. An example would be a stand for a camera.

quadruped   An animal with four feet, such as a dog or cat.

hexapod — There are over five million species of insects in the world. The total insect population of the world is at least 1 quintillion (1 followed by 18 zeros).

hexapod   An organism with six feet, such as an insect. Why aren't spiders *hexapods?* Because they have eight feet.

unicorn   That mythical animal with one horn.

unison   An instance of sounding the same note at the same time.

monopoly   A company that has no competition is called a *monopoly.* The electric and gas companies in your area are probably *monopolies* because they are the only companies allowed to give you service.

monolog(ue)   *Log* means "to speak," so a *monolog* is one person speaking without anyone responding. Jay Leno and David Letterman give *monologs* at the beginning of their shows. Why is the "ue" in parentheses? Words such as *monologue, dialogue,* and *catalogue* are in the process of losing their last two letters. As time passes, there is a tendency to drop

biplane — The first plane flight by Orville Wright lasted 12 seconds, went to a height of 8 to 12 feet, and traveled 120 feet. The name of this plane, flown at Kitty Hawk, North Carolina, was Bird of Prey.

unneeded letters from words. A dictionary 50 years from now will probably not list any of these words with the "ue" at the end.

lateral	Toward the side, sideways. The quarterback threw a *lateral* pass.
unilateral	One-sided. The mother made a *unilateral* decision and told her child to go to bed. This was not a decision that was made by discussing it with the child.
bilateral	Two-sided. We signed a *bilateral* agreement with Russia.
bicuspids	Your teeth with two points.
dual	Two of a kind, such as *dual* mufflers.
duel	A formal combat with weapons fought between two people in the presence of witnesses.
duet	A musical composition written for two musicians to perform simultaneously.
duo	Two musical performers; a pair.
trio	Three people in a group.
quartet	Four people in a group. A jazz *quartet* has four musicians.
quintuplets	Five children of the same mother born at one time.
sextuplets	Six children of the same mother born at one time.
septuplets	Seven children of the same mother born at one time. Bobbi and Kenny McCaughey of Carlisle, Iowa, had *septuplets* in 1997.
monoxide	One oxygen atom, as in carbon *monoxide* (CO).
dioxide	Two oxygen atoms, as in carbon *dioxide* (CO_2).
biplane	A plane with two sets of wings, one over the other, such as the one the Wright brothers flew.

A Typical Triplane

Pentagon — The Pentagon has 17.5 miles of corridors, 7,754 windows, and 23,000 people working there.

The Pentagon

Tetrahedron

hexagon — All snow crystals are hexagonal.

triathlon — The oldest participant in the Hawaii Triathlon was 73-year-old Walt Stack, who participated in 1981. His time of 26 hours and 20 minutes was also the longest time for any participant in this event.

triplane	A plane with three sets of wings, one over the other. The Germans, and specifically the "Red Baron," flew *triplanes* for a short period during World War I, but they were not practical for combat.
tetrahedron	A four-sided, three-dimensional object.
pentagon	A five-sided figure. The Defense Department has its headquarters in this five-sided building located in Virginia just across the Potomac River from Washington, DC.
Pentateuch	The first five books of the Old Testament (Genesis, Exodus, Leviticus, Numbers, and Deuteronomy) are called the *Pentateuch*. The Jews consider these books central to their faith and call them the Torah (law).
hexagon	A six-sided figure.
octagon	An eight-sided figure.
octave	Eight notes of the musical scale.
octane	You know it has to do with gas, but *octane* acquired its name because it has eight carbon atoms in its chemical formula (C_8H_{18}).
decade	A 10-year period.
decimal	Our numbering system is called a *decimal* system because it is based on units of 10.
September	Originally the seventh month.
October	Originally the eighth month.
November	Originally the ninth month.
December	Originally the tenth month.
biathlon	Two events, usually sporting.
triathlon	An endurance race combining three consecutive events, usually swimming, bicycling, and running. The Hawaii *Triathlon* requires participants to swim 2 miles, ride a bike 100 miles, and, last but not least, run 26 miles—all of which is done in one day.

heptathlon	An athletic contest for women that requires participants to take part in seven different events: 100-meter hurdles, shot put, high jump, 200-meter dash, long jump, javelin throw, and 800-meter run. Jackie Joyner-Kersee won the gold medal in the *heptathlon* at the Olympics in 1988 and 1992.
decathlon	An athletic contest in which each contestant takes part in 10 different events: 100-meter dash, 400-meter dash, long jump, 16-pound shot put, high jump, 110-meter hurdles, discus throw, pole vault, javelin throw, and 1500-meter run. The decathlon winner is usually proclaimed "the world's greatest athlete."
sexagenarian	A person in his or her sixties.
septuagenarian	A person in his or her seventies.
octogenarian	A person in his or her eighties.
nonagenarian	A person in his or her nineties.

Exercise 1

Directions: Write the definition of each prefix.

1. di   two
2. quad   four
3. oct   eight
4. ped   foot
5. tetra   four
6. duo   two
7. dec   ten
8. lat   side
9. nov   nine
10. pod   foot
11. bi   two

Directions: Read the definition and then write the correct prefix(es).

12. seven—(2)   sept   hept
13. five—(2)   quint   pent
14. one—(2)   mono   uni
15. three—(1)   tri   _____
16. six—(2)   sex   hex

Exercise 2: A "Prefixed" Fairy Tale

Directions: Replace the prefix with its definition, and write it in the blank provided.

Once upon a time there was a young (pent, _____) -year-old girl named

Little Red Riding Hood. She had a grandmother who was (nov × nov,

_____) years old. Grandmother lived in a house (dec, _____) blocks from

Little Red's home. (Mono, _____) day Little Red set off for Grandma's house. She took a route that was only (di, _____) miles long instead of (tri, _____) miles. Before she left, she packed a basket filled with (sept, _____) or (oct, _____) goodies. She had gone almost (bi, _____) miles, and had been walking about (hept × hept), _____) minutes when she came upon a large wolf. He put out his paw and leaned against her (lat, _____). After a brief struggle of (quad, _____) or (quint, _____) minutes, she noticed Grandma and the woodman. The (duo, _____) of them quickly came to her rescue. The woodman knocked out the wolf, and soon the wolf slept peacefully for (hex, _____) hours under a tree. Finally, Little Red was happy after all, but she wouldn't go for a walk on (pod, _____) again for at least (tetra, _____) to (sex, _____) weeks.

Exercise 3: Vocabulary in Context

Directions: In the blanks below, write the word that best completes the sentence. Use each word only once.

bicuspid	biped	decade	dual	monolog
monopoly	nonagenarian	octagon	pentagon	quartet

1. A stop sign is called an _____ because it has eight sides.

2. Bill Gates, the chair of Microsoft, was accused of creating a(n) _____ in the software industry.

3. The opening act of the play featured a(n) _____ spoken by one of the actors.

4. The _____ teeth arrive when a child is about 10–12 years old.

5. The _____ houses the offices of the five U.S. military services: the Air Force, Army, Navy, Marines, and Coast Guard.

6. A kangaroo is considered to be a(n) _____ because it has two feet.

7. Together, John, Paul, George, and Ringo formed the Beatles, the famous musical _____ of the 60s.

8. Carlos has _____ citizenship; he has legal rights in both Spain and the United States.

9. A(n) _____ is more likely than someone younger to suffer from Alzheimer's disease.

10. The Roaring Twenties was a(n) _____ of jalopies, flappers, speakeasies, and jazz.

Exercise 4: Vocabulary in Context

Directions: In the blanks below, write the word that best completes the sentence. Use each word only once.

bilateral	decathlon	duo	hexagonal
lateral	monoxide	octane	octave
quadrupeds	triathlon	triplane	unison

1. Many quartz crystals have a(n) _____ shape.

2. At the football game, the crowd yelled in _____, "Defense, defense, defense!"

3. After failing to be promoted to assistant principal, the teacher made a(n) _____ move to a teaching position at another school.

4. The _____ was a popular flying machine from about 1905 to 1910.

5. Dogs, cats, and horses are all examples of _____.

6. Batman and Robin are a dynamic, crime-fighting _____.

7. The Beatles' song "Can't Buy Me Love" (1964) sounds entirely different when sung a(n) _____ lower.

8. The winner of the grueling _____ is often featured on the cover of Wheaties, Breakfast of Champions.

9. The old Plymouth needed high- _____ gas to run well.

10. Because of a gas leak and poor ventilation, the family died of carbon _____ poisoning.

11. In 1987, a historic _____ disarmament agreement was reached between Ronald Reagan of the United States and Mikhail Gorbachev of the Soviet Union.

12. In the _____, Frank placed high in swimming and bicycling but made a poor showing in distance running.

Now that you have studied Vocabulary Unit 2, practice your new knowledge by trying the crossword puzzle.

Vocabulary Unit 2 Crossword

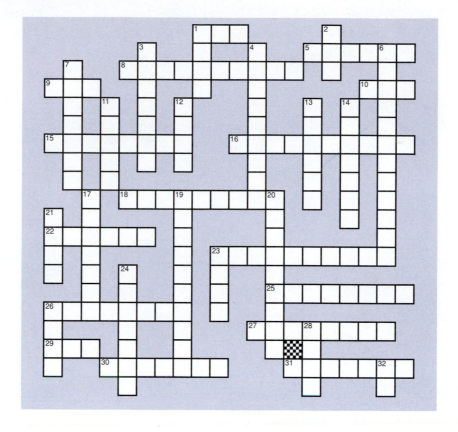

ACROSS CLUES

1. The abbreviation for what was once the 10th month.
5. A chemical found in gas.
8. The Torah, or first five books of the Old Testament.
9. A word part meaning "side."
10. A word part meaning "one."
15. What the Red Baron flew in World War I.
16. One of five children born at one time.
18. Teeth with two points.
22. All the voices or instruments together.
23. A contest involving seven track events.
25. A business that has no competition.
26. Carbon _____ is one thing that comes out of a car exhaust pipe.
27. The building in Washington, DC, where the military has its headquarters.
29. The abbreviation for what was once the 9th month.
30. What Jay Leno delivers at the start of the show.
31. We exhale carbon _____.

DOWN CLUES

1. Two of a kind.
2. The abbreviation for what was once the 8th month.
3. A numbering system that is based on units of 10.
4. An animal with four legs.
6. A person in his or her nineties is a(n) _____.
7. Passing the ball to the side is a(n) _____.
11. An animal with two legs.
12. What Aaron Burr and Alexander Hamilton fought.
13. The eight notes of the musical scale.
14. What the Wright Brothers flew.
17. The mythical animal with one horn.
19. A decision made without consulting the other party is _____.
20. What was originally the 7th month.
21. A musical piece written for two musicians to perform at the same time.
23. A word part meaning "seven."
24. A scientific name for insects.
26. A word part meaning "one."
28. Three in a group.
32. A word part meaning "two."

4

Transition Words and Patterns of Organization

CHAPTER PREVIEW

In this chapter, you will

- Learn about transition words and phrases.
- Learn about patterns of paragraph organization.

Introduction to Transition Words and Patterns of Organization

In your reading it is important to pay close attention to **transition words.** These special words help show the relationships between ideas within sentences and ideas within paragraphs. Good drivers learn to closely watch the road ahead, using signposts or markers to make their trips easier and safer. Good readers learn to use the author's transition words, which signal what is ahead.

Look at the sentences below. The addition of a transition word signaling a contrast makes a big difference in our ability to understand Tom's situation.

1. Tom was very eager to leave for college. The thought of leaving familiar surroundings filled him with dread.
2. Tom was eager to leave for college. **However,** the thought of leaving familiar surroundings filled him with dread.

The first example doesn't really make a lot of sense. If Tom is so eager to leave, why is he filled with dread? The addition of the transition word makes the situation clear in the second example. Although Tom wants to leave for college, he is understandably reluctant to give up his safe and comfortable surroundings.

Now look at these two sentences:

1. Karla did poorly in her English classes. She decided to switch her major to communication.
2. **Because** Karla did poorly in her English classes, she decided to switch her major to communication.

The first example makes us guess at the relationship between the two sentences. The addition of the transition word clarifies this relationship.

Transition Words

Words that can be used to show **classification or division (categories):**

break down	combine	lump
categorize	divide	split
class and subclass	group	type
classify	kind	

Words that can be used to show **cause-and-effect** relationships:

as a consequence	due to	resulting
as a result	for	since
because	for this reason	so
begin	hence	then
bring about	lead to	therefore
consequently	reaction	thus

Words that can be used to show **comparison:**

all	both	like
and	in comparison	likewise
as	just as	similarly

Words that can be used to show **contrast:**

although	in contrast	on the other hand
but	in opposition	rather than
despite	instead	though
even so	nevertheless	unlike
however	on the contrary	yet

Words that can be used to show **steps in a process:**

after	finally	process
afterward	first, second, third	step
at this point	next	then
at this stage	now	

Words that can be used to show **examples:**

for example	specifically	to illustrate
for instance	such as	
in particular	to demonstrate	

Words that can be used to **define:**

is defined as	is called	refers to
is described by	means	term or concept
originates from	derives from	

Words that can be used to show **chronological order:**

after	first, second, third	next
at last	finally	seasons
before	following	soon
currently	in a year, month, day	then
during	in the meantime	until

Words and symbols that can be used to show **listing (enumeration):**		
follow, following	bullets(•)	functions
first, second, third	asterisks(*)	characteristics
colon (:)	numbers (1, 2, 3)	in addition
also	letters (a, b, c)	next, finally

Practice Exercise 1: Transitions

Directions: In the following sentences, provide an appropriate transition word. If you need help, use the transition words chart. Be sure your completed sentence makes sense.

1. (contrast) _Although_ he was failing all of his classes, he still had a positive attitude about school.

2. (cause) _because_ she worked so many hours at her job, she had no time left for a social life.

3. We can (classification or division) _classify_ parents into two categories: those who are willing to use physical punishment on their children and those who are not.

4. Aggression is (definition) _described by_ any physical or verbal behavior that is directly intended to hurt someone.

5. (example) _demonstrate_ a slap, a punch, and even a direct insult are all considered forms of aggression.

6. Suppose your boss insults you; (steps in a process) _first_ you go home and yell at your wife, _Next_ she yells at your son, _then_ he kicks his baby sister, _new_ she pulls the dog's tail, and _finally_ the dog bites the mail carrier.

7. In the winter months of (months of the year in order) _dec_, _Janury_, and _feb_, assaults are at an all-time low. In the hotter seasons of _Jun_, _July_, and _august_, violent crimes are more likely to occur.

Writers organize their supporting sentences and ideas in ways called **patterns of organization.** The most common kinds of patterns of organization are (1) classification and division, (2) cause and effect, (3) comparison-contrast, (4) steps in a process, (5) examples, (6) definition, (7) chronological order, and (8) listing. A writer's chosen pattern of organization will affect the sort of transition words he or she uses. In the sections that follow, we will discuss patterns of organization and the relationships between patterns of organization and transition words.

Classification and Division

Classification is the process of organizing information into categories. We create a category by noting and defining group characteristics. The categories we create make it easier to analyze, discuss, and draw conclusions.

Have you ever scanned the classified ads section of the newspaper? If you have, you are already familiar with classification and division. Ads are not arranged randomly in the newspaper; otherwise, you would never be able to quickly locate the information you need. Instead, ads are grouped into categories, with each category further subdivided as much as needed.

For instance, if you wanted to buy your son a dog for his birthday, you would first locate the section titled "Livestock/Pets/Produce." Under this heading, you would locate the section on "Dogs." In some newspapers, the category "Dogs" may be so large that it is further subdivided into "Beagles," "Boxers," "Poodles," and other breeds of dogs.

LIVESTOCK/PETS/PRODUCE

The details in many paragraphs are also organized using classification. Look at the three short paragraphs describing unhealthy expressions of anger. The author uses two specific categories to make it easier for us to understand the information being presented.

"Self-control is the quality that distinguishes the fittest to survive."

— George Bernard Shaw

According to University of Arizona psychologist Roger J. Daldrup, there are **two classic ways** of expressing anger in an unhealthy way: misdirecting it, and suppressing it completely.

Misdirected anger, Daldrup says, "is the classic kicking the cat because you're angry at your spouse maneuver. Though people who misdirect their anger seem to be expressing it, they are just burying the real problem and creating more problems along the way."

The other classic response, complete suppression of anger, doesn't work either, because, says Daldrup, it creates what he calls "the keyboard effect." When a person starts repressing one emotion, he begins repressing them all, something he likens to pressing down the soft pedal on the piano: "That pedal will soften all the notes on the piano, just as dulling one emotion will dull them all."

From *Mind/Body Health* by Brent Q. Hafen, Keith J. Karren, Kathryn J. Frandsen, and N. Lee Smith, p. 172. Copyright © 1996 by Allyn & Bacon. Reprinted by permission of Pearson Education, Inc.

Now look at the following outline to gain a better understanding of major and minor supporting details. Here, MI refers to the main idea, MSD to major supporting details, and msd to minor supporting details.

I. There are two classic ways of expressing anger in an unhealthy way. (MI)
   A. A person can misdirect anger. (MSD)
      1. It just buries the problem and creates more problems. (msd)
      2. It is the classic kicking the cat because you're angry at a spouse. (msd)
   B. A person can suppress anger. (MSD)
      1. This method doesn't work either. (msd)
      2. It creates a keyboard effect. (msd)

In recent years, many Americans have become fascinated with investigating their ancestral background. They use the information they gather to assemble family trees or genealogy charts showing the names, birth dates, marriages, and deaths of ancestors. In addition to being fun, studying the details of a family's medical past can provide early warning of health problems that might lie ahead for current family members. Many ailments are known to have genetic links, including cancer, diabetes, and alcoholism.

To practice classification, try making a genealogy chart or family tree. Talk with family members to try to gather information about your ancestors. Then record the information on a genealogical chart like the one below.

Your family tree shows your pedigree. The word *pedigree* came to English in the 15th century from the French phrase *pied de grue,* meaning "foot of a crane." The lines showing descent (in the earliest genealogies) strongly resembled the footprint of a crane. In time, the symbol came to represent the study of genealogy itself.

Written Assignment

In the process of doing your research, you may discover some interesting stories about your family. Some of these stories are likely true, but others may be part family myth. Write three of these stories in paragraph format, and share them with the class.

FOUR-GENERATION GENEALOGICAL CHART

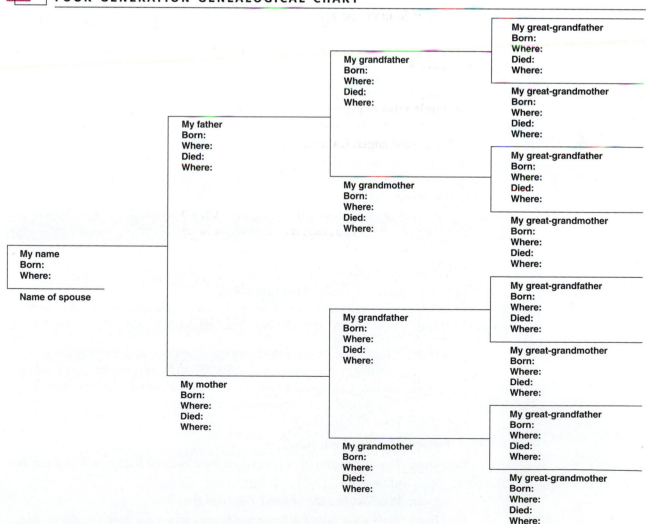

Internet Activity

Genealogy Web sites are available on the Internet. The following Web sites are especially helpful in looking up family tree information:

www.cyndislist.com

www.familysearch.org

www.rootsweb.com

www.ancestry.com

www.ellisislandrecords.org

Practice Exercise 2: Classification and Division

Directions: Fill in the blank with an appropriate transition word or phrase from the list below. Some of the transition words will fit in more than one of the sentences, but try to use a different transition word in each sentence. Make sure the sentence makes sense with the transition word you choose.

break down	classify	combine	divide	group

1. We can ___classify___ cohabitating relationships into five types.

2. The first ___group___ is called *temporary casual* and involves two people sharing living space simply because it is convenient and less expensive. Neither party is romantically involved.

3. If we ___combine___ all those who have cohabitated at some point in their lives, we discover that the figure is about 50 percent.

4. We can ___divide___ this category into those who expect to eventually marry their partners and those who do not.

5. We can further ___break down___ those couples into those who intend to have children and those who do not.

Cause and Effect

In a **cause-and-effect** relationship, one thing causes another thing to happen. The second event is the effect or result of the first event.

Try reading the following anecdote to locate cause-and-effect relationships. You will need people to read the narrator's, the farmer's, and the field hand's parts.

Narrator: It happened in the days before mail service and telephones. A wealthy farmer took a long trip. When he arrived home, he asked the first field hand he saw what had happened while he was away. This is how their conversation went:

Field hand: Well, the dog died.

Farmer: The dog died! How?

Field hand: The horses ran over him when they became frightened and ran out of the barn.

Farmer: What scared the horses? Why did they run?

Field hand: They were running from the flames when the barn caught on fire.

> *Farmer:* My God! How did the barn catch on fire?
>
> *Field hand:* Well, sir, flames jumped from the house and caught the barn on fire.
>
> *Farmer:* From the house! Did the house burn down, too?
>
> *Field hand:* Yep. The house is gone, too.
>
> *Farmer:* How on earth did the house burn down?
>
> *Field hand:* You see, one of the candles around your wife's casket fell over and caught the house on fire.

Adapted from *Contemporary's Building Basic Skills in Reading, Book I*, pp. 93–94. Copyright © 1988 by The McGraw-Hill Companies, Inc. Reprinted with permission.

Now complete the cause-and-effect sentences.

1. Because the candles on the wife's casket fell over, the _____.

2. Because flames jumped from the house, the _____.

3. Because the horses were scared, they _____.

You will encounter many cause-and-effect relationships in the textbooks you read for your various classes. The following paragraphs from a health textbook illustrate a cause-and-effect relationship; transition words are set in bold. Read the paragraphs and then study the outline that follows.

"Angers are the sinners of the soul."

—Robert Fuller

Anger has as many different causes as there are situations and people. The most common **cause** is physical or psychological restraint—being held back from something we intensely want or want to do. Others include being forced to do something against our will, being taken advantage of, being frustrated, being insulted, being ridiculed, or having plans defeated. Sometimes other emotions (such as distress, sorrow, or fear) can **lead to** anger.

The most recent research shows that the **effects** of anger are diverse and widespread. Consider the wide range of physiological **reactions** that go with it: changes in muscle tension, scowling, grinding of teeth, glaring, clenching of fists, flushing, goose bumps, chills and shudders, prickly sensations, numbness, choking, twitching, sweating, losing control, or feeling hot or cold. One of the major physiological **effects** of anger is on the release of chemicals and hormones, principally adrenaline and noradrenaline. When the release of adrenaline and noradrenaline is chronic or prolonged, **resulting** in chronic or prolonged anger, some of the most serious **effects** are high blood pressure, headache, heart attack, stroke, and kidney problems. If there's enough anger, almost any part of the body can be harmed. The **effects** can be as serious as cancer and heart disease or as minor (but annoying) as the common cold or skin disorders.

From *Mind/Body Health* by Brent Q. Hafen, Keith J. Karren, Kathryn J. Frandsen, and N. Lee Smith, pp. 174–75. Copyright © 1996 by Allyn & Bacon. Reprinted by permission of Pearson Education, Inc.

I. Anger has many different causes. (MI)
   A. One cause is physical or psychological restraint. (MSD)
   B. Other causes include being forced to do something, being taken advantage of, being frustrated, insulted, ridiculed. (MSD)
   C. Other emotions can sometimes cause anger. (MSD)

II. The effects of anger are diverse and widespread. (MI)
    A. There are a wide range of physiological reactions. (MSD)
        1. Examples are changes in muscle tension, scowling, clenching. (msd)
        2. More examples are flushing, chills, and shudders. (msd)
    B. Anger affects the release of chemicals and hormones. (MSD)
        1. Adrenaline (msd)
        2. Noradrenaline (msd)
    C. Chronic or prolonged anger causes health problems. (MSD)
        1. Effects can be major like cancer and heart disease. (msd)
        2. Effects can be minor like the common cold or skin disorders. (msd)

Practice Exercise 3: Cause and Effect

Directions: Fill in the blank with an appropriate transition word or phrase from the list below. Some of the transition words will fit in more than one of the sentences, but try to use a different transition word in each sentence. Make sure the sentence makes sense with the transition you choose.

| as a result | because | bring about | therefore | reaction |

1. __*Because*__ working moms with children under the age of five want a familiar face to care for their children, many are turning to grandparents and other relatives for help with child care.

2. Teens who begin drinking before they are old enough to drive have a higher chance of becoming alcoholics at some time in their lives. __*therefore*__, many organizations want to begin early-intervention programs with those teens who begin drinking early.

3. Last year, U.S. residents spent $207 billion on meals prepared by restaurants, with 51 percent of that total for takeout and delivery; __*as a result*__, online food order companies are beginning to see the potential for big business.

4. In __*reaction*__ to criticism by the Food and Drug Administration, R. J. Reynolds Tobacco Co. discontinued the use of Joe Camel, the cartoon character, in its ads.

5. In order to __*bring about*__ positive changes in race relations, more and more open forums discussing problems are being held around the country.

Comparison-Contrast

A **comparison** shows the similarities between two or more things, while a **contrast** shows the differences. Sometimes a writer both compares (tells the similarities) and contrasts (tells the differences) at the same time. The following information from the Internet on Presidents Lincoln and Kennedy illustrates comparison-contrast, with transition words in bold.

There are many curious parallels in the deaths of Presidents Abraham Lincoln and John Fitzgerald Kennedy. President Lincoln was elected in 1860. **And** exactly 100 years later, in 1960, Kennedy was elected president. **Both** were assassinated on a Friday in the presence of their wives. **Both** presidents were deeply involved in civil rights for blacks. **Both** President Lincoln and President Kennedy were succeeded by vice presidents named

Johnson who were southern Democrats and former senators. **Both** men were killed by a bullet that entered the head from behind. Lincoln was killed in Ford's Theater. Kennedy met his death while riding in a Lincoln convertible made by the Ford Motor Company. **Both** assassins died before they could be brought to trial. In turn, each assassin's slayer died before he could be punished. Many believe that **both** assassinations were part of a giant conspiracy extending far beyond the one gunman.

On the other hand, there are significant dissimilarities between the two. To name just a few: Lincoln, largely self-educated, was born poor and was raised by his father and a stepmother. **In contrast,** Kennedy was born to a wealthy family and attended elite private schools. Lincoln was president when the country was at war with itself during the Civil War. **In contrast,** Kennedy served during the Cold War when the country was unified against an enemy outside the United States.

To learn more about Ford's Theater and the Lincoln assassination, go to www.nps.gov/foth. To learn more about Kennedy, go to www.jfklibrary.org and take a virtual tour of the John Fitzgerald Kennedy Library and Museum in Boston.

In the two paragraphs that follow, the author explores how different cultures deal with anger. Again, transition words are set in bold. The first paragraph is outlined for you as an example. Try to complete the outline of the second paragraph.

Besides individual **differences** in the way we feel and express anger, there are also some important cultural **differences.** In a number of Latin and Arab cultures the free expression of anger is heartily endorsed; two who are angry at each other may fight because they figure that a strong third party (such as a neighbor or family member) will intervene before things go too far. The Utku Eskimos fall at the **opposite** end of the spectrum: They ostracize anyone who loses his temper, regardless of the reason. Between these two extremes are all kinds of middle ground. The Japanese don't display anger as their traditional Western counterparts do; **instead** of lashing out verbally, the Japanese assume a neutral expression and a polite demeanor when angry. The Mbuti hunter-gatherers of the Democratic Republic of the Congo take it a step further; when angry, they laugh. Some individual disputes have become "full-scale tribal laugh fests."

There are also profoundly **different** "rules" from one culture to another for the way anger is choreographed. Members of Anglo societies follow a fairly predictable course of action: hints, indirect efforts, involvement of a third party, direct confrontation, escalating anger, lawsuits, and, when all else fails, violence. The steps are quite **different, however,** in Iran, Latin America, and some American Indian cultures: There you might observe silent brooding (for five years or even five hundred years) while the tribe decides what to do; or an act of violent revenge, then more resolute measures, such as discussion, direct negotiation, or the involvement of a third party.

From *Mind/Body Health* by Brent Q. Hafen, Keith J. Karren, Kathryn J. Frandsen, and N. Lee Smith, p. 171. Copyright © 1996 by Allyn & Bacon. Reprinted by permission of Pearson Education, Inc.

I. There are cultural differences in the way anger is expressed. (MI)
   A. In Latin and Arabic cultures expressing anger is heartily endorsed. (MSD)
      1. Two who are angry at each other may fight with each other. (msd)
      2. They expect to be interrupted by a third party. (msd)
   B. The Utku Eskimos ostracize those who lose their tempers. (MSD)

C. The Japanese assume a neutral expression and polite demeanor when angry. (MSD)

D. The Mbuti laugh when they are angry.

II. There are different rules for the way anger is choreographed depending on the culture. (MI)

A. Anglo societies follow a predictable course of action. (MSD)

1. _hints, indirect efforts_ (msd)

2. _involvement of third party_ (msd)

3. _direct confrontation_ (msd)

B. In Iran, Latin America, and some Indian cultures, the steps are different. (MSD)

1. _You might observe silent brooding_ (msd)

2. _tribe decide what to do_ (msd)

3. _act of violent revenge_ (msd)

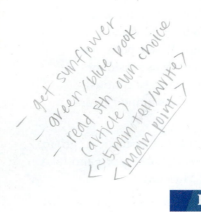

(handwritten margin note: get sunflower / green/blue book / read 5th own choice / (article) / ~15min tell/write / main point)

Practice Exercise 4: Comparison-Contrast

Directions: Fill in the blank with an appropriate transition word or phrase from the list below. Some of the transition words will fit in more than one of the sentences, but try to use a different transition word in each sentence. Make sure the sentence makes sense with the transition you choose.

| although | both | however | just as | on the other hand |

1. In order to live a healthy lifestyle, people are increasingly being told to ___*both*___ eat right and exercise.

2. Joan's advisor gave her some good reasons for going to graduate school, but, ___*on the other hand,*___ he also gave her some good reasons for directly starting her career.

3. There are two ways to go to get to the mall, and one way is ___*just as*___ good as the other.

4. ___*Although*___ linemen on a professional football team need to be large, they also need to be fast.

5. Judging by all the dark clouds in the sky, it looked like it was going to rain. ___*However*___, around noontime the sun came out.

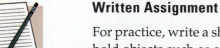

Written Assignment

For practice, write a short paragraph comparing and contrasting two ordinary household objects such as a pencil and a pen, or a fork and a spoon. Or you might want to try comparing and contrasting a typewriter and a computer. Include some of the "compare and contrast" words found in the transitions word chart.

Steps in a Process

In the **steps-in-a-process** pattern, something is explained or described in a step-by-step manner. The sequences are clearly identified by specific transition words. A lot of scientific writing uses this particular pattern. In addition, anytime we try to show

how to make or do something, we are probably using this pattern of organization. Just for fun, try following these directions explaining how to draw cartoon characters. (You will need a separate piece of paper for your sketches.)

It's easy to draw a cartoon. Just take it step by step. First, start by drawing a shape in pencil, and then lightly sketch in the features. Remember to exaggerate!

Step 1. Draw a basic shape lightly and loosely in pencil.

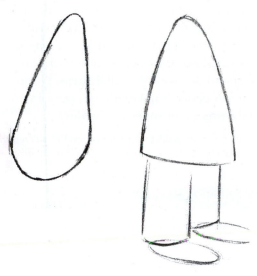

Step 2. Lightly sketch in the features.

Step 3. Go back over the drawing darkening some of your lines.

Step 4. Erase pencil lines and add details to make your drawing personal.

From *Cartooning* by Loyd Littlepage © 1994. Reprinted by permission. All rights reserved.

In the two paragraphs that follow, the author gives a step-by-step account of the physical changes that accompany anger; transition words are in bold. Try creating your own outline on a separate sheet of paper.

Medical research shows that no matter how many times you work out at the gym or how careful you are to eat correctly, you're putting yourself at risk if you don't manage your anger effectively. The body reacts to anger with immediate physical changes. **First,** blood rushes to the face, the heartbeat speeds up, and the body undergoes a physical reaction much like that of stress. **Next,** respiration speeds up, blood pressure rises, the digestive **process** slows down, and the muscles tense up, all in readiness for action. Our blood "boils," our muscles tense up, our stomach feels like it's tied up in knots, and our cheeks feel like they're burning up. **At this point,** the more angry we become, the stronger and more powerful we feel—and the more pressed to "strike out." Back when people needed the fight-or-flight response to defend themselves against aggressors, they needed anger. It was important to survival. The surge of energy helped early people defend themselves. Anger enabled them to fight with vigor and great strength.

Our culture evolved much more rapidly than our bodies. We are now a society and a civilization who are expected to deal calmly and rationally with each other. We don't need to fight saber-toothed tigers; our battles are waged in boardrooms and bedrooms. **At this stage,** we no longer need the fight-or-flight response, but our bodies still respond that way. We call it stress. We no longer need the physical stimulus of anger either, but we still get angry. Instead of being a benefit, most regard the process of anger as a liability.

From *Mind/Body Health* by Brent Q. Hafen, Keith J. Karren, Kathryn J. Frandsen, and N. Lee Smith, pp. 174, 170–71. Copyright © 1996 by Allyn & Bacon. Reprinted by permission of Pearson Education, Inc.

Practice Exercise 5: Steps in a Process

Directions: Fill in the blank with an appropriate transition word or phrase from the list below. Some of the transition words will fit in more than one of the sentences, but try to use a different transition word in each sentence. Make sure the sentence makes sense with the transition you choose.

at this point	final	first	process	second	stages

1. The ___*process*___ of sleeping is complicated, with people progressing through four distinct, 90-minute stages during a night's rest.

2. Each of these sleep ___*stages*___ is associated with a unique pattern of brain waves.

3. In the ___*first*___ stage, as people begin to go to sleep, images sometimes appear, as if they were viewing still photos.

4. It is ___*at this point*___, in stage 1, that rapid eye movement, or REM, sleep occurs. REM sleep is usually accompanied by dreams, which, whether people remember them or not, are experienced by *everyone* during some part of the night.

5. As sleep becomes deeper, people enter the ___*second*___ stage, which is characterized by a slower, more regular wave pattern.

6. By the time sleepers arrive at the ___*final*___ stage, they are least responsive to outside stimulation. Stage 4 sleep is most likely to occur during the early part of the night.

Adapted from Robert S. Feldman, *Essentials of Understanding Psychology*, 6th Edition, pp. 141–42. Copyright © 2005 by The McGraw-Hill Companies, Inc. Reprinted with permission.

Examples

A paragraph of **examples** usually gives a general statement of the main idea and then presents one or more concrete examples to provide support for this idea. Many writers place the most important or convincing example either first, as an attention-getter, or last, as a dramatic climax. While the terms *example* and *illustration* often are used interchangeably, an illustration is usually longer, and there may be only one in the paragraph.

In this poem, Richard Armour gives a series of short examples about the different ways people relate to money.

Money
Workers earn it,
Spendthrifts burn it,
Bankers lend it,
Women spend it,
Forgers fake it,
Taxes take it,
Dying leave it,
Heirs receive it,
Thrifty save it,
Misers crave it,
Robbers seize it,
Rich increase it,
Gamblers lose it,
I could use it.

Richard Armour, "Money" from *Light Armour: Playful Poems on Practically Everything.* New York: McGraw-Hill, 1954. Reprinted by permission of Geoffrey Armour.

The following paragraphs are on aggression, which is defined as "hostile assault intended to inflict harm." The main ideas in paragraphs 2 and 3 on aggression are underlined. Create your own outline of paragraphs 2 and 3 on a separate sheet of paper.

1. We need look no further than the daily paper or the nightly news to be bombarded with **examples** of aggression, both on a societal level (war, invasion, assassination) and on an individual level (crime, child abuse, and the many petty cruelties that humans are capable of inflicting on one another).

2. Sometimes aggressive behavior is a reaction to frustration. **For example,** suppose you've been working on a paper that is due for a class early the next morning, and your computer printer runs out of ink just before you can print out the paper. You rush to the store to buy more ink, only to find the sales clerk locking the door for the day. Even though the clerk can see you gesturing and begging him to open the door, he refuses, shrugging his shoulders and pointing to a sign that indicates when the store will open the next day. At that moment, the feelings you experience toward the sales clerk probably place you on the verge of real aggression, and you are undoubtedly seething inside. Frustration produces anger, leading to a *readiness* to act aggressively.

From Robert S. Feldman, *Understanding Psychology*, 8th Edition, pp. 612, 614. Copyright © 2008 by The McGraw-Hill Companies, Inc. Reprinted with permission.

3. It appears that temporary climate changes can affect human behavior. **For example,** William Griffitt found that compared with students who answered questionnaires in a room with normal temperature, those who did so in an uncomfortably hot room (over 90°F) reported feeling more tired and aggressive and expressed more hostility to strangers. In the real world, drivers without air conditioning in heat-stricken Phoenix,

Arizona, are much more likely to honk at a stalled car. And, **in another instance,** during the 1986–1988 major league baseball seasons, the number of batters hit by a pitch was two-thirds greater for games played above 90°F than for games played below 80°F. Pitchers weren't wilder on hot days—they had no more walks and wild pitches. They just clobbered more batters! Across the Northern Hemisphere, not only do hotter days have more violent crimes, so do hotter seasons of the year, hotter summers, hotter years, hotter cities, and hotter regions. If a 4-degree Fahrenheit global warming occurs, scientists project that the United States alone would actually see at least 50,000 more serious assaults.

From David G. Myers, *Social Psychology*, 9th Edition, pp. 355–56. Copyright © 2008 by The McGraw-Hill Companies, Inc. Reprinted with permission.

Practice Exercise 6: Examples

Directions: Fill in the blank with an appropriate transition word or phrase from the list below. Some of the transition words will fit in more than one of the sentences, but try to use a different transition word in each sentence. Make sure the sentence makes sense with the transition you choose.

| for example | for instance | in particular | specifically | such as |

1. Today's college classrooms include many different kinds of students, _Such as_ Donna, who entered college after working for eight years following high school.

2. One avenue of self-discovery in college is the exploration of new career choices. _for example_, James was originally interested in a career in teaching, but has since decided to pursue a career in business.

3. _Specifically_ James has decided to become a marketing major.

4. In the 1970s, high school girls were less likely to go to college. Today, girls _in particularly_ are more likely than boys to go to college.

5. However, even today many women avoid taking academic risks. _for instance_, they stay away from taking mathematics and science classes.

interchangeable

read

Definition

A paragraph of **definition** will define, clarify, or explain a key term. Definitions can be developed by providing dictionary meanings or personal meanings. They can also be developed by means of examples or by comparing and contrasting the key word to other words.

> In *The Adventures of Tom Sawyer*, Mark Twain **defines** work as "whatever a body is obliged to do while play consists of whatever a body is not obliged to do."

In the following paragraphs, the authors of *Mind/Body Health* attempt to clarify the meaning of anger by providing concrete illustrations, describing its distinguishing characteristics, and comparing and contrasting it to other, similar expressions. After reading the paragraphs, complete the outline that follows.

Everyone experiences it. Just watch two toddlers fighting over a favorite set of blocks, a teenager challenging an unreasonable curfew, an executive whose car gets rear-ended on the way to an important business presentation.

Anger is an emotion. It's temporary. It combines physiological arousal with emotional arousal. It can range in severity all the way from intense rage to "cool" anger that doesn't really involve arousal at all (and might more accurately be **described** as an *attitude,* such as resentment). People express anger in all sorts of ways such as hurling verbal insults, using profanity, slamming doors, or smashing a fist into the nearest available object.

The words we use **to describe** our anger strongly hint at the turmoil that is going on inside our bodies when we're angry. Some of the most common ones were pointed out by social psychologist and anger expert Carol Tavris:

> You make my *blood boil.*
> His pent-up anger *welled up* inside him.
> He was *bursting with anger.*
> I *blew my stack.*
> She *flipped her lid.*
> He *hit the ceiling.*

The **terms** *anger* and *hostility* are often used interchangeably **to describe** a set of negative emotions, but they are not the same. Anger has been **defined** as a temporary emotion that may or may not be accompanied by outward expression (physical or verbal). Hostility, on the other hand, is not a temporary emotion, but rather an attitude. It is anger that is expressed in aggressive behavior motivated by animosity and hatefulness. "Anger is generally considered to be a simpler concept than hostility or aggression," explain researchers Margaret A. Chesney and Ray H. Rosenman.

The **concept** of anger usually refers to an emotional state that consists of feelings that vary in intensity, from mild irritation or annoyance to fury and rage.

From *Mind/Body Health* by Brent Q. Hafen, Keith J. Karren, Kathryn J. Frandsen, and N. Lee Smith, pp. 169–70. Copyright © 1996 by Allyn & Bacon. Reprinted by permission of Pearson Education, Inc.

I. Anger is an emotion experienced by everyone. (MI)
   A. It has certain characteristics. (MSD)
      1. It is temporary. (msd)
      2. It combines _physiological arousal w/ emotional arousal_ (msd)
      3. It can range _in severity all the way from intense rage to_ (msd) _cool anger._
   B. People express anger in many different ways. (MSD)
      1. Examples of verbal anger are _hurling insults, using profanity_ (msd)
      2. Examples of physical anger are _smashing a fist, slamming doors_ (msd)
II. The words used to describe anger show the turmoil it causes. (MI)
III. Anger and hostility are not the same. (MI)
   A. Anger is a temporary emotion that may or may not be expressed outwardly. (MSD)
   B. Hostility is an attitude that is expressed in aggressive behavior. (MSD)
   C. Anger is a simpler concept than hostility. (MSD)
IV. Anger is an emotional state with feelings that vary in intensity. (MI)
   A. It can be expressed as _mild irritation or annoyance_ (MSD)
   B. Or it can be expressed as _fury and rage_. (MSD)

Do exercise outline fill in chrono—read

do

Practice Exercise 7: Definition

Directions: Fill in the blank with an appropriate transition word or phrase from the list below. Some of the transition words will fit in more than one of the sentences, but try to use a different transition word in each sentence. Make sure the sentence makes sense with the transition you choose.

described as	is called	is defined as	means	term

1. Middle adulthood _is defined as_ the years between 40 and 65.

2. A middle-aged person is sometimes _described as_ someone with grown children and/or elderly parents.

3. Many people age 40 and older need reading glasses for presbyopia, a lessened ability to focus on near objects—a condition associated with aging. (The prefix *presby* _means_ "with age.")

4. The pressures created by a society that believes in looking young, acting young, and being young—added to the real physical losses that people may suffer as they get older—may contribute to what _is called_ the midlife crisis.

5. The _term_ *empty nest* refers to the period when the last child leaves home.

From Diane E. Papalia and Sally Wendkos Olds, *Human Development*, 9th Edition, pp. 528–30. Copyright © 2004 by The McGraw-Hill Companies, Inc. Reprinted with permission.

read

Chronological Order

The word *chronological* comes from the Greek root *chron,* which means "time." The **chronological** pattern of organization involves arranging events in time in the order that they actually happened. For this reason, historical essays and articles that are date oriented are usually organized by this method. Paragraphs written with this pattern are usually very easy to recognize.

This short poem illustrates the key elements of the chronological pattern because the events are ordered by time.

> **Solomon Grundy**
> Solomon Grundy
> Born on a **Monday,**
> Christened on **Tuesday,**
> Married on **Wednesday,**
> Took ill on **Thursday,**
> Worse on **Friday,**
> Died on **Saturday,**
> Buried on **Sunday,**
> This is the end
> Of Solomon Grundy.
> —Anonymous

The following paragraphs from *Anger, The Misunderstood Emotion* are in the chronological order pattern.

Popular opinion has it that time heals all wounds, that human beings are naturally resilient. But some people do not heal from the wounds of divorce. In **1971,** Judith Wallerstein, then working with Joan Kelly, began a study of 131 children and adolescents from sixty families, and their divorcing parents, in Marin County, California. The researchers reinterviewed all family members **eighteen months later,** again **five years after** divorce, and again **ten and fifteen years after** divorce. The parents were upper-middle-class, mostly white, and had been married anywhere from four to twenty-three years. The children were all developmentally normal, doing well in school, and in good psychological health—**until** the divorce hit them.

Wallerstein found that even **after ten years,** half of the women and one-third of the men in her study were still intensely angry at their former spouses, and that the consequences of this anger and conflict for their children were often disastrous.

From Carol Tavris, *Anger: The Misunderstood Emotion*. New York: Touchstone Books/Simon & Schuster, 1989, p. 300.

 Do

Practice Exercise 8: Chronological Order

Directions: Fill in the blank with an appropriate transition word or phrase from the list below. Some of the transition words will fit in more than one of the sentences, but try to use a different transition word in each sentence. Make sure the sentence makes sense with the transition you choose.

following	frequently	1853	1890	then	until

1. In ___1853___, Vincent van Gogh was born to a Dutch Protestant minister in the town of Groot-Zundert, in Holland.

2. His early life was spent as a lay preacher to the miners of the region and so not ___until___ the age of 27 did he begin to take a serious interest in art.

3. ___then___ he went to live with his brother Theo, an art dealer in France, where he met the painter Paul Gauguin.

4. The two artists ___frequently___ quarreled, and after one very intense argument, van Gogh cut off a portion of his ear.

5. ___following___ that bizarre incident, van Gogh committed himself to an asylum where much of the work we now admire, including *Starry Night*, was created.

6. Unfortunately, his despair deepened, and so in July of ___1890___ he shot himself to death.

From Mark Getlein, *Gilbert's Living with Art*, 6th Edition, p. 11. Copyright © 2002 by The McGraw-Hill Companies, Inc. Reprinted with permission.

 read

Listing

When an author simply lists information without regard to order, the pattern of organization is referred to as simple **listing** or enumeration. Sometimes authors use numbers (1, 2, 3), letters (a, b, c), bullets (•), or asterisks (*) to show the individual items in the list. At other times, they will say *first, second, third,* and so on. Sometimes they use words such as *in addition, next,* or *finally.* Often a colon will be used as punctuation at the start of a list. A variation of the word *follow* may indicate that a list is about to begin.

In the list that follows, the author enumerates the types of behaviors associated with potential batterers.

Dear Ann: Please print this list of warning signals to help women determine if a mate or date is a potential (or actual) batterer:

- **Jealousy of your time with coworkers, friends, and family.**
- **Controlling behavior.** (Controls your comings and goings and your money and insists on "helping" you make personal decisions.)
- **Isolation.** (Cuts you off from all supportive resources such as telephone pals, colleagues at work, and close family members.)
- **Blames others for his problems.**
- **Hypersensitivity.** (Easily upset by annoyances that are a part of daily life, such as being asked to work overtime, criticism of any kind, being asked to help with chores or child care.)
- **Cruelty to animals or children.**
- **"Playful" use of force in sex.**
- **Verbal abuse.**
- **Dr. Jekyll and Mr. Hyde personality.** (Sudden mood swings and unpredictable behavior—one minute loving, the next angry and punitive.)
- **Past history of battering.**
- **Threats of violence.** (Says, "I'll slap you," "I'll kill you," or "I'll break your neck.")
- **Breaking or striking objects.** (Breaks your possessions, beats on the table with fists, throws objects near or at you or your children.)
- **Uses force during an argument.**

Ann Landers, June 30, 1997. By permission of Esther P. Lederer Trust and Creators Syndicate, Inc.

Internet Activity

There is a great deal of material on the Internet on the topic of anger. Locate two Web sites that discuss anger, and determine the purpose of each site. The following sites might be a good place to start your search:

www.apa.org (then type in "anger")

www.angermgmt.com

The last three letters of any Internet address indicate the type of the site: "org" stands for organization, "net" for networking, and "com" for commercial. Other site types are "edu" for education, "gov" for government, and "mil" for military. This information may help you determine the sort of information found on each site.

Exercise 9: Patterns of Organization

Directions: Writers often use patterns of organization to organize the supporting details of their paragraphs. In the following paragraphs, the key transition words are printed in italics. After noting these transition words, write the dominant pattern of organization on the line below each paragraph. Choose from the following: *example, contrast, comparison, definition, steps in a process,* or *cause and effect.*

1.   When the English finally got rid of their Danish occupiers in the 11th century, they entertained themselves by digging up battlefields and booting around the skulls of Danish soldiers. *Since* the skulls were tough on their toes, they eventually were forced to switch to inflated cow bladders. King Henry banned the game in the 12th century *because* it kept his soldiers from arrow-shooting practice. But, *as a result* of its early origins, the popular game was already known as "futballe."

     _____Cause and effect_____

2.   Back in the dark ages (before microphones), referees developed a series of gestures to symbolize the various penalties, so after they had thrown the flags, everybody would know what the player had done to deserve the penalty. *For example,* if the referee had one hand on his head, it meant that somebody was in the wrong place on the field. *In yet another example,* if the referee had two hands on his head, it meant that there were too many players on the field or a loss of a down.

     _____example_____

3.   A gridiron, another name for the field, was *defined* when the 100 yards was divided every five yards by lines giving an overhead view not unlike the flat iron grills used to sear meat. (Gridiron and griddle are *derived from* the same root.) And speaking of synonyms, the poles in the end zone *are called* goal posts unless they're called uprights or sticks.

     _____definition_____

4.   When the quarterback throws the ball down the field, it is a forward pass. *Similarly* it is referred to *as* a "throw," "a bomb," *and* if it's not likely to be caught without divine intervention, a "Hail Mary."

     _____comparison_____

5.   *First,* there are 32 teams in the National Football League. Half of them are in the National Football Conference (N.F.C.), and half of them are in the American Football Conference (A.F.C.). *Next,* within these groups are four geographic divisions, East, North, South, and West. *After* 16 regular season games, the teams in these geographic divisions with the most wins get to go to the playoffs. At this point, four more wild card teams get to compete. *Finally,* playoff champs go to the Super Bowl.

     _____steps in a process_____

6.   Winning the Super Bowl means more money for owners and players. By winning the Super Bowl, every player gets a cash bonus of $68,000. In *contrast,* the losers get only $36,500. What's more, the winner also gets a ring to commemorate the victory, *but* the loser gets nothing else. These rings tend to be large, gaudy affairs, usually sporting lots of diamonds, so that from across a room, the flash on a finger will let everyone know that here stands a man who can run fast, tackle hard, and explain why this strange hodgepodge of rules and rituals is always advertised as a metaphor for life.

     _____contrast_____

Exercise 10: More Patterns of Organization

Directions: Identify the dominant pattern of organization for each paragraph. You may look at the transition words chart if necessary.

1. Quick French Onion Soup (serves 4–6)

   In medium fry pan, first saute onion in butter until golden and tender, about 15 minutes. Next, stir in flour. Then add remaining ingredients. Simmer uncovered at least 20 minutes, stirring occasionally. Serve piping hot. For a final touch, if desired, top with melba toast and shredded Gruyere cheese.

   Steps in process

   Clues: _first, next, final_

2. In ancient Rome, whenever a man wished to be elected to a public office, he canvassed for votes wearing a white robe or toga. The purpose of this was to enable the populace to easily recognize him. The Latin word for white is *candidus*, so the potential official came to be known as a *candidatus*, which means "a person clothed in white." From this derivation comes our English word *candidate*.

   define

   Clues: _recognize_

3. If you were a child growing up in the 50s and you used the f-word, there would probably have been at least a discussion, and more than likely, a bar of soap would have been put to good use. In contrast, today this word is uttered routinely just about everywhere. Kids hear the word riding the bus to school, in class, in the lyrics of many songs, and on regular network TV. In the 50s, profanity was a shocking rarity. But, in the 2000s, profanity has become part of our language. Some psychologists even say using curse words is healthy because it allows us to express our deepest emotions. Young people of today are so used to hearing the f-word that many linguists predict it will end up meaning as little as the standard curse word of the 50s, "hell."

   comparison conparson

   Clues: _compare to te 50's and now_

4. One hundred years ago, no one "exercised" because their daily life was strenuous enough. As a direct result of the many labor-saving devices we have today, the typical American's weight is rising. Most Americans don't participate in athletics, and many hire others to do their routine home-maintenance chores. Thus, they get almost no vigorous exercise. The most exercise many get is changing the channel on the remote control. The sad consequence of becoming a sedentary, TV-watching nation is that one in three adults is currently overweight.

   comparson cause and effect

   Clues: _exercised one hundered years ago & now_

5. The Ripley's Museum in Orlando, Florida, is apparently the place to go for those seeking to start a family. In late 1994, two ebony fertility statues were placed in the office lobby. Three employees immediately became pregnant after rubbing the belly of the statue. In another instance, three wives of office personnel all became pregnant despite the fact one was using birth-control pills. In another example, eight women who visited the office became pregnant, including a woman who accidentally bumped into the statue while delivering a package. One Texas woman with five daughters recently came to make the pilgrimage in the hope of having a son. She's convinced the "reproductive magic" will work for her.

example

Clues: _using one story to define another_

6. In a study of workaholics, those people who work too much, Marilyn Machlowitz found that workaholics exhibited the following characteristics:
    1. Tend to be intense and energetic,
    2. Sleep less than most people,
    3. Have difficulty taking vacations,
    4. Spend most of their waking time working,
    5. Frequently eat while they work,
    6. Prefer work to play,
    7. Work hard at making the most of their time,
    8. Tend to blur the distinction between work and play,
    9. Can and do work anywhere and everywhere.

    Adapted from Jerrold S. Greenberg, _Comprehensive Stress Management_, 8th Edition. New York: McGraw-Hill, 2004, pp. 283–85.

cause and effect (listing)

Clues: _in a study_

7. Consider the gender differences market researchers observe when studying the food preferences of men and women. Women eat more fruit. On the other hand, men are more likely to eat meat. As one food writer put it, "Boy food doesn't grow. It is hunted or killed." Men are more likely to eat Frosted Flakes or Corn Pops, but women prefer multigrain cereals. Men are big root beer drinkers, but women account for the bulk of sales of bottled water.

    From Michael R. Solomon, _Consumer Behavior_, 6th Ed., Upper Saddle River, NJ: Pearson/Prentice-Hall, 2004, p. 159.

comparison and contrast

Clues: _on the other hand_

Exercise 11: More Patterns of Organization

Directions: Choose the correct pattern of organization by noting the transition words.

1. As the "global village" expands and Americans are exposed to an ever-greater variety of cultures and traditions, we find ourselves increasingly joining in the rituals of many ethnic groups and nations. Perhaps the most obvious example is St. Patrick's Day. On every 17th of March, a sea of green engulfs the streets, offices, retail establishments, and bars of all fifty states—and many "wearers o' the green" have not a trace of Irish in their background. Cinco de Mayo ("the fifth of May") is an example of a Mexican-American holiday just now coming into its own. The celebration commemorates Mexico's defeat of the French in the battle of Puebla in 1862. Cinco de Mayo is drawing ever-larger crowds of non-Hispanics who enjoy sharing traditional foods like tamales, roasted corn, and other ethnic specialties, and who love to sway to the beat of mariachi, ranchera, and banda music. Street vendors can't keep up with the demand for spicy Mexican food—and the taps flow freely with Dos Equis, Corona, and other popular Mexican beers.

    From Wayne A. Payne and Dale B. Hahn, _Understanding Your Health_, 6th Edition, p. 36. Copyright © 2000 by The McGraw-Hill Companies, Inc. Reprinted with permission.

example

Clues: _____

2.   If you want to break the caffeine habit, the following steps may help you to achieve your goal. First, gradually switch from regular to decaffeinated coffee by mixing them before brewing, or substitute decaffeinated instant coffee for some of the caffeinated instant you drink. Then, increase the decaffeinated proportion each day while using more low-fat milk in your coffee to reduce the amount of caffeinated beverage you consume. Next, switch little by little to smaller cups from larger mugs and glasses. If your favorite mug is a comfort to you, don't discard it, but fill it with a caffeine-free beverage. Change your daily routine by taking a walk instead of your usual coffee break. At this stage, if you find your coffee paraphernalia to be a temptation, get rid of those mugs, pots, filters, and grinders. If you get enough sleep, exercise regularly, and follow a healthy diet, you'll be less reliant on the artificial "pep" that caffeine provides.

From Wayne A. Payne and Dale B. Hahn, *Understanding Your Health*, 6th Edition, pp. 230–31. Copyright © 2000 by The McGraw-Hill Companies, Inc. Reprinted with permission.

Steps in a pross

Clues: *first, then, steps*

3.   Many of us experience anger and frustration at one time or another, but for some people these feelings represent a pervasive, characteristic set of personality traits defined as the Type A behavior pattern. Type A individuals are described by experts as being competitive, aggressive, and hostile, both verbally and nonverbally—especially when interrupted while trying to complete a task. They exhibit a driven quality regarding their work and show a constant sense of urgency about time.

From Robert S. Feldman, *Understanding Psychology*, 8th Edition, p. 500. Copyright © 2008 by The McGraw-Hill Companies, Inc. Reprinted with permission.

Classify and divide defined

Clues: _____

4.   On a more general level, the Internet has brought us both positive and negative consequences. On the one hand, it entertains us, informs us, links us with friends and family, provides us with the world's greatest reference library, and stimulates commerce. On the other hand, it opens up whole new areas of concern: identity theft, fraud, deceptive advertising, pornography, and invasion of privacy.

From Joseph R. Dominick, *The Dynamics of Mass Communication*, 8th Edition, pp. 294–95. Copyright © 2005 by The McGraw-Hill Companies, Inc. Reprinted with permission.

Cause and effect   contras

Clues: *both, on the other hand*

5.   Because you are always the "author" of your dreams, it is not surprising that you often play a leading role. Thus, you have an active role in nearly three-fourths of your dreams, and you are absent from your own dreams only 10 percent of the time. About half of the other characters in your dreams are friends, acquaintances, or family members. The other half are people you do not know or cannot recognize—or are animals.

From Benjamin B. Lahey, *Psychology*, 8th Edition. New York: McGraw-Hill, 2004, p. 171.

Cause and effect

Clues: *because*

6.   How many times have you asked yourself questions such as "Am I as smart as Jill?" "Is Bob better-looking than I am?" or "Is my taste as good as Carmen's?" We gain self-knowledge by comparing ourselves with others. We are more likely to compare ourselves with others who are similar to us. We develop more accurate self-perceptions by comparing ourselves with people in communities similar to where we live, with people who have similar family backgrounds, and with people of the same sex or sexual orientation.

From John W. Santrock, *Psychology*, 7th Edition, pp. 650–51. Copyright © 2003 by The McGraw-Hill Companies, Inc. Reprinted with permission.

~~Definition~~ comparing

Clues: _____ by comparing ourselves. _____

7.   If you're a traditional age student, ask some older students what they ate when they were growing up. You're likely to hear about American favorites that include meatloaf, mashed potatoes and gravy, chicken pot pie, hearty beef stew, and homemade fudge layer cake. Back then big meals served "family style," featuring red meat and lots of side dishes—plus a rich dessert—were considered healthy, as well as essential for growing, active children. Today, in contrast, our food focus is firmly on ethnic dishes, with their novel flavors and textures, their exotic spices, their alluringly foreign names. Unlike the meals of the past, ethnic cuisines feature generous servings of vegetables, with just a bit of fish, meat, or poultry, plus spices for flavor. Dishes are often cooked with heart-healthy olive oil instead of cholesterol-heavy butter, shortening, or lard. Protein is more likely to come from legumes than from meat, and dessert may be a small wedge of cheese instead of seven-layer fudge cake or rocky road ice cream.

From Wayne A. Payne and Dale B. Hahn, *Understanding Your Health*, 6th Edition, p. 139. Copyright © 2000 by The McGraw-Hill Companies, Inc. Reprinted with permission.

_____ Comparison – Contrast _____

Clues: both talking about foods but different time periods

8.   One of America's fastest-growing crimes, identity theft, is causing havoc for innocent people across the country. In a recent example, Theresa May, an English professor in Georgia, was victimized by a California woman of the same name who obtained her Social Security number and then applied for loans, defaulted on the payments, and filed for bankruptcy—all in the professor's name. In yet another example, in Ohio, a successful businesswoman's Social Security number was stolen by a thief who escaped to another state, where she used the Ohio woman's identity to obtain a driver's license and several credit cards, on which she ran up a slew of charges.

From Stephen E. Lucas, *The Art of Public Speaking*, 8th Edition, p. 440. Copyright © 2004 by The McGraw-Hill Companies, Inc. Reprinted with permission.

_____ Examples _____

Clues: In a recent example an/

Exercise 12: More Patterns of Organization

Directions: Choose the correct pattern of organization by noting the transition words.

1.   At birth, most infants can turn their heads from side to side while lying on their backs. While lying chest down, many can lift their heads enough to turn them. Within the first two to three months, they lift their heads higher and

higher, sometimes to the point where they lose their balance and roll over on their backs. After three months, the average infant begins to roll over deliberately—first from front to back and then from back to front. The average baby can sit without support by 6 months of age and can assume a sitting position without help about two and a half months later. Between 6 and 20 months, most babies begin to get around under their own power by means of creeping or crawling. By holding onto a helping hand or a piece of furniture, the average baby can stand at a little past 7 months of age. A little more than four months later, most babies let go and stand alone. The average baby can stand well about two weeks or so before the first birthday. Soon after they can stand alone well, most infants take their first unaided steps. Within a few weeks, soon after the first birthday, the average child is walking well.

From Diane E. Papalia, Sally Wendkos Olds, and Ruth Duskin Feldman, *Human Development*, 10th Edition, pp. 142–43. Copyright © 2007 by The McGraw-Hill Companies, Inc. Reprinted with permission.

Chronological order

Clues: *decribing how a baby grows*

2.　　　Our daily lives are enriched by other countries and by the diversity of American society. Consider this example of a typical American citizen. Each morning she wakes up in a bed (an invention from the Near East). She puts on clothes made in Taiwan, Mexico, and Jamaica, shoes from Spain and a wristwatch from Switzerland, jewelry from Kenya and perfume from France. She eats breakfast at a table made in Sweden, using plates from Korea and a tablecloth from India. Her breakfast includes a banana from Honduras and coffee from Colombia. While driving to work in a car made in Japan, she listens to music performed by a band from Cuba. For lunch at a restaurant, she can choose from a wide variety of ethnic cuisines—Thai, Italian, Chinese, Mexican, Korean, Vietnamese, Egyptian, and so on. Throughout the day, she is likely to use or benefit from products invented by immigrants to the United States and their descendants. Her health, for example, is protected by an oral polio vaccine, developed by Albert B. Sabin, a Polish immigrant.

From Hamilton Gregory, *Public Speaking for College and Career*, 7th Edition, pp. 75–76. Copyright © 2005 by The McGraw-Hill Companies, Inc. Reprinted with permission.

example of a typical

Clues: _____

3.　　　Medical researchers have found that the average human needs about eight hours of sleep each night in order to function well on the job, on the highway, in school, and in the home. But the majority of Americans try to get by on less than eight hours; in fact, 80 percent get six hours of sleep or less each night. Perhaps the most insidious consequence of skimping on sleep is the irritability that increasingly pervades society. Weariness corrodes civility and erases humor, traits that ease the myriad daily frustrations, from standing in supermarket lines to refereeing the kids' squabbles. Because people go without sufficient sleep, tempers flare faster and hotter at the slightest offense.

From Hamilton Gregory, *Public Speaking for College and Career*, 7th Edition, p. 32. Copyright © 2005 by The McGraw-Hill Companies, Inc. Reprinted with permission.

cause and effect

Clues: *if we don't have 9 hours of sleep we are frustrating*

4.　　　One way we simplify our environment is to categorize—to organize the world by clustering objects into groups. A biologist classifies plants and animals.

A human classifies people. Ethnicity and sex are, in our current world, powerful ways of categorizing people. Imagine Gina, a 45-year-old, New Orleans real estate agent. Your categories might be "female," "middle-aged," "businessperson," and "southerner."

From David G. Myers, *Social Psychology*, 9th Edition, p. 324. Copyright © 2008 by The McGraw-Hill Companies, Inc. Reprinted with permission.

_____classified comparison._____

Clues: _____

5.   Indian and U.S. cultures have produced different approaches to love and marriage. In India, about 95 percent of marriages are still arranged by the parents. In the U.S., individual mate selection matches the core values of individuality and independence, while arranged marriages match the Indian value of children's deference to parental authority. For Indians, love is a peaceful emotion, based on long-term commitment and devotion to family. Indians think of love as something that can be "created" between two people. For Indians, marriage produces love—however for Americans love produces marriage. Americans see love as having a mysterious element, a passion that suddenly seizes an individual. In contrast, Indians see love as a peaceful feeling that develops when a man and a woman are united in intimacy and share common interests and goals in life.

Adapted from James M. Henslin, *Essentials of Sociology: A Down-to-Earth Approach*, 7th Edition, p. 320. © 2007 Pearson Education, Inc. Reproduced by permission of Pearson Education, Inc.

_____Comparison – contrast_____

Clues: _____

Transition Words and Patterns of Organization (Continued)

Writers ordinarily try to write so that their thoughts flow smoothly and logically. They try to connect one idea with another in such a way that readers can easily understand what they are saying. They connect their ideas by means of transition words. In Latin, the prefix *trans* means "across." Transition words enable the author to carry you from one place in your reading "across" to another. Study the two sentences below. Which one is easier to read and understand?

1. Bill did everything he could think of to get a good grade in chemistry. He always attended class, did all of his homework assignments, and studied long hours. He hired a tutor.
2. Bill did everything he could think of to get a good grade in chemistry. He always attended class, did all of his homework assignments, and studied long hours. **In addition,** he hired a tutor.

The transition words *in addition* make the author's meaning easier to understand. Now look at the next example.

1. Mary did not like to go to the dentist to have her teeth cleaned. She went anyway because she knew that it would be better for her in the long run.
2. **Although** Mary did not like to go to the dentist to have her teeth cleaned, she went anyway because she knew that it would be better for her in the long run.

The transition word *although* helps clarify the relationship between the two thoughts.

Exercise 13: Transitions Words and Patterns of Organization

Directions: In the following sentences, provide an appropriate transition word. If you need help, refer to the chart below. Be sure your completed sentences make sense.

1. A shepherd boy tended his flock of sheep (spatial order) _near_ a village.

2. He used to amuse himself by crying out "Wolf! Wolf!" Each time he did this, the whole village turned out to rescue him. But (reversal) _instead_ of thanks, they were rewarded with laughter for their pains.

3. (summary) _therefore_, his trick succeeded two or three times.

4. One day the wolf really did come, (addition) _And_ the boy cried out in earnest.

5. The neighbors, thinking that he was up to his old tricks, paid no attention to his cries. (conclusion) _Although_, the sheep were left at the mercy of the wolf.

6. (emphasis) _without a doubt_ even when liars tell the truth, they are never believed.

7. (conclusion) _Finally_ this story illustrates how difficult it is to distinguish a lie from the truth.

Additional Transition Words

While lists of transition words are helpful, the groupings of the words given in this section are not perfect, and many of these words may be placed in more than one category. The only way to truly determine the function of a transition word is by studying the context of the sentence and the paragraph.

Words that can be used to show **summary and conclusion:**

finally	hence	to conclude
in brief	so	to sum up
in short	therefore	in summary
overall	thus	in conclusion

Words that can be used to show **spatial order:**

above	underneath	center
below	near	left
beyond	next to	right
on top	front	

Words that can be used to show **reversal:**

unlike	instead	still
nevertheless	yet	granted that

Words that can be used to show **emphasis:**

as indicated	to repeat	certainly
as noted	it's important	without a doubt
here again	to remember	unquestionably
once again	truly	to emphasize

Words that can be used to show **addition:**

again	further	as well as
also	furthermore	besides
and	in addition	too
another	moreover	

Words that can be used to show **concession:**

despite	in spite of
although	even though

READING

"Road rage now results in more highway deaths than drunk driving."

TUNING IN TO READING

Widespread publicity campaigns emphasizing slogans such as "Steer clear of aggressive driving" and "Instead of trying to make good time, try to make time good" have failed to prevent aggressive driving. What kinds of things do you think will help law enforcement rid the streets and highways of the menace of aggressive driving? Do you think it would help if people were encouraged to have and use "I'm Sorry" placards? Or is it simply time for law enforcement to "get tough" on those who willfully endanger the lives of others?

BIO-SKETCH

Freda Adler and Gerhard O. W. Mueller are both distinguished professors of criminal justice at Rutgers University. William S. Laufer is associate professor of legal studies at the Wharton School of the University of Pennsylvania. All three authors have written books and articles on criminal justice. Drs. Adler and Mueller have also been advisors in criminal justice to the United Nations.

NOTES ON VOCABULARY

boil over   erupt in anger. The phrase alludes to the fact that when something is vigorously boiling, it is apt to spill over unless it is watched carefully or the heat is reduced.

anonymous   with no name either known or acknowledged. *Anonymous* is derived from the Greek words *an* meaning "without" and *onoma* meaning "name." In ancient Greece, *anonymous* was used whenever an author was unknown.

aggressive driving   the operation of a motor vehicle in an unsafe and hostile manner, without regard for others.

Directions: For additional practice with transitions, read the following selection and then answer the questions that follow. You may need to refer to both transition word charts.

Road Rage

Freda Adler, Gerhard O. W. Mueller, and William S. Laufer

It has been known for years as aggressive driving. It is a factor in 28,000 highway deaths per year. It is a disorder that is said to affect over half of all drivers. Symptoms include speeding, tailgating, weaving in and out of busy traffic, passing on the right, making unsafe or improper lane changes, running stop signs and red lights, flashing lights or high beams at other drivers, using obscene gestures, swearing and yelling insults, honking or screaming at other drivers, throwing items at other vehicles, and shooting other drivers or passengers. "The symptoms are incredibly commonplace and sometimes boil over into actual assault and life-threatening situations," explains John Hagerty of the New Jersey State Police.

2   Road rage now results in more highway deaths than drunk driving. A national study by the AAA Foundation for Traffic Safety found that the majority of aggressive drivers were men aged eighteen to twenty-six, but that dangerous driving behavior is present in women also, and across age levels and economic classes. The same study concluded that from 1990 to 1996, "violent aggressive driving" increased by 7 percent per year. The reasons for this growth depend on whom you ask.

3   Psychiatrists look to deep-seated personal causes such as stress disorders, which result in impaired judgment. Sociologists see a connection between problems

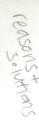

in society and aggressive driving. Others say that the car shields drivers, in effect making them anonymous. This anonymity allows those who become frustrated while driving to ignore society's rules for proper behavior and to behave recklessly. Some claim that drivers see the car as an extension of themselves, and they react angrily when cut off, passed on the highway, or forced to slow down.

4   As a consequence of young men "dueling" with their cars, two eerily similar accidents happened. The first occurred on the George Washington Memorial Parkway in the nation's capital region. As the two cars raced each other along the parkway, one car crossed the median and hit an oncoming car. Three people were killed. Two of them were drivers not involved in the duel. The second happened as two cars on the New Jersey Turnpike chased each other at speeds of up to 100 miles per hour. The cars wove in and out of lanes of traffic, until the occupant of one of the vehicles allegedly threw an object at the other car. This caused the car to slam into a tree and resulted in the death of two men.

5   Ricardo Martinez is head of the National Highway Traffic Safety Administration. He blames aggressive driving on a combination of an increase in a "me first" philosophy and reduced levels of traffic enforcement arising from budget cuts, as well as increased congestion and traffic in urban areas. Since 1987, traffic has increased by 35 percent, but new road construction has only increased 1 percent. Pam Fischer, spokeswoman for the New Jersey Automobile Club, also sees congestion on the roadways as a contributing factor. "Any time there is an accident or construction that slows down traffic, people tend to get more aggravated, and normal and rational people do some dumb things because they are running late or just don't want to sit there."

6   What can be done to prevent this carnage on our highways? In New Jersey, state troopers and municipal police first use plainclothes officers in unmarked cars to cruise dangerous highways during rush hours and spot aggressive drivers. Then, they relay the information to police in marked cars who stop the deviant motorists and give them tickets. In the District of Columbia, Maryland, and Virginia, police have a program called Smooth Operator. In two one-week periods, they issued 28,958 summonses and warnings, including nearly 12,000 for speeding, 3,300 for failing to obey traffic signals, 2,000 for failing to wear a seat belt, and 1,800 for failing to obey a traffic sign.

7   Another approach calls for making roads bigger. The reasoning is that wider roads reduce traffic congestion and the resulting frustration. But, as noted by Congressman Earl Blumenauer, a Democrat from Oregon, building more roads is "the equivalent of giving a wife beater more room to swing." Instead, he advocates building bicycle lanes and planting trees. These are "features that soften the streets and let drivers know they have to share the road."

8   It's important to remember that America has faced a deadly threat on its roadways before—drunk driving. Emphasis was placed on changing the laws and making it socially unacceptable to drink and drive. The experts say aggressive driving should be treated the same way. "We have to enforce the law, take bad drivers off the road, and make them pay for their mistakes," urged Colonel Peter J. O'Hagan, director of the New Jersey Division of Highway Safety. The time has come to address aggressive driving through better education, better enforcement, and a get-tough policy. Dr. Martinez warns that "aggressive drivers must get the message that their behavior will not be tolerated, and that they will be prosecuted."

COMPREHENSION CHECKUP

Short Answer

Directions: Answer the following questions briefly, using no more than a sentence or two.

1. What is the main idea of the selection? _Road Rage Leads to bad judgements_

2. What is the author's overall purpose? _to inform_

3. What is the cause-and-effect relationship in the last two sentences of paragraph 4?

   Cause: _two men were racing one car crossed the median_

   Effect: _hit oncoming car 3 people were killed_

4. What is the cause-and-effect relationship in the last sentence of paragraph 5?

   Cause: _Traffice slows._

   Effect: _People get more aggravated, and tend to act on impuls_

5. Paragraph 7 contains this analogy: Building more roads is "the equivalent of giving a wife beater more room to swing." In your own words, explain what this analogy means. _More oppurtunities for road Rage_

6. Here are some sentences from the selection. Paraphrase them by writing each one in your own words in the space provided.

   a. "This anonymity allows those who become frustrated while driving to ignore society's rules for proper behavior and to behave recklessly."

      People Drivers do not want to be seen, so they behive they can act recklessly

   b. "He blames aggressive driving on a combination of an increase in a 'me first' philosophy and reduced levels of traffic enforcement arising from budget cuts, as well as increased congestion and traffic in urban areas."

      _____

      _____

Multiple Choice

Directions: For each item, write the letter corresponding to the best answer. You may refer to the transition word charts on pages 178–179 and 205.

_b_ 1. A key idea expressed in this selection is that

   a. the stress of modern society is solely responsible for road rage.
   b. to get the message across to the public that aggressive driving is unsafe, law enforcement needs to deal with the problem in a manner similar to the way it has with drunk driving.
   c. making roads bigger is the answer to the problem of road rage.
   d. road rage will be alleviated when there are fewer 16-year-olds and senior citizens on the highways.

 2. The transition word *but* in paragraph 2 indicates

   a. conclusion.
   b. contrast.

c. emphasis.
d. spatial order.

_____ 3. The transition word *also* in paragraph 2 indicates
   a. reversal.
   b. concession.
   c. addition.
   d. both a and c.

_____ 4. In paragraph 3, all of the following are given as possible reasons for the growth in aggressive driving *except*
   a. intoxication.
   b. anonymity.
   c. problems in society.
   d. stress disorders.

_____ 5. Read the first sentence of paragraph 4. What do the transition words *as a consequence* signal?
   a. summary and conclusion
   b. spatial order
   c. cause and effect
   d. comparison-contrast

_____ 6. Paragraph 6 uses the transition words *first* and *then*. What pattern of organization do these words signal?
   a. chronological order
   b. examples
   c. cause and effect
   d. comparison-contrast

True or False

Directions: Indicate whether each statement is true or false by writing **T** or **F** in the space provided.

_____ 7. Road rage affects men and women in equal numbers.

_____ 8. Drunk driving is the leading cause of highway deaths.

_____ 9. Road construction has failed to keep pace with the increase in traffic.

_____ 10. Experts give various reasons to account for aggressive driving.

_____ 11. "Dueling" with cars can result in the loss of innocent lives.

Vocabulary in Context

Directions: Use context clues from the article to determine the meaning of the italicized words, and write a definition in the space provided. Then consult your dictionary to see how accurate your definition is.

1. Stress disorders, which result in *impaired* judgment (paragraph 3)

   Definition: Not able disability of a specified kind

2. The car *shields* drivers, in effect making them anonymous (paragraph 3)

   Definition: Protect Protection from object and hiding drivers identity

3. See the car as an *extension* of themselves (paragraph 3)

   Definition: _A part that is added or prolong._

4. Two *eerily* similar accidents happened (paragraph 4)

   Definition: _Spricy_

5. Drivers not involved in the *duel* (paragraph 4)

   Definition: _Raceng_

6. Increased *congestion* and traffic in urban areas (paragraph 5)

   Definition: _being congested_

7. What can be done to prevent this *carnage* (paragraph 6)

   Definition: _The kining of a large number of people_

8. Stop the *deviant* motorists and give them tickets (paragraph 6)

   Definition: _Person or thing_

9. Their behavior will not be *tolerated* (paragraph 8)

   Definition: _will won't put up with_

In Your Own Words

1. Have you ever engaged or been tempted to engage in aggressive driving? Have you ever been affected by someone else's aggressive driving? What do you think led to the behavior? How could it have been prevented?

2. Picture the area around your campus. Are there any problems with aggressive driving in this vicinity? What concrete steps could the college and local police take to address these problems?

3. What is a suitable punishment for someone who speeds? How about someone who screams obscenities at other drivers? Do you think it is possible to reduce or eliminate such misconduct through law enforcement?

Written Assignment

The following are three basic guiding principles from the AAA Foundation for Traffic Safety for avoiding the rage of other motorists. What's your opinion of these suggestions? Are they likely to help deter aggressive driving?

1. **Don't offend.** When surveys ask drivers what angers them most, the results are remarkably consistent. A few specific behaviors seem unusually likely to enrage other drivers:
   a. Cutting off
   b. Driving slowly in the left lane
   c. Tailgating

2. **Watch gestures.** Almost nothing makes another driver angrier than an obscene gesture. Keep your hands on the wheel. Avoid making any gestures that might anger another driver, even "harmless" expressions of irritation like shaking your head.

3. **Don't engage.** One angry driver can't start a fight unless another driver is willing to join in. You can protect yourself against aggressive drivers by refusing to become angry at them.

Internet Activity

Consult the following Web site for tips on not becoming the victim of aggressive driving:

www.danesheriff.com/roadrage.htm

Do you think these tips are likely to be effective? Can you think of other tips that might be effective?

REVIEW TEST: *Main Idea, Details, Purpose, Transitions, and Patterns of Organization*

Directions: Each of the following paragraphs related to aggressive behavior was adapted from commonly used psychology textbooks. Read each passage. Then choose the best answer for each item.

A.   Psychologists define *aggression* as physical or verbal behavior intended to hurt someone. Throughout the world, hunting, fighting, and warring are primarily men's activities. In surveys, men admit to more aggression than women do. In laboratory experiments, men exhibit more physical aggression by administering what they believe are hurtful shocks. In Canada, the male-to-female arrest rate is 7 to 1 for murder and 6 to 1 for assault. In the United States, it is 9 to 1 for murder and 4 to 1 for assault. Across the world murder rates vary. Yet in all regions, men are roughly 20 times more likely to murder men than women are to murder women. However, in less violent forms of aggression—say, slapping a family member or verbally attacking someone—women are no less aggressive than men.

From David G. Myers, *Social Psychology*, 7th Edition, p. 184. Copyright © 2002 by The McGraw-Hill Companies, Inc. Reprinted with permission.

  1. In the first sentence of this paragraph, the author uses a(n)
   a. cause-and-effect relationship.
   b. definition.
   c. example.
   d. contrast.

  2. The body of the paragraph is organized to
   a. make a contrast.
   b. show steps in a process.
   c. show events in chronological order.
   d. give a definition.

  3. The last sentence of the paragraph is written to
   a. define what was described above it.
   b. show a cause-and-effect relationship.
   c. show steps in a process.
   d. show a contrast with the body of the paragraph.

B.   It is a warm evening. Tired and thirsty after two hours of studying, you borrow some change from a friend and head for the nearest soft-drink machine. As the machine devours the change, you can almost taste the cold, refreshing cola. But when you push the button, nothing happens. You push it again. Then you flip the coin return button. Still nothing. Again, you hit the buttons. You slam them. And finally you shake and whack the machine. You stomp back to your studies empty-handed and shortchanged. Should your roommate beware? Are you now more likely to say or do something hurtful?

From David G. Myers, *Social Psychology*, 9th Edition, p. 349. Copyright © 2008 by The McGraw-Hill Companies, Inc. Reprinted with permission.

_____ 4. The author has written this paragraph using which method?
    a. definition
    b. comparison
    c. classification
    d. chronological order

_____ 5. The example of the student and the vending machine was used to illustrate
    a. the difficulties of a student's life.
    b. the relationship between frustration and aggression.
    c. the problems with vending machines.
    d. the wide variety of things that can go wrong in a day.

C.   One of the first psychological theories of aggression, the popular frustration–aggression theory, says that a person who has suffered frustration is more likely to do or say something harmful. "Frustration always leads to some form of aggression," said John Dollard and his colleagues. *Frustration* is anything (such as the malfunctioning vending machine) that blocks our attaining a goal. Frustration grows when our motivation to achieve a goal is very strong, when we expected satisfaction, and when the blocking is complete.

From David G. Myers, *Social Psychology*, 9th Edition, p. 349. Copyright © 2008 by The McGraw-Hill Companies, Inc. Reprinted with permission.

_____ 6. The main purpose of this paragraph is to
    a. entertain.
    b. inform or explain.
    c. persuade.
    d. criticize.

_____ 7. Which of the following best describes the organizational pattern of this paragraph?
    a. definition and explanation
    b. examples and classification
    c. comparison and contrast
    d. classification and division

D.   Our aggressive energy need not explode directly against its source. We learn to inhibit direct retaliation, especially when others might disapprove of us or punish us; instead we displace our hostilities to safer targets. Displacement occurs in the old anecdote about a man who, because he is humiliated by his boss, berates his wife, who yells at their son, who kicks the dog, which bites the mail carrier.

From David G. Myers, *Social Psychology*, 9th Edition, p. 349. Copyright © 2008 by The McGraw-Hill Companies, Inc. Reprinted with permission.

_____ 8. The author in the last sentence of this paragraph uses which of the following?
    a. comparison
    b. classification
    c. cause and effect
    d. definition

E.   What kinds of stimuli act as aggressive cues? They can range from the most obvious, such as the presence of weapons, to the subtlest, such as the mere mention of the name of an individual who has behaved violently in the past. For example, in one experiment, angered subjects were more aggressive when in the presence of a rifle and a revolver than in a similar situation in which no guns were present. It appears, then, that frustration does lead to aggression, at least when aggressive cues are present.

From Robert S. Feldman, *Understanding Psychology*, 8th Edition, p. 614. Copyright © 2008 by The McGraw-Hill Companies, Inc. Reprinted with permission.

 ____ 9. Which of the following does the author *not* use in this paragraph?
a. an example
b. a contrast
c. a definition
d. a cause-and-effect statement

 ____ 10. The main idea expressed in this passage is that
a. frustration can more easily lead to aggression when aggressive cues are present.
b. aggressive cues can be subtle or obvious.
c. people behave more aggressively when in the presence of weapons.
d. psychologists don't know what kind of stimuli act as aggressive cues.

READING

"Identity theft is a much larger problem than even the experts suspected."

TUNING IN TO READING

Identity theft is a crime that is considered to be on the rise. This is probably because many people don't understand how widespread it is and as a result don't take proper precautions to protect themselves. Today it is relatively easy for a vigilant criminal to obtain personal data without going to the trouble of breaking into someone's home. Sometimes thieves simply eavesdrop on phone conversations when you give your credit card numbers to hotels, rental car companies, or others who request them. The following selection describes the magnitude of the problem and gives suggestions on ways to combat it.

BIO-SKETCH

Robert M. Bohm is a professor of criminal justice and legal studies at the University of Central Florida. He has published widely in the areas of criminal justice and criminology.

NOTES ON VOCABULARY

felony   a serious crime punishable by death or by imprisonment (usually for one year or longer) in a federal or state penitentiary.

READING *continued*

aid or abet to assist another, by words or conduct, in the commission of a crime.

bombardment the rapid and continuous delivery of communication either spoken or written.

bogus not genuine; counterfeit; sham.

Identity Theft: When Bad Things Happen to Your Good Name

Robert M. Bohm and Keith N. Haley

Tania Collins of Apopka, Florida, had her purse snatched. Among the items lost were her driver's license, Social Security card, and about $25 in cash. Although the incident scared her and the loss of her personal belongings was an inconvenience, the theft of her purse and its contents was only the beginning of what would become a much bigger problem. Not long after the purse snatching, Tania discovered that someone else had been using her identity to accumulate more than $20,000 in credit card charges, bogus checks, grocery bills, phone bills, and other unpaid debt. Tania Collins had become a victim of identity theft.

2 Tania Collins is not alone. Identity theft is a much larger problem than even the experts suspected. According to a recent survey commissioned by the Federal Trade Commission (FTC), nearly 10 million Americans may have been victims of some type of identity theft in 2002.

3 Identity theft became a federal crime in 1998 when Congress passed the Identity Theft and Assumption Deterrence Act. The law stipulates that **identity theft** is committed "when anyone knowingly transfers or uses without legal authority the identification documentation of another person with the intent to commit, aid, or abet any unlawful activity that constitutes a felony."

4 There are three general types of identity theft that vary in seriousness of victimization. From the most serious to the least serious, identity theft may involve (1) the misuse of personal information to open new credit accounts, take out new loans, or engage in other types of fraud; (2) the misuse of existing accounts other than credit cards, such as checking or saving accounts or telephone accounts; and (3) the misuse of one or more existing credit cards or credit card account numbers.

5 Identity theft cost its victims about $50 billion in 2002. The bulk of that loss was from the misuse of a victim's personal information. The average annual loss per victim for all types of identity theft was approximately $4,800. Businesses and financial institutions and not individuals incur most of the losses from identity theft because a variety of laws protect individuals from the fraudulent actions of identity thieves. Thus, of the approximately $50 billion lost to identity theft in 2002, only about 10 percent of the loss was borne by individuals.

6 In 2002, victims of personal information misuse spent 60 hours, on average, attempting to resolve their problems. As a group, Americans spent almost 300 million hours resolving problems related to identity theft.

7 When a victim's identity was stolen, 27 percent of the personal information stolen was misused for at least six months. On the other hand, 36 percent of cases involving existing credit cards and card numbers were misused for only one day. The more quickly an identify theft was discovered, the smaller the loss incurred.

8 About a quarter of the victims report that the identity thief got their personal information from a lost or stolen wallet or purse or theft of mail. About half of the victims did nor know how the thief stole their identities.

9   Among common techniques used in identity theft are "dumpster diving," "shoulder surfing," "spamming," and "phishing." Thieves who "dumpster dive" go through dumpsters or trash cans to get copies of checks, credit card and bank statements, credit card applications, or other records with identifying information. "Shoulder surfers" look over victims' shoulders as they enter personal information into phones, computers, and ATMs. "Spammers" send unsolicited e-mail messages to victims, usually advertising a product, service, or get-rich-quick scheme, and ask the victim to provide identifying information in order to receive whatever is being advertised. "Phishers" send consumers e-mail messages claiming that there was a problem with their AOL account, for example. The messages warn consumers to update their billing information or risk losing their accounts and Internet access. The message directs consumers to click on a hyperlink to connect to the "AOL Billing Center." When consumers click on the link, they are sent to a look-alike AOL Web page, where they are asked to enter the numbers from the credit card they used to open the account and the numbers from a new credit card to correct the problem. They are also asked for additional identifying information. Identifying information can also be found on the Internet by accessing public record sites and fee-based information broker sites. The following is an example of the type of personal information obtainable on the Internet for a fee of $39.95.

Current and previous addresses

Possible aliases

Phone numbers

Liens

Small Claims/Civil judgments for or against them

Property ownership

Bankruptcies

Drug enforcement agency actions against them

Marriage status

Divorce status

10   Other ways of obtaining personal information are by getting credit card reports fraudulently by posing as an employer, loan officer, or landlord, or by obtaining names and Social Security numbers from personnel or customer files in the workplace.

11   For many victims, identity theft can be a traumatic experience. It can provoke a host of emotions such as feelings of loss, helplessness, hopelessness, vulnerability, fear, denial, anger, isolation, betrayal, rage, and embarrassment. A particularly common emotion felt by identity theft victims is frustration with the very people to whom the victims turn for help, especially law enforcement and criminal justice personnel. Identity theft can be life altering. Many victims never see the world in the same way again. They lose their innocence.

12   When asked what could be done to improve their victimization experience, identity theft victims wanted the police to (1) make a greater commitment to catch the thief or thieves, (2) follow up and communicate better with the victim, and (3) increase the assistance they provide victims. Victims also wanted offenders to receive stiffer penalties.

13   Many victims noted that people need to be more aware of identity theft and better prepared to prevent [it] and to respond to it when it occurs. They recommended that people (1) use greater security precautions when handling personal information (for example, they should destroy materials containing personal information instead of putting them in the trash); (2) should not place personal information on the Internet, (3) should secure personal information in homes and at work, (4) should

more carefully monitor their mail, billing cycles, and credit reports, and (5) should know whom to contact and notify the affected companies and credit reporting agencies more quickly when something wrong is detected.

14   Some victims wanted financial institutions to do a better job of preventing and detecting the crime. They suggested having photos on credit cards, better monitoring of account activity and notification of irregularities, and treating victims with understanding instead of suspicion.

15   Few things in life are worse than losing your good name. However, with the inevitable increase of financial transactions over the Internet, the continual bombardment of people with pre-approved credit card applications, and new, yet unknown ways of obtaining personal identifying information by thieves, identity theft is likely to become an even greater problem and headache for victims and law enforcement agencies than it currently is.

From Robert M. Bohm and Keith N. Haley, *Introduction to Criminal Justice*, 5th Edition, pp. 525–32. Copyright © 2008 by The McGraw-Hill Companies, Inc. Reprinted with permission.

COMPREHENSION CHECKUP

Multiple Choice

Directions: For each item, write the letter corresponding to the best answer.

_____ 1. Which of the following best states the main idea of the selection?
- a. Tania Collins was an unwitting victim of identity theft.
- b. Identity theft is a larger problem than experts suspected.
- c. Identity theft is likely to become an even greater problem in the future for both victims and law enforcement agencies, but there are ways to help combat it.
- d. Identity theft is a federal crime.

_____ 2. Which of the following is the most serious form of identity theft?
- a. misusing personal information to open new credit card accounts or new loans
- b. misusing existing checking or saving accounts
- c. misusing existing telephone accounts
- d. misusing existing credit card account numbers

_____ 3. A person who sends an unsolicited e-mail message advertising a get-rich-quick scheme and asks for identifying information is called a
- a. spammer.
- b. junker.
- c. diver.
- d. phisher.

_____ 4. The victims of identity theft suggest all of the following ways to combat it *except* for which?
- a. Destroy materials containing personal information.
- b. Refrain from putting personal information on the Internet.
- c. Don't carry personal information in your wallet or purse.
- d. Keep personal information at home and work secure.

_____ 5. According to the author, a dumpster diver
- a. goes through garbage cans, dumpsters, and trash bins.
- b. wishes to obtain copies of checks and credit card or bank statements.

   c. wants records that bear your name, address, and phone number.
   d. all of the above.

_____ 6. The transition words *such as* in paragraph 4 are used to signal
   a. an example.
   b. a comparison.
   c. a definition.
   d. a list.

_____ 7. In paragraph 5 the transition word *thus* indicates
   a. addition.
   b. spatial order.
   c. reversal.
   d. conclusion.

_____ 8. The transition words *on the other hand* in paragraph 7 indicate
   a. conclusion.
   b. contrast.
   c. comparison.
   d. cause and effect.

_____ 9. The organizational pattern in paragraphs 12 and 13 could be described as
   a. classification and division.
   b. comparison and contrast.
   c. listing.
   d. chronological order.

_____ 10. The transition word *however* in paragraph 15 indicates a
   a. contrast.
   b. comparison.
   c. definition.
   d. list.

True or False

Directions: Indicate whether each statement is true or false by writing **T** or **F** in the space provided.

_F_ 1. Individuals suffer a greater loss to identity theft than do business establishments.

_F_ 2. If an individual's identity is stolen, he or she can expect to have personal information misused for at least a year.

_T_ 3. Identity theft is currently a federal crime.

_T_ 4. The least serious form of identity theft involves credit cards.

_T_ 5. The person who stole Tania Collins's purse ran up $20,000 in debt.

_T_ 6. Approximately half of the victims of identity theft don't know how the thief obtained their personal information.

_T_ 7. If you are using an ATM, it is advisable to be on the lookout for shoulder surfers.

_T_ 8. Many victims are traumatized by having their identity stolen.

_T_ 9. The author predicts that identity theft is likely to become an even greater problem than it already is.

_T_ 10. Some victims are in favor of having photos on credit cards.

Vocabulary Matching

Directions: Match the vocabulary words in Column A with their definitions in Column B. Place the correct letter in the space provided.

Column A	Column B
_d_ 1. provoke	a. deceitful
_f_ 2. monitor	b. not requested
_h_ 3. bulk	c. makes up; composes
_a_ 4. fraudulent	d. to stir up purposely
_g_ 5. incur	e. to amass; to increase gradually
_i_ 6. traumatic	f. to mind; watch
_e_ 7. accumulate	g. to bring down on oneself
_c_ 8. constitutes	h. the main or greater part
_j_ 9. resolve	i. deeply distressing
_b_ 10. unsolicited	j. to clear up; deal with successfully

In Your Own Words

In an effort to thwart identity theft, the Mississippi Department of Public Safety is using special software that allows its driver's license examiners to compare a driver's previous photograph with a newly taken one. Do you think this will make much difference?

Written Assignment

Write a short paragraph discussing the meaning of the following quotation from Shakespeare's *Othello*. How does the quotation relate to the concept of identity theft?

> "But he that filches from me my good name robs me of that which not enriches him and makes me poor indeed."

Internet Activity

1. The Federal Trade Commission's identity theft site provides information to help you "deter, detect, and defend" against identity theft. You can access it at www.consumer.gov/idtheft. Which suggestions are most valuable to your personal life?

2. Another government site is sponsored by the Department of Justice. You can access it at www.usdoj.gov/criminal/fraud/websites/idtheft.html. Which of the two government sites do you think provides the best information on the topic?

3. To check out scam alerts, consult the Identity Theft Resource Center at www.idtheftcenter.org. Its slogan is "Who's in your wallet?" Write a short paragraph describing a recent scam.

Chapter Summary and Review

In this chapter, you learned about the patterns of organization that authors use. You also learned to recognize transition words and phrases. Based on the material in Chapter 3, answer the following.

Short Answer

Directions: List three or four transition words that signal the following patterns of paragraph organization.

1. Comparison __Like,_____

2. Cause and effect ___as a result_____

3. Chronological order __First, next_____

4. Classification __group classify_____

Vocabulary in Context

Directions: Choose one of the following words to complete the sentences below. Use each word only once.

chronological	conclusion	contrast	definitions	examples

5. When you write a paper for class, you may want to give specific __examples___ that illustrate your point.

6. On a history test, you might be asked to place the major events leading up to World War II in __chronological__ order.

7. A speaker at a graduation ceremony usually ends the speech with a(n) __conclusion__

8. When minor league baseball players make it to the Major Leagues for the first time, they are sometimes surprised at the huge __contrast__ between how the game is played in the major and minor leagues.

9. Sometimes authors of textbooks will give __definition__ for unusual words that they use.

Interpreting What We Read

Erykah Badu

In jazz, each player must be a clever musician, an originator as well as an interpreter.

—Carl Engel, head of the music division of the Library of Congress

Just as musicians interpret a piece of music, so readers interpret written material. The author of a written piece tries to use words in the way that best communicates the intended meaning. In seeking to understand an author's meaning, readers must interpret the words the author has written down, and the only way readers can do this is through the filter of their own skills, experiences, and personalities. While no two readers end up with precisely the same understanding of what the author meant, some interpretations will be better than others in relation to the author's intended meaning. Being a good interpreter requires a knowledge of inference, figurative language, and tone, and the purpose of Part 3 is to increase your understanding of these topics.

5

Inference

CHAPTER PREVIEW
In this chapter, you will

● Practice drawing inferences from a variety of sources.

Introduction to Drawing Inferences

We make inferences, or intelligent guesses, every day of our lives. If a teacher sees a student looking at his watch and tapping his foot, the teacher will likely assume the student is anxious to leave class. If someone comes home from work and slams the door, most of us will deduce that the person is upset about something. If Maria's dog doesn't move all day, she's likely to assume her pet is sick and needs to see the vet.

We negotiate through life by means of "cues." We are constantly "reading" situations and adjusting our actions. If we see a car weaving down the road late at night, most of us will become concerned that the driver may be intoxicated, and so we try to stay out of the way.

Study the cartoon *Bent Offerings*. The clerk at the cash register is using observed details about the items the man in the checkout line is purchasing to come to conclusions about him.

The clerk might be wrong about the man in the checkout line, of course. He could be a married man who just happens to like TV dinners. Or he might be buying deodorant for work. In fact, the clerk cannot prove or disprove her observations without the man's help. But her inferences might be considered reasonable deductions based on the available clues and her knowledge and experience with people.

Now, look at the picture on the next page and see if you can make some logical inferences.

Bent Offerings
by Don Addis

Don Addis. *St. Petersburg Times.* Reprinted with permission.

218

1. _____

2. _____

3. _____

4. _____

We can infer that the scene is a child's birthday party at a fast-food restaurant, even though no birthday cake is present. We note the tables and chairs, the decor, the age of the children, the paper hats, and especially the balloons, which usually indicate a celebration of some sort. Our inference could be wrong, but we took the available evidence and put it together in a plausible way. We do the exact same thing in our reading.

In prose or poetry, we must be alert for cues to determine the writer's true meaning. In the following paragraph, Elliott Roosevelt, a son of President Franklin Delano Roosevelt, used to tell this story about his mother, Eleanor Roosevelt:

> At a state dinner at the White House, Eleanor, who was seated next to him, leaned over and whispered into his ear. A friend later asked Elliott, then in his forties, what she had said. "She told me to eat my peas," he answered.

From Diane E. Papalia, and Sally Wendkos Olds, *Human Development*, 9th Edition, p. 589. Copyright © 2004 by The McGraw-Hill Companies, Inc. Reprinted with permission.

The key to understanding this anecdote is Elliott Roosevelt's age. It is normal behavior for a mother to tell a 4-year-old to clean his plate, but not a 40-year-old, and definitely not at a formal state dinner in the White House. We can infer that Eleanor Roosevelt had difficulty treating Elliott like an adult.

Now read the first stanza from the poem "Indian Names," by Lydia Sigourney, and record the inferences you can make.

"No matter how old a mother is, she watches her middle-age children for signs of improvement."

—Florida Scott-Maxwell

Ye say they all have pass'd away

   That noble race and brave;

That their light canoes have vanish'd

   From off the crested wave;

That mid the forests where they roam'd,

   There rings no hunter's shout;

But their name is on your waters,

   Ye may not wash it out . . .

From Lydia Huntley Sigourney, "Indian Names" (1834), in Donald Hall, ed., *The Oxford Book of Children's Verse in America.* New York: Oxford University Press, 1985, p. 24.

1. _____

2. _____

3. _____

4. _____

We can infer that the speaker is not a Native American, or is writing as though she is not one, because she uses the pronoun "their." It also appears as if a conversation is occurring between two or more people because the speaker says, "Ye say." Because of the speaker's use of the word "but," signaling a contrast, it seems likely that an opposing viewpoint is being expressed. The speaker is challenging the ideas of either another person or society in general. We can also infer from the tone of the poem, and the use of the word "noble," that the speaker's attitude toward Native Americans is respectful. At the end, the speaker reminds us that even though particular Native American tribes may have vanished, their influence is present in the names of many places (for example, Lake Huron).

You have probably heard the expression "to read between the lines." This means figuring out an idea that is not directly stated in what you are reading. When you "draw inferences," you make educated guesses using the clues provided by the writer, your own experience, and logic.

In order to understand the next passage, you must determine the meaning of the word *hora*, which can only be accomplished by reading the last two sentences of the paragraph. After reading the passage, circle the letter of the most logical answer to the questions.

A corporate president recently made a visit to a nearby reservation as part of his firm's public relations program. "We realize that we have not hired any Native Americans in the five years our company has been located in this area," he told those assembled, "but we are looking into the matter very carefully." "Hora, hora," said some of the audience. "We would like to eventually hire 5 percent of our total workforce from this reservation," he said. "Hora, hora," shouted more of the audience. Encouraged by their enthusiasm, the president closed his short speech by telling them that he hoped his firm would be able to take some hiring action within the next couple of years. "Hora, hora, hora," cried the total group. With a feeling of satisfaction the president left the hall and was taken on a tour of the reservation. Stepping in a field to admire some of the horses grazing there, the president asked if he could walk up closer to the animals. "Certainly," said his driver, "but be careful not to step in the hora."

From John Langan, *Ten Steps to Improving Reading Skills,* 4th Ed., Marlton, NJ: Townsend Press, 2003, p. 301.

_____ 1. To get the main point of the passage, we must infer
   a. the location of the reservation.
   b. the kind of company the president headed.
   c. the meaning of the word *hora.*

_____ 2. From the president's speech, we can infer that
   a. his firm had great interest in hiring Native Americans.
   b. his firm had little interest in hiring Native Americans.

_____ 3. From the passage, we can infer that
   a. the audience believed the president's speech.
   b. the audience did not believe the president's speech.

_____ 4. From the passage, we can infer that the president
   a. thought the Native Americans deserved to be hired.
   b. thought his company should not hire the Native Americans.
   c. misinterpreted the Native Americans' reaction to his speech.

_____ 5. From the passage, we can infer that the main reason the president
   spoke to the Native Americans about jobs was that
   a. they needed the jobs.
   b. he thought promising jobs to Native Americans would make his
      company look good.
   c. he thought hiring Native Americans would be good for his
      company.

If we understand the meaning of the word *hora,* we realize that the Native Americans recognized early on that the corporate president was engaging in "empty promises" and had no intention of hiring very many of them. We noted the fact that the firm had been in the area for five years and had not yet hired a single Native American. Moreover, the president was not promising to remedy the situation immediately, but was promising 5 percent employment within "the next couple of years," again indicating no real commitment on his firm's part.

You can see how experience can play a role in our ability to understand inferences. Those of us who know more about how businesses sometimes handle problems with community relations may more easily see the cues indicating the president's lack of sincerity. In this case, the joke was on the corporate president, whose feeling of satisfaction with his speech was completely unjustified.

In your reading, you are more likely to need to draw inferences in imaginative literature, that is, poetry and fiction. Nonfiction is likely to rely on direct statements calling for no interpretation on your part. In the first sentence below, the happiness described is not open to debate. In the second sentence, we must infer Marilyn's happiness based on our experience, which tells us that a smile usually indicates happiness.

Example:

1. Marilyn was happy.
2. Marilyn's face was wreathed with a smile.

In the exercises that follow, you will be given an opportunity to practice making inferences.

Exercise 1: Drawing Inferences from Cartoons

Directions: After reading the dialogue in the cartoon, try to answer the following questions. Write down the clues that helped you. If there are not enough clues in the cartoon to enable you to answer the question, write "Can't tell."

Doonesbury

DOONESBURY © 1995 G. B. Trudeau. Reprinted with permission of Universal Press Syndicate. All rights reserved.

Clues

1. What class is the student writing a paper for? — History

2. What is the student using for reference material? — History Book

3. Is the student working in the library? — No in his home

4. Is the student guilty of plagiarism? — Yes

5. Is the student showing his paper to a teacher? — No to his Mom

6. Does the adult believe the paper is the student's own work? — Yes she does

Exercise 2: More Drawing Inferences from Cartoons

Directions: Try to analyze the following cartoons just as we did before. Remember to read between the lines to discover the attitudes and values that are expressed indirectly.

1. What kind of booth is the smoker expecting to get? a smoking booth

2. Why did the maitre d' send him to a phone booth? so he wouldn't smoke inside

Shoe

Shoe © MacNelly. King Features Syndicate

3. Does the cartoon reflect a positive or a negative view of smoking? _negative_

4. Could proponents of smoking find something in this cartoon to support their viewpoint? _Not at All smoker get tired wrong_

THE FAR SIDE®   BY GARY LARSON

The real reason dinosaurs became extinct

5. According to the cartoon, why did dinosaurs become extinct? _From smoking_

6. Is the cartoonist making a positive or negative comment about smoking?
he is making a negative comment about smoking

Exercise 3: Drawing Inferences from Proverbs

A proverb is a traditional saying that offers advice or presents a moral. In order to understand proverbs, you must be able to read between the lines. Proverbs cannot be read in the literal sense. For example, the proverb "Don't put all your eggs in one basket" is not really concerned with collecting eggs. What it implies is that it is not a good idea to rely on just one thing.

Directions: What can you logically infer about the meaning of these proverbs? Working with a partner, see how well you can explain them.

1. The leopard does not change his spots. *like you can not change the person*
2. The early bird catches the worm. *be on time*
3. The squeaky wheel gets the grease. _____
4. Every cloud has a silver lining. *There is always good when there is bad*
5. Don't cross the bridge till you come to it. *do not work ahead of your self / don't count on something that might not be there*
6. A bad workman blames his tools. *the who doesn't take responsibility for his actions.*
7. You can lead a horse to water, but you can't make him drink. *you can show the person the way but doesn't mean he will take it*

Now try to identify these well-known proverbs, which have been rewritten with synonyms for key words. Use your dictionary if necessary.

8. Birds of similar plumage assemble. *Birds of a feather flock together*
9. Sanitation is next to piousness. _____
10. An examined kettle does not bubble. *a cold kettle doesn't boil*
11. It is not possible to instruct ancient canines in fresh wiles. _____

   _____

12. Where there are fumes, there is blaze. *where there is smoke there is fire*
13. Inspect before you bound. _____
14. Persons who dwell in crystal domiciles should not fling pebbles. *Persons who lives in a glass should not throw stones*

Exercise 4: Drawing Inferences from Popular Literature

Directions: Read each of the following excerpts from popular literature, and use inferential reasoning to answer the questions that follow.

A.   I suppose it was inevitable that my brother and I would get into one big fight which also would be the last one. When it came, given our theories about street fighting, it was like the Battle Hymn, terrible and swift. There are parts of it I did not see. I did not see our mother walk between us to try to stop us. She was short and wore glasses and, even with them on, did not have good vision. She had never seen a fight before or had any notion of how bad you can get hurt by becoming mixed up in one. Evidently, she just walked between her sons. The first I saw of her was the gray top of her head, the hair tied in a big knot with a big comb in it; but what was most noticeable was that her head was so close to Paul I couldn't get a good punch at him. Then I didn't see her anymore.

From Norman Maclean, *A River Runs Through It*. New York: PocketBooks, 1992, p. 9.

1. What happened to the boys' mother? _She was hit_

B.   All he would have to do would be to slip the translation out of his desk, copy it, put it away, and he would pass the examination. All of his worries would be over. His father would be happy that he passed the examination. He wouldn't have to go to summer school. He and Charlie could go out to Colorado together to work on that dude ranch. He would be through with Latin forever. The Latin grade would never pull his average down again. Everything would be all right. Everything would be fine. All he would have to do would be to copy that one paragraph. Everyone cheated. Maybe not at V.P.S. But in other schools they bragged about it. . . . Everyone cheated in one way or another. Why should that one passage ruin everything? Who cared what problems the Romans had!

From C.D.B Bryan, "So Much Unfairness of Things" in *Ten Top Stories,* ed., David A. Sohn. New York: Bantam Books, 1964, p. 55 from *The New Yorker Magazine*, 1962.

1. What subject is the student having difficulty with? _Latin_

2. How is he rationalizing his decision? _(cheated)_

C.   "C'mon, mama's boy," Bull whispered. "Bring little mama's boy up to Daddy Bull." Right hand, left hand, right hand, left hand, the ball drummed against the cement as Ben waited for his father to move out against him and Bull held back, fearing the drive to the basket. At the foul line, Ben left his feet for the jump shot, eyed the basket at the top of his leap, let it go softly, the wrist snapping, the fingers pointing at the rim and the ball spinning away from him as Bull lunged forward and drove his shoulder into Ben's stomach, knocking him to the ground. Though he did not see the ball go in, he heard the shouts of his mother and sisters; he saw Matthew leaping up and down on the porch. He felt his father rise off him slowly, coming up beaten by a son for the first time in his life. Screaming with joy, Ben jumped up and was immediately flooded by his family, who hugged, slapped, pummeled, and kissed him.

From Pat Conroy, *The Great Santini*. New York: Bantam Books, 1994, p. 121.

1. What kind of relationship does Ben have with his father? _Great_

2. Is the family rooting for the father or the son? _Son_

3. What can we infer about Bull's character from this excerpt? _Bull is his partner_

D.   A blur outside the car . . . Sherman grabbed the door pull and with a tremendous adrenal burst banged it shut. Out of the corner of his eye, the big one— almost to the door on Maria's side. Sherman hit the lock mechanism. *Rap!* He was yanking on the door handle—CELTICS inches from Maria's head with only the glass in between. Maria shoved the Mercedes into gear and squealed forward. The youth leaped to one side. The car was heading straight for the trash cans. Maria hit the brakes. Sherman was thrown against the dash. A vanity case landed on top of the gear shift. Sherman pulled it off. Now it was on his lap. Maria threw the car into reverse. It shot backward. He glanced to his right. The skinny one. . . . The skinny boy was standing there staring at him . . . pure fear on his delicate face. . . . Maria shoved it into first gear again. . . . She was breathing in huge gulps, as if she were drowning. . . .

Sherman yelled, "Look out!"

The big one was coming toward the car. He had the tire up over his head. Maria squealed the car forward, right at him. He lurched out of the way . . . a blur . . . a terrific jolt. The tire hit the windshield and bounced off, without breaking the glass. . . .

Maria cut the wheel to the left, to keep from hitting the cans. . . . The skinny one standing right there. . . . The rear end fishtailed . . . *thok!* . . . The skinny boy was no longer standing. . . . Maria fought the steering wheel . . . a clear shot between the guard rail and the trash cans. . . . She floored it. . . . A furious squeal. . . . The Mercedes shot up the ramp.

From Tom Wolfe, *The Bonfire of the Vanities.* New York: Bantam Books, 1987, p. 50.

1. Which person is wearing something that says "CELTICS"? _Sherman_

2. How many people are inside the car? _2_

3. Who is driving the car? _Maria_

4. Describe the two people outside the car. Give an identifiable characteristic for each one. _The big one, the skinny_

5. What happened to the skinny boy? _got hit by the car_

6. What is the probable location of this incident? _nairborhood_

7. What is the likely emotion of those in the car? _fear_
   How do you know? _breathing in huge gulps._

8. What can we infer about the motives of the two outside the car? _fear and angry_

9. Write a title that is descriptive of the contents of the passage. _____

Exercise 5: Drawing Inferences from Personal Ads

In the United States, personal ads have become increasingly popular as a way of meeting people. These ads appear in many newspapers and magazines, and online, throughout the country.

The following ads are all from men seeking women:

WANT TO MEET a terrific, communicative, bright, very educated man in time for the holidays? If you are under 40, educated, bright, sophisticated, and slender, Santa may have a wonderful gift for you.

WANTED: CLASSY, FINANCIALLY independent, easygoing F to enjoy life and to dabble in business, 25–45 SM, 40s, financially secure, 5'11"/187, fit and healthy. No close relatives or dependents.

NEW ON THE MARKET, won't last long, DM, 39, 6/180, brown/blue, fun-loving, down-to-earth; seeks slender F, under 40, who likes Harleys.

007's WOMAN, Yes, I have the savoir faire of James. You have the beauty of his women. Let's make life an adventure. I'm 35, great black hair, athletic build, love life. Get everything you desire in one great package. A dream come true.

✝**PERFECT MATCH,** If you were born on any of the following dates: 2-1-66, 2-2-66, 3-1-75, 4-8-79, 4-9-79, 3-5-83. A kindred soul searches for you—let's talk.

The following ads are from women seeking men:

DEAR SANTA, This year, instead of a turkey, please bring me a dashing reindeer. Any color coat OK. Please make him 30s to 40s and nonsmoking and well-employed. But not too well-fed or with a red nose. Thanks, Santa.

✝ **GO BULLS & A SF,** The Bulls are down by 3 but I'm up by 5'5". My number is 36 and I enjoy traveling around. My uniform is attractive and I'm in shape for the season. My special draft pick is a professional SM; a team player whose number is 33–39. Extra points given if you're attractive, fun-loving, and enjoy bicycling and tennis. Take a time-out and call. Shot clock's a ticking.

ATTRACTIVE & ADVENTUROUS SF, 35 is seeking physically fit, attractive man with a professional degree. Nonsmokers ONLY. Please send phone number and a recent photo.

Directions: What can you logically infer from these ads? Include the specific details that help you make your inferences.

1. Which ads are from people who are likely to be health conscious? *Go bulls & A SF,*

2. Which ads demonstrate that the individual has a sense of humor? *DOT's woman,*

3. Although it is generally considered to be unwise to meet people through personal ads, which ad conveys a special sense of danger? *Classy, Financially*

4. In which ad does the individual appear to be familiar with astrology? *Perfect match*

5. Which ads convey a sense of self-importance, or a touch of the egotistical? *Perfect match Go bulls*

6. What characteristics are emphasized in the ads? *New on the market*

Exercise 6: Drawing Inferences from the Social Sciences

A good reader makes educated guesses based on observable details. We use our intuition and experiences to create a likely interpretation of what is happening in a story, while being careful that our interpretation is logical and realistic.

Directions: Read the following excerpt, answer the questions at the end of the passage, and then write the clue on which your inference is based. To answer the questions, you must read between the lines.

> Even from the glow of the faded red-and-white exit sign, its faint light barely illuminating the upper bunk, I could see that the sheet was filthy. Resigned to another night of fitful sleep, I reluctantly crawled into bed, tucking my clothes securely around my body, like a protective cocoon.
>
> The next morning, I joined the long line of disheveled men leaning against the chain-link fence. Their faces were as downcast as their clothes were dirty. Not a glimmer of hope among them.
>
> No one spoke as the line slowly inched forward. When my turn came, I was handed a Styrofoam cup of coffee, some utensils, and a bowl of

semi-liquid that I couldn't identify. It didn't look like any food I had seen before. Nor did it taste like anything I had ever eaten.

My stomach fought the foul taste, every spoonful a battle. But I was determined. "I will experience what they experience," I kept telling myself. My stomach reluctantly gave in and accepted its morning nourishment.

The room was eerily silent. Hundreds of men were eating, each immersed in his own private hell, his head awash with disappointment, remorse, bitterness.

As I stared at the Styrofoam cup of coffee, grateful at least for this small pleasure, I noticed what looked like teeth marks. I shrugged off the thought, . . . concluding, "That must be some sort of crease from handling."

I joined the silent ranks of men turning in their bowls and cups. When I saw the man behind the counter swishing out Styrofoam cups in a washtub of water, I began to feel sick to my stomach. I knew then that the jagged marks on my cup really had come from a previous mouth.

How much longer did this research have to last? I felt a deep longing to return to my family, to a world of clean sheets, healthy food, and "normal" conversations.

Adapted from James M. Henslin, *Essentials of Sociology: A Down-to-Earth Approach*, 7th Edition, p. 3. © 2007 Pearson Education, Inc. Reproduced by permission of Pearson Education, Inc.

1. What is the likely sex of the writer? _____

2. Where is the writer? What is the writer's location? _____

   _____

3. What is the writer's purpose? _____

4. What is the likely occupation or profession of the writer? _____

   _____

5. How do we know the writer is accustomed to a better life? _____

   _____

   _____

6. Use one word to describe the demeanor of the men in line. _____

   _____

Exercise 7: Drawing Inferences from Literature

Directions: The following paragraphs are taken from the short story "Flight" by John Steinbeck; intervening paragraphs have been omitted. Answer the questions following each paragraph by using the clues provided by the author.

A.   Without warning Pepe's horse screamed and fell on its side. He was almost down before the rifle crash echoed up from the valley. From a hole behind the struggling shoulder, a stream of bright crimson blood pumped and stopped and pumped and stopped. The hooves threshed on the ground. Pepe lay half stunned beside the horse. He looked slowly down the hill. A piece of sage clipped off beside his head and another crash echoed up from side to side of the canyon. Pepe flung himself frantically behind a bush.

   1. What is the probable fate of the horse? _____

      _____

   2. Why is Pepe behaving in a frantic manner? _____

B.   The whole side of the slope grew still. No more movement. And then a white streak cut into the granite of the slit and a bullet whined away and a crash sounded up from below. Pepe felt a sharp pain in his right hand. A sliver of granite was sticking out from between his first and his second knuckles and the point protruded from his palm. Carefully he pulled out the sliver of stone. The wound bled evenly and gently. No vein nor artery was cut.

3. What is the likely setting of the story? _____

4. How has Pepe been injured? _____

5. Is the injury life-threatening? _____

_____

C.   A moment later Pepe heard the sound, the faint far crash of horses' hooves on gravel. And he heard something else, a high whining yelp of a dog.

6. In what way has Pepe's situation become more desperate? _____

_____

D.   He sat up and dragged his great arm into his lap and nursed it, rocking his body and moaning in his throat. He threw back his head and looked up into the pale sky. A big black bird circled nearly out of sight, and far to the left another was sailing near.

7. What can we infer about the status of his injury? _____

_____

8. What is the significance of the circling birds? _____

_____

E.   Pepe bowed his head quickly. He tried to speak rapid words but only a thick hiss came from his lips. He drew a shaky cross on his breast with his left hand. It was a long struggle to get to his feet. He crawled slowly and mechanically to the top of a big rock on the ridge peak. Once there, he arose slowly, swaying to his feet, and stood erect. Far below he could see the dark brush where he had slept. He braced his feet and stood there, black against the morning sky.

9. What can we infer about how Pepe is feeling physically? _____

_____

10. Is Pepe religious? _____

11. What is Pepe's solution to his dilemma? _____

_____

F.   There came a ripping sound at his feet. A piece of stone flew up and a bullet droned off into the next gorge. The hollow crash echoed up from below. Pepe looked down for a moment and then pulled himself straight again.

12. Why did Pepe stand erect again? _____

G.   His body jarred back. His left hand fluttered helplessly toward his breast. The second crash sounded from below.

13. What was the end result of Pepe's flight? _____

"Flight," from *The Long Valley* by John Steinbeck, pp. 62, 63–64, 67, 69. Copyright 1938, renewed © 1966 by John Steinbeck. Used by permission of Viking Penguin, a division of Penguin Group (USA) Inc. For on-line information about other Penguin Group (USA) books and authors, see the Internet website at: http://www.penguin.com

READING

"We are going to take the winning speckled trout out of the freezer tonight."

TUNING IN TO READING

The old sayings "The apple never falls far from the tree" and "Like father like son" are used to illustrate the continuity of family traits. Do you think bad characteristics are passed down from generation to generation? Do you think that it is possible to learn from the mistakes of those who came before us?

BIO-SKETCH

Fannie Flagg is the author of the national best seller *Fried Green Tomatoes at the Whistle Stop Cafe,* which was made into a movie. She is also the author of *Welcome to the World, Baby Girl, A Redbird Christmas,* and *Daisy Fay and the Miracle Man,* from which this excerpt is taken. Writing may not have been a natural career choice for Flagg because, as she says, "I was, *am,* severely dyslexic and couldn't spell, still can't spell, and so I was discouraged from writing and embarrassed." Flagg has been more than just a writer. She has also been an actress, screenwriter, director, and comedienne.

NOTES ON VOCABULARY

caviar   the salted eggs of sturgeon, salmon, or certain other fish, eaten as an appetizer. The word originally came from the Turkish *havyar.* Russian beluga and huso, which are types of sturgeon, are widely thought to be the source of the best *caviar. Caviar* is so expensive that it is often referred to as "black gold."

Excerpt from *Daisy Fay and the Miracle Man*

Fannie Flagg

September 6

DADDY AND I ARE EXCITED because the Big Speckled Rodeo Trout Contest is next week and he and I are going to enter and we are going to win. I know that for a fact.

2   Daddy already bought the winning fish off Harvey Underwood a month ago and put it in the freezer. He told Momma it was a fish he was going to stuff later on this year. It weighs twelve pounds and two ounces. I don't see how anybody could catch a fish bigger than that. The all-time record holder weighed thirteen pounds and that was six years ago. Our chances are excellent!

3   The person who catches the biggest speckled trout during three days of fishing wins first prize and first prize is an Evinrude outboard motor, valued at $146.90 and second prize is a Ply-Flex fishing rod valued at $36. Now all we need is a boat to go with it!

September 15

4   Tomorrow is the last day of the Speckled Trout rodeo and everything is going just as Daddy and I planned. We went down to the Speckled Trout Rodeo Headquarters the first day and registered early in the morning and headed on up to our spot on the river. Daddy made a big show of how he didn't expect to win, but thought it would be fun for his little girl since he had been so busy all summer and hadn't had a chance to spend any time with her. He made me paddle up and down the river for a while every day so people could see us fishing.

5   Then every day we went and napped and didn't even fish at all. I took my Red Ryder BB gun and shot at snakes. I ate candy and Daddy drank his beer and told me war stories. At five o'clock we would go back to the Speckled Trout Rodeo Headquarters at the live bait shop. Daddy would say, "Well no luck today. Those fish just aren't biting," and act real disappointed to throw them off the track. . . .

6   We are going to take the winning speckled trout out of the freezer tonight before we go to bed so it will be good and thawed for tomorrow.

September 18

7   The trout was still frozen stiff as a board when we took it out of the freezer. So Daddy put it in a pan of boiling water and locked it in the trunk of the car. When we got up to the Speckled Trout Rodeo Headquarters, Daddy carried on some more how he had not caught one fish and how he hoped he caught something today. What kind of fisherman would his little girl think he was? We rowed up and down the river long enough for everyone to see us, just as we always did. Then we went back up to our spot and waited for that trout to thaw out. . . . About two o'clock in the afternoon the trout finally thawed, but putting it in the hot water had turned his eyes all cloudy. It didn't look like a fresh fish to me. Daddy didn't think so either and started cussing. Then he got an idea.

8   He said, "Don't move from this spot. If anybody comes up here, tell them I have gone to the bathroom." I sat there and waited and I tell you nothing smells worse than a dead trout.

9   About an hour later he came sneaking through the bushes and nearly scared me half to death. He had me drag the fish up to the bushes where he'd brought his whole taxidermy kit, right down to the artificial eyes, and some airplane glue. It took us forever, but we found some trout eyes. They were a little too big and the wrong color, but he said he didn't think the judges would notice. He cut the real eyes out of that trout and glued those plastic eyes in their place. We sat there and blew on them so they'd dry and at about four o'clock that fish started to look pretty good. The glue had dried funny, but Daddy said it made it appear like the trout had died terrified. I told you my Daddy likes to see the bright side of things.

10   We were just getting ready to go when some old country man came by in a boat and saw us and yelled out, "I heard Emmet Weaverly caught a thirteen-pounder this morning." Our trout was only twelve pounds and two ounces. I thought Daddy was going to be sick. But he's a quick thinker. He grabbed my box of BBs and stuffed every one of them down that trout's throat. By the time we got to the headquarters, everyone had weighed in but us.

11   So far the winner was Emmet Weaverly's fish that weighed twelve pounds and eight ounces, not thirteen like that man had said.

12   When Daddy got in the room, do you know what he did? He handed me that trout and said, "Hey, folks, look what my little girl just caught."

13   I couldn't believe it. I said, "Oh, no, Daddy. You're the one who really caught it."

14   He said, "No, honey, you caught it. Run up there and have it weighed."

15   If looks could kill, he'd be deader than that fish with the plastic eyes. I knew what he was doing. He was acting like he really caught it, but he was letting his little girl get all the glory. I tried to hand it back to him, but by then everybody thought the idea was so cute they pushed me up to where the scales were. I put the fish down on the scales very carefully. I didn't want those plastic eyes making a noise if they hit anything.

16   Our trout weighed twelve pounds and nine ounces. I did some fast figuring in my head; that was seven ounces of BBs. Everybody started applauding and saying "Bill Harper's little girl won." I looked around and there was Daddy, smiling, getting patted on the back, taking all the credit. . . .

17   I never took my eyes off the trout. Just as a judge was about to pick it up, I grabbed it in the nick of time. The official Speckled Trout Rodeo photographer started posing me for the picture for the paper. They said for me to hold it up by the tail and smile real big. It was hard to smile because if one of those plastic eyes fell out on the floor and they found out that fish had been dead for a month, I would go to jail. . . . The more I thought about it, the worse it got. My heart started pounding and my lips began to tremble. I couldn't smile if my life depended on it. They made me stand there longer and said, "We're not going to let you go until you give us a big smile. So smile big, honey." My hands started to shake and that trout was shaking like crazy, too. I just knew those eyes were going to fall out. One had slipped a little anyway, but I needn't have worried about the eyes because at that moment the BBs started coming out of that trout's mouth one by one all over the floor. I was in a cold sweat, but you never saw anybody smile as big as I did.

18   I knew they had to get that picture fast! Mrs. Dot said, "Oh look she caught a female fish, it's just full of caviar!" I sure was glad she didn't know the difference between BBs and caviar. Thank goodness Daddy came over and grabbed the fish out of my hand and turned it right side up and said, "I'm taking this trout home and stuffing it to make it into a trophy to donate to the Speckled Trout Rodeo as a gift." Everybody thought that was a fine idea, especially me. He said he had to get it home right away before the trout went bad.

19   Momma was waiting up for us. Daddy said, "Look what Daisy caught," and didn't even give her time to look at it good before he threw it back in the freezer. He told Momma not to open the freezer until at least twenty-four hours because it would ruin the trout if she did. She believed him. . . .

20   Daddy won't have a hard time stuffing the fish. He's already got the eyes in. . . . [Now] my daddy has an outboard motor in the shack out by the side of the malt shop. He doesn't have a boat yet, so I don't know what good it is doing him. Momma and I want him to sell it. We need the money for the payment on the malt shop, but Daddy says as soon as he starts stuffing his animals, he will have enough money to pay the note and buy a boat besides.

"You can fool all of the people some of the time, you can fool some of the people all the time, but you can't fool all the people all the time."

—Abraham Lincoln

Reprinted by permission of The Wendy Weil Agency, Inc. First published by William Morrow & Co. as *Coming Attractions*; reissued by Warner Books and Ballantine Books as *Daisy Fay and the Miracle Man.* © 1981, 2005 by Fannie Flagg.

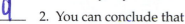 **COMPREHENSION CHECKUP**

Multiple Choice

Directions: For each item, write the letter corresponding to the best answer.

_A_ 1. You can infer from the article that
   a. Daisy Fay's daddy didn't see anything wrong with using a frozen trout.
   b. Daisy Fay's daddy was an excellent fisherman.
   c. Daisy Fay's daddy thought "Momma" would readily agree with his scheme to use the frozen fish.
   d. Daisy Fay was initially opposed to her daddy's scheme.

_d_ 2. You can conclude that
   a. Daisy Fay's daddy will be able to use the Evinrude outboard motor right away.
   b. Daisy Fay's daddy was counting on making his old fish look like a fresh fish.
   c. Daisy Fay's daddy may never have a boat to put the motor on.
   d. both b and c.

_d_ 3. Daisy Fay's general attitude toward her daddy is one of
   a. hatred.
   b. fear.
   c. affection.
   d. indifference.

_b_ 4. The words "if looks could kill" suggest that
   a. Daisy Fay was terrified of her father's anger.
   b. Daisy Fay was frustrated and embarrassed.
   c. Daisy Fay was going to kill her father later.
   d. Daisy Fay was happy to have all of the attention focused on her.

_c_ 5. The main idea of paragraph 4 is found in the
   a. first sentence.
   b. second sentence.
   c. third sentence.
   d. last sentence.

_d_ 6. The article suggests that Daisy Fay's father
   a. is not very honest.
   b. is clever and resourceful.
   c. is not very successful.
   d. all of the above.

True or False

Directions: Indicate whether each statement is true or false by writing **T** or **F** in the space provided.

_T_ 7. Emmet Weaverly should have won the fishing contest.

_T_ 8. Daisy Fay was afraid she might go to jail.

_T_ 9. Daisy Fay laughed when the BBs started falling out of the fish's mouth.

_F_ 10. Daisy Fay's daddy wanted her to pose with the fish so that she would feel good about catching it.

In Your Own Words

1. What could you infer about Bill Harper's character? List the details from the story that support your conclusions.
2. Would Daisy Fay's mother have approved of the scheme to win the fishing contest? What evidence do you have for your answer?
3. Bill Harper would probably be considered an optimist. What details in the story show that he always looks on the bright side of things.
4. What evidence shows that Bill Harper is resourceful?
5. How do we know that Daisy Fay was not comfortable with the scheme?

Internet Activity

To learn more about Fannie Flagg, including her career as an actress and writer, read an interview of her reported at the following Web site:

www.randomhouse.com/features/fannieflagg/bookshelf.html

Then write a summary of what you learned about her.

Bring the "Sunflower" get blue/green booklet

separate paper DO

REVIEW TEST: *Drawing Inferences: "Too Much of a Good Thing"*

Directions: This article by Geoffrey Cowley on antibiotics demonstrates that the need to draw inferences is not restricted to literature and the social sciences. Read each paragraph, and then write the letter of the sentence that can be directly inferred from the passage.

A.   Like any internist, Dr. Robert Moellering of Boston's Deaconess Hospital has felt the pressure to hand out antibiotics on demand. When he served as director of student health services at Emerson College, he saw a steady stream of students with colds and flus, and many knew just which drug they wanted. Instead of dashing off prescriptions, Moellering would dutifully explain that their ailments were caused by viruses, and that no antibiotic—however new or expensive—can kill a virus. His campaign didn't get very far. As he now recalls, the kids would return days later waving bottles of pills in his face. "They'd tell me, 'My doctor said I almost had pneumonia.'"

_____ 1. We can infer that
   a. students were willing to follow the advice of Dr. Moellering.
   b. students were able to obtain antibiotics from their own personal physicians.
   c. Dr. Moellering acceded to the demands of the college students.

B.   If the golden age of antibiotics is ending, the reasons should be no mystery. Bacteria gradually adapt to any antibiotic, and when one is misused, its power to heal is squandered. "If I give my patient too much hypertensive medicine, I might hurt that patient but there's no way I'm going to hurt the next patient," says Dr. Frank Rhame, director of infection control at the University of Minnesota Hospital and Clinic. "If I use an antibiotic too much, I'm making it less useful for everyone." Unfortunately, doctors have been slow to act on that insight. Confronted with a miserable patient, they tend to write a prescription. Antibiotic sales are soaring as a result (sales have already doubled since the mid-1980s), and so are drug-resistant infections.

2. We can infer that

    a. overuse of antibiotics by one person has repercussions for many others.

    b. overuse of heart medication by one person causes problems for others.

    c. doctors are unlikely to prescribe antibiotics to those with a viral infection.

C.   The misuse of antibiotics isn't a new problem. Since the 1970s, various studies have concluded that 50 to 60 percent of all outpatient prescriptions are inappropriate. Other studies have found that 7 in 10 Americans receive antibiotics when they seek treatment for common colds. "Essentially," says Dr. Lee Green, a family practitioner at the University of Michigan, "we have a tradition of prescribing antibiotics to anybody who looks sick."

    _C_ 3. We can infer that

    a. doctors are unlikely to prescribe antibiotics to relieve the symptoms of the common cold.

    b. the problem of misusing antibiotics is a relatively new phenomenon.

    c. a large percentage of prescriptions for antibiotics are unnecessary.

D.   There's plenty of blame to go around. As Moellering has learned in Boston, Americans like quick fixes, and when a doctor doesn't offer one, they look for a doctor who will. Patients aren't the only culprits. When insurance companies fail to cover bacterial tests, they encourage sloppy prescribing. Drug companies, for their part, promote the use of their products by advertising them widely and supplying doctors with free samples. Experts in health policy agree that the latest patented medications, which can cost 10 times as much as older generics, should be reserved for uniquely stubborn infections. "The more widely you use these newer antibiotics," says Dr. David Kessler, commissioner of the U.S. Food and Drug Administration, "the greater the chances that [bacteria] will develop resistance." But when a manufacturer touts a new product as a high-octane alternative that every patient deserves, doctors can feel duty-bound to prescribe it. "It's another form of defensive medicine," says Dr. Thomas O'Brien of Harvard.

    _B_ 4. We can infer that

    a. doctors are unlikely to feel pressure to prescribe the newest "wonder drugs."

    b. promotion on the part of drug companies increases the likelihood of abuse of antibiotics.

    c. overusing the new "high-octane" antibiotics increases their effectiveness.

E.   Even when doctors dispense antibiotics properly, there is no guarantee they'll be used that way. Studies suggest that a third of all patients fail to use the drugs as prescribed. Many stop taking their medication after just a few days, when it has killed the most susceptible invaders but left hardened survivors to flourish. Besides being harder to treat, those resistant germs can then spread through the community. Besides quitting treatments early, some patients save unused drugs to take later, or pass them around like vitamins.

"I've heard of people on trips who take a fellow traveler's antibiotic, thinking it will protect them from illness," says Dr. Stuart Levy of Tufts University. "It just causes widespread resistance."

_____ 5. We can infer that

     a. patients closely follow the directions on their antibiotic prescriptions.

     b. doctors are entirely to blame for the current antibiotic dilemma.

     c. a few days of antibiotic treatment kills off only the least-resistant bacteria.

F.   Drug-resistant microbes don't threaten us all equally. A healthy immune system easily repels most bacterial invaders, regardless of their susceptibility to drugs. But when resistant bugs take hold among the weak, the sick or the elderly, they're hellishly hard to control. "I believe resistant infections are present in every hospital and nursing home," says Dr. Thomas Beam of the Buffalo, N.Y., VA Medical Center. "The only question is whether the institution is releasing that information."

_____ 6. We can infer that

     a. it is unlikely that a patient can contract a bacterial infection in a hospital.

     b. the elderly are more susceptible to resistant bacterial infections.

     c. hospitals and nursing homes are likely to inform the patients of any outbreak of drug-resistant infections.

G.   Penicillin and tetracycline lost their power over staph back in the 1950s and 60s. Another antibiotic, methicillin, provided a backup for a while, but methicillin-resistant staph is now common in hospitals and nursing homes worldwide. "If it's not in your hospital already," says Dr. David Shlaes of Cleveland's Case Western Reserve University, "the only way to keep it out is to screen patients and keep [carriers] in some kind of holding center until you treat them." In the past, officials at the VA nursing home in Sioux Falls, SD, quarantined half of the facility's 42 residents to control an outbreak of drug-resistant staph.

_____ 7. We can infer that

     a. staph infections are uncommon in hospitals and nursing homes.

     b. antibiotics never lose their effectiveness against bacteria.

     c. a return to isolating patients is sometimes the only way to control infection.

H.   Like staph infections, bugs known as *enterococci* flourish among weak and elderly hospital patients. Shlaes recalls that when a resistant strain of *enterococci* took hold in a Pittsburgh liver-transplant unit, 50 people were infected over the course of two years. The only survivors were patients whose infected tissues could be removed surgically (a trick from the pre-antibiotic era), or whose infections were confined to the urinary tract, where drugs can be used in high concentrations.

_____ 8. We can infer that

     a. prior to the availability of antibiotics, doctors used to excise the infected body part.

     b. it is unwise to administer high concentrations of antibiotics in the treatment of urinary tract infections to save the life of a patient.

     c. *Staphylococcus* is the only bacterium likely to be a problem for elderly people.

I.   Though they're concentrated in hospitals and nursing homes, the superbugs aren't confined to such settings. Out in the community, many bacterial diseases are becoming even harder to treat. Some 20 percent of the nation's gonorrhea is now resistant to one or more antibiotics. A similar proportion of TB now resists the drug isoniazid. As any doctor who has spent a winter throwing one drug after another at a toddler's ear infection can tell you, resistance is common in other bugs as well. But because the government doesn't track drug resistance, clinicians rarely know when to expect it.

9. We can infer that

    a. clinicians are not kept well informed of outbreaks of resistant infections.

    b. you are not as likely to encounter a resistant form of bacteria in the community at large.

    c. gonorrhea and TB are no longer serious health threats.

"One of the first duties of the physician is to educate the masses not to take medicine."

—William Osler

J.   To give doctors a better sense of what germs are circulating in their communities, the Centers for Disease Control and Prevention now encourage local health officials to conduct regular surveys for drug resistance. Meanwhile, the World Health Organization is funding a global computer database that doctors can use to report drug-resistant outbreaks. Surveillance alone won't stop the erosion of the wonder drugs. "The classic response has been to develop new and more powerful antibiotics," says Moellering. With luck and perseverance, scientists will discover unimagined new weapons. But the immediate challenge is to get doctors, and patients, to stop abusing the weapons we still have.

10. We can infer that

    a. keeping a closer watch on drug-resistant outbreaks is likely to alleviate the problem.

    b. new and powerful antibiotics are readily available.

    c. something must be done to educate both doctors and the populace at large to the danger of using antibiotics inappropriately.

Geoffrey Cowley, "Too Much of a Good Thing." From *Newsweek*, March 28, 1994. © 1994 Newsweek, Inc. All rights reserved. Used by permission and protected by the Copyright Laws of the United States. The printing, copying, redistribution, or retransmission of the Material without express written permission is prohibited. www.newsweek.com

In Your Own Words

1. The use of antibacterial products is widespread. We have antibacterial soaps, sponges, cleaning products, and even toys. Some experts believe that we are killing off the good bacteria as well as the bad, thereby promoting the growth of drug-resistant strains. Do you routinely use antibacterial products in your home? Do you have an opinion about whether the widespread use of antibacterial products is a good idea?

2. Many scientists are concerned about the use of antibiotics in the food supply. For instance, farmers use antibiotics to prevent disease in livestock. In 1998, over 5,000 Americans were made ill by drug-resistant bacteria that had infected chickens. The sick people were immune to the antibiotics that doctors prescribed.

Do you think the Food and Drug Administration should consider banning the use of antibiotics to treat poultry and other livestock?

Internet Activity

The following Web sites offer information on the appropriate use of antibiotics:

www.apua.org (Alliance for the Prudent Use of Antibiotics)

www.familydoctor.org/handouts/680.html

Pull up either site and write a list of things the average person can do to help prevent drug-resistant bacterial diseases.

Jim Hensen, who was the creator of the Muppets and the voice of Kermit the Frog, died from a drug-resistant infection produced by Group A *Streptococcus*, or GAS for short. To find out more information about this disease, go to the following Web site:

www.astdhpphe.org/infect/strepa.html

Summarize your findings.

Do a search for information about "MRSA" on the Internet. Explain briefly what it is.

The last section on inference skills combines an excerpt from a history textbook describing the discovery of the World War II concentration camps and an excerpt from Tom Brokaw's *The Greatest Generation*. Both selections have the effects of war as a theme.

READING

"It was by chance that Allied forces first stumbled upon the camps, and the GIs . . . were totally unprepared for what they found."

TUNING IN TO READING

Have you seen Stephen Speilberg's movie *Saving Private Ryan*? This movie graphically depicts the horrors of World War II.

BIO-SKETCH

The lead author of *America Past and Present* is Robert Divine. Before retiring, he taught American diplomatic history for 42 years at the University of Texas at Austin. He is now an emeritus professor at UT and continues to teach in the UT Extension Program and the Organization of American Historians Distinguished Lectureship Program. His latest book, *Perpetual War for Perpetual Peace*, is an analysis of the U.S. involvement in wars during the 20th century.

NOTES ON VOCABULARY

holocaust　slaughter and destruction on a very wide scale, especially by fire. When used with a capital *H*, it refers to the Nazi slaughter of Jews in World War II. In pre-Christian times, a *holocaust* was a sacrificial burnt offering to pagan gods. It is derived from the Greek words *holos*, meaning "whole," and *kaustos*, meaning "burnt."

Liberation of Auschwitz Prisoners of Auschwitz, the Nazi concentration camp in Poland, greet the troops freeing them.

Inside the Vicious Heart

Robert Divine

The liberation of the Nazi death camps near the end of World War II was not a priority objective; nor was it a planned operation. Convinced that military victory was the surest way to end Nazi oppression, Allied strategists organized their campaigns without specific reference to the camps; they staged no daring commando raids to rescue the survivors of Nazi genocide. It was by chance that Allied forces first stumbled upon the camps, and the GIs who threw open the gates to that living hell were totally unprepared for what they found.

2   Not until November 1944 did the U.S. Army discover its first camp, Natzwiller-Struthof, which had been abandoned by the Germans months before. Viewing Natzwiller from a distance, Milton Bracker of the *New York Times* noted its deceptive similarity to an American Civilian Conservation Corps camp: "The sturdy green barracks buildings looked exactly like those that housed forestry trainees in the U.S. during the early New Deal."

3   As he toured the grounds, however, he faced a starker reality and slowly came to think the unthinkable. In the crematorium, he reported, "I cranked the elevator tray a few times and slid the furnace tray a few times, and even at that moment, I did not believe what I was doing was real."

4   "There were no prisoners," he wrote, "no screams, no burly guards, no taint of death in the air as on a battlefield." Bracker had to stretch his imagination to its limits to comprehend the camp's silent testimony to the Nazi attempt to exterminate the Jews of Europe. U.S. military personnel who toured Natzwiller shared this sense of the surreal. In their report to headquarters, they carefully qualified every observation. They described "what appeared to be a disinfection unit," a room "allegedly used as a lethal gas chamber," "a cellar room with a special type elevator," and "an incinerator room with equipment obviously intended for the burning of human bodies." They saw before them the evidence of German atrocities, but the

truth was so horrible, they could not quite bring themselves to draw the obvious conclusions.

5   *Inside the Vicious Heart,* Robert Abzug's study of the liberation of the concentration camps, refers to this phenomenon as "double vision." Faced with a revelation so terrible, witnesses could not fully comprehend the evidence of systematic murder of more than six million men, women, and children. But as the Allied armies advanced into Germany, the shocking evidence mounted. On April 4, 1945, the Fourth Armored Division of the Third Army unexpectedly discovered Ohrdruf, a relatively small concentration camp. Ohrdruf's liberation had a tremendous impact on American forces. It was the first camp discovered intact, with its grisly array of the dead and dying. Inside the compound, corpses were piled in heaps in the barracks. An infantryman recalled, "I guess the most vivid recollection of the whole camp is the pyre that was located on the edge of the camp. It was a big pit, where they stacked bodies—stacked bodies and wood and burned them."

6   On April 12, Generals Eisenhower, Bradley, and Patton toured Ohrdruf. The generals, professional soldiers familiar with the devastation of battle, had never seen its like. Years later, Bradley recalled, "The smell of death overwhelmed us even before we passed through the stockade. More than 3,200 naked, emaciated bodies had been flung into shallow graves. Others lay in the street where they had fallen."

7   Eisenhower ordered every available armed forces unit in the area to visit Ohrdruf. "We are told that the American soldier does not know what he is fighting for," said Eisenhower. "Now at least he will know what he is fighting against." He urged government officials and journalists to visit the camps and tell the world. In an official message Eisenhower summed it up:

8   *We are constantly finding German camps in which they have placed political prisoners where unspeakable conditions exist. From my own personal observation, I can state unequivocally that all written statements up to now do not paint the full horrors.*

9   On April 11, the Timberwolf Division of the Third Army uncovered Nordhausen. They found 3,000 dead and only 700 survivors. The scene sickened battle-hardened veterans.

10   *The odors, well there is no way to describe the odors. . . . Many of the boys I am talking about now—these were tough soldiers, there were combat men who had been all the way through the invasion—were ill and vomiting, throwing up, just at the sight of this. . . .*

11   For some, the liberation of Nordhausen changed the meaning of the war.

12   *I must also say that my fellow GIs, most thought that any stories they had read in the paper . . . were either not true or at least exaggerated. And it did not sink in, what this was all about, until we got into Nordhausen.*

13   If the experience at Nordhausen gave many GIs a new sense of mission in battle, it also forced them to distance themselves from the realities of the camps. Only by closing off their emotions could they go about the grim task of sorting out the living from the dead and tending to the survivors. Margaret Bourke-White, whose *Life* magazine photographs brought the horrors of the death camps to millions on the home front, recalled working "with a veil over my mind."

14   *People often ask me how it is possible to photograph such atrocities. In photographing the murder camps, the protective veil was so tightly drawn that I hardly knew what I had taken until I saw prints of my own photographs.*

15   By the end of 1945, most of the liberators had come home and returned to civilian life. Once home, their experiences produced no common moral responses. No particular pattern emerged in their occupational, political, and religious behavior,

beyond a fear of the rise of postwar totalitarianism shared by most Americans. Few spoke publicly about their role in the liberation of the camps; most found that after a short period of grim fascination, their friends and families preferred to forget. Some had nightmares, but most were not tormented by memories. For the liberators the ordeal was over. For the survivors of the Holocaust, liberation was but the first step in the tortuous process of rebuilding broken bodies and shattered lives.

From Divine, Robert A.; Breen, T. H. H.; Fredrickson, George M.; Williams, R. Hal; Gross, Ariela J.; and Brands, H. W.; *America Past and Present, Single Volume Edition,* 7th Edition, pp. 800-01. © 2005. Reproduced in print and electronically by permission of Pearson Education, Inc., Upper Saddle River, New Jersey.

 COMPREHENSION CHECKUP

Multiple Choice

Directions: For each item, write the letter corresponding to the best answer.

_____ 1. You could infer from the article that
   a. the United States was fully aware of the existence of concentration camps throughout the war.
   b. U.S. soldiers did not know much about concentration camps until their discovery.
   c. inmates were still alive in the Natzwiller-Struthof concentration camp.
   d. U.S. soldiers who entered the concentration camps were "fresh" troops who had not yet experienced the horrors of battle.

_____ 2. The primary organizational pattern used in this article is
   a. classification and division.
   b. definition.
   c. chronological order.
   d. steps in a process.

_____ 3. The author's primary purpose in writing this article was to
   a. explain what happened when U.S. soldiers discovered the concentration camps.
   b. persuade people to become more interested in the Holocaust.
   c. give a summary of one person's account of what he saw when he entered the camps.
   d. explain the causes of the Holocaust.

_____ 4. The best definition of the word *atrocities* as used in paragraph 4 is
   a. good deeds.
   b. mistakes.
   c. plans.
   d. acts of cruelty.

_____ 5. The purpose of the first paragraph is to
   a. give an example.
   b. discuss the strategy of the Allies.
   c. draw conclusions.
   d. discuss Nazi oppression.

_____ 6. When American GIs entered Natzwiller-Struthof,
   a. they discovered dying prisoners.
   b. they had to fight German guards.
   c. they found a prison that had been completely deserted.
   d. they rejoiced at finally being able to liberate some prisoners.

___ 7. Photographer Margaret Bourke-White stated that she worked with "a veil" over her mind. From this we can conclude that
   a. she wore a veil over her head.
   b. she closed off her emotions.
   c. she tried to find something positive in a depressing situation.
   d. she did not find the concentration camps morally offensive.

___ 8. The author implies that
   a. the people in the surrounding countryside were aware of what was occurring inside the camps.
   b. the green barracks were designed to look innocuous.
   c. every effort was made to provide for the prisoners' comfort and well-being.
   d. at the close of the war the camps served to house German prisoners of war.

___ 9. The author implies that
   a. the World War II veterans liked to talk publicly about the concentration camps.
   b. the prisoners who survived the experience of the concentration camp were able to easily adjust to life after their liberation.
   c. many GIs put the past and the horrors they had witnessed in the concentration camps behind them.
   d. GIs who entered the concentration camps tended to become more religious.

___ 10. General Eisenhower
   a. made Ohrdruf off-limits to American soldiers.
   b. prohibited journalists from visiting Ohrdruf.
   c. did not enter Ohrdruf until more than a week after its discovery.
   d. heard about Ohrdruf on news reports but never visited it.

True or False

Directions: Indicate whether each statement is true or false by writing **T** or **F** in the space provided.

___ 11. The Allies discovered more than 3,000 dead bodies in the Ohrdruf concentration camp.

___ 12. General Eisenhower did not want government officials or journalists to visit the camps.

___ 13. Liberating the camps was a high priority for the Allies.

___ 14. Allied forces staged a daring raid to rescue prisoners at Natzwiller-Struthof.

___ 15. The discovery of Ohrdruf had a tremendous effect on American forces because it was the first concentration camp discovered intact.

Vocabulary in Context

Directions: Use the context clues in the sentences below to determine the meaning of the italicized word, and write the letter corresponding to the best answer.

___ 1. "The liberation of the Nazi death camps near the end of World War II was not a *priority* objective. . . ." (paragraph 1)

The student had to decide whether her *priority* concern was going to be studying or watching TV.

Priority means
a. insignificant.
b. believable.
c. more important.
d. historical.

b 2. "Viewing Natzwiller from a distance, Milton Bracker of the *New York Times* noted its *deceptive* similarity to an American Civilian Conservation Corps camp. . . ." (paragraph 2)

The clear sky in the morning was *deceptive* because by noon a bad storm had blown in.

Deceptive means
a. truthful.
b. misleading.
c. dangerous.
d. ornamental.

c 3. "The *sturdy* green barracks buildings . . ." (paragraph 2)

The old woman, despite her recent hospitalization, was still very *sturdy* on her feet.

Sturdy means
a. practical.
b. weak.
c. strong or stable.
d. attractive.

c 4. "There were no prisoners," he wrote, "no screams, no *burly* guards. . . ." (paragraph 4)

In the football game, the *burly* linebacker was making a lot of tackles.

Burly means
a. weak.
b. relaxed.
c. big and strong.
d. handsome.

b 5. "U.S. military personnel who toured Natzwiller shared this sense of the *surreal*." (paragraph 4)

The *surreal* painting *The Persistence of Memory*, by Salvador Dali, which shows one watch hanging limply from a tree, others covered by flies and ants, and the final watch melted over a form representing the artist, illustrates the decay of time.

Surreal means
a. romantic.
b. realistic.
c. funny.
d. unreal; fantastic.

d 6. "a room 'allegedly used as a *lethal* gas chamber' . . ." (paragraph 4)

If you are a boxer like Mike Tyson, your fists can be considered *lethal* weapons.

Lethal means
a. useful.
b. simple.
c. mild.
d. deadly.

_____ ✓ *b* 7. "It was the first camp discovered intact, with its *grisly* array of the dead and dying." (paragraph 5)

The movie *Silence of the Lambs* and its sequel *Hannibal* portray a *grisly* killer.

Grisly means
a. pleasing.
b. frightful.
c. unusual.
d. well known.

_____ *c* 8. "I can state *unequivocally* that all written statements up to now do not paint the full horrors." (paragraph 8)

He stated *unequivocally* that he was innocent of his wife's murder.

Unequivocally means
a. proudly.
b. humorously.
c. with certainty.
d. doubtfully.

In Your Own Words

Directions: Use supporting details from the essay to answer the following questions.

1. Why did the soldiers who discovered the camps have difficulty believing what they were seeing? In their reports, why did they qualify their observations about the camps? Lee Miller, a former model for *Vogue,* became a war correspondent in 1944. While on assignment, she photographed Dachau, the German concentration camp. She sent her photographs to British *Vogue* and followed with a telegram that said: "I IMPLORE YOU TO BELIEVE THIS IS TRUE." Why would she find it necessary to have a cable like this accompany her photographs? How do comments like this help explain America's initial reluctance to believe in the existence of the camps?

2. Do you think the concentration camps were deliberately designed to look like American Civilian Conservation Corps camps? Why might they have been designed that way?

3. What did Eisenhower mean when he said that even if the Americans did not know what they were fighting for, they at least now knew what they were fighting against?

Internet Activity

Find out more about the U.S. Holocaust Museum in Washington, DC, by visiting its Web site at www.ushmm.org. The museum maintains an online exhibit. Write a short paragraph about your reaction to the online exhibit.

READING

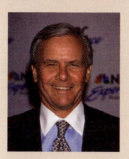

"Tom Broderick in so many ways embodies the best qualities of his generation. . . . He didn't blame the world for his condition."

TUNING IN TO READING

Tom Brokaw wrote the book *The Greatest Generation* to "pay tribute to those men and women who have given us the lives we have today." These individuals from the World War II era are now in their seventies and eighties and are, according to the Department of Veterans' Affairs, dying at the rate of about 32,000 a month. Brokaw dedicated himself to memorializing their stories of sacrifice, honor, and courage before it was too late.

BIO-SKETCH

Tom Brokaw anchored the *NBC Nightly News* for 21 years and is now retired from that position. He has received many journalism awards, including the Peabody Award for a report called "To Be an American," and seven Emmy Awards. He considers the publication of *The Greatest Generation,* from which this article is taken, to be one of his greatest achievements.

NOTES ON VOCABULARY

abundant   plentiful; more than enough. The word comes from the Latin word *abundo,* meaning "to overflow." In Latin, *ab* means "from" and *unda* means "to billow, wave, or surge." The word *abundant* refers to a profusion of things "as plentiful as the waves of the sea."

cocky   conceited; arrogant. The word refers to a rooster's proud strut around the barnyard and his early morning cry of "cock-a-doodle-doo" as he surveys his domain.

appalled   caused to feel shock or horror. The word *appalled* is derived from the Latin words *ad,* meaning "to," and *palleo,* meaning "to be pale."

braille   a system of printing and writing for the blind that relies on raised dots that represent numbers and letters that can be identified by touch. This type of writing was developed in a primitive form by the French military. It consisted of a series of raised marks on cardboard that could be passed in darkness and decoded by sentries on duty without resorting to illumination. Later, the inventor, Louis Braille, refined the system that bears his name.

Thomas Broderick

Tom Brokaw

IN WORLD WAR II, MORE THAN 292,000 Americans were killed in battle, and more than 1.7 million returned home physically affected in some way, from minor afflictions to blindness or missing limbs or paralysis, battle-scarred and exhausted, but oh so happy and relieved to be home. They had survived an extraordinary ordeal, but now they were eager to reclaim their ordinary lives of work, family, church,

The National World War II Memorial
The memorial in Washington, DC, was opened in 2004.

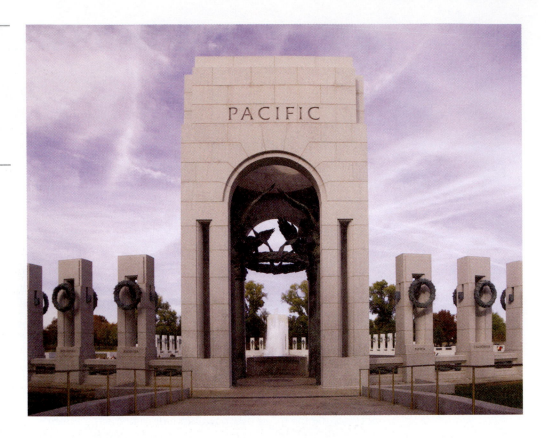

and community. The war had taught them what mattered most in their lives, and they wanted now to settle down and live.

2   Thomas Broderick was a nineteen-year-old premed student at Xavier College in Cincinnati in 1942, trying to decide which branch of the service fit his sense of adventure. This son of a south Chicago working-class family was bright and ambitious, so he enlisted in the Merchant Marine. "They gave us the best deal," he said. "If you didn't like it, you could quit." After ten weeks of training, he went on a mission to North Africa on a supply ship. The pay was excellent. The food was abundant. He had a private room on the officers' deck of his ship, the *John W. Brown,* but the trip was long and boring. He wanted out of the Merchant Marine. He wanted to join the Airborne so he could be like those cocky paratroopers he saw stationed in Algiers. "I'd never even been in a plane before," he says, "but it was the challenge I wanted."

3   His superiors in the Merchant Marine were astonished. Here he was, ready to go back to the security of the Merchant Marine Academy for another eighteen months of accelerated training, and he wanted to quit to join one of the most dangerous outfits in the service. His officer offered him a thirty-day furlough to think it over. Broderick said, "No, my mind's made up." When he returned home, his parents were equally appalled. When he told his draft board what he wanted, the clerk said, "You're nuts. I'll give you another month before we draft you, so you can change your mind." Broderick declined, saying he wanted in now.

4   Tom Broderick spent seventeen weeks in basic training for the infantry in Mineral Wells, Texas, before heading to Fort Benning, Georgia, to become a member of the 82nd Airborne. When he finished his training, a captain offered him an instructor's job and the rank of sergeant. Again Broderick refused the safer alternative, saying he wanted to stay with his outfit and go overseas.

5 Broderick's unit shipped out to England as replacements for the 82nd Airborne men lost in the Normandy invasion. In September, Broderick made his first jump into combat, in Holland. He was in the thick of it immediately, the battle of Arnhem. It was a joint mission of American and British paratroopers, and their objective was to take the Nijmegen bridge to help pave the Allies' way into Germany and to discourage any German counterattack. "We jumped at about five hundred feet because we wanted to be a low target. It was one-thirty in the afternoon."

6 "The first German I saw I couldn't shoot, because he was riding a bicycle away from me. I couldn't shoot at him because he wasn't shooting at me. Things were different ten minutes later. There were Germans all over the place—they outnumbered us about forty thousand to twenty-eight thousand. It was combat morning, noon, and night."

7 On the fifth day, Broderick made a mistake that would alter his life forever. "I remember being in the foxhole and . . . I was lining up my aim on a German. I got a little high in the foxhole and I got shot clean through the head—through the left temple."

8 A Catholic chaplain arrived to administer the last rites, but after slipping into unconsciousness, Broderick somehow managed to stay alive until he awoke a few days later in a British hospital. He was relieved to be out of combat, but he had a problem: he couldn't see. Why not? he asked. His doctors told him, "When the hemorrhage clears up, you'll be all right." Broderick continued to believe them until he was sent to Dibble General Hospital in Menlo Park, California, one of the two facilities in the nation treating blind veterans.

9 Finally a doctor told him the truth. He would be blind forever. "I was stunned. I cried, 'Aren't you going to do anything?'" He rushed to a fellow veteran who had been hospitalized with him in England, a man recovering from shrapnel in one of his eyes. "I just cried and cried, and he said to me, 'We knew the whole time, Tom; we just didn't want to tell you.'"

10 Broderick was angry and disoriented. When the Army made him take a rehabilitation course in Connecticut, he said, "I rebelled—I just didn't want to learn braille. I told them I was going to work in my dad's trucking business just so I could get out of there."

11 It didn't get much better when he returned to Chicago. He enrolled in Loyola University, and the Veterans Administration hired a reader for him. But after only seven weeks, Broderick dropped out and went to work for his father. His downslide continued. "They didn't know what to do with me. Dad had me taking orders on the phone because I could still write. But then I heard of people having to call back to get the orders straightened out. I thought, 'Hell, I'm screwing up.'" He quit after a month.

12 Broderick realized he'd have to learn braille. His Veterans Administration counselor also recommended he enroll in a class in insurance sales, a fast-growing field in postwar America. He learned the insurance business by day and braille by night. Before long the VA found him a job with an elderly insurance broker in his neighborhood. Not too long after that, Broderick had established his own insurance business. He was no longer the young man angry at his fate. He was now prepared to accept his blindness and get on with his life.

13 Broderick worked six days a week. When he wasn't taking orders by phone with his braille machine and dictating them to his secretary, he was making house calls at

night. He quickly developed a very keen audio sense; many customers he dealt with on the phone were astonished when they finally met him. He'd quickly call out their name when he heard their voice. Until that point, they had no idea he was blind.

14   Tom met his wife, Eileen, on a blind date, no irony intended. Eileen was a twenty-three-year-old nurse and Tom was twenty-seven. She fell in love instantly. "You didn't think about his blindness. It just didn't seem to matter. He was so unique. He ran a business by himself and didn't need help from anyone, although it was a little tricky when we went out alone. I'd have to take him to the men's room and ask someone to take him in. I'd stand outside. I think, being a nurse, I was a little more flexible. I understood that it was all just mechanics."

15   During his introduction to the world of the blind at the rehabilitation center in Connecticut, Broderick and his friends formed an informal organization to help each other adjust to their new realities. It became the Blinded Veterans Association, and Broderick decided that he should share the lessons of his new life with other veterans who were struggling with their blindness. He began making trips to Chicago-area rehabilitation programs, counseling sightless veterans on the career possibilities in insurance, mortgage sales, and car financing—the hot financial service fields as America exploded out of the cities and into the suburbs.

16   "I'd tell them about my own struggle—how I was young when I became blind and I knew how they felt. I brought some of them down to my office so they could see the braille machine and what was possible. I don't feel any special bond with other blind organizations or blind people, but I wanted to help veterans. You have to do it. It was no big deal, really."

17   Tom's son Dan remembers that, during Vietnam, the nearby Veterans Administration office would send over young men who'd lost their sight in the war. "When you first saw them you thought you were at a wake—some of them were suicidal, with their eyes blown out. Mom would go out and get a case of beer, and they'd sit on the porch with my dad and listen to the White Sox game. Then he'd navigate 'em around our house to show them what we had—five bedrooms, a big house. By the end of the night they'd be back on the porch, drinking beer but laughing now."

18   Another son, Scott: "You know how everyone says their dad is the best. Well do you know how many people I've heard that from about my dad? Friends, neighbors, clients. Every kid thinks it, but to hear it from other people is so gratifying. He never let his disability get in the way of anything."

19   Tom Broderick in so many ways embodies the best qualities of his generation. He was so eager to get involved in the war that he enlisted in two branches of the service. He was gravely wounded, but once he got over the initial understandable anger, he set out to be the best husband, father, businessman, and citizen he could be—sight or no sight. He didn't grow bitter and dependent on others. He didn't blame the world for his condition.

20   A common lament of the World War II generation is the absence today of personal responsibility. Broderick remembers listening to an NPR broadcast and hearing an account of how two boys found a loaded gun in one of their homes. The visiting boy accidentally shot his friend. The victim's father was on the radio, talking about suing the gun manufacturer. That got to Tom Broderick. "So," he said, "here's this man talking about suing and he's not accepting responsibility for having a loaded gun in the house."

21   Tom knows something about personal responsibility. He's been forced to live as a blind man for more than fifty years, and when asked about the moment when the lights were literally shot out of his eyes, he says only, "It was my fault for getting too high in the foxhole. That happens sometimes."

From *The Greatest Generation* by Tom Brokaw. Copyright © 1998 by Tom Brokaw. Used by permission of Random House, Inc.

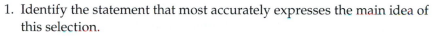 **COMPREHENSION CHECKUP**

Directions: List some inferences you can make about how Brokaw feels about Broderick.

_____

_____

Multiple Choice

Directions: For each item, write the letter corresponding to the best answer.

_**A**_   1. Identify the statement that most accurately expresses the main idea of this selection.
    a. After a war injury caused Thomas Broderick to lose his sight, his strength and determination enabled him to lead a productive and prosperous life.
    b. War injuries can be devastating.
    c. Many heroic individuals served during World War II.
    d. Thomas Broderick was involved in founding the Blinded Veterans Association.

_**d**_   2. The reference to Broderick's efforts to learn the insurance business during the day and braille at night was used to illustrate
    a. Broderick's determination to stand on his own two feet.
    b. Broderick's acceptance of his fate and willingness to get on with his life.
    c. Broderick's willingness to take advantage of the resources of the Veterans Administration.
    d. all of the above.

_**b d**_   3. All of the following could help account for Broderick's success as a businessman *except*
    a. Broderick's decision to not let his disability get in the way of his goals.
    b. Broderick's decision to work six days a week and make house calls at night.
    c. Broderick's entrance into a fast-growing new field.
    d. Broderick's reluctance to learn braille.

_**b**_   4. Paragraph 17 contrasts
    a. the difference between the Vietnam veterans and the World War II veterans.
    b. the Vietnam veterans' feelings at the beginning and at the end of a visit with Broderick.
    c. the difference between the young and the old.
    d. none of the above.

_**A**_   5. As used in paragraph 3, the word *furlough* most nearly means
    a. leave of absence.
    b. tour of duty.

c. paid vacation at a resort.
d. sightseeing trip.

_____ 6. The author's primary purpose in writing this selection is
    a. to illustrate the need for continued benefits for veterans who suffer disabilities during a war.
    b. to persuade young people to avoid enlisting in dangerous branches of the armed services.
    c. to inform readers of the life of a unique member of the World War II generation.
    d. to convince readers of the importance of avoiding World War III.

_____ 7. Which one of the following statements best expresses the viewpoint of Thomas Broderick?
    a. "I had a good time in combat."
    b. "I was able to become self-sufficient with no help from anyone."
    c. "I won't let my blindness stop me from achieving satisfaction in life."
    d. "All I care about is running a successful business."

_____ 8. From this selection, you could infer that
    a. Broderick is sorry he got involved in the war.
    b. Broderick has the respect, love, and support of his family.
    c. Broderick feels a real need to support blind veterans.
    d. both b and c.

_____ 9. The author of this selection probably feels that
    a. it's a mistake to become a mentor to others who are struggling to accept a limitation.
    b. accepting personal responsibility for one's own actions is an admirable trait.
    c. wars are best fought by the young and the reckless.
    d. Thomas Broderick should have stayed in the Merchant Marine.

_____ 10. From this selection you could conclude that
    a. Broderick is well satisfied with his life.
    b. Broderick feels that war is a mistake.
    c. Broderick is bitter about his inability to become a doctor.
    d. Broderick is reluctant to offer advice to others who find themselves in a similar situation.

True or False

Directions: Indicate whether each statement is true or false by writing **T** or **F** in the space provided.

_____ 11. The Merchant Marine suited Thomas Broderick's need for a challenge.

_____ 12. Broderick's parents, superiors in the Merchant Marine, and draft board were amazed by his desire to join the Airborne.

_____ 13. Broderick had participated in actual combat for only a short time before he was injured.

_____ 14. Broderick was initially angry and confused about his injury.

_____ 15. After his accident, Broderick achieved success in his father's trucking business.

Vocabulary in Context

Directions: Try to define the following vocabulary words by using context clues from the selection. See if you can come up with your own definition before consulting a dictionary. The number in parentheses indicates the paragraph in which the vocabulary word is located.

1. afflictions (1) _____
2. rites (8) _____
3. shrapnel (9) _____
4. straightened (11) _____
5. dictating (13) _____
6. unique (14) _____
7. lament (20) _____

Written Assignment

Have you ever found your life headed in the wrong direction? If you have, what did you do to turn your life around? Did anyone help you put your life on a more positive path? How has this change in direction affected your life today? Write a couple of paragraphs describing your experience.

Internet Activity

1. The Braille Institute, founded in 1919, has provided services to people who are visually impaired. Consult its Web site at:

   www.brailleinstitute.org

   Write a paragraph describing its history and services.

2. The National World War II Memorial in Washington, DC, opened to the public in April 2004. It is dedicated to all who served in World War II and all other citizens, corporations, and foundations that helped in the war effort. To obtain more information about the memorial, go to:

   www.wwiimemorial.com

   Print a page you find interesting. State the main idea and several supporting details. What inferences or conclusions can you logically make about the material you have read?

Chapter Summary and Review

In Chapter 5, you learned how to draw inferences from a variety of sources, such as textbook material, literature, and cartoons. Based on the material in Chapter 5, answer the following.

Short Answer

Directions: Answer the following briefly, in a few words or phrases.

1. Explain what an inference is. __Geeks_____

   ____Guess_____

Vocabulary in Context

Directions: Choose one of the following words to complete the sentences. Use each word only once.

directly	experiences	inferences	lines

2. In drawing inferences, we make use of our _____ in life.

3. To figure out an idea that is not _____ stated, we have to read between the _____.

4. We draw _____ every day of our lives.

VOCABULARY   **Unit 3**

What does the word *quadricentennial* mean?

_____

When will your state celebrate its quadricentennial?

_____

In this unit, we will continue working with word parts involving number and amount.

centi—100   milli—1,000

century	100 years. In the year 2001, we entered the 21st *century*.
centennial	A 100-year anniversary. *Ann* and *enn* mean "year." Since *centi* means "100" and *enn* means "year," we are simply putting word parts together to make a word meaning 100 years. In 1876, we celebrated the first *centennial* of our independence from England.
bicentennial	A 200-year anniversary.
tricentennial	A 300-year anniversary.
cent	A penny is called a *cent* because it is 1/100 of a dollar.

centipede—The largest centipede in the world, *Himantarum gabrielis*, has 171 to 177 pairs of legs and is found in southern Europe.

centipede   *Centi* means "100" and *ped* means "foot," so a *centipede* would be an animal with 100 feet. *Actually, centipedes don't have 100 feet; they just look like they do.*

Giant Centipede

centigrade   Divided into 100 parts. On the centigrade, or Celsius, scale, water freezes at 0 degrees and boils at 100 degrees. While most other nations use the *centigrade* scale, the United States uses the Fahrenheit scale. On this scale, water freezes at 32 degrees and boils at 212 degrees.

TRIVIA QUESTION

On the *centigrade* scale, at what temperature does beer freeze? (Answer at the end of this unit.)

centimeter	A unit of length in the metric system; 1/100 of a meter, or approximately two-fifths of an inch.
centenarian	A 100-year-old person. There are more women who are *centenarians* than there are men.
millennium	A period of 1,000 years.
millipede	An animal that looks like it has 1,000 feet. The technical difference between a *centipede* and a *millipede* is that a *millipede* has two pairs of legs on each segment, while a *centipede* has only one pair of legs on each segment.
millimeter	1/1000 of a meter. Metric wrenches used for working on bikes and cars made in Europe and Asia are measured in *millimeters*.
million	The word *million* was probably derived by multiplying 1,000 × 1,000. Maybe this will help you remember that *milli* means "1,000."

multi—many   graph—write

poly—many   gam—marriage

multiply	A system of repeating addition many times ($3 \times 3 = 3 + 3 + 3$).
multimedia	A combination of many media. A *multimedia* computer presentation might appeal to more than one of our senses simultaneously, with film, music, and special lighting all in one performance.
multilateral	Many-sided. Remember that *lat* means "side." A treaty signed by more than two nations would be a *multilateral* treaty.
polygon	A many-sided figure. A decagon is a *polygon* that has 10 sides and 10 angles. The simplest *polygon* is the triangle.
polygraph	You probably know that *polygraph* machines are used on someone suspected of lying. *Graph* means "write." The machine works by recording (writing) the many bodily changes (blood pressure, respiration, pulse rate, perspiration) thought to occur when a person lies in answering questions.
polygamy	Being married to more than one person at the same time.
polyglot	Speaking or writing several languages.

polyglot—Ziad Fazah of Brazil is a true polyglot. He can speak and write in 58 languages.

semi—half   demi—half   hemi—half

semester	Half an academic year.
semicircle	Half a circle.
semiprofessional	Not fully professional. The baseball player was not good enough to play professionally, so he played in a *semiprofessional* league, or what is commonly called the semipros.
semicentennial	Half of 100 years, or 50 years; a 50th anniversary. Here you are just putting together *semi* meaning "half," *cent* meaning "100," and *enn* meaning "year."
semilunar	Shaped like a half-moon; crescent-shaped.
hemisphere	Half of a sphere or a globe. We live in the Western *Hemisphere*. The word *hemisphere* is also used when referring to the left half or right half of our brain.
demitasse	A small (half) cup. This cup is used for drinking very strong black coffee similar to espresso. A *demitasse* is usually served following dinner.

equator—The earth is not a perfect sphere because it is slightly flattened at the poles. The greatest circumference of the earth is at the equator and is 24,902 miles.

equi—equal

Don't get *equi* confused with *equus,* which means "horse." *Equestrian* competition involves horse-riding.

equal	Evenly proportioned.
equator	The imaginary line around the middle of the earth that splits it into two equal parts.
equidistant	Equally distant.

equinox	*Equi* meaning "equal" and *nox* meaning "night." The *equinox* happens twice a year, once in March and then again in September, when day and night are of exactly *equal* length.
equilibrium	The state of being evenly balanced. Your *equilibrium,* or balance, is controlled by your inner ear.
equilateral	A figure having *equal* sides. A square is an *equilateral*.

omni—all

omnivorous	Eating all sorts of food, especially both animal and vegetable food. Human beings are *omnivorous*.
omnipotent	All-powerful. Many religions consider God to be *omnipotent*.
omniscient	All-knowing. The professor thought he was *omniscient* in his subject area.
omnipresent	Present in all places at the same time. Cartoons are *omnipresent* on TV on Saturday mornings.

ambi, amphi—both; around

These two word parts have the same meaning, one coming from Latin and the other from Greek.

ambidextrous	Able to use both hands equally well.
ambiguous	Vague; having two or more meanings. Because the teacher's directions were *ambiguous,* many students failed to complete the assignment correctly.
ambivalent	*Ambi* means "both" and *valens* means "worth," so *ambivalent* means "an inability to decide between two conflicting feelings or thoughts." My parents are *ambivalent* about my getting a job. On the one hand, they would like me to earn money; on the other, they think my grades will suffer.
amphibian	An organism that is able to live or operate on land and in the water. A salamander is an *amphibian*.

An Outdoor Amphitheater in Greece

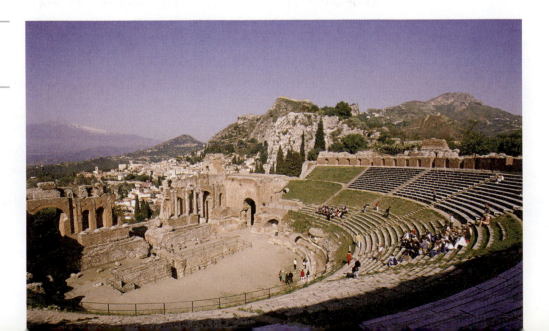

amphitheater	A type of theater or stadium that has seats going all around the stage or arena. The Greeks and Romans built outdoor *amphitheaters,* many of which are still in use today. You may have an *amphitheater* in your hometown for summer concerts.

Exercise 1

Directions: In the blanks below, write the word from the list that best completes the sentence. Use each word only once.

ambidextrous	amphitheater	centenarian	century	equal
equilibrium	million	multilateral	polygraph	semester

1. Sarah Delany, the co-author of *Having Our Say—The Delany Sisters' First 100 Years,* is a good example of a _____.

2. While many religions consider the wife to be _____ to the husband in the spousal relationship, some religions say a wife "should submit herself graciously" to her husband's leadership.

3. Because of her work for the poor of India, *Time* magazine named Mother Teresa one of the most inspirational people of the 20th _____.

4. The special prosecutor wants those individuals requesting immunity from prosecution to submit to a complete _____ examination.

5. If a basketball player can dribble and pass the ball equally well with either hand, we would probably call the player _____.

6. Marcus was relieved to have the spring _____ of college over so that he could relax over a long summer break.

7. A retired couple just won over a(n) _____ dollars in the New Jersey Lottery.

8. The old movie classic *Ben-Hur* has a famous chariot race that takes place in a Roman _____.

9. A(n) _____ environmental treaty was signed by six nations.

10. In order to perform well on the balance beam, a gymnast must have a superb sense of _____.

Exercise 2

Directions: In the blanks below, write the word from the list that best completes the sentence. Use each word only once.

ambiguous	centigrade	centimeters	centipede	equator
hemisphere	omnipresent	omniscient	omnivorous	polygamy
polyglot	semiprofessional			

1. We turned down the wrong street because the directions that the attendant at the gas station gave us were _____.

2. Young children believe their parents to be _____ because they expect them to know the answers to any question that they ask.

3. The _____ thermometer, devised by Swedish astronomer Anders Celsius, is now used throughout most of the world.

4. The United States and Canada are located in the Western _____.

5. If _____ were allowed in the United States, do you think many men would have more than one wife?

6. Ants seem to be _____ at most picnics.

7. The _____ is a segmented, nocturnal animal known for its poisonous bite.

8. The _____ is equidistant from the North Pole and the South Pole.

9. My dog Cookie is _____; she'll eat anything.

10. A college teacher who speaks five languages fluently qualifies as a(n) _____.

11. The movie *Bull Durham*, starring Kevin Costner, is about a(n) _____ baseball team.

12. A typical pencil is 19 _____ long.

Vocabulary Unit 3

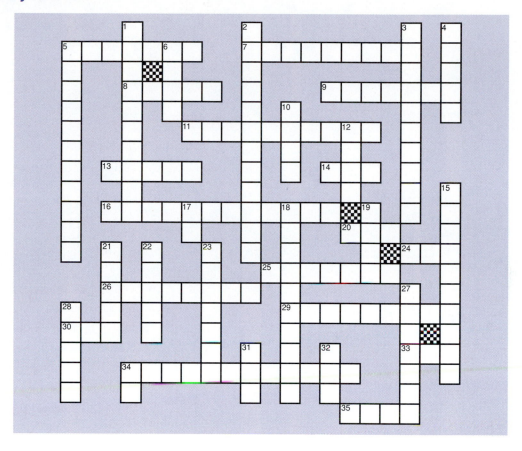

ACROSS CLUES

5. This event happens in September and March.

7. This "critter" has two pairs of legs on each of its segments.

8. A root word meaning "moon."

9. The imaginary line dividing the Northern and Southern Hemispheres.

11. 1/100 of a meter.

13. A word part meaning "1,000."

14. A word part meaning "two."

16. Being able to use both hands equally well.

20. The abbreviation for what was once the ninth month.

24. The abbreviation for what was once the eighth month.

25. 1,000 × 1,000.

26. A person who can speak many languages.

29. A "critter" that appears to have 100 legs.

30. A word part meaning "one."

33. A word part meaning "three."

34. 200-year anniversary.

35. A word part meaning "many."

DOWN CLUES

1. 1,000 years.

2. In ancient Greece, you might have gone to a(n) _____ to watch a play.

3. Water freezes at 0 degrees on this scale.

4. A word part meaning "four."

5. A square is a(n) _____ figure.

6. Word part meaning "all."

10. A word part meaning "both."

12. A word part meaning "equal."

15. Movies are _____ experiences because they combine images and sound.

17. A word part meaning "two."

18. All-knowing.

19. A word part meaning "one."

21. A word part meaning "both."

22. A word part for "many."

23. A figure with many sides.

27. In the year 2001, we entered the 21st _____.

28. A word part meaning "five."

31. An abbreviation for what was once the 10th month.

32. A word part meaning "marriage."

34. A word part meaning "two."

6

Figurative Language

CHAPTER PREVIEW

In this chapter, you will

- Learn the difference between literal and figurative comparisons.

- Learn about similes, metaphors, and personification.

- Learn about extended metaphors.

- Become familiar with the use of symbolism in writing.

- Become familiar with literary allusions.

- Become familiar with imagery.

Figures of Speech—Similes, Metaphors, and Personification

In order to read well, you must become a *critical* reader. This means understanding not only the author's literal meaning but also the author's implied or inferential meaning. Many authors use figures of speech or figurative language to make their writing more colorful and interesting. These **figures of speech** are expressions in which words are

Figurative Language Chart

COMPARISONS

Literal
(Compares things from the same category)
1. Angie is as skinny as her sister.

Figurative
(Compares things from different categories)
1. Angie is as skinny as a telephone pole.
   (Simile: A is like B.)
   Uses *like*, *as*, or *as if* to make the comparison
2. Angie is a telephone pole.
   (Metaphor: A is B.)
   Uses a state of being verb to make the comparison—
   am, is, are, was, were
3. The telephone pole reaches its long arms to the sky.
   (Personification: Something that is not alive takes on human attributes or "person" characteristics.)
   Note: Personification is a special kind of metaphor.

used regardless of their true meanings in order to create a special meaning or effect. Often this specialized language enables the author to more clearly convey meaning by making a comparison to something that is more familiar or readily understood.

When words are used conventionally and mean exactly what they say, they are being used *literally*. In figurative language, the words have been stretched to mean something beyond what they say. As an illustration of the difference between literal and figurative, study the *Shoe* cartoon below. In it, Loon takes something literally that is meant to be a figurative expression.

Shoe

Shoe. © MacNelly. King Features Syndicate

Although writers provide clues to the meaning of their figurative expressions, the critical reader must study the entire context of the expression in order to infer the meaning.

Some frequently used figures of speech are similes, metaphors, and personification. A **simile** is a figure of speech that compares two dissimilar things. Similes usually use the words *like, as,* or *as if* to show the comparison. "Sam is as energetic as Mary" is a comparison, not a simile. "Sam is as energetic as the Energizer bunny" is a simile. Both poems and prose contain similes.

Explain the meaning of each of these similes:

1. She is as confused as a rat in a maze. _She doesn't know what to do_

2. His muscles are like iron bands. _he has strong muscles_

3. The fullback charged as if he were a locomotive. _charged with a lot of pow_

A **metaphor** connects two unlike things directly without using *like, as,* or *as if*. One thing is spoken of as though it were something else. In "Dreams," the poet Langston Hughes uses a metaphor to show the hopelessness of a life without any dreams:

> Hold fast to dreams
> For if dreams die
> **Life is a broken-winged bird**
> **That cannot fly.**
>
> Hold fast to dreams
> For when dreams go
> **Life is a barren field**
> **Frozen with snow.**

"Dreams," from *The Collected Poems of Langston Hughes* by Langston Hughes, edited by Arnold Rampersad with David Roessel, Associate Editor, copyright © 1994 by The Estate of Langston Hughes. Used by permission of Alfred A. Knopf, a division of Random House, Inc., and Harold Ober Associates Incorporated.

An **extended metaphor** sustains the comparison for several lines or for the entire poem or story.

In the following excerpt from *How Good Do We Have to Be?*, Rabbi Harold S. Kushner uses an extended metaphor to express his feelings about life. What comparison is he making?

> Life is not a spelling bee, where no matter how many words you have gotten right, if you make one mistake you are disqualified. Life is more like a baseball season, where even the best team loses one-third of its games and even the worst team has its days of brilliance. Our goal is not to go all year without ever losing a game. Our goal is to win more than we lose, and if we can do that consistently enough, then when the end comes, we will have won it all.

> From Rabbi Harold S. Kushner, *How Good Do We Have to Be?* Boston: Little, Brown, 1996, pp. 180–181.

Now create your own metaphor for life. Include a short explanation of why you have chosen this metaphor.

Example: Life is a tidal wave; it doesn't stop for anybody or anything.

Life is a blind fold, you never know whats going to happen untill you take it off

Personification is a type of figurative language that gives human attributes to a nonhuman subject. When Longfellow said, "Time has laid his hand upon my heart, gently," he was personifying the concept of time and his feelings about growing old. In the poem "The Eagle" by Alfred, Lord Tennyson, the first line of each stanza makes use of personification:

> **He clasps the crag with crooked hands;**
> Close to the sun in lonely lands,
> Ringed with the azure world he stands.

> **The wrinkled sea beneath him crawls;**
> He watches from his mountain walls,
> And like a thunderbolt he falls.

1. What figure of speech is the last line of the poem? *Simile*
2. What does it mean to fall like a thunderbolt? *to fall fast and hard*

Now choose five inanimate objects, and write a sentence giving each object a human attribute.

Example: My computer sighed, wheezed, and then expired.

1. _____
2. _____
3. _____
4. _____
5. _____

Finally, can you find the figures of speech in the cartoon below?

Shoe by Chris Cassatt and Gary Brookins

Shoe. © MacNelly. King Features Syndicate

Exercise 1: Literal or Figurative Comparisons

Directions: Indicate whether the comparison is literal or figurative by writing **L** or **F** in the space provided.

Reminder: Not all comparisons are figures of speech. A *figure of speech* makes a comparison between unlike things. A *literal comparison* compares things that are from the same category.

Example:
Lucille is as thin as a bookmark. (F) Different categories
Lucille is as thin as her grandmother. (L) Same category

_F_   1. Evergreen trees bent *like people leaning out of the window.*

_F_   2. The baby's breathing was choked and rough, like something pulled through tightly packed gravel.

_L_   3. She was as strong-willed as her father.

_F_   4. The animal was as white as cream cheese.

_L_   5. He was eating as well and sleeping as well as the other students.

_F_   6. I am a willow swaying gently in the wind.

____   7. The waves beside them danced.

_L_   8. He complained all day as if no one had anything better to do than listen to him.

_L_   9. Like her brother before her, she chose to live at home while attending college.

_L_ 10. A gray mist rose on the sea's face.

List the numbers of the sentences containing a personification. _5_

List the number of the sentence containing a metaphor. _4_

Change the words in italics in sentence 1 to make an original simile.

Reminder: You need something that bends or is bent.

New simile: _____

Exercise 2: Creating Original Comparisons

Comparisons are considered to be **clichés** when they are trite, overused, worn, or hackneyed. To better understand a cliché, read the following riddles. What do these riddles have in common?

1. Why did the judge wear a catcher's mitt?

   The ball was in his court.

2. How come a pickle doesn't sweat?

   It's cool as a cucumber.

3. When does a tea bag tremble?

   When it's in hot water.

Answer: They all have clichés as punch lines.

From Patricia T. O'Conner, *Woe Is I Jr.* New York: Penguin, 2007, p. 122.

Directions: Read the following clichés and try to create a fresh or original comparison.

1. thin as a rail _He is thin as a rail_
2. red as a beet _The teacher had him red as a beet_
3. flat as a pancake _That bug was flat as a pancake_
4. nutty as a fruitcake _You are as nutty as a fruitcake_
5. light as a feather _That board is light as a feather_

Now rewrite this paragraph by substituting original comparisons of your own for the italicized trite expressions.

It was late at night, and I was working alone at the office. *Quick as a flash,*

fast as lightning

a robber dashed in and pulled a gun on me, demanding that I open the office safe. I managed to stay *cool as a cucumber* despite his gun at my temple

cold as ice

and his *grip like a vise* around my chest. Unfortunately, while escorting me

grasp like a constrictor

over to the wall safe, he knocked my glasses off my face and stepped on them with a resounding crunch. There I was *blind as a bat,* unable to see

the numbers well enough to open the lock. I began to *sweat like a pig,*

sweat bullets

realizing I would soon be *dead as a doornail,* when without any warning

dead as a corpse

the police came to my rescue. To conclude my story, I am now as *happy as a lark.*

happy as a bat eating bug

A special type of comparison is called an **analogy.** A writer uses an analogy to make something understandable or clear by comparing it to something that is different from it but that has something in common with it. Sometimes, however, an attempt to create a fresh and original comparison can go too far. These analogies recently posted on the Internet were labeled "the worst ever written in high-school essays." Try conveying the same information in a meaningful comparison of your own.

1. Her hair glistened in the rain like nose hair after a sneeze.

   _____

2. He was as tall as a six-foot-three-inch tree.

   _____

3. The politician was gone but unnoticed, like the period after the Dr. on a Dr. Pepper can.

   _____

4. His thoughts tumbled in his head, making and breaking alliances like underpants in a dryer without Cling Free.

   _____

5. The little boat gently drifted across the pond exactly the way a bowling ball wouldn't.

   _____

Exercise 3: Analyzing Figurative Comparisons

Directions: Each of the following sentences contains a figurative comparison. In the space provided, write down the real subject, what it is compared to, and the meaning of the sentence.

Example

Oliver Wendell Holmes once attended a meeting in which he was the shortest man present. "Doctor Holmes," quipped a friend, "I should think you'd feel rather small among us big fellows."

"I do," retorted Holmes, "I feel like a dime among a lot of pennies."

Subject: Dr. Holmes

Compared to: dime among pennies

Meaning: Dr. Holmes did not let his short stature bother him. Just as a dime, though smaller than a penny, is worth more, Holmes is "worth more" than his friends.

1. Whenever I try to speak to him, his mind wanders everywhere, like a cow following green grass.

   Subject: _I try to speak to him_

   Compared to: _Cow following Green grass_

   Meaning: _he can not focus on one thing_

2. Her face looked like it had just come out of a dryer and needed to be pressed.

   Subject: _Her face_

   Compared to: _dryer_

   Meaning: _____

3. He bobbed through life's turbulences like driftwood on the sea.

   Subject: _He_

Compared to: _drift wood_

Meaning: _he didn't let turbulences get to him_

4. His grandparents' home was like a giant security blanket.

Subject: _his grand parents home_

Compared to: _giant security blanket_

Meaning: _his grand parent's house was a place of refuge_

5. He struggled to extricate himself from the powerful undertow like a fly caught in a spider's web.

Subject: _him_

Compared to: _fly caught in a spider web_

Meaning: _trying to get out of a under tow_

6. The car ran the red light like a bull charging a matador.

Subject: _the car_

Compared to: _bull charging a matador_

Meaning: _____

Exercise 4: Figurative Comparisons in Fiction

Directions: The figurative expressions (set in **boldface**) in the following excerpts were chosen by the authors because they create a fresh effect or demonstrate a new insight. Determine whether the expression is a metaphor, simile, or personification, and then decide what image or insight the author is trying to convey.

A.   For speech is so much more than words and sentences. It seemed to me that regional speech is in the process of disappearing, not gone but going. Forty years of radio and twenty years of television must have this impact. Communications must destroy localness, by a slow, inevitable process. I can remember a time when I could almost pinpoint a man's place of origin by his speech. That is growing more difficult now and will in some foreseeable future become impossible. **It is a rare house or building that is not rigged with spiky combers of the air.** Radio and television speech becomes standardized, perhaps better English than we have ever used. **Just as our bread, mixed and baked, packaged and sold without benefit of accident or human frailty, is uniformly good and uniformly tasteless, so will our speech become one speech.**

From John Steinbeck, *Travels with Charlie.* New York: Bantam Books, 1972, p. 106.

1. What is Steinbeck referring to when he uses the expression "spiky combers of the air"? _____

2. Do you think Steinbeck is in favor of a uniform manner of speaking?
   no. he believes "speech is so much more then words in a sentence."

B.   Until I was thirteen and left Arkansas for good, the Store was my favorite place to be. Alone and empty in the mornings, **it looked like an unopened present from a stranger. Opening the front doors was pulling the ribbon off the unexpected gift.** The light would come in softly (we faced north), easing itself over the shelves of mackerel, salmon, tobacco, thread. It fell flat on the big vat of lard and by noontime during the summer the grease had softened to a thick soup. **Whenever I walked into the Store in the afternoon, I sensed that it was tired. I alone could hear the slow pulse of its job half done.** But just before bedtime, after numerous people had walked in and out, had argued over their bills, or joked about their neighbors, or just dropped in "to give Sister Henderson a 'Hi y'all,'" the promise of magic mornings returned to the Store and spread itself over the family in washed life waves.

From Maya Angelou, *I Know Why the Caged Bird Sings.* New York: Bantam Books, 1970, p. 13.

1. What does Angelou mean when she refers to the Store as "an unopened present"? Is this a simile or a metaphor? *Simile* "ever time it feels like the first time.*

2. To what does Angelou compare the opening of the front doors? Does this comparison involve a simile or a metaphor? *metaphor.*

3. What figurative device does the following phrase use: "I sensed that it [the Store] was tired"? *everyone in the store is tired*

C. **A Description of Grandma Mazur**
    Once a week Grandma Mazur went to the beauty parlor and had her hair shampooed and set. Sometimes Dolly would use a rinse and Grandma would have hair the color of an anemic apricot, but mostly Grandma lived with her natural color of steel gray. Grandma kept her hair short and permed with orderly rows of curls marching across her shiny pink scalp. The curls stayed miraculously tidy until the end of the week, when they'd begin to flatten and blend together.
    I'd always wondered how Grandma had managed this feat. And now I knew. Grandma rolled her pillow under her neck so barely any skull touched the bed. And Grandma slept like the dead. Arms crossed over her chest, body straight as a board, mouth open. Grandma never moved a muscle, and she snored like a drunken lumberjack.

From Janet Evanovich, *Four to Score.* New York: St. Martin's Press, 1998, p. 231.

1. To what does Evanovich compare her grandmother's curls? Is this comparison a simile, metaphor, or personification? *Personification.*

2. What are three similes in this excerpt?
    Grandma slept like the dead
    Body straight as a board
    Snored like a drunken lumberjack

Exercise 5: Figurative Comparisons in Nonfiction

It is important to realize that not all figures of speech come from fiction. Many writers of nonfiction also use figurative language in their writing. For example, to convey information to readers who are not well versed in scientific procedures, a science writer will often construct an appropriate metaphor. Keeping in mind that the word *metaphor* literally means "to transfer or bring across," Ted Anton and Rick McCourt, editors of *The New Science Journalists,* state that "almost every piece of really good science writing will connect its subject to an unexpected object or larger meaning."

Directions: Each of these figures of speech is taken from a scientific article. Determine what the figurative language suggests in each example, and then indicate whether the statements that follow are true or false by writing **T** or **F** in the space provided.

A. A Description of a Common Roundworm

Through a microscope, they look like tiny crystal serpents, curving and slithering across the dish with an almost drugged sluggishness, doubling back on themselves as though discovering their tails for the first time, or bumping up against a neighbor clumsily and then slowly recoiling.

Excerpt from "The Very Pulse of the Machine" from *The Beauty of the Beastly* by Natalie Angier, p. 53. Copyright © 1995 by Natalie Angier. Reprinted by permission of Houghton Mifflin Harcourt Publishing Company. All rights reserved.

_F_ 1. The roundworm moves quickly in a purposeful fashion.

_F_ 2. The roundworm appears well coordinated.

B. A Description of Proteins

The concentration of proteins in the cell is as thick as honey, and young proteins must be sequestered from the surrounding ooze. During the early stages of folding, the polypeptide may form characteristic corkscrew shapes, or linked loops that resemble a Christmas bow, or slender fingerlike projections.

Excerpt from "Chaperoning Proteins" from *The Beauty of the Beastly* by Natalie Angier, p. 70. Copyright © 1995 by Natalie Angier. Reprinted by permission of Houghton Mifflin Harcourt Publishing Company. All rights reserved.

_T_ 1. The ooze might jeopardize the development of the young proteins.

_T_ 2. Proteins are highly concentrated in cells.

C. A Description of a Bat Cave

The air screams, rustling movements feather against the skin, squeaks and screeches bounce off the stone walls, and a sweet acrid stench rolls across the room. My mouth chews the darkness like a thick paste. . . . The rock walls feel like cloth to the touch. . . . The feces and urine continue to shower down, the mites tickle the surface of my body, the atmosphere tastes like a bad meal and always the air drifting like a thick fog promises the whisper of rabies.

From Charles Bowden, "Bats" in *The New Science Journalists,* ed., Ted Anton and Rich McCourt. New York: Ballantine Books, 1995, pp. 284, 285.

_F_ 1. Bat caves are quiet, pleasant-smelling environments.

_F_ 2. Visibility is good inside the cave.

_T_ 3. Visitors emerging from a bat cave are likely to be covered in excrement.

D. A Description of the Brain

Brain is easy to define: It is the wet, oatmeal-colored organ, weighing about three pounds, that resides inside the skull. . . . Mind is not the all-knowing ruler of the brain, but a little circle of firelight in a dark, Australia-sized continent where the unconscious brain processes carry on.

From Timothy Ferris, "The Interpreter" in *The New Science Journalists,* ed., Ted Anton and Rick McCourt. New York: Ballantine Books, 1995, p. 31.

_F_ 1. The conscious mind forms a much smaller part of the operations of the brain than the unconscious.

_T_ 2. The mind is not really "running the show."

E. **A Description of Chromosomes**

Human chromosomes, shaped like cinch-waisted sausages and sequestered in nearly every cell of the body, are famed as the place where human genes reside.

Excerpt from "A Clue to Longevity" from *The Beauty of the Beastly* by Natalie Angier, p. 72. Copyright © 1995 by Natalie Angier. Reprinted by permission of Houghton Mifflin Harcourt Publishing Company. All rights reserved.

____T____ 1. The chromosomes contain human genetic material.

____F____ 2. Chromosomes reside in only a few dominant areas of the human body.

____F____ 3. The chromosome is smallest at the top and at the bottom.

F. **A Description of the Yellow Jacket**

August is official yellow jacket month, as a number of entomologists have proclaimed on their Internet Web pages, and as anybody within range of a public trash can will attest. This is the season when the wretched little biblical plagues boil forth in force, bobbing and weaving like drunken marionettes, poking in fruit stands, crash-landing on soda cans, and haughtily, viciously, wickedly stinging any human who dares to protest. Actually, it turns out that yellow jackets are not the mean-spirited vermin their victims assume them to be, but instead are family values types that struggle selflessly to support and defend their kin. They just happen to crave the same junk food we do.

From Natalie Angier, "Selfless, Helpful and Intelligent: The Wasp." From *The New York Times,* August 17, 1999. © 1999 The New York Times. All rights reserved. Used by permission and protected by the Copyright Laws of the United States. The printing, copying, redistribution, or retransmission of the Material without express written permission is prohibited. www.nytimes.com.

____T____ 1. August is the month when yellow jackets are out in force.

____F____ 2. Yellow jackets fly in direct routes.

Exercise 6: Extended Metaphors

In an extended metaphor, the figurative comparison is developed throughout the entire article. This lengthy comparison helps readers visualize the event much more clearly. As you read the following article, note the extended metaphor and then answer the questions that follow.

READING

"It became a love/hate relationship."

TUNING IN TO READING

What do you know about group support networks such as Weight Watchers and Alcoholics Anonymous? What techniques do these organizations use to help people change their destructive behaviors?

The following letter, by Robert L. Rodgers, made a powerful impression on the readers of the late syndicated advice columnist Ann Landers. It is included in *The Best of Ann Landers.*

BIO-SKETCH

Until her death in 2002, Ann Landers (Eppie Lederer) was the most widely syndicated columnist in the world. During the course of her long career (1955–2002), she dispensed witty advice to help solve the personal problems of millions of people. Her column, which ran seven days a week, ended with her death. Reflecting on her long career, she said that "while it can be a headache, it's never a bore."

READING *continued*

NOTES ON VOCABULARY

heart-breaking   causing severe emotional pain or grief. This form of hyperbole (exaggeration) first appeared in the works of Chaucer and Shakespeare. In 1913, George Bernard Shaw wrote a play titled *Heartbreak House.* And of course there is the song recorded by the king himself, Elvis Presley, titled "Heartbreak Hotel."

guts   pluck and perseverance in the face of opposition or adversity. The term dates from the mid-1900s.

been around   been present or active; gained experience or sophistication. The term dates from the first half of the 1900s and over time has acquired a negative meaning.

common-law   a marriage without a civil or religious ceremony based on a couple's living together continuously as husband and wife.

The Love of My Life

DEAR ANN LANDERS: I first met her in high school. She was older than I, and exciting. She'd been around. My parents warned me to have nothing to do with her. They claimed no good could come from our relationship.

2   But I kept meeting her on the sly. She was so sophisticated and worldly. It made me feel grown up just being with her. It was fun to take her to a party in those days. She was almost always the center of attention.

3   We began seeing more of each other after I started college. When I got a place of my own, she was a frequent guest. It wasn't long before she moved in with me. It may have been common-law, but it was heart-breaking for my parents. I kept reminding myself I wasn't a kid anymore. Besides, it was legal.

4   We lived together right through college and into my early days in business. I seldom went anywhere without her, but I wasn't blind. I knew she was unfaithful to me. What's worse, I didn't care. As long as she was there for me when I needed her (and she always was), it didn't matter.

5   The longer we lived together, the more attached I became. But it wasn't mutual. She began to delight in making me look foolish in front of my friends. But still I couldn't give her up.

6   It became a love/hate relationship. I figured out that her glamour was nothing more than a cheap mask to hide her spite and cynicism. I could no longer see her beauty after I came to know her true character.

7   But old habits are hard to break. We had invested many years in each other. Even though my relationship with her made me lose a little respect for myself, she had become the center of my life. We didn't go anywhere. We didn't do anything. We didn't have friends over. It was just the two of us. I became deeply depressed and knew that she was responsible for my misery. I finally told her I was leaving for good. It took a lot of guts, but I left.

8   I still see her around. She's as beautiful as when we met. I still miss her now and then. I'm not boasting when I say she'd take me back in a minute. But by the grace of God, I'll never take up with her again.

9   If you see her, give her my regards. I don't hate her. I just loved her too much.

Forty percent of eighth graders have consumed an alcoholic beverage.

10   Chances are you know her family. The name is Alcohol.

Robert L. Rodgers, Waco, Texas

11 **Dear Robert L. Rodgers:** I have never met her personally, but a great many people who have been intimately involved with your old love have written to say she ruined their lives. She has no class and no character and is totally ruthless.

12   You didn't mention one of the main problems she creates. It's financial. Almost everyone who becomes a victim of her charms ends up with money trouble. She's an expensive "hobby."

13   Nor did you mention what your companion of the past did to your health. Many of her close friends develop heart trouble, stomach problems, and cirrhosis of the liver.

14   I'm glad you had the strength to end the relationship. You didn't say whether you had help from Alcoholics Anonymous. Thousands of readers have told me it was the only way they could get out of her clutches.

15   Incidentally, I heard from a good source that she hated to lose you but she's not lonesome. She's on millions of guest lists around the country. In fact, they wouldn't dream of having a party without her! Funny that someone so evil and destructive continues to be so popular.

By permission of Esther P. Lederer Trust and Creators Syndicate, Inc. From *The Best of Ann Landers.* New York: Bantam Books, 1996, pp. 269–70.

  COMPREHENSION CHECKUP

Multiple Choice

Directions: For each item, write the letter corresponding to the best answer.

_____ 1. Rodgers is comparing "Alcohol" to
   a. his parents.
   b. a girlfriend.
   c. a trusted friend.
   d. none of the above.

_____ 2. Rodgers began drinking in
   a. elementary school.
   b. high school.
   c. college.
   d. his twenties.

_____ 3. Rodgers rationalized his drinking by saying that
   a. as an adult he was legally able to drink.
   b. alcohol made him feel mature.
   c. alcohol made things exciting.
   d. all of the above.

_____ 4. Which of the following does Ann Landers wonder about?
   a. Did Rodgers consult a self-help group for assistance in overcoming his addiction?
   b. Did Rodgers's alcoholism cause him health problems?

c. Did Rodgers get into trouble with the law?

d. Both a and b.

_____ 5. Which of the following is not mentioned specifically by either Rodgers or Landers as a possible consequence of misuse of alcohol?

a. financial difficulties

b. health complications

c. looking foolish in front of others

d. causing accidents

_____ 6. The idiomatic expression "on the sly" means that

a. Rodgers was using alcohol secretly.

b. Rodgers was using alcohol furtively.

c. Rodgers was using alcohol frequently.

d. both a and b.

_____ 7. The phrase that most closely means the opposite of "sophisticated and worldly" is

a. inexperienced and naive.

b. smart and powerful.

c. lazy and ignorant.

d. cheerful and knowledgeable.

_____ 8. When Rodgers says that "he wasn't blind," he means that

a. he was in a no-win situation.

b. he was ignorant of what was going on.

c. he was aware of what was going on.

d. he was feeling his way in the relationship.

_____ 9. Ann Landers implies that

a. she has never used alcohol.

b. she uses alcohol on an infrequent basis.

c. she is a frequent user of alcohol.

d. she fails to understand how someone could become addicted to alcohol.

_____ 10. Why does Ann Landers put the word *hobby* in quotation marks in paragraph 12?

a. She is quoting from someone.

b. She likes the way the word looks.

c. She means that alcohol is not really a hobby because it is destructive.

d. She doesn't approve of hobbies.

In Your Own Words

1. "It is estimated that between 9 and 10 million Americans are either alcoholics or problem drinkers" (*Targeting Wellness*, p. 246). What are some factors mentioned by Rodgers that influence the use of alcohol? How did alcohol help Rodgers relate to people?

2. Although it is often desirable to change patterns of behavior, it is seldom easy. In what ways does the letter from Rodgers illustrate the hidden pressures *not* to change?

3. Neither Rodgers nor Ann Landers mentioned two other destructive effects of alcohol: accidents and violence. Are you aware of any recent situations in which alcohol led to a serious accident? Are you aware of any recent situations in which alcohol was associated with violent or antisocial conduct? What should be the punishment for driving while intoxicated?

4. "A number of psychological traits have been closely associated with alcoholism, including deep-seated feelings of inadequacy, anxiety, and depression." How does Rodgers's letter illustrate these traits?

5. Do you think that Ann Landers's answer is what Rodgers expected? Why or why not?

6. What do you think the expression "love/hate relationship" means?

7. A surprisingly large number of young people are first exposed to either alcohol or drugs by relatives. What is your reaction to such incidents? If the child becomes addicted, should the relatives be held responsible?

Written Assignment

Directions: Complete one of the following:

1. Break into groups of four. Two students will write a paraphrase of Rodgers's letter, and two will write a paraphrase of Ann Landers's response. When you are finished, read your completed paraphrases to the class.

2. Give a short description of the consequences of being addicted to "Alcohol" that Rodgers mentions in his letter. What additional consequences are mentioned by Ann Landers?

3. The Oscar-nominated actor Robert Downey, Jr., was first introduced to marijuana at the age of 6 by his father Robert Downey, Sr. Since then he has waged a very public battle with drug addiction that has included numerous stays in drug rehabilitation facilities and increasingly longer jail sentences. What do you think should be done with individuals such as Robert Downey, Jr., who are nonviolent drug offenders? Write a few paragraphs giving your opinion.

4. Write a short letter to someone giving him or her your advice on how to deal with drug or alcohol addiction.

5. Do you personally know anyone who has had a problem with either alcohol or drugs? How did that person first get involved? Did the person seek help? Was he or she able to conquer that addiction? If so, how did he or she succeed?

Internet Activity

1. A major problem on college campuses is binge drinking. Using a search engine, type in "college binge drinking." Locate a Web site that discusses the problems associated with this type of drinking, and then write a paragraph summarizing the information. What is the relevance of this article for you, your friends, or your college?

2. In the past few years, many resource and support groups have become available to help problem drinkers. However, Alcoholics Anonymous still sets the standard for self-help groups. The Web site for this organization is:

   www.alcoholics-anonymous.org

   Go to this Web site to take an alcohol assessment test. For other self-assessment tests related to alcohol, go to a search engine and type in "tests for alcoholism."

The Use of Symbols

A **symbol** is a person, object, or event that stands for more than its literal meaning. It is representative of something else. A good symbol captures in a simple form a more complicated reality. For example, a white dove symbolizes peace, a flag symbolizes a country's values and aspirations, a budding flower may symbolize birth and new beginnings, and a logo on a shirt may signify wealth and status. Writers use symbols to create a particular mood or to reinforce a specific theme.

In his poem "The Road Not Taken," Robert Frost uses an extended metaphor to compare life to a journey along a road.

The Road Not Taken
Two roads diverged in a yellow wood,
And sorry I could not travel both
And be one traveler, long I stood
And looked down one as far as I could
To where it bent in the undergrowth;

Then took the other, as just as fair,
And having perhaps the better claim,
Because it was grassy and wanted wear;
Though as for that the passing there
Had worn them really about the same,

And both that morning equally lay
In leaves no step had trodden black.
Oh, I kept the first for another day!
Yet knowing how way leads on to way,
I doubted if I should ever come back.

I shall be telling this with a sigh
Somewhere ages and ages hence:
Two roads diverged in a wood, and I—
I took the road less traveled by,
And that has made all the difference.

The fork in the road is a more specific symbol that represents a major decision in life—a decision that must be made and that likely cannot be taken back. To preserve its symbolic value, the poem does not discuss the particulars of a decision or choice. In this way, the choice made in the poem can stand for any important choice made in life.

The ancient Greeks started the tradition of wearing wedding rings around the third finger of the left hand. They believed that finger contained a vein of love that runs directly to the heart. In actuality, blood flows to the heart through veins in all fingers on both hands.

Exercise 7: Identifying Symbols

Directions: Identify what each of these common symbols represents.

1. wedding ring _____

2. white wedding dress _____

3. rabbit's foot _____

4. American flag _____

5. Lexus or Infiniti _____

6. Springtime _____

7. skull and crossbones _____

8. gavel _____

READING

"The Germans bombed the town of Guernica. . . . Guernica was devastated and its civilian population massacred."

TUNING IN TO READING

To learn more about one of the greatest achievements of 20th-century art, read the following selection from an art history textbook.

BIO-SKETCH

Although Pablo Picasso (1881–1973) was born in Spain, he spent most of his adult life in France. His early works revealed his strong compassion for those who were poor and suffering. He once said, "Painting is stronger than me, it makes me do what it wants." One of Picasso's finest paintings, *Guernica*, is a passionate expression of social protest, which Picasso painted during the Spanish Civil War (1937). It is hard to view *Guernica* (pictured below) without vicariously experiencing the agony and destruction of war. Picasso was a dominant figure in Western art in the 20th century and is credited with helping to bring back storytelling to art.

"The more horrifying the world becomes, the more art becomes abstract."
—Pablo Picasso

NOTES ON VOCABULARY

fury   from Latin *furia* meaning "violent passion, rage, or madness." In classical mythology, the three Furies were winged female monsters with snakes for hair. Their goal was to pursue and punish those who had committed evil deeds.

procrastinate   to put off doing something unpleasant or burdensome until a future time. The word *procrastinate* can be broken down into parts, *pro* meaning "toward" and *cras* meaning "tomorrow." So when you *procrastinate,* you are pushing something toward tomorrow.

Guernica © 2003 Estate of Pablo Picasso/Artists Rights Society (ARS), New York/© Giraudon/Art Resource, NY.

Guernica

Rita Gilbert

[*Guernica*] was created by an artist whose sympathies lay with those not in power, an artist who took up his brush with a sense of fury at the "ins" who caused devastation. From his fury came one of the great masterpieces of 20th-century art. The artist was Picasso, and the painting is called *Guernica*.

2 It is necessary to know the story behind *Guernica* to understand its power. In 1937 Europe was moving toward war, and a trial run, so to speak, occurred in Spain, where the forces of General Francisco Franco waged civil war against the established government. Franco willingly accepted aid from Hitler, and in exchange he allowed the Nazis to test their developing air power. On April 28, 1937, the Germans bombed the town of Guernica, the old Basque capital in northern Spain. There was no real military reason for the raid; it was simply an experiment to see whether aerial bombing could wipe out a whole city. Being totally defenseless, Guernica was devastated and its civilian population massacred.

3 At the time Picasso, himself a Spaniard, was working in Paris and had been commissioned by his government to paint a mural for the Spanish Pavilion of the Paris World's Fair of 1937. For some time he had procrastinated about fulfilling the commission; then, within days after news of the bombing reached Paris, he started *Guernica* and completed it in little over a month. Despite the speedy execution, however, this was no unreasoning outburst of anger. Picasso controlled his rage, perhaps knowing that it could have better effect in a carefully planned canvas, and he made many preliminary drawings. The finished mural had a shocking effect on those who saw it; it remains today a chillingly dramatic protest against the brutality of war.

4 At first encounter with *Guernica* the viewer is overwhelmed by its presence. The painting is huge—more than 25 feet long and 12 feet high—and its stark, powerful imagery seems to reach out and engulf the observer. Picasso used no colors; the whole painting is done in white and black and shades of gray, possibly to create a "newsprint" quality in reporting the event. Although the artist's symbolism is very personal (and he declined to explain it in detail), we cannot misunderstand the scenes of extreme pain and anguish throughout the canvas. At far left a shrieking mother holds her dead child, and at far right another woman, in a burning house, screams in agony. The gaping mouths and clenched hands speak of disbelief at such mindless cruelty.

5 Another victim is the dying horse to the left of center, speared from above and just as stunned by the carnage as any of the human sufferers. Various writers have interpreted the bull at upper left in different ways. Picasso drew much of his imagery from the bullfight, an ingrained part of his Spanish heritage. Perhaps the bull symbolizes the brutal victory of the Nazis; perhaps it, like the horse, is also a victim of carnage. There is even more confusion about the symbols of the lamp and the light bulb at top center. These may be indications that light is being cast on the horrors of war, or they may be signals of hope. Picasso did not tell us, so we are free to make our own associations.

6 *Guernica* is like no other painting in the world. Enormous in size, stark in its black-and-white tones, shocking in its images of brutality, vehement in its political protest—Picasso's great work stands alone in the history of art. Although Picasso was prolific as an artist, he never made another picture like *Guernica*. This uniqueness, then, presents a problem: How can the painting be kept from harm? How does one protect a one-of-a-kind masterpiece?

7 Picasso always intended *Guernica* as a gift to the people of Spain, his homeland, but at the time of its creation in 1937, he did not trust the Spanish government. So, he shipped the picture off to the Museum of Modern Art in New York, where it was to be held "on extended loan" until such time as a "democratic" government was established in Spain.

8 In New York, *Guernica* was simply hung on a wall—a large wall to be sure. Its impact was staggering when the viewer came around a corner and, suddenly, there it was. If the museum guards decided you were all right, and if you held your breath carefully, you could get quite close to the canvas. Or you could stand far back to take in the whole work at a gulp. So the situation remained for forty years. Only one unpleasant event marred the open relationship between artwork and viewers. In 1974 an Iranian artist splashed the *Guernica* with red paint as a political protest, but no permanent damage was done.

9   By 1981, eight years after Picasso's death, there was general agreement that Spain's government had become sufficiently "democratic" to satisfy the artist's conditions. Under tight security *Guernica* was sent to Madrid, where it was installed in an annex of the Prado museum. The Prado was taking no chances with its newly acquired masterpiece. *Guernica* was quickly sealed up in what some observers called a "cage"—an immense riot-resistant enclosure under an armor-plated ceiling, with bulletproof glass set some 14 feet in front of the canvas's surface. Obviously, one could no longer move in close to study details. Museum visitors complained that glare on the glass prevented any overall view of the painting. Some grumbled that the protective box dominated the picture, making even a 25-foot-wide painting seem puny. *Guernica* was safe, all right, but at what cost to its expression?

10   The controversy escalated in 1992, when *Guernica* was moved yet again, this time to the Reina Sofia museum a mile or so from the Prado. This new journey had all the drama of a spy movie. A special steel box, climate-controlled and weighing 3,500 pounds, was built to carry the painting. The transport company practiced its run down the road for weeks in advance, using stand-in paintings. Finally, on the fateful day, an armored truck carried *Guernica* through heavily guarded streets to its new home. The trip took half an hour and cost $200,000. Arriving intact at the Reina Sofia, *Guernica* was once again secured behind bulletproof glass.

11   One cannot help wondering what Picasso would have thought about all this hullabaloo. His eldest daughter has accused the Spanish art ministry of "murdering" *Guernica.* Perhaps "jailing" it would be a better term. The issue is one of balance. If *Guernica* should be damaged or destroyed, there is no way ever to replace it. But what is the point of keeping this masterpiece so very safe that no one can properly see it? [After many complaints, the glass was removed in 1995.]

From Rita Gilbert, *Living with Art,* 5th Edition, pp. 56–58. Copyright © 1998 by The McGraw-Hill Companies, Inc. Reprinted with permission.

 COMPREHENSION CHECKUP

True or False

Directions: Indicate whether each statement is true or false by writing **T** or **F** in the space provided.

_____ 1. Franco's collaboration with Hitler resulted in the bombing of Guernica.

_____ 2. Picasso's painting required many months to complete.

_____ 3. The colorful painting is generally thought to be very large.

_____ 4. Picasso was a Spaniard by birth.

_____ 5. The light bulb at the top of the painting may be seen as a sign of hope.

_____ 6. Picasso intended *Guernica* to be a gift from him to the people of Spain.

_____ 7. Originally *Guernica* was loaned to the Louvre in France.

_____ 8. *Guernica* survived an incident in which red paint was splashed on it.

_____ 9. Today *Guernica* is secured behind glass.

_____ 10. Picasso's oldest daughter feels that the painting has been "murdered."

Vocabulary in Context

Directions: Indicate whether the italicized word is used correctly or incorrectly by writing **C** or **I** in the space provided.

_____ 1. The cruel loss of his five children was *devastating*.

_____ 2. Because the price of gas in the United States keeps *escalating*, people are no longer going on long car trips.

_____ 3. When someone has an *outburst*, they are especially calm.

_____ 4. If you cannot swim and are *engulfed* by a wave, you might need a life-guard immediately.

_____ 5. It is considered to be especially polite to *gape* at someone.

_____ 6. At car speeds of over 100 miles an hour, an *impact* with a wall can cause serious injury.

_____ 7. Stephen King is a *prolific* writer who has written over 30 best sellers.

_____ 8. AIDS, a worldwide epidemic, has killed a *staggering* number of human beings.

_____ 9. His *clenched* fist and scowling face indicated his happiness with his math grade.

_____ 10. Millions of bats were *massacred* because the townspeople feared rabies.

In Your Own Words

1. How does Rita Gilbert feel about the way the Spanish government chose to exhibit Picasso's *Guernica* prior to 1995? What clues enable you to make this inference?

2. How do you think Picasso might feel about the safe-keeping of his masterpiece?

3. The author suggests that Picasso might have painted *Guernica* in black, white, and shades of gray to create a "newsprint" effect. What other reasons might Picasso have had for using this color scheme?

4. Picasso was fascinated by the ancient sport of bullfighting. The author mentions several things that the bull in the painting might symbolically represent. What do you think the bull in *Guernica* represents?

Internet Activity

View some of Picasso's paintings by visiting the Online Picasso Project at:

www.tamu.edu/mocl/picasso

The Web site is officially recognized by the Pablo Ruiz Picasso Foundation. Additional Web sites that feature examples of his work are:

www.abcgallery.com/P/picasso/picasso.html (Olga's Gallery)

www.mcs.csuhayward.edu/~malek/Pablo.html (Hayward Collection)

To learn more about Pablo Picasso, visit his official Web site at:

www.picasso.fr

Then choose a favorite painting and write a brief description of it.

READING

*"If you can't do the time,
don't do the crime"*

TUNING IN TO READING

Today, many people use yellow ribbons to welcome home soldiers or to serve as a reminder for those who are missing. What does a yellow ribbon symbolize to returning soldiers? Why do families with soldiers who are POWs or MIAs wear or display yellow ribbons?

BIO-SKETCH

Pete Hamill (1935–   ) was born in Brooklyn and attended Catholic schools as a child. He left school at the age of 16 to become a sheet-metal worker and later joined the United States Navy. The G.I. Bill of Rights helped him pay for his education at Mexico City College. In 1960, he began his career in journalism at the *New York Post* and later served as its editor in chief. He also became editor in chief for the *New York Daily News*. As a journalist, he covered wars in Vietnam, Nicaragua, Lebanon, and Northern Ireland. He has written several fiction and nonfiction books, including *The Drinking Life* and *Downtown: My Manhattan*. "The Yellow Ribbon," originally written for the *Post*, became the inspiration for a TV movie and a song by Tony Orlando titled "Tie a Yellow Ribbon 'Round the Old Oak Tree."

NOTES ON VOCABULARY

solitude   the state of being solitary or alone. It comes from the Latin word *solus*, meaning "sole" or "alone." It is often used to describe the state of being cut off from human contact. The loneliness of such a situation is sometimes stressed.

THE YELLOW RIBBON   BY PETE HAMILL

They were going to Ft. Lauderdale, the girl remembered later. There were six of them, three boys and three girls, and they picked up the bus at the old terminal on 34th Street, carrying sandwiches and wine in paper bags, dreaming of golden beaches and the tides of the sea as the gray cold spring of New York vanished behind them. Vingo was on board from the beginning.

2   As the bus passed through Jersey and into Philly, they began to notice that Vingo never moved. He sat in front of the young people, his dusty face masking his age, dressed in a plain brown ill-fitting suit. His fingers were stained from cigarettes and he chewed the inside of his lip a lot, frozen into some personal cocoon of silence.

3   Somewhere outside of Washington deep into the night, the bus pulled into a Howard Johnson's, and everybody got off except Vingo. He sat rooted in his seat, and the young people began to wonder about him, trying to imagine his life: Perhaps he was a sea captain, maybe he had run away from his wife, he could be an old soldier going home. When they went back to the bus, the girl sat beside him and introduced herself.

4   "We're going to Florida," the girl said brightly. "You going that far?"

5   "I don't know." Vingo said.

6   "I've never been there," she said. "I hear it's beautiful."

7   "It is," he said quietly, as if remembering something he had tried to forget.

8   "You live there?"

9   "I did some time there in the Navy. Jacksonville."

10   "Want some wine?" she said. He smiled and took the bottle of Chianti and took a swig. He thanked her and retreated again into his silence. After a while, she went back to the others, as Vingo nodded in sleep.

In 1513, the Spanish explorer Ponce de Leon landed in what we now call Florida. He named this new territory after the Pascua Florida, or Spanish Festival of Flowers, which is a celebration that occurs during the Easter season.

Chianti—Did you know that this red wine is called "Chianti" because it was originally produced in the Chianti Mountains of Italy?

11 In the morning they awoke outside another Howard Johnson's, and this time Vingo went in. The girl insisted that he join them. He seemed very shy and ordered black coffee and smoked nervously, as the young people chattered about sleeping on the beaches. When they went back on the bus, the girl sat with Vingo again, and after a while, slowly and painfully and with great hesitation, he began to tell his story. He had been in jail in New York for the last four years, and now he was going home.

12 "Four years!" the girl said. "What did you do?"

13 "It doesn't matter," he said with quiet bluntness. "I did it and I went to jail. If you can't do the time, don't do the crime. That's what they say and they're right."

14 "Are you married?"

15 "I don't know."

16 "You don't know?" she said.

17 "Well, when I was in the can I wrote to my wife," he said. "I told her, I said, Martha, I understand if you can't stay married to me. I told her that. I said I was gonna be away a long time, and that if she couldn't stand it, if the kids kept askin' questions, if it hurt her too much, well, she could just forget me. Get a new guy—she's a wonderful woman, really something—and forget about me. I told her she didn't have to write me or nothing. And she didn't. Not for three-and-a-half years."

18 "And you're going home now, not knowing?"

19 "Yeah," he said shyly. "Well, last week, when I was sure the parole was coming through I wrote her. I told her that if she had a new guy, I understood. But if she didn't, if she would take me back she should let me know. We used to live in this town, Brunswick, just before Jacksonville, and

there's a great big oak tree just as you come into town, a very famous tree, huge. I told her if she would take me back, she should put a yellow handkerchief on the tree, and I would get off and come home. If she didn't want me, forget it, no handkerchief, and I'd keep going on through."

20 "Wow," the girl said. "Wow."

21 She told the others, and soon all of them were in it, caught up in the approach of Brunswick, looking at the pictures Vingo showed them of his wife and three children, the woman handsome in a plain way, the children still unformed in a cracked, much-handled snapshot. Now they were 20 miles from Brunswick and the young people took over window seats on the right side, waiting for the approach of the great oak tree. Vingo stopped looking, tightening his face into the ex-con's mask, as if fortifying himself against still another disappointment. Then it was 10 miles, and then 5 and the bus acquired a dark hushed mood, full of silence, of absence, of lost years, of the woman's plain face, of the sudden letter on the breakfast table, of the wonder of children, of the iron bars of solitude.

22 Then suddenly all of the young people were up out of their seats, screaming and shouting and crying, doing small dances, shaking clenched fists in triumph and exaltation. All except Vingo.

23 Vingo sat there stunned, looking at the oak tree. It was covered with yellow handkerchiefs, 20 of them, 30 of them, maybe hundreds, a tree that stood like a banner of welcome blowing and billowing in the wind, turned into a gorgeous yellow blur by the passing bus. As the young people shouted, the old con slowly rose from his seat, holding himself tightly, and made his way to the front of the bus to go home.

"The Yellow Ribbon" Pete Hamill. Reprinted by permission of International Creative Management, Inc. Copyright © 1972 by Pete Hamill.

COMPREHENSION CHECKUP

Multiple Choice

Directions: For each item, write the letter corresponding to the best answer.

_____ 1. The main idea expressed in this article is that

    a. a prison sentence can easily ruin a marriage.

    b. young people on vacation can meet interesting people.

    c. love is better the second time around.

    d. after serving his time in prison, Vingo returned to Brunswick and discovered that his wife wanted him back after all.

_____ 2. The author's primary purpose in writing this article is to

    a. inform readers about unjust prison sentences.

    b. explain to readers how prison disrupts family life.

    c. entertain readers with a heartwarming story.

    d. persuade readers to show compassion for those returning from prison.

_____ 3. The pattern of organization used in this article is

    a. classification and division.

    b. comparison-contrast.

    c. chronological order.

    d. cause and effect.

_____ 4. You can conclude that Pete Hamill obtained the information needed to write this article by

    a. interviewing Vingo.

    b. interviewing a girl who was on the bus with Vingo.

    c. interviewing Vingo's family and friends.

    d. interviewing the boys who were riding on the bus.

_____ 5. We can infer that the young people aboard the bus are going to Florida

    a. to visit relatives.

    b. to get married.

    c. to interview for jobs.

    d. to take a vacation.

_____ 6. We can infer that Vingo's wife was

    a. willing to forgive Vingo.

    b. angry for having to raise their children alone.

    c. a compassionate and caring woman.

    d. both a and c.

_____ 7. We can infer that the young people began their trip in

    a. Washington, DC.

    b. New York.

    c. Florida.

    d. Pennsylvania.

_____ 8. In paragraph 3, the word *rooted* in "He sat rooted in his seat" means

    a. to become established or anchored.

    b. to search about.

    c. to work hard.

    d. to dig.

_____ 9. In paragraph 21, the word *fortifying* in "as if fortifying himself against still another disappointment" means

    a. strengthening.

    b. weakening.

    c. praising.

    d. condemning.

True or False

Directions: Indicate whether each statement is true or false by writing **T** or **F** in the space provided.

_____ 10. Vingo was in prison for four years before being paroled.

_____ 11. There were eight young people and two chaperones making the trip.

_____ 12. Vingo had never been to Jacksonville before.

_____ 13. Vingo looked at the pictures of his wife and children a lot.

_____ 14. Vingo felt that you shouldn't commit crimes if you aren't willing to do the time.

In Your Own Words

1. In the last paragraph, Hamill says that the tree covered with yellow handkerchiefs "stood like a banner of welcome." In Vingo's case, what does the tree symbolically represent?

2. Make a profile sketch of Vingo by listing his key character traits. Some traits are directly stated in the text, and others must be inferred from the evidence presented. Be able to justify each of your traits by citing specific passages.

3. What does it mean to be "frozen into some personal cocoon of silence"?

4. What does Vingo's face look like when he tightens it "into the ex-con's mask"?

5. What inference can you make about why Vingo's wife did not keep in regular contact with him while he was in prison? What kind of woman do you think she is?

Written Assignment

All of us make assumptions about other people just by looking at them. We also judge people by their friends. You can often tell a lot about a person from the people he or she associates with. What do your friends "say" about you? That is, what can someone tell *about you* from knowing or observing your friends? Write a paragraph about yourself from this perspective.

Internet Activity

Many people wear ribbons or bracelets to support various causes. Can you think of some examples? What colors are used? Many people across the United States display yellow ribbons as an expression of solidarity with our troops. Others display these ribbons as a reminder of loved ones in danger and a desire for their safe return home. To learn more about the tradition of wearing yellow ribbons, go to

www.loc.gov/folklife/ribbons

or type "origins of yellow ribbons" into a search engine. Write a paragraph summarizing the information you find.

Literary Allusions

A **literary allusion** is a reference to something that is supposed to be common cultural knowledge. Allusions are a technique writers use to quickly express a complex thought or evoke a certain image or reaction. In this sense, they are much like symbols. To fully understand a literary work, you need to be able to recognize and understand the allusions used by the author. Often, research must be done to discover the meaning of an allusion.

Study the following example from the opening stanza of "Travel" by Robert Louis Stevenson:

> I should like to rise and go
> Where the golden apples grow;—
> Where below another sky
> Parrot islands anchored lie,
> And, watched by cockatoos and goats,
> Lonely Crusoes building boats;—

The word *Crusoe* refers to the main character of Daniel Defoe's 18th-century novel *Robinson Crusoe*. In the novel, Crusoe is shipwrecked and washed ashore on an uninhabited island. Crusoe has come to symbolize a person who can overcome hardships and survive in isolation. The second literary allusion, Parrot islands, refers to the Canary Islands, located in the Atlantic Ocean directly off the northwest coast of Africa. The Canaries, because of their beauty and relative isolation, symbolize serenity. Thus, in the beginning of this poem, the poet is expressing a longing to journey to a remote area.

Cultural Literacy Assignment

Directions: Form groups of four. Each group will then be assigned either Quiz A or Quiz B. You are allowed to help each other.

Cultural Literacy Quiz A

Mythology and Folklore

1. A weak or sore point in a person's character. A_____ h_____

2. A magician who acted as King Arthur's primary advisor. M_____

Proverbs

3. Physical beauty is superficial. B_____ is _____ _____ d_____.

4. If we want to achieve our goal, we must get an early start. The _____ b_____ catches the w_____.

Idioms

5. A disgrace to the family. B_____ sh_____

6. If something can go wrong, it will. M_____ L_____

Literature

7. Author of *Diary of a Young Girl*. A_____ F_____

8. "I'll huff and I'll puff, and I'll blow your house down." T_____ _____ P_____

9. A novel by J. D. Salinger recounting the adventures of the young Holden Caulfield. *The Catcher in the R*_____

Art

10. The creator of the paintings on the ceiling of the Sistine Chapel. M_____

11. The statue features the words "Give me your tired, your poor, your huddled masses." S_____ of L_____

History

12. A king of England who beheaded two wives. H_____ the _____

13. A Roman emperor alleged to have fiddled while Rome burned. N_____

14. The inventor of the lightning rod, bifocal glasses, and a stove. B_____

    F_____

15. A seamstress who made flags in Philadelphia during the Revolutionary War.

    B_____ R_____

16. A battle between Custer and Native Americans. L_____ B_____

17. The championship game of the NFL held in January. S_____ B_____

Bible

18. The principle of justice that requires punishment equal in kind to the offense.

    An _____ for an _____

19. "Do unto others as you would have them do unto you." The G_____ R_____

Science

20. Large, white, puffy clouds—some carry rain. C_____

21. A shuttle that exploded in space. C_____/_____

Cultural Literacy Quiz B

Mythology and Folklore

1. A very handsome man. A_____

2. Small men who resemble elves capable of revealing the whereabouts of a pot of

   gold at the end of the rainbow. L_____

Proverbs

3. Apples keep us healthy. An _____ a day k_____ the d_____ a_____.

4. Don't assume that you'll get the things you want until you have them.

   D_____ c_____ y_____ ch_____ b_____ they h_____.

Idioms

5. Smooth, flattering talk (Irish derivation). B_____

6. To blow an event out of proportion. Don't m_____ a m_____ out of a

   m_____ h_____.

Literature

7. Ali Baba and the _____ Thieves.

8. "All animals are equal, but some animals are more equal than others."

   A_____ F_____

9. "Elementary, my dear Watson." Sh_____ H_____

Art

10. A painting by Leonardo da Vinci of a woman with a mysterious smile.

    M_____ L_____

11. The Spanish painter of *Guernica*. P_____

History

12. The queen of Egypt famed for her beauty; lover of Marc Antony. C_____

13. A female French military leader who claimed God spoke to her in voices.

    J_____ of A_____

14. An English nurse of the 19th century, and a symbol for all nursing.

    F_____ N_____

15. The commander of the Confederate troops. R_____ E. L_____

16. His most famous speech is "I Have a Dream." M_____ L_____ K_____, Jr.

17. The oldest and most famous of the college "bowl games." R_____ B_____

Bible

18. The reason people of the earth speak different languages. The T_____ of

    B_____

19. The first children of Adam and Eve. C_____ and A_____

Science

20. Lacy or wispy clouds that form at high altitudes. C_____

21. A very "unlucky" space mission. A_____

Imagery

In addition to the figures of speech mentioned earlier, writers use **imagery** to create word pictures. This means that they describe a person, object, or setting by relying on sensory images. The words or phrases that they use may emphasize any one, or all, of our five senses—sight, sound, taste, touch, and smell. Readers must not only be able to recognize these images but also understand the author's intent in presenting a particular image. For example, in "The Runner," the poet Walt Whitman uses imagery to convey the sensation of running. The descriptive words in the poem primarily appeal to our visual sense.

> On a flat road runs the well-train'd runner;
> He is lean and sinewy, with muscular legs;
> He is thinly clothed—he leans forward as he runs,
> With lightly closed fists, and arms partially rais'd.

The excerpt below creates a visual picture of the 2004 tsunami disaster:

> Women shrieking and what sounded like the roar of a freight train awakened me. I jumped out of bed and ran to the balcony door of our second-floor guest room to see water—filled with wood and cars and pieces of twisted metal—swirling below us. Damika, the owner of the inn, and some of his family had run up the stairs to our balcony. I looked over their shoulders at the rising waves and went cold with fear.
>
> Now I realize that the strange calm I felt at the time was shock. The scene outside had become increasingly more terrifying, more surreal. The water was slowly receding, but now buildings were starting to collapse around us, and the noise brought fresh waves of panic. Half of Damika's house, right in front of our balcony, came crashing down. Would our building be next? The mantra I repeated to myself would continue for the next four days: "I want to go home. I want to see my family. I don't want to die."

The Great Wave Off Kanagawa by Hokusai

Below us, the water was teeming with all the objects that once held so much importance: televisions, furniture, cars, shoes. Life was the only thing that mattered now, and people were screaming out for the ones who had lost it.

We wanted to be higher still, and, with the help of a local man, struggled up the cliff behind the hotel. Halfway up we heard shouts from below and then the dreaded sound that I still listen for. It was the sound of the ocean as it pelted its entire being, once again, onto the battered shore, traveling farther inland as there was less resistance from the fallen buildings. We ran, stumbling, over logs and up embankments, through the jungle, helping the injured and shocked, to get to higher ground. At the top, we turned and watched the sea enfold the once sleepy tourist-filled village. Only the palm trees were visible.

From Laura Dunham, "Amid the Ruin and Sorrow on Sri Lanka, the Reservoir of Kindness Remains." From *The New York Times*, January 16, 2005. © 2005 The New York Times. All rights reserved. Used by permission and protected by the Copyright Laws of the United States. The printing, copying, redistribution, or retransmission of the Material without express written permission is prohibited. www.nytimes.com

Study the painting by Hokusai titled *The Great Wave Off Kanagawa*. In what way does the painting express the sensory images conveyed by the tsunami disaster?

READING

"I hunt Black Widow. I have never been bitten."

TUNING IN TO READING

What do you know about spiders? Did you know that they have been on Earth for millions of years and are important to our survival because of the large numbers of insects they consume? While all spiders are poisonous, most species don't cause serious harm to humans. The black widow, though generally shy and retiring, has a very toxic bite. To learn more about the habits of the black widow, read the following selection.

READING *continued*

BIO-SKETCH

Gordon Grice is the author of *The Red Hourglass* and *The Deadly Kingdom*. He has written for *The New Yorker*, *Harper's*, and other magazines. His work has been anthologized in *The Best American Essays* and *The Art of the Essay*. His published work includes memoirs, essays, short stories, and poems.

NOTES ON VOCABULARY

gargoyle   a sculpture or decoration depicting grotesque human shapes, beasts, or evil spirits and placed on many buildings in the Middle Ages, especially churches and cathedrals. Some gargoyles acted as spouts that drained rainwater from the roof of the building. The Gothic gargoyle was usually a grotesque bird or animal sitting on the back of a cornice and projecting forward for several feet in order to throw the water far from the building. This form of sculpture declined with the introduction of lead drainpipes in the 16th century. The term originates from the French *gargouille,* meaning "the throat or waterspout."

arthropods   animals with jointed legs and segmented bodies, such as insects, centipedes, scorpions, crustaceans, and spiders.

The Black Widow

Gordon Grice

I HUNT BLACK WIDOW. When I find one, I capture it. I have found them in discarded wheels and tires and under railroad ties. I have found them in house foundations and cellars, in automotive shops and toolsheds, in water meters and rock gardens, against fences and in cinderblock walls. I have found them in a hospital and in the den of a rattlesnake, and once at the bottom of a chair I was sitting in.

2   Sometimes I raise a generation or two in captivity. The egg sacs produce a hundred or more pinpoint cannibals, each leaving a trail of gleaming light in the air, the group of them eventually producing a glimmering tangle in which most of them die, eaten by stronger sibs. Finally I separate the three or four survivors and feed them bigger game.

3   Once I let several egg sacs hatch out in a container about eighteen inches on a side, a tight wooden box with a sliding glass top. As I tried to move the box one day, the lid slid off and I fell, hands first, into the mass of young widows. Most were still translucent newborns, their bodies a swirl of brown and cream. A few of the females had eaten enough to molt; they had the beginnings of their blackness. Their tangle of broken web clung to my forearms. They felt like trickling water in my arm hairs.

4   The black widow has the ugliest web of any spider. It is a messy-looking tangle in the corners and bends of things and under logs and debris. Often the web is littered with leaves. Beneath it lie the husks of insect prey, their antennae still as gargoyle horns, cut loose and dropped; on them and the surrounding ground are splashes of the spider's white urine, which looks like bird guano and smells of ammonia even at a distance of

several feet. This fetid material draws scavengers—ants, sow bugs, crickets, roaches, and so on—which become tangled in vertical strands of silk reaching from the ground up into the web. The widow comes down and, with a bicycling of the hind pair of legs, throws gummy silk onto this new prey.

5   When the prey is seriously tangled but still struggling, the widow cautiously descends and bites the creature, usually on a leg joint. This is a killing bite; it pumps neurotoxin into the victim. The widow will deliver a series of bites as the creature dies, injecting substances that liquefy the organs. Finally it will settle down to suck the liquefied innards out of the prey, changing position two or three times to get it all.

6   Before the eating begins, and sometimes before the victim dies from the slow venom, the widow usually moves it higher into the web. It attaches some line to the prey with a leg-bicycling toss, moves up the vertical web strand, and here secures the line. It has thus dragged the prey's body up off the ground. The whole operation is like that of a person moving a load with block and tackle.

7   You can't watch the widow in this activity very long without realizing that the web is not a mess at all but an efficient machine. It allows complicated use of leverage and also, because of its complexity of connections, lets the spider feel a disturbance anywhere in the web—usually with enough accuracy to tell the difference at a distance between a raindrop or leaf and viable prey. The web is also constructed in a certain relationship to movements of air so that flying insects are drawn into it. An insect that is clumsy and flies in random hops, such as a June beetle, is especially vulnerable to this trap.

8   The architectural complexities of the widow web do not particularly impress the widows. They move around in these webs almost blind, yet they never misstep or get lost. Furthermore, widows never snare themselves, even though every strand of the web is a potential trap. A widow will spend a few minutes every day coating the clawed tips of its legs with the oil that lets it walk the sticky strands. It secretes the oil from its mouth, coating its legs like a cat cleaning its paws.

9   Widows reportedly eat mice, toads, tarantulas—anything that wanders into that remarkable web. I have seen them eat scarab beetles heavy as pecans; cockroaches more than an inch long; and hundreds of other arthropods of various sizes. Widows begin life by eating their siblings. An adult female will fight any other female; the winner often eats the loser. The widow gets her name by eating her lover, though this does not always happen.

10   The widow's venom is a soundly pragmatic reason for fear. The venom contains a neurotoxin that can produce sweats, vomiting, swelling, convulsions, and dozens of other symptoms. The variation in symptoms from one person to the next is remarkable. The constant is pain. A useful question for a doctor trying to diagnose an uncertain case: "Is this the worst pain you've ever felt?" A "yes" suggests a diagnosis of black widow bite. Occasionally people die from widow bites. The very young and the very old are especially vulnerable. Some people seem to die not from the venom but from the infection that may follow; because of its habitat, the widow carries dangerous microbes.

11   I have never been bitten.

From Gordon Grice, "The Black Widow." First published in *High Plains Literary Review*. Copyright © 1995 by Gordon Grice. Reprinted by permission of the author.

COMPREHENSION CHECKUP

Multiple Choice

Directions: For each item, write the letter corresponding to the best answer on the line provided.

__b__ 1. The author's purpose in writing this selection was to
  a. describe how black widows are a threat to human beings.
  b. explain how black widows are well suited to survive in their particular environments.
  c. persuade the reader to exercise extreme caution in handling black widows.
  d. entertain the reader with scary stories about the black widow.

__b__ 2. "They felt like trickling water in my arm hairs." This is an example of a
  a. simile.
  b. metaphor.
  c. personification.
  d. symbol.

_____ 3. "It secretes the oil from its mouth, coating its legs like a cat cleaning its paws." This sentence makes use of
  a. simile.
  b. symbolism.
  c. literary allusion.
  d. metaphor.

_____ 4. The author suggests all of the following *except* that
  a. the black widow preys on insects.
  b. the female black widow may eat the male.
  c. the black widow has a venomous bite that is always fatal to humans.
  d. the web of a black widow looks messy.

_____ 5. By describing baby black widow spiders as *pinpoint cannibals,* the author is implying that they
  a. are exceedingly small.
  b. feed on each other.
  c. are warriors.
  d. both a and b.

_____ 6. From this excerpt you could conclude that the widow's web is all of the following *except*
  a. capable of ensnaring the black widow in a trap.
  b. ugly.
  c. messy but efficient.
  d. architecturally complex.

_____ 7. The black widow does all of the following to its prey *except*
  a. throw gummy silk on its prey.
  b. kill the prey by biting it.
  c. lower the prey to the ground.
  d. suck the liquified innards from the prey.

Vocabulary in Context

Directions: In the paragraphs indicated in parentheses, find a word that correctly matches the definition given, and write it in the space provided. Answers may vary.

1. cast-off (1)   _____

2. extremely small (2)   _____

3. allowing light to pass through (3)   _____

4. shed part or all of a coat or outer covering (3) _____

5. the outer layers or shells (4)   _____

6. upright (4)   _____

7. foul-smelling (4)   _____

8. sufficiently developed; living (7)   _____

9. having no specific pattern or purpose (7)   _____

10. practical (10)   _____

11. capable of being wounded or hurt (10)   _____

12. an environment providing the food and   _____
    shelter required for an animal to survive (10)

In Your Own Words

1. How many cultural references or literary allusions can you think of in regard to the spider? Here are a few to get you started.
   a. Charlotte in *Charlotte's Web* by E. B. White—In this children's book, Charlotte weaves wonderful webs in order to save her pal Wilbur (a pig) from slaughter.
   b. "Little Miss Muffet"—a nursery rhyme about a little girl frightened by a spider:

   > Little Miss Muffett sat on a tuffet
   > Eating her curds and whey.
   > Along came a spider,
   > Who sat down beside her
   > And frightened Miss Muffet away.

   c. "The Spider and the Fly"—a poem by Mary Howitt:

   > "Will you walk into my parlor? said the Spider to the Fly,
   > It's the prettiest little parlor that ever you did spy;
   > The way into my parlor is up a winding stair,
   > And I've many curious things to show when you are there."
   > "Oh no, no," said the little Fly, "to ask me is in vain,
   > For who goes up your winding stair can never come down again."

   d. Anansi—a spider who is a trickster in many African folk tales.
   e. "The Itsy Bitsy Spider"—a children's song about a spider who went up a water spout.
   f. Spider-man—a superhero of comics, cartoons, and action movies. A man is bitten by a spider and acquires spiderlike superpowers.
   g. Shelob (*The Lord of the Rings*) and Aragog (*Harry Potter*)—giant, nasty spiders from popular children's literature.
   h. *Arachnophobia*—a 1990 movie featuring evil venomous spiders.
   i. Spiders and webs are featured as creepy Halloween decorations.
2. Taken collectively, what do these references tell us about spiders?
3. Arachnophobia is an abnormal and persistent fear of spiders. It is among the most common of all phobias. People with arachnophobia feel uneasy in any area they believe could harbor spiders or that has signs of their webs. Their fear of spiders can produce panic attacks. Do you have any specific phobias? How do you think phobias are created? Could there be any advantages to having a specific phobia?

4. What are your feelings about spiders? Do you think learning about spiders can help us appreciate them better and reduce the fear factor?

Written Assignment

Directions: After reading "The Story of Arachne," write a paragraph responding to the questions that follow.

A myth is a traditional story of anonymous origin that deals with the activities of gods, goddesses, heroes, and supernatural events. The word *myth* derives from the word *mythos,* which is the Greek word for "story." The Greek myths tell stories of gods and goddesses, their lives on Mt. Olympus, and their interactions with human beings. Many myths attempt to explain natural phenomena or cultural practices. The story that follows takes place in Greece in the days when the gods and goddesses of Greek mythology were thought to rule the lives of mortals. It concerns Athena the Greek goddess of wisdom, household arts, and crafts.

Athena, goddess of wisdom, was a proud and talented young goddess. She was a skillful weaver and taught the local people many of her talents. She always took pride in her pupils' work, as long as they respected her. One of Athena's pupils was Arachne, a poor girl who lived in the country. Arachne wove beautiful fabrics of delicate designs, and people began to comment to her that surely she had been taught by the patron goddess of weaving, Athena herself. The proud Arachne scoffed at this and stated that she was a better weaver than Athena and that she had learned little or nothing from Athena's teachings. Arachne said, "I have achieved this marvelous skill due to my own talent, hard work, and efforts."

Soon Athena heard of the boastings of Arachne and decided to speak to her privately. Disguised as an old woman, Athena visited Arachne saying, "It is foolish to pretend that you are like one of the gods. You're simply a mortal whose talents are paltry in comparison to those of the goddess Athena." Arachne responded by saying, "If Athena doesn't like my words, then let her show her skills in a weaving contest." Suddenly, the old woman removed her disguise and there stood the goddess Athena ready for the challenge. As the contest began, it was clear that both Athena's and Arachne's tapestries were lovely. However, the goddess worked more quickly and skillfully. Still, Arachne felt her weaving was superior, but Athena viewed her efforts as an insult to the gods. This angered Arachne, especially because Athena requested an apology from her. Arachne arrogantly refused, and as a result Athena touched Arachne's forehead. Almost immediately Arachne felt her head begin to shrink and her nimble fingers grow into long, thin legs. Athena spoke to her saying, "Vain girl, since you love to weave so much, why don't you go and spin forever?" Athena had turned Arachne into a spider. From that day on, all spiders (arachnids) have been punished for Arachne's boasting, since they are required to live within their own webs.

1. What does this myth tell us about ancient Greek culture?
2. What does the myth have to say about vanity or hubris (excessive pride)?
3. Does this ancient myth have any relevance today?
4. What is the moral or lesson in this myth?

Internet Activity

1. Check out the following Web site to read an interview with Gordon Grice. Among other things, he discusses what led to his interest in spiders and how he came to marry his wife. You might want to read a fascinating excerpt from his

"We can't imagine what a spider thinks, Louisa, because it's a whole different life style."

book *The Red Hourglass*, describing the effects of a black widow bite. Write a paragraph discussing what you found most interesting about his interview:

www.randomhouse.com/boldtype/0598/grice/interview.html

2. Locate information about the black widow by typing "information about black widow spiders" into Google, or use one of the following Web sites:

www.animals.nationalgeographic.com/animals/bugs/black-widow-spider.html

www.desertusa.com/july97/du_bwindow.html

Try to find information that was not covered in the reading selection. Briefly summarize your findings.

3. Do a search of Anansi tales and summarize your favorite. What is the moral or message of the tale that you selected?

READING

"When everything in your life is uncertain, there's nothing quite like the clarity and precision of fresh snow and blue sky."

TUNING IN TO READING

In "A Blizzard Under Blue Sky," Pam Houston describes the curative powers of nature. Her character, at a crossroads in life, is suffering from depression. Rather than resort to pills, she seeks to heal herself by being self-reliant in the great outdoors. Houston

READING *continued*

uses many sensory details to describe her character's experience camping out in Utah in winter with her two dogs as her only companions.

As you read Houston's short story, be sure to notice the descriptive elements used to convey the key character's loneliness, as well as those used to describe the beauty of her surroundings.

BIO-SKETCH

The short story "A Blizzard Under Blue Sky" comes from a collection of short stories titled *Cowboys Are My Weakness,* by Pam Houston. The collection was named a *New York Times* Notable Book in 1992 and is the 1993 winner of the Western States Book Award. Her second collection of short stories, titled *Waltzing the Cat,* was published in 1998 to great acclaim. A licensed river guide and accomplished equestrian, Houston is often asked if her female characters are based on her own life. To this she replies, "My fiction begins in autobiography and then shapes itself into something invented." Her recent works include *A Little More about Me* and *Sighthound,* a story about a three-legged dog.

NOTES ON VOCABULARY

rampant   spreading unchecked; widespread.

inversion-cloaked   obscured by a temperature inversion. Salt Lake City sits in a valley surrounded by high mountains. In the winter, an inversion layer, or a layer of warmer air over cooler air, often forms over this region. The combination of the mountains around the valley and the inversion layer over the top traps the pollution in, leading to high levels of smog.

translucent   shining through. Something that is *translucent* allows some light through, but not as much as clear glass. Stained glass windows are *translucent* because they allow light through, but you cannot see through them.

yin and yang   In Chinese philosophy, *yin* is the passive female principle of the universe associated with earth, darkness, and coldness. In contrast, *yang* is the male principle of the universe associated with heaven, heat, and light.

A Blizzard Under Blue Sky

Pam Houston

THE DOCTOR SAID I WAS CLINICALLY DEPRESSED. It was February, the month in which depression runs rampant in the inversion–cloaked Salt Lake Valley and the city dwellers escape to Park City, where the snow is fresh and the sun is shining and everybody is happy, except me. In truth, my life was on the verge of more spectacular and satisfying discoveries than I had ever imagined, but of course I couldn't see that far ahead. What I saw was work that wasn't getting done, bills that weren't getting paid, and a man I'd given my heart to weekending in the desert with his ex.

2   The doctor said, "I can give you drugs."

3   I said, "No way."

4   She said, "The machine that drives you is broken. You need something to help you get it fixed."

5   I said, "Winter camping."

6   She said, "Whatever floats your boat."

7   One of the things I love the most about the natural world is the way it gives you what's good for you even if you don't know it at the time. I had never been winter camping before, at least not in the high country, and the weekend I chose to try and fix my machine was the same weekend the air mass they called the Alaska Clipper showed up. It was thirty-two degrees below zero in town on the night I spent in my snow cave. I don't know how cold it was out on Beaver Creek. I had listened to the weather forecast, and to the advice of my housemate, Alex, who was an experienced winter camper.

8   "I don't know what you think you're going to prove by freezing to death," Alex said, "but if you've got to go, take my bivvy sack; it's warmer than anything you have."

9   "Thanks," I said.

10   "If you mix Kool-Aid with your water it won't freeze up," he said, "and don't forget lighting paste for your stove."

11   "Okay," I said.

12   "I hope it turns out to be worth it," he said, "because you are going to freeze your butt."

13   When everything in your life is uncertain, there's nothing quite like the clarity and precision of fresh snow and blue sky. That was the first thought I had on Saturday morning as I stepped away from the warmth of my truck and let my skis slap the snow in front of me. There was no wind and no clouds that morning, just still air and cold sunshine. The hair in my nostrils froze almost immediately. When I took a deep breath, my lungs only filled up halfway.

14   I opened the tailgate to excited whines and whimpers. I never go skiing without Jackson and Hailey: my two best friends, my yin and yang of dogs. Some of you might know Jackson. He's the oversized sheepdog-and-something-else with the great big nose and the bark that will shatter glass. He gets out and about more than I do. People I've never seen before come by my house daily and call him by name. He's all grace, and he's tireless; he won't go skiing with me unless I let him lead. Hailey is not so graceful, and her body seems in constant indecision when she runs. When we ski, she stays behind me, and on the downhills she tries to sneak rides on my skis.

15   The dogs ran circles in the chest-high snow while I inventoried my backpack one more time to make sure I had everything I needed. My sleeping bag, my Thermarest, my stove, Alex's bivvy sack, matches, lighting paste, flashlight, knife. I brought three pairs of long underwear—tops and bottoms—so I could change once before I went to bed, and once again in the morning, so I wouldn't get chilled by my own sweat. I brought paper and pen, and Kool-Aid to mix with my water. I brought Mountain House chicken stew, and some freeze-dried green peas, some peanut butter and honey, lots of dried apricots, coffee and Carnation Instant Breakfast for morning.

16   Jackson stood very still while I adjusted his backpack. He carries the dog food and enough water for all of us. He takes himself very seriously when he's got his pack on. He won't step off the trail for any reason, not even to chase rabbits, and he gets nervous

and angry if I do. That morning he was impatient with me. "Miles to go, Mom," he said over his shoulder. I snapped my boots into my skis and we were off.

17   There are not too many good things you can say about temperatures that dip past twenty below zero, except this: They turn the landscape into a crystal palace and they turn your vision into Superman's. In the cold thin morning air the trees and mountains, even the twigs and shadows, seemed to leap out of the background like a 3-D movie, only it was better than 3-D because I could feel the sharpness of the air.

18   I have a friend in Moab who swears that Utah is the center of the fourth dimension, and although I know he has in mind something much different and more complicated than subzero weather, it was there, on that ice-edged morning, that I felt on the verge of seeing something more than depth perception in the brutal clarity of the morning sun.

19   As I kicked along the first couple of miles, I noticed the sun crawling higher in the sky and yet the day wasn't really warming, and I wondered if I should have brought another vest, another layer to put between me and the cold night ahead.

20   It was utterly quiet out there, and what minimal noise we made intruded on the morning like a brass band: the squeaking of my bindings, the slosh of the water in Jackson's pack, the whoosh of nylon, the jangle of dog tags. It was the bass line and percussion to some primal song, and I kept wanting to sing it, but I didn't know the words.

21   Jackson and I crested the top of a hill and stopped to wait for Hailey. The trail stretched out as far as we could see into the meadow below us and beyond, a double track and pole plants carving through softer trails of rabbit and deer.

22   "Nice place," I said to Jackson, and his tail thumped the snow underneath him without sound.

23   We stopped for lunch near something that looked like it could be a lake in its other life, or maybe just a womb-shaped meadow. I made peanut butter and honey sandwiches for all of us, and we opened the apricots.

24   "It's fabulous here," I told the dogs. "But so far it's not working."

25   There had never been anything wrong with my life that a few good days in the wilderness wouldn't cure, but there I sat in the middle of all those crystal-coated trees, all that diamond-studded sunshine, and I didn't feel any better. Apparently clinical depression was not like having a bad day, it wasn't even like having a lot of bad days, it was more like a house of mirrors, it was like being in a room full of one-way glass.

26   "Come on, Mom," Jackson said. "Ski harder, go faster, climb higher."

27   Hailey turned her belly to the sun and groaned.

28   "He's right," I told her. "It's all we can do."

29   After lunch the sun had moved behind our backs, throwing a whole different light on the path ahead of us. The snow we moved through stopped being simply white and became translucent, hinting at other colors, reflections of blues and purples and grays. I thought of Moby Dick, you know, the whiteness of the whale, where white is really the absence of all color, and whiteness equals truth, and Ahab's search is finally futile, as he finds nothing but his own reflection.

30   "Put your mind where your skis are," Jackson said, and we made considerably better time after that.

31   The sun was getting quite low in the sky when I asked Jackson if he thought we should stop to build the snow cave, and he said he'd look for the next bank. About one hundred yards down the trail we found it, a gentle slope with eastern exposure that didn't look like it would cave in under any circumstances. Jackson started to dig first.

32   Let me make one thing clear. I knew only slightly more about building snow caves than Jackson, having never built one, and all my knowledge coming from disaster tales of winter camping fatalities. I knew several things not to do when building a snow cave, but I was having a hard time knowing what exactly to do. But Jackson helped, and Hailey supervised, and before too long we had a little cave built, just big enough for three. We ate dinner quite pleased with our accomplishments and set the bivvy sack up inside the cave just as the sun slipped away and dusk came over Beaver Creek.

33   The temperature, which hadn't exactly soared during the day, dropped twenty degrees in as many minutes, and suddenly it didn't seem like such a great idea to change my long underwear. The original plan was to sleep with the dogs inside the bivvy sack but outside the sleeping bag, which was okay with Jackson, the supermetabolizer, but not so with Hailey, the couch potato. She whined and wriggled and managed to stuff her entire fat body down inside my mummy bag, and Jackson stretched out full-length on top.

34   One of the unfortunate things about winter camping is that it has to happen when the days are so short. Fourteen hours is a long time to lie in a snow cave under the most perfect of circumstances. And when it's thirty-two below, or forty, fourteen hours seems like weeks.

35   I wish I could tell you I dropped right off to sleep. In truth, fear crept into my spine with the cold and I never closed my eyes. Cuddled there, amid my dogs and water bottles, I spent half of the night chastising myself for thinking I was Wonder Woman, not only risking my own life but the lives of my dogs, and the other half trying to keep the numbness in my feet from crawling up to my knees. When I did doze off, which was actually more like blacking out than dozing off, I'd come back to my senses wondering if I had frozen to death, but the alternating pain and numbness that started in my extremities and worked its way into my bones convinced me I must still be alive.

36   It was a clear night, and every now and again I would poke my head out of its nest of down and nylon to watch the progress of the moon across the sky. There is no doubt that it was the longest and most uncomfortable night of my life.

37   But then the sky began to get gray, and then it began to get pink, and before too long the sun was on my bivvy sack, not warm, exactly, but holding the promise of warmth later in the day. And I ate apricots and drank Kool-Aid flavored coffee and celebrated the rebirth of my fingers and toes, and the survival of many more important parts of my body. I sang "Rocky Mountain High" and "If I Had a Hammer," and yodeled and whistled, and even danced the two-step with Jackson and let him lick my face. And when Hailey finally emerged from the sleeping bag a full hour after I did, we shared a peanut butter and honey sandwich and she said nothing ever tasted so good.

38   We broke camp and packed up and kicked in the snow cave with something resembling glee.

39   I was five miles down the trail before I realized what had happened. Not once in that fourteen-hour night did I think about deadlines, or bills, or the man in the desert. For the first time in many months I was happy to see a day beginning. The morning sunshine was like a present from the gods. What really happened, of course, is that I remembered about joy.

40   I know that one night out at thirty-two below doesn't sound like much to those of you who have climbed Everest or run the Iditarod or kayaked to Antarctica, and I won't try to convince you that my life was like the movies where depression goes away in one weekend, and all of life's problems vanish with a moment's clear sight. The simple truth of the matter is this: On Sunday I had a glimpse outside of the house of mirrors, on Saturday I couldn't have seen my way out of a paper bag. And while I was skiing back toward the truck that morning, a wind came up behind us and swirled the snow around our bodies like a blizzard under blue sky. And I was struck by the simple perfection of the snowflakes, and startled by the hopefulness of sun on frozen trees.

 COMPREHENSION CHECKUP

Short Answer

Directions: Answer the questions briefly, using a word, phrase, or sentence as appropriate.

1. At the outset of the story, the narrator is feeling _____.

2. List three things that have gone wrong in the narrator's life. _____,
   _____, and _____

3. In the first paragraph, what sentence demonstrates to the reader that the narrator
   feels self-pity? _____

4. What analogy does the doctor use to describe the narrator's condition?

   _____

5. What does this analogy mean? _____

   _____

Multiple Choice

Directions: For each item, write the letter corresponding to the best answer.

_____ 1. The narrator's purpose in writing this selection was to
         a. recommend that we all go to the mountains to fix our "machines."
         b. show how her life has changed since her weekend experience in the mountains.
         c. give readers a visual and sensory understanding about her weekend experience.
         d. explain how to survive in cold weather.

_____ 2. A likely title for this selection would be
   a. "A Tale of Two Dogs."
   b. "Utah in the Winter."
   c. "A Weekend to Remember."
   d. "How to Keep Warm in Subzero Temperatures."

_____ 3. The organizational pattern of paragraph 15 is
   a. main idea sentence followed by details.
   b. details followed by the main idea in the last sentence.
   c. details, main idea sentence in the middle, followed by more details.
   d. just details with no stated main idea.

_____ 4. "I noticed the sun crawling higher in the sky" is an example of a
   a. simile.
   b. metaphor.
   c. personification.
   d. symbol.

_____ 5. "What minimal noise we made intruded on the morning like a brass band." This sentence makes use of
   a. simile.
   b. symbolism.
   c. literary allusion.
   d. metaphor.

_____ 6. The imagery in the sentence above refers to
   a. the beauty of the surrounding area.
   b. the silence of the woods before their arrival.
   c. the bitter cold of the woods.
   d. the life-and-death situation they were facing.

_____ 7. The squeaking of bindings, slosh of water, whoosh of nylon, and jangle of dog tags are all images that appeal to our sense of
   a. smell.
   b. taste.
   c. touch.
   d. hearing.

_____ 8. The narrator refers to clinical depression by saying it was "like a house of mirrors, it was like being in a room full of one-way glass." These similes suggest that the narrator
   a. feels hopeful.
   b. is unmoved by the beauty of her surroundings.
   c. feels a great deal better.
   d. is having a good time in the wilderness.

_____ 9. When the narrator refers to Superman, Moby Dick, Captain Ahab, and Wonder Woman, she is using a
   a. simile.
   b. metaphor.
   c. literary allusion.
   d. personification.

_____ 10. What is the narrator saying in this sentence: "The morning sunshine was like a present from the gods"?
   a. She has rediscovered her joy in being alive.
   b. She is glad it is morning and she has survived the night.
   c. Her personal problems no longer seem as important.
   d. All of the above.

True or False

Directions: Indicate whether each statement is true or false by writing **T** or **F** in the space provided.

_____ 11. The narrator took along Kool-Aid to keep her water from freezing.

_____ 12. The narrator's two dogs have similar personalities.

_____ 13. The narrator believes her pets act and think like human beings.

_____ 14. The narrator used drugs to cure her depression.

_____ 15. Hailey likes to be "in charge."

Matching

Directions: Match the vocabulary words in Column A with their definition in Column B.

Column A

1. __h__ verge
2. __a__ clarity
3. __c__ utterly
4. __g__ futile
5. __i__ fatality
6. __e__ amid
7. __d__ chastising
8. __f__ primal
9. __b__ glimpse

Column B

a. clearness; lucidity

b. brief passing look; glance

c. in the middle of; among

d. severely criticizing

e. completely

f. first in time; primary

g. ineffective; useless

h. brink

i. death

In Your Own Words

1. Compare and contrast Jackson's and Hailey's personalities. What does the narrator mean when she refers to Jackson and Hailey as "my two best friends, my yin and yang of dogs." Use specific details from the story to support your answers.

2. Referring to specific details from the story, describe what the landscape looks like at 20 degrees below zero.

3. Explain the meaning of the title "A Blizzard Under Blue Sky."

Written Assignment

Directions: Write one or two paragraphs about one of the following.

1. Have you ever felt as depressed as the narrator's description? What did you do to restore the "joy" in your life?

2. Have you ever been on a winter or summer camping trip? If you have, describe the preparations you made for the trip and what you saw and how you felt while actually camping.

3. Do you have pets? What kind of relationship do you have with them? Do you think your animals are capable of thinking and feeling?

Internet Activity

Each of the following four Web sites gives information related to depression, but each site has a slightly different purpose. The first two sites look the same, but the domains are different (.com versus .org). The third site is also .org, while the fourth site is .gov. Which of these sites would likely give you the most impartial information and which would be the least objective? Go to all four sites, find out who sponsors them, and write a summary about what you found out about the purpose of each site.

www.depression.com

www.depression.org.nz

www.nmha.org

www.nimh.nih.gov

Chapter Summary and Review

In Chapter 6, you learned about the use of figurative language, including similes, metaphors, and personification. You also became familiar with extended metaphors, literary allusions, and imagery.

Short Answer

Directions: Give an example for each of the following.

1. Simile: _____

2. Metaphor: _____

3. Personification: _____

Vocabulary in Context

Directions: Choose one of the following words to complete the sentences below. Use each word only once.

inanimate	language	literally	personification	unlike	visual

4. _____ occurs when human characteristics are assigned to _____ objects.

5. Both fiction and nonfiction writers use figurative _____ in their writing.

6. Descriptive poems often appeal to readers' _____ sense.

7. Figures of speech should not be taken _____.

8. Similes and metaphors find a similarity in two _____ things.

Tone

CHAPTER PREVIEW

In this chapter, you will

- Learn to recognize an author's tone.
- Become familiar with ironic devices.
- Become familiar with satirical devices.

Inferring Tone

The word **tone** refers specifically to the emotional quality of an article. Just as a speaker's voice can convey a wide range of feelings, so can a writer's **voice.** Because tone reveals an author's attitude toward a subject, understanding it is crucial to interpreting what the author has written. Tone is expressed by the words and details an author selects and can often be described by a single adjective.

Here is a list of words that are sometimes used to describe tone. Brief definitions are provided.

1. admiring (thinking of with delight or approval; respecting)
2. alarmed (suddenly afraid or anxious; frightened)
3. amazed (feeling great wonder; astonished)
4. ambivalent (uncertain about a choice; showing mixed feelings)
5. amused (entertained; playful; humorous)
6. angry (feeling strong resentment)
7. appreciative (thankful; grateful)
8. arrogant (feeling superior or self-important)
9. befuddled (confused)
10. bitter (extremely resentful)
11. charming (very pleasing; attractive; delightful)
12. cheerful (full of cheer; glad; joyful)
13. compassionate (full of sympathy)
14. contemptuous (disdainful; scornful; showing little respect)
15. critical (finding fault with; disapproving)
16. cruel (causing great pain; brutal)
17. cynical (doubting that people are ever sincere, honest, or good)

18. depressed (sad; gloomy; discouraged)
19. dictatorial (inclined to be domineering; overbearing; tyrannical)
20. disgusted (feeling strong distaste; nausea; loathing)
21. excited (stirred up)
22. formal (not relaxed or familiar; stiff)
23. humorous (funny or amusing; comical)
24. informal (casual; familiar)
25. ironic (meaning the opposite of what is expected or said)
26. irreverent (not showing respect)
27. loving (warmly affectionate)
28. nostalgic (longing for something that happened long ago or is now far away)
29. objective (without bias; neutral)
30. optimistic (looking on the bright side)
31. outraged (great anger aroused by something seen as an injury, insult, or injustice)
32. peevish (cross or irritable)
33. perplexed (filled with doubt; puzzled)
34. pessimistic (expecting the worst)
35. playful (lively; said in fun)
36. remorseful (feeling great guilt or sorrow)
37. sarcastic (mocking, sneering, or cutting speech)
38. scolding (using sharp, angry words to find fault with someone; rebuking)
39. self-pitying (a self-indulgent attitude concerning one's own difficulties)
40. sentimental (having tender, gentle feelings)
41. serious (showing deep thought; not joking or fooling around)
42. solemn (very serious or grave)
43. sorrowful (filled with sadness or grief)
44. surprised (struck by a sudden feeling of wonder by something unexpected)
45. tragic (mournful; dreadful)
46. vindictive (said in revenge; wanting to get even)
47. whiny (complaining or begging in a way that lacks dignity)
48. witty (clever in an amusing way)

Exercise 1: Tone—At the Restaurant

Directions: The following conversations took place at a local restaurant at lunchtime. Choose one of the following words to identify the tone in each numbered passage. Use key words and punctuation as clues, and be able to justify your choices.

amazed	appreciative	cheerful	dictatorial	disgusted
nostalgic	outraged	perplexed	scolding	sorrowful

scolding 1. "Don't you dare talk to me like that! I'm your mother and you owe me a little respect. Sit up straight, stop slouching, and please chew with your mouth closed. Don't you have any manners?"

Amazed 2. "Wow! This is really a nice restaurant. From the outside it certainly doesn't look like much."

perplexed 3. Mike looks up at the servers singing Happy Birthday and says, "What is this? What's going on? It's not my birthday."

srroufal 4. "Mommy, I hate this macaroni," Susie said with a sob. "I don't want to be here anymore," she cried. "Please take me home."

outraged 5. "I'd like to speak to your manager. You've completely ignored me while you've flirted with the young men at the next table. I want you to know I've never been treated like this before. You're going to be sorry your behavior was so rude when you're out of a job."

dictator 6. "Gene, clean up the spill at table 6 and then take four glasses of water to table 7."

appreal 7. "We hope you had a pleasant time and will come back soon. Please tell all your friends about us. We've only been open for two weeks and are grateful for all new customers."

cheerful 8. "Hello, everybody! How are you all today? I'm Susan, your server! The tuna looks terrific today! Can I get you an appetizer to start off?"

disgusted 9. "This food is awful! My lettuce is soggy and it's turning brown. There's a hair in my tomato soup and my sandwich is burnt!"

nostalgic 10. "Oh, honey. Look at that picture on the wall. Remember when we were in Italy? We were so young then and we had such a wonderful time. I wish we could go back to those carefree days."

Exercise 2: Tone—The Lost Dog

Directions: Choose one of the following words to identify the tone in each numbered passage. Use key words and punctuation as clues, and be able to justify your choices.

arrogant	befuddled	critical	depressed	loving
optimistic	pessimistic	remorseful	sentimental	surprised

remorseful 1. "Oh, my poor little dog Cookie is gone!" shrieked Mrs. Carter. "It's all my fault. I forgot to close the gate this morning! I feel so guilty about this. How could I have been so stupid? I can never forgive myself. What kind of dog mommy am I?"

sentimental 2. "Little sweet Cookie means so much to me. I remember when we got her as a puppy at the pet store. She came right up and gave each one of us a lick. She was the tiniest little thing and so loving. Cookie personally picked us out to be her owners."

depressed 3. "This is so sad. Without her here, I feel like there's a big dark cloud sitting on my head. I can't go in to work today. I'm just going to sit here and wait till I hear something."

optimistic 4. "Maybe somebody will see my posters about the reward for her return. She couldn't have wandered very far. After all, she's only been gone for a short while. Anyway, I'll bet she can find her own way back home. We take her on long walks every evening. I know she's coming back to me. I'm sure she'll be back really soon."

surprised 5. "Oh my goodness, Cookie! Is that really you? What are you doing here?"

bedtubbing 6. "Have you been here inside the house all this time? How could that happen? I thought you were gone. Did you go away and then come back? What's going on here? Is somebody playing a trick on me?"

loving 7. "Come here, my sweet little doggy. Your mommy is so glad to see you. How's my little precious? Here, sweet Cookie girl. Mommy's got a goodie for you."

critical 8. "Helen, you really need to be a lot more careful," said Mr. Carter. "You need to pay attention to what you're doing. You could've lost Cookie forever just because you didn't take enough time to check the gates."

arrogant 9. "Young man, here's a dollar for you. I'm sure you have nothing better to do today. Go around the neighborhood and remove all of the reward posters. I expect you back here promptly in 10 minutes. Get a move on."

Pessimistic 10. "That young boy will probably mess it up. If you want something done right, you have to do it yourself. I'll probably spend the rest of the day receiving phone calls asking about the reward. And people are going to be bringing small dogs to my door and asking me if it's Cookie. What a lousy day this is going to turn out to be."

Exercise 3: Tone—At the Movie Theater

Directions: Choose one of the following words to identify the tone in each numbered passage. Use key words and punctuation as clues, and be able to justify your choices.

admiring	alarmed	angry	appreciative	compassionate
dictatorial	disgusted	ironic	self-pitying	whining

compassionate 1. "I know this has been an especially difficult time for you. This movie will be good for you. You won't have to concentrate on a complex plot. It's just pure light-hearted entertainment. Relax and enjoy yourself and let me take care of everything."

ironic 2. "Is this seat taken? Whoops, I didn't mean to step on your foot. I'm as graceful as a dancing elephant!"

admiring 3. "What a wonderful actress. No matter what role she plays, she always does a beautiful job. It's such a pleasure to attend one of her movies. I don't think she's ever been in a bad one. And she's so lovely, too. Her smile lights up the screen."

alarmed 4. "Oh my goodness. I don't think I remembered to lock the door. I had the key right there in my hand, but I don't think I used it. What am I going to do?"

self-pitying 5. "What is the matter with me? I can't seem to do even the simplest thing right. Things certainly haven't been easy for me lately. Car problems, school problems, health problems, and now this."

dictatorial 6. "Sit there and hold our seats. Don't move. I'll go get the popcorn and drinks."

whining   7. "What's this? I like plain popcorn not buttered. And I don't like Junior Mints at all. I like to eat Raisinettes at the movies. And this drink. You know I don't like diet drinks."

disgusted   8. "Ooh yuck. Somebody must have spilled their drink. There's something sticky all over the floor. And now it's on my shoes. This place is a pit. Doesn't anybody clean up in here. Look, even the seats are a mess."

Angry   9. "Are you the manager? Listen here, young man, I want my money back. I demand a refund. This whole evening has been a disaster."

app   10. "Thank you so much for going with me to the movie. This is just what I needed. You are such a good friend to think of me. I don't know what I'd do without you."

Exercise 4: Tone—Do Any of These Sound Familiar?

Directions: For each question, write the letter for the word that best describes the tone of the passage quoted.

_____ 1. "Hey, it's not my problem. It's your problem. I'm going to do what I'm going to do. You don't like it, that's just tough."
a. excited
b. self-pitying
c. contemptuous

_____ 2. "I can't decide if I should stay in school or drop out and get a job."
a. peevish
b. ambivalent
c. playful

_____ 3. "Oh, thank you for the necklace. It's lovely. It's just what I've always wanted."
a. informal
b. appreciative
c. objective

_____ 4. "Don't feel bad about forgetting my birthday, sweetie. I know you've been busy. It's really not that important."
a. forgiving
b. amused
c. bitter

_____ 5. "You're late to pick me up again. This is the fifth time this week! Don't give me your excuses. I don't want to hear it."
a. tragic
b. surprised
c. outraged

_____ 6. "Well, of course you're right and I'm wrong. I keep forgetting that someone as brilliant as you say you are is never wrong."
a. informal
b. sarcastic
c. humorous

_____ 7. "Of all the nerve. Can you believe some people? Hey, lady! I'm next in line. Wait your turn."
   a. angry
   b. befuddled
   c. sorrowful

_____ 8. "Mike, you're making far too many errors in your papers. I suggest you proofread them more carefully."
   a. surprised
   b. witty
   c. critical

_____ 9. "He's had all kinds of problems and yet he just keeps on trying. I have nothing but respect for the guy."
   a. admiring
   b. solemn
   c. cheerful

_____ 10. "Tina was so sweet. She used to make little flowers and smiley faces for me when she was three. She was such a loving child."
   a. charming
   b. nostalgic
   c. amused

_____ 11. "Mommy, why does Ann always get to sit next to the window? I want to sit next to the window. You never let me sit there. It's not fair! And I'm hungry, too."
   a. optimistic
   b. formal
   c. whining

_____ 12. "I hate to loan you my car. Something bad always happens to it. I know it's not going to be any different this time either. Why should it be?"
   a. ironic
   b. nostalgic
   c. cynical

READING

"His hideous crumpled wings lay glued and rucked on his back."

TUNING IN TO READING

The section of Annie Dillard's book that you will be reading is drawn from her childhood memories. How much of your early childhood can you remember? Do you think that events that happened in your childhood can affect your choice of a vocation?

BIO-SKETCH

Annie Dillard was born in 1945 in Pittsburgh, Pennsylvania, and received her BA and MA degrees from Hollins College in Roanoke, Virginia. She has received numerous awards for her writings, which include essays, poetry, memoirs, literary criticism, and even a western novel. Dillard taught for several years as an adjunct professor at Wesleyan University in Middletown, Connecticut, where she is currently professor emeritus.

The following selection is taken from *Pilgrim at Tinker Creek*, for which she won the 1975 Pulitzer Prize for Nonfiction Writing. This book was the result of her stay on Tinker

READING *continued*

Creek in Virginia's Roanoke Valley, where she observed the natural world while exploring the subjects of theology, philosophy, and science. Many have compared this work to Thoreau's *Walden*.

NOTES ON VOCABULARY

doily   a small ornamental mat of lace, or paper made to look like lace, used as decoration.

Polyphemus moth   a large yellowish brown American moth having a prominent eyespot on each hind wing.

pupa   an insect in the nonfeeding transformation stage between larva and adult.

wracked   wrecked; miserable. Derived from the Old English word *wraec*, meaning "misery."

rucked   folded; wrinkled; creased. Derived from the Old Norse word *hrukka*, meaning "a wrinkle."

The Fixed

Annie Dillard

O NCE, WHEN I WAS 10 OR 11 YEARS OLD, my friend Judy brought in a Polyphemus moth cocoon. It was January; there were doily snowflakes taped to the schoolroom panes. The teacher kept the cocoon in her desk all morning and brought it out when we were getting restless before recess. In a book we found what the adult moth would look like; it would be beautiful. With a wingspread of up to six inches, the Polyphemus is one of the few huge American silk moths, much larger than, say, a giant or tiger swallowtail butterfly. The moth's enormous wings are velveted in a rich, warm brown, and edged in bands of blue and pink delicate as a watercolor wash. A startling "eyespot," immense, and deep blue melding to an almost translucent yellow, luxuriates in the center of each hind wing. The effect is one of masculine splendor foreign to the butterflies, a fragility unfurled to strength. The Polyphemus moth in the picture looked like a mighty wraith, a beating essence of the hardwood forest, alien-skinned and brown, with spread, blind eyes. This was the giant moth packed in the faded cocoon. We closed the book and turned to the cocoon. It was an oak leaf sewn into a plump oval bundle; Judy had found it in a pile of frozen leaves.

2   We passed the cocoon around; it was heavy. As we held it in our hands, the creature within warmed and squirmed. We were delighted, and wrapped it tighter in our fists. The pupa began to jerk violently, in heart-stopping knocks. Who's there? I can

The Polyphemus Moth

still feel those thumps, urgent through a muffling of spun silk and leaf, urgent through the swaddling of many years, against the curve of my palm. We kept passing it around. When it came to me again it was hot as a bun; it jumped half out of my hand. The teacher intervened. She put it, heaving and banging, in the ubiquitous Mason jar.

3   It was coming. There was no stopping it now. January or not. One end of the cocoon dampened and gradually frayed in a furious battle. The whole cocoon twisted and slapped around in the bottom of the jar. The teacher fades, the classmates fade, I fade: I don't remember anything but that thing's struggle to be a moth or die trying. It emerged at last, a sodden crumple. It was a male; his long antennae were thickly plumed, as wide as his fat abdomen. His body was very thick, over an inch long, and deeply furred. A gray, furlike plush covered his head; a long, tan furlike hair hung from his wide thorax over his brown-furred, segmented abdomen. His multijointed legs, pale and powerful, were shaggy as a bear's. He stood still, but he breathed.

4   He couldn't spread his wings. There was no room. The chemical that coated his wings like varnish, stiffening them permanently, dried, and hardened his wings as they were. He was a monster in a Mason jar. Those huge wings stuck on his back in a torture of random pleats and folds, wrinkled as a dirty tissue, rigid as leather. They made a single nightmare clump still wracked with useless, frantic convulsions.

5   The next thing I remember, it was recess. The school was in Shadyside, a busy residential part of Pittsburgh. Everyone was playing dodgeball in the fenced playground or racing around the concrete schoolyard by the swings. Next to the playground a long delivery drive sloped downhill to the sidewalk and street. Someone—it must have been the teacher—had let the moth out. I was standing in the driveway, alone, stockstill, but shivering. Someone had given the Polyphemus moth his freedom, and he was walking away.

6   He heaved himself down the asphalt driveway by infinite degrees, unwavering. His hideous crumpled wings lay glued and rucked on his back, perfectly still now, like a collapsed tent. The bell rang twice; I had to go. The moth was receding down the driveway, dragging on. I went; I ran inside. The Polyphemus moth is still crawling down the driveway, crawling down the driveway hunched, crawling down the driveway on six furred feet, forever.

Annie Dillard, "The Fixed" from *Pilgrim at Tinker Creek*, pp. 59–61. Copyright © 1974 by Annie Dillard. Reprinted by permission of HarperCollins Publishers.

 COMPREHENSION CHECKUP

Identifying Tone

Directions: Answer the questions briefly, with a word, phrase, or sentence, as appropriate.

1. Describe the young Annie Dillard's mood (a) at first and (b) by the end of the essay.

    a. _Excited_

    b. _Sad._

2. At what point in the essay does Dillard's reaction to what is happening in the classroom change?

    When the Mouth Escaped

3. How can we tell that the other children were not as concerned as Dillard about the moth's fate?

   Because She Stays As Long As She Can To watch it.

4. To what does Dillard compare the moth in paragraph 4?

   a monster

5. What do you suppose caused the moth to start working its way out of the cocoon?

   Because it was Taken Out of its Enviroment

6. When was the moth supposed to be born?

   When the PUPA becomes worm

7. Why do you think Dillard felt guilty about what happened?

   Because it Died + She was Amused by it.

8. Does this essay have any symbolic value for humankind's relationship to the environment?

   yes

9. By use of context in paragraph 2, give a definition of the word "intervened."

   Came in between.

10. List the similes and metaphors Dillard uses to describe the body parts of the moth. What part of the moth's body is described most vividly? What overall image is created by Dillard's figures of speech?

   _____

   _____

   _____

Vocabulary in Context

Directions: In the paragraphs indicated, find a word that matches the definition given, and write that word in the space provided.

Paragraph 1

   1. *doily* _____ partially transparent; clear

   Splendor 2. *eyespot* _____ brightness; brilliance; glory

   3. _____ delicateness; the state of being easily damaged

   4. _____ open or spread out

   5. _____ a ghost; a spectral vision seen before death

   6. _____ foreign; strange

Paragraph 2

   7. _____ calling for haste; insistent

   8. _____ present everywhere

Paragraph 3

   9. *Thorax* _____ the body segment between the head and abdomen

Paragraph 6

   10. *Infinite* _____ endless; very great

   11. *Unwavering* showing no doubt or indecision

Written Assignment

In *The Scalpel and the Silver Bear,* Dr. Lori Arviso Alford, who is a Native American, expresses the following viewpoint: "Navajos believe in *hozho* or *hozhoni*—'walking in beauty'—a worldview in which everything in life is connected and influences everything else. A stone thrown into a pond can influence the life of a deer in the forest, a human voice and the spoken word can influence events around the world, and all things possess spirit and power. So Navajos make every effort to live in harmony and balance with everyone and everything else"

From Dr. Lori Arviso Alvord, *The Scalpel and the Silver Bear.* New York: Bantam Books, 1999, p. 14, quoted in Richard T. Schaefer, *Sociology,* 11th ed. New York: McGraw-Hill, 2008, p. 465.

Write a few paragraphs discussing how this Navajo philosophy relates to the incident with the moth described by Annie Dillard.

Irony

When there is a contrast between what people say and what they actually mean, they are using **verbal irony.** Since the meaning is usually expressed indirectly, you must use inference to understand this *reversed* meaning, or you will misinterpret the author.

Another form of irony is **situational.** In this form, there is a contrast between what is expected to occur and what actually does happen. Many stories or poems that end with an unexpected twist are based on this type of irony.

Directions: Examine the cartoon below and then answer the following questions.

RUBES. © 1995 by Leigh Rubin. By permission of Leigh Rubin and Creators Syndicate, Inc.

1. Locate the word in the cartoon that best expresses irony. _____
2. What can you infer has happened in the cartoon?

   _____

3. What key point is being made in the cartoon? What situation is being criticized?

   _____

4. Describe the tone or attitude you think is really being expressed in the cartoon.

   _____

The "Forest" cartoon concerns the environment. The sign proclaims the new headquarters of a forest conservation group. This cartoon is ironic because, instead of preserving timberland, the foundation has cleared ground to erect another building. The foundation has destroyed what it was supposed to be protecting. This action has defeated the group's fundamental goal. This is the exact *opposite* of what we would reasonably expect. In the cartoon, the meaning is expressed indirectly, so you must use inference to decipher the reversed meaning.

Look at the sign in the photo below. What inferences can be drawn from the words and the picture? In what way is the sign ironic?

Exercise 5: Detecting Irony

Directions: Read the fable and then answer the questions that follow.

> "The only two things in life that are guaranteed are death and taxes."
>
> —Benjamin Franklin

Once, a long time ago, Death came riding into the city of Baghdad looking for Ali Haj, a proud and wealthy merchant. Death was in no hurry to meet Ali Haj, for he had many other old friends whom he wished to honor by a visit. On hearing that Death was in the town and had already called on some of his friends, Ali Haj, who had not gained his riches by stupidity, spoke to his old, blind servant:

"There is a great prince come to town, whom I am eager to see, for I wish to give him a rare jewel to win his friendship. Unfortunately, I cannot hope he would visit the poor home of a humble merchant like myself. Therefore I shall go to seek him. But if he should by chance come here while I am away, welcome him with the choicest of food and drink, and beg him only to wait for me a little while. But see you keep him here."

Then Ali Haj gathered his favorite treasures, his wives and children, and fled on his swiftest horses to Damascus.

When Death knocked at his door the next day, the blind servant appeared. "I seek your master, Ali Haj," Death said.

"He has gone out to seek a great prince to give him a precious jewel," answered the servant. "But if you, my lord, are that prince, then my master begs you to consider this house your own and to stay only a little while till he returns."

"There are many who call me Prince," said Death, "but few so joyful to greet me as Ali Haj. But that is what I expected of him." Then he stared at the ancient man, who was indeed rich in white hairs and wrinkles. "Since you are sure to see him soon, kindly remind him that he need not have gone out today to seek me, for I wished only to ask him to meet me tomorrow in Damascus."

Multiple Choice

Directions: For each item, write the letter corresponding to the best answer.

_____ 1. Ali Haj succeeds in fooling all of the following *except*
   a. himself.
   b. the old, blind servant.
   c. Death.
   d. his wives and children.

_____ 2. All of the following are true statements according to the fable *except* for which?
   a. Death had many old friends whom he wished to visit.
   b. The old servant is going to die soon.
   c. Ali Haj is trying to avoid Death.
   d. Ali Haj is going to be able to outsmart Death.

_____ 3. The main organizational pattern used in this fable is
   a. comparison-contrast.
   b. example.
   c. chronological order.
   d. definition.

_____ 4. The author's purpose in writing this fable is to
   a. inform.
   b. persuade.
   c. entertain.
   d. convince.

_____ 5. All of the following are descriptive of Ali Haj *except*
   a. he is clever.
   b. he is rich.
   c. he is proud.
   d. he is brave.

_____ 6. In context the word *rich* (paragraph 6) means
   a. owning much money and property.
   b. deep and brilliant.

c. having a lot.

d. full and mellow.

In Your Own Words

1. What is the fable saying about Death?

2. What is ironic about Ali Haj's departure? Why does he ask the servant to keep Death well entertained in Baghdad? What does Death mean when he says he expected this type of welcome from Ali Haj?

3. Is Ali Haj going to succeed in avoiding Death? Explain your answer.

4. What does Death mean when he tells the old servant that he is sure to see his master, Ali Haj, soon?

READING

"God: of the money that I asked for, only seventy pesos reached me. Send me the rest, since I need it very much."

TUNING IN TO READING

Irony is a form of commentary by an author. In this story, pay close attention to the situation described by the author.

BIO-SKETCH

Gregorio Lopez y Fuentes (1897–1966) was a highly acclaimed author who received Mexico's National Prize for Literature in 1935. As the son of a small farmer, he understood the difficulties farmers faced in trying to make a living off the land. This story was translated from Spanish by Donald A. Yates.

NOTES ON VOCABULARY

mortify   the word *mortify* comes from the Latin words *mortis*, meaning "death," and *facere* meaning "to make." Today, *mortify* means "to humiliate or shame."

locusts   migratory grasshoppers that strip vegetation from large areas.

prodigy   something that excites wonder or amazement.

A Letter to God

Gregorio Lopez y Fuentes

THE HOUSE—THE ONLY ONE IN THE ENTIRE VALLEY—sat on the crest of a low hill. From this height one could see the river and, next to the corral, the field of ripe corn dotted with the kidney-bean flowers that always promised a good harvest.

2   The only thing the earth needed was a rainfall, or at least a shower. Throughout the morning Lencho—who knew his fields intimately—had done nothing else but scan the sky toward the northeast.

3   "Now we're really going to get some water, woman."

4   The woman, who was preparing supper, replied:

5   "Yes, God willing."

6   The oldest boys were working in the field, while the smaller ones were playing near the house, until the woman called to them all:

7   "Come for dinner . . ."

8   It was during the meal that, just as Lencho had predicted, big drops of rain began to fall. In the northeast, huge mountains of clouds could be seen approaching. The air was fresh and sweet.

9   The man went out to look for something in the corral for no other reason than to allow himself the pleasure of feeling the rain on his body, and when he returned he exclaimed:

10   "Those aren't raindrops falling from the sky, they're new coins. The big drops are ten-centavo pieces and the little ones are fives. . . ."

11   With a satisfied expression he regarded the field of ripe corn with its kidney-bean flowers, draped in a curtain of rain. But suddenly a strong wind began to blow and together with the rain very large hailstones began to fall. These truly did resemble new silver coins. The boys, exposing themselves to the rain, ran out to collect the frozen pearls.

12   "It's really getting bad now," exclaimed the man, mortified. "I hope it passes quickly."

13   It did not pass quickly. For an hour the hail rained on the house, the garden, the hillside, the cornfield, on the whole valley. The field was white, as if covered with salt. Not a leaf remained on the trees. The corn was totally destroyed. The flowers were gone from the kidney-bean plants. Lencho's soul was filled with sadness. When the storm had passed, he stood in the middle of the field and said to his sons:

14   "A plague of locusts would have left more than this. . . . The hail has left nothing: this year we will have no corn or beans. . . ."

15   That night was a sorrowful one:

16   "All our work, for nothing!"

17   "There's no one who can help us!"

18   "We'll all go hungry this year. . . ."

19   But in the hearts of all who lived in that solitary house in the middle of the valley, there was a single hope: help from God.

20   "Don't be so upset, even though this seems like a total loss. Remember, no one dies of hunger!"

21   "That's what they say: no one dies of hunger. . . ."

22   All through the night, Lencho thought only of his one hope: the help of God, whose eyes, as he had been instructed, see everything, even what is deep in one's conscience.

23   Lencho was an ox of a man, working like an animal in the fields, but still he knew how to write. The following Sunday, at daybreak, after having convinced himself that

there is a protecting spirit, he began to write a letter which he himself would carry to town and place in the mail.

24   It was nothing less than a letter to God.

25   "God," he wrote, "if you don't help me, my family and I will go hungry this year. I need a hundred pesos in order to resow the field and to live until the crop comes, because the hailstorm . . ."

26   He wrote "To God" on the envelope, put the letter inside and, still troubled, went to town. At the post office he placed a stamp on the letter and dropped it into the mailbox.

27   One of the employees, who was a postman and also helped at the post office, went to his boss laughing heartily and showed him the letter to God. Never in his career as a postman had he known that address. The postmaster—a fat amiable fellow—also broke out laughing, but almost immediately he turned serious and, tapping the letter on his desk, commented:

28   "What faith! I wish I had the faith of the man who wrote this letter. To believe the way he believes. To hope with the confidence that he knows how to hope with. Starting up a correspondence with God!"

29   So in order not to disillusion that prodigy of faith, revealed by a letter that could not be delivered, the postmaster came up with an idea: answer the letter. But when he opened it, it was evident that to answer it he needed something more than good will, ink and paper. But he stuck to his resolution: he asked for money from his employee, he himself gave part of his salary, and several friends of his were obliged to give something "for an act of charity."

30   It was impossible for him to gather together the hundred pesos, so he was able to send the farmer only a little more than half. He put the bills in an envelope addressed to Lencho and with them a letter containing only a single word as a signature: GOD.

31   The following Sunday Lencho came a bit earlier than usual to ask if there was a letter for him. It was the postman himself who handed the letter to him, while the postmaster, experiencing the contentment of a man who has performed a good deed, looked on from the doorway of his office.

32   Lencho showed not the slightest surprise on seeing the bills—such was his confidence—but he became angry when he counted the money. . . . God could not have made a mistake, nor could he have denied Lencho what he had requested!

33   Immediately, Lencho went up to the window to ask for paper and ink. On the public writing table, he started in to write, with much wrinkling of his brow, caused by the effort he had to make to express his ideas. When he finished, he went to the window to buy a stamp which he licked and then affixed to the envelope with a blow of his fist.

34   The moment that the letter fell into the mailbox the postmaster went to open it. It said:

"Better to accept whatever happens."

—Horace

35   "God: of the money that I asked for, only seventy pesos reached me. Send me the rest, since I need it very much. But don't send it to me through the mail, because the post-office employees are a bunch of crooks. Lencho."

From "A Letter to God," by Gregorio López y Fuentes, translated by Donald A. Yates. Reprinted by permission.

COMPREHENSION CHECKUP

Recognizing Irony

Directions: Answer the questions briefly, in a few words, phrases, or sentences, as appropriate.

1. Record your first impressions about Lencho, his wife, the postman, and the post-master. Give a brief description of each.

   _____

   _____

2. Study the following list of key details and explain what could reasonably be inferred from each.

   a. Lencho knows his fields "intimately."

   _____

   b. Lencho's only hope is "the help of God."

   _____

   c. The postman goes to his boss "laughing heartily."

   _____

   d. Never had the postman "known that address."

   _____

   e. The postmaster answers the letter "in order not to disillusion that prodigy of faith."

   _____

   f. The postmaster experiences "the contentment of a man who has performed a good deed."

   _____

   g. Lencho affixes the stamp "with a blow of his fist."

   _____

3. Why does Lencho react the way he does? Would you react as Lencho does? Explain why or why not.

   _____

4. Identify and explain a simile and a metaphor in the story.

   _____

   _____

5. In what way is the story ironic? Explain your answer.

   _____

   _____

Written Assignment

Have you ever tried to help someone, and it turned out that the person resented your efforts? If so, how did you feel about that person? Describe your experience in a short paragraph.

Satire

Satire is a kind of writing that uses ridicule to create awareness of flaws and to bring about change. Almost anything can be satirized, including people, institutions, and ideas. Because it relies on exaggeration and distortion, satire often has a humorous effect.

Caricature is a form of satire in which certain characteristics, such as physical features, are exaggerated. In the 15th century, when Leonardo da Vinci sketched the faces of clerics and nobles, the "charged portrait" was an important means of political and social criticism. Biting portraits provided a way to tear down a public figure. But the social impact of the political cartoon is not as potent as it used to be. As the 20th century wore on, politicians and other targets of political cartoons began to embrace and benefit from their own caricatures. Most U.S. presidents have become ardent collectors of political cartoons about themselves. President Lyndon Johnson reportedly liked seeing himself in cartoons so much that he didn't care whether they were flattering or not.[1] Look at the following caricature of President George Washington. Which of the features are distorted?

Hyperbole is language that exaggerates. It comes from the Greek word *hyperbole,* meaning "excess or extravagance." We are using hyperbole when we say, "He is as strong as a bull." In Mark Twain's classic novel *The Adventures of Huckleberry Finn,* the author uses hyperbole when he gives readers the following warning at the start of the book:

> NOTICE: *Persons attempting to find a motive in this narrative will be prosecuted; persons attempting to find a moral in it will be banished; persons attempting to find a plot in it will be shot.—By Order Of The Author*

---

[1]Information from Week in Review, *New York Times,* June 17, 2001, section 4, p. 16.

Another word for hyperbole is **overstatement.** In overstatement the subject is magnified beyond reality by using adjectives (*big, longer, best*) and sweeping generalizations (*every, always, never*). Look at this example:

He stood there, tall and proud—taller than Mount Everest and prouder than New England on the day the Patriots won their first Super Bowl.

Much of our humor is comic overstatement. Look at the following example:

Virginia's young son had been living in the back of his pickup truck for so long she decided to give it an address.

The satirist may also use **understatement,** which is saying less about something than is expected. As an example of understatement, consider Mark Twain's comment in the following story. In 1897, Samuel Clemens (Mark Twain) was staying in London at the same time as his cousin, Dr. James Ross Clemens. Dr. Clemens became ill and died, but the press mistakenly reported that it was Mark Twain who had died. To untangle the mix-up, Twain sent a cable from London to the Associated Press that read, "The reports of my death are greatly exaggerated."

"*A satirist is a man who discovers unpleasant things about himself and then applies it to other people.*"

—Peter McArthur

Jonathan Swift, well-known satirist of the 18th century and author of *Gulliver's Travels* and *A Modest Proposal,* gave this example:

Last week I saw a woman flayed alive, and you will hardly believe how it altered her appearance for the worse.

The long-running TV show *The Simpsons* received the prestigious George Foster Peabody Award for excellence in television. *The Simpsons* was cited for satire and social commentary. If you have not seen the show, try watching an episode or two. What kinds of things does Matt Groening, creator of *The Simpsons,* satirize? For example, using the "Grandpa" character, what is Groening saying about how elderly people are treated in this country?

The *Calvin and Hobbes* cartoon below uses satire to demonstrate how powerful the popular media are in influencing behavior. Even Calvin, who is portrayed as being very sophisticated about the media, is not immune. Is the cartoonist making a valid point about the media? Do you think young children are easily influenced by messages they receive from television? Why or why not?

When reading satire, pay close attention to the goals of the satirist, the devices used to accomplish his or her goals, and the tone. While a satire can have any tone, the most common is irony.

Calvin and Hobbes

CALVIN AND HOBBES © 1995 Watterson. Dist. By Universal Press Syndicate. Reprinted with permission. All rights reserved.

Exercise 6: Detecting Satire

Directions: Read this short satire and then answer the questions that follow.

The Animal School: The Administration of the School Curriculum with References to Individual Differences

by Dr. George H. Reavis, Assistant Superintendent, Cincinnati Public Schools, 1939–1948

Once upon a time, the animals decided they must do something heroic to meet the problems of "a new world." So they organized a school.

They adopted an activity curriculum consisting of running, climbing, swimming, and flying. To make it easier to administer the curriculum *all* the animals took *all* the subjects.

The duck was excellent in swimming, in fact better than his instructor; but he made only passing grades in flying and was very poor in running. Since he was slow in running, he had to stay after school and also drop swimming in order to practice running. This was kept up until his web feet were badly worn and he was only average in swimming. *But average was acceptable in school so nobody worried about that except the duck.*

The rabbit started at the top of the class in running, but had a nervous breakdown because of so much make-up work in swimming.

The squirrel was excellent in climbing until he developed frustration in the flying class where his teacher made him start from the ground up instead of from the treetop down. He also developed a "charlie horse" from overexertion and then got a C in climbing and a D in running.

The eagle was a problem child and was disciplined severely. In the climbing class he beat all the others to the top of the tree, but insisted on using his own way to get there.

At the end of the year, an abnormal eel that could swim exceedingly well, and also run, climb, and fly a little, had the highest average and was valedictorian.

The prairie dogs stayed out of school and fought the tax levy because the administration would not add digging and burrowing to the curriculum. They apprenticed their children to a badger and later joined the groundhogs and gophers to start a successful private school.

In Your Own Words

1. What makes this story satirical?
2. With regard to the school system, what changes would Reavis like to see implemented?
3. What criticism is the author making about the way schools are run?
4. Why was the eel chosen as the valedictorian?
5. What is the significance of this choice?
6. Is the prairie dogs' course of action similar to any contemporary trends in education?
7. Does this fable have a moral?

Exercise 7: Detecting Satire

In addition to *The Simpsons*, Matt Groening created *Life in Hell,* a comic book describing life in Los Angeles. This book led to a syndicated comic strip by the same name that appears in about 250 newspapers. He has authored at least seven other *Life in Hell* books.

Directions: Answer the following questions briefly.

1. Study Matt Groening's satirical cartoon. What is he saying about the current school situation?

2. What attitude about learning does the cartoon express?

3. Do you see yourself in this cartoon? Has your school experience been similar? Explain.

4. What attitude about adults does the cartoon express?

READING

> *"'There are a lot of people in this country who only use a handgun once or twice a year. . . . So we'll rent them a gun for a day or two.'"*

TUNING IN TO READING

This article, written in a satirical style, argues for stronger gun-control legislation.

BIO-SKETCH

Art Buchwald was one of the foremost humorists in the United States. His job, as he saw it, was to expose us to our failings as human beings and as members of society. Buchwald wrote numerous books and was a regular contributor to a syndicated newspaper column. He was also a recipient of the Pulitzer Prize.

NOTES ON VOCABULARY

chicken out   lose one's nerve; back out of something because of fear. *Chicken* is a slang term for "cowardly."

Russian roulette   loading a bullet into one chamber of a revolver, spinning the cylinder, and then pulling the trigger while pointing the gun at one's own head.

gutted   destroyed; removed the vital or essential parts from something.

dream come true   wild fancy or hope that is realized.

What is the play on words in Hurts Rent-A-Gun?

Hurts Rent-A-Gun

BY ART BUCHWALD

Is Buchwald optimistic or pessimistic about the possibility of gun control? (paragraph 1)

THE SENATE RECENTLY passed a new gun-control bill, which some observers consider worse than no bill at all. Any serious attempt at handgun registration was gutted, and Senate gun lovers even managed to repeal a 1968 gun law controlling the purchase of .22 rim-fire ammunition.

Why does Buchwald make the last name of his friend "Hurts"? (paragraph 2)

2 After the Senate got finished with its work on the gun-control bill, I received a telephone call from my friend Bromley Hurts, who told me he had a business proposition to discuss with me. I met him for lunch at a pistol range in Maryland.

3 "I think I've got a fantastic idea," he said, "I want to start a new business called Hurts Rent-A-Gun."

4 "What on earth for?" I asked.

Is Buchwald serious about proposing rent-a-gun counters at gas stations? (paragraph 8)

5 "There are a lot of people in this country who only use a handgun once or twice a year, and they don't want to go to all the expense of buying one. So we'll rent them a gun for a day or two. By leasing a firearm from us, they won't have to tie up all their money."

6 "That makes sense," I admitted.

7 "Say a guy is away from home on a trip, and he doesn't want to carry his own gun with him. He can rent a gun from us and then return it when he's finished with his business."

8 "You could set up rent-a-gun counters at gas stations," I said excitedly.

9 "And we could have stores in town where someone could rent a gun to settle a bet," Hurts said.

10 "A lot of people would want to rent a gun for a domestic quarrel," I said.

11 "Right. Say a jealous husband suspects there is someone at home with his wife. He rents a pistol from us and tries to catch them in the act. If he discovers his wife is alone, he isn't out the eighty dollars it would cost him to buy a gun."

12 "Don't forget the kids who want to play Russian roulette. They could pool their allowances and rent a gun for a couple of hours," I said.

13 "Our market surveys indicate," Hurts said, "that there are also a lot of kids who claim their parents don't listen to them. If they could rent a gun, they feel they could arrive at an understanding with their folks in no time."

14 "There's no end to the business," I said. "How would you charge for Hurts Rent-A-Gun?"

15 "There would be hourly rates, day rates, and weekly rates, plus ten cents for each bullet fired. Our guns would be the latest models, and we would guarantee clean barrels and the latest safety devices. If a gun malfunctions through no fault of the user we will give him another gun absolutely free."

16 "For many Americans it's a dream come true," I said.

17 "We've also made it possible for people to return the gun in another town. For example, if you rent the gun in Chicago and want to use it in Salt Lake City, you can drop it off there at no extra charge."

18 "Why didn't you start this before?"

19 "We wanted to see what happened with the gun-control legislation. We were pretty sure the Senate and the White House would not do anything about strong gun control, especially during an election year. But we didn't want to invest a lot of money until we were certain they would all chicken out."

20 "I'd like the franchise for Washington's National Airport," I said.

21 "You've got it. It's a great location," Hurts said. "You'll make a fortune in hijackings alone."

From Art Buchwald, *I Never Danced at the White House.* New York: Putman, 1973. Appeared originally in *The Washington Post,* August 17, 1972. © Tribune Media Services, Inc. All Rights Reserved. Reprinted with permission.

What is Buchwald saying in paragraphs 12 and 13?

_____

_____

_____

_____

What is Buchwald's concern here? (paragraphs 20–21)

_____

_____

_____

_____

   COMPREHENSION CHECKUP

Multiple Choice

Directions: For each item, circle the letter corresponding to the best answer.

_b_ 1. The topic of the article is
   a. car rental agencies.
   b. gun control.
   c. domestic violence.
   d. free enterprise.

_b_ 2. Buchwald chose the name Bromley Hurts because
   a. his wife's cousin has the same name.
   b. it is a "play" on Hertz Rent-A-Car.
   c. it indicates that guns can cause "hurt."
   d. both b and c.

_____ 3. The author's primary purpose in writing this satire is to
   a. persuade readers to stop buying guns.
   b. condemn the new gun-control bill.
   c. persuade readers to buy handguns.
   d. describe a lucrative business opportunity.

_b_   4. The tone of this article could best be described as
   a. sentimental and sad.
   b. humorous and ironic.
   c. angry and vindictive.
   d. cautious and logical.

_d_   5. According to the article, which of the following people would benefit
   from the fictitious Hurts Rent-A-Gun?
   a. a jealous spouse
   b. a man away from home on a trip
   c. a person wanting to settle a bet
   d. all of the above

 6. You can infer from the article that Buchwald believes that
   a. people can be trusted to use guns responsibly.
   b. people cannot be trusted to use guns responsibly.
   c. people who use guns should practice at pistol ranges.
   d. disposable guns are the wave of the future.

_____   7. The statement "for many Americans it's a dream come true" is an
   example of
   a. literary allusion.
   b. caricature.
   c. ironic exaggeration.
   d. understatement.

True or False

Directions: Indicate whether the following statements are true or false by writing **T** or
F in the space provided.

_F_   8. Buchwald likely favors strong gun-control legislation.

_T_   9. Buchwald is really happy with the new gun-control bill.

_T_   10. Leasing a gun is the same as owning one.

Short Answer

Directions: Answer the following questions briefly, in a few words, phrases, or sentences, as appropriate.

1. What details indicate Buchwald's desire for a stronger gun-control bill?

2. Who is Buchwald most critical of in this article?

3. Describe the tone of Buchwald's satire.

4. Buchwald implies an analogy between renting a gun and renting a car. List the details that show how Hertz Rent-A-Car, or any other car rental agency, is similar to Hurts Rent-A-Gun.

5. Hurts and Buchwald mention several specific uses for rental guns. What are they? Why did Buchwald include these reasons in his story?

6. Does Buchwald believe that the country will be a less or more dangerous place if handguns are more closely regulated? Give supporting reasons.

Vocabulary in Context

Directions: Underline the word or phrase in the second sentence that helps explain the meaning of the italicized word in the first sentence.

1. I can't imagine that Stephanie would fall for Joshua's _proposition._ After all, she already suffered from his last proposed scheme.

2. Do you think it is likely that they are going to *repeal* that law? They should revoke it because it makes no sense.

3. Doing *domestic* chores is one of my least favorite activities. However, if you don't take care of your home, it will fall apart.

4. Greg's computer *malfunctioned* again causing the loss of valuable data. If it fails to work one more time, I think he should get a new computer.

5. Sutin has the *franchise* for three Baskin-Robbins ice cream stores. As the owner of the right to operate the stores, he is expecting to make a lot of money.

6. Let's *pool* our money and buy some lottery tickets. We'll increase our chances of winning by putting our money together.

In Your Own Words

Do you think the easy availability of guns contributes to the higher rates of violent crime in the United States? Are you in favor of more gun control? Why or why not?

Internet Activity

You can find newspaper columns and articles written by Art Buchwald at www.washingtonpost.com. Type in "Buchwald." Select one of his pieces, print it, and explain what he is satirizing.

Exercise 8: Detecting Satire

Directions: The following cartoon offers an opposing viewpoint to the one expressed by Art Buchwald in the previous article. On the line provided, give the main idea of the cartoon.

Jerry Barnett, *The Indianapolis Star*. Reprinted with permission.

The main idea of this cartoon is: We wouldn't have our Independents if we had gun control laws.

Internet Activity

1. To obtain additional information about the issue of gun control, visit both of the following Web sites. One site presents the pro position to gun control, and the other site presents the con position. Write a summary paragraph contrasting these two viewpoints on this issue. Which viewpoint do you find more appealing?

   www.bradycampaign.org (The Brady Campaign to Prevent Gun Violence)

   www.nra.org (National Rifle Association)

2. You must be able to draw inferences to understand any cartoon, but political or editorial cartoons require a level of sophistication about current events. Find an editorial cartoon on one of the two Web sites given below, print it, and identify the cartoonist's main idea. What background knowledge on your part was required to interpret the cartoon? What inferences were you able to draw about the cartoonist's viewpoint?

   www.comicspage.com

   www.creators.com

Chapter Summary and Review

In Chapter 7, you learned how to recognize the tone of an article. You also became familiar with irony, satire, hyperbole, caricature, and understatement. Based on the material in Chapter 7, answer the following.

Short Answer

Directions: Give synonyms for each of the following tone words.

1. arrogant _cocky_
2. whining _complaining_
3. optimistic _spontaneous_
4. pessimistic _worryer_
5. vindictive _bitter_
6. dictatorial _smart_

Directions: Define the following word.

7. Satire _Sarcastic_ _____

Vocabulary in Context

Directions: Choose one of the following words to complete the sentences below. Use each word only once.

caricatures	emotional	hyperbole	satire

8. The phrase "strong as an ox" is usually an example of _hyperbole_

9. Tone refers to the _emotional_ quality of an article.

10. Political cartoonists often like to draw _caricature_ of our presidents.

11. _satire_ relies on exaggeration and distortion and often has a humorous effect.

In Vocabulary Unit 3, you learned that *enn* and *ann* mean "year." In this unit, you will study some more words using these word parts. We will also introduce word parts related to the five senses, size, and writing.

Sunflower

ann—year   enn—year

anniversary	The yearly return of a date or event, as in a wedding *anniversary*.
annual	*Annual* usually means "yearly," but it is also a term used to describe a plant living only one year or season. A sunflower is an example of an *annual* because it completes its life cycle, produces seeds, and dies after growing only one season. *Annual* flowers will not bloom again.
biannual	Happening twice a year. The equinox is a *biannual* event.
biennial	Happening every two years; also a plant that lasts for two years. Congressional elections take place *biennially*.
perennial	Continuing for a long time; year after year; also a plant that has roots that remain alive during the winter and that blooms year after year, such as the iris. The New York Yankees are *perennially* a good baseball team.
anno Domini (A.D.)	*Anno* means "year," and *Domini* means "Lord," so *A.D.* does not mean "after death," but "Year of Our Lord." The Civil War began in *A.D.* 1860.

The largest television audience for a live broadcast was the worldwide audience that listened to and watched the funeral of Princess Diana on September 6, 1997, estimated at 2.5 billion.

spectators—The largest number of spectators at a one-day sporting event is the approximately 2.5 million people who line the streets of New York every year to watch the New York Marathon.

audio—hear   ology—the study of; the science of   spec(t)—to see

audience	A group of people gathered to hear (and see) a speaker, play, or concert; also a formal interview with someone in a high position. The local parish priest was granted an *audience* with the pope.
audiology	The science of hearing.
auditorium	A room where an audience usually gathers to listen.
audition	A hearing to judge the skills of a musician or actor for a job. When you *audition* for a part in a play, the director will be interested in hearing how you read your lines. There were no microphones in ancient Greece, so actors who were in plays had to be able to say their lines loud enough so that the people in the back row of the amphitheaters could hear them.
auditory	Having to do with the sense of hearing; also your listening skills. In the first part of this textbook, you discovered whether you were an *auditory* learner.
spectator	A person who sees or watches something without being an active participant. You might be a *spectator* at a football game.

spectrum—One beautiful spectrum, the rainbow, occurs when light hits moisture in the air at a certain angle.

speculate   To mentally see something in a serious way.   Are you *speculating* about what you are going to do tonight?

spectrum   A *spectrum* is a range of color, as in a rainbow or in light shining through a prism. The word also sometimes refers to a range of ideas.   In the college classroom, there was a wide *spectrum* of opinion on the subject of abortion.

vis—see   in—not; into, within

visible   Capable of being seen.   The mountains were *visible* from a great distance.

invisible   Not capable of being seen. Here *in* means "not." The Latin prefix *in* appears in many English words. Sometimes it means "not," and other times it means "into." When you come to a word using *in*, you may need to use context clues or your dictionary to determine the correct meaning.

"Vision is the art of seeing things invisible."

—Jonathan Swift

vista   A view or outlook seen from some distance.

visionary   Looking into the future.   He had a *visionary* scheme to create human colonies on Mars. *Visionary* also means a prophet or seer. In the Old Testament, prophets were *visionaries* because they looked into the future.

audio-visual   Involving both hearing and seeing.   DVD recorders are examples of *audio-visual* equipment.

phono—sound

phonograph   A device for reproducing sound recorded in a turning record. The word literally means "sound written down."   We used to listen to records on a *phonograph*. What's the modern-day equivalent of the *phonograph*?

phonics   The study of speech sounds and their written symbols (letters).   Your teacher might have taught you *phonics* when you were learning to read.

Frank and Ernest

FRANK & ERNEST: © Thaves/Dist. by Newspaper Enterprise Association, Inc.

macro—large   micro—small, or one-millionth part; enlarging, amplifying
bio—life   scope—an instrument for seeing

microwave   A small electromagnetic wave; also an oven that cooks with *microwaves*. The literal meaning is "small wave."

	micrometer	One-millionth of a meter.
microphone—The smallest microphone is 0.06 by 0.03 inch.	**microphone**	An instrument for amplifying sound. In this word *micro* means "amplifying what is small or weak."
	microscope	An instrument for making very small objects look larger. In this word *micro* means "enlarging what is small."
	microeconomics	An economic analysis of small-scale parts of the economy, such as the growth of a single industry or demand for a single product.
	macroeconomics	The part of economic theory that deals with the larger picture, such as national income, total employment, and total consumption.
	microbiology	The branch of biology that deals with small life organisms.

magna—large   mega—large; one million   tele—distance

	magnify	To make larger.
	megaphone	A device for magnifying the voice; literally means "large sound." Police may use *megaphones* to be heard over the noise of the crowd.
telescope—The largest telescope in the world is located on Mauna Kea, Hawaii. Its mirror is 394 inches wide.	**megabyte**	One million pieces of information; loosely one million bytes.
	telescope	An optical device for seeing distant objects; use of a *telescope* makes these distant objects appear to be closer.
	telephone	A device for transmitting speech or computerized information over distances; "sound from a distance."
telephone—The first telephone book was published in 1878 in New Haven, Connecticut. It listed only 50 names.	**telephoto**	A camera lens that magnifies a distant object so that it appears to be close. A photographer working for a tabloid magazine was able to get a picture of Prince William by using a camera equipped with a *telephoto* lens.
	telepathy	Mind reading; knowledge communicated from one person to another without using any of the five senses; "feeling from a distance."
	teleconference	A conference of persons in different locations by means of the telephone or TV.
television—"All television is educational television. The question is: what is it teaching?"	**television**	"Seeing from a distance."

scribe, script—write   biblio—book   pre—before   post—after

	scribble	To write carelessly, quickly.
—Nicholas Johnson	**inscription**	Something engraved; a short, signed message. (Here *in* means "into.") Because Thomas Jefferson wanted to be remembered for the things he had left to the people, and not for the high offices he had held, the *inscription* on his tomb reads: "Here was buried Thomas Jefferson, author of the Declaration of American Independence, of the Statute of Virginia for religious freedom, and father of the University of Virginia."
	prescription	Something advised or ordered; a written direction for the preparation and use of medicine; "written before." Following her attack of the flu, her doctor's *prescription* was lots of fluids and complete bed rest.

postscript	A note written after the signature in a letter (P.S.).
scribe	A writer, author, or secretary. Before the invention of printing, the *scribes* were professional penmen who copied manuscripts and documents.
Scripture	Any sacred writing or book; a Bible passage.
Bible	The sacred book of Christianity; the Old Testament and New Testament.
bibliography	Since *graph* means "write," a *bibliography* literally means "books written down." A *bibliography* is a list of sources of information on a particular subject. When you write a research paper for one of your classes, you will include a *bibliography* at the end of your paper listing the books and articles you used for your research.

Exercise 1: Word Parts

Directions: Write sentences using the following words. Add whatever endings are necessary.

1. audiologist _____

_____

2. perennial _____

_____

3. speculate _____

_____

4. scribe _____

_____

5. biennial _____

_____

6. visionary _____

_____

7. telepathy _____

_____

8. scribble _____

Exercise 2: Word Parts

Directions: In the blanks below, write the word from the list that best completes the sentence. Use each word only once.

audition	biannual	bibliography	inscription	invisible
magnify	microwave	perennial	phonics	scribbles

1. Marco decided to fill his garden with _____ plants that don't have to be replaced year after year.

2. The former employees of the department store hold a(n) _____ luncheon in January and July of every year.

3. Educators have not decided whether it is better to teach young children to read by the whole-language approach or to use _____ to teach them the sounds the letters make.

4. The mother saved all of her child's drawings, although most were little more than colorful _____.

5. Marla's research paper was excellent, but she received a D because she forgot to include a complete list of her sources in a(n) _____.

6. The _____ on the wedding ring read, "To my beloved Luz, the light of my life."

7. Millions of baby boomers need glasses to _____ the small print in books.

8. The young actor's _____ for the play apparently did not go well because he did not get the role.

9. A chameleon can make itself almost _____ by changing colors to match its surroundings.

10. The _____ is a more popular appliance than the dishwasher.

Exercise 3: Word Parts

Directions: In the blanks below, write the word from the list that best completes the sentence. Use each word only once.

biennial	megaphone	microphones	postscript	spectators
spectrum	teleconference	telepathy	visionary	vista

1. I would think that if anyone could communicate by means of _____ it would be identical twins.

2. The police officer, who was using a _____ to be heard over the crowd, urged the soccer fans to disperse quickly and quietly.

3. Rather than waste time, energy, and money flying to New York to go over the details of the will, all of the parties agreed to hold a _____ instead.

4. Marta's daughter wrote her a wonderful letter for Mother's Day, and as a _____ she wrote, "I love you."

5. Although the number of _____ actually attending the World Series has not declined, the number of viewers watching on TV certainly has.

6. During the televised debate, both candidates' _____ went dead for over 10 minutes.

7. The pansy is a _____ plant that produces a flower in the second year.

8. After the arduous climb to the top of Mount Everest, we were rewarded with a sweeping _____ of Southeast Asia.

9. The polls certainly revealed a wide _____ of opinion about future tax cuts.

10. In his book *The Road Ahead*, Bill Gates clearly demonstrates why he is the leading communications _____ of the 21st century.

Vocabulary Unit 4 Crossword

ACROSS CLUES

1. A word part meaning "two."
2. Written before.
7. Instrument to see from a distance.
10. Roses are _____ flowers. They bloom year after year.
11. A word part meaning "year."
12. A word part meaning "side."
14. "Year of Our Lord" (no space between words).
15. The sacred book of Christianity.
16. A word part meaning "to see."
20. A person who looks into the future.
22. The _____ for the Opening Ceremony of the Winter Olympics was one of the largest in history.
25. View seen from a distance.
26. A list of books or references at the end of a paper.
27. A writer.
28. A word part meaning "half."
29. Your listening skills.
30. P.S.
31. A range of light or ideas.

DOWN CLUES

1. Every other year.
3. A group that watches an event.
4. Sound from a distance.
5. Police might use one of these.
6. Seeing from a distance.
8. An instrument for amplifying sound.
9. A word part meaning "1,000,000."
10. A word part meaning "sound."
13. The equinox is a(n) _____ event.
17. A word part meaning "the same amount or size."
18. A word part meaning "three."
19. Happening once a year, such as a wedding _____.
21. Sacred writing.
23. A word part meaning "write."
24. A word part meaning "marriage."

Recognizing Modes of Writing

Carlos Santana

Music is a collection of sounds that are arranged into patterns. These sounds, or notes, may be produced by human voices, instruments, or even nature itself. When sound, or noise, is organized or manipulated by a person into some kind of pattern it may become music.

— **Caroline Grimshaw, from** *Music Connections*

Even jazz—that glorification of the senses . . . is organized [and] obeys the principles of form and structure.

—**Andre Hodeir, from** *The Forms of Music*

CHAPTERS IN PART 4

It may surprise you that jazz, which often seems so lively and creative, has structure. Writing, too, has structure. On a general level, writing is structured into what we will call modes of writing. These modes of writing are narrative, descriptive, expository, and persuasive. And within these general structures are more specific structures, which we will call modes of organization. Understanding the ways in which writing may be structured will make you a better, more efficient reader. The purpose of Part 4 is to develop your understanding of modes of writing and modes of organization.

8

Four Primary Modes of Writing

CHAPTER PREVIEW

In this chapter, you will

- Become familiar with the four modes of writing: narrative, descriptive, expository, and persuasive.

An Introduction to Modes of Writing (Rhetorical Modes)

In longer reading selections, the main idea is often referred to as the **thesis.** The thesis, just like the main idea in paragraphs, expresses the most important point the writer is trying to make. You may also hear the thesis referred to as the *controlling idea* because its primary purpose is to hold the essay or story together.

In the process of creating written work, most writers select a **mode of writing** (sometimes called a *rhetorical mode*) that helps them achieve their purpose. There are four primary modes of writing: narrative, descriptive, expository, and persuasive.

Narrative Mode

Material written in a **narrative mode** tells a story, either true or fictional. In narrative writing, the events of a story are usually ordered by time. The excerpt below is an example of narrative writing. In this excerpt, who is narrating the significant events of the story? What key point is she making?

> The click of the door handle seems entirely too loud as I pull open the door to check the breathing of my three sleeping children. They look so peaceful, sleeping there in the back of my station wagon under the yellow light of a flickering street lamp.
>
> I smooth the curls on Lydia's scarred face and gently close the door. Those scars—they are just one of the reasons I am seeing my children to sleep in my car. Walking through the backdoor of the kitchen, I look back once and then, all right, just once more. I smile at the cooks as I rush through the kitchen and grab the food for my customers from under the warmers. They'll keep an eye out the door for me.
>
> It's after 1:00 A.M. when my last table leaves. I thought they would never finish. Oh, to have that kind of time to linger over a meal. It's been so long since I've had that kind of freedom. I carefully place the wineglasses in the

bus tub next to the dessert plates and haul it all down the stairs. My mother would tell me to take more than one trip, but I'd always rather make one long, painful trip than two or three.

I tip out the bartender and head for the small parking lot behind the restaurant, where, I am told, my children are still blissfully asleep. I realize that I am tiptoeing my way out to the car, which makes no sense at all. I carefully open the car door and sink into the front seat. I let my head fall onto the steering wheel. I am so tired.

I am home.

"Hi, Mom," I hear from behind me. Startled, I whip around to find Matthew, the oldest, who is all of five, blinking his eyes awake.

"How was work?" he asks.

"It was fine," I reply. "Very busy. It's late though—you should go back to sleep. We'll talk in the morning."

"OK," he says, and within seconds he is out again, snuggled up against Alex, who is just fourteen months old. Living in the car doesn't seem to faze any of them in the slightest. Oh sure, they ask why we have to keep sleeping in the car, but the answer seems to suffice, and they don't whine about not having a television. Well, we do have a television, actually. It was a graduation present years before, and it's tucked in front of the passenger seat. I tried to sell it, but it wasn't worth much, so I decided to keep it. A last vestige of middle-class life, if you will. I was a middle-class housewife once upon a time. . . .

Making the leap from given-every-opportunity, spoiled-in-every-way middle-class child to boring middle-class housewife and eventually to homeless single mother should be harder than it is. In reality, it doesn't take much more than a series of bad judgment calls and wrong decisions that, at the time, appear to be perfectly reasonable and in most cases for the better.

My own journey into homelessness did not begin with drug use, alcoholism, or any of the other things we, as a society, so often attribute to such a downward spiral. Instead, I followed my bliss right into the back of a Subaru station wagon.

At eighteen, I was a promising freshman at American University in Washington, D.C. At nineteen, I was married and pregnant with my first child. By the time I was twenty-five, I had three children and within a year, I was separated from my husband and living out of the backseat of my car, my three children all under the age of six.

This is the story of how we were homeless while I simultaneously tried to hide it from my family, my friends, and the rest of the world. By day, I walked the streets of Stone Harbor, Maine, as the completely normal mother of three children, looking in shop windows and going to the library and the Laundromat. By night, however, I was driving around town, looking for a place to sleep and park, bathing at the truck stop, and boiling ramen noodle dinners on public grills.

I had a decent job waiting tables and, although I did my best to hide my situation, I found that revealing myself, even in small amounts, gained me not only a cadre of friends, but an occasional helping hand. In time, I pulled us out of homelessness and returned us to a more normal lifestyle, but the hot days of that summer will never leave me. Neither will what I learned from them.

"Prologue," from *Without a Net* by Michelle Kennedy, pp. 1–3. Copyright © 2005 by Michelle Kennedy. Used by permission of Viking Penguin, a division of Penguin Group (USA) Inc. For on-line information about other Penguin Group (USA) books and authors, see the Internet website at: http://www.penguin.com

Descriptive Mode

With material written in a **descriptive mode,** the emphasis is on providing details that describe a person, place, object, concept, or experience. The writing may employ the use of figurative language and include material that appeals to one or more of the five senses. Descriptive writing most commonly deals with visual perceptions but not always. The excerpt below is an example of descriptive writing. What details does the writer use to give you the sensation of actually experiencing poverty? Name four vivid details the author uses to describe the poverty. After reading the excerpt, what is your overall impression of poverty?

> Poverty is getting up every morning from a dirt- and illness-stained mattress. The sheets have long since been used for diapers. Poverty is living in a smell that never leaves. This is a smell of urine, sour milk, and spoiling food sometimes joined with the strong smell of long-cooked onions. Onions are cheap. If you have smelled this smell, you did not know how it came. It is the smell of the outdoor privy. It is the smell of young children who cannot walk the long dark way in the night. It is the smell of the mattresses where years of "accidents" have happened. It is the smell of the milk which has gone sour because the refrigerator long has not worked, and it costs money to get it fixed. It is the smell of rotting garbage. I could bury it, but where is the shovel? Shovels cost money.

From Jo Goodwin Parker, "What Is Poverty?" in *America's Other Children: Public Schools Outside Suburbia,* ed. George Henderson, p. 216. Copyright © 1971 by University of Oklahoma Press, Norman, OK. Reprinted by permission. All rights reserved.

Expository Mode

An author who is trying to explain something will likely use an **expository mode.** Expository writing explains ideas and how things work. It is more likely to be logical and factual. Much of the material that you read in your textbooks follows an expository mode. The excerpt below is an example of expository writing. What is being explained to you? What are some factual details that are intended to inform you?

The Poor: Who and How Many?

The U.S. government defines the poverty line as the annual cost of a thrifty food budget for an urban family of four, multiplied by three to include the cost of housing, clothes, and other necessities. Families whose incomes fall below that line are officially considered poor. In 2007, the poverty line was set at an annual income of roughly $20,000 for a family of four. One in eight Americans—roughly thirty-five million people, including more than ten million children—lives below the poverty line. If they could all join hands, they would form a line stretching from New York to Los Angeles and back again.

America's poor include individuals of all ages, races, religions, and regions, but poverty is concentrated among certain groups. Children are one of the largest groups of poor Americans. One in every five children lives in poverty. Most poor children live in single-parent families, usually with the mother. In fact, a high proportion of Americans residing in families headed by divorced, separated, or unmarried women live below the poverty line. These families are at a disadvantage because most women earn less than men for comparable work, especially in nonprofessional fields. Women without higher education or special skills often cannot find jobs that pay significantly more than the child-care expenses they incur if they work outside the home. Single-parent, female-headed families are roughly five times as likely as two-income families to fall below the poverty line, a situation referred to as "the feminization of poverty."

From Thomas Patterson, *We the People*, 7th Edition, p. 577. Copyright © 2008 by The McGraw-Hill Companies, Inc. Reprinted with permission.

Persuasive Mode

Material written in a **persuasive mode** is meant to convince you of something. Persuasive writing tends to be about controversial topics. It presents an argument and offers evidence. It is writing that is considered to be biased. The excerpt below is an example of persuasive writing. What idea is the author trying to convince you to accept? What course of action is she recommending?

> It is common among the non-poor to think of poverty as a sustainable condition—austere, perhaps, but they get by somehow, don't they? They are "always with us." What is harder for the non-poor to see is poverty as acute distress. The lunch that consists of Doritos or hot dog rolls, leading to faintness before the end of the shift. The "home" that is also a car or a van. The illness or injury that must be "worked through," with gritted teeth because there's no sick pay or health insurance and the loss of one day's pay will mean no groceries for the next.
>
> These experiences are not part of a sustainable lifestyle, even a lifestyle of chronic deprivation and relentlessly low-level punishment. They are, by almost any standard of subsistence, emergency situations. And that is how we should see the poverty of so many millions of low-wage Americans—as a state of emergency.

Excerpt from "Poverty" in *Nickel and Dimed: On (Not) Getting By in America* by Barbara Ehrenreich, p. 214. Copyright © 2001 by Barbara Ehrenreich. Reprinted by permission of Henry Holt and Company, LLC.

The reading selections that follow illustrate modes of writing. Though these selections come from a variety of sources, they all, either directly or indirectly, concern the topic of relationships.

Narrative

READING

> "The woman said, 'Pick up my pocketbook, boy, and give it here.'"

TUNING IN TO READING

What would you do if someone attempted to steal your purse or wallet? After reading the first paragraph of this short story, what do you think is going to happen next?

As you read this narrative, notice how the action of the story is told in sequence, with a clear beginning, middle, and end. Try to discover the larger message about relationships that the author is illustrating.

BIO-SKETCH

Langston Hughes (1902–1967) is one of the best-known African American writers of the 20th century and the first to live solely from his writings and lectures. Shortly after his birth in Joplin, Missouri, his parents were divorced. As a result, Hughes spent much

READING *continued*

of his early childhood living in poverty with his maternal grandmother. In the following short story, the character of Mrs. Jones is most probably based on his grandmother. Hughes, a graduate of Lincoln University, was a prolific writer of poems, short stories, and plays. He also wrote two books. Throughout his literary career, he was sharply criticized by other African American writers who believed that he portrayed an unattractive view of African American life.

NOTES ON VOCABULARY

thank you, ma'm   a small bump in the road sometimes put there to force drivers to go slowly. In earlier times, if a young couple went out riding, the male was entitled to a kiss every time he hit one of the bumps. He acknowledged that kiss with a polite *"Thank you, ma'm."*

pocketbook   the original *pocketbook* was a man's purse that resembled an open book with a clasp at the top and that conveniently fit into the owner's pocket.

Thank You, Ma'm   BY LANGSTON HUGHES

She was a large woman with a large purse that had everything in it but a hammer and nails. It had a long strap, and she carried it slung across her shoulder. It was about eleven o'clock at night, dark, and she was walking alone, when a boy ran up behind her and tried to snatch her purse. The strap broke with the sudden single tug the boy gave it from behind. But the boy's weight and the weight of the purse combined caused him to lose his balance. Instead of taking off full blast as he had hoped, the boy fell on his back on the sidewalk and his legs flew up. The large woman simply turned around and kicked him right square in his blue-jeaned sitter. Then she reached down, picked the boy up by his shirt front, and shook him until his teeth rattled.

2   After that the woman said, "Pick up my pocketbook, boy, and give it here."

3   She still held him tightly. But she bent down enough to permit him to stoop and pick up her purse. Then she said, "Now ain't you ashamed of yourself?"

4   Firmly gripped by his shirt front, the boy said, "Yes'm."

5   The woman said, "What did you want to do it for?"

6   The boy said, "I didn't aim to."

7   She said, "You a lie!"

8   By that time two or three people passed, stopped, turned to look, and some stood watching.

9   "If I turn you loose, will you run?" asked the woman.

10   "Yes'm," said the boy.

11   "Then I won't turn you loose," said the woman. She did not release him.

12   "Lady, I'm sorry," whispered the boy.

13   "Um-hum! Your face is dirty. I got a great mind to wash your face for you. Ain't you got nobody home to tell you to wash your face?"

14   "No'm," said the boy.

15   "Then it will get washed this evening," said the large woman, starting up the street, dragging the frightened boy behind her.

16   He looked as if he were fourteen or fifteen, frail and willow-wild, in tennis shoes and blue jeans.

17   The woman said, "You ought to be my son. I would teach you right from wrong. Least I can do right now is to wash your face. Are you hungry?"

18   "No'm," said the being-dragged boy. "I just want you to turn me loose."

19   "Was I bothering *you* when I turned that corner?" asked the woman.

20   "No'm."

21   "But you put yourself in contact with *me*," said the woman. "If you think that

that contact is not going to last awhile, you got another thought coming. When I get through with you, sir, you are going to remember Mrs. Luella Bates Washington Jones."

22   Sweat popped out on the boy's face and he began to struggle. Mrs. Jones stopped, jerked him around in front of her, put a half nelson about his neck, and continued to drag him up the street. When she got to her door, she dragged the boy inside, down a hall, and into a large kitchenette-furnished room at the rear of the house. She switched on the light and left the door open. The boy could hear other roomers laughing and talking in the large house. Some of their doors were open, too, so he knew he and the woman were not alone. The woman still had him by the neck in the middle of her room.

23   She said, "What is your name?"

24   "Roger," answered the boy.

25   "Then, Roger you go to that sink and wash your face," said the woman, whereupon she turned him loose—at last. Roger looked at the door—looked at the woman—looked at the door—*and went to the sink.*

26   "Let the water run until it gets warm," she said. "Here's a clean towel."

27   "You gonna take me to jail?" asked the boy, bending over the sink.

28   "Not with that face, I would not take you nowhere," said the woman. "Here I am trying to get home to cook me a bite to eat, and you snatch my pocketbook! Maybe you ain't been to your supper either, late as it be. Have you?"

29   "There's nobody home at my house," said the boy.

30   "Then we'll eat," said the woman. "I believe you're hungry—or been hungry—to try to snatch my pocketbook!"

31   "I want a pair of blue suede shoes," said the boy.

32   "Well, you didn't have to snatch *my* pocketbook to get some suede shoes," said Mrs. Luella Bates Washington Jones. "You could of asked me."

33   "M'am?"

34   The water dripping from his face, the boy looked at her. There was a long pause. A very long pause. After he had dried his face, and not knowing what else to do, dried it again, the boy turned around, wondering what next. The door was open. He could make a dash for it down the hall. He could run, run, run, *run!*

35   The woman was sitting on the daybed. After a while she said, "I were young once and I wanted things I could not get."

36   There was another long pause. The boy's mouth opened. Then he frowned, not knowing he frowned.

37   The woman said, "Um-hum! You thought I was going to say *but,* didn't you? You thought I was going to say, *but I didn't snatch people's pocketbooks.* Well, I wasn't going to say that." Pause. Silence. "I have done things, too, which I would not tell you, son—neither tell God, if He didn't already know. Everybody's got something in common. So you set down while I fix us something to eat. You might run that comb through your hair so you will look presentable."

38   In another corner of the room behind a screen was a gas plate and an icebox. Mrs. Jones got up and went behind the screen. The woman did not watch the boy to see if he was going to run now, nor did she watch her purse, which she left behind her on the daybed. But the boy took care to sit on the far side of the room, away from the purse, where he thought she could easily see him out of the corner of her eye if she wanted to. He did not trust the woman *not* to trust him. And he did not want to be mistrusted now.

39   "Do you need somebody to go to the store," asked the boy, "maybe to get some milk or something?"

40   "Don't believe I do," said the woman, "unless you just want sweet milk yourself. I was going to make cocoa out of this canned milk I got here."

41   "That will be fine," said the boy.

42   She heated some lima beans and ham she had in the icebox, made the cocoa, and set the table. The woman did not ask the boy anything about where he lived, or his folks, or anything else that would embarrass him. Instead, as they ate, she told him about her job in a hotel beauty shop that stayed open late, what the work was like, and how all kinds of women came in and out, blonds,

An ice box was what people used before electricity. It literally held a block of ice to keep food cold.

Suede was first used in gloves in Sweden and France in the 1880s.

red–heads, and Spanish. Then she cut him a half of her ten–cent cake.

43 "Eat some more, son," she said.

44 When they were finished eating, she got up and said, "Now here. Take this ten dollars and buy yourself some blue suede shoes. And next time, do not make the mistake of latching onto *my* pocketbook *nor nobody else's*—because shoes got by dev–ilish ways will burn your feet. I got to get my rest now. But from here on in, son, I hope you will behave yourself."

45 She led him down the hall to the front door and opened it. "Good night! Behave yourself, boy!" she said, looking out into the street as he went down the steps.

46 The boy wanted to say something else other than, "Thank you, Ma'm," to Mrs. Luella Bates Washington Jones, but he couldn't do so as he turned at the barren stoop and looked back at the large woman in the door. He barely managed to say, "Thank you," before she shut the door. And he never saw her again.

✓ COMPREHENSION CHECKUP

Short Answer

Directions: Answer the question briefly, in no more than a sentence or two.

What is the main idea the author is trying to convey?

_____

Sequencing

Directions: Number the sentences to put the events in the correct chronological (or *time*) sequence.

_____ Roger tells Mrs. Jones that he wants some blue suede shoes.

_____ Roger thanks Mrs. Jones.

_____ Roger combs his hair.

_____ Roger offers to go to the store for Mrs. Jones.

_____ Mrs. Jones kicks Roger and shakes him roughly.

_____ Mrs. Jones serves Roger dinner and tells him about her job.

_____ Mrs. Jones drags Roger behind her.

_____ Roger washes his face.

_____ Mrs. Jones gives Roger ten dollars to buy some blue suede shoes.

_____ Roger tries to steal Mrs. Jones's purse.

In Your Own Words

In Your Own Words

1. When did Mrs. Jones decide to take Roger home to her house?

2. Why didn't Mrs. Jones call the police? Do you think Roger had tried to steal anything before?

3. Why didn't Roger run when he finally was given the opportunity?

4. When they were finally at her home, why did Mrs. Jones give Roger the chance to steal her purse?

5. Why does Mrs. Jones want Roger to make himself "presentable"? How are her suggestions interpreted by Roger?

6. At the end of their meal together, why did Mrs. Jones give Roger the money to buy his blue suede shoes?

7. What lesson do you think Mrs. Jones was trying to teach Roger?

8. Look at the "Notes on Vocabulary" for an unusual meaning of the phrase "thank you, ma'm." What do you think Hughes means to imply by the title of this story? Do you think he made use of this special meaning?

9. Do you think a similar incident could happen today? Or are people too frightened to get involved in another person's life?

Written Assignment

1. Describe the character of Mrs. Jones. Use as many descriptive details as possible.

2. Trace the character development of Roger. How does his behavior change as the result of Mrs. Jones's actions?

3. Discuss how you helped someone or someone helped you. Give details about what happened and how you felt.

Internet Activity

Discover more about Langston Hughes by going to the following Web site:

www.poets.org/poets/

Type in his name, read a short biography about him, and then read one of his poems. Print the poem and write a short paragraph discussing the tone of the poem and its use of figurative language.

Descriptive

READING

"What I had was a frail and failing old woman who couldn't take a shower on her own."

TUNING IN TO READING

Have you ever helped someone who was very ill for an extended period of time? Do you recall what the experience was like?

While reading this descriptive essay, notice how the key details describe both the author's mother and the author's experience giving her a shower. Because of the emphasis on sensory images, readers can visualize the scene being depicted.

BIO-SKETCH

John Daniel is a poet and essayist living in Oregon. He is the author of two books of poetry, *Common Ground* (1988) and *All Things Touched by Wind* (1994). He is also the author of a work of nonfiction titled *Rogue River Journal: A Winter Alone* (2005). His mother, described in the selection below, died in 1992.

NOTES ON VOCABULARY

Alzheimer's a progressive, irreversible disease characterized by deterioration or loss of function of brain cells causing severe dementia. Former President Ronald Reagan was an acknowledged sufferer of Alzheimer's, which has been called "the disease of the century." The disease is named after Alois Alzheimer, the German physician who first described the condition.

A Son's Memoir

John Daniel

M Y MOTHER WAS TOUGH AS LOBSTER SHELL, solid as New England granite, lively as the wind. . . .

2   In 1988, when she was 80, my mother agreed to leave her home on the Maine coast and live with my wife and me in Portland, Oregon. She was frail, slowed to a stooped-back shuffle. Her memory was failing. She was frequently disoriented and confused. She lived her last four years with us, and it was to understand those years, their burdens and their blessings, that I wrote *Looking After.* The story that follows is composed of an excerpt from the book.

"The only gift is a portion of thyself."
—Ralph Waldo Emerson

3   I never looked forward to helping my mother with her shower. She wasn't the least self-conscious about baring her body in my presence, but something in me shrank from it. To be with her in her nakedness seemed too intimate for a grown son. And some other part of me, the child who wants always to be cared for and never burdened with responsibility, felt put upon and put out. Why was I having to do this? It seemed an indignity, and it touched an open wound. I had no child to bathe, to make faces at, to splash and laugh with. Most likely I never would. What I had was a frail and failing old woman who couldn't take a shower on her own.

4   Talking her into it was the first challenge. "Oh, I don't need a shower," she would say. "I just had one yesterday, didn't I?"

5   "You haven't had one for a week."

6   "But I don't *do* anything. Why do I need a shower?"

7   It wasn't only bad memory and lapsing judgment that made her resist, of course. It was also that the shower was strenuous for her, and she didn't want to acknowledge, or couldn't, that she needed help with anything so simple. In her own mind, the mind I believe she inhabited most of the time, she was perfectly capable of taking a shower by herself if she wanted to. In this mind, she was still the woman she had been five years ago, a woman who came and went and drove a car, a woman who lived on her own on the coast of Maine and was only temporarily exiled in a distant place. This woman was honestly perplexed when we bought her a cane and asked her, over and over again, to use it. What need had Zilla Daniel for a cane? Somewhere inside her she was not only an able-bodied woman but still a Sea Scout, climbing the rigging in a bright clear wind.

8   But in her present mind she knew, whenever she leaned far forward in a chair and tried to stiff-arm herself to her feet, whenever she steadied herself with a hand on the wall as she shuffled to the bathroom, just how incapable she had become. She knew, and she hated it. How could she not have hated it? And if she had to bear it, she didn't want me or my wife, Marilyn, or anyone else to have to help her bear it. She wanted to carry herself on her own stooped shoulders. I can still hear her making her way to the toilet with her left hand pulling her nightgown tight behind her, disgustedly whispering "No, no" to her bladder that

could not hold back what it should have held back. As if she were castigating an unbroken puppy, but without the tolerance she would have granted an innocent thing. Standing for any length of time was hard for my mother, and so the shower was a kind of siege. She would grip the soap tray with both hands as I got the water temperature right—"Aaant!" she would holler, "too cold!"—and soaped a washcloth to scrub her sway-spined back. Even the soap met resistance.

9 . . . "It's just one more thing that has to come off."

10 "Well, it does come off," I answered, peeling open a bar of Dial. "It rinses off."

11 "My dear, it leaves a residue. Plain water is enough."

12 "Mother, for God's sake. . . . You need soap to get clean."

13 "Yes, Father," she said with a scowl.

14 Eventually we worked out a mulish compromise. We used Ivory, which we both agreed was the most natural. I washed her back and buttocks with a soaped washcloth, she held the cloth for a few seconds in the shower spray before washing her front. . . . Then I helped her down to the bath stool, where she rested a while and washed her lower legs and feet. The skin of her shins was dry and papery, perpetually blotched with dark purple—not impact bruises but bruises of age.

15 As I lathered shampoo into her wet white curls, her head would bow from the pressure of my fingers. I'd ask her to hold it up and she would for a second or two, then it would slowly sink again. It must have taken a major effort just to hold herself as upright as she did in her last years. All the while she was slowly bending, slowly folding, curling toward the fetal comfort of the grave.

16 She squeezed her eyes shut as I rinsed her hair in the shower stream. She scrunched up her face, stuck her lips out, and sputtered through the soapy runoff. It was in that recurring moment of her life with us, her hair flattened to her head, darkened a little with that soaking spray, that I could almost see my mother as a girl—swimming the cold swells off Hancock Park, splashing and laughing, shouting something toward shore, laying into the water with strong, even strokes that would take her where she wanted to go.

17 She would let me stop rinsing only when she could rub a bit of her hair between finger and thumb and make it squeak. Then I would steady her out of the shower stall, her two hands in mine. It felt at moments like a kind of dance, a dance that maybe I knew how to do and needed to do. Who was that, doing the dance? Who was it who allowed himself those moments of pleasure helping his mother from the shower? When I look back at that scene in the bathroom, I see a boy in my place. A solemn boy with a bit of a smile, a boy attending his mother out of love and duty blended as one. The boy was there, and he was there now and then at other times in those years my mother was with us. He was there when I'd let him be there.

18 I helped my mother down into a straight-backed chair and left her in the bathroom with towels, clean underwear, and a little space heater to keep her warm. She took her time, as with everything. Often it was half an hour or longer before she emerged in her dressing gown, her hair beginning to fluff, her face smiling. No matter how hard she might have resisted the idea, a bath or shower always seemed to renew her. Soap, or no soap, the old woman came forth cleaner of spirit.

19 "She was pure as the driven snow," she usually quoted, gaily, then a pause: "But she drifted."

20   I guess I came out of the bathroom cleaner of spirit myself. Soap or no soap, whatever the tenor of our conversation, I appreciate now what a privilege it was to help my mother with her shower. I wish I'd seen it more clearly at the time. We don't get to choose our privileges, and the ones that come to us aren't always the ones we would choose, and each of them is as much burden as joy. But they do come, and it's important to know them for what they are.

21   One morning as my mother came out of her shower she paused at the bottom of the stairs. I was reading the paper in the living room.

22   "Do you feel them sprouting?" she said, smiling in her white gown.

23   "Do I feel what sprouting?"

24   "Your wings," she said. She stood there, barefooted and bright, smiling right at me and through me, smiling as though she weren't feeble of body and failing of mind but filled with an uncanny power that saw things I could only glimpse.

25   "Mother, I don't have wings," I said.

26   But she was still smiling as she headed up the stairs, gripping the banister hand over hand, hauling herself up 15 carpeted steps to her room and her bed made of sea-weathered posts and boards, where she would read for a while, gaze out her window at sky and treetops, then drift into sleep.

From *Looking After: A Son's Memoir.* Copyright © 1997 by John Daniel. Reprinted by permission of Counterpoint.

 COMPREHENSION CHECKUP

Multiple Choice

Directions: For each item, write the letter corresponding to the best answer.

_____ 1. The author implies that in the past his mother
    a. was strong in mind and body.
    b. was highly independent.
    c. was often depressed.
    d. both a and b.

_____ 2. The author's purpose in writing this selection was to
    a. entertain readers with amusing anecdotes about his mother.
    b. describe and share an important experience in his life.
    c. persuade readers that we need more funding for preventing and treating Alzheimer's.
    d. convince readers that Alzheimer's patients should be cared for in the home by family members rather than in health care facilities.

_____ 3. We can conclude from the selection that
    a. the relationship of the son and mother has not changed since the author was a young boy.
    b. the son is comfortable with viewing his mother's naked body.
    c. the son was somewhat resentful of having to care for his mother.
    d. the things we are forced to do by circumstances rarely turn out to be worthwhile experiences.

———— 4. How is paragraph 8 related to paragraph 7?
    a. It provides a contrast to the events described in paragraph 7.
    b. It provides an explanation for the son's dislike of his mother.
    c. It clarifies Daniel's relationship with his mother.
    d. It provides a list of activities to assist caregivers in entertaining their charges.

———— 5. In paragraph 3 the author's tone could be described as
    a. self-pitying.
    b. vindictive.
    c. bitter.
    d. both a and c.

Vocabulary in Context

Directions: Use the context clues from the sentences below to determine the meaning of the italicized words, and write a definition in the space provided. Then consult your dictionary to check how closely you came to the correct definition.

1. "It was also that the shower was *strenuous* for her, and she didn't want to acknowledge, or couldn't, that she needed help with anything so simple."

   After engaging in a *strenuous* workout at the Y, he would come home and take a long nap.

   strenuous: ———————————————————— Your guess
   ———————————————————————— Dictionary meaning

2. "As if she were *castigating* an unbroken puppy, but without the tolerance she would have granted an innocent thing."

   After the teacher finished *castigating* the student for his sloppy classwork, she made him stay after class for an hour.

   castigating: ———————————————————— Your guess
   ———————————————————————— Dictionary meaning

3. "The skin of her shins was dry and papery, *perpetually* blotched with dark purple—not impact bruises but bruises of age."

   He was *perpetually* late to class even though he got up early enough each morning.

   perpetually: ———————————————————— Your guess
   ———————————————————————— Dictionary meaning

4. "A *solemn* boy with a bit of a smile, a boy attending his mother out of love and duty blended as one."

   When she was naturalized as a new citizen of the United States, she *solemnly* swore her allegiance to her new country.

   solemn: ———————————————————— Your guess
   ———————————————————————— Dictionary meaning

5. "Soap or no soap, whatever the *tenor* of our conversation, I appreciate now what a privilege it was to help my mother with her shower."

If you persist in taking that *tenor* with me, I'll have to ask you to leave my house.

tenor: _____ Your guess

_____ Dictionary meaning

6. "In this mind, she was still the woman she had been five years ago, a woman who came and went and drove a car, a woman who lived on her own on the coast of Maine and was only temporarily *exiled* in a distant place."

When Juan Peron lost political power in Argentina, lived in *exile* in Spain.

exile: _____ Your guess

_____ Dictionary meaning

In Your Own Words

1. What is the main idea of this selection?
2. Why does Daniel feel resentful about having to help his mother with her shower?
3. Why does his mother initially resist taking a shower? What is the larger issue in their battle over the soap? What is the implication of his mother saying "Yes, Father" to him?
4. When does Daniel catch a glimpse of his mother as she might have been as a young girl?
5. What is the son implying when he describes attending to his mother as a kind of "dance"?
6. What image does the author use to describe his mother's impending death?
7. How do both mother and son feel at the conclusion of the shower?
8. What is the mother implying by her comment about "wings sprouting"?

Written Assignment

In the poem "Sailing to Byzantium," W. B. Yeats cautions that, unless his soul is enlivened by appreciation of immortal works of art, "An aged man is but a paltry thing, a tattered coat upon a stick." Explain the meaning of this quotation. How are elderly people treated in the United States? How much deference is shown to older people in the United States? In other countries?

A Short Poem

Maya Angelou is best known as the author of *I Know Why the Caged Bird Sings,* an account of the early years of her life. She has published five collections of poetry, including the inspirational poem "On the Pulse of Morning," which she read at the inauguration of President Clinton. Angelou is currently a professor at Wake Forest University in North Carolina.

What view on aging is expressed by Maya Angelou in the following poem?

On Aging

Maya Angelou

When you see me sitting quietly,
Like a sack left on the shelf,
Don't think I need your chattering.
I'm listening to myself.
Hold! Stop! Don't pity me!
Hold! Stop your sympathy!
Understanding if you got it,
Otherwise I'll do without it!

When my bones are stiff and aching
And my feet won't climb the stair,
I will only ask one favor:
Don't bring me no rocking chair.

When you see me walking, stumbling,
Don't study and get it wrong.
'Cause tired don't mean lazy
And every goodbye ain't gone.
I'm the same person I was back then,
A little less hair, a little less chin,
A lot less lungs and much less wind.
But ain't I lucky I can still breathe in.

Maya Angelou, "On Aging" from *And Still I Rise* by Maya Angelou. Copyright © 1978 by Maya Angelou,
Used by permission of Random House, Inc.

Maya Angelou

 **COMPREHENSION CHECKUP**

Multiple Choice

Directions: For each item, write the letter corresponding to the best answer.

_____ 1. The topic of this poem is
   a. old age.
   b. the good life.
   c. death.
   d. rebirth.

_____ 2. The speaker in the poem is
   a. a youth.
   b. a criminal.
   c. an old person.
   d. a member of the clergy.

_____ 3. The main idea of "On Aging" is that
   a. elderly people deserve our respect as they struggle to deal with their infirmities.
   b. we should treat elderly people as if they were a fragile glass that could break at any moment.
   c. the minute elderly people show signs of frailty we should put them in a rest home.
   d. elderly people need constant attention and care.

_____ 4. The tone of "On Aging" can best be described as
   a. sorrowful and fearful.
   b. amused and appreciative.
   c. scolding and assertive.
   d. excited and cheerful.

_____ 5. The "rocking chair" is used as a symbol for
   a. playfulness.
   b. wisdom.
   c. surrender.
   d. contentment.

_____ 6. The reader can infer that the speaker feels
   a. wearied by the monotony of life.
   b. defeated by personal burdens.
   c. tormented by visions of death.
   d. resentful of pity.

_____ 7. "Like a sack left on the shelf" is a simile used by the speaker to express
   a. a sense of strength.
   b. a sense of abandonment.
   c. a sense of hostility.
   d. a sense of acceptance.

_____ 8. The poem is
   a. a prayer to God.
   b. an appeal to friends and family.
   c. a symptom of depression.
   d. a longing for death.

_____ 9. The speaker of "On Aging" wishes people would stop treating elderly people
   a. as though they were lazy.
   b. as though they were useless.
   c. as though they were dying.
   d. all of the above.

_____ 10. At the end of the poem, the speaker expresses a feeling of
   a. compassion.
   b. self-pity.
   c. disgust.
   d. gratitude.

In Your Own Words

1. Does the poem express conflicting attitudes toward growing old? If so, what are they?

2. The speaker's comment "and every goodbye ain't gone" criticizes what specific attitude on the part of family and friends?

Written Assignment

Compare and contrast the viewpoints toward elderly people expressed in the previous reading to the viewpoints expressed by Angelou in her poem. What do the authors agree on concerning the treatment of older persons? What do they disagree about?

Internet Activity

Further information about Alzheimer's may be obtained from the Web sites given below:

   www.alz.org (Alzheimer's Association)

   www.alzheimers.org (Alzheimer's Disease Education and Referral Center)

The first site provides general information about Alzheimer's, and the second more technical information. Print a page that gives good information about Alzheimer's, and summarize the information.

Expository

READING

"In some instances, siblings may be stronger socializing influences on the child than parents are."

TUNING IN TO READING

It appears that siblings as well as parents have a profound effect on people's lives, shaping their personalities and affecting their views of the world. In a recent Gallup poll of incoming first-year college students, many felt they had either been physically abused (kicked, punched, or bitten) or mentally abused (criticized, berated, and put down) by their siblings. Between the two types of abuse, most felt that mental abuse had caused more lasting "scars." What was the situation in your family? Did your siblings set the stage for your later relationships with others? Do you think having siblings helps you learn how to deal with others? More than 80 percent of American children have one or more siblings (brothers or sisters).

READING *continued*

BIO-SKETCH

John Santrock, a professor at the University of Texas, is the author of textbooks in the areas of psychology, child development, and life-span development.

NOTES ON VOCABULARY

sibling   one of two or more persons born of the same parents, or sometimes having only one parent in common. The word can refer to either a brother or a sister. *Sibling* comes from the Old English *sibb,* meaning "kinship," and can be traced back to the heroic poem *Beowulf* (approximately A.D. 725), the earliest long work of literature in English.

sibling rivalry   competition between children in a family.

Sibling Relationships and Birth Order

John Santrock

A mother's anecdote captures some of the many possibilities of sibling relationships:

> Jamie and Andy were fighting over wooden building blocks and began throwing them at each other. The stress was depleting my strength and ability to cope. I didn't know what to do so I sent them to their bedrooms while I took time to think.
>
> Then a curious thing happened. While still in their rooms, the kids began talking to each other. Jamie thought of a way they could solve the problem. Andy vetoed it. They continued talking back and forth until a settlement was reached, all without my saying a word!

2   Of course, many sibling interactions involve less civilized endings. Sandra describes to her mother what happened in a conflict with her sister:

3   We had just come home from the ball game. I sat down on the sofa next to the light so I could read. Sally [the sister] said, "Get up. I was sitting there first. I just got up for a second to get a drink." I told her I was not going to get up and that I didn't see her name on the chair. I got mad and started pushing her. Her drink spilled all over her. Then she got really mad. She shoved me against the wall, hitting and clawing at me. I managed to grab a handful of hair. At this point, Sally comes into the room and begins to tell her side of the story. Sandra interrupts, "Mother, you always take her side."

4   Does this sound familiar? Any of you who have grown up with siblings probably have a rich memory of aggressive, hostile interchanges. But sibling relationships . . . have many pleasant, caring moments as well. Children's sibling relationships include helping, sharing, teaching, fighting, and playing. Children can act as emotional supports, rivals, and communication partners.

5   Is sibling interaction different from parent–child interaction? There is some evidence that it is. Observations indicate that children interact more positively and in more varied ways with their parents than with their siblings. Children also follow their parents' dictates more than those of their siblings, and they behave more negatively and punitively with their siblings than with their parents.

6 In some instances, siblings may be stronger socializing influences on the child than parents are. Someone close in age to the child—such as a sibling—may be able to understand the child's problems and be able to communicate more effectively than parents can. In dealing with peers, coping with difficult teachers, and discussing taboo subjects such as sex, siblings may be more influential to the socialization process than parents.

7 Is sibling interaction the same around the world? In industrialized societies, such as the United States, parents tend to delegate responsibility for younger siblings to older siblings primarily to give the parents freedom to pursue other activities. However, in non-industrialized countries, such as Kenya, the older sibling's role as caregiver to younger siblings has much more importance. In industrialized countries, the older sibling's caregiving role is often discretionary; in non-industrialized countries, it is more obligatory.

8 Because there are so many possible sibling combinations, it is difficult to generalize about sibling influences. Among the factors to consider are the number of siblings, the ages of siblings, birth order, age spacing, and the sex of siblings. There is something unique about same-sex sibling relationships. Aggression, dominance, and rivalry occur more in same-sex sibling relationships than opposite-sex sibling relationships.

9 Temperamental traits ("easy" and "difficult," for example), as well as different treatment of siblings by parents, influence how siblings get along. Siblings with "easy" temperaments who are treated in relatively equal ways by parents tend to get along with each other the best. By contrast, siblings with "difficult" temperaments, or whose parents have given one of them preferential treatment, get along the worst. Variations in sibling relationships are also linked to birth order.

10 Birth order is a special interest of sibling researchers. The oldest sibling is expected to exercise self-control and show responsibility in interacting with younger siblings. When the oldest sibling is jealous or hostile, parents often protect the younger siblings. The oldest sibling is more dominant, competent, and powerful than the younger siblings. The oldest sibling is also expected to assist and teach younger siblings. Indeed, researchers have shown that older siblings are both more antagonistic—hitting, kicking, and biting—*and* more nurturant toward their younger siblings than [younger sibling are toward older].

11 The influence of birth order goes well beyond its link with sibling relationships. Indeed, many people are fascinated by links between birth order and personality. For example, firstborn children are more adult oriented, helpful, conforming, anxious, and self-controlled than their siblings. Firstborns excel in academic and professional endeavors. Firstborns are overrepresented in *Who's Who* and Rhodes scholars, for example. They also have more guilt, anxiety, difficulty in coping with stressful situations, as well as higher admission to child guidance clinics, than other children.

12 What accounts for such differences related to birth order? Proposed explanations usually point to variations in interactions with parents and siblings associated with being in a particular position in the family. This is especially true in the case of the firstborn child. The oldest child is the only one who does not have to share parental love and affection with other siblings—until another sibling comes along. An infant requires more attention than an older child; this means that the firstborn sibling now gets less attention than before the newborn arrived. Does this result in conflict between parents and the firstborn? In one research study, mothers became more negative, coercive, and restraining and played less with the firstborn following the birth of a second child.

13 Even though a new infant requires more attention from parents than does an older child, parents and firstborns often maintain an especially intense relationship throughout the life span. Parents have higher expectations for firstborn children than for later-born children. They put more pressure on them for achievement and responsibility. They also interfere more with their activities. The extra

attention that firstborns receive has been linked to firstborns' nurturant behavior. Parental demands and high standards established for firstborns have been associated with both their achievements and their difficulties, such as anxiety and guilt. Given the differences in family dynamics involved in birth order, it is not surprising that firstborns and later-borns have different characteristics.

14   What is the only child like? The popular conception is that the only child is a "spoiled brat" with such undesirable characteristics as dependency, lack of self-control, and self-centered behavior. But researchers present a more positive portrayal of the only child. Only children often are achievement-oriented and display a desirable personality, especially in comparison with later-borns and children from large families.

15   So far our consideration of birth-order effects suggests that birth order might be a strong predictor of behavior. However, an increasing number of family researchers believe that birth order has been overdramatized and overemphasized. The critics argue that, when all of the factors that influence behavior are considered, birth order itself shows limited ability to predict behavior. Consider just sibling relationships alone. They vary not only in birth order, but also in number of siblings, age of siblings, age spacing of siblings, and sex of siblings.

16   Think about some of the other important factors in children's lives that influence their behavior beyond birth order. They include heredity, models of competency or incompetency that parents present to children on a daily basis, peer influences, school influences, socioeconomic factors, socio-historical factors, and cultural variations. When someone says firstborns are always like this, but last-borns are always like that, you know that the person is making overly simplistic statements that do not adequately take into account the complexity of influences on a child's behavior. Keep in mind, though, that, although birth order itself may not be a good predictor of children's behavior, sibling relationships and interaction are important dimensions of family processes.

From John W. Santrock, *Child Development: An Introduction,* 11th Edition, pp. 476–78. Copyright © 2007 by The McGraw-Hill Companies, Inc. Reprinted with permission.

COMPREHENSION CHECKUP

Multiple Choice

Directions: For each item, write the letter corresponding to the best answer.

_____ 1. Which of the following would be the best subtitle for this selection?
   a. "The Roles Siblings Play"
   b. "The Lonely Only"
   c. "Firstborns and Success"
   d. "The Forgotten Sibling"

_____ 2. The author's purpose is to
   a. entertain.
   b. persuade.
   c. explain.
   d. show steps in a process.

_____ 3. The tone of the selection is
   a. objective.
   b. excited.
   c. argumentative.
   d. both a and b.

_____ 4. All of the following would probably be considered positive sibling interactions *except*
   a. helping.
   b. sharing.
   c. bickering.
   d. teaching.

_____ 5. All of the following statements *except* one are true about parent–child interactions. Which is *not* true?
   a. Siblings may be a stronger socialization influence on a child than the parents in the area of dealing with peers.
   b. Children are likely to interact more positively with their parents than their siblings.
   c. Children are likely to follow the dictates of their parents over those of their siblings.
   d. Children interact in more varied ways with their siblings than with their parents.

_____ 6. All of the following are likely to be considered industrialized countries *except*
   a. Kenya.
   b. the United States.
   c. Japan.
   d. Germany.

_____ 7. Sibling relationships are influenced by
   a. birth order.
   b. different treatment of siblings by parents.
   c. temperamental traits of siblings.
   d. all of the above.

_____ 8. Researchers have concluded that only children are often
   a. achievement oriented.
   b. lacking in self-control.
   c. possessors of a desirable personality.
   d. both a and c.

_____ 9. The selection mentions all of the following variables affecting sibling relationships *except*
   a. number and age of siblings.
   b. sex of siblings.
   c. degree of material possessions.
   d. spacing between siblings.

_____ 10. Children's behavior can be influenced by
   a. birth order and heredity.
   b. parental incompetency or competency.
   c. peer and school influences.
   d. all of the above.

Identifying Key Characteristics

Directions: Put a check beside the descriptions that are most likely to apply to a first-born child.

_____ 1. He or she is likely to tell the other siblings what they need to do and when they need to do it.

_____ 2. He or she has difficulty abiding by the rules.

_____ 3. He or she acts helpless and is always on the lookout for potential saviors.

_____ 4. He or she is likely to say, "I've always felt invisible."

_____ 5. He or she is likely to say, "Competition is everything! Being number one is who I am."

_____ 6. He or she is likely to get good grades.

True or False

Directions: Indicate whether each statement is true or false by writing **T** or **F** in the space provided.

_____ 1. Sibling interaction is different from parent–child interaction.

_____ 2. Sibling interaction is the same around the world.

_____ 3. Aggression and dominance are more likely to occur in opposite-sex sibling relationships.

_____ 4. Parents expect the oldest sibling to be irresponsible and exhibit little self-control.

_____ 5. Older siblings are more likely to be both nurturant and antagonistic toward younger siblings.

_____ 6. Younger siblings are more likely to exhibit guilt and anxiety than firstborns.

_____ 7. In general, parents have higher expectations for firstborn children than for later-born children.

_____ 8. Research has determined that only children tend to be "spoiled brats."

_____ 9. Only children tend to be achievement oriented.

_____ 10. Many researchers feel that birth order is overemphasized.

Vocabulary in Context

Directions: Choose one of the following words to complete each of the sentences below. Use each word only once.

anecdote	discretionary	obligatory	simplistic
antagonistic	hostile	preferential	vetoed
depleting	nurturant		

1. The students' assignment in the speech class was to share a personal _____ about their first day on a college campus.

2. Marla's budget was so strict that she had no money left over for _____ spending.

3. The Arctic, with its frigid temperatures, is considered by most to be a _____ environment.

4. Despite being urged by his advisors to sign the bill, the president followed his conscience and _____ it.

5. Environmental groups are especially concerned that we are _____ our natural resources.

6. In most states, attending high school is _____ until age 16.

7. Mike was chosen so often by the teacher to be line leader that the other children complained about his obvious _____ treatment.

8. The problem was far too complicated for any _____ solution.

9. Bill and Todd were always getting into schoolyard fights and had a competitive, _____ relationship.

10. The kindergarten teacher was popular with her young charges because of her kind and _____ behavior.

In Your Own Words

1. Do you think position in the family (first, middle, last child) influences certain personality traits? Do you think birth order can affect a person's future lifestyle?

2. The following is a summary about what some researchers have to say about birth order. Do you agree with the information presented? Or do you think that the information in birth-order books sounds a lot like that provided in horoscopes?

Firstborn Children

There have been more firstborn U.S. presidents and Nobel Prize winners than any other birth ranking. They are overrepresented in professions requiring higher education such as medicine, engineering, and law. In terms of personality, they tend to be conscientious, ambitious, aggressive, good at problem solving, strong-willed, determined, controlling, jealous, and moralistic.

Middle Children

Middle children are easygoing and peer oriented. Because they mediate between siblings they tend to have excellent people skills. They are flexible and giving. They have lots of friends, but they can also be manipulative. Many feel forced to assume roles that their older siblings for one reason or another are unable to fulfill, and this may leave them with a chip on their shoulder.

Youngest Children

Later-born children always have someone ahead of them to compete against. Parents are more relaxed and less strict with later-born children, who can be rebellious but are also pleasant, agreeable, and easygoing. They tend to be creative, unconventional, and often feel like the "baby," even when they are adults.

3. Dr. Toni Falbo, professor of educational psychology at the University of Texas, has focused her research on only children and one-child families. She has determined that "onlies" are as normal as their peers in larger family units. In fact, she has discovered that instead of being at a disadvantage, they actually have advantages in certain areas. For instance, their educational attainment is somewhat higher than that of other children, and they tend to have close relationships with their parents. What characteristics of an only child's environment would likely account for this?

4. The one-child family is common in China because of the strong motivation to limit population growth. In China, there is a lot of discussion about having a nation of "little emperors." What do you think the effects of this policy are likely to be on the Chinese nation as a whole?

5. Frank Sulloway, a professor at the University of California, Berkeley, developed a theory about birth-order effects, which he calls "de-identification." Siblings who want to stand out in their families do so by observing what the eldest child does and then doing the exact opposite. For instance, if the eldest child gets good grades, the second child may become a "slacker." What do you think about this theory? Can you think of any examples from your personal experience?

6. What kinds of lessons do you think are learned from living with siblings? Do you think understanding the role that your siblings played in your life will help you lead a more productive and happy life?

7. If you grew up with a sibling, you likely showed some jealousy of your sibling and vice versa. What can parents do to help children reduce their jealousy toward a sibling?

Written Assignment

Directions: Write a short paragraph responding to one of the following quotations.

1. "Big sisters are the crab grass in the lawn of life." (Charles Schulz, American cartoonist, 20th century)

2. "In general parents serve the same big-picture role as doctors on grand rounds. Siblings are like the nurses on the ward. They're there every day." (Daniel Shaw, psychologist at the University of Pittsburgh)

3. "Overall, 65% of mothers and 70% of fathers have a favorite child." (Katherine Conger, sociologist at the University of California, Davis)

4. "After the shooting stops, even the fiercest sibling wars leave little lasting damage. Indeed, siblings who battled a lot as kids may become closer as adults." (Thomas O'Connor, professor of psychiatry at the University of Rochester Medical Center)

Internet Activity

Two good Web sites on the topic of sibling rivalry are:

www.kidshealth.org/parent/emotions/feelings/sibling_rivalry.html

www.med.umich.edu/1libr/yourchild/sibriv.htm

Consult one of them to learn more about what causes sibling rivalry and how to control it. Write a few paragraphs discussing your favorite tips on helping kids get along better.

Persuasion/Argumentation

READING

"On television things that are not visually interesting, such as thinking, reading and talking, are ignored."

TUNING IN TO READING

How has TV affected you positively? Negatively? How much TV do you watch in a typical day? In the following excerpt, written in a persuasive mode, the author compares and contrasts the community of the past with the new MTV community. She offers personal and other evidence in an effort to change how we think about the media.

READING   *continued*

BIO-SKETCH

Dr. Mary Pipher is a clinical psychologist, part-time instructor at the University of Nebraska, nationwide lecturer, and best-selling author. Her book *Reviving Ophelia*, published in 1994, explored the stresses placed on teenage girls by modern society. In 1999, Pipher published *Another Country,* a book about elderly people in America. She observes that "to grow old in the U.S. is to inhabit a foreign country, isolated, disconnected, and misunderstood." In her 1996 book *The Shelter of Each Other,* from which this excerpt is taken, Pipher turns her attention to the stresses placed on the family as a whole. In Pipher's view, the family is so burdened with problems that it can no longer protect family members from the "enemy within," which she defines as inappropriate stimulation from a variety of sources, with TV being at the top of her list.

NOTES ON VOCABULARY

Romeo and Juliet   a tragedy by William Shakespeare about two ill-fated lovers whose romance ends in death because of the feud between their two families.

persona   a character in a fictional work; the public role or personality a person assumes. In Latin, the word for "mask" was *persona.* In ancient Rome, actors wore masks that covered the entire face. Each Roman god was represented by a particular mask so that the audience always knew what god an actor was portraying.

nuance   a slight difference or distinction. The term was borrowed from French and originally referred to a slightly different shade of color.

decry   to denounce or disparage openly.

rule of thumb   a practical method or principle that is based on the wisdom of experience. The expression dates from the 1600s and originally referred to making rough estimates of measurements by using one's thumb.

Tonga Islands   a group of islands in the southwest Pacific Ocean slightly east of Fiji. They are also known as the Friendly Islands.

According to the A. C. Nielsen Company, the average American watches 3 hours and 46 minutes of television each day (more than 52 days of nonstop television watching per year). By age 65, the average American will have spent nearly 9 years glued to the tube.

TV

Mary Pipher

IN A COLLEGE CLASS I ASKED, "What would it be like to grow up in a world without media?" A student from the Tonga Islands answered, "I never saw television or heard rock and roll until I came to the United States in high school." She paused and looked around the room. "I had a happy childhood. I felt safe all the time. I didn't know I was poor. Or that parents hurt their children or that children hated their parents. I thought I was pretty."

2   Television has probably been the most powerful medium in shaping the new community. The electronic community gives us our mutual friends, our significant events and our daily chats. The "produced" relationships of television families become our models for intimacy. We know media stars better than we know our neighbors. Most

of us can discuss their lives better than we can discuss those of our relatives. We confuse personas and persons. That is, we think a man who plays a doctor on TV actually knows something about medicine. We think a chatty talk show host is truly good-natured. This confusion is especially common with young children, who are developmentally incapable of distinguishing between reality and fantasy. But even adults get mixed up about this.

3   Most real life is rather quiet and routine. Most pleasures are small pleasures—a hot shower, a sunset, a bowl of good soup or a good book. Television suggests that life is high drama, love and sex. TV families are radically different from real families. Things happen much faster to them. On television things that are not visually interesting, such as thinking, reading and talking, are ignored. Activities such as housework, fund raising and teaching children to read are vastly underreported. Instead of ennobling our ordinary experiences, television suggests that they are not of sufficient interest to document.

4   These generalizations even fit the way TV portrays the animal kingdom. Specials on animals feature sex, births and killing. Dangerous and cuddly-looking animals are favored. But in reality, most animals are neither dangerous nor cute. Sharks and panda bears are not the main species on the planet. Most animals, like most people, spend most of their time in rather simple ways. They forage *eat* and sleep.

> *"Television has proved that people will look at anything rather than each other."*
>
> —Ann Landers

5   TV isolates people in their leisure time. People spend more time watching music videos but less time making music with each other. People in small towns now watch international cable networks instead of driving to their neighbor's house for cards. Women watch soaps instead of attending church circles or book clubs. When company comes, the kids are sent to the TV room with videos. Television is on during meals and kids study to television or radio.

> *Forty percent of 2-year-olds watch three or more hours of TV every day.*

6   Parents are not the main influences in the lives of their children. Some of the first voices children hear are from the television; the first street they know is Sesame Street. A child playing Nintendo is learning different lessons than a child playing along a creek or playing dominoes with a grandfather. Many children have been conditioned via the media into having highly dysfunctional attention spans.

7   Adults too have diminished concentration. Neil Postman in *Amusing Ourselves to Death* writes of the 1858 Lincoln/Douglas debates. The average citizen sat for up to seven hours in the heat and listened to these two men discuss issues. People grasped the legal and constitutional issues, moral nuances and political implications. In addition, they could listen to and appreciate intricate and complex sentences. In the 1990s President Clinton's speeches were decried by the press and the public when they lasted more than an hour. To an audience socialized to information via sound bite, an hour seems like a long time.

8   The time devoted to violence on TV in no way reflects its importance in real life. In real life, most of us exercise, work, visit our friends, read, cook and eat and shop. Few of us spend any significant amount of our time solving murders or fleeing psychotic killers. On television there are many more detectives and murderers than exist in the real world. A rule of thumb about violence is "If it bleeds, it leads." Violence captures viewer attention. Our movies have become increasingly violent, and as James Wolcott wrote in *The New Yorker,* "Violence is the real sex now."

9   Some might argue that there is nothing new under the sun. Of course, in a narrow sense, they are correct. There have always been murderers and rapists, and stories

about violence have been themes of literature and song. But things are different now. Children, including toddlers, are exposed to hundreds of examples of violence every day. The frequency and intensity of these images is unprecedented in the history of humanity. We have ample documentation that this exposure desensitizes children, makes it more likely they will be violent and increases their fear levels about potential violence.

10   Another difference is in the attitudes about violence. *Romeo and Juliet,* for example, was a tragedy. The deaths in the play were presented as a cause of enormous suffering to friends and families and as a terrible waste. When Juliet and Romeo died, something momentous happened in the universe. The very gods were upset. Often today, death is a minor event, of no more consequence than, say the kicking of a flat tire. It's even presented as a joke.

11   It is one thing to read Shakespeare, which at least requires that the person can read. It's another to, day after day, see blood splattered across a screen by "action heroes." It is one thing to show, as Shakespeare did, that violence can be the tragic consequence of misunderstandings, and another to show violence as a thrill, as a solution to human problems or merely as something that happens when people are slightly frustrated or men need to prove they are men.

12   Of course, one could argue that parents can keep televisions out of their homes. This is extremely hard for the average parent to do. Even if they succeed, their children go from these "protected environments" to play with children who have watched lots of TV and who behave accordingly.

13   I don't often go to violent movies, but I do have a stake in them. I don't like living in a world where thousands of teenage boys, some of whom own guns, have been reared on them. Walking city streets, I may be accosted by a youth who has spent most of his life watching violent media. Unfortunately, needy children are the ones most affected. Children with the least available parents watch the most TV. Violent television is like secondhand smoke; it affects all of us.

14   Heavy viewers develop the "mean world syndrome." This leads to a vicious-cycle phenomenon. Because children are afraid and the streets are not safe, they come home right after school and stay indoors. They watch more TV, which makes them more afraid and thus more likely to stay indoors. With everyone indoors the streets are less safe. Families watch more TV and are more fearful and so on.

15   Television and electronic media have created a new community with entirely different rules and structures than the kinds of communities that have existed for millions of years. Families gather around the glow of the TV as the Lakota once gathered around the glow of a fire on the Great Plains or as the Vikings once huddled around fires in the caves of Scandinavia. They gather as New England families gathered in the 1800s around a fireplace that kept them warm and safe. But our TVs do not keep us warm, safe and together. Rapidly our technology is creating a new kind of human being, one who is plugged into machines instead of relationships, one who lives in a virtual reality rather than a family.

COMPREHENSION CHECKUP

Short Answer

Directions: Answer the following questions briefly, in no more than a sentence or two.

1. Write the main idea in paragraph 1.

   _____

2. Write the main idea that is directly stated in paragraph 2. Explain what Pipher means when she says we have trouble distinguishing between "personas and persons." Are children the only ones who have trouble with this?

   _____

   _____

   _____

3. Summarize the key points that Pipher makes in paragraph 3. How does what you see on the evening local or national news reinforce Pipher's argument?

   _____

   _____

4. In paragraph 4, Pipher says that TV distorts our impression of animals. How does TV do this?

   _____

5. What does Pipher say in paragraph 5 about what is happening to our sense of belonging to a community? Is the Internet likely to create strong community ties or weaken them?

   _____

   _____

6. Do you agree with Pipher's assertion that parents are not the primary influences in their children's lives? Why or why not? How do the media contribute to children's short attention spans?

   _____

   _____

7. Paragraphs 8–13 are devoted to a discussion of violence on TV. Why does television portray so much violence? What are some of the effects of violent TV programs on the young?

   _____

   _____

8. Pipher compares and contrasts the modern media's attitude to violence and death to that portrayed in *Romeo and Juliet*. What is the difference she perceives?

   _____

   _____

9. Many people would suggest that parents are responsible for their own children and so should restrict the amount of time their kids spend watching TV. What is Pipher's response to these critics?

_____

_____

10. Explain the cause-and-effect relationships in paragraph 14.

    Cause: _____

    Effect: _____

    Cause: _____

    Effect: _____

11. This article is written in the persuasive mode. What are the key points that Pipher is trying to persuade readers to accept?

    _____

    _____

12. Paragraph 15 compares and contrasts two communities. List the similarities and differences between the two. Then fill in the Venn diagram below with your details.

    _____

    _____

Venn Diagram

Directions: Making a Venn diagram is a good way to compare and contrast two things. Create a Venn diagram to compare and contrast pre-TV and post-TV communities. First, list everything about the pre-TV community in area A. Next, do the same with the post-TV community in area C. Then, list everything that A and C have in common in area B. When you are finished, the outer areas will show how the two communities are different, and the overlapping area in the middle will show the similarities between the two communities. Use the information in your Venn diagram to write a paragraph comparing and contrasting the two communities.

A   B   C

1. _____   1. _____   1. _____

   _____   _____   _____

2. _____   2. _____   2. _____

   _____   _____   _____

3. _____   3. _____   3. _____

   _____   _____   _____

4. _____   4. _____

   _____   _____

Family of the past   Family of today

Multiple Choice

Directions: For each item, write the letter corresponding to the best answer.

_____ 1. The organizational pattern used in paragraph 2 is
   a. main idea, details.
   b. details, main idea, details.
   c. details, main idea.
   d. no directly stated main idea.

_____ 2. What does Pipher mean by the term "protected environments" in paragraph 12?
   a. She is referring to homes that are middle class.
   b. She is referring to homes in gated communities.
   c. She is referring to homes that have only one television.
   d. She is referring to homes that do not have a television.

_____ 3. From this selection you could conclude that
   a. no one should watch TV.
   b. people should limit the amount of television they and their families watch.
   c. people should spend more time on the Internet.
   d. the government should regulate the content of TV programs.

_____ 4. A likely title for this selection would be
   a. "TV—The Cause of Violence."
   b. "TV versus Shakespeare."
   c. "TV in the Tonga Islands."
   d. "TV and Its Effects on Relationships."

_____ 5. If the author was reading this selection orally, her tone of voice would probably be
   a. admiring.
   b. optimistic.
   c. critical.
   d. amused.

_____ 6. What does Pipher mean when she says that "Violent television is like secondhand smoke" (paragraph 13)?
   a. She means that the effects of violence on television quickly disappear like cigarette smoke.
   b. She means that people who don't watch violence on television are affected by people who do.
   c. She means that there's too much violence on television.
   d. She means that the networks should curb violence on television.

True or False

Directions: Indicate whether each statement is true or false by writing **T** or **F** in the space provided.

_____ 7. Pipher suggests that children whose parents are most available watch the least TV.

_____ 8. Watching television is likely to significantly increase a person's ability to concentrate.

_____ 9. According to Pipher, things happen much more quickly in real life.

_____ 10. Pipher believes that violence on television causes children to view the world as mean and unsafe.

Vocabulary in Context

Directions: Use the context clues to determine the meaning of the italicized word, and then write a definition for the word in the space provided.

1. Roxana is living a *fantasy* life, buying clothes, cars, and jewelry she cannot afford.

   _____

2. Gladys is such a *chatty* person that Yoko feels a deep need for solitude after spending only a short while with her.

   _____

3. Wild animals sometimes enter towns to *forage* for food.

   _____

4. Children like to sleep with their cute and *cuddly* teddy bears.

   _____

5. The *implication* of running a red light could be a car accident or a ticket.

   _____

6. She was trying to pretend that she was not angry, but *nuances* in her behavior told you that she was.

   _____

7. Something *momentous* happened to Tamotsu yesterday—he won the lottery!

   _____

8. Sandy decided to give up jogging late at night after she was *accosted* by a stranger for the second time in a week.

   _____

Drawing Inferences

Directions: Study the following cartoon carefully, then consider the statements below. If the statement appears to be a valid inference based on the details found in the cartoon, mark it **Y** for yes. If it seems to be an unlikely conclusion, mark it **N** for no.

_____ 1. The people standing in line are purchasing tickets to a violent movie.

_____ 2. They are expecting the film to foster decent values.

Non Sequitur

_____ 3. The cartoonist feels the general public is responsible for the decline in high moral standards in the entertainment industry.

A Song
"The Sound of Silence"
Paul Simon

"The Sound of Silence" was recently included in the Rock and Roll Hall of Fame. It is considered to be one of the 500 most influential songs of the 20th century. As you read the song, note the figurative language and then answer the questions that follow. Do this song and the previous selection by Mary Pipher have a similar message?

Hello darkness, my old friend,
I've come to talk with you again,
Because a vision softly creeping,
Left its seeds while I was sleeping,
And the vision that was planted in my brain
Still remains
Within the sound of silence.

In restless dreams I walked alone
Narrow streets of cobblestone,
'Neath the halo of a street lamp,
I turned my collar to the cold and damp
When my eyes were stabbed by the flash of a neon light
That split the night
And touched the sound of silence

And in the naked light I saw
Ten thousand people, maybe more.
People talking without speaking,
People hearing without listening,
People writing songs that voices never share
And no one dared
Disturb the sound of silence.

"Fools" said I, "You do not know
Silence like a cancer grows.
Hear my words that I might teach you,
Take my arms that I might reach you."
But my words like silent raindrops fell,
And echoed
In the wells of silence

And the people bowed and prayed
To the neon god they made.
And the sign flashed out its warning,
In the words that it was forming.
And the sign said, "The words of the prophets
are written on the subway walls
And tenement halls."
And whispered in the sounds of silence.

_____ 1. "Because a vision softly creeping" (line 3) would best be described as an example of
   a. symbol.
   b. simile.
   c. personification.
   d. allegory.

_____ 2. "Silence like a cancer grows" (line 23) would best be described as an example of
   a. irony.
   b. simile.
   c. metaphor.
   d. inference.

_____ 3. "But my words like silent raindrops fell" (line 26) would best be described as an example of
   a. simile.
   b. cliché.
   c. metaphor.
   d. personification.

_____ 4. The poem implies that
   a. human beings fail to communicate with each other.
   b. modern society is increasingly plagued by violence.
   c. no one listens to the lyrics of songs anymore.
   d. people today are less likely to attend church regularly.

_____ 5. In the fifth stanza, the "neon god" the people are worshiping is most likely
   a. the National Football League.
   b. the *Sports Illustrated* swimsuit models.
   c. rock stars.
   d. TV.

In Your Own Words

1. A paradox can be a statement that seems contradictory but that actually presents a truth. Explain why the title "The Sound of Silence" is a paradox.

2. What is the author describing in the third stanza?

3. Prophets, in the tradition of Amos of the Old Testament, have often warned people about worshiping false gods and ignoring the needs of the poor. What message is Simon trying to convey in the last stanza?

Written Assignment

Directions: Write a paragraph or two in response to one of the following.

1. Summarize the information presented in a local news show. Identify the subject of each story (murder, robbery, fire, accident, etc.) and the approximate amount of time given to coverage of the story.

2. Watch a TV drama, detective show, soap opera, or movie, and keep track of how many specific acts of violence the show portrays.

3. Find a cartoon in a magazine or newspaper, and write down all that you can logically infer from it. Share the cartoon with a classmate and see if your inferences "match."

4. How does the cartoon on page 363 support Mary Pipher's thesis?

Internet Activity

If you have children at home, you may want to limit the amount of time they spend watching TV. The site below, sponsored by the Kansas National Education Association, has some information that may help you. Print out a page and highlight the tips that you think might work.

http://ks.nea.org/parents/tvviewing.html

Chapter Summary and Review

In Chapter 8, you became familiar with the four modes of writing: narrative, descriptive, expository, and persuasive. Based on the material in Chapter 8, answer the following.

Short Answer

Directions: Find an example for each of the modes of writing from previous selections in this book. Explain your choices.

1. Narrative: _____

   Reasons for choice: _____

2. Descriptive: _____

   Reasons for choice:_____

3. Expository: _____

   Reasons for choice: _____

4. Persuasive: _____

   Reasons for choice: _____

Vocabulary in Context

Directions: Choose one of the following words to complete the sentences below. Use each word only once.

arguments	controversial	expository	mode	time-order	visual

5. Textbook material is usually written in a(n) _____ mode.

6. Persuasive writing often presents _____ about _____ topics.

7. An article written in the descriptive mode usually draws on _____ perceptions.

8. Stories written in the narrative mode often follow a(n) _____ sequence.

9. Sometimes an author will use more than one _____ of writing.

VOCABULARY   Unit 5 Word Parts: Direction and Position

supersonic—Chuck Yaeger made the first supersonic flight October 14, 1947, over Edwards Air Force Base in California.

All of the word parts in this unit are related to either direction or position.

super—above or over
sub—under, below, beneath

supersonic   *Super* means "above," and *sonus* means "sound," so *supersonic* means moving at a speed greater than that of sound.

supervisor	A person who oversees or directs work or workers. The original meaning of the word was "to see from above."
superscript	A figure, letter, or symbol written above the line. In math, 10 squared would be written 10^2, with the 2 being a *superscript*.
subscript	A figure, letter, or symbol written below the line. The chemical formula for water, H_2O, has a *subscript*.
subscribe	To agree to pay for a service or periodical. Originally, when you *subscribed* to a magazine, you signed your name at the bottom of the contract on the dotted line.
subliminal	*Limen* means "threshold." If something is *subliminal*, it is below the threshold of consciousness. The sale of audiocassette tapes with *subliminal* self-help messages is a big business in the United States. While you are sleeping, you could listen to a weight-loss tape with a *subliminal* message saying "eat less."

retro—backward, back, behind

retroactive	Having an effect on things that are past; going back in time. If you received *retroactive* pay, you would be paid for work that was done in the past.
retrorocket	A small rocket that produces a backward thrust in order to reduce speed.
retrogress	To move backward toward an earlier or worse condition; to decline. After learning new study techniques, the student *retrogressed* to her old methods of studying and just read the chapter the night before the quiz.
retrospect	To see back in time; hindsight. In *retrospect*, the cook should have added more garlic to her soup.

> **TRIVIA QUESTION 1**
>
> Which space vehicle does not use retrorockets to reduce speed? (Answer at the end of this unit.)

ante(i)—before, in front of, prior to
ad—toward

Sometimes spellings of word parts change over the years. In the word part *anti*, sometimes the "e" changes to "i." This causes confusion with the word part *anti* meaning "opposite of." What do you think was the original meaning of the word *antifreeze*? Sometimes you have to use the context of a sentence to determine the meaning of a word part. When in doubt, consult a dictionary.

anticipate	To look forward to something before it happens. She was *anticipating* a pleasant two-week vacation in Hawaii.
ante	In poker, each player must *ante* up (place a bet) before receiving cards.
anteroom	A small room before a larger or more important room. *Anterooms* can be lobbies, vestibules, or waiting rooms.
antecedent	Coming before in time, order, or logic. In English grammar, the *antecedent* of a pronoun is the noun to which the pronoun refers. In the sentence "The team will win the game if it plays well," the *antecedent* of the pronoun "it" is the word "team."
antebellum	*Bellum* means "war," so *antebellum* means "before the war." The word is often used in relation to the American Civil War. The *antebellum* days of the South were approximately 1820–1860.
advance	*"Ance"* originally came from *ante*, and so the word *advance* literally translates as "toward before." The hurricane rapidly *advanced* on the helpless town.

adolescent	A person moving toward adulthood or maturity.
advent	*Ven* means "come," so *advent* means "to come toward." To Christians, the season of *Advent* includes the four Sundays before Christmas.
advertise	*Vert* means "to turn," so *advertise* means "to turn toward." *Advertising* praises a service or product so that people will want to turn toward it, or buy it.

circ—ring; around   cycle—circle; wheel

circle	A *circle* is a plane figure, but the word also means "to surround" or "move around."
circulate	To move in a circle and return to the same point; to move around freely. Blood *circulates* through the body.
circumference	The measure of the distance around a circle.
circumnavigate	To sail or fly around, as in *circumnavigating* the earth. Magellan's crew was the first to *circumnavigate* the earth. Magellan himself was killed on the voyage.
circumscribe	To draw a line around. The student *circumscribed* the correct answer on the quiz by drawing a circle around it.
circumspect	To look all around or to consider all circumstances before deciding.
circadian	Relating to a person's daily biological cycle.
circa	*Circa* means "around" or "approximately," in reference to a period of time or the date of an event, especially when the exact dates are not known. Jazz began in the United States *circa* 1920.
bicycle	To ride or travel on a two-wheeled vehicle.
cyclorama	No, not a track for bicycles. A *cyclorama* is a series of large pictures put on the wall of a circular room so that a spectator standing in the middle can see all around (360 degrees). If you have been to Disneyland, you might have seen a movie in a *cyclorama*.
cyclical	Moving or occurring in a circular pattern. Fashions in clothing tend to be *cyclical*. Men's ties gradually become wider, and then gradually become narrower, and then start the cycle over.

pan—all; every; around   peri—around; about

Panavision®	See all around. The movie was in *Panavision*. Movies in *Panavision* are not really all around you, but are simply on a large screen.
Panasonic®	Sound all around. Do you think you really get sound all around you from a *Panasonic* transistor radio?
panorama	A wide view. A synonym for *panorama* is *vista*. From the top of the mountain, the sunset produced a beautiful *panorama*.
panacea	A cure-all; or the act of going around the problem. Owners of sports teams often resort to firing the coach as a *panacea* for the team's failure to win enough games. Some people view building more prisons as a *panacea* to the crime problem.
Pan-American	Common to North, South, and Central America together. The diplomats negotiated a *Pan-American* treaty to deal with poaching of endangered species.

circulate—In one year, the human heart circulates 770,000 to 1.6 million gallons of blood. This is enough to fill 200 tank cars, each with a capacity of 8,000 gallons.

circumference—The circumference of a quarter has 119 grooves; a dime has one less.

TRIVIA QUESTION 2

Who was the first American to circumnavigate the earth in a space vehicle? Hint: He served as a U.S. senator from Ohio. (Answer at the end of this unit.)

bicycle—The longest true tandem bicycle with just two wheels measures 72.96 feet. In 1988, it was ridden 807 feet by four riders. Needless to say, turning corners presented problems.

Pan-American—The Pan-Am Highway is the longest driveable road in the world. It is 15,000 miles long. It goes from northwest Alaska, down through Santiago, Chile, east through Argentina, and ends in Brasilia, Brazil.

perimeter	The outer boundary or measurement around a figure or area. The soldiers guarding the camp walked along its *perimeter.*
peripheral	Lying at the outside. Because he has so much money already, it is of only *peripheral* importance to him whether he gets a job. You might have your driver's license revoked if you have poor *peripheral* vision.
periscope	An optical instrument used on submarines that goes up to the surface and allows a person to "look around."

Exercise 1

Directions: In the blanks below, write the word from the list that best completes the sentence. Use each word only once.

adolescent	anteroom	anticipating	circulate	circumspect
panacea	perimeter	retrospect	subscribe	supervisor

1. Ginny can't seem to get along with her _____ at work, so she's going to have to start looking for another job.

2. Oscar was _____ his 21st birthday because his friends were taking him to Las Vegas to celebrate.

3. There is no easy _____ for the problem of poverty in the United States because every possible solution creates a host of unforeseen complications.

4. In trying to win a sweepstakes award, many people _____ to a large number of magazines they don't really want.

5. In _____, Herminia should have known that the free, all-expenses-paid vacation to the Bahamas was too good to be true.

6. The legislator waited in the _____ for about 30 minutes talking to the president's secretary before being admitted to the president's private study.

7. At a wedding reception, it's considered good manners for the bride and groom to _____ among all of their guests.

8. Many parents find it difficult to understand and cope with a(n) _____ and are glad when the teenage years finally end.

9. Since his last brush with the law, Mark has behaved in a very _____ manner, going out of his way to stay out of trouble.

10. Bandit patrols the _____ of his yard to make sure no other dog has dared trespass.

Exercise 2

Directions: Write the word from the list that best completes the sentence. Use each word only once.

advent	antebellum	antecedent	circa	circumference
circumscribe	cyclical	panorama	peripheral	retroactive

1. The most famous and probably most photographed _____ mansion in Louisiana is Oak Alley, where parts of *Interview with a Vampire* and *Primary Colors* were filmed.

2. Does the _____ of a person's head have anything to do with how smart the person is? Some studies suggest there may be a correlation.

3. Only one item has been in the White House since the very beginning—the Gilbert Stuart painting of George Washington _____ 1800.

4. The cab crashed because of a number of _____ events, including the cab company's failure to replace faulty brakes and its hiring of a careless driver.

5. With the _____ of winter, Victor knew he would soon have to put snow tires on his car.

6. After a six-month training period at Bank of America, Diarra received a salary of $9 an hour. She also got some back pay, because her new salary was _____ to when she first started her training.

7. Watching her young daughter go out the door in a tank top and bell bottoms reminded Charlene of clothes she had worn as an adolescent. She realized just how _____ fashion is.

8. Edwin stood on the edge of the Grand Canyon and looked at the _____ spread before him. The breathtaking view filled him with awe.

9. My father, who is in his eighties, is no longer allowed to drive because of an impairment of his _____ vision.

10. The teacher told the student to look on the map of California and _____ Santa Clara County in red ink.

Vocabulary Unit 5 Crossword

ACROSS CLUES

1. What you might do at the beginning of a poker game before receiving your cards.
5. A word part meaning "toward."
6. _____ vision is to the side.
9. You might see a beautiful _____ (synonym for *vista*) from the top of a mountain.
12. The _____ days of the South were those preceding the Civil War.
13. A cure-all.
15. To sign your name at the bottom of a contract.
18. A person who oversees.
21. John Glenn was able to _____ the earth.
26. A lobby or vestibule.
27. Your daily biological rhythm is your _____ cycle.

28. The formula for carbon dioxide has a(n) _____ in it.
30. An outer boundary is called a(n) _____.
32. Occurring in cycles.
33. The literal meaning is "to turn toward."

DOWN CLUES

1. The period of time before Christmas.
2. The abbreviation for what was once the 10th month.
3. The distance around a circle.
4. A word part meaning "large."
7. A word part meaning "under."
8. The movie was in _____.
10. A word part meaning "all."
11. Large pictures all around you in a circular room.

14. A word part meaning "see."
16. A word part meaning "half."
17. A word part meaning "hear."
19. Back pay is _____.
20. The antique was _____ 1900.
22. In hindsight or _____.
23. The abbreviation for what was once the 8th month.
24. A word part meaning "three."
25. A word part meaning "one."
28. A word part meaning "six."
29. A word part meaning "100."
31. A word part meaning "around."
34. A word part meaning "two."

9

Modes of Organization

CHAPTER PREVIEW
In this chapter, you will

- Become familiar with the following modes, or patterns, of organization: comparison-contrast, examples, chronological order, classification or division (categories), steps in a process, cause and effect, and listing.

- Practice writing summaries of longer selections.

Introduction to Modes of Organization

Once a writer has selected a mode of writing, he or she needs to select one or more **modes of organization.** The modes of organization are (1) comparison-contrast, (2) examples, (3) chronological order, (4) classification or division (categories), (5) steps in a process, (6) cause and effect, and (7) listing. These categories should be familiar to you because they previously appeared in this book as patterns of organization for paragraphs.

A writer who wishes to write in a persuasive mode might choose as modes of organization comparison-contrast, definition, and examples. A writer who wishes to write in a descriptive mode might select examples and chronological order. Sometimes an author may organize an entire selection using only one mode of organization.

Writers select the modes of writing and organization that will best enable them to communicate with their audience. Being able to recognize the different modes of writing and organization will help you become a better reader.

Happiness

What makes for a happy life is an age-old question, and this section of the book seeks to shed some light on the issue.

There is an ancient fable about happiness that is common in many cultures. Once upon a time there was an old king who was greatly worried about his son. The young prince was terribly unhappy, and although the king tried everything in his power, he could not convince his son to enjoy life. In despair, the king called his advisors to him. They counseled him by saying that the only cure for unhappiness was to obtain the shirt of a happy man and present it to the young prince. The king, thinking this to be a simple task, was greatly relieved. He eagerly sent his messengers out to search. For two years, they roved far and wide throughout the kingdom, visiting every town and village. At last, they rejoiced in locating one supremely happy man. Unfortunately, for the king and the young prince, the poor farmer, though gloriously happy, possessed no shirt.

The moral of this fable is that happiness does not depend upon material possessions, can't be given to another, and, above all, is elusive. The writer Nathaniel Hawthorne once said, "Happiness is a butterfly, which when pursued, is always just beyond your grasp, but which, if you will sit down quietly, may alight upon you."

The reading selections that follow illustrate various modes of organization. Though these selections come from a variety of sources, they all, either directly or indirectly, address the topic of happiness. When you finish reading the selections, try to come to some sort of conclusion about what happiness means to you.

Comparison-Contrast

READING

"Not surprisingly, people who like themselves tend to be happier than those who do not."

TUNING IN TO READING

While the Declaration of Independence says that everyone has the right to "life, liberty, and the pursuit of happiness," only recently have psychologists begun to explore what makes people happy. A 2002 study conducted at the University of Illinois by Edward Diener and Martin Seligman found that students reporting the highest levels of happiness had strong ties to friends and family. The researchers concluded that close relationships with others are important in order to be happy. They also discovered that some people are more likely to be happy than others. In general, those who have an optimistic personality are more likely to label themselves as happy. Read the following selection to find out what else correlates with happiness. As you read, note the primary mode of organization: comparison-contrast.

BIO-SKETCH

Wayne Weiten, a professor of psychology at the University of Nevada, Las Vegas, is a trained social psychologist with a research interest in stress and health psychology. He has received many awards for excellence in teaching and research, and is the author and coauthor of several best-selling psychology textbooks.

Margaret A. Lloyd retired from teaching in 2004. She is currently professor emerita and chair of psychology at Georgia Southern University and has been a recipient of that institution's Award for Excellence for Contributions to Instruction. She was also very active in the establishment and development of the Women's and Gender Studies program at Georgia Southern.

NOTES ON VOCABULARY

commonsense exhibiting sound practical judgment. Coming in out of the rain is considered a *commonsense* action.

heartfelt deeply or sincerely felt. An Academy Award winner might give *heartfelt* thanks to the movie's producer and director.

voracious insatiable; greedy. From the Latin *vorare*, meaning "to devour." Many dogs have *voracious* appetites.

The Roots of Happiness: An Empirical Analysis

Wayne Weiten and Margaret A. Lloyd

What exactly makes a person happy? This question has been the subject of much speculation. Commonsense theories about the roots of happiness abound. For example, you have no doubt heard that money cannot buy happiness. But do you believe it? A television commercial says, "If you've got your health, you've got just about everything." Is health indeed the key? What if you're healthy but poor, unemployed, and lonely? We often hear about the joys of parenthood, the joys of youth, and the joys of the simple, rural life. Are these the factors that promote happiness?

2   In recent years, social scientists have begun putting these and other theories to empirical test. Quite a number of survey studies have been conducted to explore the determinants of happiness. The findings of these studies are quite interesting. As you will see, many commonsense notions about happiness appear to be inaccurate.

3   The first of these is the apparently widespread assumption that most people are relatively unhappy. Writers, social scientists, and the general public seem to believe that people around the world are predominantly dissatisfied, yet surveys consistently find that the vast majority of respondents characterize themselves as fairly happy. When people are asked to rate their happiness, only a small minority place themselves below the neutral point on the various scales used. The overall picture seems rosier than anticipated.

What Isn't Very Important?

Money.

4   There is a positive correlation between income and feelings of happiness, but the association is surprisingly weak. Admittedly, being very poor can make people unhappy, but once people ascend above the poverty level, there is little relation between income and happiness. On the average, even wealthy people are only slightly happier than those in the middle classes. The problem with money is that in this era of voracious consumption, most people find a way to spend all their money and come out short, no matter how much they make. Complaints about not having enough money are routine even among affluent people who earn six-figure incomes.

Age.

5   Age and happiness are consistently found to be unrelated. Age accounts for less than 1 percent of the variation in people's happiness. The key factors influencing people's thoughts about their own well-being may shift some as people grow older—work becomes less important, health more so—but people's average level of happiness tends to remain remarkably stable over the life span.

Gender.

6   Women are treated for depressive disorders about twice as often as men, so one might expect that women are less happy on the average. However, like age, gender accounts for less than 1 percent of the variation in people's happiness.

Parenthood.

7   Children can be a tremendous source of joy and fulfillment, but they also can be a tremendous source of headaches and hassles. Compared to childless couples, parents worry more and experience more marital problems. Apparently the good and bad aspects of parenthood balance each other out, because the evidence indicates that people who have children are neither more nor less happy than people without children.

Intelligence.

8   Intelligence is a highly valued trait in modern society, but researchers have not found an association between IQ scores and happiness. Educational attainment also appears to be unrelated to life satisfaction.

Physical Attractiveness.

9   Good-looking people enjoy a variety of advantages in comparison to unattractive people. Given that physical attractiveness is an important resource in Western society, we might expect attractive people to be happier than others, but the available data indicate that the correlation between attractiveness and happiness is negligible.

What Is Somewhat Important?

10   Research has identified three facets of life that appear to have a moderate impact on subjective well-being: health, social activity, and religious belief.

Health.

11   Good physical health would seem to be an essential requirement for happiness, but people adapt to health problems. Research reveals that individuals who develop serious, disabling health conditions aren't as unhappy as one might guess. Furthermore, good health does not, by itself, produce happiness, because people tend to take good health for granted. Researchers found only a moderate positive correlation between health status and subjective well-being.

Social Activity.

12   Humans are social beings, and people's interpersonal relations do appear to contribute to their happiness. People who are satisfied with their friendship networks and who are socially active report above-average levels of happiness. At the other end of the spectrum, people troubled by loneliness tend to be very unhappy.

Religion.

13   A number of large-scale surveys suggest that people with heartfelt religious convictions are more likely to be happy than people who characterize themselves as nonreligious.

What Is Very Important?

14   The list of factors that turn out to be very important ingredients of happiness is surprisingly short. Only a few variables are strongly related to overall happiness.

Love and Marriage.

15   Romantic relationships can be stressful, but people consistently rate being in love as one of the most critical ingredients of happiness. Furthermore, although people complain a lot about their marriages, the evidence indicates that marital status is a key correlate of happiness. Among both men and women, married people are happier than people who are single or divorced.

Work.

16   Given the way people often complain about their jobs, we might not expect work to be a key source of happiness, but it is. Although less critical than love and marriage, job satisfaction is strongly related to general happiness. Studies also show that unemployment has devastating effects on subjective well-being.

Personality.

17   The best predictor of individuals' future happiness is their past happiness. Some people seem destined to be happy and others unhappy, regardless of their triumphs or setbacks. Several studies suggest that happiness does not depend on

external circumstances—having a nice house, good friends, and an enjoyable job—as much as internal factors, such as one's outlook on life. With this reality in mind, researchers have begun to look for links between personality and subjective well-being, and they have found some relatively strong connections. For example, self-esteem is one of the best predictors of happiness. Not surprisingly, people who like themselves tend to be happier than those who do not. Other personality correlates of happiness include extraversion, optimism, and a sense of personal control over one's life.

From Wayne Weiten and Margaret A. Lloyd, *Psychology Applied to Modern Life*, 7th Edition, pp. 17–21. © 2003 Wadsworth, a part of Cengage Learning, Inc. Reproduced by permission. www.cengage.com/permissions.

 COMPREHENSION CHECKUP

True or False

Directions: Indicate whether each statement is true or false by writing **T** or **F** in the space provided.

_____ 1. Happy people like themselves.

_____ 2. Happy people feel in control of the events in their lives.

_____ 3. Happy people are pessimistic.

_____ 4. Single people are happier than married people.

_____ 5. Most people are moderately unhappy most of the time.

_____ 6. Being very poor can make people unhappy.

_____ 7. Men and women are about equally happy.

_____ 8. Job satisfaction correlates favorably with happiness.

_____ 9. An extravert is more likely to be happy than an introvert.

_____ 10. People tend to take good health for granted.

Vocabulary in Context

Directions: In the blanks below, write the word from the list that best completes the sentence. Use each word only once.

above-average	adapt	childless	correlation	depressive
essential	ingredients	internal	loneliness	marital
negligible	nonreligious	satisfaction	weak	

1. There is a positive association between income and feelings of happiness, but the association is surprisingly _____.

2. Women are treated for _____ disorders about twice as often as men.

3. Compared to _____ couples, parents worry more and experience more _____ problems.

4. We might expect attractive people to be happier than others, but the available data indicate that the _____ between attractiveness and happiness is _____.

5. Good physical health would seem to be a(n) _____ requirement for hap-piness, but people _____ to health problems.

6. People satisfied with their friendship networks report _____ levels of happiness, but people troubled by _____ tend to be very unhappy.

7. People with heartfelt religious convictions are more likely to be happy than people who characterize themselves as _____.

8. While romantic relationships can be stressful, people rate being in love as a crit-ical _____ of happiness.

9. Although less critical than love and marriage, job _____ is strongly re-lated to general happiness.

10. Studies suggest that happiness does not depend on external circumstances as much as on _____ factors.

Vocabulary Matching

Directions: Match the vocabulary words in Column A with their antonyms in Col-umn B. Place the correct letter in the space provided.

	Column A	Column B
_____	1. rosier	a. objective
_____	2. affluent	b. incidental
_____	3. routine	c. unsocial
_____	4. negligible	d. unusual
_____	5. subjective	e. pessimism
_____	6. essential	f. gloomier
_____	7. moderate	g. significant
_____	8. interpersonal	h. disaster
_____	9. optimism	i. impoverished
_____	10. triumph	j. extreme

In Your Own Words

1. Professor Martin Seligman believes that "interpersonal virtues like kindness and gratitude are strongly tied to happiness." According to research, he says, "giving puts meaning into your life." This premise is illustrated in the success of *Extreme Makeover Home Edition*, a popular reality show in which a lucky individual re-ceives a completely remodeled house. In some cases, hundreds of volunteers have participated in the makeovers. Dubbed "Good Samaritan" TV, the program is just the first in a list of similar programs. What's your opinion? Does practicing "random acts of kindness" really lead to happiness?

2. Why do you think the loss of a job can be so devastating to a person's sense of well-being? Does it help that a person is able to turn life's lemons into lemonade?

3. Are you surprised that parenthood is in the category "What Isn't Very Impor-tant"? What kinds of stresses do parents face today? Do you think raising chil-dren today is harder or easier than it was a generation ago?

4. Are you surprised that "wealthy people are only slightly happier than those in the middle classes"? Does it surprise you that people who win the lottery soon revert to their level of happiness before their big win? How do you account for this?

5. Does acting happy or putting on a happy face actually help you feel happy?

Written Assignment

Rank the following traits for their importance to happiness: wealth, parenthood, health, social activity, religious commitment, marriage, and work. Explain your ranking.

Internet Activity

Ed Diener, a psychology professor at the University of Illinois, has developed "The Satisfaction with Life" scale. To take the quiz, go to:

www.psych.uiuc.edu/~ediener/hottopic/hottopic.html

Explain what you learned about yourself. Did the quiz confirm what you already knew about yourself? Did it give you new insight into your personality?

Examples

READING

"In other words, sudden wealth poses a threat that has to be guarded against."

TUNING IN TO READING

What would you do if you won a million dollars? Do you think it would make you happy? Or do you think suddenly acquiring considerable wealth might cause problems in your life? The following selection from a sociology textbook gives examples of individuals who won a great deal of money in the lottery, but then didn't exactly live "happily ever after."

BIO-SKETCH

James M. Henslin is a professor emeritus in the department of sociology at Southern Illinois University. He has written textbooks and published extensively in sociology journals. His two favorite activities are writing and traveling.

NOTES ON VOCABULARY

lottery   a way of raising money by selling numbered tickets and giving prizes to the holders of the numbers drawn at random.

scratch-off ticket   With this particular type of ticket, you don't have to wait for a specific date and time to find out if you're a winner. You buy a ticket and scratch a special coating off. If it's a winning ticket you'll know right away.

anomie   a personal state of isolation and anxiety that comes from a lack of purpose or ideals.

status inconsistency   According to sociologists, there are three dimensions of social class: property, prestige, and power. If people have a mixture of high and low ranks, the condition is called status inconsistency. Instant wealth can often cause status inconsistency.

The Big Win: Life after the Lottery

James M. Henslin

1   "If I just win the lottery, life will be good. These problems I've got, they'll be gone. I can just see myself now."

2   So goes the dream. And many Americans shell out megabucks every week, with the glimmering hope that "Maybe this week, I'll hit it big."

3   Most are lucky to hit for $10, or maybe just another scratch-off ticket.

4   But there are the big hits. What happens to these winners? Are their lives all roses and chocolate afterwards?

5   Unfortunately, we don't have any systematic studies of the big winners, so I can't tell you what life is like for the average winner. But several themes are apparent from reporters' interviews.

6   The most common consequence of hitting it big is that life becomes topsy-turvy. All of us are rooted somewhere. We have connections with others that provide the basis for our orientations to life and how we feel about the world. Sudden wealth can rip these moorings apart, and the resulting *status inconsistency* can lead to a condition sociologists call *anomie*.

7   First, comes the shock. As Mary Sanderson, a telephone operator in Dover, New Hampshire, who won $66 million, said, "I was afraid to believe it was real, and afraid to believe it wasn't." Mary says she never slept worse than her first night as a multimillionaire. "I spent the whole time crying—and throwing up."

8   Reporters and TV cameras appear on your doorstep. "What are you going to do with all that money?" they demand. You haven't the slightest idea, but in a daze you mumble something.

9   Then come the calls. Some are welcome. Your mom and dad call to congratulate you. But long-forgotten friends and distant relatives suddenly remember how close they really are to you—and strangely enough, they all have emergencies that your money can solve. You even get calls from strangers who have sick mothers, sick kids, sick dogs . . .

10   You have to unplug the phone and get an unlisted number.

11   Some lottery winners are flooded with marriage proposals. These individuals certainly didn't become more attractive or sexy overnight—or did they? Maybe money makes people sexy.

12   You can no longer trust people. You don't know what their real motives are. Before, no one could be after your money because you didn't have any. You may even fear kidnappers. Before, this wasn't a problem—unless some kidnapper wanted the ransom of a seven-year-old car.

13   The normal becomes abnormal. Even picking out a wedding gift is a problem. If you give the usual toaster, everyone will think you're stingy. But should you write a check for $25,000? If you do, you'll be invited to every wedding in town—and everyone will expect the same.

14   Here is what happened to some lottery winners:

15   As a tip, a customer gave a lottery ticket to Tonda Dickerson, a waitress at the Waffle House in Grand Bay, Alabama. She won $10 million. Her co-workers sued her, saying they had always agreed to split such winnings.

16   Then there is Michael Klingebiel of Rahway, New Jersey. When he won $2 million, his mother Phyllis, said they had pooled $20 a month for years to play the lottery. He said that was true, but his winning ticket wasn't from their pool. He bought this one on his own. Phyllis sued her son.

17   Frank Capaci, a retired electrician in Streamwood, Illinois, who won $195 million, is no longer welcome at his neighborhood bar, where he had hung out for years. Two bartenders had collected $5 from customers and driven an hour to Wisconsin to buy tickets. When Frank won, he gave $10,000 to each of them. They said he promised them more. Also, his former friends say that Capaci started to

act "like a big shot," buying rounds of drinks but saying, "Except him," while point-ing to someone he didn't like.

18   Those who avoid *anomie* seem to be people who don't make sudden changes in their lifestyles or their behavior. They hold on to their old friends, routines, and other moorings in life that give them identity. Some even keep their old jobs—not for the money, of course, but because it anchors them to an identity with which they are familiar and comfortable.

19   In other words, sudden wealth poses a threat that has to be guarded against.

20   And I can just hear you say, "I'll take the risk!"

From James M. Henslin, *Essentials of Sociology: A Down-to-Earth Approach*, 7th Edition, p. 201. © 2007 Pearson Education, Inc. Reproduced by permission of Pearson Education, Inc.

 COMPREHENSION CHECKUP

Multiple Choice

Directions: For each item, write the letter corresponding to the best answer.

_____   1. A *systematic* study is one that is
   a. methodical.
   b. orderly.
   c. both a and b.
   d. none of the above.

_____   2. What is the meaning of "average winner" as used in paragraph 5?
   a. equitable
   b. intermediate
   c. usual or typical
   d. mediocre

_____   3. What is the meaning of "all roses and chocolate" as used in paragraph 4?
   a. happiness and prosperity
   b. petals and thorns
   c. hard work and trouble
   d. gardens and candy stores

_____   4. In paragraph 4, the transition word *but* implies a
   a. contrast.
   b. definition.
   c. conclusion.
   d. comparison.

_____   5. What is the relationship between the sentence beginning in paragraph 7 ("First, comes the shock") and the sentence beginning in paragraph 9 ("Then come the calls")?
   a. cause and effect
   b. comparison-contrast
   c. definition and example
   d. steps in a process

_____   6. The author describes all of the following events happening to lottery winners *except*
   a. being besieged by requests from various people.
   b. being sued by coworkers who claimed to be cowinners.
   c. being forced to file for bankruptcy within a few years.
   d. being inundated by marriage proposals.

_____ 7. Identify the statement that most accurately states the main idea.
   a. Money makes people sexy.
   b. Winning the lottery makes life good.
   c. Sudden wealth creates problems that have to be managed.
   d. For a lottery winner, wise financial investments are essential.

_____ 8. From the selection, we can conclude all of the following about winning a lottery _except_ that
   a. it can cause stress.
   b. it can cause the loss of friendships.
   c. it can cause a lack of trust.
   d. it can cause a desire to give vast amounts of money to charity.

_____ 9. The examples of Tonda Dickerson, Michael Klingebiel, and Frank Capaci were used to illustrate
   a. that good things continue to happen to good people.
   b. the difficulty in maintaining relationships after a big financial windfall.
   c. the generosity of strangers.
   d. that money can solve all problems.

_____ 10. The author of this selection suggests that
   a. lottery winners will be besieged by investment companies who want to handle their money.
   b. winning the lottery may not be all good.
   c. lottery winners will have to move and begin new lives.
   d. lottery winners will spend all of their winnings in a few years.

_____ 11. The selection suggests that people who cope best with sudden wealth may do any of the following _except_
   a. keep their old friends and routines.
   b. splurge on big-ticket items like a house and then save their money thereafter.
   c. avoid making sudden changes in their behavior.
   d. keep their old jobs.

_____ 12. As used In paragraph 15, the word _tip_ means
   a. an amount of money given to someone in return for service.
   b. a helpful hint or warning.
   c. a piece of inside information.
   d. a narrow or pointed end of something.

Vocabulary Matching

Directions: Match the vocabulary words in Column A with their definitions in Column B. Place the correct letter in the space provided.

	Column A	**Column B**
_____	1. ransom	a. an indeterminately large sum of money
_____	2. apparent	b. faint
_____	3. big shot	c. in utter confusion or disorder
_____	4. consequence	d. clear
_____	5. daze	e. stabilizing influences
_____	6. flooded	f. stunned state
_____	7. glimmering	g. inundated

_____ 8. megabucks   h. put into a common fund

_____ 9. moorings   i. to utter words in a low, indistinct manner

_____ 10. mumble   j. a person of consequence or promise

_____ 11. pooled   k. result

_____ 12. topsy-turvy   o. money paid or demanded for the release of
                                       someone or something from captivity

In Your Own Words

1. Do you agree or disagree with the old adage "Be careful what you wish for be-cause you just might get it?" Do you think more money causes more problems?

2. Many psychologists say that if you were unhappy before wining a huge amount of money, then you will probably still be unhappy afterward. Apparently, money will only temporarily cover up the problems you face. How is this theory supported by the lottery winners cited in the selection? Do you think money can solve all problems?

3. Fully one-third of multimillion-dollar lottery winners become bankrupt in just a few years after their big win. Many winners immediately buy a big mansion but don't take into account the upkeep of such a home such as higher utilities, a security system, insurance, and taxes. The one thing most fail to do is learn anything about investing. How would you handle your big win? What would you do first? To whom would you turn for advice?

4. Americans spend more than $25 million a year on lottery tickets. Does that amount surprise you? Do you buy lottery tickets? If so, how much do you spend on tickets per week?

5. Experts have compiled a list of tips to help lottery winners adjust to their new wealth. Here are a few of their suggestions:
   a. Give yourself a modest initial spending spree and then invest the rest of the money wisely so that you can live on the interest.
   b. Don't quit your job. Even working part-time is better than quitting altogether. You need something to do all day besides running around spending money.

   What do you think of these suggestions? Can you think of any others?

Written Assignment

Some experts believe there is a real risk with acquiring sudden wealth. One expert says that "often lottery-winners can keep the money and lose family and friends, or lose the money and keep family and friends." Write a few paragraphs giving your opinion on this issue.

Internet Activity

1. To calculate your odds of winning the lottery, check out the following Web site:

   www.webmath.com/lottery.html

   Did you know that you have a better chance of getting into a car accident, suffering a plane accident, or being struck by lightning than of winning the lottery?

2. For information about the history of the lottery, go to:

   www.naspl.org/05/history.html

   Write a few paragraphs about what you find interesting.

Chronological Order

READING

"Over time, Charley drove stages on almost every route in Northern California."

TUNING IN TO READING

In Chapter 3, you summarized a fairly short article. You are now going to be working with a longer article about a 19th-century woman who took on a role usually reserved for a man. The information in the article is presented chronologically, making it easier to summarize.

Use the survey and question steps of SQ3R (see pages 65–66) before actually beginning to read the article. Study the bibliographic material. Who wrote the article? What is the title? What journal is it from? When was it written? All of this information will suggest what the article is about, how it is organized, and what the author's viewpoint is. In your survey, read the first two paragraphs, the last two paragraphs, and the first sentence of the other paragraphs. After completing your survey of the entire article, write the main idea below.

Main idea:_____

NOTES ON VOCABULARY

coerce   to compel by force. Derived from the Latin *coercere,* meaning "to confine or control."

rheumatism   a disease characterized by pain or stiffness in the joints or muscles.

undertaker   a person who prepares a dead body for burial or cremation. The term dates from the 17th century and originally referred to someone who undertakes to carry out some endeavor for another.

wax profane   to grow or become vulgar or irreverent; to curse. *Profane* is based on the Latin word *profanum,* meaning "outside the temple." The *profane* person is behaving in an "unholy" way.

hearsay   unverified information acquired from another; rumor.

ply the trade   to carry on; practice; pursue busily and steadily.

Charley's Secret   BY SHANNON MOON LEONETTI

On December 28, 1879, Charley Parkhurst lost his battle against crippling rheumatism and cancer. The well-known stagecoach driver had been seriously ill for weeks when he mentioned to his friend Charles Harmon, that he had something to tell him, but "there was no hurry." The tough old driver had less time than he knew, however, and died without speaking to Harmon.

2   The local undertaker, beckoned to prepare Charley's body for burial, was not prepared for what he discovered. When he started to change Charley out of his bed clothes, he was shocked to find that the tobacco-chewing man who had handled a black snake whip and a gun as well as anyone, was, in fact, a woman.

3   At first the undertaker did not know what to do. After gathering his wits, he called out for Frank Woodward, Charley's closest friend for more than 20 years. Frank had kept a daily vigil during Charley's illness and was by his side at the end. But when informed of the startling discovery, Woodward forgot his grief and started to "wax profane."

4   The truth was almost impossible to comprehend. It confounded those closest to Charley and shocked the people who had

respected their friend's prowess as a reins-man, skills that had earned Parkhurst a spot in an elite group nicknamed the "Kings of the Road." A lifetime spent within a small circle of friends had not prevented Charley Parkhurst from keeping her secret from everyone.

5 While the written history of nineteenth century America is dominated by the ex-ploits of men, the bizarre story of Charley Parkhurst is not unique. A number of women disguised themselves as men in or-der to fight in the Civil War. Whatever had motivated Charley Parkhurst, and whether or not her "secret" was one she kept will-ingly, the truth remains that opportunities for women of her day to lead the kind of lives they wanted were very limited.

6 Facts about Charley's life are difficult to come by, and harder to prove. Much of what has been written about her is based on hearsay and legend. Still, enough is known about her 67 years to categorize her life as another example of how, in the history of the American West, the truth is often more interesting than fiction.

7 Born around 1812, in Lebanon, New Hampshire, Parkhurst spent her youth in an orphanage. There is no record of who left her there, or of whether her birth name was Charlotte, as many have assumed. Orphan-ages of this era were not happy places in which to grow up. Rules were adopted for the convenience of the staff, and with so many children under one roof, child-care institutions could not supply the warmth, affection, and attention of a normal house-hold. Boys and girls often were dressed alike in easy-to-care-for overalls, with their hair cut in identical bobs. This sort of ge-neric environment must have encouraged Charley's sense of independence, and shaped her outlook on life.

8 By the time she was a teenager, Charley had had enough of the harsh, restricted life of the orphanage and decided to run away. She went to work in a livery stable in Worcester, Massachusetts, cleaning stalls, keeping the tack in good repair, washing the coaches, and currying and feeding the horses. The new stable "boy" turned out to be a natural with the horses, and his em-ployer, Ebenezar Balch began teaching him

to drive the coaches, beginning with a one-horse buggy. It was not long before he could handle as many as six horses at a time.

9 Charley moved with Balch to Provi-dence, Rhode Island, where he earned a reputation as both a smooth and careful driver and the perfect coachman for parties and dances. Long after he moved west, Charley was remembered back east as a quiet man who "struck a handsome figure when he showed up driving six grays exactly matched." He grew restless with driving livery, however, and reportedly left Rhode Island for Georgia with another driver in the mid-1840s. His exact whereabouts for this period are unclear, but presumably, he con-tinued to ply the trade at which he had be-come so skilled, until he returned to Rhode Island in 1849.

10 A pair of young businessmen and expert reinsmen from that state named Jim Birch and Frank Stevens went west to take advan-tage of the money-making opportuni-ties that followed the recent gold rush in California. In 1851, when Birch desper-ately needed good reinsmen for the rapidly growing stage and mail lines he had es-tablished, he induced Charley to come and work for him. Two years later, Birch and Stevens, in an effort to head off growing competition, formed the California Stage Company, with Charley as one of their top drivers.

11 By 1856, stagecoaching had grown enormously in the West, particularly in California, where Sacramento had become the largest stagecoach center in the world. The California Stage Company, the largest stagecoach firm in the country, dominated the business within the state, with 28 daily lines that covered nearly two thousand miles of roads. The company owned two hundred Concord stagecoaches and wagons, and employed three hundred drivers, agents, hostlers, and others. Drivers, such as the famed Frank Monk who both terrified and impressed *New York Tribune* editor Horace Greeley during an 1859 excursion, earned inflated reputations because of their speed and skill on mountain roads. A good driver, given a change of teams and a Concord coach, could cover nearly one hundred miles in 24 hours.

12   Like Monk, Charley earned a reputation of heroic proportions while driving local routes for the California Stage Company. Passengers considered it an honor to be asked by the veteran reinsman to ride up on the box with him. Parkhurst worked hard to maintain his record as one of the fastest and safest stagecoach drivers in California. His incessant tobacco chewing did nothing to diminish his high, booming voice or his loud whistle; valuable tools when it came time to shout over the clamor of the coach or signal his approach on a particularly narrow road.

13   One day, not long after Charley arrived in California, a road agent surprised and robbed his stage. From then on he carried a weapon beside him. The next time he faced a similar threat, Parkhurst, better prepared, reportedly fired a shot as he kept the stage rolling. The partner of a notorious stage robber called "Sugarfoot" was wounded in the fray; he died later, after making a deathbed confession. "Old Charley," as the nearly middle-aged reinsman was called by younger drivers, never again had serious trouble with highwaymen.

14   Over time, Charley drove stages on almost every route in northern California. Once, on a run from San Francisco to San Jose, he was said to have lost his left eye while shoeing a horse who "ungratefully kicked him in the face." From then on, Charley wore a patch over the damaged eye socket, enhancing the aura of mystery that surrounded this "unsociable feller."

15   Having only one good eye did not prevent Charley from becoming famous for feats of skill and bravery. While driving at a fast clip, he could, some claimed, run over a half dollar that was lying in the road, with the front and rear wheels of his stage. Some found his proficiency with a whip "downright spooky"; Parkhurst could, the stories went, "cut the end off an envelope held at arm's length at 15 paces, or cut the cigar from a man's mouth at the same distance without hurting anyone."

16   Sometime around the 1860s, Charley was carrying a load of liquor to the Pleasant Valley ranch owned by Andrew Jackson Clark. Charley was said to have arrived so drunk that Clark and his 14-year-old son put him to bed. The young Clark came running and told his mother that "Charley ain't no man, he's a woman." For some unknown reason, Mr. Clark chose this occasion to teach his young son a lesson in not telling stories about others, and the Clarks kept Charley's secret until after his death. Charley was never seen drunk again.

17   Around that same time, Parkhurst's rheumatism convinced him it was time to give up driving. He wanted to leave the roads before an accident or a runaway marred his clean record. In 1864, he settled on a small tract of land on the road from San Jose to Santa Cruz, built a two-room house and stable, and planted wheat, turnips, and an apple orchard. The worn-out driver noted: "I'm no better now than when I commenced. Pay's small and work's heavy. I'm getting old. Rheumatism in my bones."

18   Parkhurst continued working, however. His place became a stage stop where he changed horses and refreshed travelers. Then, joining in a venture with his good friend Frank Woodward, Charley started raising cattle. When times were slow, the pair hired themselves out as lumberjacks. Before long, however, his rheumatism forced Charley to slow down further. Heavy physical work was becoming too tough, and his limbs were starting to shrivel. Nearly sixty, he had to give up his long habit of sleeping out in the woods wrapped only in a blanket. And, he grew increasingly reticent and private.

19   Never one to talk about himself, Charley shined when the subject turned to politics. He firmly believed that it was both the right and the obligation of every citizen to pay attention to the political situation and to vote. In November 1868, Charley Parkhurst cast his first recorded vote; having lived for so long as a man, it may never have occurred to him that he did not have that right. The voting entry recorded in the Great Register of Santa Cruz County, California, lists one "Charley Darkey Parkhurst, age 55, occupation farmer, native New Hampshire, resident Soquel."

20   The country was changing rapidly as the 1870s approached, yet women still had

almost no property or inheritance rights, and the doors were just beginning to open in the job market. Only because she sacrificed her identity as a woman was Charley able to exercise one special privilege, the right to vote, almost 52 years before anyone else of her gender.

21 Sometime around 1872, Parkhurst sold off all of his cattle and property, and moved into a small vacant house on land owned by Charles Harmon. A few years later, in 1879, Charley complained of a sore throat, but refused to see a doctor. Even when the sore throat became a swelling on the side of his tongue, Charley—the person who took the best care possible of his horses—still did not seek medical attention. Nearly a year went by before he could be coerced into seeing Mr. Plumm, Soquel's "Cancer man." By then it was too late.

22 As Christmas approached, Charley's health was rapidly deteriorating. Frank Woodward started visiting him every day. The two tired old-timers mostly sat in front of the fire, sometimes breaking the silence to reminisce or to share fresh gossip.

23 Finally, death came, and word of Charley's secret spread. Shock and anger overwhelmed "his" closest friends, and much time passed before their sense of loss settled in. Woodward is said to have sworn aloud at the corpse as he accompanied it to the carpenter's shop to be fitted for a coffin. Old Charley had no money, but an acquaintance donated a plot in the Odd Fellow's cemetery in Watsonville, California. In 1880, Charles Harmon donated a small headstone.

24 Another donation provided a plaque that was hung on the Soquel, California, fire station. The inscription noted that "On this site on November 3, 1868 was cast the first vote by a woman in California. A Ballot by Charlotte 'Charley' Parkhurst who disguised herself as a man."

Shannon Moon Leonetti, "Charley's Secret." Reprinted with permission, *American History* magazine, May/June 1997, pp. 40–43, 73. Copyright Weider History Group.

Short Answer

Directions: Answer the following questions briefly.

Do you still agree with your original main idea? _____

If not, rewrite your main idea below.

Main idea: _____

_____

Chronological Order and Summaries of Longer Articles

Your ability to summarize will help you in college because summarizing information is a good way to learn it. Summarizing may also help you at work. For instance, a nurse might summarize a patient's condition, a sportswriter might summarize the action in a basketball game, and a police officer might summarize the events leading up to an accident.

You summarize a reading selection by stating the main ideas and key supporting details in your own words. A summary condenses the original material, and good summaries are about one-fourth the length of the original. If a summary is written well, you do not have to go back and read the selection again.

You just read "Charley's Secret." It is a relatively easy article to summarize because the main ideas are presented in chronological order.

First, answer the following questions about the topic. Your answers will provide you with important details about the story.

Who: _____

What: _____

Where: _____

When: _____

Why: _____

How: _____

In your own words, write four main points from the article along with two supporting details for each main point.

Point 1: _____

Details: _____

_____

Point 2: _____

Details: _____

_____

Point 3: _____

Details: _____

_____

Point 4: _____

Details: _____

_____

If you have difficulty with any of the steps, check the following examples.

Main idea of the article: *Charley Parkhurst, disguising herself as a man, became a well-known and respected stagecoach driver living a life of independence unknown to women at the time.*

Who:	*Charley Parkhurst (Charlotte?)*
What:	*became a well-known stagecoach driver*
Where:	*the West, mainly California*
When:	*middle 19th century before women had the vote*
Why:	*lived a life of great independence*
How:	*disguised herself as a man*
Point 1:	*Charley's early years in an orphanage encouraged her independence and shaped her outlook on life.*
Details:	Born 1812 and abandoned at harsh orphanage where all dressed alike; ran away to work in livery stable where learned to drive coaches

Point 2:	*Charley became a well-respected reinsman for the largest stagecoach company in the world.*
Details:	Worked for California Stage Co.; was part of "Kings of the Road"; known as fast, safe driver and hero
Point 3:	*Charley, disguised as a man, exercised the right to vote long before other women.*
Details:	In 1868, at 55, voted as man, 52 years before other females allowed; first owned stagecoach rest stop and then in 1872 moved to house
Point 4:	*When Charley became ill with cancer and died, friends were shocked and angry about the deception.*
Details:	Even after sore throat was diagnosed as cancer, failed to tell secret; fell to undertaker to announce that Charley was woman

Now you are ready to write your summary. The introductory paragraph will present the main idea of the selection. Each of the next paragraphs will focus on one of the main points. Include just enough details to support each main point. Use transitional words to smoothly connect everything together.

After writing your summary, compare your version to the student sample in the Appendices (page A-28).

Now write a summary of a previous reading. Because you have already read this selection, you can skip the survey questions.

What is the main idea of your selection?

_____

_____

Answer the following questions about the topic.

Who:_____

What: _____

Where: _____

When: _____

Why: _____

How: _____

In your own words, list three or four main points from the article along with two supporting details for each main point.

Point 1: _____

Details: _____

_____

Point 2: _____

Details: _____

_____

Point 3: _____

Details: _____

_____

Point 4: _____

Details: _____

_____

Using this information, write your summary on a separate sheet of paper.

 COMPREHENSION CHECKUP

Multiple Choice

Directions: For each item, write the letter corresponding to the best answer.

_____ 1. The author's purpose in writing this article was to
    a. encourage women to enter predominantly male occupations.
    b. inform us of the life of one woman who assumed the role of a man.
    c. explain the life of 19th-century stagecoach drivers.
    d. entertain readers with an amusing story.

_____ 2. You can infer from this article that Charley
    a. had many friends who knew she was a woman.
    b. would have been allowed to vote if her true sex had been known.
    c. probably could not have become a stagecoach driver if she had not pretended to be a man.
    d. was happy to live in an orphanage.

_____ 3. The most likely mode of organization for this article is
    a. chronological.
    b. cause and effect.
    c. classification.
    d. comparison-contrast.

_____ 4. The word *incessant* in paragraph 12 means
    a. disliked by others.
    b. off-and-on.
    c. constant or continual.
    d. frequent.

_____ 5. The last sentence of paragraph 20 indicates
    a. comparison-contrast.
    b. cause and effect.
    c. chronological order.
    d. classification/division.

True or False

Directions: Indicate whether each statement is true or false by writing **T** or **F** in the space provided.

_____ 6. Charley stopped driving stagecoaches because of cancer.

_____ 7. Charley died in poverty.

_____ 8. Charley led other women to fight for the right to vote.

_____ 9. The undertaker was the first person to discover that Charley was a woman.

_____ 10. Charley had a difficult childhood.

Vocabulary in Context

Directions: Scan the paragraphs indicated in parentheses to find a word that matches the definition given, and write it in the space provided.

1. mental faculties; good sense (3) _____
2. bewildered; confused (4) _____
3. exceptional ability, skill, or strength (4) _____
4. notable deeds; feats (5) _____
5. strange; odd (5) _____
6. classify (6) _____
7. lessen; reduce (12) _____
8. loud uproar (12) _____
9. noisy quarrel; brawl (13) _____
10. began; started (17) _____
11. to wither (18) _____
12. uncommunicative; reserved (18) _____
13. to talk about past experiences (22) _____

Creating a Time Line

Directions: When working with historical articles, or other kinds of articles that describe a sequence of events, it sometimes helps to prepare a time line. Complete the time line with information from "Charley's Secret." Additional historical dates have been added to put Charley's life in perspective.

1812	approximate birth date of Charley _____
mid-1840s	_____
1848	gold discovered in California _____
1849	_____
1851	_____
1853	Charley a top driver for the California Stage Company
1861	Civil War begins _____
1864	_____
1865	Robert E. Lee surrenders at Appomattox _____
1868	_____
1872	Charley moves to a small home owned by Charles Harmon
1879	Charley dies _____
1880	_____

Internet Activity

For more information about stagecoaches, go to:

www.over-land.com

This Internet site is a listing of several Web pages that discuss the history of stagecoaches and other types of transportation common in the late 19th century.

Categories

READING

"What we possess is, in a very real way, part of ourselves."

TUNING IN TO READING

The following expository essay makes good use of categories. When you read the essay, notice how the author organizes information into categories, defines the categories, and uses the categories to analyze and draw conclusions.

Have you ever been burglarized? If so, how did the experience make you feel?

BIO-SKETCH

Russell W. Belk, PhD, is a professor of business administration at the Graduate School of Business, University of Utah. He has published numerous books, articles, and monographs, and is in demand as a speaker. His chief area of expertise is marketing and consumer behavior.

NOTES ON VOCABULARY

donor   someone who gives something as a gift. From the Latin *don*, meaning "gift."

sedentary   characterized by remaining in one place; sitting. From the Latin word *sedeo*, meaning "sit."

vicariously   felt or enjoyed through imagined participation in the experience of others.

JACKIE'S PEARLS RING UP A LOT MORE CAMELOT CASH 1D

▶ BIDDING LIST, 6D
▶ BOSTON ACE PITCHES BID OF HIS OWN, 1C

JFK Library, Agence France-Presse
Jackie, John Jr.: Pearls, worth $700, fetched $211,500, 1D

My Possessions Myself   BY RUSSELL W. BELK

Burglary victims often say that they feel they have been personally polluted, even raped. Since they never had any personal contact with the burglar, what has been violated is the sense of self that exists in their jewelry, clothing, photographs and other personal possessions.

2   The feeling of violation goes even deeper since the burglar has also wounded the family's sense of identity by penetrating its protective skin, the family home. Clearly, the sense of self is not only individual. Heirlooms, for example, can represent and extend a family's sense of identity, while public

buildings, monuments and parks help us develop regional and national identities. Although we Americans think of ourselves as highly individualistic, aggregate identity is important to us, as the willingness to preserve and restore symbols such as the Statue of Liberty shows.

3   What we possess is, in a very real way, part of ourselves. Our thoughts and our bodies are normally the most central part of our self-concept. But next in importance are what we do—our occupations and skills—and what we have—our unique set of possessions. The fact that jewelry, weapons and domestic utensils are found in prehistoric burial sites is evidence that we have long considered possessions as part of the person, even after death.

4   We find the same identification of people with possessions in examples as diverse as the reverence religions pay to relics of saints and prophets, the intensity of autograph hounds, the emphasis auctioneers place on the previous ownership of objects up for bid and the difficulty secondhand stores have in selling used underwear and other garments worn close to the body. In each case a sense of the prior owners is thought to remain in the things that touched their lives.

5   We generally include four types of possessions in our personal sense of self: body and body parts, objects, places and time periods, persons and pets. Body parts are normally so well integrated into our identities that we think of them as "me" rather than mere "mine." But several studies have shown that body parts vary widely in their importance to us.

6   Recently, doctoral student Mark Austin and I gave 248 adults a group of cards, each of which listed a single item in one of the four categories: body parts such as kidneys, hearts and knees; objects such as a favorite dessert or the contents (other than money) of your wallet; places and times such as a favorite city or time of life; and particular people or pets.

7   We asked people to put the 96 cards in two piles, things they considered self and non self. They then sorted each of these into two piles representing a little or a lot of self or non self. We then gave each pile a "self" score (1, 2, 3, 4) and calculated average scores for each card. This gave us a rating of how central each item was to the sense of identity.

8   Eyes, hair, heart, legs, hands, fingers, genitals and skin were the most important body parts, while throat, liver, kidneys, chin, knees and nose were least essential to the sense of self. In general, women saw their bodies—particularly external parts such as eyes, hair, legs and skin—as more central to their identities than men did to theirs. In interviews, we found that many willing donors, men and women, believed that having part of themselves live on in someone else's body promised a kind of immortality.

9   Objects were somewhat less central than body parts to the sense of self. Not surprisingly, the most important material possessions were dwellings, automobiles and favorite clothes—each a kind of second skin that embellishes the self we present to others. Automobiles were particularly important to the identities of men.

10   For both houses and cars, the more recently they had been acquired and the better their condition, the more important they were to someone's sense of self; and the more important they were, the better care they got—dusting, painting, and remodeling in the case of houses; washing, waxing, and oil changing for the cars. The similarities stopped when it came to the possession's age. Here older houses and newer cars were considered more important parts of the self. It may be that houses are looked on as heirlooms, for which age is a virtue, while new cars run and look better.

11   Other objects important to a sense of self included favorite rooms, artwork, jewelry and clothing—all meaningful attachments to the body and the home. We found that academics were especially likely to cite books as favorite possessions, perhaps because they represent the knowledge on which their work is based. For other people, sporting goods represent what they can or could do, while the contents of wallets or purses were important because they indicated central characteristics such as age, sex, and organizational memberships, as well as personal power to spend (credit cards) and travel (driver's license).

12 For some, collections were a significant part of their extended selves—possessions that had been acquired through considerable personal effort. For others, heirlooms were vital parts of family self, providing a sense of the past and of continuity with prior generations.

13 The third category of possessions important to the extended self is the less tangible one of time and place. To most of the people in our study, and others we interviewed, childhood was an especially important time of life. They tended to cherish memories, accurate or otherwise, of this period. We found that older people were most likely to name nearby cities, states, and countries as important to their sense of self, while younger ones generally named places farther away.

14 Our interviews showed that people can be as acquisitive of places they visit as they are of objects they collect. We even found a sedentary form of place acquisition. An Amish man whose religion forbids him to drive a motorized vehicle collected the hometowns of people who visited his community. While speaking to us, he reeled off a list of their states and countries much as other people mention the places they have visited personally.

15 There were few surprises in the final major category of possessions—people and pets—that individuals used to define themselves. The most important were generally parents, spouses, siblings, children and favorite friend of the same sex. Prominent political figures and favorite stars of movies and television were usually at the opposite end of the "selfness" continuum, unrelated to the sense of identity.

16 The common idea that some people consider their pets part of the family (and therefore of themselves) was supported by a series of interviews with people who owned dogs, cats, ferrets, birds and various other animals. While not all owners identified strongly with their pets, some felt closer to them than to their immediate families.

17 Is the fact that we are what we possess desirable or undesirable? There is no simple answer, but certain advantages and disadvantages seem evident. Among the advantages is that possessions provide a sense of the past. Many studies have shown that the loss of possessions that follows natural disasters or that occurs when elderly people are put in institutions is often traumatic. What people feel in these circumstances is, quite literally, a loss of self. Possessions also help children develop self-esteem, and learning to share possessions may be important in the growth of both individual and aggregate senses of self.

18 Incorporating possessions deeply into the sense of self can also have undesirable consequences. Too much attachment to pets can reflect an unhealthy drive to dominate and possess power and result in less devotion to family and friends. Investing too much of the self in collections and other possessions may displace love from people to things. Regarding other people as parts of our self can lead to jealousy and excessive possessiveness. Or by identifying too strongly with a spouse or child, we may end up living vicariously, instead of developing our own potential. As Erich Fromm asked in his book *To Have or To Be,* "If I am what I have and if what I have is lost, who then am I?"

Russell W. Belk, "My Possessions, Myself." Reprinted with permission from *Psychology Today Magazine,* July/August 1988, pp. 50–53 (Copyright © 1988 Sussex Publishers, L.L.C.).

 COMPREHENSION CHECKUP

Multiple Choice

Directions: For each item, write the letter corresponding to the best answer.

_____ 1. The author's overall tone in the article could be described as
 a. critical.
 b. matter-of-fact.

    c. concerned.

    d. sympathetic.

_____ 2. In paragraph 4, the organization pattern could be described as

    a. comparison-contrast.

    b. cause and effect.

    c. chronological order.

    d. examples.

_____ 3. For paragraph 7, the author uses an organization pattern that indicates

    a. the definition of something.

    b. division and steps in a process.

    c. a cause-and-effect relationship.

    d. examples of something.

_____ 4. "We found that academics were especially likely to cite books as favorite possessions, perhaps because they represent the knowledge on which their work is based." This sentence in paragraph 11 is an example of

    a. definition.

    b. classification.

    c. cause and effect.

    d. steps in a process.

_____ 5. The author's primary purpose in the final two paragraphs of the article is to

    a. discuss the advantages and disadvantages of strong identification with possessions.

    b. discuss the loss of self that elderly people experience when they give up their possessions.

    c. discuss the problems of living through others.

    d. discuss how possessions help build self-esteem in young children.

Short Answer

Directions: Answer the following questions briefly, using no more than a few words or a sentence or two.

1. What is the main idea of the essay? In which paragraph did you find the main idea?

_____

2. What is the author's purpose in writing this article?

_____

3. Archaeologists have recovered finely worked jade artifacts and marble vessels from a series of burial caves in Honduras. What directly stated main idea from the essay does this information reinforce?

_____

_____

_____

4. When the possessions of Jacqueline Kennedy Onassis were sold at an auction at Sotheby's, people paid far more for her things than their actual appraised value. Write the directly stated main idea from the essay that helps explain why this occurred.

_____

_____

5. In Italy recently, an American family devastated by their son's untimely death donated his heart, lungs, liver, and corneas to others. What main idea from the essay supports their action?

   _____

   _____

6. Susan has a cup and saucer collection that once belonged to her maternal grandmother. What are these objects likely to represent to her?

   _____

   _____

7. An elderly woman, estranged from her family, risked her life to retrieve her dog from her burning apartment. What is positive about her attachment to her dog? What is negative?

   _____

   _____

8. A mother distraught over a diagnosis of cancer fatally wounded both her two children and herself. This incident reinforces what main idea from the essay?

   _____

   _____

Completion

Directions: In the chart below, describe each of the categories listed, and then apply the category to yourself and give examples from your own life.

Category	Application to You/Examples
Body and body parts	
Objects	
Places and time periods	
Persons and pets	

Vocabulary in Context

Directions: Use context clues to determine the meaning of the italicized word, and write a definition for that word in the space provided.

1. "Burglary victims often say that they feel they have been personally *polluted,* even raped."

   Your definition: _____

   Dictionary definition: _____

2. "Although we Americans think of ourselves as highly individualistic, *aggregate* identity is important to us, as the willingness to preserve and restore symbols such as the Statue of Liberty shows."

   Your definition: _____

   Dictionary definition: _____

3. "Body parts are so well *integrated* into our identities that we think of them as 'me' rather than merely 'mine.'"

   Your definition: _____

   Dictionary definition: _____

4. "In general, women saw their bodies—particularly *external* parts such as eyes, hair, legs and skin—as more central to their identities than men did to theirs."

   Your definition: _____

   Dictionary definition: _____

5. "In interviews, we found that many willing donors, men and women, believed that having part of themselves live on in someone else's body promised a kind of *immortality*."

   Your definition: _____

   Dictionary definition: _____

6. "We found that *academics* were especially likely to cite books as favorite possessions, perhaps because they represent the knowledge on which their work is based."

   Your definition: _____

   Dictionary definition: _____

7. "Many studies have shown that the loss of possessions that follows natural disasters or that occurs when elderly people are put in institutions is often *traumatic*."

   Your definition: _____

   Dictionary definition: _____

Written Assignment

After reading the article "My Possessions Myself," describe which possessions you would save from a fire at your own home if you could safely retrieve anything (assuming all your family members and pets were safely removed). Tell why you would save these particular items and why they are so important to you.

Steps in a Process

READING

"The integrating stage is a time when individuals give up some characteristics of their old selves and develop shared identities."

TUNING IN TO READING

The following excerpt on the stages in a relationship comes from *Looking Out/Looking In*, a textbook on interpersonal communications written by Ronald Adler, Russell Proctor, and Neil Towne. The purpose of this textbook is to aid students in communicating more effectively with the important people in their lives.

READING *continued*

BIO-SKETCH

Ronald B. Adler is a professor of communications at Santa Barbara City College. In addition to writing and teaching, Adler works with professionals to improve on-the-job communication. Russell F. Proctor II is a communications professor at Northern Kentucky University and serves as advisor to the Speech Communications Club. Neil Towne is now retired after four decades of teaching. He currently conducts communication workshops on conflict resolution.

NOTES ON VOCABULARY

goosebumps a bristling of the hair on the skin causing small raised bumps. The term compares the skin of a human who is cold or afraid to the skin of a plucked goose.

starstruck dazzled or enraptured, especially with romance; also, especially idealistic or optimistic. The term compares the shining of stars to eyes aglow with love or enthusiasm.

token of affection a sign or symbol of one's devotion. A *token* originally was a badge worn to indicate allegiance to a particular person.

handwriting is on the wall a warning of impending doom. The expression comes from the Old Testament. King Belshazzar sees a disembodied hand writing four words on his palace wall. He summons the prophet Daniel to interpret the meaning of the message and is told that the words foretell his eventual overthrow. Shortly thereafter, the king is slain.

Cathy

CATHY © 1985 Cathy Guisewite. Reprinted with permission of Universal Press Syndicate. All rights reserved.

Developmental Stages in Intimate Relationships

Ronald B. Adler, Russell F. Proctor II, and Neil Towne

The process of interpersonal attraction is only the beginning of a relationship. As attraction motivates us to seek intimacy with some people we encounter, communication passes through several stages that characterize different levels of intimacy.

2   The following stages are especially descriptive of intimate, romantic relationships and close friendships. The pattern for other intimate relationships, such as families, would follow different paths.

3   **Initiating** The goals in the first stage of a relationship are to show that you are interested in making contact and to show that you are the kind of person worth talking to. Communication during this **initiating** stage is usually brief, and it generally follows conventional formulas: handshakes, remarks about innocuous subjects like the weather, and friendly expressions. These kinds of behavior may seem superficial and meaningless, but they are a way of signaling that we're interested in building some kind of relationship with the other person. They allow us to say without saying, "I'm a friendly person, and I'd like to get to know you."

4   **Experimenting** After we have made contact with a new person, the next stage is to decide whether we are interested in pursuing the relationship further. This involves **uncertainty reduction**—the process of getting to know others by gaining more information about them. A usual part of uncertainty reduction is the search for common ground, and it involves the conversational basics such as "Where are you from?" or "What's your major?" From there we look for other similarities: "You're a runner, too? How many miles do you do a week?"

5   The hallmark of the **experimenting** stage is small talk. As Mark Knapp says, this small talk is like Listerine: "We hate it, but we take large quantities every day." Small talk serves several functions. First, it is a useful way to find out what interests we share with the other person. It also provides a way to "audition" the other person—to help us decide whether a relationship is worth pursuing. In addition, small talk is a safe way to ease into a relationship. You haven't risked much as you decide whether to proceed further.

6   **Intensifying** Several changes in communication patterns occur during intensifying. The expression of feelings toward the other becomes more common. Dating couples use a wide range of communication strategies to describe their feelings of attraction. About one-quarter of the time they express their feelings directly. More often they use less direct methods of communication: spending an increasing amount of time together, asking for support from one another, doing favors for the partner, giving tokens of affection, hinting and flirting, expressing feelings nonverbally, getting to know the partner's friends and family, and trying to look more physically attractive.

7   The **intensifying** stage is usually a time of relational excitement and even euphoria. For romantic partners, it's often filled with starstruck gazes, goosebumps, and daydreaming. As a result it's a stage that's regularly depicted in movies and romance novels—after all, we love to watch lovers in love. The problem, of course, is that the stage doesn't last forever. Sometimes romantic partners who stop feeling goosebumps begin to question whether they're still in love. Although it's possible that they're not, it's also possible that they've simply moved on to a different stage in their relationship—integrating.

8   **Integrating** As a relationship strengthens, the parties begin to take on an identity as a social unit. In romantic relationships, invitations begin to come addressed to the couple. Social circles merge. The partners begin to take on each other's commitments: "Sure, we'll spend Thanksgiving with your family." Common property may begin to be designated—our apartment, our car, our song. Partners may even begin to speak alike, using personal idioms and sentence patterns. In this sense, the **integrating** stage is a time when individuals give up some characteristics of their old selves and develop shared identities.

9   As we become more integrated with others, our sense of obligation to them grows. We feel obliged to provide a variety of resources such as class notes and money, whether or not the other person asks for them. Surprisingly, partners make fewer straightforward requests than they did in earlier relationship stages. This isn't as surprising as it might at first seem: As partners become better acquainted, their knowledge of each other makes overt requests less necessary.

Cathy

10   **Bonding** During the **bonding** stage, the parties make symbolic public gestures to show the world that their relationship exists. The most common form of bonding in romantic relationships is a wedding ceremony and the legal ties that come with it. Bonding generates social support for the relationship. Custom and law both impose certain obligations on partners who have officially bonded.

11   Bonding marks a turning point in a relationship. Up to now the relationship may have developed at a steady pace: experimenting gradually moved into intensifying and then into integrating. Now, however, there is a spurt of commitment. The public display and declaration of exclusivity make this a distinct stage in the relationship.

12   **Differentiating** Bonding is the peak of the "coming together" phase of relational development. But people in even the most committed relationships need to assert their individual identities. This **differentiating** stage is the point where the "we" orientation that has developed shifts, and more "me" messages begin to occur. Partners use a variety of strategies to gain privacy from each other. Sometimes they confront the other party directly, explaining that they don't want to continue a discussion. At other times they are less direct, offering nonverbal cues, changing the topic, or leaving the room.

13   **Differentiation** is likely to occur when a relationship begins to experience the first, inevitable feelings of stress. This need for autonomy needn't be a negative experience, however. People need to be individuals as well as parts of a relationship, and differentiation is a necessary step toward autonomy. The key to successful differentiation is maintaining a commitment to the relationship while creating the space for being an individual as well.

14   **Circumscribing** So far we have been looking at the growth of relationships. Although some reach a plateau of development, going on successfully for as long as a lifetime, others pass through several stages of decline and dissolution.

15   In the **circumscribing** stage, communication between members decreases in quantity and quality. Restrictions and restraints characterize this stage. Rather than discuss a disagreement (which requires energy on both sides), members opt for withdrawal—either mental (silence or daydreaming and fantasizing) or physical (where people spend less time together). Circumscribing doesn't involve total avoidance, which may come later. Rather, it involves a shrinking of interest and commitment—the opposite of what occurred in the integrating stage.

Cathy

CATHY © 1986 Cathy Guisewite. Reprinted with permission of Universal Press Syndicate. All rights reserved.

16 **Stagnating** If circumscribing continues, the relationship enters the **stagnating** stage. The excitement of the intensifying stage is long gone, and the partners behave toward each other in old, familiar ways without much feeling. No growth occurs. The relationship is a hollow shell of its former self. We see stagnation in many workers who have lost enthusiasm for their job yet continue to go through the motions for years. The same sad event occurs for some couples who unenthusiastically have the same conversations, see the same people, and follow the same routines without any sense of joy or novelty.

17 **Avoiding** When stagnation becomes too unpleasant, parties in a relationship begin to create physical distance between each other. This is the **avoiding** stage. Sometimes they do it indirectly under the guise of excuses ("I've been sick lately and can't see you"); sometimes they do it directly ("Please don't call me; I don't want to see you now"). In either case, by this point the handwriting is on the wall about the relationship's future.

18 The deterioration of a relationship from bonding through circumscribing, stagnating, and avoiding isn't inevitable. One of the key differences between marriages that end in separation and those that are restored to their former intimacy is the communication that occurs when the partners are unsatisfied. Unsuccessful couples deal with their problems by avoidance, indirectness, and less involvement with each other. By contrast, couples who "repair" their relationship communicate much more directly. They confront each other with their concerns (sometimes with the assistance of a counselor) and spend time and effort negotiating solutions to their problems.

19 **Terminating** Characteristics of the final stage, **terminating,** include summary dialogues of where the relationship has gone and the desire to dissociate. The relationship may end with a cordial dinner, a note left on the kitchen table, a phone call, or a legal document. Depending on each person's feelings, this stage can be quite short, or it may be drawn out over time, with bitter jabs at each other.

20 Relationships don't always move toward termination in a straight line. Rather they take a back-and-forth pattern, where the trend is toward dissolution. Regardless of how long it takes, termination doesn't have to be totally negative. Understanding each other's investments in the relationship and needs for personal growth may dilute the hard feelings. In fact, many relationships aren't so much terminated as redefined. A divorced couple, for example, may find new, less intimate ways to relate to each other.

21 In romantic relationships, the best predictor of whether the parties will become friends is whether they were friends before their emotional involvement. The way

Cathy

CATHY © 1986 Cathy Guisewite. Reprinted with permission of Universal Press Syndicate. All rights reserved.

the couple splits up also makes a difference. It's no surprise to find that friendships are most possible when communication during the breakup is positive: expressions that there are no regrets for time spent together and other attempts to minimize hard feelings. When communication during termination is negative (manipulative, complaining to third parties), friendships are less likely.

From Ronald B. Adler, Russell F. Proctor II, and Neil Towne, *Looking Out, Looking In*, 11th Edition, pp. 293–99. © 2005 Wadsworth, a part of Cengage Learning, Inc. Reproduced by permission. www.cengage.com/permissions.

✔ COMPREHENSION CHECKUP

Multiple Choice

Directions: For each item, write the letter corresponding to the best answer.

_____ 1. All of the following are examples of initiating *except*
   a. soulful kisses.
   b. handshakes.
   c. discussions about the weather.
   d. discussions about sports.

_____ 2. All of the following are typical of the experimenting stage *except*
   a. gaining more information about others.
   b. reducing uncertainty.
   c. practicing small talk.
   d. spending large amounts of time with each other.

_____ 3. All of the following were given as reasons for the use of small talk *except* for which?
   a. It is a way to discover interests in common.
   b. It is a way to interact with others.
   c. It is a way to test the commitment of a partner.
   d. It is a way to decide whether the relationship is worthwhile.

_____ 4. Which stage is marked by spending increasing amounts of time together, exchanging gifts, and making introductions to close friends and family members?

a. intensifying
b. initiating
c. experimenting
d. circumscribing

_____ 5. Paragraph 11 contains the following sentence: "Now, however, there is a spurt of commitment." What is this sentence's relationship to the preceding sentence in the paragraph?
a. comparison
b. contrast
c. cause and effect
d. definition

_____ 6. You could infer from paragraphs 12 and 13 that
a. the need to differentiate is not necessarily a negative experience.
b. some stress in relationships is inevitable.
c. couples use verbal and nonverbal strategies to communicate a need for autonomy.
d. all of the above.

_____ 7. The stagnation stage can best be described as
a. shrinking interest and commitment.
b. going through the motions with little enthusiasm.
c. confronting each other over problems and negotiating solutions.
d. continuing to grow in small, significant ways.

_____ 8. It is possible to remain friends after the final breakup if
a. communication during the breakup was positive.
b. the partners were friends prior to their romantic involvement.
c. attempts were made to minimize hard feelings.
d. all of the above.

_____ 9. The authors' tone for this selection can best be described as
a. optimistic.
b. objective.
c. sarcastic.
d. perplexed.

_____ 10. The authors' primary purpose in writing this selection is to
a. inform readers of the difficulties in maintaining successful relationships.
b. persuade readers to delay marriage until they have reached a mature age.
c. tell a story about relationships.
d. explain the communication stages in a typical relationship.

True or False

Directions: Indicate whether each statement is true or false by writing **T** or **F** in the space provided.

_____ 1. Something told in a _straightforward_ fashion can be expected to be ambiguous.

_____ 2. When you _confront_ someone, you directly challenge him.

_____ 3. Honesty is the _hallmark_ of a good judge.

_____ 4. If you _impose_ on someone, you can count on her being grateful.

_____ 5. If something is *inevitable*, you should be able to avoid it.

_____ 6. After the two countries *merged*, they remained two separate entities.

_____ 7. Once the tired climber reached the *plateau*, she could begin to walk on level ground.

_____ 8. Two students who don't like each other might try to avoid having an accidental *encounter* on campus.

_____ 9. A driver with a speeding ticket might *opt* to go to traffic school and get the ticket dismissed rather than pay a fine.

_____ 10. A boxer whose *jabs* keep missing will likely win the fight.

Vocabulary Matching

Directions: Match the vocabulary words in Column A with their antonyms in Column B. Place the correct letter in the space provided.

Column A	Column B
_____ 1. superficial	a. secret
_____ 2. conventional	b. inclusivity
_____ 3. overt	c. unfriendly
_____ 4. innocuous	d. strengthen
_____ 5. exclusivity	e. avoidable
_____ 6. cordial	f. profound
_____ 7. euphoria	g. unification
_____ 8. dilute	h. harmful
_____ 9. inevitable	i. depression
_____ 10. dissolution	j. unusual

In Your Own Words

1. Considering the information provided in this selection, do you think it's possible to live "happily ever after"? Explain your answer.

2. In your opinion, based on your own personal observations, do "opposites attract"? Or is it more likely that "birds of a feather flock together"? Explain.

3. Is living together more likely or less likely to lead to marriage? Which proverb do you think is more accurate: "Out of sight out of mind" or "Absence makes the heart grow fonder"? Give reasons for your answers.

4. What kind of personality traits lead to success in marriage? What factors are associated with increased likelihood of divorce? Why do you think there is more divorce today?

5. What do you think of the practice of arranged marriages? Do you see any advantages to an arranged marriage?

Written Assignment

1. Look at each of the *Cathy* cartoons in the reading, and write the main idea from the selection that each cartoon illustrates.

2. Write a one- or two-sentence summary of each of the stages in a relationship.

3. In the initiating stage, two people are probably attracted to each other on the basis of characteristics such as physical appearance, social standing, reputation, dress, race, age, education, and religion. Which of these characteristics do you feel is most important to the typical male? To the typical female? Which are most important to you?

Internet Activity

Robert Sternberg of Yale University developed the widely used three-dimensional theory of love based on the components of intimacy, commitment, and passion. Recently, his research has sought to determine why so many relationships fail. Consult his Web site at:

www.psy.pdx.edu/PsiCafe/KeyTheorists/Sternberg.htm

From that site, you can link to Sternberg's homepage to read about his research projects. There is also a "Measure Your Love" questionnaire that you might wish to take.

You might also take an Internet relationships test. Go to a search engine and type in "relationships tests." Take a test that suits your needs (and make sure it's free!). Write a paragraph about what you found out about your relationships. Does the test correlate with the stages of relationships you read about in the reading selection?

Cause and Effect

READING

> *"'Is it true,' asked Alan, 'that you have a certain mixture
> that has—er—quite extraordinary effects?'"*

TUNING IN TO READING

This short story, a descriptive narrative, demonstrates a cause-and-effect relationship. Alan, the young man, wishes to change his beloved Diana forever by making her more responsive to him. He pursues his dream without ever realizing the unintended, or ironic, effects.

Try to determine the personality of the old man after reading the first three paragraphs of the story. Do you think Alan is being "suckered" into doing something against his will?

BIO-SKETCH

John Collier was born in London in 1901 and died in California in 1980. In his lengthy career, he was a successful novelist, playwright, and screenwriter, but he is primarily remembered today for his sinister short stories. Many of these stories, though focused on evil, were written with great wit and irony. Each word in a Collier short story was carefully chosen to heighten a particular effect. Most critics consider Collier's particular strength his use of dialogue.

NOTES ON VOCABULARY

sinister ominous; threatening harm or evil. The original Latin meaning was simply "left" or "on the left." The origins of this word have to do with an ancient prejudice favoring what is to the right over what is to the left. So, the more important guests at a banquet would be seated to the right of the host or hostess.

au revoir　a French interjection meaning "until we see each other again; good-bye for the present."

chaser　a milder beverage taken after a drink of liquor.

draught　a current of air in any enclosed space; the British spelling of *draft*.

phial　a small glass bottle or vial.

siren　a beautiful or tempting woman. In classical mythology, *sirens* were evil creatures who sang in beautiful voices, luring sailors to shipwreck and death. The word's origin is Greek.

The Chaser

John Collier

ALAN AUSTEN, AS NERVOUS AS A KITTEN, went up certain dark and creaky stairs in the neighborhood of Pell Street, and peered about for a long time on the dim landing before he found the name he wanted written obscurely on one of the doors.

2　He pushed open this door, as he had been told to do, and found himself in a tiny room, which contained no furniture but a plain kitchen table, a rocking-chair, and an ordinary chair. On one of the dirty buff-coloured walls were a couple of shelves, containing in all perhaps a dozen bottles and jars.

3　An old man sat in the rocking-chair, reading a newspaper. Alan, without a word, handed him the card he had been given. "Sit down, Mr. Austen," said the old man very politely. "I am glad to make your acquaintance."

4　"Is it true," asked Alan, "that you have a certain mixture that has—er—quite extraordinary effects?"

5　"My dear sir," replied the old man, "my stock in trade is not very large—I don't deal in laxatives and teething mixtures—but such as it is, it is varied. I think nothing I sell has effects which could be precisely described as ordinary."

6　"Well, the fact is . . ." began Alan.

7　"Here, for example," interrupted the old man, reaching for a bottle from the shelf. "Here is a liquid as colourless as water, almost tasteless, quite imperceptible in coffee, wine, or any other beverage. It is also quite imperceptible to any known method of autopsy."

8　"Do you mean it is a poison?" cried Alan, very much horrified.

9　"Call it a glove-cleaner if you like," said the old man indifferently. "Maybe it will clean gloves. I have never tried. One might call it a life-cleaner. Lives need cleaning sometimes."

10　"I want nothing of that sort," said Alan.

11 "Probably it is just as well," said the old man. "Do you know the price of this? For one teaspoonful, which is sufficient, I ask five thousand dollars. Never less. Not a penny less."

12 "I hope all your mixtures are not as expensive," said Alan apprehensively.

13 "Oh dear, no," said the old man. "It would be no good charging that sort of price for a love potion, for example." Young people who need a love potion very seldom have five thousand dollars. Otherwise they would not need a love potion."

14 "I am glad to hear that," said Alan.

15 "I look at it like this," said the old man. "Please a customer with one article, and he will come back when he needs another. Even if it is more costly. He will save up for it, if necessary."

16 "So," said Alan, "you really do sell love potions?"

17 "If I did not sell love potions," said the old man, reaching for another bottle, "I should not have mentioned the other matter to you. It is only when one is in a position to oblige that one can afford to be so confidential."

18 "And these potions," said Alan. "They are not just—just—er—"

19 "Oh, no," said the old man. "Their effects are permanent, and extend far beyond the mere casual impulse. But they include it. Oh, yes, they include it. Bountifully, insistently. Everlastingly."

20 "Dear me!" said Alan, attempting a look of scientific detachment. "How very interesting!"

21 "But consider the spiritual side," said the old man.

22 "I do, indeed," said Alan.

23 "For indifference," said the old man, "they substitute devotion. For scorn, adoration. Give one tiny measure of this to the young lady—its flavour is imperceptible in orange juice, soup, or cocktails—and however gay and giddy she is, she will change altogether. She will want nothing but solitude and you."

24 "I can hardly believe it," said Alan. "She is so fond of parties."

25 "She will not like them anymore," said the old man. "She will be afraid of the pretty girls you may meet."

26 "She will actually be jealous?" cried Alan in a rapture. "Of me?"

27 "Yes, she will want to be everything to you."

28 "She *is,* already. Only she doesn't care about it."

29 "She will, when she has taken this. She will care intensely. You will be her sole interest in life."

30 "Wonderful!" cried Alan.

31 "She will want to know all you do," said the old man. "All that has happened to you during the day. Every word of it. She will want to know what you are thinking about, why you smile suddenly, why you are looking sad."

32 "That *is* love!" cried Alan.

33 "Yes," said the old man. "How carefully she will look after you! She will never allow you to be tired, to sit in a draught, to neglect your food. If you are an hour late, she will be terrified. She will think you are killed, or that some siren has caught you."

34 "I can hardly imagine Diana like that!" cried Alan, overwhelmed with joy.

35   "You will not have to use your imagination," said the old man. "And, by the way, since there are always sirens, if by any chance you *should,* later on, slip a little, you need not worry. She will forgive you, in the end. She will be terribly hurt, of course, but she will forgive you—in the end."

36   "That will not happen," said Alan fervently.

37   "Of course not," said the old man. "But if it did, you need not worry. She would never divorce you. Oh, no! And, of course, she will never give you the least, the very least grounds for—uneasiness."

38   "And how much," said Alan, "is this wonderful mixture?"

39   "It is not as dear," said the old man, "as the glove-cleaner, or life-cleaner, as I sometimes call it. No. That is five thousand dollars, never a penny less. One has to be older than you are, to indulge in that sort of thing. One has to save up for it."

40   "But the love potion?" said Alan.

41   "Oh, that," said the old man, opening the drawer in the kitchen table, and taking out a tiny, rather dirty-looking phial. "That is just a dollar."

42   "I can't tell you how grateful I am," said Alan, watching him fill it.

43   "I like to oblige," said the old man. "Then customers come back, later in life, when they are better off, and want more expensive things. Here you are. You will find it very effective."

44   "Thank you again," said Alan. "Good-bye."

45   "*Au Revoir,*" said the old man. [Good-bye. Until we meet again.]

John Collier, "The Chaser." Originally appeared in *The New Yorker*, 1940. © 1951 by John Collier.
© Renewed 1979 by John Collier. Permission to reprint granted by Harold Matson Co., Inc.

COMPREHENSION CHECKUP

Multiple Choice

Directions: For each item, write the letter corresponding to the best answer.

_____ 1. A chaser is a drink that takes away the taste of another drink. What is Diana's likely chaser?
   a. orange juice
   b. milk
   c. poison
   d. beer

_____ 2. The old man describes the glove-cleaner as having all of the following qualities *except* for which?
   a. It is colorless as water.
   b. It is almost tasteless.
   c. It is imperceptible in most beverages.
   d. It is ordinary.

True or False

Directions: Indicate whether each statement is true or false by writing **T** or **F** in the space provided.

_____ 3. The old man says that if Alan becomes tempted by another woman, Diana will never forgive him.

_____ 4. The old man implies that at some point in Alan's life he will grow tired of Diana.

_____ 5. Someone referred Alan to the old man.

_____ 6. The old man sells many items that could be considered ordinary.

_____ 7. The old man's shop is in an affluent area.

_____ 8. The mixture referred to as a "glove-cleaner" is actually poison.

_____ 9. In contrast to the "glove-cleaner," the love potion is inexpensive.

_____ 10. The old man makes his money on customers returning for more-expensive items.

_____ 11. The love potion will cause Diana to be incapable of anything but permanent devotion to Alan.

_____ 12. The old man indicates that he likes to please his customers.

Completion

Directions: Complete the following cause-and-effect diagram.

Cause (Why?)

Alan purchases a love potion to make Diana "love" him.

Effect (What result?)

1. Diana will fall "head over heels" in love with Alan.

2. Alan will eventually feel suffocated by Diana's devotion.

3. Alan will _____.

Vocabulary in Context

Directions: In the blanks below, write the word from the list that best completes each sentence. Use each word only once.

autopsy	confidential	creaky	detachment	imperceptible	indulge
obscure	peered		scorn	sole	solitude

1. Although I try to stay away from rich foods, every once in a while I _____ myself by having a hot fudge sundae with nuts, whipped cream, and a cherry.

2. A tiny baby was the _____ survivor of American Airlines Flight 209.

3. Sue wanted to surprise her husband on his birthday with a special present, and so she looked everywhere for a(n) _____ hood ornament for his 1965 Corvette.

4. Unable to see a thing without his glasses, the old man _____ closely at the bus schedule in his hand.

5. Although Raymond tried to be a fair and open-minded person, he felt only revulsion and _____ for the man who had cut off the young girl's arms.

6. The _____ revealed that the young child had died of a fractured skull.

7. Investigative reporters who work for _The National Enquirer_ claim that they frequently search people's garbage in order to obtain private, _____ information.

8. Although she had her heart set on a sleek, modern home with up-to-date conveniences, her husband was resolved to own the Victorian mansion with the _____ stairs.

9. There was so much chaos at the rock concert, that Tom found himself longing for the peace and _____ of his home.

10. Because our dog Bandit didn't like to swallow pills, they had to be hidden in the middle of a hot dog where they became _____ to his taste and sight.

11. The judge tried not to be biased in favor of one side or the other, and so maintained a level of professional _____.

In Your Own Words

1. In the very first sentence of this story, what descriptive words give the setting a sinister aspect?

2. What word or words are used to describe Alan?

3. What effects does Alan think the potion will have? Why does Alan want to purchase it? How will the potion actually affect Diana?

4. Does the old man think that Alan will return later in life? Refer to specific details in the story to support your answer. At the end of the story, what does the old man mean by "more expensive things"?

5. What does the old man mean when he says: "Young people who need a love potion very seldom have five thousand dollars. Otherwise they would not need a love potion"? What viewpoint about love is he expressing?

6. What point is Collier making about love? How can something that we want very badly end up causing us grief?

7. Why is one bottle referred to by words such as a "glove-cleaner," or a "life-cleaner"?

8. What is ironic about this story? What does Alan expect to happen? What is really going to happen?

Optional: The dialog in this story reads very much like a play. Have two people in your class act out the part of Alan and the old man.

Written Assignment

Breaking up is always hard to do, and doing it in person is almost always better than using a phone call, an instant message, or an e-mail. However, for those who just can't cope with the in-person ordeal, the authors of the popular *Dating and Sex Handbook* provide an example of a rejection letter. The trick, according to them, is to be kind, but firm.

Dear _____, [their name]

I won't be able to make it this Saturday, or any Saturday, in fact. The truth is, I just can't be in a committed relationship right now. It's not you, it's me. I'm just not able to appreciate all that you have to give.

I feel like we've been spinning our wheels these last few years/months/ weeks/days. I can't believe how wonderful you've been to me and how much you've put up with. You deserve better. I can't put you through this anymore and I can't give you what you need/want/deserve right now. I need more space, and I need time to figure out who the real [your name here] is.

It may take some time, but I hope we can still be friends.

Sincerely,

_____ [your name here]

Just for fun, try writing your own rejection letter. Use concrete examples, but don't be too nasty!

Listing

READING

"Mass media are very powerful socialization agents."

TUNING IN TO READING

Test yourself on the following Mass Media Love Quiz. Answer true or false to each statement to indicate your own personal belief.

BIO-SKETCH

Dr. Mary-Lou Galician, author of several books about this essay's topic, is head of Media Analysis & Criticism in the Walter Cronkite School of Journalism and Mass Communication at Arizona State University, where thousands of students of all majors have learned how to be "media literate" in her popular classes. Known internationally by her nickname "Dr. FUN" (because of her musical motivation program *FUN-dynamics!—The FUN-damentals of DYNAMIC Living*®), she is the creator of *Realistic Romance*®—*The Thinking Person's Relationship Remedy* and maintains the media literacy website www.RealisticRomance.com, where you can take her *Dr. FUN's Mass Media Love Quiz* © and get her *Dr. Galician's Prescriptions* ©.

NOTES ON VOCABULARY

Prince Charming   The fairy tale *Cinderella* by Charles Perrault (1856) featured the hero Prince Charming. The term has come to refer to a man who fulfills all the romantic expectations of a woman.

Snow White   The fairy tale was written by the Brothers Grimm and was the basis of a 1937 animated feature by Walt Disney. Snow White, pursued by a jealous queen, hides with the Seven Dwarfs. The queen locates Snow White and feeds her a poison apple, but Prince Charming awakens her with a kiss.

Beauty and the Beast   The 1991 Walt Disney movie was based on a classic French fairy tale. To break the spell placed upon him and his servants, a beast (in reality, an enchanted prince) must earn the love of Belle or risk remaining a beast forever.

Tarzan and Jane   Tarzan is a fictional character created by Edgar Rice Burroughs (1914). Although Tarzan is the son of an English lord, he was raised in the African jungle by apes. Jane Porter, rescued by Tarzan, becomes his wife and the mother of his son.

Pretty Woman   This popular 1990 movie starred Richard Gere as Edward Lewis, a successful, wealthy lawyer, who hires the beautiful Vivian Ward, a prostitute played by Julia Roberts. They fall in love, and in the process Edward changes into a better person and Vivian gets a chance to start a new life.

Jerry Maguire   Jerry Maguire, a sports agent played by Tom Cruise, wants to lead a more ethical life. His new moral sense isn't welcome at his firm and he is fired. Left with only one client and the love of Dorothy Boyd, played by Renée Zellweger, he discovers what's really important in life.

Media Literacy: Portrayals of Sex, Love, and Romance in the Mass Media

Dr. Mary-Lou Galician*

TEST YOURSELF by taking *Dr. FUN's Mass Media Love Quiz* ©, based on my media literacy teaching and research:

For each statement, select "TRUE" or "FALSE" to indicate YOUR belief.

1. Your perfect partner is cosmically pre-destined, so nothing/nobody can ultimately separate you.
2. There's such a thing as "love at first sight."
3. Your true soul mate should KNOW what you're thinking or feeling without your having to tell.
4. If your partner is truly meant for you, sex is easy and wonderful.
5. To attract and keep a man, a woman should look like a model or a centerfold.
6. The man should NOT be shorter, weaker, younger, poorer, or less successful than the woman.
7. The love of a good and faithful true woman can change a man from a "beast" into a "prince."
8. Bickering and fighting a lot mean that a man and a woman really love each other passionately.
9. All you really need is love, so it doesn't matter if you and your lover have very different values.
10. The right mate "completes you"—filling your needs and making your dreams come true.
11. In real life, actors and actresses are often very much like the romantic characters they portray.
12. Since mass media portrayals of romance aren't "real," they don't really affect you.

Dr. FUN's Mass Media Love Quiz © 1995, 2000 by Dr. Mary-Lou Galician. All Rights Reserved. Used by permission.

Your Answers

I hope you answered "FALSE" to ALL 12 statements of my *"Dr. FUN's Mass Media Love Quiz©,"* based on my research and teaching focused on what we learn about sex, love, and romance from the mass media and how these portrayals affect us. All 12 are myths and stereotypes perpetuated by the mass media.

If you answered "TRUE" to some of them, don't worry: You're like most people who take the quiz. The problem is that while most of us know the right responses, we still believe the unrealistic ones our popular culture presents to us.

Mass media are very powerful socialization agents. From the time we're very young, we're barraged with fairy-tale depictions of romantic love in the popular culture—movies and television, books and magazines, recordings and radio, the Internet, advertising, and even the news—so we shouldn't feel too bad if we wind up with some unrealistic expectations. Remember: Mass media rely on simplification, distortions of reality, and dramatic symbols, and myths and stereotypes to communicate their messages.

Unfortunately, false-love images and scripts of coupleship put pressure on *both* women and men to measure up to what I call "media-myth P.C."—Playboy Centerfolds and Prince Charmings. Some media-constructed unrealistic expectations can even lead to depression and other dysfunctions, and several can be downright dangerous. So it's smart to become aware and change our unhealthy views.

With this in mind, let's look more closely at the mass media myths and stereotypes in my quiz, for each of which I have a corresponding media literacy "antidote"—the 12 *Dr. Galician's Prescriptions© (Rxs),* which the media rarely present:

Myth 1. While you're seeking your one-and-only Mr. or Ms. "Right" (by the way, I prefer the term "appropriate partner"), your blinders prevent you from seeing a whole spectrum of candidates who could make an excellent match. And a partner who is "perfect" would be less than fully human, even though media myths glorify the unrealistically ideal.

> *Rx 1. CONSIDER COUNTLESS CANDIDATES.*

Myth 2. There's attraction-at-first-sight; real love takes real time. Too many movies and TV shows give us the opposite idea. But they have only two hours to spin their tales. And advertisers have only 30 seconds. How long have you known each other? Take your time. You have lots more of it in real life.

> *Rx 2. CONSULT YOUR CALENDAR AND COUNT CAREFULLY.*

Myth 3. Mind-readers function only in circuses—and romance novels, which feed our fantasy of having a perfect relationship without really working at it. Realistically romantic partners learn about each other by daring to be open and honest (and courteous) about what they want.

> *Rx 3. COMMUNICATE COURAGEOUSLY.*

Myth 4. As with all intimacy, genuinely good sex takes time, trust, and togetherness. In real life (unlike in the pages of Playboy and Cosmo), the essential element of love is NOT sex: It's committed long-term relationships.

> *Rx 4. CONCENTRATE ON COMMITMENT AND CONSTANCY.*

Myth 5. Real love doesn't superficially turn a person into an object. Nevertheless, even though they might not realize it, many males subconsciously use actresses, models, and centerfolds as a standard for their own real-life partners, who cannot help disappointing them (unless they, too, have the surgical and photographic enhancements that pop culture icons get). What's worse is that even women's magazines reinforce unhealthy female body images.

> *Rx 5. CHERISH COMPLETENESS IN COMPANIONS (NOT JUST THE COVER).*

Myth 6. To fit the "Me-Tarzan, You-Jane" cultural stereotypes that mass media perpetuate, many leading men in movies and TV shows have to stand on boxes to appear taller than their leading ladies. Even news anchor "couples" are usually an older male-younger female duo. These images reinforce sexual inequality and block many potentially wonderful relationships from ever getting started. Studies show that peer couples are the happiest.

> *Rx 6. CREAT COEQUALITY; COOPERATE.*

Myth 7. Children who see "Beauty and the Beast" should be warned that Belle's attempts to reform her captor would be most unwise in real-life. We cannot change others—especially not abusive "heroes" (or "heroines"!) who have some good inside if only their partner can be "good enough" to bring it out. This fallacy underlies domestic violence. We *can* see the myth as a metaphor for fixing our own "beastly" side.

> *Rx 7. CEASE CORRECTING AND CONTROLLING; YOU CAN'T CHANGE OTHERS (ONLY YOURSELF).*

Myth 8. Invariably in mass media, a male and female who take an instant strong dislike to each other will (eventually) discover that they're made for each other—despite their continual bickering. Respectful disagreement is healthy, but these constant combatants need conflict-resolution training. Don't confuse fighting with passion: Love is about peace, not war.

Rx 8. COURTESY COUNTS; CONSTANT CONFLICTS CREATE CHAOS.

Myth 9. Opposites frequently attract—but they don't stay together very long except in mass media mythology, including Paula Abdul's song. Can you image a reallife dinner party mixing the street friends of "Pretty Woman" and her stockbroker boyfriend? Though rarely demonstrated by the mass media, shared values (not "interests") form the basis of lasting romantic relationships.

Rx 9. CRAVE COMMON CORE-VALUES.

Myth 10. Although "love" songs cultivate this "Snow White" syndrome (Her big Disney solo was "Someday My Prince Will Come"!), using your partner as a completer, fixer, or rescuer—someone from whom you "take" or "get"—is robbery not romance. (And that goes for "incomplete" MEN like Jerry Maguire!) But where's the dramatic conflict in well-adjusted self-sufficient individuals who choose to share their already-full lives?

Rx 10. CULTIVATE YOUR OWN COMPLETENESS.

Myth 11. Many men and women are less than satisfied with their real-life romantic partners because they aren't like their idealized image of a celebrity they think they know. When countless adolescent girls wanted "Twilight"'s star to "bite them" at publicity events for the film, the actor who portrayed the hero-vampire was amazed.

Rx 11. DE-CONSRUCT CELEBRITIES.

Myth 12. Though we might not be aware of the all-pervasive media culture, we subconsciously incorporate its messages and myths into our own lives. In my own studies of Baby Boomers and Generation Xers, I've found that avid consumers of movies and fashion and fitness magazines tend to have more unrealistic and stereotypical expectations about coupleship, and, correspondingly, less satisfaction in their own real romantic relationships.

Rx 12. CALCULATE THE VERY REAL CONSEQUENCES OF UNREAL MEDIA.

Does all this mean we should avoid romantic media entirely?

We can still enjoy the metaphoric meanings and pure "escape" that romantic media myths offer us (though stereotypes are always harmful to us and others), but it's not wise to use media myths—or media celebrities—as models in our real lives. It's much healthier and smarter to make yourself the hero or heroine of your own true love story.

My ultimate advice: "Get real about romance!"

COMPREHENSION CHECKUP

Multiple Choice

Directions: For each item, write the letter corresponding to the best answer.

_____ 1. All of the following are myths about romantic love *except* for which one?
   a. True love always happens quickly, even at first sight.
   b. True love happens only to women who look like models or centerfolds.

      c. Couples with similar values have a better chance of staying together.

      d. Continual fighting and bickering is a sign of true love.

_____ 2. According to the selection, all of the following are true *except* for which one?

      a. Even though we can recognize myths about romantic love portrayed in the media, they still affect us.

      b. Images about romantic love in the mass media affect only women.

      c. The mass media are full of images about romantic love.

      d. Unrealistic expectations about romantic love in the mass media can sometimes lead to depression.

_____ 3. A good title for this selection would be

      a. "Love at First Sight."

      b. "The Perfect Partner."

      c. "Recognizing Myths of Romantic Love."

      d. "How to Find Your One and Only."

_____ 4. Which statement below best reflects the main idea of the selection?

      a. The way we view ourselves and our expectations for romantic relationships are often shaped by our exposure to the mass media.

      b. Unrealistic beliefs about romantic love cause difficulties in finding a good partner.

      c. There are many potential partners available for everyone.

      d. Romantic love rarely leads to marriage.

_____ 5. The author is likely to agree with which of the following statements?

      a. Love can overcome every obstacle.

      b. Love at first sight is how most good romantic relationships begin.

      c. It is reasonable to expect perfection in a potential mate.

      d. True love is not likely to change an abusive partner.

True or False

Directions: Indicate whether each statement is true or false by writing **T** or **F** in the space provided.

_____ 6. Everyone has a perfect partner who will appear at the right moment.

_____ 7. The author believes that mass media can influence the way we think and feel about ourselves.

_____ 8. Mass media can communicate messages by means of stereotypes.

_____ 9. Mass media can put pressure on women to "measure up" to *Playboy* centerfolds.

_____ 10. The author urges us to become aware of the media's power to manipulate our views.

_____ 11. Honesty and openness cause romantic couples to break up.

_____ 12. Women's magazines, as well as men's magazines, can foster unhealthy body images.

_____ 13. If people are truly opposites, they have a better chance of succeeding in a long-term romantic relationship.

_____ 14. Love has more in common with peace than with war.

_____ 15. It is a good idea to model your romantic relationships on how celebrities behave.

Vocabulary Matching

Directions: Match the vocabulary words in Column A with their definitions in Column B. Place the correct letter in the space provided.

	Column A	**Column B**

_____ 1. predestined   a. brawlers; fighters

_____ 2. soulmate   b. bombarded; attacked

_____ 3. barraged   c. foreordained

_____ 4. depictions   d. variety; a broad range

_____ 5. dysfunctions   e. final; conclusive

_____ 6. blinders   f. improvements

_____ 7. spectrum   g. strengthen

_____ 8. perpetuate   h. objects of devotion

_____ 9. duo   i. something that impedes vision or discernment

_____ 10. enhancements   j. impairments

_____ 11. icons   k. a person with whom one has a strong affinity or connection

_____ 12. abusive   l. portrayals

_____ 13. combatants   m. to make continual

_____ 14. ultimate   n. physically harmful

_____ 15. reinforce   o. a couple

In Your Own Words

1. Can you think of any recent movies or TV shows where the "romantic" relationships depicted were unrealistic? In what ways were they unrealistic?
2. At a very young age, many children start watching Disney classic movies such as *The Little Mermaid, Cinderella, Sleeping Beauty, Lady and the Tramp,* and *Snow White.* A common theme in these movies is the heroine being rescued by the hero. Do you think this sets the stage for later unrealistic expectations about romance?

Written Assignment

Many teenagers appear to want breast enlargement surgery in an attempt to copy their celebrity idols. However, experts warn that young people are putting themselves at mental and physical risk, because in many cases their bodies have not finished developing. Write a few paragraphs giving your opinion on this subject. Do you think celebrities and the media are mainly responsible for this trend? Or do you think there are other influences?

Internet Activity

Many girls and young women have eating disorders. A recent poll suggests that 40 percent of first-, second-, and third-grade girls want to be thinner, and 80 percent of 10-year-old girls are worried about being fat. Do some research about eating disorders at the National Institutes of Mental Health Web site (www.nimh.nih.gov/). Write a paragraph summarizing your findings.

REVIEW TEST: *Recognizing Modes of Writing*

The following paragraphs are taken from college textbooks. The general purpose of each author is to present information about the topic or to explain a specific idea.

Directions: Read each paragraph. Then circle the best answer for each question.

A.   Psychologist John Reisman divides enduring friendships into three types: "associative," "receptive," and "reciprocal." An *associative friendship* endures because of circumstances that bring the partners together. Associative friendships include relationships with colleagues at work, at church, at school and members of the same club, athletic team, fraternity, or sorority. The sense of commitment that each partner feels toward the other is due to the situation (belonging to the same club). A *receptive friendship* is based on a difference in status or control. One member is the giver and the other is the taker. Leaders and followers create receptive friendships, as do instructors and students, mentors and trainees, masters and apprentices, or any sets of people whose relationship is based on a relational difference of complementary roles in which one person is the giver and the other is the receiver. A very close relationship is most likely to be a *reciprocal friendship* rather than an associative or receptive one. Partners in a reciprocal friendship feel a commitment specifically to their interpersonal relationship. Moreover, reciprocal friends tend to consider themselves as equals in the relationship. They will switch back and forth between giving and receiving roles and will typically not maintain one role throughout the relationship.

From B. Aubrey Fisher and Katherine L. Adams, *Interpersonal Communication*, 2nd Edition. New York: McGraw-Hill, 1994, p. 392.

_____ 1. The organizational patterns used in this paragraph are
    a. persuasion, and cause and effect.
    b. expository, and classification and division.
    c. narrative and comparison-contrast.
    d. description and chronological order.

_____ 2. Your relationship with a supervisor at work would be an example of which type of friendship?
    a. associative
    b. receptive
    c. reciprocal

_____ 3. You work as a teacher's aide at a local high school and have become friends with a fellow teacher's aide. The two of you often take lunch and recess breaks together. This is an example of a(n) _____ friendship.
    a. associative
    b. receptive
    c. reciprocal

B.   The Beatles—the singer-guitarists Paul McCartney, John Lennon, and George Harrison, and the drummer Ringo Starr—have been the most influential performing group in the history of rock. Their music, hairstyle, dress, and lifestyle were imitated all over the world, resulting in a phenomenon known as Beatlemania. All four Beatles were born during the early 1940s in Liverpool, England, and dropped out of school in their teens to devote themselves to rock.

Lennon and McCartney, the main songwriters of the group, began working together in 1956 and were joined by Harrison about two years later. In 1962 Ringo Starr became their new drummer. The group gained experience by performing in Hamburg, Germany; and in Liverpool, a port to which sailors brought the latest American rock, rhythm-and-blues, and country-and-western records. In 1961, the Beatles made their first record, and by 1963 they were England's top rock group. In 1964, they triumphed in the United States, breaking attendance records everywhere and dominating the record market. Audiences often became hysterical, and the police had to protect the Beatles from their fans. Beatle dolls, wigs, sweatshirts, and jackets flooded the market. Along with a steady flow of successful records, the Beatles made several hit movies: *A Hard Day's Night, Help!,* and *Yellow Submarine.*

From Roger Kamien, *Music: An Appreciation,* 9th Edition, pp. 570–71. Copyright © 2008 by The McGraw-Hill Companies, Inc. Reprinted with permission.

_____ 1. For this paragraph, the author uses an organizational pattern that
   a. gives examples to support a point.
   b. describes a series of events in chronological order.
   c. compares and contrasts key details.
   d. defines key terms.

_____ 2. You can infer from this paragraph that the Beatles
   a. took college classes in music theory.
   b. had little effect on rock music.
   c. were well-known musicians before joining the group.
   d. changed the course of rock music.

_____ 3. Ringo Starr
   a. was the Beatles' first drummer.
   b. was born in the late 1940s.
   c. joined the group after the Beatles released their first record.
   d. was one of the group's main songwriters.

C.　　Appearance counts when you are communicating on the Internet. You won't be judged by your physical appearance, your race, your hair color, or your age. But you will be judged by how you appear *in your writings.* You never know who might be lurking or how looking your best could benefit you. People have received job offers, internship and study opportunities, book contracts, and even marriage proposals, all based on their appearance on the Net.

Here is a list of some guidelines for looking your best when you send a personal e-mail message or post a message to a discussion group:

(1) Be professional about what you say and how you say it. Know what you are talking about and be sure that what you are saying is correct to the best of your knowledge.

(2) Make sure that your message is clear and logical. Focus on one subject per message. Don't be long-winded.

(3) Use informative subject headings and present the most important information in your first several sentences.

(4) Keep your paragraphs short and to the point. Include line breaks between your paragraphs.

(5) Add some color. Using *asterisks* around words and phrases to empha-size a point, or a smiley :-) to indicate an emotion, can make your post more interesting to read. But don't overdo it and PLEASE AVOID SHOUTING.

(6) Be careful when using sarcasm and humor. In the absence of face-to-face communication, your joke could cause offense. It can also be very difficult for people from other cultures to understand "native" humor.

From Nancy E. Willard, *The Cyber Ethics Reader*, pp. 9–11. Copyright © 1997 by The McGraw-Hill Companies, Inc. Reprinted with permission.

_____ 1. The organizational pattern used in this paragraph could be described as
   a. description.
   b. comparison-contrast.
   c. cause and effect.
   d. listing.

_____ 2. The main idea expressed in this paragraph is that
   a. although you will not be judged by your physical appearance on the Internet, you will be judged by your written appearance.
   b. humor is cultural and can easily be misunderstood.
   c. brevity counts on the Internet.
   d. presenting a good appearance on the Internet can lead to finan-cial success.

_____ 3. The author's primary purpose is to
   a. warn readers about the dangers of e-mail.
   b. inform readers of proper behavior for communicating on the Internet.
   c. explain the meaning of communication.
   d. entertain readers by comparing the Internet to face-to-face communication.

_____ 4. The author would agree with all of the following *except* for which?
   a. Sloppiness in writing on the Internet does not make a good impression.
   b. We should not use all capital letters.
   c. It's not necessary to include a subject heading.
   d. We should be careful when using jokes or wisecracks as they are easily misunderstood.

D.   When you are a *speaker*, you are the source, or originator, of a message that is transmitted to a listener. Whether you are speaking to a dozen people or 500, you bear a great responsibility for the success of the communication. The key ques-tion that you must constantly ask yourself is not "Am I giving out good informa-tion?" or "Am I performing well?" but rather "Am I getting through to my listeners?" The *listener* is defined as the recipient of the message sent by the speaker. The true test of communication is not whether a message is delivered by the speaker, but whether it is accurately received by the listener. The message is whatever the speaker communicates to the listeners. The message is sent in the form of *symbols*—either *verbal* or *nonverbal*. The *channel* refers to the medium used to communicate the message. A speech can reach an audience by means of a variety of channels: radio, television, the Internet, a public address system, or direct voice communication. *Feedback* means the response that the listeners give the speaker. Sometimes it is *verbal,* as when a listener asks questions or makes comments during a lecture. Listeners also give *nonverbal* feedback. If they are smiling and nodding their heads, they are obviously in agreement with your remarks. If they are frowning and sitting with their arms folded, they more than likely disagree with what you are saying. *Interference* refers to anything that blocks or hinders the accurate communication of a message. When you are a speaker, watch for any signs of interference and if possible take steps to overcome the problem.

From Hamilton Gregory, *Public Speaking for College and Career*, 7th Edition, pp. 8–12. Copyright © 2005 by The McGraw-Hill Companies, Inc. Reprinted with permission.

_____ 1. The organizational pattern used in this paragraph is
a. sequence/process.
b. time order.
c. definition and example.
d. cause and effect.

_____ 2. The author implies that
a. successful communication requires a listener to accurately receive a message.
b. a speaker need only be concerned with presenting a message.
c. a message can be expressed either verbally or nonverbally.
d. both a and c.

_____ 3. According to the author, feedback
a. can be negative as when a listener frowns at something the speaker says.
b. can be positive as when a listener nods to agree with a speaker.
c. can be verbal as when a listener asks questions.
d. all of the above.

E.   One of the most striking contrasts between the United States and Brazil, the two most populous nations of the Western Hemisphere, is in the meaning and role of the family. Contemporary North American adults usually define their families as consisting of their husbands or wives and their children. However, when middle-class Brazilians talk about their families, they mean their parents, siblings, aunts, uncles, grandparents, and cousins. Later they add their children, but rarely the husband or wife, who has his or her own family. The children are shared by the two families. Because middle-class Americans lack an extended family support system, marriage assumes more importance. The husband–wife relationship is supposed to take precedence over either spouse's relationship with his or her own parents. This places a significant strain on North American marriages. Living in a less mobile society, Brazilians stay in closer contact with their relatives, including members of the extended family. Residents of Rio de Janeiro and São Paulo, two of South America's largest cities, are reluctant to leave those urban centers to live away from family and friends. Brazilians find it hard to imagine, and unpleasant to live in, social worlds without relatives. Contrast this with a characteristic American theme: learning to live with strangers.

From Conrad Phillip Kottak, *Anthropology: The Exploration of Human Diversity*, 12th Edition, p. 416. Copyright © 2008 by The McGraw-Hill Companies, Inc. Reprinted with permission.

_____ 1. The dominant pattern of organization in this paragraph is
   a. cause and effect.
   b. contrast.
   c. classification.
   d. listing.

_____ 2. The writer of this paragraph probably believes that
   a. spouses in the United States are not as involved with their own extended families as spouses in Brazil.
   b. Brazilians find it more difficult to live away from their relatives than persons in the United States.
   c. the father's side has more involvement with the children in a Brazilian family than the mother's side.
   d. both a and b.

_____ 3. The author's main idea in this paragraph is that
   a. the Brazilian system of marriage stands in contrast to the prevailing system in the United States.
   b. Brazilians don't like to work too far away from their relatives.
   c. an extended family is important to the Brazilians.
   d. the U.S. system of families should become more like the Brazilian system.

F.   Among the middle and upper classes of the industrialized nations, some people suffer from a condition called anorexia nervosa. Anorexic individuals suffer from a mistaken perception of their body size. Because they imagine themselves to be heavier than they really are, they desire to be thinner as a result. Anorexia is most common among Caucasian women between the ages of 15 and 30 with an average or above-average level of education. Anorexia is all but unknown among people living in poverty or in undernourished populations anywhere. It never seems to occur where food is scarce, or in times of famine. Anorexia was once extremely rare. Several experts say its marked increase in the United States since World War II is caused by a general standard of beauty that has increasingly glorified thinness, as measured by such criteria as waist and hip measurements of Miss America contestants, _Playboy_ centerfolds, and models and ballet dancers generally. In fact, women in professions like modeling and ballet dancing are particularly likely to develop anorexia. Also, female athletes in sports like rowing where competition is organized by weight classes are at high risk for developing anorexia.

From Eli Minkoff and Pamela J. Baker, _Biology Today_, 1996, pp. 244–245. McGraw-Hill, 1996.

_____ 1. The author suggests that
   a. anorexia is a frequent disease of the poor.
   b. anorexia primarily occurs among well-fed populations.
   c. anorexia rarely occurs in times of famine.
   d. both b and c.

_____ 2. The writer of this paragraph probably believes that anorexia might be caused by
   a. an inability to accurately "see" one's size.
   b. an identification of thinness with beauty.

    c. the mass media's reliance on role models who are inappropri-
       ately thin.

    d. all of the above.

_____ 3. According to the author, the person most likely to suffer from
          anorexia is

    a. a Black female age 15–30.

    b. a Caucasian male with an above-average education.

    c. a middle-class Caucasian female age 15–30.

    d. a person who participates in aerobics.

_____ 4. The dominant pattern of organization in this paragraph is

    a. cause and effect.

    b. time order.

    c. listing.

    d. classification.

G.   Innocent victims trigger more compassion if personalized. In a week when
a soon-forgotten earthquake in Iran kills 3,000 people, a lone boy dies, trapped
in a well shaft in Italy, and the whole world grieves. The projected death statistics of a nuclear war are impersonal to the point of being incomprehensible.
So international law professor Roger Fisher proposed a way to personalize the
victims:

It so happens that a young man, usually a navy officer, accompanies the President wherever he goes. This young man has a black attaché case which contains the codes that are needed to fire nuclear weapons.

    I can see the President at a staff meeting considering nuclear war as an ab-
stract question. He might conclude, "On SIOP Plan One, the decision is
affirmative. Communicate the Alpha line XYZ." Such jargon keeps what is involved at a distance.

    My suggestion, then, is quite simple. Put that needed code number in
a little capsule and implant that capsule right next to the heart of a volunteer.
The volunteer will carry with him a big, heavy butcher knife as he accompanies the President. If ever the President wants to fire nuclear weapons,
the only way he can do so is by first, with his own hands, killing one human
being.

    "George," the President would say, "I'm sorry, but tens of millions must
die." The President then would have to look at someone and realize what death
is—what an *innocent* death is. Blood on the White House carpet: it's reality
brought home.

    When I suggested this to friends in the Pentagon, they said, "My God,
that's terrible. Having to kill someone would distort the President's judgment.
He might never push the button."

From David G. Myers, *Social Psychology*, 9th Edition, p. 398. Copyright © 2008 by The McGraw-Hill
Companies, Inc. Reprinted with permission. Quote from Roger Fisher, "Preventing Nuclear War,"
The Bulletin of the Atomic Scientists, March 1981, pp. 11–17.

_____ 1. The organization pattern used by the author in this paragraph

    a. gives an illustration to support a point.

    b. demonstrates a cause-and-effect relationship.

c. lists ideas without regard to order.

d. defines key terms.

_____ 2. International law professor Roger Fisher probably believes that

a. in times of war, jargon is used to create distance from one's actions.

b. it may be easier to bomb an entire village from 40,000 feet than to shoot a single helpless villager face-to-face.

c. people responsible for killing other people are sometimes emotionally detached from the human reality of their decisions.

d. all of the above.

_____ 3. The main idea expressed in this paragraph is that

a. personalizing the destruction that a nuclear war would cause may help prevent one.

b. people are sometimes unresponsive to great tragedies.

c. people are more likely to treat compassionately those they personally relate to.

d. people are least likely to be compassionate to persons they bomb from the air.

Chapter Summary and Review

In Chapter 9, you became familiar with several modes of organization. You also practiced summarizing longer reading passages. Based on the material in Chapter 9, answer the following questions.

Short Answer

Directions: Answer the following questions briefly, in a few words or sentences as appropriate.

1. What questions must you ask yourself in writing a summary? _____?

_____? _____? _____? _____? and _____?

2. When you survey a selection, what parts of it should you look at first?

_____

Vocabulary in Context

Directions: Choose one of the following words to complete the sentences below. Use each word only once.

| categories   cause   chronological   effect   modes |

3. When you fail to study for a test and do poorly, your lack of preparation is a(n)

_____ and your poor performance is a(n) _____.

4. People usually tell stories in _____ order.

5. Chronological order and cause and effect are _____ that describe _____ of organization.

Reading Critically

John Scofield

The jazz of any period needs critical comment and evaluation, but criticism must be based on something more than personal preference or personal opinion. Discussion and debate over the relative merits of different kinds of jazz can be healthy and rewarding provided they are based not merely on opinion but on significant analysis and interpretation.

—Leroy Ostransky, from *Understanding Jazz*

When we hear a musical piece played, most of us have an opinion on whether we like it. Few of us, though, have the knowledge necessary to evaluate the piece on its technical merits. Only someone with enough expertise about music can do that. Often we need to critically evaluate reading selections, especially those that are meant to explain or persuade. The purpose of Part 5 is to teach you some techniques for performing such an evaluation. Specifically, we will discuss the difference between fact and opinion, what it means for a writer to have a bias and how to identify a writer's bias, and how to look at the evidence presented to determine whether it supports the writer's conclusions.

425

10

Fact and Opinion

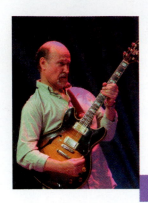

CHAPTER PREVIEW

In this chapter, you will

- Develop strategies to help you tell the difference between fact and opinion.

Learning to Read Critically

Listening: To Tell Fact from Opinion

You spend a good part of your day listening to other people—teachers, friends, parents, radio and TV announcers. Sometimes they tell you facts; other times they offer their opinions. Can you tell the difference? If you cannot, you will have a hard time knowing what to believe.

Fact

A fact is a statement that can be proved. You can prove it yourself, or you can use a reliable authority. Here are some examples of facts and how they can be proved.

Statements of Fact	Sources of Proof
Abraham Lincoln was assassinated.	History book
Mr. Guthrie teaches math.	Experience
Jeff won the election.	Number of votes
Your kitchen table is 52 inches long.	Measurement

Laws and observations are also forms of fact. A law may be based on science (the law of gravity) or an established government authority (the speed limit). You can prove an observation, such as "Some stars are brighter than others," by pointing it out yourself or by testing it scientifically.

"So many men, so many opinions."

—Terence

Opinion

An opinion cannot be proved. It is based only on someone's thoughts, feelings, or judgment.

Opinions: Abraham Lincoln was a great man.

Mr. Guthrie works his students too hard.

Jeff is the better candidate.

You should have a larger table.

Some people may think that these statements are true; others may disagree. Listen for words like *good, nice, bad, wonderful,* and *should.* They can help you identify opinions.

Some opinions, however, are sounder than others. While they cannot be proved, they can be backed up with facts. Someone who tells you that Jeff is the better candidate can support this opinion by giving facts about Jeff's experience and past actions. Historians who believe Lincoln was great can support their opinion with facts about his achievements.

A **hypothesis** is a form of opinion. It is a reasonable guess made to explain an observation. Each hypothesis must be tested to make sure it is a good guess.

Hypotheses: Objects move only when they are pushed or pulled.

The car stopped because it ran out of gas.

Green food makes me sneeze.

You can test the last hypothesis by seeing if you really do sneeze whenever you eat something green. If you also sneeze when you eat something yellow, you may have to change your hypothesis.

A **theory** is also an opinion, but it is not a guess. A theory is an accepted explanation of a set of observations. A theory often includes several hypotheses that belong together and have been tested successfully. If a theory is good, it can be used to explain other things.

Theories: Heat results from the movement of tiny particles.

All the forces of nature are interrelated.

Here are some examples of some other kinds of opinions.

Speculative Statement: Allison Packer is going to win the seat in the state legislature.

Value Judgment: She is the best candidate.

Exaggeration: Allison Packer will get billions of votes.

Belief: She will change the government as she has promised.

When you listen to someone—in a lecture, a commercial, an election campaign, or even just conversation—be aware of the difference between a fact and an opinion. Do not be persuaded by an opinion unless the speaker supports it with facts.

From *Houghton Mifflin English,* Level 8 by Shirley Haley-James, et al., pp. 356–57. Copyright © 1988 by Houghton Mifflin Company. Reprinted by permission of Houghton Mifflin Harcourt Publishing Company. All rights reserved.

Note: It is important to realize that **facts** can change over time for a variety of reasons. At one time in the past, it was considered to be a "fact" that the earth was at the center of the universe. Of course, we now know that this is not true. Until recently, the following statement was considered to be a fact:

Star Wars is the top domestic money-earner of all time.

This is no longer a "fact" because in 1997 the movie *Titanic* surpassed *Star Wars* in box office receipts.

Some statements of "fact" are false because the information on which they are based is erroneous. Comedians like to joke that if you ask most women over 40 their age, you're going to get a false answer. Other "facts" that are based on numbers and statistics may be false because numbers and statistics can be easily manipulated. In evaluating factual information, it is best to keep in mind what Mark Twain famously said: "There are lies, damn lies, and statistics."

Clues to Identifying an Opinion

Opinions are beliefs or judgments that cannot be proved by any objective means. Any statement that deals with probabilities or future events is considered to be an opinion because it cannot be proved. Opinions rely on abstract words that are not quantifiable, such as value judgment words. Below are some examples of typical opinion words.

Words and Phrases That Signal an Opinion

I believe	Perhaps	This suggests
Apparently	In my view	Presumably
It seems likely	Many experts agree	In my opinion
One interpretation is	One possibility is	

In addition, any word that indicates a value judgment on someone's part signals an opinion. Many people disagree about what is the best or the worst, and so forth. Because of our different values, the use of these words makes any statement that contains them impossible to prove.

Value Judgment Words

necessary	interesting	effective
beautiful/attractive, etc.	highest/lowest	most/least
best/worst	bad	nice
greatest	successful	

Most of what we read and hear is a combination of fact and opinion. Because of this, it is important to be able to distinguish between the two. Remember, not all opinions are of equal validity. Poorly supported opinions are of little value, while opinions from an expert, or someone knowledgeable in the field, are far more reliable.

Exercise 1: Thinking about Facts and Opinions

Directions: Using complete sentences, write six facts about yourself. Then think about some opinions you have, and write down six of them.

Facts about You

1. _____
2. _____
3. _____
4. _____
5. _____
6. _____

Your Opinions

1. _____
2. _____
3. _____
4. _____

5. _____

6. _____

Exercise 2: Recognizing Facts and Opinions

Directions: Place an **F** in the blank for those statements that are mostly factual and an **O** in the blank for those statements that are mostly opinion. Circle the abstract or value judgment words in the statements of opinion.

_____O_____ 1. The community college is a better place to attend school for the first two years than a university or a four-year school.

_____F_____ 2. *U.S. News & World Report* found that 100 percent of the students at Harvard University were in the top quarter of their high school graduating class.

_____O_____ 3. David McCullough's *John Adams* is a convincing portrait of one of the dominant men of the Revolutionary War.

_____F_____ 4. According to Sharon Thompson's 2008 research study, teenagers' rates of drug use, eating disorders, depression, and suicide are rising.

_____F_____ 5. Sue Grafton's book *T is for Trespass,* is number one after its second week on the *New York Times* fiction best-seller list.

_____O_____ 6. At $13.95 a copy, the book is a real bargain.

_____F_____ 7. In a 2008 study, the American Medical Association reported that drinking is heaviest among singles and the newly divorced.

_____F_____ 8. A 2008 study by A. C. Nielsen Company showed that home use of the Internet has cut TV viewing, with wired homes watching an average of 13 percent less television.

_____F_____ 9. According to data reported in *Retirement Places Rated,* Las Vegas, with a grade of 84.5, is America's no. 1 retirement destination.

_____F_____ 10. Researchers from the University of Arizona recently tested 500 used kitchen dishcloths and found that two-thirds contain bacteria that can make people sick.

_____O_____ 11. Toothpaste containing peroxide and baking soda is far better at producing clean and attractive teeth.

_____F_____ 12. Researchers at Ohio State University found that women experience anxiety and depression about 30 percent more often than men.

_____O_____ 13. Women have greater burdens and limitations placed on them in both the workplace and the family.

Exercise 3: More Recognizing Facts and Opinions

Directions: Read the following sentences and put an **O** in the blank if the statement is an opinion or an **F** if the statement is a fact. Circle the opinion words that indicate probabilities or future events.

_____F_____ 1. The Victoria's Secret catalog offers 45 items in satin.

_____O_____ 2. You will learn more from reading books than you will from watching television.

_____F_____ 3. By the year 2020, we will be unable to function as a society without computers.

_____F_____   4. A recent Ohio State study showed that playing the violin or cello burns 40 percent more calories than watching TV.

_____F_____   5. In 1923, F. Scott Fitzgerald called a collection of his short stories *Tales of the Jazz Age.*

_____F_____   6. The National Highway Department, in its 2009 study, concluded that elderly drivers (those over the age of 70) are responsible for the majority of driving fatalities in the United States.

_____O_____   7. The United States is certain to do better in the next Olympic competition.

_____F_____   8. The United Nations Human Development Program reports that the divorce rate in the United States is now the highest of any major industrialized nation.

_____F_____   9. An Education Department survey showed that 70 percent of 5,500 secondary school principals approve of requiring school uniforms.

_____O_____ 10. Schools that maintain a dress code will tend to have fewer instances of assault, robbery, and vandalism, and at the same time will tend to report improved academic performance.

Exercise 4: Rewriting Opinion Statements

Directions: Working in a group, determine whether the given statement is a fact (**F**) or an opinion (**O**), and write your answer on the line provided. Then on a separate piece of paper rewrite all statements of opinion as statements of fact. Be sure to eliminate all abstract and value judgment words. Your fact sentence should use concrete words and be verifiable.

> *Example:*
>
> Opinion: My current house is **too small** for my family.
>
> Fact: I have a one-bedroom house and 10 people in my family.
>
> or
>
> Fact: I have a 900-square foot home and 10 people in my family.

_____F_____   1. My husband and I took a three-mile hike on Sunday.

_____O_____   2. My spring break was much too short.

_____O_____   3. My Honda Accord gets excellent gas mileage.

_____F_____   4. The yearly salary for the principal of John F. Kennedy School is $75,000.

_____O_____   5. He is a reckless and irresponsible driver.

_____O_____   6. The iMac computer was very reasonably priced.

_____F_____   7. The temperature in the oven is 375 degrees.

_____O_____   8. My English teacher graded my last essay unfairly.

_____O_____   9. Of all my college classes, my computer class has been the most helpful.

_____O_____ 10. Tiger Woods is the best golfer in Professional Golf Association (PGA) history.

Exercise 5: Recognizing Facts and Opinions in Movie Reviews

Best American Films

The American Film Institute picked its list of the 100 greatest American movies of all time in 1998, in honor of the 100th anniversary of American filmmaking. While the list was controversial, most critics agree about the top 10 films.

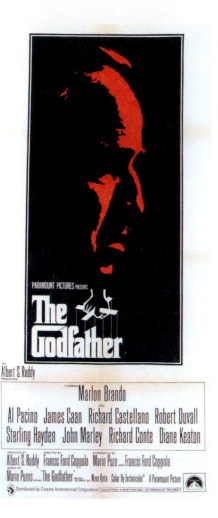

Four of the Top 10 Movies

Directions: Study the reviews for the top 10 titles from the list. If the review is entirely factual, place an **F** in the blank provided. If the review is entirely opinion, place an **O** in the blank. For the reviews containing both facts and opinions write **FO** in the blank.

 1. *Citizen Kane*, 1941. (1) This classic film by Orson Welles about the rise and fall of a media titan was based on the life of William Randolph Hearst. (2) The film was made when Welles was only 25. (3) Despite favorable reviews, it was not a commercial success, at least in part because Hearst used his power as a newspaper magnate to demand negative reviews and to force theater owners to boycott the film. (4) The film features stunning visual effects and a first-rate cast including Joseph Cotten as Kane's friend Jed Leland, Agnes Moorehead as Kane's mother, and Dorothy Comingore in a brilliant performance as Kane's wife Susan. (5) Welles himself is entirely convincing as he portrays Kane from a brash young man to a bitter 75-year-old.

 2. *Casablanca*, 1942. (1) Humphrey Bogart (Rick) and Ingrid Bergman (Ilsa) star as two sides of a lovers' triangle in World War II Morocco. (2) This film won Oscars for best picture, best director, and best screenplay.

3. *The Godfather*, 1972. (1) Francis Ford Coppola's story of the life and times of a Mafia family. (2) It won Oscars for best picture, best actor (Marlon Brando), and best screenplay (Coppola and Mario Puzo, from whose novel the film was adapted).

 4. *Gone with the Wind*, 1939. (1) Produced by David O. Selznick, this magnificient soap opera set during the Civil War won eight Oscars, including best picture, best actress (Vivian Leigh, as the indestructible Scarlett O'Hara), best director (Victor Fleming), and best screenplay (Sidney Howard). (2) The movie is divided by an intermission into two halves. (3) The first half, featuring glorious visuals, covers the beginning of the Civil War and ends with Sherman's march through Atlanta. (4) The weaker second half deals with the Reconstruction era.

 5. *Lawrence of Arabia*, 1962. (1) David Lean's magnificent, intelligent blockbuster starred Peter O'Toole as the adventurer T. E. Lawrence, an officer in the British Army serving in the Middle East during World War I. (2) The movie won Oscars for best picture, best director, best cinematographer, best score, best editing, and best art direction.

 6. *The Wizard of Oz*, 1939. (1) Victor Fleming directed "Oz" based on L. Frank Baum's story. (2) The movie stars Judy Garland as Dorothy Gale, Ray Bolger as the Scarecrow, Bert Lahr as the Cowardly Lion, Jack Haley as the Tin Man, and Margaret Hamilton as the Wicked Witch of the West. (3) Judy Garland's song "Over the Rainbow" won an Oscar.

7. *The Graduate*, 1967. (1) Mike Nichols's tribute to the 1960s included actor Dustin Hoffman's breakthrough role as a naïve college grad who has affairs with his beautiful childhood friend (Katharine Ross) and her sexy mother (Anne Bancroft as Mrs. Robinson). (2) Paul Simon and Art Garfunkel provided the outstanding musical score. (3) Nichols received a well-deserved Oscar for best director.

 8. *On the Waterfront*, 1954. (1) Marlon Brando stars as a longshoreman in a New York City harbor union. (2) The film garnered eight Oscars, including best picture, best director (Elia Kazan), best actor (Brando), best supporting actress (Eva Marie Saint), and best screenplay (Budd Schulberg).

(3) The movie was filmed in and around the docks of New York and New Jersey.

9. *Schindler's List,* 1993. (1) The story of Oscar Schindler, who saved more than 1,000 Jewish people during World War II, earned seven Oscars, including best picture, best director (Steven Spielberg), and best screenplay.

10. *Singin' in the Rain,* 1952. (1) Gene Kelly directed and starred in one of the greatest Hollywood musicals ever made. (2) The story features the talented Gene Kelly as Don Lockwood, the spunky Debbie Reynolds as Kathy Selden, and the hilarious Jean Hagen as Kelley's silent screen costar, who was having a difficult time getting into the new industry because her voice could shatter glass. (3) One of the highlights is the performance of Donald O'Connor (Lockwood's pal Cosmo Brown), in the "make 'em laugh" dance number.

Adapted from George Rodman, *Mass Media in a Changing World,* p. 158. Copyright © 2006 by The McGraw-Hill Companies, Inc. Reprinted with permission.

Exercise 6: Distinguishing Fact from Opinion

Many writers try to convince readers of the wisdom of their arguments by combining both facts and opinions, often within the same sentence. The following sentences contain both fact and opinion. The facts have been italicized.

1. *With half of all American marriages failing,* it appears that "till death do us part" simply means until the going gets rough.
2. *A USA Today poll showed that 65 percent of Americans were unable to identify* the Bill of Rights, thus demonstrating the widespread ignorance of the population at large.

Directions: After reading each sentence, underline only the facts.

1. With the National Institute on Drug Abuse estimating that at least 500,000 high school students use or have used steroids, it is obvious that something needs to be done about the growing drug threat among teens.

2. Immediately after divorce, the income of households with kids declines by 21 percent, thereby creating an unfortunate new class of people in poverty—divorced women with children.

3. Male adults who enjoy light or moderate drinking should keep right on enjoying imbibing since research by Serge Renaud of the National Institutes of Health on 36,000 middle-age men demonstrated that those who drank two to four glasses of wine a day had a 30–40 percent reduction in mortality from all causes.

4. In the state of Illinois, the delicate balance between a boss's right to know what's going on in the office and an employee's right to privacy has been upset by a 1995 state law that permits bosses to eavesdrop on employees' work telephones.

5. California, the state where 1.8 million civil lawsuits were filed in 2007, perhaps should have a new motto emblazoned on all license plates—Home of Litigators.

6. In 1981, the product NutraSweet was introduced to the public as a boon to the overweight, yet the Centers for Disease Control and Prevention recently reported that U.S. obesity rates have actually increased since that time.

7. Despite the fact that many physicians, scientists, and consumer advocates regard homeopathic medicines as ineffective at best and dangerous at worst, the National Center for Homeopathy reports that Americans are spending more than $165 million annually on homeopathic preparations.

READING

"People like to think that their opinions are supported by the 'facts.' However, they sometimes form their opinions first and then devise 'facts' that support those opinions."

TUNING IN TO READING

Can you think of a recent issue that has attracted a lot of attention? Today when public officials want to gauge the public's feelings about an issue, they commission a public opinion poll. It may surprise you to know that pollsters arrive at their results after polling only a small group of people. They assume that the opinions of this small group will reflect the opinions of the public at large. Most of the time, polling leads to fairly accurate results. But this is not always true. Can you think of any recent instances when what pollsters were saying about public opinion turned out to be misleading or wrong?

BIO-SKETCH

Thomas Patterson is Bradlee Professor of Government and the Press in the John F. Kennedy School of Government at Harvard University. Previously he was a Distinguished Professor of Political Science at Syracuse University. He has received many awards for his books and articles.

NOTES ON VOCABULARY

Jeremy Bentham is best known as the founder of the utilitarian philosophy. He developed the principle of utility, which states that action is acceptable if it promotes an increased amount of pleasure and is unacceptable if it promotes an increased amount of pain.

entails makes necessary; requires; involves.

The Nature of Public Opinion
Thomas Patterson

Public opinion is a relatively new concept in the history of political thought. Not until pressures began to mount in the 1700s for representative government was there a need for a term to refer to what ordinary people thought about politics.

In the 1948 presidential election, Gallup polls had predicted that challenger Thomas E. Dewey would defeat the incumbent, Harry S Truman. But a hard-fought campaign gave Truman a slight edge on the eve of the election. Unfortunately for Chicago's *Daily Tribune,* the editors went with what they believed would happen, rather than waiting for election returns—and so they went with the wrong headline. This photo shows Truman holding a copy of the early edition of the Chicago paper.

The first English-speaking philosopher to write at length about public opinion was Jeremy Bentham (1748–1832). Originally an advocate of government by an enlightened elite, Bentham came to believe that the public's views had to be taken into account if leaders were to govern properly.

2   *Public opinion* is now a widely used term, but it is a term that is often used inexactly. A common mistake is the assumption that "the public"—meaning the whole citizenry—actually has an opinion on most issues of public policy. In fact, most issues do not attract the attention of even a majority of citizens. Agricultural conservation programs, for example, are of intense interest to some farmers, hunters, and environmentalists but of little interest to most people. This pattern is so pervasive that opinion analysts have described America as having *many* publics.

3   Hence, any definition of the term *public opinion* cannot be based on the assumption that all citizens, or even a majority, are actively interested in and hold a preference about all aspects of political life. **Public opinion** can be defined as the politically relevant opinions held by ordinary citizens that they express openly. This expression need not be verbal. It could also take the form, for example, of a protest demonstration or a vote for one candidate rather than another. The crucial point is that a person's private thoughts on an issue become public opinion when they are expressed openly.

How Informed Is Public Opinion?

4   A practical obstacle to government by public opinion is that people have differing opinions; in responding to one side of an issue, government is compelled to reject other preferences. Public opinion can also be contradictory. Polls indicate, for example, that most Americans would like better schools, health care, and other public services, while also favoring a reduction in taxes. Which opinion of the people should govern—their desire for more services, or their desire for lower taxes?

5   Another limitation is that people's opinions, even on issues of great importance, are often misinformed. In the buildup to the U.S. invasion of Iraq in 2003, for example, polls revealed that more than half of the American public wrongly believed that Iraqis were among the nineteen terrorists who had flown airplanes into the World Trade Center and Pentagon on September 11, 2001. Moreover, despite opposition to the war on the part of most Europeans, Asians, South Americans, and Africans, one-fourth of Americans wrongly believed that world opinion favored the war. Americans who held such views were more supportive of the Iraq war than were other Americans.

6   The public's relatively low level of accurate information is due partly to what is called "the will to believe." People like to think that their opinions are supported by the "facts." However, they sometimes form their opinions first and then devise "facts" that support those opinions.

7   Moreover, most Americans are not closely attentive to politics and therefore do not possess a lot of factual information. Americans are not unique in this respect, but in some areas they are less informed than citizens of most other Western democracies. In a seven-country survey, Americans ranked next to last in their ability to respond correctly to five factual questions about prominent world leaders and developments. Despite America's leading role in the world, most Americans are less informed about global affairs than are most Europeans. Analysts suggest that America's "ocean isolation" is a reason why its citizens are insular. Unlike Europeans, Americans are not surrounded by a host of other countries. But ocean isolation is not a complete explanation. Americans share a border with Canadians and Mexicans, for example, but know much less about Canada and Mexico than Canadians and Mexicans know about the United States.

8   Even many college-educated Americans lack basic information about public affairs. A survey of Ivy League students found that one-third could not identify the British prime minister, half could not name both U.S. senators from their state, and three-fourths could not identify Abraham Lincoln as the author of the phrase "a government of the people, by the people, and for the people."

9   Of course, citizens do not always have to be well informed about an issue to have a reasonable opinion about it. Opinions derive largely from people's values and interests. People can have sound opinions on the abortion issue, for example, without precise knowledge of what courts and lawmakers have done on the issue. Nevertheless, the public's lack of information limits the role that public opinion can play in policy formation. The choice among policy options in some cases requires an understanding of the consequences of the different opinions. Citizens usually lack this type of information.

10   Citizenship entails responsibilities, one of which is to stay informed about problems and developments that affect the community, the state, and the nation. As an informed citizen, you will be better able to make judgments about policy issues, to choose wisely when voting during elections, and to recognize situations that call for greater personal involvement. Fortunately, you have access to one of the most substantial news systems in the world. News about public affairs is virtually at your fingertips—through your computer, on television, and in the newspaper. Spending only a small amount of time each day following the news will enable you to be a more effective and involved citizen.

COMPREHENSION CHECKUP

Fact and Opinion

Directions: Indicate whether each statement is a fact or an opinion by writing **F** or **O** in the blank provided.

_____ 1. Another limitation is that people's opinions, even on issues of great importance, often are misinformed.

_____ 2. People like to think that their opinions are supported by the "facts."

_____ 3. Moreover, most Americans are not closely attentive to politics and therefore do not possess a lot of factual information.

_____ 4. *Public opinion* is now a widely used term, but it is a term that is often used inexactly.

_____ 5. In a seven-country survey, Americans ranked next to last in their ability to respond correctly to five factual questions about prominent world leaders and developments.

_____ 6. A survey of Ivy League students found that one-third could not identify the British prime minister, half could not name both U.S. senators from their state, and three-fourths could not identify Abraham Lincoln as the author of the phrase "a government of the people, by the people, and for the people."

_____ 7. Spending only a small amount of time each day following the news will enable you to be a more effective and involved citizen.

_____ 8. Of course, citizens do not always have to be well informed about an issue to have a reasonable opinion about it.

_____ 9. People can have sound opinions on the abortion issue, for example, without precise knowledge of what courts and lawmakers have done on the issue.

_____ 10. Citizens usually lack this type of information.

Directions: Determine whether the paragraph indicated is primarily one of fact (**F**) or opinion (**O**).

_____ 11. Paragraph 5

_____ 12. Paragraph 6

_____ 13. Paragraph 9

_____ 14. Paragraph 10

Vocabulary in Context

Directions: Cross out the incorrect word in each sentence, and replace it with its antonym from the box below.

attentive	global	informed	limitation	opposition
precise	prominent	reduction	relevant	unique

_____ 1. Only insignificant dignitaries were selected to accompany the president to the pope's funeral in Rome.

_____ 2. The world today is so interconnected that many problems, such as air pollution, are of local concern.

_____ 3. Her directions, which were vague and to the point, enabled me to find the party easily.

_____ 4. As a performer, he was especially grateful whenever he had distracted audiences.

_____ 5. There is only one Mark Twain. He is ordinary, an American original.

_____ 6. The political party in power will usually encounter support from the party out of power.

_____ 7. Generally considered to be an authority in his field, all of his comments on the subject were immaterial.

_____ 8. The library was going to be closed on the Fourth of July. The librarian repeatedly misinformed the students of this fact so that they could plan their studying accordingly.

_____ 9. Many people credit gastric-bypass surgery for a big increase in their weight.

_____ 10. His chief strength as a sales representative is his shyness.

In Your Own Words

1. Is government sufficiently responsive to public opinion? Can you cite examples when the government has responded by aligning itself with public opinion? What about times when the government has ignored public opinion?

2. Do you think it is important that people base their opinions on facts? Or should people pay more attention to their values and feelings when forming opinions?

3. Analyze the following quotations: Do you agree with either one? Why or why not?

   "I have learned to hold popular opinion of no value." —Alexander Hamilton

   "Public opinion in this country is everything." —Abraham Lincoln

   "We are concerned in public affairs, but immersed in our private ones." —Walter Lippmann

4. Many countries around the world have higher rates of voter turnout at elections than the United States. Why do you suppose the United States has a lower rate? What do you think could be done to improve voter participation?

Written Assignment

The following is a popular song by singer and songwriter John Mayer. Identify the main ideas of each stanza of the song. How does the song attempt to explain the lack of involvement of young people in the political process? Write a few short paragraphs giving your reaction to the song's main ideas. Do you agree or disagree with Mayer's overall thesis?

Waiting on the World to Change

John Mayer

Me and all my friends
We're all misunderstood
They say we stand for nothing and
There's no way we ever could
Now we see everything is going wrong
With the world and those who lead it

We just feel like we don't have the means
To rise above and beat it
So we keep waiting (waiting)
Waiting on the world to change
We keep on waiting (waiting)
Waiting on the world to change
It's hard to beat the system
When we're standing at a distance
So we keep waiting (waiting)
Waiting on the world to change

Now if we had the power
To bring our neighbors home from war
They would've never missed a Christmas
No more ribbons on their door
When you trust your television
What you get is what you got
Cuz when they own the information ooohhh,
They can bend it all they want

So while we're waiting (waiting)
Waiting on the world to change
We keep on waiting (waiting)
Waiting on the world to change
It's not that we don't care
We just know that the fight ain't fair
So we keep on waiting (waiting)
Waiting on the world to change
We're still waiting (waiting)
Waiting on the world to change
We keep on waiting (waiting)
Waiting on the world to change
One day our generation
Is gonna rule the population

So we keep on waiting (waiting)
Waiting on the world to change
No, we keep on waiting (waiting)
Waiting on the world to change
We keep on waiting (waiting)
Waiting on the world to change
Waiting on the world to change
Waiting on the world to change
Waiting on the world to change

Internet Activity

The Pew Research Center is a nonprofit organization that researches public opinion on current subjects. Go to its Web site at:

http://people-press.org/

Click on "About the Center." Can you find a listing of current issues the center is studying? Write a summary of what you found out about the center.

Fact and Opinion Quiz 1

Directions: Indicate whether the statement is a fact or an opinion by writing **F** or **O** in the blank provided.

___F___ 1. According to a study of kids age 12–17 conducted by the Pew Internet & American Life Project, 73 percent of kids in the United States are online.

___F___ 2. Using fire department and medical examiner reports, the *New England Journal of Medicine* found that risk of harm from house fires was 2.8 times higher for elderly people.

___O___ 3. The simplest way to have psychologically healthy children is to avoid divorce.

___O___ 4. Rudeness is the worst problem in the U.S. workplace because it damages the mental health and productivity of employees.

___F___ 5. The National Fatherhood Initiative reports that about 4 out of 10 first marriages end in divorce.

___O___ 6. Workers who bring their lunches from home and eat them at their desks make a big mistake because they end up working longer hours without a break.

___F___ 7. Over half of criminal behavior nationally is committed by individuals under the influence of drugs, according to studies by the National Institute of Justice.

___O___ 8. Astrology is a good method for predicting future events and identifying individual characteristics.

___F___ 9. In a government survey of 5,001 youngsters, one in five adolescents who regularly socialize on the Internet encountered a stranger who wanted "cybersex."

___O___ 10. Women who date strangers should hire a private detective to run a background check on potential suitors.

___O___ 11. Capital punishment is immoral.

___O___ 12. The Internet is not likely to become as essential as the telephone and television are today.

___F___ 13. The research of California State University psychologist Diane Halpern demonstrates that men are likely to be better than women at finding their destinations in unfamiliar settings.

___O___ 14. Oprah Winfrey is a positive role model for television watchers.

___F___ 15. According to the Bureau of Justice Statistics, the number of local, state, and federal prisoners has risen by 676,000 since 1990.

Fact and Opinion Quiz 2

Directions: Indicate whether the statement is a fact or an opinion by writing **F** or **O** in the blank provided.

___O___ 1. Sixteen-year-olds shouldn't be allowed to drive because they are involved in too many accidents.

_F_   2. The Insurance Institute for Highway Safety reported that the death rate for 16-year-old drivers has nearly doubled.

_F_   3. According to a recent study by Dr. Bruce Pomeranz, bad reactions to prescription and over-the-counter medicines kill more than 100,000 Americans and seriously injure 2.5 million more each year.

_O_   4. Middle-class families with children have a lot less money to spend.

_O_   5. If young children know the difference between right and wrong, they won't be bothered by violence on TV.

_F_   6. The U.S. Justice Department survey showed that 78 percent of all jail inmates reported using marijuana at some point in their lives.

_O_   7. The most difficult job for the working parent is balancing the demands of work with those of family.

_O_   8. Many people make the mistake of not becoming vegetarians until they have experienced a major health crisis.

_F_   9. In 1997 Diana, Princess of Wales, was killed in a car crash.

_O_ 10. Today's workers have to work harder and faster, and they never seem to have enough time to get everything done.

_O_ 11. Compact cars are a lot more practical than full-size cars.

_F_ 12. Recent proposals by elementary school districts across the country to eliminate recess are part of an alarming trend in education.

_F_ 13. According to the Census Bureau, nearly a third of young children under the age of 5 are cared for in day care centers.

_O_ 14. Parents should search a teenager's bedroom only if they suspect the teen has been abusing drugs.

_F_ 15. Researchers in Scotland cloned an adult mammal, a lamb named Dolly, who is a genetic copy of her mother.

READING

"Most striking is the hold that superstition has for those who are trained to be highly rational."

TUNING IN TO READING

Many of us engage in superstitious behavior. We are careful to avoid opening an umbrella in the house and breaking mirrors. We may try to avoid crossing in front of a black cat or walking under a ladder. We may be extra cautious on Friday the 13th. And some of us even knock on wood. Read the following selection to gain a new appreciation of superstitions.

NOTES ON VOCABULARY

placebo effect   the effect caused by a fake remedy; a beneficial reaction to a pill, medicine, or procedure that has been prescribed for the psychological benefit of the patient, and that otherwise has no medical value.

Pascal   (1623–1662) a French mathematician, physicist, and religious thinker of the 17th century who founded the theory of probabilities.

READING *continued*

debunk   to expose as being false or exaggerated. William E. Woodward created the word *debunk* when he exposed the vices of some of our famous early statesmen, including presidents George Washington and Ulysses S. Grant.

epitomize   to serve as a typical or perfect example.

reincarnation   being reborn in another body. *Reincarnation* refers to the belief that the soul upon the death of the body returns to earth in different forms again and again as it strives for perfection.

enchanted   delighted; captivated. In the early days of England, approximately 1300, an enchantress practiced "the evil arts." To *enchant* meant to place under a spell or to bewitch.

Superstitions Help Us Cope   BY PATRICIA WEN

In the middle of the most rapid expansion of scientific knowledge in history, Americans may be more superstitious today than they were a generation ago. Indeed, just as Americans abandon old superstitions such as the fear of the number "13," they embrace new ones like the belief that how furniture is arranged can somehow channel good luck into the room. Studies show these magical beliefs persist—even flourish—despite this scientific age that debunks fears of black cats and broken mirrors as nonsense.

2   In a curious way, the expansion of technology may even promote superstitious beliefs. New high-tech gadgets, such as cell phones and computers, work in ways that seem "indistinguishable from magic" to most people, and may enhance beliefs in the supernatural, according to astrophysicist Jonathan McDowell.

3   And while humans always have a baseline of worry about the future, some psychologists suggest that today's rapid technological changes have created a heightened sense of anxiety, an emotional swirl in which good luck charms and other superstitions thrive.

4   "Superstitions emerge whenever there is uncertainty and anxiety about something that people want," says Stuart Vyse, a psychologist and author of *Believing in Magic: The Psychology of Superstitions*. "Our world today is just as full of anxiety as it ever was."

5   It's not that superstitions don't have value for some people in helping them cope with stress. It's that they have no basis in scientific fact: No study has ever shown a link between walking under a ladder and bad luck, or that a rabbit's foot is lucky at all.

6   Most striking is the hold that superstition has for those who are trained to be highly rational. While athletes and movie stars are notorious for knocking on wood and phoning astrologers, scientists, for example, are supposed to know better. Yet at the Massachusetts Institute of Technology, generations of students have passed the bronze plaque of inventor George Eastman in the department hallway, and rubbed his nose for good luck on a test. "You never know if it will help," says graduate chemistry student Sarah Aeilts.

7   But many people, especially scientists, know that superstitions are a guilty pleasure. Like adults who crave Kellogg's Frosted Flakes, they often keep to themselves the superstitions that they hold dearest.

8   Only on the condition of anonymity would one MIT scientist admit that he avoids black cats. Like many people, he prefers to describe these habits as traditions passed down from his family, and he added with emphasis, "I'd never defend these from a scientific point of view."

9   Surveys show that, if anything, Americans are increasingly enchanted with superstitions

and other forms of non-rational thinking. For example, a study by Yankelovich Partners, a marketing research firm, showed 37 percent of Americans believed in astrology in 1997, up from 17 percent in 1976. In the same two-decade period, belief in reincarnation grew from 9 percent to 25 percent, while people who believe in the value of fortune telling increased from 4 percent to 14 percent.

10   Studies also indicate superstition has increased. A Gallup poll showed that, in 1996, 25 percent of Americans described themselves as very or somewhat superstitious, up from 18 percent in 1990. When it comes to measuring common dread, 13 percent of Americans fear black cats, 11 percent worry about broken mirrors, and 9 percent don't like 13.

11   It's easy to see how superstitions can develop. Humans are prone to look for cause and effect in everyday life, though sometimes the two are coincidental. Still, a man who aces a test every time he wears purple sneakers may think the shoes are like a charm even though he knows that's irrational, said Steve Grossberg, a Boston University professor of cognitive and neural systems.

12   Why do people keep superstitions once they fail? Grossberg explained that people prone to superstitions have a way of rationalizing why they don't always work. Perhaps the person didn't tie the shoelaces right on those purple sneakers.

13   Grossberg said education plays a key role in helping people understand what factors can actually enhance a good result, and which are superfluous. For instance, if the student understood the role between a healthy breakfast and mental performance, he might rightly assume his food helped his test, not what he wore.

14   But even many years of education, even scientific training, often can't overcome the power of old superstitious habits.

15   Dr. Laura Riley, an obstetrician at Massachusetts General Hospital, said she wears a charm bracelet whenever she flies to keep the plane from crashing. She also doesn't like to reuse a hospital room where she has overseen a complicated birth, fearing that there's some kind of bad aura in that room.

16   Psychologists say many superstitions, even if they have no scientific basis, can actually be helpful if they have a kind of placebo effect of relaxing someone in a tense situation.

17   It's hard to find harm when a baseball star insists on eating chicken before every game to boost his hitting. In the same way, it's hard to find fault with a computer systems manager who insists on scratching lottery tickets with an 1867 3-cent coin.

18   But superstitions become dangerous when they lead to destructive choices, such as when sick people avoid medical care because they believe in unproven remedies. Some new superstitions involve beliefs that crystals or magnets heal illness, which could be harmful if sick people choose these treatments over a visit to a conventional doctor.

19   In 1998, the *Journal of the American Medical Association* reported that superstitions—such as a belief that mystical spells cause cancer—kept some low-income Black women from seeking medical treatment when they had lumps in their breasts.

20   Steven Pinker, a psychology professor at MIT, said many people passively go along with superstitions, just as an insurance policy or a kind of "Pascal's wager" in life. The 17th century French philosopher Blaise Pascal believed that it was rational to believe in God, just in case he existed. If you believed, you'd lead a moral life and have the benefit of going to heaven if God did exist. But if you rejected God and acted immorally, you were doomed in this life and thereafter.

21   "Lots of people figure, 'What do I lose if I walk around the ladder rather than underneath it?'"

From Patricia Wen, "The New Superstitions," *Boston Globe*, January 2, 2001, p. E1. Copyright 2001 by Globe Newspaper Company—MA. Reproduced with permission of Globe Newspaper Company—MA in the format Textbook via Copyright Clearance Center.

COMPREHENSION CHECKUP

Fact or Opinion

Directions: Indicate whether each statement is a fact or an opinion by writing **F** or **O** in the blank provided.

_____ 1. "Our world today is just as full of anxiety as it ever was."

_____ 2. While athletes and movie stars are notorious for knocking on wood and phoning astrologers, scientists, for example, are supposed to know better.

_____ 3. Only on the condition of anonymity would one MIT scientist admit that he avoids black cats.

_____ 4. A Gallup poll showed that, in 1996, 25 percent of Americans described themselves as very or somewhat superstitious, up from 18 percent in 1990.

_____ 5. It's easy to see how superstitions can develop.

_____ 6. Humans are prone to look for cause and effect in everyday life, though sometimes the two are coincidental.

_____ 7. Dr. Laura Riley, an obstetrician at Massachusetts General Hospital, said she wears a charm bracelet whenever she flies to keep the plane from crashing.

_____ 8. It's hard to find harm when a baseball star insists on eating chicken before every game to boost his hitting.

_____ 9. In the same way, it's hard to find fault with a computer systems manager who insists on scratching lottery tickets with an 1867 3-cent coin.

Directions: Determine whether the paragraph indicated is primarily one of fact (**F**) or opinion (**O**).

_____ 10. Paragraph 4

_____ 11. Paragraph 9

_____ 12. Paragraph 10

_____ 13. Paragraph 16

_____ 14. Paragraph 18

_____ 15. Paragraph 19

Multiple Choice

Directions: For each item, write the letter corresponding to the best answer.

_____ 1. Which statement below best states the main idea of the article?
  a. Superstitious behavior is all bad.
  b. Only the uneducated are likely to be superstitious.
  c. Our modern world encourages superstitious behavior in various ways.
  d. Very few people are superstitious.

_____ 2. The purpose of this article is to
  a. persuade readers that superstitions are foolish.
  b. provide a historical background to the study of superstitious behavior.

      c. entertain readers with interesting anecdotes about foolish, superstitious people.

      d. inform readers about the phenomenon of superstition.

_____ 3. The author cites the example of furniture arrangement in the first paragraph to show that

      a. as people abandon old superstitions they acquire new ones.

      b. new superstitions work better than old ones.

      c. some superstitions have a scientific basis.

      d. none of the above.

_____ 4. The example of Dr. Laura Riley in paragraph 15 is used to illustrate the idea that

      a. lucky charms keep planes from crashing.

      b. education reduces or eliminates superstitious behavior.

      c. education and training do not prevent superstitious behavior.

      d. doctors tend to be very superstitious.

_____ 5. In paragraph 18, the author cites the examples of crystals and magnets to show that

      a. superstitions can be practical.

      b. superstitions can cause harm.

      c. superstitions bring bad luck.

      d. superstitions bring good luck.

True or False

Directions: Indicate whether each statement is true or false by writing **T** or **F** in the space provided.

_____ 6. According to the author, high-tech gadgets may promote superstitious behavior.

_____ 7. Surveys show Americans are increasingly enchanted with superstitions.

_____ 8. Among Americans there has been an increased interest in astrology in recent years.

_____ 9. There is a strong correlation between carrying a rabbit's foot and having good luck.

_____ 10. Many people practice superstitious behavior as a kind of "insurance policy."

Vocabulary in Context

Directions: Decide whether the word in italics is used correctly in the following sentences. Write **C** if it is used correctly and **I** if it used incorrectly.

_____ 1. Plants are likely to *flourish* if you deprive them of sufficient water.

_____ 2. If you are *prone* to asthma attacks, you need to take care to avoid breathing polluted air.

_____ 3. The police officer successfully *coped* with the loud and angry crowd at the soccer match.

_____ 4. Her suitcase was filled with *superfluous* items; everything in it was absolutely essential.

_____ 5. Yvette was *notorious* on campus for causing disruptions in the classroom.

_____ 6. The business *thrived* under his care and as a result he filed for bankruptcy in August.

_____ 7. The father was filled with *dread* when he realized he couldn't find his daughter.

_____ 8. The populace had a *heightened* sense of anxiety after the earthquake.

_____ 9. Nearly two hours late, the star finally *emerged* on stage to face the audience.

_____ 10. Antolin bought some new clothes to *enhance* his appearance.

In Your Own Words

1. Do you have any superstitions? Do you avoid letting black cats cross your path? Or avoid walking under ladders? Are there things you do or say to bring yourself good luck?

2. Can you think of any superstitions that belong to particular cultures? For instance, the belief that a four-leaf clover brings good luck is associated with Irish culture.

Written Assignment

At one time, some people believed that gods lived in the trunks of trees. If you wanted to ask a favor of a god, you would go to a tree and knock politely on the trunk before making your request. Then, if your favor was granted, you would return to the tree and knock on the trunk again to thank the god. This old superstition may still exist in a different form. Many people today knock on wood to ensure the continuation of good luck. Write a list of common superstitions and some possible explanations of their origin.

Internet Activity

Many superstitions are associated with weddings. For instance, why do guests at a wedding throw rice at the bride and groom as they are leaving? Why does the bride want to have "something borrowed and something blue"? Why are tin cans often tied to the couple's car? Use the Internet to research a wedding superstition. Two interesting sites that offer information about wedding superstitions are:

www.weddings.co.uk/info/tradsup.htm

www.blissweddings.com/library/superstitions.asp

READING

"Toothpaste manufacture is a very lucrative occupation."

TUNING IN TO READING

Most of us attempt to maintain healthy teeth and good oral hygiene by brushing at least once a day. But have you ever stopped to consider what's actually in the toothpaste we're using? Are those ingredients that we can't pronounce good for us, or at least not causing us harm?

In June 2007, the U.S. Food and Drug Administration (FDA) advised consumers to avoid certain brands of toothpaste manufactured in China after batches of Chinese-made toothpaste were found to contain the poisonous chemicals diethylene glycol (also called diglycol or DEG). The chemical is used in antifreeze as a solvent, and ingesting it is potentially fatal. As stated on most tubes, toothpaste is not intended to be swallowed. In fact, it can be harmful especially to children.

When you examine the ingredients on the label of your own tube of toothpaste, you may see the following: hydrated silica (sand), which is the abrasive found in most gel toothpastes; common detergents such as sodium lauryl sulfates and lauryl sarcosinate; sodium carbonate peroxide or titanium dioxide for whitening; and triclosan, a controversial chemical, which is found in some brands.

BIO-SKETCH

David Bodanis earned a degree in mathematics from the University of Chicago. Bodanis has a talent for explaining complex topics in simple, easy-to-understand language. Some of the books he has written are *E = MC²*, *The Secret Family*, *The Secret Garden*, *The Body Book*, and *The Secret House*, from which this excerpt is taken.

NOTES ON VOCABULARY

hunker down   to settle in a location for an extended period; hide out; hold firm. The phrase is from the Old Norse word *hokra*, meaning "to crouch."

errant   straying; wayward. From Old French *errer*, meaning "to travel about."

dollop   a small portion or amount. From the Norwegian word *dolp*, meaning "lump."

gustatory   of or relating to the sense of taste. From the Latin *gustare*, meaning "to taste."

What's in Your Toothpaste?

David Bodanis

I NTO THE BATHROOM GOES OUR MALE RESIDENT, and after the most pressing need is satisfied, it's time to brush the teeth. The tube of toothpaste is squeezed, its pinched metal seams are splayed, pressure waves are generated inside, and the paste begins to flow. But what's in this toothpaste, so carefully being extruded . . .?

2   Water mostly, 30 to 45 percent in most brands: ordinary, everyday simple tap water. It's there because people like to have a big glob of toothpaste to spread on the brush, and water is the cheapest stuff there is when it comes to making big globs. Dripping a bit from the tap onto your brush would cost virtually nothing. Whipped in with the rest of the toothpaste, the manufacturers can sell it at a neat and accountant-pleasing $4 per pound equivalent. Toothpaste manufacture is a very lucrative occupation.

3   Second to water in quantity is chalk: exactly the same material children use to draw on sidewalks. It is collected from the crushed remains of long-dead ocean creatures. In

the Cretaceous seas, chalk particles served as part of the wickedly sharp outer skeletons that these creatures had to wrap around themselves to keep from getting chomped by all the slightly larger ocean creatures they met. Their massed graves are our present chalk deposits.

4   The individual chalk particles—the size of the smallest mud particles in your garden—have kept their toughness over the eons, and now on the toothbrush they'll need it. The enamel outer coating of the tooth they'll have to face is the hardest substance in the body—tougher than skull, or bone, or nail. Only the chalk particles in toothpaste can successfully grind into the teeth during brushing, ripping off the surface layers like an abrading wheel grinding down a boulder in a quarry.

5   The craters, slashes, and channels that the chalk tears into the teeth will also remove a certain amount of built-up yellow in carnage, and it is for that polishing function that it's there. A certain amount of unduly enlarged extra-abrasive chalk fragments tear such cavernous pits into the teeth that future decay bacteria will be able to hunker down there and thrive; the quality control people find it almost impossible to screen out these errant super-chalk pieces, and government regulations allow them to stay in.

6   In case even the gouging doesn't get all the yellow off, another substance is worked into the toothpaste cream. This is titanium dioxide. It comes in tiny spheres, and it's the stuff bobbing around in white wall paint to make it come out white. Splashed around onto your teeth during the brushing, it coats much of the yellow that remains. Being water soluble, it leaks off in the next few hours and is swallowed, but at least for the quick glance up in the mirror after finishing, it will make the user think his teeth are truly white. Some manufacturers add optical whitening dyes—the stuff more commonly found in washing machine bleach—to make extra sure that the glance in the mirror shows reassuring white.

7   These ingredients alone would not make a very attractive concoction. They would stick in the tube like a sloppy white plastic lump, hard to squeeze out as well as revolting to the touch. Few consumers would savor rubbing in a mixture of water, ground-up blackboard chalk, and the whitener from latex paint first thing in the morning. To get around that finicky distaste the manufacturers have mixed in a host of other goodies.

8   To keep the glop from drying out, a mixture including glycerine glycol—related to the most common anti-freeze ingredient—is whipped in with the chalk and water, and to give *that* concoction a bit of substance (all we really have so far is wet colored chalk), a large helping is added of gummy molecules from the seaweed *Chondrus crispus*. This seaweed ooze spreads in among the chalk, paint, and anti-freeze, then stretches itself in all directions to hold the whole mass together. A bit of paraffin oil (like fuel that flickers in camping lamps) is pumped in with it to help the moss ooze keep the whole substance smooth.

9   With the glycol, ooze, and paraffin we're almost there. Only two major chemicals are left to make the refreshing, cleansing substance we know as toothpaste. The ingredients so far are fine for cleaning, but they wouldn't make much of the satisfying foam we have come to expect in the morning brushing.

10   To remedy that, every toothpaste on the market has a big dollop of detergent added too. You've seen the suds detergent will make in the washing machine. The same substance added here will duplicate that inside the mouth. It's not particularly necessary, but it sells.

11   The only problem is that by itself this ingredient tastes, well, too like detergent. It's horribly bitter and harsh. The chalk put in toothpaste is pretty foul-tasting too for that matter. It's to get around that gustatory discomfort that the manufacturers put in the ingredient they tout perhaps the most of all. This is the flavoring, and it has to be strong. Double rectified peppermint oil is used—a flavor so powerful that chemists know better than to sniff it in the raw state in the laboratory. Menthol crystals and saccharine or other sugar simulators are added to complete the camouflage operation.

12   Is that it? Chalk, water, paint, seaweed, anti-freeze, paraffin oil, detergent, and peppermint? Not quite. A mix like that would be irresistible to the hundreds of thousands of individual bacteria lying on the surface of even an immaculately cleaned bathroom sink. They would get in, float in the water bubbles, ingest the ooze and paraffin, maybe even spray out enzymes to break down the chalk. The result would be an uninviting mess. The way manufacturers avoid that final obstacle is by putting something in it to kill the bacteria. Something good and strong is needed, something that will zap any accidentally intrudant bacteria into oblivion. And that something is formaldehyde—the disinfectant used in anatomy labs.

13   So it's chalk, water, paint, seaweed, anti-freeze, paraffin oil, detergent, peppermint, formaldehyde, and fluoride (which can go some ways towards preserving children's teeth)—that's the usual mixture raised to the mouth on the toothbrush for a fresh morning's clean. If it sounds too unfortunate, take heart. Studies show that thorough brushing with just plain water will often do as good a job.

From David Bodanis, *The Secret House*, pp. 10–15. Copyright © 2003 by David Bodanis. Reprinted with permission of the Carol Mann Agency.

COMPREHENSION CHECKUP

Short Answer

Directions: Answer the questions briefly.

1. What is the topic of the selection? _____

2. What is the selection's main idea? _____

   _____

3. List three details supporting the author's main idea. _____

   _____

   _____

Fact and Opinion

Directions: Determine whether the paragraph indicated is primarily one of fact (**F**) or opinion (**O**).

_____   4. Paragraph 3

_____   5. Paragraph 7

Directions: Identify each numbered sentence in the following paragraphs as either a fact (**F**) or an opinion (**O**).

(1) "With the glycol, ooze, and paraffin we're almost there." (2) "Only two major chemicals are left to make the refreshing, cleansing substance we know as toothpaste."

(3) "The ingredients so far are fine for cleaning, but they wouldn't make much of the satisfying foam we have come to expect in the morning brushing."

_____   6. Sentence 1

_____   7. Sentence 2

_____   8. Sentence 3

(1) "So it's chalk, water, paint, seaweed, anti-freeze, paraffin oil, detergent, peppermint, formaldehyde, and fluoride (which can go some ways towards preserving children's teeth)—that's the usual mixture raised to the mouth on the toothbrush for a fresh morning's clean." (2) "If it sounds too unfortunate, take heart. (3) Studies show that thorough brushing with just plain water will often do as good a job."

_____   9. Sentence 1

_____ 10. Sentence 2

_____ 11. Sentence 3

Directions: In each of the following sentences, underline the words that indicate an opinion.

12. "Only two major chemicals are left to make the refreshing, cleansing substance we know as toothpaste."

13. "Whipped in with the rest of the toothpaste, the manufacturers can sell it at a

neat and accountant-pleasing $4 per pound equivalent."

14. "Toothpaste manufacture is a very lucrative occupation."

Multiple Choice

Directions: For each item, write the letter corresponding to the best answer.

_____   1. The main ingredient in toothpaste is
    a. water.
    b. chalk.
    c. formaldehyde.
    d. none of the above.

_____   2. Which of the following is true, according to the selection?
    a. The chalk in toothpaste comes from long-dead ocean creatures.
    b. Toothpaste gels are healthier than regular paste.
    c. It's a good idea to brush after each meal.
    d. Children should be encouraged to chew gum to clean their teeth.

_____   3. From the selection, you could conclude that
    a. toothpaste contains only harmful ingredients.
    b. toothpaste contains only healthful ingredients.
    c. Toothpaste contains many unappetizing ingredients.
    d. Toothpaste contains lead and other metals.

_____   4. According to the selection, the enamel in teeth
    a. is very prone to yellowish stains.
    b. is water soluble.
    c. is the hardest substance in the body.
    d. should be scraped clean on a regular basis.

_____   5. According to information presented in the selection
    a. seaweed is added to toothpaste to create a refreshing taste.
    b. the chalk in toothpaste is unlike the kind children play with.

    c. titanium dioxide is found in Windex.

    d. detergent is added to toothpaste to create foam.

True or False

Directions: Indicate whether each statement is true or false by writing **T** or **F** in the space provided.

_____ 6. Formaldehyde is added to toothpaste to kill bacteria.

_____ 7. Peppermint oil is added to toothpaste to counter the taste of detergent and chalk.

_____ 8. Chalk particles may be responsible for creating holes in teeth.

_____ 9. Whitening agents added to toothpaste make teeth permanently white.

_____ 10. Toothpaste manufacturers add some ingredients to camouflage the taste of other ingredients.

Vocabulary in Context 1

Directions: Use the context clues from the paragraph indicated to determine the meaning of the italicized words. (Remember, no looking in the dictionary.)

1. Paragraph 1: *pressing*

    Definition: _____

2. Paragraph 2: *extruded*

    Definition: _____

3. Paragraph 2: *lucrative*

    Definition: _____

4. Paragraph 5: *unduly*

    Definition: _____

5. Paragraph 5: *cavernous*

    Definition: _____

6. Paragraph 6: *bobbing*

    Definition: _____

7. Paragraph 6: *soluble*

    Definition: _____

8. Paragraph 6: *reassuring*

    Definition: _____

9. Paragraph 7: *revolting*

    Definition: _____

10. Paragraph 10: *remedy*

    Definition: _____

11. Paragraph 10: *duplicate*

    Definition: _____

12. Paragraph 12: *immaculately*

    Definition: _____

Vocabulary in Context 2

Directions: Choose one of the following words to complete each of the sentences below. Use each word only once. Be sure to pay close attention to the context clues provided.

camouflage	eons	ingests	screen out
carnage	finicky	oblivion	thrive
concoction	gouging	savor	tout

1. No longer heard on the radio, many songs from the 1930s and 1940s have passed into _____.

2. If a child _____ poison, it may be necessary to induce vomiting.

3. Dinosaurs roamed the earth _____ ago.

4. Most house plants will _____ if they receive enough water and proper light.

5. The goal of the company was to _____ half of the applicants after the initial interview.

6 Using only the ingredients she had on hand, Stella created a savory _____ for dinner.

7. After winning the primary, the politician took time to _____ his success.

8. She was so _____ about her food that she ended up eating very little.

9. Many studies _____ the benefits of adding fluoride to toothpaste.

10. The army wanted to _____ the tanks with green and brown paint to help them blend into their surroundings.

11. The battle at Gettysburg resulted in dreadful _____ with thousands of soldiers killed or wounded.

12. The little children were _____ out enough sand on the beach to make a castle.

In Your Own Words

1. If you couldn't brush your teeth with toothpaste, how else would you do it?
2. Do you think the FDA should be more zealous in evaluating toothpaste and other products manufactured in foreign countries?
3. Would you be willing to brush your teeth with a foul-tasting substance if it had all-natural ingredients and would not harm your health?
4. What do you think the author's toward toothpaste attitude is? Do you think he uses toothpaste himself?

Written Assignment

Do you think it's a good idea to know more about the ingredients of everyday products? Write a paragraph giving your opinion.

Internet Activity

1. Try to find out who invented toothpaste or who first marketed it successfully. Use your favorite search engine to discover the facts, and write a brief paragraph summarizing your findings.

2. Toothpaste has a history that stretches back thousands of years. Do some research to determine what the ancient Egyptians and Chinese used to clean their teeth. Write a paragraph presenting a brief history.

Chapter Summary and Review

In Chapter 10, you learned how to tell the difference between fact and opinion. Based on the material in Chapter 10, answer the following.

Short Answer

Directions: Answer the following briefly.

1. Write three factual statements.

   a. _____

   b. _____

   c. _____

2. Write three opinion statements.

   a. _____

   b. _____

   c. _____

Vocabulary in Context

Directions: Choose one of the following words to complete the sentences below. Use each word only once.

fact	opinion	signal	value

3. *Perhaps, presumably,* and *apparently* are words that _____ a(n) _____.

4. It is a(n) _____ that the title of this book is *Reading and All That Jazz.*

5. If you said that *Titanic* was the best movie of all time, you would be making a(n)

   _____ judgment.

VOCABULARY   **Unit 6 Word Parts: Opposing Meanings**

TRIVIA QUESTION 1

Who invented the automobile? (Answer at the end of this unit.)

This unit begins with the word part *auto,* found in many English words. It then looks at word parts having opposing meanings, such as "over" and "under," and "same" and "different." The last section covers some words that are commonly confused.

auto—self or same

automobile	*Auto* means "self," so an *automobile* is a self-moving vehicle.
autograph	*Graph* means "write," and *auto* means "self," so an *autograph* is a person's own signature. The literal meaning is self-written.

automobile—The largest car is 100 feet long and has 26 wheels. Inside this limousine is a swimming pool with diving board and a king-sized bed.

automaton   Acting unthinkingly or automatically, like a robot. After the police officer had informed the Millers of their daughter's murder, the couple acted like *automatons* in making arrangements for her funeral.

autonomous   *Auto* means "self" and *nomos* means "law," so the literal meaning of *autonomous* is "self law." The word refers to self-government or being independent.   The United States is an *autonomous* country. Individual states in the United States are not totally *autonomous* because they are part of the United States. Are individual citizens in the United States *autonomous*?

co, com, con—with, together
contra—against; opposite

cooperate   To act or work together with another or others.

committee   A group of people chosen to work together on a particular matter.

consensus   Comes from *con* meaning "with" and *sentire* meaning "to think or feel." It refers to a thinking together or a general agreement.

compare   *Par* means "make equal," so if you *compare* two things, you are technically showing their similarities. But people, including college instructors, often use this word when they really mean to show similarities and differences. If one of your instructors asks you to do a *comparison,* find out whether the instructor wants you to show similarities only, or really wants you to show similarities and differences.

contrast   *Contra* means "against," so *contrast* means "to point out differences," or how one thing goes against another.

contradict   Comes from *contra* meaning "against" and *dict* meaning "say," as in *diction* and *predict.* The literal meaning of *contradict* is "say against." To *contradict* means "to deny the statement" of another person.

contraband   *Ban* originally meant "to officially forbid," so *contraband* means "to forbid against." Today it refers to something that is illegal to import or export.   Cocaine would be considered *contraband.*

extra—over; more than; beyond
ultra—over; more; beyond
infra—under, below, beneath

extramarital   Relating to a sexual relationship with someone other than one's spouse.

extraterrestrial *Terra* means "earth," so an *extraterrestrial* is a being from outside the earth's limits. The title character from the movie *E.T.* was an *extraterrestrial.* Scientists are actively searching for signs of *extraterrestrial* intelligence.

extrasensory   Some people believe that they have a power of perception beyond the normal senses. They credit this *extrasensory* perception, or ESP, for their ability to predict the future, read someone else's thoughts, or visualize an unknown event. For example, have you ever felt that something tragic has happened to a close friend, and it turned out you were right? That might be ESP. Scientists, though, are very skeptical about the validity of ESP.

ultraviolet	*Ultraviolet* light is above violet on the color spectrum. It is invisible because its wavelengths are too short. The ozone layer blocks most, but not all, of the harmful *ultraviolet* radiation, which is what causes sunburns.
ultramicroscope	An instrument that allows a person to see things too small to be seen by an ordinary microscope.
infrared	*Infrared* light is below red on the color spectrum. It is invisible because its wavelengths are too long for the human eye. The army uses *infrared* light to see at night. TV remote controls use *infrared* light.
infrastructure	The basic structure or underlying foundation of something. The *infrastructure* of a house is its foundation and framing. The *infrastructure* of a community is its roads, schools, power plants, and transportation and communication systems.

trans—across

transportation	*Port,* as in portable, port-a-potties, and import, means "to carry." So, *transportation* refers to the act of carrying something from one place to another.
transmission	*Mis,* as in missile and missionary, means "to send," so *transmission* means "the act of sending across." The *transmission* of a car sends energy from the engine across the drive shaft to the wheels. You can also *transmit* a message to another person by writing a letter, using e-mail, voice mail, or text messaging.
transsexual	A person who undergoes surgery and hormone treatments to change his or her sex. So, it could be said that a *transsexual* goes across sexual boundaries.
transvestite	A *transvestite* dresses in the clothing of the opposite sex. So, a *transvestite* dresses across sexual boundaries. If you can't remember the difference between this word and the one above, keep in mind that a vest is a piece of clothing. It comes from *vestire,* which means "to dress."

homo—same; equal; like
hetero—different

homosexual	Having sexual desire for the same sex.
heterosexual	Having sexual desire for the opposite sex.
homogeneous	The same in structure or quality; having similar parts. Your class is fairly *homogeneous* in terms of age if you are all of a comparable age.
heterogeneous	Dissimilar; composed of unlike parts. Your class may be *heterogeneous* because you come from different backgrounds, cultures, and countries.
homogenization	The *homogenization* process of milk mixes the fat particles of the cream evenly throughout so that the cream doesn't separate.

TRIVIA QUESTION 2

On what liquid did Pasteur conduct his initial experiments? (Answer at the end of this unit.)

In milk taken straight from the cow, the lighter cream rises to the top. This is different from the process of pasteurization, named after inventor Louis Pasteur, which uses heat to kill bacteria.

Here are some words that are often confused with one another. Though some may appear to use the word parts mentioned in this unit, they really do not.

compliment	Something said in praise; to make a nice remark about someone.
complement	That which completes or makes whole or perfect; to balance. The team plays well because the players *complement* each other; they fit together well. Steve needs to get his date a corsage that will *complement* the color of her dress.
supplement	Comes from *sub* meaning "under" and *plere* meaning "to fill," and refers to something added to make up for a lack. Physicians often prescribe vitamin *supplements* to pregnant women.
council	A group of people called together to make decisions, such as a city council.
counsel	A mutual exchange of ideas; to give or take advice.
consul	A government official appointed to live in a foreign country and look after his or her country's citizens who are in the foreign country. If you were in a foreign country and having passport problems, you might go to the U.S. *consulate* for help. If you are from another country, you may wish to visit your country's *consulate*.
continuous	Going on without any interruption; unbroken. Think of "ous" to help you remember the meaning of this word, as in "one uninterrupted sequence." The cars backed up in a *continuous* line on the freeway.
continual	Repeated often; over and over again but with interruptions. The weather forecaster predicted *continual* showers over the Labor Day weekend.

Exercise 1: Writing Sentences

Make up your own sentences using each of the following words:

complement _____

_____

homogeneous _____

_____

autonomous _____

_____

infrastructure _____

_____

continuous _____

_____

extrasensory _____

_____

automaton _____

_____

ANSWER TO TRIVIA QUESTION 1

Henry Ford did not invent the automobile; rather, his contribution was to mass-produce it. The two persons commonly given much credit for the invention of the automobile are the German engineers Gottlieb Daimler and Karl Benz.

ANSWER TO TRIVIA QUESTION 2

Pasteur conducted his original experiments on beer. Most of our beer is pasteurized. Nonpasteurized beer, such as keg beer, needs to be kept cold to prevent the growth of bacteria.

Exercise 2 Word Parts: Opposing Meanings

Directions: In the blanks below, write the word from the list that best completes the sentence. Use each word only once.

autograph	automaton	committee	compare	complement
consul	contraband	extramarital	heterogeneous	homogeneous

1. After Duy's daughter was killed in a drive-by shooting, he performed his job like a(n) _____, just going through the motions.

2. To address morale problems in the school district, a(n) _____ was formed composed of teachers, parents, administrators, and students.

3. Many educators believe that a national test in reading and math is needed so that people can _____ student performance in their state with what is happening in other states.

4. Many major league baseball stars will only sign a(n) _____ for a child.

5. Drug traffickers often use "mules" to transport _____ into the United States.

6. People who form successful partnerships often have individual traits that _____ each other.

7. Stranded in Brazil with no money and no passport, Kathleen sought help from the U.S. _____.

8. In the workplace today, diversity is widespread, creating a(n) _____ mix of people and ideas.

9. In the past few years, the media has often exposed the _____ affairs of leading political candidates.

10. A high school composed solely of Catholic boys age 14–18 would have a(n) _____ student body.

Exercise 3 Word Parts: More Opposing Meanings

Directions: In the blanks below, write the word from the list that best completes the sentence. Use each word only once.

autonomous	complimented	consensus	continual	continuously
contradict	council	counsel	extraterrestrials	supplement

1. We all _____ my daughter-in-law, Bonnie, and her friend, Kathleen, on the outstanding meal they had prepared.

2. The teacher was not going to be able to attend class on Monday. She told her students that if they could achieve a(n) _____ about doing an extra assignment, she would agree to cancel class. Otherwise, she would have to get a substitute.

3. Betsy, a battered wife, sought _____ on how to get a restraining order against her husband.

4. The city _____ passed an ordinance requiring those under the age of 18 to be home by 10:00 P.M. on weekdays and by midnight on weekends.

5. While working at the preschool with the two- and three-year olds, Elvira had a(n) _____ headache.

6. The Colorado River flows _____.

7. If Bart wanted to be completely _____ and his own man, why did he call his parents every Sunday asking for money?

8. A president needs to have advisors willing to _____ him. It is not a good idea for him to be surrounded by a bunch of "yes men."

9. Many police officers _____ their incomes by working in department stores as security guards on their days off.

10. He won an award for his science fiction story about _____ on Mars.

Vocabulary Unit 6 Crossword

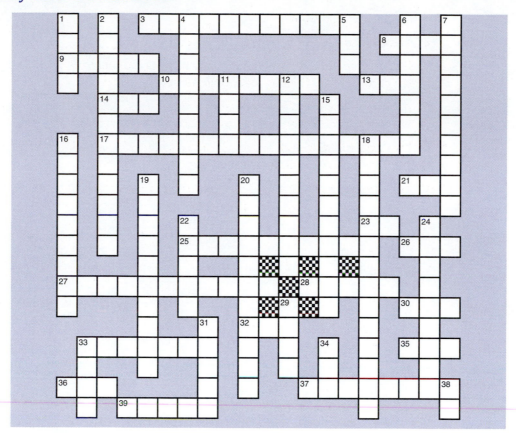

ACROSS CLUES

3. A person who has had a sex change operation.
8. A word part meaning "same."
9. A word part meaning "across."
10. To point out differences.
13. A word part meaning "around."
14. A word part meaning "below."
17. E.T.
21. An abbreviation for what was once the 10th month.
23. A word part meaning "toward."
25. Your state is not _____ because it is part of the United States.
26. A word part meaning "two."
27. _____ milk has been heated to kill bacteria.
28. A word part meaning "back."
30. An abbreviation for what was once the 8th month.
32. A word part meaning "year."
33. A group called together for discussion.
35. A word part meaning "see."
36. A word part meaning "three."
37. _____ light has wavelengths longer than ordinary light.
39. A word part meaning "over, more, beyond."

DOWN CLUES

1. A word part meaning "self."
2. A person who wears the clothing of the opposite sex.
4. Self-written.
5. A word part meaning "side."
6. To give advice.
7. To deny the statement of someone.
11. A word part meaning "distance."
12. A person who directs work or workers.
15. Light that causes sunburn.
16. The chemical formula for water has a(n) _____ in it.
18. The foundation and frame of a building.
19. That which completes; to balance.
20. In a(n) _____ group, the members are alike.
22. A word part meaning "large."
24. To sign your name at the bottom of a document.
29. A word part meaning "before."
31. A word part meaning "more or over."
33. A word part meaning "around."
34. A word part meaning "with."
38. A word part meaning "two."

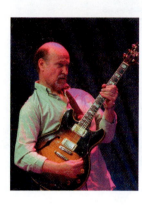

CHAPTER PREVIEW
In this chapter, you will

- Learn to distinguish between denotative and connotative meanings.

- Learn to identify positive and negative connotations.

- Learn to recognize an author's personal bias.

- Develop familiarity with writing that has a biased viewpoint.

Introduction to Bias

In the previous chapter, we learned how important it is to be able to distinguish between fact and opinion. In order to be a critical reader, we also need to be aware of our biases and the biases of others. A **bias** is defined as a strong leaning in either a positive or a negative direction.

Authors have biases, and it is the critical reader's job to discover what they are. A careful reader will study the author's line of reasoning, notice whether opinions have been supported by facts and reasons, and then decide if the author's bias has prevented the making of a good argument.

In the drawing "The Investigation" on the next page, the suspect in the investigation is in the center. Each of the individuals (and the Martian life-form?) briefly describes the suspect's appearance and gives his or her point of view. **Point of view** is defined as an opinion, attitude, or judgment on the part of an individual.

Notice how the descriptions they give the interviewer reflect their personal biases. Can you list some of these biases? Now read the essay "The Defendant's Characteristics" while noting the effect bias can have on legal judgments.

John Jonik. Reprinted with permission.

READING

> *"There is a physical attractiveness stereotype:*
> *Beautiful people seem like good people."*

TUNING IN TO READING

Have you ever served on a jury? Did you enjoy the experience? Can you think of any instances when a jury verdict was not popular with the public? Was the defendant found guilty or not guilty? Can you explain the difference between popular perception and the verdict?

BIO-SKETCH

David G. Myers is an active writer with many articles and books to his credit, including the textbook *Social Psychology,* from which this excerpt is taken. He is the John Dirk Werkman Professor of Psychology at Hope University in Michigan.

NOTES ON VOCABULARY

Clarence Darrow   a lawyer known for his legal writings and for his defense of unpopular causes in the late 19th and early 20th centuries. Darrow was the defense attorney in the famous *Scopes* trial of 1925. John Scopes, a high school biology teacher, was arrested for teaching the theory of evolution to his students. Although

Scopes was eventually found guilty and had to pay a $100 fine, Darrow was considered to be the winner in the trial.

Cicero   a famous orator and statesman who lived in Rome from 106 B.C. to 43 B.C. He is known as one of ancient Rome's finest writers of prose. Many of his essays on philosophy are based on the works of Aristotle and Plato.

The Defendant's Characteristics

David G. Myers

According to the famed trial attorney Clarence Darrow, jurors seldom convict a person they like or acquit one they dislike. He argued that the main job of the trial attorney is to make the jury like the defendant. Was he right? And is it true, as Darrow also said, that "facts regarding the crime are relatively unimportant"?

2   Darrow overstated the case. One study of more than 3,500 criminal cases and some 4,000 civil cases found that 4 times in 5 the judge agreed with the jury's decision. Although both may have been wrong, the evidence usually is clear enough that jurors can set aside their biases, focus on the facts, and agree on a verdict. Darrow was too cynical; facts do matter.

3   Nevertheless, when jurors are asked to make social judgments—would *this* defendant commit *this* offense? intentionally?—facts are not all that matter. Communicators are more persuasive if they seem credible and attractive. Jurors cannot help forming impressions of the defendant. Can they put these impressions aside and decide the case based on the facts alone? To judge from the more lenient treatment often received by high-status defendants it seems that some cultural bias lingers. But actual cases vary in so many ways—in the type of crime, in the status, age, gender, and race of the defendant—that it's hard to isolate the factors that influence jurors. So experimenters have controlled such factors by giving mock jurors the same basic facts of a case while varying, say, the defendant's attractiveness or similarity to the jurors.

4   There is a physical attractiveness stereotype: Beautiful people seem like good people. Michael Efran wondered whether this stereotype would bias students' judgments of someone accused of cheating. He asked some of his University of Toronto students whether attractiveness should affect presumption of guilt. They answered: "No, it shouldn't." But did it? Yes. When Efran gave other students a description of the case with a photograph of either an attractive or an unattractive defendant, they judged the most attractive as least guilty and recommended that person for the least punishment.

5   To see if these findings extend to the real world, Chris Downs and Phillip Lyons asked police escorts to rate the physical attractiveness of 1,742 defendants appearing before 40 Texas judges in misdemeanor cases. Whether the misdemeanor was serious (such as forgery), moderate (such as harassment), or minor (such as public intoxication), the judges set higher bails and fines for less-attractive defendants. What explains this dramatic effect? Are unattractive people also lower in status? Are they indeed more likely to flee or to commit crime, as the judges perhaps suppose? Or do judges simply ignore the Roman statesman Cicero's advice: "The final good and the supreme duty of the wise man is to resist appearance."

6   If Clarence Darrow was even partly right in his declaration that liking or disliking a defendant colors judgments, then other factors that influence liking should also matter. Among such influences is the principle that likeness (similarity) leads to liking. When people pretend they are jurors, they are indeed more sympathetic

to a defendant who shares their attitudes, religion, race, or (in cases of sexual assault) gender. For example, when Cookie Stephan and Walter Stephan had English-speaking people judge someone accused of assault, they were more likely to think the person not guilty if the defendant's testimony was in English, rather than translated from Spanish or Thai.

7   So it seems we are more sympathetic toward a defendant with whom we can identify. If we think *we* wouldn't have committed that criminal act, we may assume that someone like us is also unlikely to have done it.

8   Ideally, jurors would leave their biases outside the courtroom and begin a trial with open minds. So implies the Sixth Amendment to the U.S. Constitution: "The accused shall enjoy the right to a speedy and public trial by impartial jury." In its concern for objectivity, the judicial system is similar to science: Both scientists and jurors are supposed to sift and weigh the evidence. Both the courts and science have rules about what evidence is relevant. Both keep careful records and assume that others given the same evidence would decide similarly.

9   When the evidence is clear and jurors focus on it, their biases are indeed minimal. The quality of the evidence matters more than the prejudices of the individual jurors.

From David G. Myers, *Social Psychology*, 9th Edition, pp. 555–58. Copyright © 2008 by The McGraw-Hill Companies, Inc. Reprinted with permission.

 COMPREHENSION CHECKUP

Multiple Choice

Directions: For each item, write the letter corresponding to the best answer.

_____ 1. The main idea expressed in this selection is that
    a. jurors can be influenced by the physical appearance and actions of a defendant.
    b. jurors are unlikely to pay attention to the physical characteristics of a defendant.
    c. in Texas, judges were affected by the attractiveness of the defendants.
    d. jurors are unlikely to be sympathetic to those who are like them.

_____ 2. Paragraph 2 contains the following statement: "Darrow overstated the case." This is a statement of
    a. fact.
    b. opinion.

_____ 3. As used in paragraph 3, the word *credible* means
    a. easily deceived.
    b. believable.
    c. childish.
    d. doubtful.

_____ 4. In paragraph 4, the example of Efran's University of Toronto students was used to illustrate that
    a. attractive people receive more lenient sentences in court.
    b. the way we treat attractive and unattractive people shapes the way they think about themselves.
    c. attractive people are thought to be less likely to have committed a crime.

_____ 5. In paragraph 5, the author helps readers understand the different types of misdemeanors by providing
    a. definitions.
    b. examples.

   c. cause-and-effect relationships.
   d. chronological order.

_____ 6. Based on Cicero's statement, readers can conclude that he would advise
jurors to
   a. carefully consider the appearance of the defendant during jury
      deliberations.
   b. disregard the appearance of the defendant during jury deliberations.

_____ 7. Paragraph 8 contains the following statement: "Ideally, jurors would
leave their biases outside the courtroom and begin a trial with open
minds." This is a statement of
   a. fact.
   b. opinion.

_____ 8. The mode of writing used in this selection is
   a. narrative.
   b. descriptive.
   c. expository.
   d. persuasive.

Short Answer

Directions: Answer the following questions briefly.

1. According to the selection, what are some biases that can affect a jury's ability to

   reach a fair decision? _____

   _____.

2. What key point made by famed trial attorney Clarence Darrow is illustrated by

   this cartoon? _____.

THE FAR SIDE®   By GARY LARSON

"And so I ask the jury—is that the face of a
mass murderer?"

3. According to the context clues in paragraph 2, what does the word *cynical* mean? "Darrow was too *cynical;* facts do matter."

   Cynical means ___mean___ ___hurtful_____.

4. In paragraph 3, what does the transition word *nevertheless* signal?

   Nevertheless signals ___don't forget_____.

5. According to the context clues in paragraph 6, what does the word *colors* mean? "If Clarence Darrow was even partly right in his declaration that liking or disliking a defendant *colors* judgments . . ."

   Colors means ___diff people skin tone_____.

6. What two things are being compared in paragraph 8?

   ___sustain system___ and ___science_____.

7. According to the context clues in paragraph 8, what does the word *objectivity* mean?

   "In its concern for *objectivity* . . ."

   Objectivity means ___Judgment Based on observable___.

Denotation and Connotation

When you look up a word in your dictionary, you are determining its **denotation,** or dictionary meaning. However, words also have **connotations,** or meanings beyond simple dictionary definitions. These words carry an extra emotional "charge." We can think of these words as being positive, negative, or neutral.

For example, even though the words *thin, slender,* and *skinny* all have similar dictionary definitions, they have different connotative meanings. Most of us think *slender* has a positive connotation and *skinny* a negative one. *Thin* has a more neutral meaning. In using words that have connotative meanings, we reveal our personal biases.

Authors can do exactly the same thing as speakers by choosing one particular word over another. If an author begins a novel by referring to the title character as someone who is *thrifty,* what picture of that person comes to your mind? How about if the author refers to the title character as *cheap* or *stingy?*

In the following cartoon, the word *problems* and the word *challenges* have very similar denotative meanings. However, as the son points out to his dad, they have very different connotative meanings.

One Big Happy

(One Big Happy) © 1998 Creators Syndicate, Inc. By permission of Rick Detorie and Creators Syndicate, Inc.

Exercise 1: Spotting Biased Words

Directions: Read the following comments from a parent–teacher conference and, for each word pair, circle the word with the most positive connotation.

I am very proud of Tommy and his *diligent / plodding* effort to improve his arithmetic grade. He does seem to have a(n) *self-confident / arrogant* approach toward the work at this grade level. However, he is not placing enough emphasis on producing quality homework. It is done in a(n) *sloppy / untidy* way. In general, he is a very *able / gifted* child. He does, however, need to improve his social and emotional conduct. His contributions to the class are made in a(n) *enthusiastic / hyperactive* way, and he is sometimes *rude / insensitive* in his comments to others. He does seem *eager / willing* to participate in most activities in the classroom, but he needs to learn to do so in a less *assertive / aggressive* manner. On the playground and in his relations with his peers, he is often *shy / reserved*, but he is beginning to be asked to enter into new activities. I enjoy having Tommy in my room and I hope we can make the rest of the year a pleasant one.

Exercise 2: Positive and Negative Connotation

Directions: Below are two versions of the same speech. One uses positive words to favor Senator X and the other uses words slanted against him. Read both speeches and circle all of the biased words or phrases. Then rewrite the speech as a neutral observer reporting only facts rather than giving opinions or making value judgments. As a guideline answer *who, what, where, when, why,* and *how* questions. Be careful not to substitute your own biased words for the ones you eliminate.

In Favor of Senator X

In a well-reasoned statement to an admiring audience, the dignified and courtly Senator X today forcefully argued for his proposal to limit violence in the media. The auditorium filled with laughter as the esteemed senator showed his trademark dry wit. By disarming the opposition, it looks like the senator will emerge triumphant and his insightful proposal will carry the day.

Against Senator X

In his usual dour style, the aging Senator X today sought to persuade the crowd in the auditorium to accept his proposal to limit violence in the media. The audience, clearly repulsed by his crude, cynical attempts at humor, appeared to be laughing more at the senator than with him. Frightened by his threats, the opposition will probably be goaded into backing his program.

Neutral Version

_____

_____

_____

_____

_____

Euphemisms

When we substitute inoffensive words or phrases for ones that are likely to offend someone, we are using **euphemisms.** Generally, we use euphemisms to be polite or to avoid controversy. For example, a euphemism like "passed away" might be substituted for the word "died."

The use of euphemisms to purposely mislead others and obscure the truth is called **doublespeak.** In the working world, layoffs have become commonplace, but because the word "layoff" has a negative connotation, many new euphemisms have been created both to appease the person being fired and to mislead the general public. Thus, when a company fires a large group of workers and announces a "force reduction program," they are guilty of doublespeak. Read the following information on doublespeak and inflated language from Hamilton Gregory's *Public Speaking for College and Career.*

Beware of Doublespeak

When some federal and state legislators raise taxes, they don't refer to their action as "raising taxes." To do so might anger taxpayers. No, timidly and sneakily, they say they voted for "revenue enhancement."

"Revenue enhancement" is an example of **doublespeak.** Here are some additional examples:

- After one of its planes crashed, National Airlines described the event—in its annual report to stockholders—as an "involuntary conversion of a 727," a legal term designed to conceal the truth.
- When politicians in Washington, DC, slashed funding for national parks in 2004, they asked park superintendents to call the budget cuts "service level adjustments."
- A British teachers' association campaigned to ban the word "fail" from classrooms, saying that it was demoralizing to students. Instead, they argued, teachers should use the term "deferred success."

Euphemisms become harmful when they mask a problem that should be dealt with. When homeless people are called "urban nomads," does this romantic euphemism cause the public to turn its eyes from a problem that needs attention?

The best advice is this: Use euphemisms if tact and kindness require them, and avoid them if they serve to deceive or confuse.

In his book *The New Doublespeak,* William Lutz discusses another type of doublespeak called **inflated language.** Lutz says, "inflated language is designed to make the ordinary seem extraordinary; to make everyday things seem impressive; to give an air of importance to people, situations, or things that would not normally be considered important." For example:

- A used car is advertised as a *preowned car* or *pre-enjoyed automobile.*
- A clothing store calls its salespeople *wardrobe consultants.*
- A national pizza delivery chain announces that its drivers will henceforth be known as *delivery ambassadors.*

Some inflated language seems harmless. If garbage collectors prefer to be called *sanitation engineers,* most people will not criticize too strenuously. If they believe that the term dignifies their valuable but unglamorous work, most won't object to the use of the term. But the problem is that inflated language is spreading rapidly into all areas of life, causing misunderstanding and confusion. If you saw an advertisement for a *grief therapist,* wouldn't you envision a counselor for a mourning individual whose loved one has just died? If so, you'd be wrong, because *grief therapist* is an inflated term for an undertaker. How are we to know that an *excavation technician* is a ditch digger? That a *communications monitor* is a switchboard operator? That a *customer engineer* is a salesperson? That a *corrosion control specialist* is the person who sends your car through a car wash?

An inflated term may begin in kindness, but it often ends in confusion. Avoid its use unless you know that it is clearly understood. In other words call a spade a spade—unless you are military personnel who prefer the official name *entrenching tool.*

From Hamilton Gregory, *Public Speaking for College and Career,* 8th Edition, pp. 285–86. Copyright © 2008 by The McGraw-Hill Companies, Inc. Reprinted with permission.

Note: William Lutz suggests that people fight doublespeak by becoming "first-rate crap detectors." One way to accomplish this is to start collecting and trading examples of doublespeak. Try to bring in examples to your class on a topic like the economy, unemployment, or foreign aid.

The *Far Side* cartoon below shows a "swamp thing" that would rather be referred to as a "wetlands-challenged mutant" because it has a more positive connotation. Is this an example of doublespeak or inflated language?

THE FAR SIDE By GARY LARSON

"Well, actually, Doreen, I rather resent being called a 'swamp thing.' ... I prefer the term 'wetlands-challenged mutant.'"

Exercise 1: Euphemisms

Directions: Give euphemisms for each of the following words or phrases.

1. older person ___ senior citizen ___
2. toilet ___ restroom ___
3. drunk ___ intoxicated. ___
4. pregnant ___
5. lazy ___ unmovited ___
6. pornography ___

Directions: Turn these euphemistic words or phrases into regular words.

1. to be temporarily without funds ___
2. lingerie ___
3. cemetery ___
4. mixed-breed dog ___
5. preowned vehicle ___
6. chemically dependent ___
7. to misappropriate the company's funds ___
8. night club ___
9. telemarketing ___
10. to score below average on a test ___
11. vertically challenged ___
12. to stretch the truth somewhat ___
13. learning resources center ___
14. to depart from this life ___

Exercise 2: Detecting Bias in Magazines and Newspapers

Directions: For each passage, write the letter corresponding to words that suggest the writer's bias on the line provided.

___ 1.   Citizenship today is in a precarious state. Citizen involvement in community and government has been declining. Government responsiveness to citizens may also be on the wane. Some scholars believe the reciprocal bonds of citizenship are fraying. Although we believe that the low level of citizen involvement in government today gives us cause for concern about the health of our democracy, we are not overly pessimistic. Once we understand the reasons for low levels of participation and open a dialogue about how we might change this relationship for the better, we can do something about it.

From Joseph Losco, *AM GOV*. New York: McGraw-Hill, 2008, p. 2.

a. health, overly, understand, citizen
b. reciprocal, involvement, state, responsiveness
c. precarious, wane, fraying, declining

_____ 2.   Who ever would have thought that good old PB&J could be a health hazard? Sad but true: the peanut-butter-and-jelly sandwich is under assault, along with its cousin the fluffer nutter, the peanut-butter cracker, the Reese's Piece, the peanut M&M and all the other delectable forms the humble peanut comes in. At the Breck School in Minneapolis, PB&J sandwiches must now be eaten at separate tables. The Bradstreet Early Childhood Center in North Andover, Massachusetts, is one of many kindergartens to have created peanut-free classrooms this fall, and the Trinity School in New York City has expelled all forms of the peanut from the premises. Why the frenzy over goobers? Because 1 percent of American children are now estimated to have a peanut allergy.

From John Sedgwick, "Goodbye to the Goober," *Newsweek*, October 14, 1996. Reprinted by permission of International Creative Management, Inc. Copyright © 1996 by John Sedgwick for Newsweek.

   a. hazard, sad, expelled, frenzy, assault
   b. goobers, separate, peanut-free, premises
   c. cracker, estimated, allergy, health

_____ 3.   Any work is potentially censorable by someone, someplace, sometime, for some reason. Nothing is permanently safe from censorship, not even most books most teachers and librarians would regard as far removed from censorial eyes—not *Hamlet, Julius Caesar, Treasure Island*, or anything else. If one book is removed from a classroom or library, no book is safe any longer. If a censor succeeds in getting one book out, every other person in the community who objects to another book should, in courtesy, be granted the same privilege. When everyone has walked out of the library carrying all those objectionable books, nothing of any consequence will be left no matter how many books remain. Some books are certain to offend some people and be ardently defended by others. Indeed, every library has books offensive to someone, maybe everyone. After all, ideas do offend many people.

From Alleen Pace Nilsen and Kenneth L. Donelson, *Literature for Today's Young Adults*, 8th Edition. Boston: Pearson, 2009, pp. 394–95.

   a. offend, offensive, objectionable, censorship
   b. courtesy, granted, someplace, potentially
   c. classroom, library, removed, reason

_____ 4.   There was blood, sweat, and a puddle of tears on kitchen tables across America this morning, the detritus of a long afternoon, stretching into evening, of yesterday's homework. Sure, some students probably whipped out their perfectly organized assignment pad, did each task cheerfully and finished with time to spare for reading, television, or play. We just don't know any. Something that infuriates parents, sabotages family time, and crowds out so much else in a child's life might be tolerable if it also helped kids learn and if it imbued them with good study habits and a lifelong love of learning. Unfortunately, "for elementary-school students the effect of homework on achievement is trivial, if it exists at all," concludes psychologist Harris Cooper of the University of Missouri, whose analysis of more than 100 studies has stood up for 10 years.

From Sharon Begley, "Homework Doesn't Help." From *Newsweek*, March 30, 1998. © 1998 Newsweek, Inc. All rights reserved. Used by permission and protected by the Copyright Laws of the United States. The printing, copying, redistribution, or retransmission of the Material without express written permission is prohibited. www.newsweek.com

   a. infuriates, sabotages, crowds out, trivial
   b. puddle, learning, imbued, exists
   c. analysis, sweat, task, family

_b_ 5.   Querulous, funny, serious, playful, fearless, caring, and curious—the roadrunner sports a jaunty outlook wrapped in a bundle of tan, white, black, and metallic bronze. The roadrunner earned its name when settlers traveling westward first discovered that this odd, vivacious bird liked to race their wagons. But Mexicans were calling the bird *corre camino* ("it runs the road") long before Europeans settled the lands in the southwestern United States. It measures just 22 to 24 inches in length—half of which is tail—but has earned quite a reputation and many names from many cultures. In Texas, it goes by the name "chaparral cock," in New Mexico it's known as "snake eater," and in Mexico it's dubbed *paisano* ("compatriot" or "countryman"). Confident and crowned with a feather crest, the roadrunner earns king-of-the-road bragging rights. So swift of foot that it rarely takes flight, this clever member of the cuckoo family snatches airborne insects and smaller birds with leaps up to 6 feet in the air.

From Carrie M. Miner, "Roadrunner Facts & Fantasy," *Arizona Highways*, April 2001, p. 16.

a. jaunty, vivacious, confident, clever
(b.) wrapped, reputation, names, dubbed
c. outlook, metallic, crest, rights

 6.   White-coated experts at the Faster Living Institute, alarmed by a nationwide study that showed the average American constantly running behind schedule, have just announced the results of their drive to isolate the cause and find a solution. Where does all the time go? It's stolen, is the institute's shocking answer, by our own medicine chests and the obsolete nineteenth-century medication-taking process. "Don't let that innocent-looking little bathroom cabinet fool you," says one college-trained researcher. "It's a diabolical time trap. You can finally stop torturing yourself about always running late when you realize that two minutes per day, fourteen minutes per week, fifty-six minutes per month, or twelve hours per year, are wasted in finding, selecting, uncapping, and ingesting medication."

From Bruce McCall, "Hurry-Up Experts Say Medicine Chest Doomed," *My Generation*, May–June 2001, p. 14.

a. white-coated, constantly, isolate
(b.) stolen, shocking, diabolical
c. nationwide, average, ingesting

_____ 7.   The taunts from the parents and the coaches always got to him. They rained like showers of sparks from the sidelines: Get your fat body down the field. You're blind. You're just doing this for the money. Last summer, Mr. Lazarevic, who has worked for 18 years as a referee in basketball, soccer, and baseball in suburban Chicago, hung up his whistle. "When people started saying personal things about me, about what I was as a person, I decided it was time to get out," he said. Mr. Lazarevic, a 32-year-old middle school science teacher, is among thousands of referees who have left high school and youth sports in recent years because of poor sportsmanship on the part of spectators, said Bob Still, a spokesman for the National Association of Sports Officials. But that is only one of the many results of what players, coaches, scholars, and sports psychologists say is a rising tide of misbehavior at high school and youth sports especially among adult spectators. Some call it "sideline rage." From hockey arenas in Maine to soccer fields in New Mexico, parents and amateur coaches are yelling and jeering—even spitting and brawling—as never before, experts say.

a. sparks, personal, thousands, sportsmanship
b. taunts, misbehavior, rage, jeering
c. spectators, tide, amateur, experts

Exercise 3: Detecting Bias: "Who Gets In?"

The college can admit only 5 more students. As a member of the board, it is your responsibility to rank the 10 students listed below according to who most deserves to be accepted. Descriptions of their precollege situation and performance are given.

In your group, keep in mind the following factors as you select the **5** you consider the most deserving:

1. The person's potential, abilities, or capabilities
2. The person's motivation to perform
3. The probability of successful completion of a college education

Your group must be in complete agreement about your choices. After selecting your 5, write a brief sentence or two explaining the rationale for your choices. When everyone has completed the assignment, the group leader should write the selections on the board. Be prepared to defend your selections to the rest of the class.

L'Tisha

Very intelligent; senior class valedictorian; has won awards in the National Science Fair for exhibits; has definite plans to major in chemistry; high school counselor says she has difficulty relating to others; she was involved in several disputes with high school classmates over chemistry experiments.

Julio

An all-state center in high school; plans to play college basketball and would help the team; scored poorly on the college admittance test although his high school grades were average; plans to become a physical therapist.

Jill

Ranked in the middle of her graduating class; did well in high school math; has good study habits; high school counselor says she has interfering, confrontational parents.

Carolyn

A divorced mother with two children; 24 years old, trying to return to college to continue her education after dropping out six years ago; works and raises her family; no financial support from her former husband; will need financial aid; wishes to become an elementary schoolteacher.

Dominique

An applicant from Venezuela; has already earned a degree in her own country; did very well academically; she wants to enroll to experience our lifestyle and perfect her English; not interested in any specific subject; plans to return home.

Juan Carlos

High school counselor says he is outgoing and well-liked among his peers; poor grades; studied little in high school and has poor study skills; test results reveal a very high IQ.

Howard

Ranked in the top 5 percent of his graduating class; high school counselor says he is a loner who lacks social skills; had no extracurricular activities in high school; has a great deal of academic potential; wants to be a doctor like his father.

Jiao

Had attendance problems in high school; grades were mediocre; worked in excess of 40 hours a week; IQ in gifted range; will need financial aid.

Evelyn

She is 58 years old; worked in a day care center for the past 15 years; prior to that she was a housewife and mother; wants to earn a degree in child psychology; high test scores.

Dakin

Average grades; works 28 hours a week to pay for his education; is aiming for a degree in engineering; high potential in math; a very hard worker.

From David B. Ellis, *Becoming a Master Student: Course Manual*, 7th Edition. © 1994 Wadsworth, a part of Cengage Learning, Inc. Reproduced by permission. www.cengage.com/permissions

Exercise 4: Point of View

This story by Katherine Brush is told from the point of view of an observer seated in a restaurant watching the action unfold.

A Birthday Party

They were a couple in their late thirties, and they looked unmistakably married. They sat on the banquette opposite us in a little narrow restaurant, having dinner. The man had a round, self-satisfied face, with glasses on it; the woman was fadingly pretty, in a big hat. There was nothing conspicuous about them, nothing particularly noticeable, until the end of their meal, when it suddenly became obvious that this was an Occasion—in fact, the husband's birthday, and the wife had planned a little surprise for him.

It arrived, in the form of a small but glossy birthday cake, with one pink candle burning in the center. The headwaiter brought it in and placed it before the husband, and meanwhile the violin-and-piano orchestra played "Happy Birthday to You" and the wife beamed with shy pride over her little surprise, and such few people as there were in the restaurant tried to help out with a pattering of applause. It became clear at once that help was needed, because the husband was not pleased. Instead he was hotly embarrassed, and indignant at his wife for embarrassing him.

You looked at him and you saw this and you thought, "Oh now don't *be* like that!" But he was like that, and as soon as the little cake had been deposited on the table, and the orchestra had finished the birthday piece, and the general attention had shifted from the man and the woman, I saw him say something to her under his breath—some punishing thing, quick and curt and unkind. I couldn't bear to look at the woman then, so I stared at my plate and waited for quite a long time. Not long enough, though. She was still crying when I finally glanced over there again. Crying quietly and heartbrokenly and hopelessly, all to herself, under the gay big brim of her best hat.

Katherine Brush, "A Birthday Party." Copyright © 1946 Condé Nast Publications. All rights reserved. Originally published in *The New Yorker,* March 16, 1946. Reprinted by permission.

After reading the story, most people feel that the narrator is clearly sympathetic to the wife's feelings and is solely representing the wife's point of view. But is this true? Try reading the story again looking at the situation from the husband's perspective. The narrator indirectly tells the reader a great deal about these particular characters and their relationship to each other. Look specifically at the details of physical description that are given.

In Your Own Words

1. Why is the wife who is "fadingly pretty" wearing a "big hat" in a "little, narrow restaurant"?
2. Why does the narrator note that they "looked unmistakably married"? Should the wife have been aware of the type of surprise her husband would have enjoyed?
3. What does it say about the husband that he waits until the "general attention had shifted" before he says "some punishing thing" to her "under his breath"?
4. The narrator states that he/she waited "quite a long time," and yet the woman continued "crying quietly and heartbrokenly and hopelessly." Is there another more appropriate action that the wife could have taken? What is her crying in a public place likely to do?
5. Do you think the "one pink candle" suggests for whom the wife really planned the surprise? Which of the two is more likely to enjoy this type of attention?
6. The author reveals her point of view by the words she chose to use to tell the story. What is the author's point of view about the birthday party? Is she sympathetic toward the husband or the wife? Or both?

Exercise 5: Detecting Bias—Sex-Based Words

A. Each word or phrase below is usually associated with only one sex. Using your knowledge of cultural history, determine why these phrases are associated with one sex but not with the other.

Feminine Based	Masculine Based
1. mother nature _____	1. old man winter _____
2. black widow spider _____	2. daddy longlegs spider _____
3. lazy Susan serving tray _____	3. LA-Z-BOY lounging chair _____
4. *The Clarissa* (clipper ship) _____	4. man-of-war (battleship) _____
5. the statue of justice _____	5. a father of modern science _____
6. a ladybug _____	

THE FAMILY CIRCUS. By Bil Keane

2-5
©2001 Bil Keane, Inc.
Dist. by King Features Synd.
www.familycircus.com

"How come we don't hear anything about FATHER Nature?"

© Bil Keane, Inc. King Features Syndicate.

Write a general statement about your findings.

_____

_____

B. The (animal) words listed below are nearly always associated with one sex or the other. Mark **M** for the terms you would most likely use with males and **F** for terms you would most likely use with females. See if you can come to any conclusions as to how the two lists differ and what they show about cultural expectations for males and females.

_M_ 1. a beast	_M_ 1. to be mousy
_F_ 2. a bird	_M_ 2. a rat
_M_ 3. to be bullheaded	_M_ 3. a loan shark
_F_ 4. a social butterfly	_F_ 4. a fox
_F_ 5. to be catty	_M_ 5. a tiger
_F_ 6. a chick	_F_ 6. a tigress
_M_ 7. a donkey	_F_ 7. a vixen
_F_ 8. to be kittenish	_M_ 8. a vulture
_M_ 9. a hog	_M_ 9. a wolf
_F_ 10. a lamb	_F_ 10. doe eyes

Conclusions: _____

_____

_____

C. Change the following "man words" to "gender-inclusive" alternatives.

Example: congressman—congressional representative

Herman

"We're living in very strange times, Martha."

1. mankind _Humans_
2. manmade _People_
3. the best man for the job _best person_
4. man-hours _People hours_
5. foreman _fore person_
6. businessman _business person_
7. salesman _sales person_
8. mailman _mail driver_
9. insurance man _insurance company_
10. fireman _fire fighter_
11. cameraman _camera person_
12. freshman _first year_
13. manpower _someone strong_
14. man-sized job _Big job_
15. sportsmanship _better player_

D. Change the following "female words" to "gender-inclusive" alternatives.

1. cleaning lady _house keeper_
2. housewife _stay at home spous_
3. ladylike _kind like_

E. Change the following titles, used to distinguish female workers from males, to neutral terms for both men and women.

1. lady doctor _doctor_
2. stewardess _host_
3. policewoman _Police_
4. waitress _waitering_

F. What is the problem with using language that is sexist or biased?
People want to be treted equiley.

Adapted from material by Alleen Pace Nilsen, *Changing Words in a Changing World*. Washington, DC: Women's Educational Equity Act Program, U.S. Department of Education, 1980, pp. 40, 55.

Exercise 6: Bias in Publications

Directions: Study the list of publications and the given topic. Would you expect the publication to be biased or objective (neutral) on this particular topic? Write an **O** for objective or a **B** for biased in the space provided.

Publication	Topic	
1. *Los Angeles Times* editorial	marijuana	O
2. *The New England Journal of Medicine*	marijuana	O
3. *The Catholic Star Church Newsletter*	marijuana	B
4. *American Medical Association Complete Medical Encyclopedia*	marijuana	O
5. *The Partnership for a Drug-Free America Newsletter*	marijuana	B
6. *The Scourge of Drugs* by Wendell Collins	marijuana	B
7. *Sociology* by James N. Henslin	marijuana	B
8. *Understanding Psychology* by Charles G. Morris	marijuana	O

READING

"The public image of policing is heavily influenced by stereotypes about police officers: about who they are, what they believe, and how they act."

TUNING IN TO READING

Almost all of us have a point of view about the police that is dependent on our own personal experiences or the experiences of people we know. What image of the police springs to your mind? Is it of the officer pulling someone over to write a ticket for speeding? Is it of the cop breaking up a party of underage drinkers? Is it of a police officer hitting someone with a nightstick? Is it of a detective tracking down a killer or robber or rapist? Are your feelings about the police in the United States largely negative, positive, or neutral?

BIO-SKETCH

Dr. Samuel Walker is Isaacson Professor of Criminal Justice at the University of Nebraska at Omaha. He is the author of numerous books and journal articles on policing, criminal justice, and civil liberties. He is currently engaged in research on police accountability systems. Dr. Charles Katz is an associate professor in the Department of Criminal Justice and Criminology at Arizona State University West. He is currently engaged in research on the police response to gangs and police organizational theory.

NOTES ON VOCABULARY

Rorschach   The Rorschach inkblot test was developed by the Swiss psychiatrist Hermann Rorschach. A series of inkblots are presented to the individual being tested. He or she then suggests what the inkblots represent. The therapist analyzes the results and makes an assessment about the patient's personality traits.

Beyond Stereotypes of Cops

Samuel Walker and Charles Katz

How many times have you heard someone make a statement such as "All cops are _____"? How many jokes have you heard about police officers spending all their time at donut shops? How often have you heard someone say that people became cops because they like to use force? Statements and jokes of this sort reflect negative stereotypes about police officers.

2   At the same time, how many times have you heard someone say that police officers do no wrong or, more likely, that they have such dangerous and stressful jobs that we should never criticize them for maybe using a little too much force in some situation? This point of view reflects a positive stereotype about police officers.

3   The public image of policing is heavily influenced by stereotypes about police officers: about who they are, what they believe, and how they act. These stereotypes fall into two categories. On the one side, a negative stereotype views officers as uneducated, untrained, prejudiced, brutal, and corrupt. On the other side, a positive stereotype views them as heroic saints, risking their lives in the face of hostility from the public, the media, and the courts. Arthur Niederhoffer characterizes the police officer as a "Rorschach in uniform." "To people in trouble the police officer is a 'savior,' but to others he is a 'fierce ogre.'"

4   Neither stereotype is accurate. As Bayley and Mendelsohn conclude in their study of police-community relations in Denver, the average police officer is a rather average person in terms of values and political beliefs, although a little more conservative than the population as a whole. The special nature of police work does, however, encourage certain attitudes and behavior, and there is a distinct police subculture among officers. No studies, however, have concluded that police officers are fundamentally different from other people in any important respect.

5   Inaccurate stereotypes about policing affect the recruitment of new officers. The National Center on Women and Policing argues that stereotypes emphasizing officer use of force and the need for physical size and strength discourage women from considering careers in policing. In reality, most police work is uneventful, and police-citizen encounters primarily require communication skills.

Reality Shock: Beginning Police Work

6   Police officer attitudes toward the public change significantly during the first weeks and months on the job. McNamara found that the percentage of officers agreeing with the statement "Patrolmen almost never receive the cooperation from the public that is needed to handle police work properly" rose from 35 percent at the beginning of academy training to 50 percent after two years on the job. Meanwhile, at the start of academy training, 31 percent agreed that it was necessary to use force to gain respect in "tough" neighborhoods, while two years later 55 percent agreed.

7   Changes in officers' attitudes are the result of several different aspects of police work. Officers encounter some hostility from citizens. This is a shock because officers tend to choose law enforcement as a career because they want to work with people and help the community. Officers also experience being stereotyped, with citizens reacting to the uniform, the badge, and the gun. As is the case with racial stereotyping, it is an unpleasant experience to have people react to you as a category rather than as an individual. In still other instances, citizens feel discomfort at being around a person with arrest powers. To avoid the discomfort of these incidents, police officers tend to socialize primarily with other officers, thereby increasing their isolation from the public.

8   Police officers' attitudes also change because they perform society's "dirty work," handling unpleasant tasks that no one else wants to perform or is able to handle. The police see humanity at its worst. They are the first people to find the murder victim, for example. Officers encounter the victims of serious domestic abuse, child abuse, and rape firsthand. These kinds of situations accumulate over time, affecting their attitudes about people in general. In one study, for example, officers ranked dealing with an abused child as the most stressful kind of situation they encounter.

Police–Community Relations

9   Conflict between the police and racial and ethnic minority communities is one of the most serious problems in American policing. The focus of the problem in recent years has been the controversy over "driving while black" or "driving while brown" (DWB)—the allegation that the police single out African-American or Hispanic drivers for traffic stops on the basis of their race or ethnicity rather than suspected criminal conduct.

10   In a survey of Cincinnati residents, 46.6 percent of African-Americans indicated they had been personally hassled by the police, compared with only 9.6 percent of whites. Hassled was defined as being "stopped or watched closely by a police officer, even when you had done nothing wrong." Among many African-American families there is much fear of the police. A *New York Times* article in 1997 described how some African-American and Hispanic parents made a special effort to teach their children to be very respectful of police officers, primarily because they were afraid their children might be arrested, beaten, or even shot if they displayed any disrespect to an officer.

11   The use of deadly force has been the source of major conflict between minorities and the police. James Fyfe concluded that "blacks and Hispanics are everywhere overrepresented among those on the other side of police guns." One of the most controversial incidents in recent years was the fatal shooting of Amadou Diallo by New York City police officers in 1999 (and the subsequent acquittal of officers on criminal charges). Diallo was unarmed and apparently reaching for his wallet when he was shot. This shooting, together with other incidents of police misconduct, created a strong feeling among many minorities in the city that they are the target of systematic police abuse.

12   Allegations of police brutality, defined as the use of excessive physical force, represent the most common complaint voiced by minorities about the police. The videotaped beating of Rodney King in 1991 by Los Angeles police officers provided dramatic visual evidence of this problem.

13   The issue of excessive physical force is particularly complex. Police officers are authorized by law to use force in certain situations: to protect themselves, to effect an arrest, to overcome resistance, and to bring a dangerous situation under control. The relevant question is, "when is the use of force excessive?" Officers are supposed to "use only the force necessary to accomplish lawful objectives."

14   Whether or not a certain level of force is necessary in a particular situation is frequently a matter of opinion. It often involves conflicting perceptions of whether a person was resisting arrest, or whether he or she posed a threat to the safety of

the officer. The Bureau of Justice Statistics found that police officers used some kind of force in less than 1 percent of all encounters with citizens. About two-thirds of all uses of force are justified, given the circumstances, and about one-third are unjustified, or excessive. Thus, police use excessive force in an estimated one-third of 1 percent (0.3 percent) of all encounters with citizens.

15 The 1 percent figure acquires a different meaning when examined more closely. The Bureau of Justice Statistics estimate of 421,000 force incidents per year translates into 1,100 per day. Thus, there are about 360 excessive force incidents every day of the year. The result is that a sizable number of racial and ethnic minorities experience police misconduct at one time or another.

Summary

16 Conflict between the police and racial and ethnic communities remains a serious problem in American policing. This problem persists despite general improvements in policing. Many of these problems are the responsibility of the police themselves. At the same time, conflict between police and minorities is a product of the larger structure of racial discrimination in American society.

From Samuel Walker and Charles M. Katz, *The Police in America: An Introduction,* 6th Edition, pp. 122–23, 219, 385, 394, 404–6, 157–58. Copyright © 2008 by The McGraw-Hill Companies, Inc. Reprinted with permission.

 COMPREHENSION CHECKUP

Multiple Choice

Directions: For each item, write the letter corresponding to the best answer on the line provided.

_____ 1. In paragraph 3, the authors
    a. discuss positive and negative stereotypes of police officers.
    b. mention that the public's view of the police is influenced by stereotypes.
    c. use antonyms to describe officers as either savior or ogre.
    d. all of the above.

_____ 2. The authors present information that supports all of the following *except* for which?
    a. The police are only slightly more conservative than the populace as a whole.
    b. The majority of police work is high-risk and exciting.
    c. A distinct police subculture does exist.
    d. Women are discouraged from applying for positions as police officers because of the emphasis on brute strength.

_____ 3. Police attitudes toward the public at large
    a. change little over the course of their careers.
    b. change about the need for the use of force.
    c. become more positive.
    d. none of the above.

_____ 4. All of the following are true about police officers *except* for which?
    a. Officers frequently encounter hostility from the citizenry they are hired to protect.
    b. Officers tend to choose police work for altruistic reasons.
    c. Officers are treated as individuals.
    d. Officers frequently socialize with other officers.

_____ 5. The police are called upon
    a. to do society's unpleasant tasks.
    b. to deal with victims of domestic abuse.
    c. to deal with murder victims.
    d. all of the above.

_____ 6. Minorities frequently say that they are
    a. stopped or watched closely by a police officer even when they have committed no crime.
    b. the victims of excessive force on the part of the police.
    c. treated in a fair and equitable manner by the police.
    d. both a and b.

_____ 7. Officers are authorized by law to use force
    a. to protect themselves from danger.
    b. to bring control to a possibly dangerous situation.
    c. to overcome resistance on the part of a suspect.
    d. all of the above.

_____ 8. The authors mention Amadou Diallo and Rodney King to illustrate
    a. videotaped beatings.
    b. excessive physical force.
    c. problems with New York City police officers.
    d. problems with the Los Angeles Police Department.

True or False

Directions: Indicate whether each statement is true or false by writing **T** or **F** in the space provided.

_____ 9. The job of policing tends to isolate the police from the public at large.

_____ 10. Among officers there is a distinct police subculture.

_____ 11. African Americans are more likely to be hassled by the police than Whites.

_____ 11. An officer may properly use as much force as the officer wants regardless of the circumstances.

Fact and Opinion

Directions: Indicate whether the statement is a fact or an opinion by writing **F** or **O** in the blank provided.

_____ 1. Neither stereotype [about police officers] is accurate.

_____ 2. As Bayley and Mendelsohn conclude in their study of police-community relations in Denver, the average police officer is a rather average person in terms of values and political beliefs.

_____ 3. No studies, however, have concluded that police officers are fundamentally different from other people in any important respect.

_____ 4. At the start of academy training, 31 percent agreed that it was necessary to use force to gain respect in "tough" neighborhoods, while two years later 55 percent agreed.

_____ 5. As is the case with racial stereotyping, it is an unpleasant experience to have people react to you as a category rather than as an individual.

_____ 6. In one study, for example, officers ranked dealing with an abused child as the most stressful kind of situation they encounter.

_____ 7. In a survey of Cincinnati residents, 46.6 percent of African-Americans indicated they had been personally hassled by the police, compared with only 9.6 percent of whites.

_____ 8. The issue of excessive physical force is particularly complex.

_____ 9. The Bureau of Justice Statistics found that police officers used some kind of force in less than 1 percent of all encounters with citizens.

_____ 10. At the same time, conflict between police and minorities is a product of the larger structure of racial discrimination in American society.

Vocabulary in Context

Directions: Match each word to its definition. Use each word only once.

acquittal	controversy	corrupt	excessive	hassled
heroic	incidents	isolation	ogre	relevant

1. in fairy tales, a flesh-eating monster or giant _____

2. found not guilty in a court of law _____

3. too much or too great _____

4. by itself; separated _____

5. pertinent; to the point _____

6. dispute or disagreement _____

7. larger than life; brave _____

8. dishonest; debased _____

9. annoyed, harassed, disturbed _____

10. occurrences _____

In Your Own Words

In Your Own Words

1. Will putting more police officers on the streets help solve the U.S. crime problem? Or will it turn the United States into a "police state"? Why or why not?

2. Although the United States already has the highest percentage of its population in prison of any country in the world, many people say we need to get tougher on crime. What is your opinion?

3. In Youngstown, Ohio, seven principles were established to guide police forces in both established and emerging democracies around the world. Principle 7 is: "The police are expected to discharge their duties in a nondiscriminatory manner." Do you think American police forces are successful in respecting this principle? Why or why not?

4. What is your opinion of reality-based police television shows? Do these shows help the public understand the nature of police work? Or do they offer a one-sided view of police work?

5. How important do you think it is to have a police department that mirrors America? Should police departments strive to actively recruit more women and minorities? How important is it to have bilingual officers?

Written Assignment

In *The Police in America* by Walker and Katz, Herman Goldstein says, "The police, by the very nature of their function, are an anomaly in a free society. On the one hand, we expect them to exercise coercive force: to restrain people when they are out of control, to arrest them when they break the law, and in some extreme cases to use deadly force. At the same time, however, we expect the police to protect the individual freedoms that are the essential part of a democratic society. The tension between freedom and constraint is one of the central problems in American policing" (p. 10). Write a short essay discussing this issue.

Internet Activity

Consult the following Web site that serves police officers:

www.officer.com

Pull up material of interest to you and write a few paragraphs about it. Does the Web site reflect a general bias? Can you find a more specific bias in each of the topics discussed?

READING

"We all had a drink together, native and European alike,
quite amicably. The dead man was a hundred yards away."

Archive Photos/Getty Images

TUNING IN TO READING

All of us have strong opinions on a variety of subjects. Our particular backgrounds and experiences influence our points of view.

Authors also have a point of view that may be directly expressed in their work or simply implied. As you read "A Hanging" by George Orwell, keep in mind that he is presenting a classic argument against capital punishment. Look at the following questions before you read the essay to begin familiarizing yourself with the issue of capital punishment. Put a check mark next to the statements you agree with.

_____ 1. Society has a right to execute its "mad dogs."

_____ 2. Not using the death penalty signals a lessened regard for the victim's life.

_____ 3. The death penalty is nothing more than state-sponsored murder.

_____ 4. The death penalty is a fair and just punishment for reprehensible crimes.

_____ 5. Two wrongs do not make a right.

_____ 6. It is more humane to sentence murderers to life imprisonment without parole.

_____ 7. Although the death penalty is not flawless, it is a necessary evil.

_____ 8. The death penalty is necessary to prevent individuals from taking the law into their own hands to avenge the murder of a loved one.

READING *continued*

_____ 9. The death penalty is applied in a way that discriminates against minorities and the poor.

_____ 10. Only the death penalty can prevent a murderer from being pardoned and possibly murdering others.

BIO-SKETCH

George Orwell (1903–1950) is best known as the author of the novels *1984* and *Animal Farm. 1984* is Orwell's version of the future and was meant to serve as a warning to humankind. It was completed just before his death at the age of 46. *Animal Farm,* a clever satire of dictatorships, was published in 1945 just after the end of World War II. During his lifetime, Orwell published 10 books and two collections of essays. The essay "A Hanging," originally published in 1931, is considered to be a classic. It is the only surviving example of his early years as a writer, and the only work originally published under his real name of Eric Blair.

Blair was born in Bengal, a province of British India, to a father who was a minor official in the Indian customs office. From 1917 to 1921, he attended Eton, a preparatory school in England, and then, instead of going on to a university, he served with the British Imperial Police in Burma, the setting of "A Hanging." It is obvious from the details carefully described in the essay that the incident of the hanging made a deep impression on him.

"A Hanging" takes place at Insein, where the second-largest prison in Burma was located. At the time of the essay, the prison held approximately 2,000 inmates. It was while he was serving as a police officer that Orwell's lifelong hatred of imperialism began. His experiences in Burma allowed him to see "the dirty work of the Empire at close quarters." What was especially painful to him was the power of life and death that the British officials held over their subjects. He agonized when he saw human beings being treated as though they were "things." Blair felt that in order to hang a man for a crime, one had to see him as less than human. Otherwise, one would be forced to admit the "unspeakable wrongness" of taking his life.

Upon his return from Burma, Orwell struggled with his need to be a writer, and his need to rid himself of the guilt he felt over his Burma experiences. At first he lived in Paris, writing stories that he later destroyed. Later, when his money ran out, he washed dishes and performed other odd jobs. Finally, he returned to London, where he held a series of teaching positions.

When "A Hanging" was published in the *Adelphi,* it received such good critical reviews that Orwell's career as a writer was launched. In the essay, the now-mature Blair is reflecting on an event that took place five years before. The story is deceptively simple. A condemned man, a Hindu, is taken out of his cell and escorted across the jail yard where the gallows are located. During his walk, two things of importance occur. First, he is greeted by a large, friendly dog, and second, he steps aside to avoid a puddle in his path. Years later, Blair, now using the pen name of George Orwell, wrote: "I watched a man hanged once; it seemed to me worse than a thousand murders. I never went into a jail without feeling that my place was on the other side of the bars."

NOTES ON VOCABULARY

Burma   formerly, the name of a country in Southeast Asia on the Bay of Bengal. Burma was colonized by the British in 1824. In 1948, Burma overthrew its colonial government and became an independent nation. Today, the official name for Burma is Union of Myanmar.

pariah   Today, the word *pariah* means any person (or animal) who is a social outcast. However, originally, *Pariahs* were members of one of the lowest castes in India, who served as slaves to the higher castes. The word is derived from a Tamil word meaning "drummer." Members of the *Pariah* caste frequently beat the drum (*parai*) at various festivals. At the time of Orwell's essay, the *Pariahs* served as household servants to the British, and the term *pariah* was used to designate anyone of low caste.

warder   a person who guards something. *Warder* is the British term for a prison guard or officer.

rupee   the basic monetary unit of India, Pakistan, Nepal, and Burma (Myanmar).

A Hanging

George Orwell

I T WAS IN BURMA, A SODDEN MORNING of the rains. A sickly light, like yellow tinfoil, was slanting over the high walls into the jail yard. We were waiting outside the condemned cells, a row of sheds fronted with double bars, like small animal cages. Each cell measured about ten feet by ten and was quite bare within except for a plank bed and a pot for drinking water. In some of them brown silent men were squatting at the inner bars, with their blankets draped round them. These were the condemned men, due to be hanged within the next week or two.

2   One prisoner had been brought out of his cell. He was a Hindu, a puny wisp of a man, with a shaven head and vague liquid eyes. He had a thick, sprouting moustache, absurdly too big for his body, rather like the moustache of a comic man in films. Six tall Indian warders were guarding him and getting him ready for the gallows. Two of them stood by with rifles and fixed bayonets, while the others handcuffed him, passed a chain through his handcuffs and fixed it to their belts, and lashed his arms tightly to his sides. They crowded very close about him, with their hands always on him in a careful, caressing grip, as though all the while feeling him to make sure he was there. It was like men handling a fish which is still alive and may jump back into the water. But he stood quite unresisting, yielding his arms limply to the ropes, as though he hardly noticed what was happening.

3   Eight o'clock struck and a bugle call, desolately thin in the wet air, floated from the distant barracks. The superintendent of the jail, who was standing apart from the rest of us, moodily prodding the gravel with his stick, raised his head at the sound. He was an army doctor, with a gray toothbrush moustache and a gruff voice. "For God's sake hurry up, Francis," he said irritably. "The man ought to have been dead by this time. Aren't you ready yet?"

4   Francis, the head jailer, a fat Dravidian in a white drill suit and gold spectacles, waved his black hand. "Yes sir, yes sir," he bubbled. "All iss satisfactorily prepared. The hangman iss waiting. We shall proceed."

5   "Well, quick march, then. The prisoners can't get their breakfast till this job's over."

6   We set out for the gallows. Two warders marched on either side of the prisoner, with their rifles at the slope; two others marched close against him, gripping him by arm and shoulder, as though at once pushing him and supporting him. The rest of us, magistrates and the like, followed behind. Suddenly, when we had gone 10 yards, the procession stopped short without any order or warning. A dreadful thing had happened—a dog, come goodness knows whence, had appeared in the yard. It came bounding among us with a loud volley of barks and leapt round us wagging its whole body, wild with glee at finding so many human beings together. It was a large woolly dog, half Airedale, half pariah. For a moment it pranced round us, and then, before anyone could stop it, made a dash for the prisoner and, jumping up, tried to lick his face. Everyone stood aghast, too taken aback even to grab at the dog.

7   "Who let the bloody brute in here?" said the superintendent angrily. "Catch it, someone!"

8   A warder, detached from the escort, charged clumsily after the dog, but it danced and gamboled just out of his reach, taking everything as part of the game. A young Eurasian jailer picked up a handful of gravel and tried to stone the dog away, but it dodged the stones and came after us again. Its yaps echoed from the jail walls. The prisoner, in the grasp of the two warders, looked on incuriously, as though this was another formality of the hanging. It was several minutes before someone managed to catch the dog. Then we put my handkerchief through its collar and moved off once more, with the dog still straining and whimpering.

9   It was about 40 yards to the gallows. I watched the bare brown back of the prisoner marching in front of me. He walked clumsily with his bound arms, but quite steadily, with that bobbing gait of the Indian who never straightens his knees. At each step his

muscles slid neatly into place, the lock of hair on his scalp danced up and down, his feet printed themselves on the wet gravel. And once, in spite of the men who gripped him by each shoulder, he stepped lightly aside to avoid a puddle on the path.

10   It is curious, but till that moment I had never realized what it means to destroy a healthy, conscious man. When I saw the prisoner step aside to avoid the puddle I saw the mystery, the unspeakable wrongness, of cutting a life short when it is in full tide. This man was not dying, he was alive just as we were alive. All the organs of his body were working—bowels digesting food, skin renewing itself, nails growing, tissues forming—all toiling away in solemn foolery. His nails would still be growing when he stood on the drop, when he was falling through the air with a tenth of a second to live. His eyes saw the yellow gravel and the gray walls, and his brain still remembered, foresaw, reasoned—reasoned even about puddles. He and we were a party of men walking together, seeing, hearing, feeling, understanding the same world; and in two minutes, with a sudden snap, one of us would be gone—one mind less, one world less.

11   The gallows stood in a small yard, separate from the main grounds of the prison, and overgrown with tall prickly weeds. It was a brick erection like three sides of a shed, with planking on top, and above the two beams and a crossbar with the rope dangling. The hangman, a gray-haired convict in the white uniform of the prison, was waiting beside his machine. He greeted us with a servile crouch as we entered. At a word from Francis the two warders, gripping the prisoner more closely than ever, half led half pushed him to the gallows and helped him clumsily up the ladder. Then the hangman climbed up and fixed the rope around the prisoner's neck.

12   We stood waiting, five yards away. The warders had formed in a rough circle round the gallows. And then, when the noose was fixed, the prisoner began crying out to his god. It was a high, reiterated cry of "Ram! Ram! Ram! Ram!" not urgent and fearful like a prayer or a cry for help, but steady, rhythmical, almost like the tolling of a bell. The dog answered the sound with a whine. The hangman, still standing on the gallows, produced a small cotton bag like a flour bag and drew it down and over the prisoner's face. But the sound, muffled by the cloth, still persisted, over and over again: "Ram! Ram! Ram! Ram!"

13   The hangman climbed down and stood ready, holding the lever. Minutes seemed to pass. The steady, muffled crying from the prisoner went on and on, "Ram! Ram! Ram!" never faltering for an instant. The superintendent, his head on his chest, was slowly poking the ground with his stick; perhaps he was counting the cries, allowing the prisoner a fixed number—fifty, perhaps, or a hundred. Everyone had changed color. The Indians had gone gray like bad coffee, and one or two of the bayonets were wavering. We looked at the lashed, hooded man on the drop, and listened to his cries—each cry another second of life; the same thought was in all our minds; oh, kill him quickly, get it over, stop that abominable noise!

14   Suddenly the superintendent made up his mind. Throwing up his head he made a swift motion with his stick. "Chalo!" he shouted almost fiercely.

15   There was a clanking noise, and then dead silence. The prisoner had vanished, and the rope was twisting on itself. I let go of the dog, and it galloped immediately to the back of the gallows; but when it got there it stopped short, barked, and then retreated into a corner of the yard, where it stood among the weeds, looking

timorously out at us. We went round the gallows to inspect the prisoner's body. He was dangling with his toes pointed straight downward, very slowly revolving, as dead as a stone. ↩

16   The superintendent reached out with his stick and poked the bare brown body; it oscillated slightly. "*He's* all right," said the superintendent. He backed out from under the gallows, and blew out a deep breath. The moody look had gone out of his face quite suddenly. He glanced at his wristwatch. "Eight minutes past eight. Well, that's all for this morning, thank God."↩

17   The warders unfixed bayonets and marched away. The dog, sobered and conscious of having misbehaved itself, slipped after them. We walked out of the gallows yard, past the condemned cells with their waiting prisoners, into the big central yard of the prison. The convicts, under the command of warders armed with lathis, were already receiving their breakfast. They squatted in long rows, each man holding a tin pannikin, while two warders with buckets marched round ladling out rice; it seemed quite a homely, jolly scene, after the hanging. An enormous relief had come upon us now that the job was done. One felt an impulse to sing, to break into a run, to snigger. All at once everyone began chattering gaily. ↩

18   The Eurasian boy walking beside me nodded toward the way we had come, with a knowing smile: "Do you know sir, our friend [he meant the dead man] when he heard his appeal had been dismissed, he pissed on the floor of his cell. From fright. Kindly take one of my cigarettes, sir. Do you not admire my new silver case, sir? From the boxwalah, two rupees, eight annas. Classy European style."

19   Several people laughed—at what, nobody seemed certain.

20   Francis was walking by the superintendent, talking garrulously. "Well, sir, all hass passed off with the utmost satisfactoriness. It was all finished—flick! like that. It iss not always so—oah no! I have known cases where the doctor wass obliged to go beneath the gallows and pull the prisoner's legs to ensure decease. Most disagreeable!"

21   "Wriggling about, eh? That's bad," said the superintendent.

22   "Ach, sir, it iss worse when they become refractory! One man, I recall, clung to the bars of hiss cage when we went to take him out. You will scarcely credit, sir, that it took six warders to dislodge him, three pulling at each leg. We reasoned with him. 'My dear fellow,' we said, 'think of all the pain and trouble you are causing to us!' But no, he would not listen! Ach, he wass very troublesome!"

23   I found that I was laughing quite loudly. Everyone was laughing. Even the superintendent grinned in a tolerant way. "You'd better all come and have a drink," he said quite genially. "I've got a bottle of whiskey in the car. We could do with it."

24   We went through the big double gates of the prison into the road. "Pulling at his legs!" exclaimed a Burmese magistrate suddenly, and burst into a loud chuckling. We all began laughing again. At that moment Francis' anecdote seemed extraordinarily funny. We all had a drink together, native and European alike, quite amicably. The dead man was a hundred yards away.

"A Hanging" from *Shooting an Elephant and Other Essays* by George Orwell. Copyright 1950 by Sonia Brownell Orwell and renewed 1978 by Sonia Pitt-Rivers. Reprinted by permission of Houghton Mifflin Harcourt Publishing Company, and (Copyright © George Orwell, 1931) by permission of Bill Hamilton as the Literary Executor of the Estate of the Late Sonia Brownell Orwell and Secker & Warburg Ltd.

COMPREHENSION CHECKUP

Multiple Choice

Directions: For each item, write the letter corresponding to the best answer on the line provided.

_____ C _____ 1. The first paragraph of the narrative serves to
   a. express Orwell's feelings about capital punishment.
   b. introduce the reader to the person being executed.
   c. introduce the reader to the setting of the story.
   d. describe the hanging process in detail.

_____ d _____ 2. From the story, you could infer that Orwell
   a. would support the continued use of capital punishment.
   b. viewed the death penalty process as ironic.
   c. saw no problems in executing a man.
   d. had been opposed to the death penalty before he went to Burma.

_____ d _____ 3. Orwell serves as the narrator of the story. Which role does the narrator play?
   a. the person responsible for hanging the prisoner
   b. a fellow prisoner due to be executed later
   c. the superintendent of the prison
   d. an observer to the hanging process

_____ C _____ 4. The organizational pattern used in paragraph 17 is
   a. cause and effect.
   b. comparison-contrast.
   c. chronological order.
   d. definition and example.

True or False

Directions: Indicate whether each statement is true or false by writing **T** or **F** in the space provided.

_____ F _____ 5. The prisoner was accused of committing murder in a fit of rage.

_____ T _____ 6. A British official was responsible for serving as the executioner.

_____ T _____ 7. On the way to the gallows, they were interrupted by a large, friendly dog.

_____ F _____ 8. After the hanging, everyone felt a great deal of grief and began to wail and cry.

_____ T _____ 9. The men, both British and local, later drank together quite amicably.

_____ F _____ 10. It was possible to see the prisoner's face when he was executed.

Vocabulary in Context

Directions: Use the context clues to determine the meaning of the italicized words, and then write a definition for that word in the space provided.

1. a *sodden* morning of the rains (1)   _____

2. a *puny* wisp of a man (2)   _____

3. a bugle call, *desolately* thin in the wet air (3) _____

4. Everyone stood *aghast* (6)   _____

5. it danced and *gamboled* (8)   _____

6. All *toiling* away (10) _____

7. It was a high, *reiterated* cry (12) _____

8. never *faltering* for an instant (13) _____

9. looking *timorously* out at us (15) _____

10. it *oscillated* slightly (16) _____

11. Francis was . . . talking *garrulously* (20) _____

12. when they become *refractory* (22) _____

13. he said quite *genially* (23) _____

14. Francis' *anecdote* seemed extraordinarily funny (24) _____

15. native and European alike, quite *amicably* (24) _____

Short Answer

Directions: Answer the questions briefly, in a few words or sentences as appropriate.

1. What is the overall main idea of the essay?

   _____

   _____

2. What was the author's purpose in writing the essay?

   _____

3. Orwell is noted for his use of figurative language. List a few examples from the first paragraph.

   _____

4. As a writer, Orwell was often preoccupied with detail. At the beginning of the essay, he is concerned with using concrete details to set the scene for the reader. Give an example of this type of detail. What is the tone of paragraph 1?

   _____

5. Give some descriptive details about the prisoner's appearance at the start of the essay.

   _____

   _____

6. Considering Orwell's emphasis on details, why doesn't he tell us more about the prisoner, such as his name and the reason he was being hanged? How does this selective omission of key details reveal Orwell's point of view?

   _____

   _____

7. What is ironic about the dog's reaction to the prisoner? How does the dog's behavior serve as a contrast to the behavior of the human beings in the story? How does the inclusion of this incident reveal Orwell's point of view?

   _____

   _____

   _____

8. Analyze the simile Orwell uses to describe the way the guards handle the prisoner: "It was like men handling a fish which is still alive and may jump back into the water."

   Subject: _____

   Compared to: _____

   Meaning: _____

   _____

9. In paragraph 10, the author discovers that he is opposed to capital punishment. What are his reasons for opposing it? What trivial incident on the part of the prisoner brought him to this realization?

   _____

   _____

10. After the author realizes he is opposed to capital punishment, how does the way he describes the prisoner change? What words does he use to describe our common bond with the prisoner? How does his choice of words reveal his point of view?

    _____

    _____

    _____

11. Identify the similes in paragraphs 13 and 15.

    _____

12. What is ironic about the superintendent's statement in paragraph 16?

    _____

13. What is ironic about the description of the scene in paragraph 17?

    _____

14. After the hanging, what clues does the author give us indicating that those who participated in the execution were uncomfortable with their role?

    _____

15. What is the irony in paragraph 22?

    _____

Written Assignment

Have you heard about a murder in the news media that shocked you? Write an essay telling as much as you know about what happened—the circumstances of the murder, the police investigation, the trial, the sentence imposed. What is your personal reaction to those events?

Internet Activity

Visit one of the Web sites below. Find information either in favor of or opposed to the use of the death penalty, print the information, and highlight any words that demonstrate a clear bias.

www.prodeathpenalty.com

www.ncadp.org

REVIEW TEST: *Identifying Author Bias*

Directions: Use what you learned about connotation and denotation, euphemism, point of view, and fact versus opinion to identify the author's bias. Then state this bias briefly in your own words.

1.   Tropical forests (home for 66% of the plant species, 90% of nonhuman primates, 40% of birds of prey, and 90% of insects), used to cover 6–7% of the total land surface of the Earth—an area roughly equivalent to our contiguous 48 states. Every year, humans destroy an area of forest equivalent to the size of Oklahoma.

   At this rate, these forests and the species they contain will disappear completely in just a few more decades. The destruction of tropical rain forests gives only short-term benefits but is expected to cause long-term problems. If tropical rain forests are preserved, the rich diversity of plants and animals will continue to exist for scientific and pharmacological study. One fourth of the medicines we currently use come from tropical rain forests. It is hoped that many of the still unknown plants will provide medicines for other human ills. Worldwide, without tropical rain forests, there could be changes in climate that would affect the entire human race. Preserving these forests is a wise investment. Such action promotes the survival of most of the world's species—indeed, the human species, too.

   From Sylvia S. Mader, *Human Biology,* 8th Edition, p. 7. Copyright © 2004 by The McGraw-Hill Companies, Inc. Reprinted with permission.

   Bias: _____

   _____

2.   I can think of some pretty good reasons why vouchers for private schools are a bad idea. First of all, and probably most important, these schemes deprive public schools of the support they deserve. Parents who choose to send their kids to private school still have a responsibility to support public education, not the other way around. Pat Robertson, one of the biggest endorsers of voucher schemes, has said: "They say vouchers would spell the end of public schools in America. To which we say, so what?" What in the world is he thinking? Look, 42 million of our kids go to public school each day. Their future is America's future. No matter what we choose for our own kids, we all have a stake in the success of public education.

   There's something else I want you to understand. Just because vouchers are public money doesn't mean that the participating private schools will be accountable to the public. Wondering about the curriculum at the David Koresh Academy? How about the expulsion policy at the Louis Farrakhan School? Well, stop wondering. It ain't any of your business now, and it will never get to be your business, even if they used your tax dollars to send somebody to these schools.

   From James Carville, *We're Right, They're Wrong.* New York: Random House, 1996, p. 102.

   Bias: _____

   _____

3.   Girls today are much more oppressed. They are coming of age in a more dangerous, sexualized and media-saturated culture. They face incredible pressures to be beautiful and sophisticated, which in junior high means using chemicals and being sexual. As they navigate a more dangerous world, girls are less protected.

As I looked at the culture that girls enter as they come of age, I was struck by what a girl-poisoning culture it was. The more I looked around, the more I listened to today's music, watched television and movies and looked at sexist advertising, the more convinced I became that we are on the wrong path with our daughters. America today limits girls' development, truncates their wholeness, and leaves many of them traumatized.

From Mary Pipher, *Reviving Ophelia*. New York: Ballantine Books, 1994, p. 12.

Bias: _____

4.   The information age has brought us many wonders, but it has also made possible an unprecedented level of record keeping and high-tech snooping into the lives of others. While we dazzle ourselves in virtual worlds and strange new digital communities that stretch around the globe, it's easy to forget that the same technology that connects us can keep track of us as never before.

Employers have more freedom to infringe on the privacy of employees than do the police, who still need court approval to tap most telephone or data lines, notes Andre Bacard, author of the *Computer Privacy Handbook*. Supervisors, he says, "can tap an employee's phones, monitor her e-mail, watch her on closed-circuit TV, and search her computer files, without giving her notice."

From Reed Karaim, "The Invasion of Privacy," *Civilization,* October 1996.

Bias: _____

5.   As college students you are exposed to loud music and other noise all the time. You go to parties, clubs, and concerts where the volume is so loud you have to shout so the person next to you can hear what you are saying. You turn your personal CD players so high they can be heard halfway across the room. And you seldom give it a second thought. But you should, because excessive noise can have a serious impact on your health and well-being. Noise-induced hearing loss can begin as early as 10 years of age. There are now 21-year-olds walking around with hearing-loss patterns of people 40 years their senior. The problem with hearing loss is that it creeps up on you. Today's hard-rock fans won't notice the effect of their hearing loss for another 15 years. And then it will be too late. Unlike some physical conditions, hearing loss is irreversible. Loud noise damages the microscopic hairs in the inner ear that transmit sound to the auditory nerve. Once damaged, those hairs can never recover and can never be repaired. Now are you convinced? At least think about the possible consequences the next time you are set to pump up the volume on your personal CD player.

From Stephen E. Lucas, *The Art of Public Speaking*, 8th Edition, pp. 434–35. Copyright © 2004 by The McGraw-Hill Companies, Inc. Reprinted with permission.

Bias: _____

6.   Super Bowl beer ads, and beer ads in general, have for many years seemed to be directed toward juveniles. Whether or not advertisers do this intentionally, children pick up on them. This kind of advertising impact is especially troublesome because young people see nearly 2,000 commercials for beer and wine each year. For every public service announcement with a message like "Just say no," teens will view 25 to 50 beer and wine commercials that say essentially "Drinking is cool." Meanwhile, underage drinking remains a widespread problem. Many young people are beginning to consume alcohol around the age of 13, and a large majority will do their heaviest drinking before their 21st birthday. Beer advertisements in particular often glamorize drinking and provide no information about the potential negative effects alcohol has on the body, including nausea, blackouts, and liver problems.

From George Rodman, *Mass Media in a Changing World*, p. 432. Copyright © 2006 by The McGraw-Hill Companies, Inc. Reprinted with permission.

Bias: _____

_____

7.   For more than 200 years, America has been known as the "Land of Opportunity" where anyone who works hard can enjoy both material success and the freedom of living in a democracy. Indeed, millions of immigrants from all around the globe have poured into the United States eager to work, learn, and build a better future for themselves and their families. However, for many immigrants and refugees who come to America, the hard work they hope will be the path to the good life often puts them at risk for workplace-related illness and injury. Immigrants who have little education and lack work and language skills often are forced to take jobs that are low-paying, hazardous, or both. They sew for long hours in garment sweatshops, work with hazardous materials like asbestos or toxic chemicals without adequate protection, or labor in settings where they are targets of violent crime. Clearly, all workplaces should be safe and healthy environments for their workers. Just as clearly, immigrants with low levels of skill and education must be protected from a host of workplace hazards that can cause illness, injury, and even death.

From Wayne A. Payne and Dale B. Hahn, *Understanding Your Health*, 6th Edition, p. 545. Copyright © 2000 by The McGraw-Hill Companies, Inc. Reprinted with permission.

Bias: _____

8.   National attention has recently been focused on a serious and growing problem on our highways—people who talk on the phone while they drive. Police, state legislators, and local activists say that something must be done. A handful of counties and municipalities have already enacted ordinances limiting the use of cell phones for drivers and at least 40 states are considering similar bills. But the powerful cell phone lobby is battling back, stressing public education over a new generation of anti–cell phone laws. Although 80 percent of cell-phone users say they talk while driving, good numbers on how many car accidents are caused by cell phones are hard to come by. In most states, accidents filed by the police don't reflect whether cell phones played a role. The medical community has provided the most sound,

and most damning, statistics. A 1997 study published in *The New England Journal of Medicine* found that the collision rate for drivers using handheld cell phones were roughly the same as for drivers who were legally drunk.

Bias: _____

_____

Chapter Summary and Review

In Chapter 11, you learned to identify writing that has a biased viewpoint and to recognize an author's personal bias. You also learned about the difference between denotative and connotative meanings and between positive and negative connotations. Based on the material in Chapter 11, answer the following.

Short Answer

Directions: List three organizations you think may have a biased point of view, and indicate their bias.

Name of Organization	**Bias of Organization**
1. _____	_____
2. _____	_____
3. _____	_____

Vocabulary in Context

Directions: Choose one of the following words to complete the sentences below. Use each word only once.

> bias   euphemism   positive

4. Some cities do not admit that they have potholes. Instead, they use a

   _____ and call their potholes "pavement deficiencies."

5. Three driver-training teachers became part of a jury pool in a drunk-driving case. The judge dismissed them from serving as jurors because of their presumed

   _____ against drunk drivers.

6. The term *administrator* has a more _____ connotation than the term *bureaucrat*.

Propaganda Techniques

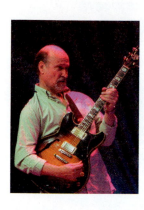

CHAPTER PREVIEW

In this chapter, you will

- Become familiar with common propaganda techniques.

- Learn to apply knowledge of propaganda techniques to reading selections.

- Learn about faulty cause and effect.

What Are Propaganda Techniques and How Are They Used?

We have learned the difference between fact and opinion, and we have also discussed bias. Now we are going to look at the related topic of propaganda.

The word *propaganda* was first used by Pope Urban VIII (1623–1644), who created a "congregation for propagating the faith." Thus, **propaganda** originally meant spreading the Christian faith with missionary activity throughout the world. Today *propaganda* refers to the spreading of ideas to further a cause. Political parties often use *propaganda* to persuade people to vote for their candidates or support their programs. Advertising is a form of propaganda designed to persuade consumers that certain products or brands are superior.

Because modern propaganda often makes use of distortion and deception, the word *propaganda* now has a negative sound to it. But propaganda is sometimes destructive and sometimes beneficial. Tobacco companies use propaganda to persuade people to smoke, and more specifically to persuade people to smoke particular brands of cigarettes. Many people would characterize this use of propaganda as destructive because smoking is damaging to health. But in recent years, propaganda has been used in antismoking campaigns to inform people of the dangers of smoking and to try to persuade them to stop smoking. These antismoking campaigns use propaganda for a positive, beneficial purpose, as illustrated by the advertisement from a box of Players cigarettes sold in Canada on the next page.

Propaganda works by using certain techniques to manipulate reason and emotion. Because propaganda is manipulative, it is important for you to be familiar with these techniques so that you will know when propaganda is being directed at you. Once you are aware that propaganda techniques are being used, your knowledge of these techniques will also help you evaluate the accuracy and fairness

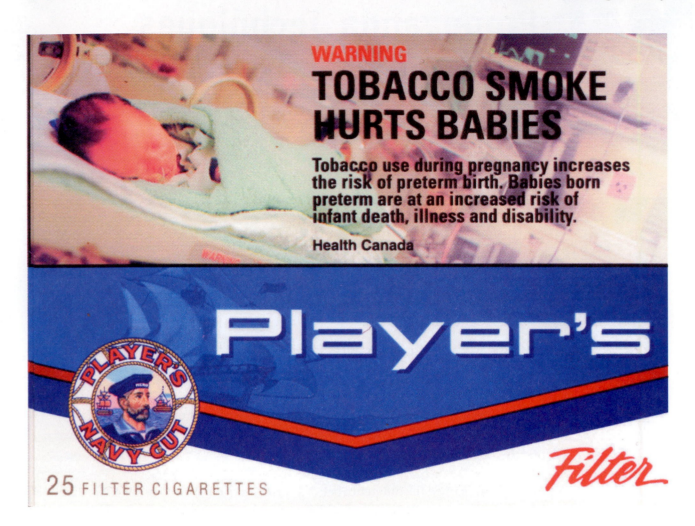

of the message. Does the message really make sense? Is the cause being promoted by the propaganda something that you want to support? Our special focus is on the use of propaganda techniques in written material. You want to know when a writer is using propaganda techniques so that you can more accurately and fairly evaluate what is being said.

The Institute for Propaganda Analysis was formed in 1937 to study propaganda and educate the American public about it. The institute identified seven propaganda techniques. Other techniques have since been added to the list. We will discuss the main propaganda techniques in this chapter and give you some practice in identifying them.

1. **Name-calling.** This technique consists of attaching a negative label to a person or a thing. During the presidential campaign of 1992, when President Bush dismissively called Bill Clinton "a bozo," he was engaging in name-calling. When politicians engage in this type of behavior, they are usually trying to avoid supporting their own positions with facts. Rather than explain what they believe in, they try to tear their opponent down. Many of us engage in the same type of technique when someone disagrees with us. We might call someone we disagree with "radical," "reactionary," "foolish," or "stupid."

2. **Glittering generalities.** This technique involves the use of important-sounding "glad words" that have little or no real meaning. These words are used in general statements that cannot be proved or disproved. Words like "good," "honest," "fair," and "best" are examples of glad words. When an automobile manufacturer

says in an advertisement that its cars are the "best," what does the manufacturer really mean? Does that particular car have the "best" safety record? The "best" warranty? Get the "best" mileage?

3. **Transfer.** In this technique, an attempt is made to transfer the prestige of a positive symbol to a person or an idea. At both the Republican and Democratic national conventions, the backdrop is always the American flag. Politicians want us to think that they are patriotic and will do what is right for the country. Advertising also makes use of transfer. Both the U.S. Postal Service Express Mail and a nationwide legal firm specializing in injury and wrongful death use an eagle in their advertisements.

4. **False analogy.** In this technique, two things that may or may not really be similar are portrayed as being similar. The store brand can of peas may look like the name brand, but is it exactly the same? We have to ask ourselves several questions in order to determine the answer. For instance, are the peas of the same quality? Are there as many peas in the can? In most false analogies, there is simply not enough evidence available to support the comparison.

5. **Testimonial.** This technique is easy to understand. Often, big-name athletes, as well as movie and TV stars, are paid huge amounts of money to endorse a product. Whenever you see someone famous endorsing a product, ask yourself how much that person knows about the product, and what he or she stands to gain by promoting it. In the area of politics, national political leaders often give ringing endorsements of members of their party running for office at the state or local level. They hope to use their prestige to influence the voting.

Exercise 1: Propaganda

Directions: The following statements make use of propaganda techniques 1–5. For each statement, identify the techniques used.

1. Vote for Jack Hazelhurst. Governor Brown is voting for him.

   _____

2. E-Z LIVING recliners are the best that money can buy.

   _____

3. My opponent has been stingy in spending the public's money, and he voted against all the bills for building a rapid transit system.

   _____

4. Yang Chow Chinese dinners are just as good and appetizing as what is served in expensive Hong Kong restaurants.

   _____

5. Before giving his speech, Senator Jones had the band play "The Star Spangled Banner." _____

6. Basketball star Michael James says, "You should buy QuickLift tennis shoes. They'll help you lift off for a great day." _____

7. The National Vehicle Insurance Association has backed the bill going through Congress allowing state governments to build new freeways with federal tax dollars. _____

8. ShopRight laundry soap has as much cleaning power as the more expensive CleanEase detergent. _____

9. Congressional candidate Fred Goodheart says that people should vote for him because he is fair, honest, and kind. _____

10. In a recent interview, Governor Herman said that those who oppose his reform measures are "misguided, arrogant fools." _____

More Propaganda Techniques

Keep in mind that there is often overlap among these propaganda techniques, and propagandists commonly use more than one of the techniques at the same time. Also, we all are propagandists at times, such as when we are trying to persuade someone to do or believe something. Understanding propaganda techniques helps us be more effective and think more clearly and logically.

6. **Plain folks.** This technique uses a folksy approach to convince us to support someone or something. At election time, politicians appear at local diners, coffee shops, or malls to prove they are just like us. A man running for president will be photographed making his own breakfast or taking out the garbage. In order to sell products such as headache remedies, cereal, or toilet bowl cleaners, advertisers will depict ordinary-looking people doing ordinary activities.

"A half truth is a whole lie."

—Jewish proverb

7. **Card stacking.** This term comes from the act of stacking a deck of cards in your favor. Propagandists effectively use card stacking to slant the message. Key-words or unfavorable statistics may be omitted in an ad or commercial, leading to a series of half-truths. An advertisement stating that "four out of five dentists surveyed recommend Zest toothpaste" may be true, but it may also fail to disclose that only five dentists were actually contacted, and of those five, four accepted money to provide an endorsement. Keep in mind that an advertiser is under no obligation "to tell the truth, the whole truth, and nothing but the truth." If you go into a car dealership to purchase a new car, the salesperson is not likely to inform you that the model you are interested in has a problem with paint discoloration. The telemarketer trying to solicit funds to feed hungry children in Asia is unlikely to reveal how much of your donation goes to pay his salary and other administrative costs.

8. **Bandwagon.** The bandwagon approach encourages you to think that because everyone else is doing something, you should do it too, or you'll be left out. Ads urging you to join the "Pepsi Generation" or to live it up because it's "Miller time" are using a bandwagon appeal. The technique embodies a "keeping up with the Joneses" philosophy. This technique got its name from the days when politicians would hire a band to play while they were seated on a horse-drawn wagon. As the wagon rolled through town, crowds of people would gather and follow, eager to be part of the action. Those who didn't immediately join in felt they might be missing something. Teenagers today often feel the same way. If they don't wear certain clothes and say and do certain things, they fear they won't be accepted by their peers. Commercials or ads, such as those for beer, exploit this fear. During World War II, Adolf Hitler, a master propagandist, would

frequently gather German citizens in large arenas. As he spoke, a type of "herd mentality" would result. Since people wanted to be accepted and not labeled as "different," they tended to follow blindly like a bunch of cattle.

9. **Either/or fallacy.** This technique is also called "black-and-white thinking" because only two choices are given. You are either for something or against it; there is no middle ground or shades of gray. People who exhibit this type of thinking have a "bumper sticker" mentality. They say things like "America—love it or leave it" and "Put up or shut up." According to this line of reasoning, you are either in favor of gun control or against it, or in favor of abortion or opposed to it. When we attempt to polarize issues, we negate all attempts to find a common ground.

Exercise 2: Propaganda

Directions: The following statements make use of propaganda techniques 6–9. For each statement, identify the technique used.

1. Hurry down to our car dealership before we sell our last sale car. _____

2. If you don't buy our SureShine kitchen polish, your floor will look dull and dirty. _____

3. Governor Swellguy put on a hardhat and took a tour of the new mining operation at National Mining Company. _____

4. McDougal's has sold 50 billion hamburgers. _____

5. You are either part of the solution or part of the problem. _____

6. All the guys down at Barney's Bar drink Blitz beer. _____

7. Brightwhite toothpaste makes your smile bright again. It gets rid of ugly discoloration caused by coffee and tea. It makes that special person in your life eager to get close. _____

8. Almost everyone in the office has given $5 to buy a present for Jim, who is retiring. Would you like to give a donation? _____

9. Mayor Walker is for the little guy. You don't see him driving an expensive car or sending his daughter to a private school. _____

One Last Propaganda Technique

10. **Faulty cause and effect.** This last propaganda technique suggests that because B follows A, A must *cause* B. When we hear people say, "I know it's going to rain today because I just washed my car," they are guilty of faulty cause and effect. Remember, just because two events or two sets of data are related does not necessarily mean that one caused the other to happen. It is important to evaluate the data carefully and not jump to the wrong conclusion. Is the man in the cartoon on the next page guilty of faulty cause and effect?

" WILL YOU SHUT THAT THING OFF ?
THE MAN IS PUTTING ! "

Bob Zahn. www.cartoonfile.net. Reprinted with permission.

Exercise 3: Propaganda

Directions: For each statement, identify the propaganda technique used.

_____ 1. Last year 20 million winners switched to EZ-JUMP athletic shoes. Isn't it time you made the switch, too?

_____ 2. Danny Moreno is our choice for Congress. He has a wife and kids, and he has worked all his life just like us.

_____ 3. Buy SHUGAR. It is a sugar substitute that is low in calories. It won't cause cavities. It has no artificial colors or preservatives.

_____ 4. Suzy Swifty, the famous track star, says that everybody needs milk.

_____ 5. Don't vote for my opponent; he avoided the draft because he was a coward. He ought to be ashamed of himself.

_____ 6. If you want an honest person for the job, someone who's going to treat the public in a fair way, give your vote to Colin, the best choice for our future.

_____ 7. Jeremy saw Mike hanging out with Tim, who has just gotten out of jail. "Now Mike will end up in jail too," he said.

_____ 8. I feel lucky today, so my favorite basketball team is going to win.

_____ 9. Buy the new Bendex watch. Just like Big Ben, it will keep you on time.

_____ 10. Either he is a genius or he is a fraud.

Exercise 4: Propaganda

What propaganda techniques does the "got milk?" ad on the next page illustrate? To whom do you think this ad is likely to appeal?

READING

*"The rush to smoke was also fueled by the fight for
suffrage; women wanted equality."*

TUNING IN TO READING

More than 172,000 Americans were diagnosed as having lung cancer in 2005. Lung cancer kills more people than the combined death toll from alcohol, cocaine, heroin, homicide, suicide, automobile accidents, and AIDS. Although smoking in the United States
has declined markedly, millions of Americans—particularly the young—still smoke.
Smoking is also more common among people who are highly stressed, divorced or
separated, unemployed, or in the military.

READING *continued*

BIO-SKETCH

Dr. Stanley J. Baran has had a long and distinguished academic career. He currently teaches at Bryant College in Rhode Island, where he is chair of the Communications Department. In addition to earning numerous awards for both research and teaching excellence, Dr. Baran has published over 10 books.

NOTES ON VOCABULARY

suffrage   the right to vote in political elections. The U.S. Constitution states, "No state shall be deprived of its equal *suffrage* in the Senate."

crusade   a vigorous movement or enterprise on behalf of a cause. Originally, the word referred to the Crusades, which were European military expeditions in the 11th–13th centuries to "recover" the Holy Lands from the Muslims.

coup   a highly successful act. *Coup* came from the French word meaning "blow" or "stroke," as in *coup d'état*. Among the Plains Indian tribes, *coup* referred to a daring deed performed by a warrior in battle against an enemy.

taboo   something prohibited or forbidden. In Fijian, a Polynesian language, the word originally meant "marked as holy." The first *taboos* were prohibitions against the use or mention of certain things. Violating a *taboo* was believed to make the gods angry.

Boosting Smoking among Women and Children

Stanley J. Baran

Before the early 1900s, smoking was seen as an unsavory habit, permissible for men, never for women. But with the turn of the century, women too wanted to light up. Advertising campaigners first began targeting female smokers in 1919. The American Tobacco Company slogan "Reach for a Lucky instead of a sweet," along with ads designed to help women understand that they could use cigarettes to keep their figures, was aimed at this new market. The rush to smoke was also fueled by the fight for suffrage; women wanted equality. The right to vote was an important goal, but if men could smoke without a fight, why couldn't women?

2   As more women began to smoke, antismoking crusades attempted to deter them. The protection of women's morality, not their health, inspired the crusaders. Many cities forbade the use of tobacco by women in public places. Yet the number of women who started smoking continued to grow. George Washington Hill, head of American Tobacco, wanted this lucrative market to continue to expand, and he wanted to own as large a part of it as possible. He turned to public relations and Edward Bernays.

3   A nephew of Sigmund Freud, Bernays was employed to conduct psychological research aimed at understanding the relationship between women and cigarettes. He learned that women saw cigarettes as symbols of freedom, as the representation of their unfair treatment in a man's world, and as a sign of their determination to be accepted as an equal.

"Reach for a Lucky – instead of a sweet"

LUCKY STRIKE
"IT'S TOASTED"
CIGARETTES

Toasting takes out every bit of bite and throat irritation

"It's toasted"

No Throat Irritation–No Cough.

© 1929, The American Tobacco Co., Manufacturers

Lucky Strike used advertising and an effective public relations campaign to break the taboo on women smokers.

4   Bernays had several objectives: (1) to let the public know that it was quite all right for women to smoke; (2) to undercut the bans on public smoking by women that existed in many places; and (3) to position Lucky Strike cigarettes as a progressive brand.

5   In meeting these goals, Bernays perpetrated a publicity stunt that is still heralded as a triumphant coup among public relations practitioners. New York City had a ban on public smoking by females. Because of, rather than despite this, Bernays arranged for 10 socially prominent young women to enter the 1929 annual Easter Parade down Fifth Avenue as "The Torches of Liberty Contingent." As they marched, the debutantes lit their Lucky "torches of freedom" and smilingly proceeded to puff and walk. For reporters on the scene, this made for much better news and photos than the usual little kids in their spring finery. The blow for female emancipation was front-page news, not only in New York, but nationally. The taboo was dead.

6   Later in his life, Bernays would argue that had he known of the link between cigarette smoking and cancer and other diseases, he would never have taken on American Tobacco as a client.

7   In the 1980s as U.S. levels of smoking continued to decline, R. J. Reynolds introduced a new campaign for its Camel brand cigarettes. The campaign featured a sun-bleached, cool, and casual camel who possessed human qualities. Joe Camel, as he was called, was debonair, in control, and the center of attention, whether in a pool hall, on a dance floor, leaning against his convertible, or lounging on the beach. He wore the hippest clothes. He sported the best sunglasses. R. J. Reynolds said it was trying a new campaign to boost brand awareness and corner a larger portion of a dwindling market. But antismoking groups saw in Joe Camel the echo of Edward Bernays' strategy to open smoking to an untapped market. They accused the company of attempting to attract young smokers—often adding that these were the lifelong customers the tobacco company needed to replace those it was killing.

8   The battle heated up in 1991, and an entire issue of the *Journal of the American Medical Association* was devoted to the impact of smoking on the culture. One of the articles reported on a study of Joe Camel's appeal to youngsters. Researcher Dr. Joseph DiFranza had discovered that Joe Camel was the single most recognizable logo in the country. Children as young as 3 years old could recognize Joe, and more kids could identify him than could identify Mickey Mouse.

9   R. J. Reynolds attempted to discredit the study and its author and claimed that it had a First Amendment right to advertise its legal product any way it wanted. Nonetheless, soon after the publication of the *JAMA* issue, antismoking activist Janet Mangini filed a lawsuit in San Francisco against the tobacco company. Several California counties and cities joined the suit, alleging that the

Joe Camel campaign violated state consumer protection laws designed to protect minors from false or misleading tobacco advertising.

10 Just before it was to go to trial in 1997, the country's second largest tobacco company, while admitting no wrongdoing, agreed to settle out of court with a payment of $10 million. It also agreed to a court order to suspend the Joe Camel campaign, the first time in history that a tobacco company had been forced to abandon an advertising campaign. What may have encouraged the cigarette company to cooperate were internal memos in the hands of the court that would later be made public. An R. J. Reynolds Tobacco memo from 1975 said: "To ensure increased and long-term growth for Camel Filter, the brand must increase its share penetration among the 14–24 age group." Other memos identified target smokers as young as 12 years old!

From Stanley J. Baran, *Introduction to Mass Communication*, 5th Edition, pp. 363, 385. Copyright © 2008 by The McGraw-Hill Companies, Inc. Reprinted with permission.

 ## COMPREHENSION CHECKUP

Multiple Choice

Directions: For each item, write the letter corresponding to the best answer on the line provided.

_____ 1. All of the following are true according to the selection *except* for which?
  a. Women wanted men to quit smoking.
  b. Women wanted to enjoy the same privileges as men.
  c. Women viewed smoking as a liberating activity.
  d. Women worried about their weight.

_____ 2. We can conclude that Edward Bernays
  a. always took pride in his association with American Tobacco.
  b. helped change public attitudes about women and smoking.
  c. masterminded a public relations success.
  d. both b and c.

_____ 3. By using "10 socially prominent young women" to smoke their "torches of freedom" in the Easter Parade, Bernays employed all of the following propaganda techniques *except*
  a. testimonial.
  b. name-calling.
  c. bandwagon.
  d. transfer.

_____ 4. For women in the early 1900s, Lucky Strike cigarettes were associated with all of the following *except*
  a. emancipation.
  b. slimness.
  c. glamour.
  d. disease.

_____ 5. In paragraph 5, "the taboo is dead" suggests that
  a. women were now permitted to vote.
  b. women were now free to smoke in public places.
  c. women no longer received less pay for the same work.
  d. women were free to work outside the home.

_____ 6. In paragraph 7, the word *debonair* means
  a. suave.
  b. careless.
  c. crotchety.
  d. none of the above.

_____ 7. In paragraph 7, the word *But* signals
  a. classification and division.
  b. definition.
  c. example.
  d. contrast.

_____ 8. As used in paragraph 7, "corner a larger portion" means to
  a. relinquish a part of.
  b. engender awareness of.
  c. push to the side.
  d. gain control of.

_____ 9. R. J. Reynolds Tobacco
  a. felt that it should be allowed to advertise cigarettes any way that it desired.
  b. tried to discredit DiFranza's study.
  c. agreed to discontinue using Joe Camel in its advertisements.
  d. all of the above.

_____ 10. The mode of writing for this selection is primarily
  a. descriptive.
  b. narrative.
  c. expository.
  d. persuasive.

True or False

Directions: Indicate whether each statement is true or false by writing **T** or **F** in the space provided.

_____ 11. Smoking was once seen as a man's activity.

_____ 12. "Cool" Joe Camel was designed to appeal to the young.

_____ 13. DiFranza discovered that Mickey Mouse was the most recognized logo in the United States.

_____ 14. Just one California city sued R. J. Reynolds.

_____ 15. R. J. Reynolds admitted to targeting children with its Joe Camel campaign.

Vocabulary in Context

Directions: Use context clues to determine the meaning of the italicized word, and then write a definition for that word in the space provided.

1. smoking was seen as an *unsavory* habit (paragraph 1)

   Definition: _____

2. the rush to smoke was also *fueled* by the fight (paragraph 1)

   Definition: _____

3. antismoking crusades attempted to *deter* them (paragraph 2)

    Definition: _____

4. wanted this *lucrative* market to continue to expand (paragraph 2)

    Definition: _____

5. a publicity stunt that is still *heralded* as a triumphant coup (paragraph 5)

    Definition: _____

6. the *echo* of Edward Bernays's strategy (paragraph 7)

    Definition: _____

7. corner a larger portion of a *dwindling* market (paragraph 7)

    Definition: _____

8. most recognizable *logo* in the country (paragraph 8)

    Definition: _____

In Your Own Words

1. Whose responsibility is it to educate young people about the dangers of smoking? Parents? The public school system? The federal government? Cigarette manufacturers?

2. Many employers pay the cost of health insurance for their employees. Since smokers are at higher risk for future illness, should employers be allowed to exclude them from coverage or charge them more? Do you think employers should be allowed to hire only nonsmokers?

3. Half of the movies released between 1990 and 2002 featured a major character who smoked. Moreover, a recent study found that tobacco use appeared in 89 percent of the 200 most popular movie rentals, including those having a G or PG rating. Since young people are frequent moviegoers, should the entertainment industry be forced to reduce the frequency of smoking in movies?

4. Although smoking has declined in the United States, it has actually increased in the rest of the world, partly due to aggressive marketing campaigns by U.S. tobacco companies. Because many of the poorest countries do not warn their citizens about the dangers of smoking, children as young as 7 and 8 smoke in these countries. Should tobacco companies be required to inform the citizens of all countries about the health risks of smoking?

Written Assignment

The Virginia Slims brand of cigarettes was introduced by Philip Morris in 1968. Throughout the 1970s and 1980s, Philip Morris promoted this product with the slogan "You've come a long way, baby." One panel of the ad would depict women stacking wood for stoves or washing the laundry by hand and then hanging it out on clotheslines to dry. The other panel would depict a stylish, sexy woman doing modern activities. Do some research on the original ad campaign. Why do you think the word "slim" was included in the brand name of the cigarette? Can you identify other brands that are designed to appeal to specific segments of society? Should tobacco companies be allowed to target particular groups?

Internet Activity

The character of Joe Chemo, a camel who wished he'd never smoked, was developed by Scott Pious, a psychology professor at Wesleyan University. Check out the Joe Chemo Web site at:

www.joechemo.org

Then test your tobacco IQ in the 10-item test to get your "smoke-o-scope." Do you think the tips on quitting are likely to help long-term smokers?

Detecting Propaganda Techniques

Directions: Select one ad and write a short description of it. When you have completed your description, answer the questions below.

1. What propaganda techniques, if any, are used in the ad?
2. What attitude toward life does the ad promote?
3. In addition to the product, what else is the ad trying to "sell"?
4. What is the ad's appeal to a man? To a woman?

Short description of the scene portrayed in the ad:

_____

_____

_____

_____

_____

Answers to questions 1–4:

1. _____

_____

_____

2. _____

_____

_____

3. _____

_____

_____

4. _____

_____

_____

Violence in the Media

Many of you will take courses in introductory psychology or sociology. An ongoing controversy in these two fields has to do with the relationship between viewing violence in the media and behaving in an aggressive manner.

"Does observing violent and antisocial acts in the media lead viewers to behave in similar ways?"

TUNING IN TO READING

The following excerpt is from *Understanding Psychology* by Robert S. Feldman. This author sees a correlation between violence in the media and aggressive behavior in children, but he hesitates to state that there is a direct cause-and-effect relationship between the two.

If a definite link between watching violent television shows or playing violent video games and subsequent aggressive acts were established, would you support a ban on such media? Why or why not? While reading the selection, be thinking of other ways to limit aggression among children who frequently watch TV or play video games.

BIO-SKETCH

Robert S. Feldman is a professor of psychology at the University of Massachusetts. Dr. Feldman has written numerous books and articles. He is also noted for his research on honesty and deception.

NOTES ON VOCABULARY

mobster   a member of a criminal gang.

henchman   originally meant "trusted attendant or follower." In the 19th century, Scottish novelist Sir Walter Scott got the word confused with "haunchman," which meant "an obedient or unscrupulous follower." Thus, *henchman* today refers to a ruthless subordinate, often a gang member.

dismember   to divide into parts; to cut up.

copycat   to imitate or mimic. The origins of this word are uncertain. *Copycat* may simply be derived from the actions of a kitten mimicking its mother.

Violence in Television and Video Games: Does the Media's Message Matter?

Robert S. Feldman

In an episode of HBO's "The Sopranos," fictional mobster Tony Soprano murdered one of his associates. To make identification of the victim's body difficult, Soprano, along with one of his henchmen, dismembered the body and dumped the body parts.

2   A few months later, two real-life half brothers in Riverside, California, strangled their mother and then cut her head and hands from her body. Victor Bautista, 20, and Matthew Montejo, 15, who were caught by police after a security guard noticed that the bundle they were attempting to throw in a dumpster had a foot sticking out of it, told police that the plan to dismember their mother was inspired by the "Sopranos" episode.

3   Like other "media copycat" killings, the brothers' cold-blooded brutality raises a critical issue: Does observing violent and antisocial acts in the media lead viewers to behave in similar ways? Because research on modeling shows that people frequently learn and imitate the aggression that they observe, this question is among the most important being addressed by psychologists.

4   Certainly, the amount of violence in the mass media is enormous. By the time of elementary school graduation, the average child in the United States will have viewed more than 8,000 murders and more than 800,000 violent acts on network television. Adult television shows also contain significant violence, with cable television leading the way with such shows as "When Animals Attack" and "World's Scariest Police Shootouts."

5   Most experts agree that watching high levels of media violence makes viewers more susceptible to acting aggressively, and recent research supports this claim. For example, a recent survey of serious and violent young male offenders incarcerated in Florida showed that one-fourth of them had attempted to commit a media-inspired copycat crime. A significant proportion of those teenage offenders noted that they paid close attention to the media.

6   Research using video games has also linked violent media with actual aggression. According to a recent series of studies by psychologist Craig Anderson and colleagues, playing violent video games is associated with later aggressive behavior. In one study, for example, they found that college students who frequently played violent video games, such as *Postal* or *Doom,* were more likely to have been involved in delinquent behavior and aggression. Furthermore, college students—particularly men—also were more apt to act aggressively toward another student if they'd played a violent video game. Frequent players also had lower academic achievement.

7   However, such results do not show that playing violent video games *causes* delinquency, aggression, and lower academic performance; the research only found that the various variables were *associated with* one another. To explore the question of whether violent game play actually caused aggression, Anderson and Dill subsequently conducted a laboratory study. In it, they had participants play either a violent video game or one that was nonviolent. The results were clear: Exposure to the graphically violent video game increased aggressive thoughts and actual aggression.

8   Several aspects of media violence may contribute to real-life aggressive behavior. For one thing, experiencing violent media content seems to lower inhibitions against carrying out aggression—watching television portrayals of violence or using violence to win a video game makes aggression seem a legitimate response to particular situations. Exposure to media violence also may distort our understanding of the meaning of others' behavior, predisposing us to view even nonaggressive acts by others as aggressive. Finally, a continuous diet of aggression may leave us desensitized to violence, and what previously would have repelled us now produces little emotional response. Our sense of the pain and suffering brought about by aggression may be diminished.

From Robert S. Feldman, *Understanding Psychology,* 8th Edition, p. 210. Copyright © 2008 by The McGraw-Hill Companies, Inc. Reprinted with permission.

 COMPREHENSION CHECKUP

Multiple Choice

Directions: For each item, write the letter corresponding to the best answer on the line provided.

_____ 1. The author's main idea is that
   a. displays of violence in the media are quite common.
   b. *The Sopranos* is a violent television program.
   c. parents should watch violent television programs with their young children rather than let them view such programs by themselves.
   d. there is a significant association between observing violent acts in the media and behaving in an aggressive manner.

_____ 2. The word *modeling* as used in paragraph 3 means
      a. imitating.
      b. observing.
      c. extending.
      d. preserving.

_____ 3. The transition word *However* in paragraph 7 indicates a
      a. comparison.
      b. contrast.
      c. addition.
      d. conclusion.

_____ 4. An *insensitive* person is one who
      a. shows consideration for others.
      b. lacks creativity.
      c. is not affected by the suffering of others.
      d. feels a great deal of pain.

_____ 5. The author would agree with all of the following *except* for which?
      a. Observing aggression in the media increases the likelihood that viewers will act aggressively.
      b. Viewing programs such as *Sesame Street* is unlikely to lead to aggressive behavior in young children.
      c. There is little actual violent material on television.
      d. Exposure to media violence desensitizes viewers to acts of aggression.

_____ 6. After watching a violent program a person might
      a. mistake a nonthreatening act for a threatening one.
      b. become overly sensitive to the suffering of others.
      c. respond in a threatening way to a slight by another person.
      d. both a and c.

_____ 7. The author's purpose in writing this selection is to
      a. explain.
      b. persuade.
      c. entertain.
      d. define.

_____ 8. According to recent research, all of the following are associated with playing violent video games *except*
      a. lower academic achievement.
      b. delinquent behavior.
      c. personal generosity.
      d. acts of aggression.

Vocabulary in Context

Directions: Choose one of the following words to complete the sentences below. Use each word only once.

| antisocial | desensitized | ~~diminished~~ | distorts | incarcerated |
| ~~inhibitions~~ | proportion | repelled | ~~subsequent~~ | susceptible |

1. Margaret has missed a great deal of school because she is especially _____ to colds and flu.

2. Because the coach frequently berated him, Nick had a(n) _____ interest in continuing with the team.

3. To be able to participate in karaoke, people need to overcome their _____ about performing in public.

4. After having been _____ for over 20 years, Carlos was set free when DNA evidence conclusively proved he could not have committed the murder.

5. His _____ behavior was responsible for his lack of close friends.

6. What _____ of the population favors tax reform?

7. After years of hearing his crude jokes, Blanca had become _____ to their impact.

8. After learning that she had failed the course after trying so hard, her _____ bursting into tears was completely understandable.

9. Duc was so _____ by the foul odor in the air that he had to leave the building immediately.

10. Presidential candidates frequently complain that the press _____ what they say.

In Your Own Words

1. Assuming that there is a cause-and-effect relationship between watching violent programs in the media and engaging in violent behavior, can you think of ways to help solve this problem? Is there anything the media could do? What about parents?

2. Can you think of some desirable traits in children that are fostered by television? By playing video games?

3. Look at the cartoon below by Bill Watterson, creator of *Calvin and Hobbes*. What position does he seem to be taking on the issue of TV and violence?

Calvin and Hobbes

CALVIN AND HOBBES © 1995 Watterson. Dist. By Universal Press Syndicate. Reprinted with permission. All rights reserved.

4. TV wrestling shows are very popular with males aged 12–34. However, Court TV produced a recent film, *Wrestling with Death*, that documented kids imitating the aggressive acts they saw performed on the TV shows in their own backyards. In these backyard wrestling matches, kids routinely hit each other with objects such

as chairs. Do you think World Wrestling Entertainment bears some responsibility for these incidents? Do you think the wrestling programs on TV glamorize violence? Are you in favor of censoring these kinds of programs?

Written Assignment

James P. Steyer is a Stanford University professor and author of *The Other Parent: The Inside Story of the Media's Effect on Our Children.* In that book, he presents the following 10 steps that parents can take to help create a safer media environment for their kids.

Top 10 Steps for Parents

1. Establish good media habits early.
2. Location, location, location: no TV or computer in your child's room.
3. Set a media diet and stick to it.
4. Teach your child to ask permission to use media.
5. Watch and listen with your kids—then tell them what you like and don't like, and why.
6. Set clear rules regarding your child's media use in other homes.
7. Have pediatricians review your kids' media use as part of their annual checkup.
8. Teach media literacy in school and at home.
9. Read to your child and share positive media experiences.
10. Switch the dial to "off."

What do you think of Steyer's suggestions? Are they likely to work? Write a short essay discussing his suggestions. Try to include a few suggestions of your own.

Internet Activity

LimiTV is a nonprofit North Carolina corporation formed in 1995 to educate parents, teachers, and children about the effects of excessive television viewing, including the relationship between TV violence and aggressive behavior. Go to its Web site at:

www.limitv.org

Find an article on the site of interest to you, and try to identify any propaganda techniques used in the presentation. List any examples you find.

REVIEW TEST: *Propaganda Techniques*

Directions: For each passage, identify the propaganda technique being used.

_____ 1. "Get behind the wheel of the most popular car on the road today!"

_____ 2. "You need a toothpaste that does it All. All toothpaste fights cavities, plaque, bad breath, and gingivitis. Plus it brightens your smile. Face your day the All-prepared way!"

_____ 3. "Either this community votes to fund mass transit or all of us will be personally affected by gridlock on our streets."

_____ 4. Sports star: "I've tried every brand of pain relief medication on the market, and, believe me, nothing out there works better than Pain-away."

_____ 5. Politician running for election: "When I was very young, my father died, leaving my mother with debt and no way to support our family. Unlike my opponent, I know what it's like to struggle to put food on the table and pay the bills. Give me your vote on election day."

_____ 6. Broncos fan watching the Super Bowl on TV: "I better go away. Every time I come in to watch the game, the Packers score a touchdown."

_____ 7. "My opponent for the school board has the morals of an alley cat. Maybe his wife can tolerate his 'affairs' but the rest of us should not allow him to become a role model to our children."

_____ 8. "A lot of us want only the best—the best house, in the best neighborhood, with the best car in our garage. Don't you think it's about time to be thinking about the best phone service. Call 1-800-BEST for a free consultation."

_____ 9. "Your sister has always gotten good grades and worked part-time to pay for her expenses. Don't you think you should be doing the same?"

_____ 10. "This is Chuck Jones standing in front of 'Old Faithful' in Yellowstone National Park. Remember to use Old Faithful laxative if you have problems with irregularity."

Chapter Summary and Review

In Chapter 12, you became familiar with different types of propaganda techniques and learned how to apply your knowledge of these techniques to reading selections. You also learned about faulty cause and effect. Based on the material in this chapter, answer the following.

Short Answer

Directions: From advertising or your own experience, give an example of the following propaganda techniques. Explain how your example illustrates the technique.

Propaganda Technique	Example	Explanation
1. Name-calling	_____	_____
2. Transfer	_____	_____
3. Glittering generalities	_____	_____
4. False analogy	_____	_____
5. Either/or fallacy	_____	_____

Vocabulary Review

Directions: Fill in the blank with an indicated propaganda technique. Use each word only once.

bandwagon   card stacking   plain folks   testimonial

6. A famous model in a commercial promoting a particular line   _____
   of cosmetics.

7. A cell phone provider telling you all of the favorable features   _____
   of the product, but failing to mention that the rate goes up in
   three months.

8. A politician putting on a hard hat and going into a coal mine.   _____

9. A commercial featuring a bar filled with people who are   _____
   drinking one particular brand of beer.

VOCABULARY   **Unit 7 Word Parts: More Opposing Meanings**

This vocabulary unit will continue with word parts having opposite or nearly opposite meanings. Some of these, such as *hyper* and *hypo,* and *inter* and *intra,* are commonly confused. The middle section discusses word parts having to do with phobias. The last section discusses a word part meaning "false."

	syn—same; together pro—for
	anti—opposite, against nym—name

synonym—There are 2,660 synonyms for being intoxicated, more than for any other condition or object.

synonym	Same name. *Synonyms* are words that have the same or similar meanings. For example, *vista* and *panorama* are synonyms.
antonym	Different name. *Antonyms* are words having opposite meanings. *Homogeneous* and *heterogeneous* are words with opposite meanings.
symphony	*Sym* means "together" and *phono* means "sound," so a *symphony* orchestra produces music by blending sounds together.

symphony—Beethoven was totally deaf when he wrote his Ninth Symphony.

antiphony	Opposition of sounds. An *antiphony* is a musical piece that has half of a choral group singing in front of the audience and half in back. Such singing was popular in the Middle Ages.
analyze	To separate into its parts. *Ana* means "up" and *lyze* means "to loosen," so the literal meaning of the word is "to loosen something up." When you *analyze* why you did not do very well on your psychology test, you try to take apart what happened to see what went wrong.

synthesize	*Syn* means "together," and so *synthesize* means to form a whole by bringing together the separate parts. What does a *synthesizer* do in music? It combines different sounds to produce a new sound.
antithesis	*Anti* means "opposite," so an *antithesis* is something that is in opposition. The *antithesis* of segregation is integration.
pro-choice	*Pro* means "in favor of," so a person who is *pro-choice* is supportive of a woman's right to *choose* legal abortion.
anti-abortion	If you are *anti-abortion*, you are opposed to legal *abortion*.
antidote	*Dote* comes from the root word meaning "to give," so an *antidote* is something given to counteract something else. If your child drinks a toxic liquid that is acidic, the container may give instructions recommending bicarbonate of soda as an *antidote*. (Remember that you should still call a doctor.)
syndicated	*Syn* means "same" and *dic* means "to say," so *syndicated* means "saying the same thing." If something is *syndicated*, it appears in many newspapers, magazines, or radio or TV stations. Dear Abby is a *syndicated* advice column that appears in newspapers around the country.

hypo—under, below   hyper—above, over, excessive

hyperactive	A *hyperactive* child is excessively active. If you were *hyperactive* as a child, there's a good chance you still are.
hypoactive	Meaning "underactive." Depressed people are often *hypoactive*.
hyperthermia	The state of being overheated or too hot; very high temperature. Long-distance runners in hot weather need to be careful to drink enough water to avoid *hyperthermia*.
hypothermia	The state of being too cold or of having a below-normal body temperature. A person lost in a snowstorm might die of *hypothermia*.
hypodermic	Many of you know that *derm* means "skin," so a *hypodermic* needle is one that goes under the skin.
hyperbole	A *hyperbole* is an exaggeration, such as "strong as an ox." In the cartoon below, Calvin says that his bad day makes him feel as though he has been run over by a train. This is an example of *hyperbole*. *Hyperbole* is discussed in the section on satire.

hypothermia—A person may die of hypothermia when the body temperature is 95 degrees or less.

Calvin and Hobbes

phobias—Twenty-five percent of women and 12 percent of men have at least one type of phobia. Some of the most common phobias are related to injections, the dentist, and heights.

mania—craving
phobia—irrational fear of something

claustrophobia	Irrational fear of small, tightly enclosed places.
acrophobia	Fear of high places. Acrobats obviously do not have this *phobia*.
monophobia	Fear of being alone.
homophobia	Fear of homosexuals (gay men and lesbians) or homosexuality.
pyromania	A compulsion to start fires.
monomania	An excessive interest in one thing. A *monomaniac* has a mental disorder characterized by preoccupation with one subject.

TRIVIA QUESTION

Why was our interstate highway system originally built? (Answer at the end of this unit.)

intra—within or inside   inter—between or among

intercollegiate	Between or among colleges or universities. Your college's *intercollegiate* baseball team plays other colleges.
intramurals	Literally, this word means "within the walls," so an *intramural* sports program would be one that takes place within the walls of your college. In *intramural* athletics, student teams play against each other.
interstate	Between or among states. The *interstate* highway system connects 48 states.
intrastate	Within a state. Your telephone bill may have a list of your *intrastate* calls.
international	Between or among nations.
intravenous	Within or directly into a vein, such as an *intravenous* injection or IV bottle.

para—alongside, beside, side; partial; similar

parallel	*Parallel* lines run side by side. *Parallel* ideas are similar thoughts.
paraphrase	Literally, a similar phrase. When you *paraphrase* something, you put it into your own words.
paraprofessional	Alongside a professional. This word refers to a person who is not a member of a given profession but who assists those who are. *Paramedics* and *paralegals* are *paraprofessionals*.
paramedic	A person with limited medical duties such as a nurse's aide; a person trained to rescue others.
paralegal	Persons trained to aid lawyers but not licensed to practice law.
paranoid	*Para* means "beside" and *noid* refers to the mind. *Paranoia* is characterized by extreme suspiciousness or delusions of persecution.
paraplegic	A *paraplegic* has a paralysis of the lower half of the body, or is partially paralyzed.
quadriplegic	Total paralysis of the body from the neck down; having all four limbs paralyzed.

pseudo—false

pseudoscience	A false science; a system of theories that presumes without warrant to have a scientific basis. Astrology, which studies the placement of the moon, sun, and stars to predict the future, is considered by many to be a *pseudoscience*. Astronomy is the real scientific study of the universe.
pseudonym	A false name; a fictitious name, such as a pen name used by a writer to preserve anonymity. The book *Primary Colors*, describing an insider's look at the American political system, was written by Joe Klein using the *pseudonym* of Anonymous. Who is the most famous American author to write under a *pseudonym*? Hint: His two most well-known books are *The Adventures of Tom Sawyer* and *The Adventures of Huckleberry Finn*.
alias	Also a false name, but usually used by criminals to disguise their identity.
misnomer	To attach the wrong name to a person or a thing. What do you call that cuddly, tree-dwelling little animal from Australia? If you called this animal a Koala bear, you have just used a *misnomer*, because Koalas aren't bears at all. They are marsupials and carry their young in pouches like a kangaroo.

pseudonym—The deceased Russian author Konstantine Arsenievich Mikhailov holds the record for the author with the most pseudonyms. He used 325 different pen names, most of which were abbreviations of his real name.

Exercise 1: Using Word Parts to Make Words

Directions: Make a word using each of the following word parts. Then, in your own words, define or explain the meaning of your word. Do not create any nonsense words.

ANSWER TO TRIVIA QUESTION

The interstate highway system was initially proposed in 1953 by Secretary of Defense Charles Wilson. The stated purpose of the plan was to have a means for moving military vehicles around the country and also for moving people out of cities in case of nuclear war. Before becoming the secretary of defense, Wilson was president of General Motors.

Word Part	Your Word	Meaning
1. hyper	_____	_____
2. hypo	_____	_____
3. syn or sym	_____	_____
4. anti	_____	_____
5. phobia	_____	_____
6. mania	_____	_____
7. inter	_____	_____
8. intra	_____	_____

Exercise 2: Using Word Parts to Understand Meaning

Directions: Choose one of the following words to complete the sentences below. Use each word only once.

anti-abortion	claustrophobia	pseudoscience	hyperactive	hyperthermia
hypodermic	hypothermia	paraplegics	synonym	ultraviolet

1. A(n) _____ for *irritate* is *annoy*.

2. Too much exposure to _____ radiation can cause skin cancer.

3. The goal of the _____ group Operation Rescue was to shut down abortion clinics.

4. _____ and other persons with disabilities who are in wheelchairs sometimes encounter physical barriers such as the lack of ramps.

5. Most of the victims of _____ are elderly people who have poorly heated homes.

6. A(n) _____ child is impulsive, is full of energy, and sleeps less than other children.

7. Many people consider palm reading and fortune telling to be a form of _____.

8. When he was 3 years old, Jeremy was locked in a closet. Now he suffers from _____ and has trouble riding in an elevator.

9. After spending three days in the Arizona-Sonora desert without water, Brandon was suffering from _____ and was transported to the Tucson Medical Center.

10. AIDS can be spread when drug users inject themselves with unsterile _____ needles.

Exercise 3: Using Word Parts to Understand Meaning

Directions: Choose one of the following words to complete the sentences below. Use each word only once.

acrophobia	antidote	antonym	hyperbole	hypoactive
misnomer	parallel	paraphrase	pseudonyms	syndicated

1. Dear Abby is a nationally _____ columnist whose column appears in hundreds of newspapers across the country.

2. The men who clean the windows on the Empire State Building most likely do not suffer from _____.

3. The chair of the Federal Reserve Board cut interest rates as a(n) _____ for a slowing economy.

4. Because a whale is a mammal, to call it a fish would be a(n) _____.

5. "Be true to yourself" is a(n) _____ of "To thine own self be true."

6. The young child diagnosed as _____ appeared to lack energy and rarely ran around and played with other children.

7. It is a(n) _____ to say that Dave is as tall as a tree.

8. *Introvert* is a(n) _____ of *extrovert*.

9. Many famous authors, such as O Henry, whose real name is William Sydney Porter, used _____ to keep their identities secret.

10. You can choose to travel on the coastal route or the interstate; both run _____ to each other.

Vocabulary Unit 7 Crossword

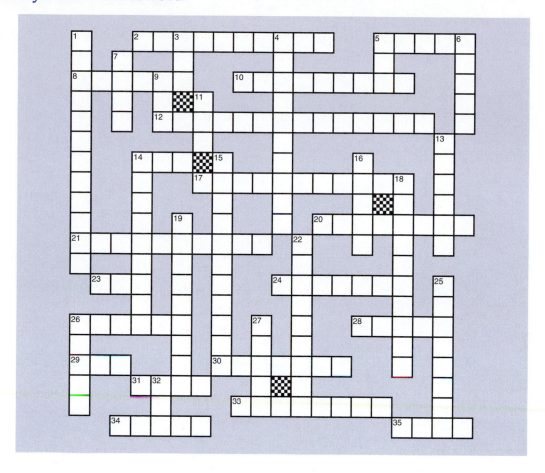

ACROSS CLUES

2. Underactive.
5. A word part meaning "above."
8. A word part meaning "false."
10. An opposition of sounds.
12. The fear of enclosed spaces.
14. A word part meaning "six."
17. Team sports on campus.
20. A person with delusions of persecution.
21. Within a state.
23. A word part meaning "two."
24. To separate into parts.
26. A word part meaning "different."
28. Used by a criminal to disguise identity.
29. A word part meaning "all around."
30. A(n) _____ for *vista* might be a *panorama*.
31. A word part meaning "same."
33. Lines running side by side.
34. A word part meaning "within" or "inside."
35. A word part meaning "alongside."

DOWN CLUES

1. Overheated.
3. A word part meaning "in favor of."
4. Between or among states.
5. A word part meaning "same."
6. A word part meaning "back."
7. A word part meaning "around" or "about."
9. An abbreviation for what was once the 10th month.
11. A word part meaning "marriage."
13. A word meaning "irrational fear."
14. An exaggeration.
15. IV.
16. A word part meaning "large."
18. To bring elements together.
19. Mark Twain is the _____ of Samuel Clemens.
22. An excessive interest in one thing.
25. The wrong name for an object.
26. A word part meaning "above" or "over."
27. A word part meaning "craving."
32. An abbreviation for what was once the 8th month.

13 Evaluating the Evidence

CHAPTER PREVIEW
In this chapter, you will

- Learn about persuasive writing techniques.
- Become familiar with inductive and deductive reasoning.
- Evaluate persuasive writing selections.

Introduction to Persuasive Techniques

Instead of using neutral, objective language, authors sometimes use language designed to arouse readers emotionally. This is often a sign of bias on the author's part and serves as a signal to you that the author is trying to influence you. Authors might use any or all of the following persuasive techniques:

1. **Emotionally loaded language** designed to appeal directly to your feelings rather than your reasoning abilities

   In the example below, the boldfaced words "have powerful connotations certain to produce strong revulsion to terrorism."

   > **Terrorists** neither listen to reason nor engage in reasoning with others. Their aim is to generate **fear**—to **frighten** people into **submission.** They measure success by the magnitude of the **fear** they generate through **brutal, savage** acts of **violence. Terrorists** are prepared to **kill** to further whatever cause they claim to be pursuing. And the **heinousness** of these **murders** is accentuated by the fact that **terrorists murder** without passion. They **murder** with **cool deliberation** and deliberate planning. They are **utterly amoral.**

   From Stephen E. Lucas, *The Art of Public Speaking,* 9th Edition, p. 274. Copyright © 2007 by The McGraw-Hill Companies, Inc. Reprinted with permission.

2. **Tear-jerking stories** or references to people and causes that you empathize with

   After the jurors found Timothy McVeigh guilty of murder and conspiracy in the bombing of the Alfred P. Murrah Federal Building in Oklahoma City, they had to determine whether he should be executed. During the first day of the penalty phase of the trial, prosecutors called upon both rescuers and relatives of the victims to tell their stories.

Father-to-be for one day:

> Mike Lenz on Thursday told jurors he saw his unborn son on an ultrasound machine and gave him a name the day before the bombing. The next day, the blast ripped through Lenz's happy life, killing his wife, Carrie, and Michael James Lenz III, the son he never met.
>
> "In one fell swoop, I went from being a husband and a daddy to realizing it was all gone," Lenz said. "I lost everything."

From www.cnn.com/us/9706/06/mcveigh.am.

3. **Figurative analogies**

A widely known death-row case concerns journalist Mumia Abu-Jamal. In 1981, Philadelphia police officer Daniel Faulkner was killed after he stopped a Volkswagen traveling in the wrong direction on a one-way street. Evidence implicated Abu-Jamal, the brother of the driver of the Volkswagen. He was convicted and sentenced to die. Since that time, he has managed to raise doubts about some of the evidence used to convict him. A stay of execution was granted in August 1995.

In his book *Live from Death Row,* Abu-Jamal used a metaphor when he said:

> Unlike other prisoners, death row inmates are not "doing time." **Freedom does not shine at the end of the tunnel.** Rather, the **end of the tunnel brings extinction.**

Mumia Abu-Jamal, *Live from Death Row.* New York: Avon Trade Books, 1996, p. 6.

4. **Manipulation of tone**

The author uses irony in the following description of an execution:

> It didn't quite go as planned in Florida recently. The humming of the electricity was joined by a more ominous crackling sound like cellophane crinkling. Then great waves of gray smoke poured out and flames leaped from the prisoner's head. The smell of cooked human flesh and burning hair became pronounced. Despite the evidence to the contrary, proponents of capital punishment hasten to insist that the execution was not "cruel and unusual."

5. **Propaganda techniques** such as bandwagon, plain folks, name-calling, testimonial

Animal rights activists are frequently at odds with medical researchers. The activists may refer to those conducting research as "cruel" or "sadistic." Researchers, on the other hand, may call the activists names like "fanatic" or "kook."

Those in support of animal research may use a testimonial such as this one from Dr. Michael E. DeBakey, chair of surgery, and director of the DeBakey Heart Center at Baylor College of Medicine in Houston, Texas:

> Even with today's technology, I could not have developed on a computer the roller pump that made open-heart surgery possible or the artificial artery that restored to health previously doomed patients with aneurysms. Nor could we have attempted the first successful coronary artery bypass or implanted the first temporary mechanical heart with which we saved a patient's life two decades ago.

From Michael E. DeBakey, Editorial, "Holding Human Health Hostage," *Journal of Investigative Surgery,* Vol. 1, 1988, in Annette T. Rottenberg, *Elements of Argument.* New York: Bedford Books of St. Martin's Press, 1991, p. 378.

When an author uses a testimonial, ask yourself the following questions:

Is the writer an authority in that particular field?

Is this the writer's specific area of competence?

Is the writer biased?

Is the writer likely to gain some advantage from the testimonial?

6. **Psychological appeals**

This technique is used frequently by the media to create ads that appeal directly to our desire for power, prestige, sex, or popularity.

For example, People for the Ethical Treatment of Animals (PETA) used "sex appeal" when it had five well-known models pose naked, "wearing only their skins," to protest the buying of fur coats.

7. **Moral appeals**

Authors may seek to appeal to your sense of morality or fair play.

C. S. Lewis was a professor of English literature at Oxford and Cambridge Universities. He is known for his writings on Christianity and morality. His tales for children include the popular *The Lion, the Witch, and the Wardrobe* in the Chronicles of Narnia series. Lewis, in arguing against experimental surgery on animals, said:

> If we cut up beasts simply because they cannot prevent us and because we are backing our own side in the struggle for existence, it is only logical to cut up imbeciles, criminals, enemies, or capitalists for the same reason.

From C. S. Lewis, "Vivisection," pamphlet by Anti-Vivisection Society, 1947, in Annette T. Rottenberg, *Elements of Argument*. New York: Bedford Books of St. Martin's Press, 1991, p. 378.

On this same issue, PETA has publicized an ad showing a bulbous-headed alien looking for humans for scientific experiments. The caption in this ad says:

> Powerful, big-brained aliens from outer space with government grants to spend seek human beings for experimentation. Although our diseases do not occur naturally in your species, we plan to infect humans to test experimental drugs. Subjects can expect to convulse, vomit, go blind, develop painful rashes, bleed internally, lose bladder and bowel control, and die. Survivors may be recycled into other tests. Among the most desirable specimens are the homeless, orphans, and other strays who have little or no protection. Your participation may help our superior species or at least satisfy our curiosity.

PETA officials say they began the campaign because laboratories that use animals for research often justify their action by assigning a superior status to human beings. PETA spokesperson Joey Penello said, "We are trying to address the issue of vivisection (surgery on living animals) in a new way. How would we feel if they did to us what we've been do-ing to animals for years?"

From Michael E. DeBakey, Editorial, "Holding Human Health Hostage," *Journal of Investigative Surgery*, Vol. 1, 1988, in Annette T. Rottenberg, *Elements of Argument*. New York: Bedford Books of St. Martin's Press, 1991, p. 383.

8. **Appeal to authority**

Authors may call attention to their integrity, intelligence, and knowledge to con-vince you to trust their judgment and believe them.

Judge Alex Kozinski wrote an article for *The New Yorker* magazine supporting the death penalty. Near the beginning of the article, he established his authority on this topic by saying:

> As a judge on the United States Court of Appeals for the Ninth Circuit, I hear cases from nine states and two territories spread over the western United States and Oceania.

In addition to the above techniques, be sure to note the author's

Affiliations. Look for information in the introduction that tells you what types of people or organizations the author associates with.

Assumptions. Be sure to note the author's principal beliefs. What ideas does the author hold that enable him or her to present this particular argument?

Organization. Authors are more likely to be trying to persuade you of some-thing when they withhold the purpose or the main idea until the end.

In summary, authors who are trying to persuade do not usually write material that is entirely objective and meant solely to inform. Instead, such authors tend to use factual material to bolster their opinions on a particular subject. By recognizing per-suasive techniques and understanding the author's motives, you can avoid being manipulated and become better able to evaluate the issue on its own merits.

Drawing Conclusions: Inductive and Deductive Reasoning

In the final step of analyzing a selection, readers must evaluate the soundness of the author's reasoning.

All of us draw conclusions based on what we think is reasonable and acceptable. Often these conclusions are based on inductive or deductive reasoning.

Inductive Reasoning

The word parts for "inductive" are *in* meaning "into" and *duc* meaning "to lead." In **inductive reasoning,** specific examples, evidence, or propositions lead to a more gen-eral conclusion. We reason inductively all the time.

An example of inductive reasoning is the following:

> It's time for me to plan my vacation. The last time Steve flew on Snoozy Air-lines, they lost his luggage. My friend Greg says Skyloft is never on time. Tony says RightAir is always too crowded. Ryan and Bonnie have flown many miles on SureFlight and have never had any problems. Therefore, I think I'll fly on SureFlight too.

As this example implies, a conclusion reached by inductive reasoning is only as valid as the specific information on which it is based. Maybe if I had talked to more people, I would have heard some critical comments about SureFlight or some flattering comments about Snoozy or SkyLoft.

So you can see that inductive reasoning leads to a conclusion that is only probably correct. A conclusion becomes more likely to be correct when the specific information on which it is based improves.

Deductive Reasoning

Deductive reasoning goes in the opposite direction from inductive reasoning. *De* means "away from," and **deductive reasoning** moves away from the general to the specific. A conclusion reached through deductive reasoning is seen as following logically from more general propositions or statements. Just as we often reason inductively, we also often reason deductively.

A **syllogism** is a common kind of deductive reasoning. The following is an example of a syllogism:

> All men are mortal.
> Harrison Ford is a man.
> Harrison Ford is mortal.

Here is another example of a syllogism:

> "All of the comedies starring Ben Stiller are really enjoyable. He's starring in the movie *Night of the Museum 2*. This movie is going to be really enjoyable."

You can see that whether the conclusion drawn by deductive reasoning is valid depends on whether the general statements on which it is based are correct. If not all Ben Stiller comedies really are enjoyable—maybe some were boring—then it does not follow that his movie *Night of the Museum 2* has to be enjoyable. Or maybe all Ben Stiller comedies are enjoyable, but he is not really starring in *Night of the Museum 2* and instead is just playing a supporting role, Again, the conclusion would not follow.

Does the *Zits* cartoon shown here make use of a syllogism? Is the conclusion a valid one?

Zits

The Scientific Process

Inductive and deductive reasoning are both involved in the **scientific process.** Scientists do research, which involves collecting and analyzing data, and then they seek to draw a general conclusion or hypothesis from their research. This process of formulating hypotheses from research involves inductive reasoning. Scientists then use deductive reasoning to test their hypotheses. A hypothesis tells a scientist what should happen when the scientist collects further data or performs another test. If the new data or test is consistent with the hypothesis, the hypothesis is confirmed; if not, the hypothesis needs to be modified or rejected. Scientists often have to revise their hypotheses to keep up with new research.

For example, suppose a friend offers to set you up on a blind date. You have some reservations about blind dates, so you decide to do a little informal scientific research on the subject. You collect data on blind dates by talking to a number of people who have been on blind dates. All of these people tell you that they had a terrible experience. So, using inductive reasoning, you formulate a hypothesis based on your research: Anyone who goes on a blind date will have a miserable time.

Then, reasoning deductively from your hypothesis, you conclude that should you accept your friend's offer of a blind date, you will have a miserable time. But you're either courageous or desperate, and you decide to go on the blind date anyway. If it turns out that you have a miserable time, your hypothesis is confirmed. But if it turns out that you have a good time, your hypothesis has been contradicted and needs some further work. You might then formulate a new hypothesis: If you go on a blind date, chances are high that you will have a miserable time, but you might get lucky and have a good time.

In the pages that follow, you, as a critical reader, will need to evaluate the author's reasoning to see how valid or persuasive it is.

READING

"A DNA fingerprint would identify with greater accuracy than any other test the biological father of Katie."

TUNING IN TO READING

This article on DNA demonstrates how scientists evaluate evidence in order to come to a reasonable conclusion. Read the article carefully, noting the inductive and deductive reasoning, and then answer the questions that follow.

NOTES ON VOCABULARY

coin   to invent. The Roman method of producing coins was to make a metal blank, place the blank upon a die that held an image, and then use a wedge-shaped tool called a *cuneus* to hammer or stamp the image into the metal. Over time, *cuneus* came to be spelled as *cuigne*, then *coing*, and finally *coin*. Later *coin* came to refer not only to currency but also to the fabrication of any unusual term or process.

DNA Fingerprinting
Ruth Bernstein and Stephen Bernstein

John and Susan Gladstone had a young child and a bad marriage. They decided to divorce, but both of them wanted to keep their three-year-old daughter, Katie. Susan shocked her husband when she claimed the child was not his. Katie's biological father, she said, was the man next door. Susan planned to move in with him and take Katie with her.

DNA, or deoxyribonucleic acid, is a protein that is a building block of life. It disappears rapidly from carcasses and thus is rarely found in fossils. However, in 1993 in Lebanon, DNA was found in a 120- to 135-million-year-old weevil.

2   John couldn't believe he wasn't Katie's father but arranged a paternity test to make sure. Samples of blood were taken from all three Gladstones as well as from the man next door, and DNA fingerprints were made of the DNA molecules in the white blood cells. A DNA fingerprint would identify with greater accuracy than any other test the biological father of Katie.

3   DNA fingerprinting was developed in 1985 by a British geneticist, Alec Jeffreys, at the University of Leicester. He coined the term *DNA fingerprinting* and was the first to use techniques of genetic engineering in paternity and murder cases.

4   Jeffreys observed that human DNA contains particular sequences of bases that are repeated many times. The repetitive sequences, which appear within genes and between genes, do not code for proteins. The number of times the sequences are repeated varies from one person to the next. Thus, when the same DNA molecule in different people is cut with the same restriction enzyme (which cuts the DNA at the same base sequences), the lengths of the fragments vary: someone with a longer fragment has more repetitive sequences than someone with a shorter fragment. Moreover, the number of repetitive sequences, and so the fragment length, is inherited. A child inherits fragment lengths from both parents. The array of fragments should contain some like the mother's array and others like the father's array.

5   DNA molecules taken from white blood cells of the Gladstones and the man next door were fragmented by restriction enzymes and the fragments lined up according to length by gel electrophoresis. The fragments were then labeled with DNA probes (built to match the repetitive sequences) so that they could be seen and photographed. The array of fragments for each person appears as a pattern of bands, similar to the bar codes used in supermarkets.

6   A DNA fingerprint is remarkably precise. Virtually everyone, except an identical twin, has a unique banding pattern. And all that is needed to identify a person is a tiny sample of blood, semen, skin, or hair.

7   Try to help unravel the mystery of Katie's parentage. Remember that Katie's fingerprint is a mixture of her mother's fragments and her father's. A child inherits half the fragment lengths from each parent.

8   The fingerprints of Susan, Katie, and John Gladstone, as well as the man next door, are shown in the figure on the next page. Each column of bars is a DNA fingerprint. Each bar in a column represents a fragment of DNA. The vertical arrangement of bars represents the DNA fragments sorted according to length. The four fragments shown are from a mother (Susan), a child (Katie), and two men (the man next door and John) who claim to be Katie's father.

9   The bars reveal that the man next door is Katie's real father. Katie's fingerprint is a mixture of her mother's fragments and fragments in the fingerprint of the man next door. Note that Katie has bands found in the fingerprint of the man next door but not found in either her mother's fingerprint and John's fingerprint. John had helped raise Katie, but the man next door gave her his genes. The court ruled that Katie should live with her biological mother and father.

From Ruth Bernstein and Stephen Bernstein, *Biology*. Dubuque, IA: Wm. C. Brown Publishers, 1996, p. 222. Reprinted by permission of the authors.

In Your Own Words

1. When Jeffreys was collecting data and drawing conclusions about their usefulness for "fingerprinting," was he thinking primarily inductively or deductively? (Hint: Keep in mind that inductive reasoning goes from the specific to the general, and deductive reasoning goes from the general to the specific.)

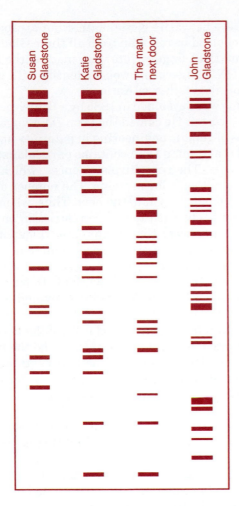

Katie's Father

2. If Jeffreys's hypothesis is correct, matching bands should exist between Katie and her mother, and Katie and her natural father. Is this conclusion—that these matching bands should be present—reached by inductive or deductive reasoning?

3. Why must a criminal be careful not to leave a single cell at the scene of the crime?

4. Can you see any potential problems with DNA evidence?

What follows is an odd tale of the use of nonhuman DNA in a murder trial. A Canadian man was convicted of murdering his former wife after hairs in a blood-stained jacket were genetically matched to his parents' cat.

The body of the ex-wife was found in a shallow grave two months after she had been reported missing. At the same site, a bloody leather jacket in a plastic sack was also discovered. Tests revealed that the bloodstains on the jacket belonged to the woman. Inside the lining of the jacket, cat hairs were discovered.

The man had been living with his parents and Snowball, a white short-haired cat. The police sent a blood sample from Snowball and the hair from the jacket to Stephen O'Brien of the National Cancer Institute in Maryland. O'Brien has studied cat genetics for over 20 years. According to O'Brien, Snowball's DNA matched genetic material from the root of one of the hairs.

In order to determine that the match was not the result of chance, a local veterinarian drew blood randomly from 19 cats. O'Brien studied the DNA in those samples and data from a survey of nine cats from the United States. His research concluded that the likelihood that the jacket hair DNA would match Snowball's DNA just by chance was about 1 in 45 million. As a result, the ex-husband was convicted of second-degree murder.

Nonhuman DNA evidence has been used to successfully prosecute other murderers. Another famous case occurred in Arizona in 1993, when a man was convicted after DNA from seed pods in his pickup truck was matched to a Palo Verde tree at the site where the victim's body was discovered.

5. What the investigators did in the case of the Canadian man was collect evidence that he had killed his former wife. Was this reasoning process primarily inductive or deductive? Explain.

6. Would you feel comfortable convicting someone of murder on the basis of a scientific analysis of nonhuman DNA? Why or why not?

7. When DNA is used to solve crimes, what assumptions about DNA are being made?

A new study reported in *Nature* magazine suggests that DNA can be found on everyday objects, such as pens, keys, telephones, and glasses that were only casually touched by our hands. We apparently leave DNA in many places that can be traced back to us. Researchers have also determined that people can pick up other people's DNA, particularly on their hands. If a person can pick up your DNA from a handshake or something you touched, that at least raises the possibility that a person could "plant" or accidentally leave your DNA at a crime scene, thus implicating you in a crime you didn't commit.

8. Look at the following cartoon. Do you think the circumstantial evidence is already enough to convict the boys of the crime? Explain.

Frank and Ernest

FRANK & ERNEST: © Thaves/Dist. by Newspaper Enterprise Association, Inc.

In the last few years, a number of prisoners have been set free because of further DNA testing. Sometimes, prosecutors remained convinced of the guilt of these prisoners despite the new testing. As a result, some prosecutors have begun to change their view of DNA testing. Instead of viewing it as something that absolutely shows guilt or innocence, they may now view it as just another important piece of evidence. As these prosecutors are beginning to realize, while DNA testing can theoretically provide positive proof of guilt or innocence, the validity of the results can be compromised by problems in handling the evidence and interpreting the results.

9. If, as some prosecutors say, DNA testing has been used to wrongly gain freedom for some prisoners, is it fair or right for prosecutors during a trial to tell jurors that DNA testing conclusively proves the defendant's guilt?

10. Do you think that DNA testing is more or less persuasive than simple fingerprinting?

11. Based on the information that has been presented here, do you think DNA evidence should be admissible in a court of law to convict people of crimes? Give your reasons.

12. Is DNA playing an important role in any criminal investigation that has recently been in the news?

Eyewitness Testimony

Read the following account of mistaken identity. Does this excerpt tell you anything about the reliability of identification evidence?

In 1984, I was a 22-year-old college student with a perfect GPA and a bright future. One dark night someone broke into my apartment, put a knife to my throat, and raped me.

During my ordeal I was determined that if, by the grace of God, I should live, I was going to make sure that my rapist was caught and punished. My mind quickly separated me from my body and began recording every detail of my attacker. I carefully studied his face: noting his hairline, his brow, his chin. I listened hard to his voice, his speech, his words. I looked for scars, for tattoos, for anything that would help me identify him. Then, after what seemed like an eternity, and in a brief moment when my rapist let down his guard, I fled from my apartment in the early morning wrapped only in a blanket. I had survived.

Later that day I began the painstaking process of trying to bring my attacker to justice. For hours I sat with a police artist and meticulously looked through books filled with hundreds of noses, eyes, eyebrows, hairlines, nostrils, and lips—reliving the attack again and again in the minute details that together made up his composite sketch. The next day the newspaper carried my rapist's image on the front page. There was a lead. The case had its first suspect. Several days later I sat before a series of photographs and picked out my attacker. I got him. I knew he was the man. I was completely confident. I was sure.

When the case went to trial six months later, I took the witness stand, put my hand on the Bible, and swore to "tell the whole truth and nothing but the truth." Based on my eyewitness testimony Ronald Junior Cotton was sentenced to prison for life. Ronald Cotton was never going to see the light of day again. Ronald Cotton would never rape another woman again.

During a 1987 retrial hearing the defense brought forward another inmate, Bobby Poole, who had bragged of raping me. In court, he denied raping me. When asked if I had ever seen this man, I emphatically answered that I had never seen him before in my life. Another victim agreed. Ronald Cotton was resentenced to two life sentences with no chance for parole.

In 1995, 11 years after I had first identified Ronald Cotton as my rapist, I was asked if I would consent to a blood sample so that DNA tests could be run on evidence from the rape. I agreed because I knew that Ronald Cotton had raped me and DNA was only going to confirm that.

I will never forget the day I learned the DNA results. I stood in my kitchen as the detective and district attorney told me: "Ronald Cotton didn't rape you. It was Bobby Poole." Their words struck me like a thunderbolt. The man I was convinced I never saw before in my life was the man who held a knife to my throat, who hurt me, who raped me, who crushed my spirit, who robbed me of my soul. The man I was positive did all those things and whose face continued to haunt me at night was innocent.

Ronald Cotton was released from prison after serving 11 years, becoming the first convicted felon in North Carolina exonerated through DNA testing. Bobby Poole, serving a life sentence of his own and dying of cancer, confessed to the rapes without remorse.

Ronald Cotton and I now shared something in the brutal crime that had pitted us against each other for years—we were both victims. My part in his conviction, though, filled me with guilt and shame. We were the same age, so I knew what he had missed during those 11 years in prison. I had had the opportunity to move on and begin to heal. To graduate from college. To find trust and love in marriage. To find self-confidence in work. And to find the hope of a bright future in the gifts of my beautiful children. Ronald Cotton, on the other hand, spent those years alone defending himself from the violence that punctuated his life in prison.

Sometime after Ronald Cotton's release I requested a meeting through our attorneys so that I might say I was very sorry and seek his forgiveness. In the end, Ron and I finally found total freedom through forgiveness. I will forever look back now through our unlikely friendship, thankful that in Ron's case of mistaken identity, I wasn't dead wrong.

Reprinted by permission of Jennifer Thompson-Cannino. Jennifer Thompson-Cannino and Ronald Cotton are the authors of *Picking Cotton: Our Memoir of Injustice and Redemption.* New York: St. Martin's Press, 2009.

Written Assignment

In a few paragraphs discuss the following: What does the excerpt tell you about the importance of DNA?

Internet Activity

Some scholars think that Thomas Jefferson fathered a child with one of his slaves, Sally Hemings. To find more information about Jefferson and this controversy, go to the following Web site:

www.monticello.org

Type the name "Sally Hemings" into the search box, or click on "plantation life" and then "lives." Summarize your findings.

Evaluating the Evidence in Editorials, Letters to the Editor, Advertisements, and Political Cartoons

Editorials

In contrast to news stories, which try to be objective, an **editorial** is a statement of personal opinion. As such, editorials are much more subjective than textbook selections or newspaper and magazine articles. The purpose of an editorial is to persuade readers to believe one thing rather than another. Editorials are found in magazines, newspapers, and also on radio and television. Editorials tend to be short and direct, and so they are particularly appealing to those who dislike lengthy articles and complex analyses. While most editorials provide a quick update of a topic, it is generally advisable to have some knowledge of the topic being discussed in advance, so that you are in a better position to evaluate the material. When you are reading or listening to an editorial, it is sometimes helpful to engage in a mental dialog with the author.

When you are having a discussion (or an argument) with a friend, you might ask such questions as "Is that so?" "Where did you get that information?" and "But, what about this?" You might try to ask similar questions when you are evaluating an editorial. Here are some additional tips for reading editorials.

1. Think about the author. How authoritative is he or she? Is this topic within the author's area of expertise? Editorials, being personal in nature, reveal a lot about the author. Is he or she someone you respect?

2. Read the title of the editorial first. The title may reveal the author's position at the outset.

3. While a good editorial is passionate, it is your job as reader to identify the author's biases and determine whether or not you agree with the positions presented. Try to determine the author's predispositions or biases as you read.

4. Consider how the author of the editorial handles opposing positions. Does he or she acknowledge other positions? Does he or she attempt to rebut the opposing arguments?

5. Consider whether the editorial writer differentiates between important and trivial arguments. Make a list to see whether you can determine which arguments are important to making the case and which are not.

6. Consider whether the author recommends a solution to the problem. If so, is the solution reasonable or practical? Can it be implemented? If the problem cannot be solved, does the author provide constructive suggestions for improving the situation?

The last section of this chapter focuses on the current U.S. policy toward marijuana. You will be reading and evaluating editorials, letters to the editor, an advertisement, and a political cartoon on this topic.

> *"The question whether marijuana has any legitimate medical*
> *uses has been hotly debated."*

Marijuana—Background Information

Paul M. Insel

Marijuana is the most widely used illegal drug in the United States (cocaine is second). More than 40% of Americans—more than 90 million—have tried marijuana at least once; among 21–25-year-olds, more than 50% have tried marijuana. In recent surveys, about 18% of college students report using marijuana within the last month.

2   Marijuana is a crude preparation of various parts of the Indian hemp plant *Cannabis sativa*, which grows in most parts of the world. THC (tetrahydrocannabinol) is the main active ingredient in marijuana. Based on THC content, the potency of marijuana preparations varies widely. Marijuana plants that grow wild often have less than 1% THC in their leaves, whereas when selected strains are cultivated, the bud leaves from the flowering tops may contain 7–8% THC. Hashish, a potent preparation made from the thick resin that exudes from the leaves, may contain up to 14% THC. These various preparations have all been known and used for centuries, so the frequently heard claim that today's marijuana is more potent than the marijuana of the 1970s is not strictly true. However,

a greater proportion of the marijuana sold today is of the higher potency; hence, the average potency of street marijuana has increased.

"In June of 2005, the United States Supreme Court ruled that federal authorities may prosecute sick people whose doctors prescribe marijuana to ease pain."

Medical Marijuana Ruling

ASSOCIATED PRESS

IN JUNE OF 2005, the United States Supreme Court ruled that federal authorities may prosecute sick people whose doctors prescribe marijuana to ease pain, concluding that state laws don't protect users from a federal ban on the drug. The court said the prosecution of marijuana users under the federal Controlled Substances Act was constitutional.

Justice John Paul Stevens, writing the 6–3 decision, said the court was not passing judgment on the potential medical benefits of marijuana. In the court's main decision, Stevens raised concerns about abuse of marijuana laws. "Our cases have taught us that there are some unscrupulous physicians who over-prescribe when it is sufficiently profitable to do so," he said.

Arguments for and against Legalizing the Use of Marijuana for Medicinal Purposes

The following two editorials from *The American Legion Magazine* discuss the issue of medical marijuana.

The first editorial was written by Ethan Nadelmann, founder and executive director of the Drug Policy Alliance, an organization that promotes alternatives to the war on drugs.

"Marijuana may be an unconventional medicine, but it works."

"For" Argument   BY ETHAN NADELMANN

Marijuana may be an unconventional medicine, but it works. Montel Williams, decorated former naval intelligence officer and talk-show host, uses medical marijuana to help him control the symptoms of multiple sclerosis. So does Keith Vines, an assistant district attorney, retired Air Force Captain and former federal narcotics prosecutor living with AIDS.

2   These men are just two of hundreds of thousands of Americans who use marijuana to treat pain from accidents or debilitating conditions such as MS; to help restore appetite during chemotherapy; to treat the symptoms of AIDS, glaucoma, and epilepsy; and for a host of other medical reasons.

3   The vast majority are law-abiding citizens who suffer from chronic pain and illness. They use marijuana as medicine because it works better than anything else, with fewer negative side effects. Many never smoked marijuana until they became sick. Dozens of scientific studies demonstrate marijuana's safety and therapeutic value.

4   More than two thirds of Americans say marijuana should be legal for medical purposes—and that's the law now in 10 states.

5   Only one big problem: the federal government. The Clinton administration was callous, and the Bush administration has been downright cruel, arresting and prosecuting patients and providers. Federal drug enforcement agents, acting at the behest of the Justice Department, even raided a hospice and handcuffed frail and elderly patients who use marijuana as medicine.

6   The crackdown represents a shameful abuse of power: punishing sick people for using the medicine that works best for them, threatening doctors who exercise responsible medical judgment, and prohibiting state governments from acting in the interests of their own citizens.

7   It's time to tell the feds to get out of the doctors' offices and medicine cabinets, and out of the way of citizens who simply want to do what's right.

The second editorial was written by John P. Walters, the federal drug czar under President George W. Bush and past deputy director for supply reduction in the Office of National Drug Control Policy.

"In America today, well-financed organizations
and individuals are exploiting the pain of sick people,
and the compassion of those who care about them,
to legalize marijuana."

Ethan Nadelmann, "Legalize Medicinal Marijuana," *The American Legion Magazine,* November 2004, p. 10. Copyright © 2004 Ethan Nadelmann. Reprinted by permission of the author.

"Against" Argument   BY JOHN P. WALTERS

In America today, well-financed organizations and individuals are exploiting the pain of sick people, and the compassion of those who care about them, to legalize marijuana. Advocating for the use of a smoked weed under the guise of medicine is dishonest, scientifically irresponsible and contradictory to the high standards of quality effectiveness guaranteed by the U.S. Food and Drug Administration.

2   Our medical system relies on proven scientific research to protect U.S. citizens from unsafe and ineffective products. Research has not demonstrated that smoked marijuana is helpful as medicine. The FDA has also stated that while marijuana use has no proven benefits, it does have long-term risks associated with it. Furthermore, the British Lung Foundation says that smoking three to four marijuana cigarettes a day is as harmful for your lungs as smoking 20 tobacco cigarettes.

3   Some claim smoking marijuana helps ease symptoms associated with certain illnesses. The fact that smoking a joint may make them feel better is not in dispute. But simply feeling better is not the standard of modern medicine. If it were, snake oils and miracle potions would still line our medicine cabinets today.

4   The reality is that modern science has afforded us safe alternatives to smoking a crude plant. The FDA-approved drug Marinol makes the component in marijuana known as THC available in pill form. A product that delivers marijuana's THC

through an inhaler is currently in development. The difference between these medicines and smoking a joint: the user does not get high.

5   Our veterans have sacrificed much to secure the blessings we enjoy today, including a safe and reliable medical system grounded in research and unparalleled in the world. We owe it to them to protect the integrity of that system and to prevent those seeking to legalize marijuana from riding on the coattails of our compassion.

John P. Walters, "Legalize Medicinal Marijuana," *The American Legion Magazine*, November 2004, p. 10.

Analyzing the Editorials—Propaganda Techniques

Editorials frequently use propaganda techniques in an effort to make their case. Try to identify the propaganda techniques used in these editorials. Below is a chart for you to fill in. First, take the argument in favor of legalizing the use of marijuana for medicinal purposes, and see how many propaganda techniques you can identify. When you find a propaganda technique being used, record it in the appropriate box. Some boxes have already been filled in for you. Then look at the arguments against legalizing the use of marijuana for medicinal purposes, and see how many propaganda techniques you can identify. Record these too. When you finish filling in the chart, answer the question that follows.

Propaganda Technique	"For" Argument	"Against" Argument
Name-calling	Clinton administration—callous; Bush administration—cruel	Advocating use of marijuana under guise of medicine is dishonest, scientifically irresponsible, and contradictory.
Glittering generalities	It works.	Safe and reliable medical system
Transfer		
False analogy		
Testimonial		
Plain folks		
Card stacking		
Bandwagon		
Either/or argument		

What conclusions can you draw about the use of propaganda techniques in these two editorials?

_____

_____

_____

_____

_____

Analyzing the Editorials—Techniques for Appealing to Readers

Now that you have read the two editorials, choose one of them and use it to answer the following questions.

1. **Author's purpose.** Is it the author's primary purpose to inform or to persuade? Why do you think so?

_____

_____

_____

_____

2. **Emotional appeals.** Where does the author use language that is meant to appeal to your emotions? Give an example of material that is included in the editorial for its emotional appeal.

_____

_____

_____

_____

3. **Ethical appeals.** Does the editorial cite any experts? What do the experts have to say about the topic of the editorial? How much trust should you put in what the experts say? Might other experts have different opinions?

_____

_____

_____

_____

4. **Logical appeals.** What logical or reasonable arguments are included in the editorial? Does the editorial make use of inductive or deductive reasoning?

_____

_____

_____

_____

5. **Psychological appeals.** Does the editorial say anything that is intended to manipulate you psychologically by appealing to your need for acceptance, power, prestige, and so forth?

_____

_____

_____

_____

6. **Tone.** What is the author's tone? Is the tone meant to influence or manipulate you? Give specific examples of how the author uses tone to affect you.

_____

_____

_____

_____

7. **Bias.** What is the author's specific bias? Where does this bias appear in the editorial—at the beginning, the middle, or the end?

_____

_____

_____

_____

War on Drugs: Opposing Viewpoints

The following two editorials are from _USA Today_. The first was written by the editorial staff and represents the viewpoint of the newspaper itself. The opposing viewpoint is by John Walters, who also wrote the opposing viewpoint presented above.

War on Drugs Gone to Pot

Our View: Massive Arrests Just Smoke Screen Hiding Impotency of Crackdown

BY _USA TODAY_ EDITORIAL STAFF

MARIJUANA IS THE MOST widely used illegal substance. About 15 million Americans smoke it, and police make nearly 7,000,000 pot related arrests each year, accounting for nearly half of all drug arrests.

2 The $35-billion-a-year war on drugs has turned largely into a war on marijuana and a losing war at that. Pot isn't harmless, but shouldn't law enforcement focus more of its resources on hard drugs—cocaine, heroin, and methamphetamines—that are

associated with violence and devastated lives.

3 According to a new study by The Sentencing Project, a liberal research group that favors alternatives to incarceration:

- Marijuana arrests increased 113 percent from 1990 through 2002, while arrests for all other drugs rose just 10 percent.
- Four of five marijuana arrests are for possession, not dealing.

4 The theory behind the war on drugs is that enough arrests will curtail both supply and demand. But the impact of increased marijuana arrests appears negligible. According to private and government studies, overall marijuana use is the same as it was in 1990, while daily use by high school seniors has nearly tripled, from 2.2 percent to 6 percent. Since 1992, the inflation-adjusted price of pot has fallen about 16 percent while potency has doubled, the studies show.

5 So the intensified crackdown has coincided with cheaper, stronger pot that's readily available. Law enforcement's efforts to arrest marijuana smokers are diverting resources from combating other crimes and those who traffic in hard drugs.

6 Few people arrested for possessing marijuana serve jail time, but the consequences they face are severe. They may not qualify for federal student loans or entry to public housing, may lose the right to vote, and face a job market with criminal records they must report to potential employers.

7 The drug war against low-level users also sparks resentment against police, particularly in the minority community. African-Americans represent 14 percent of marijuana users but account for 30 percent of arrests, The Sentencing Project study found.

8 The get-tough approach is showing cracks both at home and abroad. Twelve states have some form of decriminalization or reduced sentences. Great Britain, Canada and Russia have decriminalized possession of small amounts of the drug.

9 Today's more potent marijuana carries substantial health and social risks. It can lead to depression, thoughts of suicide and schizophrenia, especially among teens, according to government research. Its use should be discouraged. But it's a smoke screen to suggest that rising arrest numbers show the war on drugs is working. It's time for a serious debate on whether massive arrests of low-level users are worth the cost or having any benefit.

From *USA Today*, May 18, 2005, p. A10. Reprinted with permission.

 **COMPREHENSION CHECKUP**

Multiple Choice

Directions: For each item, write the letter corresponding to the best answer on the line provided.

_____ 1. Which of the following best expresses the main idea?
   a. Marijuana is a harmful drug.
   b. Marijuana does less damage to individuals and society as a whole than hard drugs do.

c. The current war on drugs is not working.
d. Marijuana use by teens should be discouraged.

_____ 2. Which of the following statements directly supports the author's main idea?
   a. African-Americans represent 14 percent of marijuana users but account for 30 percent of arrests.
   b. [Marijuana] can lead to depression, thoughts of suicide, and schizophrenia, especially among teens, according to government research.
   c. According to private and government studies, daily use by high school seniors has nearly tripled from 2.2 percent to 6 percent.
   d. None of the above.

_____ 3. "It's time for a serious debate on whether massive arrests of low-level users are worth the cost or having any benefit." This sentence makes a statement of
   a. fact.
   b. opinion.

_____ 4. An antonym for the word *potent* is
   a. weak.
   b. powerful.
   c. strong.
   d. none of the above.

_____ 5. The main purpose of the editorial is to
   a. explain.
   b. persuade.
   c. entertain.
   d. define.

_____ 6. The author chose the title "War on Drugs Gone to Pot" because
   a. it is a "play" on the word *pot*.
   b. it indicates that the war on drugs is not going well.
   c. it indicates that the focus of the war on drugs is "pot" rather than hard drugs like cocaine and heroin.
   d. all of the above.

_____ 7. The phrase "smoke screen" indicates
   a. an openness toward new information.
   b. a concealing of the truth with misleading information.
   c. the placement of a device similar to a smoke detector.
   d. none of the above.

_____ 8. The phrase "impotency of crackdown" implies that the U.S. government is
   a. winning the war on drugs.
   b. holding its own in the war on drugs.
   c. ineffective in the war on drugs.
   d. none of the above.

_____ 9. According to the editorial, all of the following statements are true about the war on drugs *except* for which?
   a. The U.S. government's position is that if enough people are arrested, both the supply of drugs and the demand for drugs will decrease.
   b. During the period of "cracking down" on drugs, marijuana has gotten cheaper and more potent, and become more readily available.

     c. Most people arrested for possessing small amounts of marijuana serve lengthy sentences.

     d. Those arrested for possession of marijuana may be ineligible for a host of government-related benefits.

_____ 10. According to the editorial, marijuana use is linked to all of the following *except*

     a. depression.

     b. suicidal thoughts.

     c. cancer.

     d. schizophrenia.

_____ 11. An antonym for the word *negligible* is

     a. irrelevant.

     b. significant.

     c. minor.

     d. infinitesimal.

True or False

Directions: Indicate whether each statement is true or false by writing **T** or **F** in the space provided.

_____ 12. Nearly half of all drug arrests are pot-related.

_____ 13. The majority of marijuana arrests are for possession, not dealing.

_____ 14. Daily use of pot by high school seniors is currently lower than in the 1990s.

_____ 15. The majority of states have decriminalized possession of marijuana.

_____ 16. Marijuana use is associated with few, if any, health risks.

Marijuana Policy Just Right

Opposing View: Focus Is Response to New Research on Drug's Potency, Use, and Risks

BY JOHN WALTERS

ASSERTIONS THAT OUR NATION'S DRUG policy minimizes cocaine and heroin while focusing on marijuana are misleading. The fallacy involves interpreting drug arrests as signals of changed drug policy, rather than as indicators of drug use. As drug use went down in the 1980s, arrests fell accordingly. When drug use climbed between 1992 and 1997, arrests followed suit. And when the cocaine epidemic struck, cocaine arrests rose steeply, only to drop as the epidemic waned.

2 The commonsense conclusion is that drug use rates and criminal justice responses are linked. Thus the key to reducing drug arrests is reducing drug use. Important progress has already occurred—youth drug use has declined 17 percent since 2001.

3 Our drug policy balances prevention, treatment and interdiction. Criminal justice sanctions are sometimes necessary, but we are not locking up low-level marijuana offenders. Rather, drug courts, which use supervised treatment to help users (rather than prison) are a

critical component of our approach. President Bush has requested an extra $30 million to expand the program.

4 We are more concerned about marijuana today. Studies long ago established marijuana as a risky substance. For youth, it is the single largest source of abuse and dependency. But compelling new research shows an increased public health threat.

5 First, marijuana potency has more than doubled within the past 10 years. Second, kids are using marijuana at younger ages, during crucial periods in their development, and thereby increasing risks

that extend into adult life. And third, research from many nations now implicates marijuana's role in mental illness.

6 Youth marijuana use elevates risks of depression, psychosis, even schizophrenia. For those with predispositions to mental disorders, the risk is compounded. Some studies show marijuana can trigger the onset or increase the severity of mental illness.

7 Coming to grips with new facts, we are focusing on marijuana. As we do so, we respond to a fundamental public health problem in a balanced and responsible manner.

From *USA Today*, May 18, 2005, p. A10.

 COMPREHENSIVE CHECKUP

Short Answer

Directions: Answer the following questions briefly, in a few words or sentences as appropriate.

1. Explain the cause-and-effect relationships in paragraph 1.

   Cause: Because drug use went down during the 1980s,

   Effect: _____

   Cause: Because drug use climbed between 1992 and 1997,

   Effect: _____

2. Because the author sees a cause-and-effect relationship between drug use and arrest rates, he believes that the key to reducing drug arrests is to

   _____

3. What does the author mean by the expression "coming to grips with new facts"?

   _____

Multiple Choice

Directions: For each item, write the letter corresponding to the best answer on the line provided.

_____ 1. The "epidemic waned" means that it
   a. increased.
   b. abated.
   c. declined.
   d. both b and c.

_____ 2. The author believes that marijuana is a public health threat for all of the following reasons *except* for which?
  a. Marijuana today is more powerful than it used to be.
  b. Children begin using marijuana at critical points in their development.
  c. Marijuana is a gateway drug that leads to harder drugs.
  d. Marijuana has been correlated to mental illness.

_____ 3. The author would agree with all of the following *except* for which?
  a. Because of the new research, the focus of the U.S. drug program should be on marijuana.
  b. The nation's current drug policy is both balanced and responsible.
  c. Little or no progress has been made in reducing youth drug abuse.
  d. Drug courts, which treat rather than imprison, are a key part of the current approach to controlling drug abuse.

_____ 4. Which of the following statements is an opinion?
  a. The commonsense conclusion is that drug use rates and criminal justice responses are linked.
  b. We are more concerned about marijuana today.
  c. When drug use climbed between 1992 and 1997, arrests followed suit.
  d. Both a and b.

_____ 5. If you have a *predisposition* to something, you are
  a. ignorant of it.
  b. angry about it.
  c. more susceptible to it.
  d. more resistant to it.

True or False

Directions: Indicate whether each statement is true or false by writing **T** or **F** in the space provided.

_____ 6. *Interdiction* means an official prohibition or restraint.

_____ 7. Youth drug use has increased since 2001.

_____ 8. More young people are dependent on marijuana than on any other drug.

_____ 9. Low-level marijuana offenders are increasingly being incarcerated.

_____ 10. Long-term studies show that marijuana is a risky substance.

_____ 11. The U.S. government favors locking up low-level marijuana offenders.

_____ 12. There is a correlation between drug-use rates and criminal justice responses.

_____ 13. Money has been requested to expand the drug court program.

Letters to the Editor

People sometimes respond to controversial issues by writing a letter to the editor stating their opinion. Read the following letters to the editor and consider their claims.

Letter 1: For Legalizing the Use of Marijuana for Medicinal Purposes

IT IS SAD THAT SOMETHING so critical to many Americans' health and well-being is being withheld by politics. Elderly patients are more likely to encounter adverse reactions from conventional medications because of slowed metabolisms and other consequences of aging. The Food and Drug Administration's litany of recalls and drug warnings point up the need for non-toxic alternatives like marijuana.

2 Washington politicians not only claim we have the best health care in the world but tout this nation's commitment to democracy, liberty and freedom. These will remain just claims until our lawmakers restore the freedom to use cannabis as medicine that they revoked with the passage of the Controlled Substances Act in 1970.

Gary Storck, cofounder,
Is My Medicine Legal YET?,
Madison, Wisconsin

Gary Storck, Letter to the Editor, *USA Today*, May 2005. Copyright © 2005 Gary Storck. Reprinted with permission.

Multiple Choice

Directions: For each item, write the letter corresponding to the best answer on the provided.

_____ 1. The principal point the writer makes is that
   a. marijuana has always been illegal.
   b. marijuana should be made available as a medicine to those who could benefit from it.
   c. marijuana alleviates the side effects of chemotherapy.
   d. none of the above.

_____ 2. The writer would probably agree with which of the following statements?
   a. Marijuana can be toxic in moderate doses.
   b. Elderly people could benefit from the availability of marijuana as a medicine.
   c. Conventional drugs are always just as effective as marijuana.
   d. Marijuana is as dangerous as cocaine.

_____ 3. The writer implies that
   a. the dangers of marijuana are greatly exaggerated.
   b. conventional drugs are not free of risk and drawbacks.
   c. withholding marijuana from the public should not happen in a country that honors liberty and freedom.
   d. all of the above.

_____ 4. An assumption the writer makes is that
   a. elderly patients should refrain from taking conventional medications.
   b. the Controlled Substances Act allows the distribution of marijuana as a legal medication.
   c. marijuana is more likely to cause problems for elderly people than conventional medications.
   d. none of the above.

Letter 2: Against Legalizing the Use of Marijuana for Medicinal Purposes

ON MARCH 28, 2005, the television show The O'Reilly Factor aired a segment on medical fraud in which a FOX News producer strolled into one of California's cannabis buyers' clubs and bought an eighth ounce of marijuana with no questions asked. The club required the producer to obtain the recommendation of a doctor. With no serious health problems, he obtained the recommendation within fifteen minutes for $250. He then walked into the buyers' club and bought the marijuana for $65. The recommendation from the doctor never expires, so this producer is free to go back as often as he wishes for more pot.

2   Our Executive Director, Calvina Fay, was a guest on the follow-up show. "This incident clearly shows the loopholes in the legislation allowing marijuana to be distributed for so-called medical purposes. It is accessible to everybody, which is the ultimate goal of the pro-legalization movement."

3   Clearly this is an example of how people are toking up under the guise of treating "serious maladies" such as premenstrual syndrome, athlete's foot, and even ingrown toenails. The reality is that people with fatal diseases are not smoking pot to treat them—they are already under the care and supervision of legitimate doctors and are receiving valid medicines to treat their ailments.

Letter to the Editor, Unsigned, Drug Free America Foundation.

Letter to Editor, Unsigned. Drug Free America Foundation.

Multiple Choice

Directions: For each item, write the letter corresponding to the best answer on the line provided.

_____ 1. Which of the following statements is an opinion?
   a. The producer was required to obtain the recommendation of a doctor.
   b. He then walked into the buyers' club and bought an eighth ounce of marijuana for $65.
   c. Our Executive Director, Calvina Fay, was a guest on the follow-up show.
   d. This incident clearly shows the loopholes in the legislation allowing marijuana to be distributed for so-called medical purposes.

_____ 2. Which of the following is a generalization the writer makes?
   a. Nearly anyone can obtain marijuana at a cannabis buyers' club in California.
   b. Smoking marijuana can prevent athlete's foot.
   c. People with fatal diseases aren't obtaining marijuana for treatment purposes.
   d. Both a and c.

_____ 3. Which of the following best describes the writer's main purpose?
   a. He wants to encourage people to avail themselves of inexpensive drugs.
   b. He wants people to understand that medical marijuana is a ruse to achieve the legalization of marijuana.

     c. He wants people with serious ailments to frequent cannabis buyers' clubs.

     d. He wants people who purchase pot illegally to serve lengthy prison sentences.

_____ 4. A reasonable inference that can be made from the writer's letter is that

     a. people with serious medical problems will stop going to doctors and start going to cannabis buyers' clubs.

     b. medical marijuana is currently being dispensed to treat trivial problems.

     c. an ingrown toenail is a serious malady.

     d. none of the above.

Letter 3: Against the Current War on Drugs

AMERICANS WILL BE disappointed to learn that the war on drugs is not what they thought it was. Many of us grew up supporting this war, thinking it would imprison high-level traffickers in hard drugs and keep cocaine and heroin off the streets. Instead, law enforcement officers devote precious hours on hundreds of thousands of arrests for possession of a little marijuana, only to have prosecutors deem the infractions too minor to take to court.

2 This tremendous waste of time and resources must stop.

Mitch Earleywine, Author,
Understanding Marijuana,
Associate Professor, Psychology,
University of Southern
California, Los Angeles

Mitch Earleywine, Letter to the Editor, *USA Today,* May 2005. Reprinted by permission of Dr. Mitch Earleywine.

Multiple Choice

Directions: For each item, write the letter corresponding to the best answer on the line provided.

_____ 1. The tone of the writer toward the war on drugs is

     a. outraged.

     b. sympathetic.

     c. indifferent.

     d. optimistic.

_____ 2. A reasonable inference that can be drawn is that

     a. the writer believes that the war on drugs has been worth the time and money allocated to it.

     b. the writer believes that the war on drugs has greatly reduced the availability of hard drugs.

     c. the writer wants the government to change its priorities in the war on drugs.

     d. the writer is pleased that small-time drug traffickers have often been imprisoned.

_____ 3. In paragraph 1, the word *deem* means

     a. consider.

     b. think.

     c. judge.

     d. all of the above.

Letter 4: Against the Current War on Drugs

IF U.S. DRUG CZAR JOHN WALTERS thinks marijuana is so harmful, why does he want it to remain completely unregulated, untaxed, and controlled by criminal gangs.

2 Only legal products of any kind can be regulated, taxed, and controlled by any government.

3 Regarding the so-called high potency of today's marijuana, in my view, if we smoked the world's most potent marijuana all day long, the worst effect would be a severe case of the munchies. On the other hand, drinking more than 80 cups of caffeinated coffee could result in a lethal dose of caffeine.

4 Perhaps we should criminalize coffee instead of marijuana.

Kirk Muse, Mesa, Arizona

Letter to the Editor, *USA Today,* May 2005. Copyright © Kirk Muse. Used with permission.

Multiple Choice

Directions: For each item, write the letter corresponding to the best answer on the line provided.

_____ 1. The author's use of the phrase "so-called" in reference to the potency of today's marijuana implies that
   a. the author feels that marijuana is far more potent today than in the past.
   b. the author has doubts about how potent today's marijuana really is.
   c. the author doesn't agree with authorities who call today's marijuana high-potency.
   d. both b and c.

_____ 2. The author makes use of the following persuasive technique when he equates drinking coffee with smoking marijuana:
   a. testimonial.
   b. plain folks.
   c. false analogy.
   d. bandwagon.

_____ 3. The author suggests criminalizing coffee instead of marijuana because
   a. he really wants to see coffee criminalized.
   b. he is being ironic.
   c. he believes that smoking marijuana is more harmful than ingesting large amounts of coffee.
   d. none of the above.

Advertisements

The advertisement on the next page was sponsored by the White House Office of National Drug Control Policy through its national youth antidrug campaign. It appeared in the *New York Times* on May 12, 2005. Study the ad carefully and then answer the following questions.

1. What is the topic of the ad? _____

2. What is the main idea of the ad? _____

_____

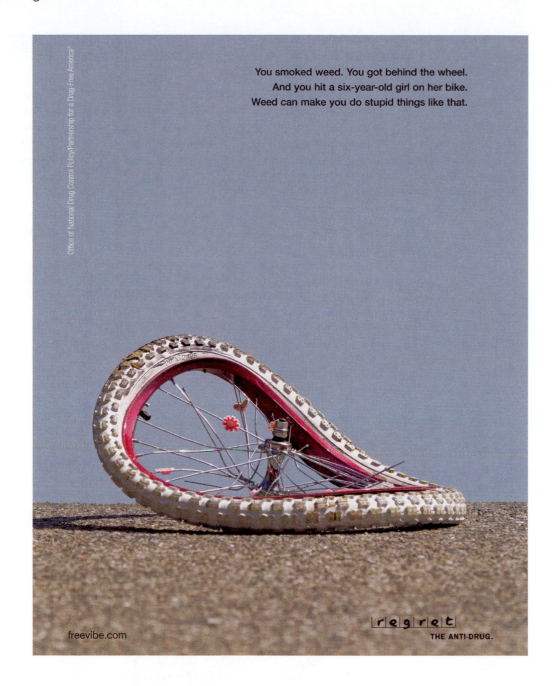

3. What is the ad's purpose? _____

4. What is the overall tone of the ad? _____

5. What is the point of view of the ad? _____

6. What support is given for the argument presented? Give specific examples.

   _____

7. Can you tell who sponsored the ad from reading the ad alone, or would you need to do further research? How might you find this information on the Internet? (Hint: Many Web sites include information about the organization; go to the Web site listed in the ad. You might want to consult the following Web sites: www.drugfree.org, www.campaigns.drugfreeamerica.org/)

Political Cartoons

A political (or editorial) cartoon is a drawing that has a political or social message. Most political cartoons employ satire or humor to communicate a specific point of view about a current event or issue. Many political cartoons feature caricatures of prominent public figures. They also often make use of common symbols. For instance, the Democratic Party is represented by a donkey, and the Republican Party by an elephant. A drawing of Uncle Sam stands for the United States as a whole.

Political cartoons can be difficult to decipher. Understanding them often requires a knowledge of current events. It also helps to be familiar with social and political issues.

Study the cartoon below to determine what the cartoonist, Scott Stantis, has to say about the war on drugs. What is his point of view on the topic? Is he for the current policy or against it?

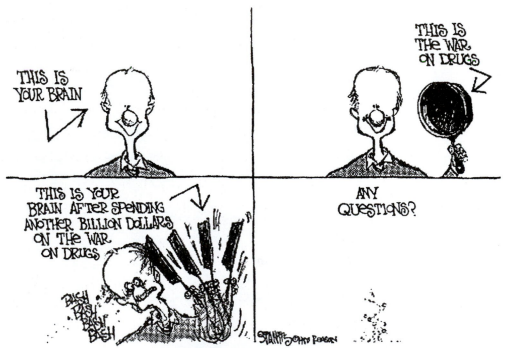

© 1998 by Scott Stantis. By permission of Scott Stantis and Creators Syndicate, Inc.

Visual Aid: Map on the Status of Medical Marijuana

One current and controversial debate over laws governing behavior is whether people should be allowed to use marijuana legally, for medical purposes. Although the majority of adults polled in national surveys support such a use, the federal government continues to regard all uses of marijuana as illegal. In 2005, the Supreme Court upheld the federal government's position. Nevertheless, 11 states have granted citizens the right to use marijuana for medical purposes—even if that privilege rests on dubious legal grounds. Look at the map and answer the questions that follow.

**The Status of
Medical Marijuana**

MAPPING LIFE
NATIONWIDE

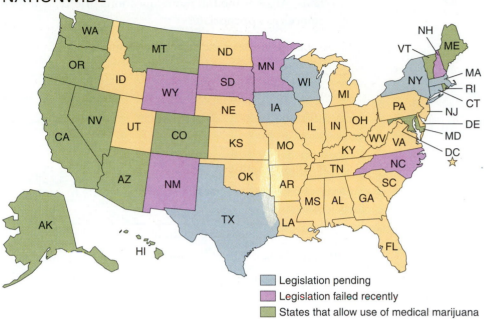

Legend:
- Legislation pending
- Legislation failed recently
- States that allow use of medical marijuana

Note: Federal law confers a one-year prison sentence on those convicted of possessing a small amount of marijuans. No exception is made for medical use, even if state law allows it, as it does in California. Maryland has not legalized medical use, but has greatly reduced the penalties.
Source: Developed by author based on data from L. Greenhouse 2005 and Marijuana Policy Project 2004, 2007.

1. How many states allow the use of medical marijuana? _____

2. Has Texas legalized the usage of medical marijuana? _____

3. Has New Mexico legalized the use of medical marijuana? _____

_____

From Richard T. Schaefer, *Sociology*, 11th Edition, p. 189. Copyright © 2008 by The McGraw-Hill Companies, Inc. Reprinted with permission.

In Your Own Words

1. Do you think that harsher penalties will deter people from using marijuana?
2. Should marijuana be legalized and regulated like cigarettes and alcohol?
3. What resources are available in your area to help people who abuse drugs?

Internet Activity

Using a search engine such as Google, Yahoo!, or MSN, find an article of interest related to the medical use of marijuana. Print out and evaluate that article in relation to the eight types of persuasive writing techniques discussed at the beginning of this chapter.

Chapter Summary and Review

In Chapter 13, you learned about persuasive writing techniques, evaluated persuasive writing selections, and became familiar with inductive and deductive reasoning. Based on the material in Chapter 13, answer the following questions.

Short Answer

Directions: Answer the following questions briefly, using no more than a few words or sentences as appropriate.

1. Give an example of inductive reasoning. _____

_____

2. Give an example of deductive reasoning. _____

_____

Vocabulary in Context

Directions: Choose one of the following words to complete the sentences below. Use each word only once.

authority	deductive	inductive	subjective

3. When a person who is giving an opinion on cloning states that she is a professor of bioethics, she is making an appeal to _____.

4. When people relate their personal feelings and opinions, they are being

_____.

5. Trying to draw conclusions from a hypothesis or general principle is _____ reasoning.

6. _____ reasoning begins with gathering evidence and then draws a conclusion from that evidence.

Becoming Ready for Content-Area Classes

In a logically organized piece of music, one thought grows from another, and all the parts are interrelated.

—**Roger Kamien, from** *Music, An Appreciation*

Look for connections. No matter what you're doing, everything is related. That's why we can relate practicing an instrument to building a house, learning a language, improving in a sport, cooking, getting along with people, and many other things. When you look for connections in life, you and your ideas don't have to be lonely. The more you discover similarities in things that seem different, the greater the world you can participate in.

—**Wynton Marsalis, from** *Marsalis on Music*

CHAPTERS IN PART 6

Wynton Marsalis

In Part 6 of this text, we will connect what you have learned in previous chapters to the kind of reading you will be called upon to do for your classes. We will begin with a chapter on skimming and scanning that will show you how to connect the skills you use every day to more challenging reading material. Our final chapter, on jazz, will introduce you to various study and test-taking skills that you can use when you are reading your own college textbooks.

14 | Scanning and Skimming

CHAPTER PREVIEW

In this chapter, you will

- Learn how to scan material quickly to locate specific information.
- Learn how to skim material to gain an overview and acquire the essential information.

Scanning

Scanning is the process of quickly searching reading material in order to locate specific bits of information. When you scan, you don't start at the beginning and read through to the end. Instead, you jump around in the text trying to find the information you need. You probably already scan when you search for a phone number in a telephone book, go through the TV guide looking for a program to watch, or look up a word in the dictionary. The purpose of this section is to improve your scanning skills.

This section has three exercises. We will first practice doing the type of scanning you are probably already familiar with. Then we will practice scanning some more difficult reading material.

Exercise 1: Scanning the Phone Book

Directions: The purpose of this exercise is to increase your scanning speed. Complete the exercise as quickly as you can by moving your eyes rapidly across the phone book listings shown on the next page to find the answers to the following questions:

1. What is Jack Holloway's telephone number? _____

2. How many people on this page have the name "Hollister"? _____

3. Where does L. E. Holly live? _____

4. Where does Barbara Hollway live? _____

5. What is Oletta Hollis's telephone number? _____

Exercise 2: Scanning the *TV Guide*

Directions: Scan the television guide listings on page 556 as quickly as you can to find the answers to the following questions.

1. How many four-star movies are being shown between 7:00 P.M. and 10:30 P.M.?

_____ Name the movie(s). _____

Hollis - Holm

HOLLIS Jeff
563 N Spanish Springs Dr CDR 480 940-9111
Jerry S 342 W Citation Ln TMP 480 897-0483
Jesse 1717 S Dorsey Ln TMP 480 219-9332
Joeseph & Devin
2049 E Cortez Dr GLBT 480 545-7942
John 2032 E Orion St TMP 480 831-2245
John W 5238 E Oak St PNX 602 286-0046
Ken & Debbie 8732 E Rose Ln SCT 480 556-6560
Leo & Martha
2246 N Calle Largo MESA 480 354-0217
M 480 358-0324
M 5201 N 24 St PNX 602 954-8945
M E 4707 N 10 St PNX 602 263-8073
Mark P 1333 E Enrose Cir MESA 480 464-1098
Merle 1050 S Longmore MESA 480 834-1268
N T 11610 N 110 Pl SCT 480 892-6418
Oletta 15440 N 71st St SCT 480 699-3751
R J 1901 E Southern Av PNX 602 276-1525
Robert 5275 W Quail Av GLDL 623 362-4105
Robert E 480 951-0918
Roy S 2458 E Cathedral Rock Dr PNX 480 759-7178
Ruth E 2555 N Price Rd CDR 480 345-1954
Ryan 12830 W Pershing St ELMRG 623 583-6856
S 1638 E Villa St PNX 602 253-1534
HOLLIST Matthew & Deonna
1051 S Dobson Rd MESA 480 557-6931
HOLLISTER A 8020 E Keats Av MESA 480 380-6235
Amy 2430 S Mill Ave TMP♦480 927-9626
B 3646 N 69 Av PNX 623 849-1575
Brett 5042 W Kesler Ln CDR 480 753-9069
Clayton 8930 E Capri Ave MESA 480 984-6580
Clyde 8220 E Garfield St SCT 480 946-9579
Dale 3403 E Main St MESA 480 218-6429
Dana 26811 N 156 St RIOV 480 471-7777
David 946 N Barkley Rd APCJ 480 982-6349
David 1420 N Spire Ct CDR 480 705-4532
Don H 8139 E Via Del Futuro SCT 480 948-1812
Dorothy E 3412 W Sells Dr PNX 602 242-6064
Elton 2311 S Farnsworth Dr MESA 480 984-1970
Gary 480 948-7636
J R 5412 E Arcadia Av MESA 480 985-1538
Jackie 7225 W Monterey Wy PNX 623 245-9985
Marsha 4698 W Folley St CDR 480 961-9608
P A 1002 W Kerry Ln PNX 623 582-5511
Randy 6125 E Larkspur Dr SCT 480 596-9086
Todd 15050 N 59 Av GLDL 602 547-9208
William 6152 W Oakland St CDR 480 893-1954
Y C 6839 N 17 Pl PNX 602 944-2927
HOLLIWAY J Harold
515 S 77th St MESA 480 984-2786
HOLLMAN Gary & June
15833 N 62 Pl PNX 480 998-0730
Gene 2929 E Main St MESA 480 396-6847
J 480 946-0054
John 4215 E Aspen Ave MESA 480 832-2300
Michelle 2115 N 115 Ln AVDL 623 907-3453
Phil 6365 E Gary St MESA 480 325-0807
Phil & Christy 3717 E Betsy Ln GLBT 480 279-6530
Vaughn 5645 W Shaw Butte Dr GLDL 623 878-4660
Walter G
17812 N Del Webb Blvd SNCY 623 974-3255
HOLLMANN Allan
18908 W Amelia Ave LTCH 623 853-1464
Vern 5747 W Missouri Ave GLDL 623 937-5287
Victor 1535 N Horne MESA 480 649-5573
Vivian 5820 W Yucca St GLDL 623 979-7432
HOLLO B PRA 623 594-0436
Brad & Heather
17722 N 79 Av GLDL 623 486-1350
HOLLOBAUGH Erik
519 W Willow Av PNX 602 896-2626
Linus 234 N Concord St GLBT 480 539-0585
S S 26602 S Maricopa Pl SNLK 480 895-1662
Thomas 845 W Lindner Ave MESA 480 820-8464
HOLLOCK Derry 19022 N 8 Av PNX 623 780-0332
HOLLOCKER S
7955 E Montebello Av SCT 480 947-8931
HOLLOMAN D 623 581-0795
Edward 3812 E Cholla St PNX 602 996-9437
L I 4124 W Virginia Ave PNX 602 233-6633
William S 5107 W Corrine Dr GLDL 602 978-8383
HOLLOMON Emily
10350 W McDowell Rd AVDL 623 936-3804
HOLLON Kimberly
3476 S 162 Ln GDYR 623 932-5716
Rose 1410 E Vineyard Rd PNX 602 304-1170
Roy MESA 480 986-0011
Tyler C 11363 W Pima St AVDL 623 478-9513
Ward 1205 E Northshore Dr TMP 480 345-1878
Wayne N Jr
10222 S Santa Fe Ln GDYR 623 386-1222
William R 11465 N 131 Wy SCT 480 614-3845
HOLLONBECK Dwight
2350 E University Dr MESA 480 668-1537
HOLLORAN Andrew D
5940 E Paisano Cir PNX 480 945-3744
D & K 12922 W Rosewood Dr ELMRG 623 974-9720
D &K 12922 W Rosewood Dr ELMRG 623 977-4326
Duane Rev 5802 N 14 Pl PNX 602 266-4653
F M 9843 N 48 Ave GLDL 623 937-1402
Patrick 5601 E Calle Tuberia PNX 480 425-8390
Thomas & Elaine
12325 W Edgemont Ave AVDL 623 535-9116
Tom 14743 N 148 Av SRPRS 623 215-7833

HOLLOWAY C L
1320 S Val Vista Dr MESA 480 219-1571
Carolyn 480 283-1281
Charles 9743 W Riviera Dr SNCY 623 583-0716
Charles M 6532 W Van Buren St PNX 623 936-3476
Clyde L 1642 W Alcott St MESA 480 964-2557
Curtis
21650 W Eagle Mountain Rd
RNBW VLY 623 386-2211
D 362 E Chicory Pl QNCK 480 888-7036
Daniel 249 S 124 Ave AVDL 623 932-3790
David 2245 N 9 St PNX 602 266-1843
Dianne 3710 W Gardenia Av PNX 602 973-1182
Don F 6706 N Dysart Rd GLDL 623 935-3167
Doug 1264 E Marconi Av PNX 602 993-0242
Doug 5435 E McLellan Rd MESA 480 985-6960
Douglas 9253 N Firebrick Dr FNTH 480 836-9815
Douglas B Ins
1619 E Guadalupe Rd TMP 480 345-0011
Edward 2222 W Maple Dr PNX 623 587-9878
Emily 623 937-8760
Erika 480 730-1221
Eugene 12016 W Joblanca Rd AVDL 623 925-1010
Eugene & Joyce
4700 E Main St MESA 480 832-2148
F K 1137 N 60 Av PNX 602 269-1724
Frances 1137 N 60th Av PNX 602 368-4954
Gary 8814 E Charter Oak Dr SCT 480 994-9052
Geoffrey L appr
2227 W Isabella Av MESA 480 730-0427
Gerald 1178 E Del Rio St GLBT 480 821-5066
Greg 706 W Gable Av MESA 480 733-4595
H W 3230 S Jackrabbit Trl BKEY 623 386-1442
J E 7505 S 13 Pl PNX 602 268-6680
J E 15320 W Echo Canyon Dr SRPRS 623 937-6350
J & J 623 879-8111
Jack 480 924-4681
James A 26434 S Lakeside Dr SNLK 480 895-2269
James S 3447 E Dennisport Av GLBT 480 963-5170
Janet 10215 N 178 Ave WDL 623 935-1002
Janice 200 E Southern Av APCJ 480 288-0920
Jason 426 E Pecan Rd PNX 602 268-3022
Jason 1821 W Marlboro Dr CDR 480 899-1816
Jeff 1175 W Pecos Rd CDR 480 219-3272
Jeffery 480 775-1006
Jerry 1864 N Barkley MESA 480 753-3729
Jerry A 7246 S 27 Ave PNX 602 305-8750
Jill 10050 E Mountainview Lake Dr SCT 480 451-1110
Jim 480 456-8701
Joel 38310 N 3 Av NWRV 623 465-1188
John 7981 E Soaring Eagle Way SCT 480 595-8335
John 30570 N Sunray Dr QNCK 480 888-8411
John & Donna
10826 E Navajo Dr SNLK 480 802-6742
K 4242 E Minton St PNX 602 438-7019
Karl 3826 W Purdue Av PNX 602 864-1876
Karole 5601 W Missouri Ave GLDL 623 939-2033
Kay 1326 E 8th St MESA 480 964-3060
Kevin 5602 N 7 St PNX 602 264-8114
Lance 3859 W Harrison St CDR 480 782-8543
Larry 854 E Tortoise Tr QNCK 480 987-1063
Larry 3110 W Mercer Ln PNX 602 942-3784
Lee 15608 N 19th St PNX 602 482-7963
Lois & Robert 12455 N 36 Dr PNX 602 789-8668
Lowell T 7714 E Akron St MESA 480 986-4943
M A 4002 W Sierra Vista Dr PNX 623 937-8390
M B 1668 W Glendale Ave PNX 602 864-0613
Mae 18031 N 129th Dr SN CY W 623 975-3472
Margaret
5027 W New World Dr GLDL 623 931-1948
Mark D 5624 E 34 Av APCJ 480 671-6887
Matt 2855 E Broadway Rd MESA 480 832-2039
Mike 8002 W Sweetwater Av PRA 623 979-1480
Mike 17941 W Tierra Del Sol Dr SRPRS 623 266-6070
Millie 5802 S 13 Pl PNX 602 243-5729
Mitchell 1034 E Lilac Dr TMP 480 994-0727
Mitchell 1317 W 7 St TMP 480 949-1542
Odis 2245 W Wayland Rd PNX 602 276-7587
P J 5733 W Windrose Dr GLDL 623 776-7944
Paul W 6711 E Camelback Rd SCT 480 994-5714
Richard 1158 E Galveston St GLBT 480 855-7835
Rick 8649 E Royal Palm Rd SCT 480 998-9670
Robert D 10215 N 178 Ave WDL 623 935-7076
Robin 480 732-0580
Ronald 1073 E Watson Dr TMP 480 491-6704
Ross 4066 E Concho Av MESA 480 396-0946
S 1009 E Myrtle Av PNX 602 674-5945
S B 2116 E Cornell Dr TMP 480 838-8068
Steffani 480 598-1753
Stephen A 6455 W Fremont Rd LVN 602 237-2004
Steve 1635 N 70 St SCT 480 990-1876
Tara 1518 N Rowen MESA 480 634-1233
Therese 3802 E Baseline Rd PNX 602 437-0064
Tim & Ingrid
12767 W Coronado Rd AVDL 623 536-2251
Tonia 14453 S 41 Pl PNX 480 759-6271
Tracie 5712 N 67 Av GLDL 623 849-8416
V 7113 N 59 Dr GLDL 623 847-7722
Willard 2175 W Southern Av APCJ 480 983-7142
William 2958 N 21 Pl PNX 602 957-9554
William E
1621 W Fairmount Ave PNX 602 266-2841
William L 6046 E Wildcat Dr CVCK 480 488-1228
William W & Joann
11059 E Juan Tabo Rd SCT 480 502-6990

HOLLWAY Albert
2101 S Meridian Rd APCJ 480 983-5915
Barbara
4219 W Misty Willow Ln PNX 623 780-3404
HOLLY Alan
1979 E Palomino Dr TMP 480 831-0061
Angela 1814 E Bell Rd PNX 602 482-0677
Barbara A Jr
21806 N Canto Ln SN CY W 623 214-1832
Bernie & Pam
17561 W Wandering Creek Rd GDYR 623 393-8300
Bret 33619 N 46 Pl PNX 480 575-3238
Chris & Grace
12615 N Columbine Dr PNX 602 942-8657
Chris & Scott
9220 W Marconi Av PRA 623 974-8399
D 7608 W Crocus Dr PRA 623 878-4219
Dan Jr 11721 E Cortez Dr SCT 480 314-9115
Daniel 9163 W Melinda Ln PRA 623 876-4071
Daniel D 8417 S Jentilly Ln TMP 480 838-0247
Detmar & Robin
20051 W Hwy 85 BKEY 623 386-7282
Dorothy 4514 W El Caminito Dr GLDL 623 435-9933
Doug & Cindy
3202 E Corrine Dr PNX 602 788-1824
E 2736 E Dry Creek Rd PNX 480 704-1796
Fred & Marian
3713 N 359 Ave TONPH 623 386-9131
Fritz L 4723 N Greenview Cir W LTCH 623 935-1218
G C Sr 4927 E Emelita Ave MESA 480 832-6076
Harlan 7473 E Bent Tree Dr SCT 480 473-0996
J 4918 W Oraibi Dr PNX 623 434-3379
J L Bud 14745 N 81 Av PRA 623 979-3519
James & Kelly 7009 E Acoma Dr SCT 480 607-5196
Jan 5832 W Campo Bello Dr GLDL 602 439-2849
John 3808 W Calavar Rd PNX 602 439-9584
John 3808 W Calavar Rd PNX 602 795-6150
L 6040 E Juniper Ave SCT 480 367-6866
L E 6252 E Billings St MESA 480 832-4182
Leonard & Harriett
11642 N 103rd Ave SNCY 623 933-1971
Lynda 5402 E Windsor Av PNX 602 468-6359
Mark 19616 W Hwy 85 BKEY 623 386-8200
Mary 10304 E Plata Av MESA 480 380-2726
Mathew 454 W Citation Ln TMP 480 756-9880
Michael 11314 W Dana Ln AVDL 623 877-4753
Michael 14425 N 45th Dr GLDL 602 863-0752
Patricia 2401 W Southern Av TMP 602 454-9095
Patrick J 8818 S Los Feliz Dr TMP 480 345-9002
Patty 5601 N 105 Ln PNX 623 872-8436
Paul J 10032 W Riviera Dr SNCY 623 977-6068
R 7120 W Country Gables Dr PRA 623 878-1433
R K 3700 S Ironwood Dr APCJ 480 474-9822
Ralph E 5020 W Thunderbird Rd PNX 602 843-3231
Robert & Dee 8745 W Potter Dr PRA 623 581-2523
Scott Ins 4014 N Goldwater Blvd SCT 480 949-7204
Susan 10101 W Forrester Dr SNCY 623 583-1542
Thomas S 204 W Surrey Av PNX 602 938-3790
Timothy 5319 W Cheryl Dr GLDL 623 939-8735
Tom & Mary 8021 E Keats Av MESA 480 984-6468
William C 18034 N 129th Dr SN CY W 623 975-0869
HOLLYER A B 2226 W Keim Dr PNX♦602 242-3152
Russ 3124 N 50 St PNX 602 956-3041
HOLLYFIELD Linette
9707 E Obispo Av MESA 480 219-8155
HOLLYWOOD Helen
14126 W Yosemite Dr SN CY W 623 546-6994
Patrick 2744 E Cortez St PNX 602 992-5417
Paul 16640 N 19 Pl PNX 602 923-2825
S 4588 E Chuckwalla Cyn PNX 480 940-4355
HOLM Andrew 480 391-0917
Andrew
15730 N Hayden D4 Pmb 184 SCT 480 767-2738
Ann
10227 W White Mountain Rd SNCY 623 266-0227
Arvilla 19350 N Cave Creek Rd PNX♦602 493-3851
Brad & Barbara
1341 N Lakeshore Dr CDR 480 345-1953
Brent 3520 E Harvard Ave GLBT 480 324-0556
C 7937 E Naranja Av MESA 480 354-1578
Cal & Gayle 8625 E Paraiso Dr SCT 480 585-7714
Calvin 12813 N 39 Dr PNX 602 978-3686
Charles L
12718 W Maplewood Dr SN CY W 623 584-5977
Christopher
2904 E Nighthawk Way PNX 480 857-6237
Craig & Judy 31231 N 43 St PNX 480 513-0193
Dale & Joy 14619 N Shiprock Dr SNCY 623 977-0455
Deanne 7977 W Wacker Rd PRA 623 486-0213
Debbie 9313 E Hobart St MESA 480 984-3804
HOLM-DEMEUSE Connie
746 E Park Ave CDR 480 782-0358
HOLM Donald & Arlene
8615 E Apache Tr MESA 480 986-1065
Dorothy 2108 Klamath APCJ 480 983-5818
Dorothy 8208 E Ebola Av MESA 480 984-3336
E&D 993 E Constitution Dr GLBT 480 722-2905
Edward 1460 E Bell Rd PNX 602 482-3911
Emma 480 456-6084
Gayland & Debbie
3060 N Ridgecrest MESA 480 830-7773
Gaylend 1759 N Sinova MESA 480 830-4188
Harold P 8600 E Broadway Rd MESA 480 354-8469
Howard 275 N Saguaro Dr APCJ 480 671-8517
Irmgard 4763 W Palmaire Ave GLDL 623 931-8914

Phoenix, Arizona telephone directory, *Dex/Qwest Official Directory, Residential Edition*. Dex Media, Inc., 2004, p. 831. Used with permission.

Saturday
8AM
9AM

MORNING

8 AM
2 12 News 2:00 84356/59608
3 Good Morning Arizona Saturday 2:00 71882
4 11 Crocodile Hunter's Croc Files —Children 38530/40630
5 13 Backyardigans 65608/57288/57288
6 America Sews with Sue Hausmann 96578
8 America Quilts Creatively 81646
9 15 Even Stevens—Comedy 1146/42/2436
10 Wild About Animals—Magazine 19004
13 Inspector Gadget's Field Trip 46714
21 McGee and Me! The Big Lie 84998
40 Jacobo Dos Dos—Aventura 856714
APL Xiaolin Showdown 75240/924240
CAR Static Shock—Cartoon 6741085
COM Duckman 77608
DIS Higglytown Heroes
EI Gastineau Girls—Reality 926608
ENC MXX *The Lord of the Rings: The Two Towers*—Fantasy 3:00 5465801
Part two of the trilogy is packed with spectacular action and dazzling effects. Elijah Wood.
ESN SportsCenter 1132882
ESZ BassCenter
FAM Battle B-Daman—Animation 933284
FSN FSN Across America—Magazine 33240
H&G DIY to the Rescue 6736153
HAL Gilligan's Island—Comedy 48530
HBO Making of 'S.W.A.T.' 9678578
HIS 20th Century 1:00 1403424
MTV Weekend Dime 1:00 997017
NTK Jimmy Neutron—Animation 861646
QVC Patio & Garden—Shopping 1:00 5762462
TBS MXX *Powder*—Drama 2:00 759462
(1995) A youth with special abilities encounters prejudice. Mary Steenburgen.
VH1 Clean Sweep 1:00 807269
VH1 Fresh: New Music 1:00 621801

8:15 HBO MXX *Starsky & Hutch*—Comedy 1:45 64387882
Underwhelming spoof of the '70s crime drama. Ben Stiller, Owen Wilson, Snoop Dogg.

8:25 DIS Go Baby 8446849

8:30 4 11 Jeff Corwin Unleashed 37801/90171
13 Dora the Explorer—Cartoon
8 Martha's Sewing Room 95849
8 Smart Gardening 60917
9 15 That's So Raven 10733/41627
10 Sonic X—Cartoon 10733/90171
13 Critter Gitters—Children 18375
21 Knock Knock Show—Children 83269
58 Xiaolin Showdown 74511/923511
BET BET.COM Countdown 303733
CAR Static Shock—Cartoon 6741085
COM Mad TV—Comedy 1:00 387733
9720756559/56559

DIS JoJo's Circus—Animation 864269
EI The Soup 958207
ESZ Timeless 1131153
FAM Power Rangers: Space Patrol Delta—Children 383725
FSN Around the Track—Auto Racing 32511
NASCAR auto racing is previewed.
H&G Fix It Up 6735424
HAL Gilligan's Island—Comedy 47801
NTK Jimmy Neutron—Animation 860917

8:45 AMC MXX *My Darling Clementine*—Western (BW) 2:15 50863801
(1946) John Ford's account of the O.K. Corral gunfight. Henry Fonda, Victor Mature.

9 AM 4 11 Scout's Safari 28153/96153
5 13 This Old House Hour 1:00 98608
9 11 Little Bill 88559/30511/30511
15 Phil of the Future 90135/65207
10 Sonic X—Cartoon 90135/96153
13 Sewing with Nancy 798601
7 Autoshow with Michael Hagerty 73627
8 This Old House Hour 1:00 98608
21 Teenage Mutant Ninja Turtles
58 61 Petkeeping with Marc Morrone 90117
40 Garden Guy 36337
21 Mr. Henry's Wild & Wacky World 96379
33 63 Teledia 1:00 224530
APL Animal Precinct 9819/947191
BET Rap City Top 10—Music 779191
CAR Codename: Kids Next Door 1:00 170066
DIS Wiggles—Children 6489085
DSC Bermuda Triangle 1:00 734714
EI TV News Weekend 1:00 365608 NEW
ESZ Auto Show 1:00 648882
FAM Super Robot Monkey Team Hyperforce Go!—Cartoon 688117
FX MXX *Operation Delta Force*—Adventure 2:00 2812207
(1997) Military experts prepare to battle terrorists armed with a deadly virus. Jeff Fahey
H&G New Spaces 6759004
HAL MXX *Big Red*—Drama 2:00 83240
(1962) Boy-and-his-dog tale featuring Walter Pidgeon as the boy's wealthy but lonely employer. Gilles Payant, Emile Genest.
HIS Heavy Metal 1:00 2913608
A look at a unique double-tailed P-38 fighter used to escort U.S. bomber formations.
MTV My Super Sweet 16 488199
NTK SpongeBob SquarePants 851269
QVC Dr. Wayne W. Dyer 'The Power of Intention'—Shopping 1:00 1532559
SCI MXX *The Clan of the Cave Bear*—Drama 2:00 8410375
(1986) Daryl Hannah as a Cro-Magnon girl.
SPR Three Stooges (BW) 1:00 552172
TCM MXX *2001: A Space Odyssey*—Science Fiction 2:30 7807269
(1968) Stanley Kubrick's epic of space travel. Keir Dullea, Gary Lockwood. [Shown in letter-box format.]

Tonight's prime-time grids begin on page 134.

TLC Trading Spaces 1:00 5447240
TMC MXX *Mrs. Dalloway*—Drama 1:45
Vanessa Redgrave in an adaptation of Virginia Woolf's book. Natascha McElhone. 9129820
USA Kojak—Crime Drama 1:00 716882
VH1 Top 20 Countdown 2:00 2276240

9:05 SHO MXX *Greedy*—Comedy 1:55 18874511
Potential heirs of an ailing tycoon (Kirk Douglas) move in for their share. Michael J. Fox.

9:25 SHO Shanna's Show 36641424

9:30 4 11 Trading Spaces: Boys vs. Girls—Renovation 60627/38627
5 13 Blue's Clues 13733/72085/72085
6 Fons & Porter's Love of Quilting 11375
9 11 Lizzie McGuire—Comedy 43559/67153
10 Critter Gitters—Children 34801
13 13 Little Bill 88559/30511/30511
21 Miss Charity's Diner 50545
58 61 The Batman—Adventure 50527/656337
CAR Codename: Kids Next Door 2368085
COM Mad TV—Comedy 1:00 333733
DIS Stanley—Children 580795
ESZ Greatest Angler Debate 7515240
FAM W.I.T.C.H.—Cartoon 779191
H&G House Detective 2353153
MAX MXX *Malibu's Most Wanted*—Comedy 1:30 865578
A toothless social satire about a white-rapper wannabe (Jamie Kennedy) who irks his wealthy father (Ryan O'Neal).
MTV My Super Sweet 16 777733
NTK SpongeBob SquarePants 593733
WGN Walgreens Health Corner 508191

10 AM 2 12 Crocodile Hunter's Croc Files —Children 87443/52795
3 Your Life A to Z 1:00 35578
4 11 Darcy's Wild Life 72511/54153
5 MXX *RoboCop*—Science Fiction 2:00
(1987) He's programmed to serve justice at any cost. Peter Weller, Nancy Allen, Ronny Cox, Miguel Ferrer. 58129
6 This Old House Hour 1:00 51530
7 Arizona Real Living 34375
8 Great Cars 32917 NEW
9 NBA Inside Stuff 69085
9 11 One Piece—Cartoon 69085/54153
13 Jack Hanna's Animal Adventures 15849
15 W.I.T.C.H.—Cartoon 69707
21 Bibleman—Religion 59849
33 63 El Reto Burundis 1:00 38882
63 Yu-Gi-Oh!—Cartoon 40191/208849
A&E Inside This Old House 116733
APL Animal Precinct 1:00 282240
BET BET Now—Music Videos 1:00 473066
DIS Rolie Polie Olie—Children 132207
DSC Unraveling the Mystery of Alien Abduction—Documentary 1:00 842646

Saturday
9AM
11AM

EI Michael Jackson Trial: Weekend Edition 1:00 914998
A wrap-up of the week's testimony.
ESN Auto Racing 3:00 110849
Indianapolis 500 time trials. (Live)
ESZ Bowling Night 1:00 8558240
The semifinal round in Miami.
FAM Digimon: Digital Monsters 372337
H&G Ground Breakers—Gardening 7882795
HBO Costas Now 1:00 299530
Debut. A panel discussion with Charles Barkley, Cris Collinsworth and John McEnroe kicks off a new Bob Costas magazine. See box on p. 124.
HIS Full Throttle—Reality 1:00 1816917
MTV My Super Sweet 16 303207
NTK Fairly OddParents—Cartoon 129207
QVC Clarks Footwear 1:00 6993424
SPR Maximum MLB 589191
TBS MXX *Message in a Bottle*—Drama 2:35 48021240
(1999) A reporter tracks down the author of a note in a bottle. Kevin Costner.
TLC White You Were Out 1:00 2025530
TNT MXX *Batman Forever*—Adventure 2:30 123801
(1995) Batman (Val Kilmer) battles Two-Face and the Riddler. Tommy Lee Jones.
USA MXX *Blue Crush*—Adventure 2:00
(2002) Tepid romantic subplot sinks this drama about a surfer (Kate Bosworth) working on a comeback in Hawaii. 111153
WGN Soul Train—Music 1:00 855646

10:30 2 12 Jeff Corwin Unleashed 39269/23207
4 11 Endurance: Hawaii 24337/92337
8 Woodcarving with Rick Butz 60153
9 11 Power Rangers: Space Patrol Delta—Children 9019/54191 NEW
9 Allen Racers—Animation 90199/92337
21 Davey and Goliath—Biblical Cartoon 96733
40 63 TodoBebé 875849/81801
A&E Ask This Old House—Restoration 877207
CAR Grim Adventures of Billy and Mandy—Cartoon 6753820
COM Comedy-Drama 2:00 243646
DIS Disney's House of Mouse 877733
FAM Dragon Booster 783581
H&G Spring! 6755088
MTV My Super Sweet 16 583563
NTK Fairly OddParents—Cartoon 840153
SPR RealTV 224627
TMC MXX *Canadian Bacon*—Comedy 1:45
The U.S. cooks up a phony cold war against Canada. Alan Alda, John Candy. 6978443

11 AM 4 11 Jack Hanna's Animal Adventures 5627

2. What time is *60 Minutes* shown? _____

3. *Sunday Night Football* is on which network? _____

4. What type of show is *Hoodwinked?* _____

5. What time is *Iron Chef of America* shown on the Food Network? _____

Exercise 3: Scanning an Essay

Directions: The following exercise makes use of a reading selection titled "The American Environment: 'Silent Spring'" (below). Scan the essay to locate the date that corresponds to each of the following statements. Write the date on the line.

Time Line for "The American Environment: 'Silent Spring'"

_____ Gypsy moths are accidentally introduced to the Boston area.

_____ Paul Muller discovers DDT's toxicity to insects.

_____ American scientists become aware of Muller's discovery.

_____ DDT is used on a typhus outbreak in Italy.

_____ DDT enters the marketplace.

_____ Muller is awarded the Nobel Prize in Medicine; DDT-resistant housefly appears.

_____ A DDT-resistant mosquito appears.

_____ Rachel Carson publishes *The Sea Around Us.*

_____ The nature sanctuary behind Olga Huckins's house is sprayed with DDT; a letter is sent to the newspaper and Rachel Carson.

_____ Rachel Carson publishes *Silent Spring.*

_____ Rachel Carson dies of cancer.

_____ The United States bans the sale of DDT.

Now carefully read the essay and answer the questions that follow.

READING

"Silent Spring became one of the most controversial books of the 1960s."

BIO-SKETCH

Alan Brinkley is the Alan Nevins Professor of History at Columbia University and the author of many books on American history, including *Voices of Protest* (1982), *The End of Reform* (1995), and *Eyes of a Nation* (1998).

The American Environment: "Silent Spring"

Alan Brinkley

One summer day in 1957, a small plane flew over the nature sanctuary behind Olga Huckins's house in Duxbury, Massachusetts. It sprayed the land below with an oily mist and then vanished. The next day, Huckins found seven dead songbirds, their beaks gaping in apparent agony. She was so furious that she wrote an angry letter to a local newspaper; as an afterthought, she sent a copy to her friend Rachel Carson. It was one of those small events that alters the course of history.

2   Carson was a biologist and a gifted writer. Educated at Johns Hopkins University at a time when few women became scientists, she had gone to work for the government as an aquatic biologist, where—despite her painful shyness—she distinguished herself as a writer able to explain scientific issues to a wider public. In the meantime, she began to write popular essays about her special love, the ocean. In 1951 she published *The Sea Around Us*. It became an international best seller, bringing Carson a fame she never imagined and enough income to retire from government. By 1957, when she received Huckins's letter, she was one of the most popular nature writers of her generation.

3   The mist that the plane had sprayed behind Huckins's house was a mixture of ordinary fuel oil and a chemical called dicholoro-diphenyl-trichloroethane: DDT. In 1939, a Swiss chemist named Paul Muller had discovered that although DDT seemed harmless to human beings and other mammals, it was extremely toxic to insects. American scientists learned of Muller's discovery in 1942, just as the army was grappling with the insect-borne tropical diseases—especially malaria and typhus—that threatened American soldiers.

4   Under these circumstances DDT seemed like a godsend. It was first used on a large scale in Italy in 1942–1944 during a typhus outbreak, which it quickly helped end. Soon it was being sprayed in mosquito-infested areas of Pacific islands where American troops were fighting the Japanese. No soldiers suffered any apparent ill effects from the spraying, and the incidence of malaria dropped precipitously. DDT quickly gained a reputation as a miraculous tool for controlling insects, and it undoubtedly saved thousands of lives. For its discovery, Paul Muller was awarded the Nobel Prize in medicine in 1948. With so many benefits and no obvious drawbacks, the new chemical was first released for public use in 1945. DDT entered the marketplace billed as an extraordinarily safe and effective poison, the ultimate weapon against destructive insects.

5   For the next decade, the new chemical continued to live up to its early billing. It helped farmers eliminate chronic pests and was widely used to control mosquitoes. One of its most impressive successes was in virtually eliminating the gypsy moth, a voracious insect that had been stripping the leaves from northeastern forests ever since being accidentally introduced to the Boston area in 1868.

6   By the time Rachel Carson received Olga Huckins's letter, however, signs of trouble were beginning to appear in areas that had been sprayed with the chemical. For one, its effectiveness against certain insects declined as they developed resistance to its effects, so that higher doses were needed to produce the same lethal effect. A resistant housefly had appeared as early as 1948, and a resistant mosquito in 1949.

7   More worrisome were the chemical's effects on larger animals. Some were killed outright, like the birds in Olga Huckins's back yard. But DDT also seemed to inhibit some animals' ability to reproduce. It would later be learned that the eggshells of certain birds were so thinned by the chemical that young birds were crushed in their nests even before they hatched. The extraordinary persistence of DDT in the environment, and its tendency to accumulate in fatty tissues, meant that animals could concentrate surprising quantities in their flesh. This was especially true of those at the top of food chains—eagles, trout, and, not least, people. Many bird lovers were noting a general reduction in bird populations, and people who fished were catching fewer fish. As the woods became emptier and more silent, DDT seemed the most likely culprit. Rachel Carson had worried about pesticides for years, but it was not until reading Olga Huckins's letter that she decided to do something about them. Meticulously gathering the best available data, she wrote a book that was published in 1962, *Silent Spring*. In it, she warned that the indiscriminate

use of pesticides was wreaking havoc with the web of life, destroying wildlife populations, and threatening human health. She wrote of a landscape in which sickness and death threatened animals and people alike, in which "a strange stillness" had replaced the familiar songs of birds. Her eloquence was made all the more urgent by her private knowledge as she finished the book that she herself was dying of cancer.

8   *Silent Spring* became one of the most controversial books of the 1960s. It sold nearly half a million copies within six months of its publication and was discussed everywhere. The chemical industry was outraged. After first trying to suppress the book's publication altogether and threatening lawsuits against its author and publisher, pesticide manufacturers began a long campaign to discredit Carson and repair the damage her book had done. In the end, though, Carson won at least a partial victory: the U.S. finally banned the sale of DDT in 1972. More important, her book raised public awareness about the threats human activities pose to the natural environment. Although she died in 1964, no single person would be more important in shaping environmental policies over the next thirty years.

From Alan Brinkley, *American History:* A Survey, 11th Edition, pp. 876–77. Copyright © 2003 by The McGraw-Hill Companies, Inc. Reprinted with permission.

 COMPREHENSION CHECKUP

True or False

Directions: Indicate whether the statement is true or false by writing **T** or **F** in the space provided.

_____ 1. Rachel Carson had a special fondness for the ocean.

_____ 2. DDT was responsible for saving thousands of lives.

_____ 3. DDT was initially thought to be both safe and effective.

_____ 4. Rachel Carson wrote *Silent Spring* to make the public aware of the helpful effects of pesticide use.

_____ 5. DDT is toxic to both beneficial and harmful species.

_____ 6. As a result of her exposure to pesticides, Rachel Carson contracted cancer.

_____ 7. DDT was first used to eradicate typhus in Germany.

_____ 8. Some mosquitoes became resistant to DDT.

_____ 9. Rachel Carson was praised by the chemical industry.

_____ 10. Rachel Carson was a nature writer.

Skimming

The purpose of **skimming** is to gain a quick overview in order to identify the main points. When skimming, you will often skip words, sentences, and paragraphs. When you are satisfied that you have a general understanding of the author's key points, you put aside the reading material. Skimming, then, serves as a substitute for careful reading.

When you are skimming, be sure to move rapidly through the material, skipping the information you are already familiar with. You may wish to read the first and last sentences of each paragraph because that is often where main ideas are located. Read the introduction and the summary if one is provided. When examples are given, you may want to read a few of them until you understand the concepts they are meant to illustrate. When skimming a textbook chapter, glance quickly at the title, subheadings, italicized words, boldface print, and illustrations.

The selection you are about to skim (see pp. 561–562) is from the textbook *Human Biology* by Sylvia Mader.

Exercise 4: Skimming a Textbook Selection

1. First, read the title and the introductory paragraph, and answer the following questions based on them.

   a. What is a pesticide?

   _____

   b. Based on the title, what point of view do you think the author is going to be taking?

   _____

   c. What effects do pesticides have on the immune system?

   _____

   d. According to the EPA, what are the effects of pesticide residues on food?

   _____

2. Now read the last paragraph. What can citizens do to promote the biological control of pests?

   a. _____

   b. _____

   c. _____

   d. _____

   e. _____

3. Now read just the first and second sentences of each paragraph and answer the following questions.

   a. Are there any alternatives to the use of pesticides?

   _____

   b. Are enough natural enemies available to be used instead of pesticides?

   _____

   c. Which method of pest control is the most sophisticated?

   _____

READING

"The argument for using pesticides at first seems attractive."

BIO-SKETCH

Dr. Sylvia Mader is the author of several college textbooks in biology, including *Inquiry into Life, Introduction to Biology, Understanding Human Anatomy and Physiology,* and *Human Biology,* from which this excerpt is taken.

Pesticides: An Asset and a Liability

Sylvia Mader

A pesticide is any one of 55,000 chemical products used to kill insects, plants, fungi, or rodents that interfere with human activities. Increasingly, we have discovered that pesticides are harmful to the environment and humans. The effect of pesticides on the immune system is a new area of concern; no testing except for skin sensitization has thus far been required before pesticide products are put on the market. Contact or respiratory allergic responses are among the most immediately obvious toxic effects of pesticides. But pesticides can also cause suppression of the immune system, leading to increased susceptibility to infection or tumor development. Lymphocyte impairment was found following the worst industrial accident in the world, which took place in India in 1984. Nerve gas used to produce an insecticide was released into the air; 3,700 people were killed, and 30,000 were injured. Vietnam veterans claim a variety of health effects due to contact with a herbicide called Agent Orange that was used as a defoliant during the Vietnam War. The Environmental Protective Agency (EPA) says that pesticide residues on food possibly cause suppression of the immune system, disorders of the nervous system, birth defects, and cancer.

2   The argument for using pesticides at first seems attractive. Pesticides are meant to kill off disease-causing agents, increase crop yield, and work quickly with minimal risk. But over time, it has been found that pesticides don't meet these claims. Instead, pests become resistant to pesticides, which kill off natural enemies in addition to the pest. Then the pest population explodes.

3   There are alternatives to the use of pesticides. Integrated pest management uses a diversified environment, mechanical and physical means, natural enemies, disruption of reproduction, and resistant plants to control rather than eradicate pest populations. Chemicals are used only as a last resort. Maintaining hedgerows, weedy patches, and certain trees can provide diverse habitats and food for predators and parasites that help control pests. The use of strip farming and crop rotation by farmers denies pests a continuous food source.

4   Natural enemies abound in the environment. When lacewings were released in cotton fields, they reduced the boll weevil population by 96% and increased cotton yield threefold. A predatory moth was used to reclaim 60 million acres in Australia overrun by the prickly pear cactus, and another type of moth is now used to control alligator weed in the southern United States. Also in the United States the *Chrysolina* beetle controls Klamath weed, except in shady places where a root-boring beetle is more effective.

5   Sex attractants and sterile insects are used in other types of biological control. In Sweden and Norway, scientists synthesized the sex pheromone of the *Ips* bark beetle, which attacks spruce trees. Almost 100,000 baited traps collected females normally attracted to males emitting this pheromone. Sterile males have also been used to reduce pest populations. The screwworm fly parasitizes cattle in the United States. Flies raised in a laboratory were made sterile by exposure to radiation. The entire Southeast was freed from this parasite when female flies mated with sterile males and then laid eggs that did not hatch.

6   In general, biological control is a more sophisticated method of controlling pests than the use of pesticides. It requires an in-depth knowledge of pests and/or their life cycles. Because it does not have an immediate effect on the pest population, the effects of biological control may not be apparent to the farmer or gardener who eventually benefits from it.

7   Citizens can promote biological control of pests by:

- Urging elected officials to support legislation to protect humans and the environment against the use of pesticides.

- Allowing native plants to grow on all or most of the land to give natural predators a place to live.
- Cutting down on the use of pesticides, herbicides, and fertilizers for the lawn, garden, and house.
- Using alternative methods such as cleanliness and good sanitation to keep household pests under control.
- Disposing of pesticides in a safe manner.

From Sylvia S. Mader, *Human Biology*, 9th Edition, p. 421. Copyright © 2006 by The McGraw-Hill Companies, Inc. Reprinted with permission.

You will find below "A Fable for Tomorrow" by Rachel Carson. Read the essay, noting the comparisons and contrasts, and then complete the chart that follows.

READING

"There once was a town in the heart of America where all life seemed to live in harmony with its surroundings. . . . Then a strange blight crept over the area and everything began to change."

TUNING IN TO READING

In 1963, Rachel Carson published *Silent Spring*, a book devoted to protecting the natural environment from pesticides. Carson, who died of breast cancer one year after the book's publication, wrote, "The beauty of the living world I was trying to save has always been uppermost in my mind—that, and anger at the senseless, brutish things that were being done."

BIO-SKETCH

Rachel Carson (1907–1964) was a biologist and best-selling author. Many consider Carson to be one of our best nature writers because of her ability to translate scientific fact into lyrical prose. The publication of *Silent Spring* was meant to serve as a wake-up call to conserve natural resources and to protect both human health and the environment. While critics objected to the book, calling it exaggerated and emotional, Carson is credited with sowing the seeds of the environmental movement. Carson is also the author of *The Sea Around Us*. The following selection is from *Silent Spring*.

NOTES ON VOCABULARY

maladies   disorders or diseases of the body. In Latin, the word *malus* means "bad." The word *maladies* is derived from an Old French word meaning "sickness."

scores   a great many. The word is derived from the Old Norse *skor*, meaning "notch." *Score* can also more specifically refer to a quantity of 20.

brooded   sat on, hatched. The word is derived from the Old English *brod*, meaning "heat or warmth."

counterpart   one person or thing that closely resembles another. From the Old French *countrepartie. Counter* means "opposite to" and *partie* means "a copy of a person or thing."

specter   an object or source of terror or dread. From the Latin word *spectrum*, meaning "appearance, vision, apparition."

A Fable for Tomorrow

Rachel Carson

THERE WAS ONCE A TOWN IN THE HEART OF AMERICA where all life seemed to live in harmony with its surroundings. The town lay in the midst of a checkerboard of prosperous farms, with fields of grain and hillsides of orchards where, in spring, white clouds of bloom drifted above the green fields. In autumn, oak and maple and birch set up a blaze of color that flamed and flickered across a backdrop of pines. Then foxes barked in the hills and deer silently crossed the fields, half hidden in the mists of the fall mornings.

2   Along the roads, laurel, viburnum and alder, great ferns and wildflowers delighted the traveler's eye through much of the year. Even in winter the roadsides were places of beauty, where countless birds came to feed on the berries and on the seed heads of the dried weeds rising above the snow. The countryside was, in fact, famous for the abundance and variety of its bird life, and when the flood of migrant birds was pouring through in spring and fall people traveled from great distances to observe them. Others came to fish the streams, which flowed clear and cold out of the hills and contained shady pools where trout lay. So it had been from the days many years ago when the first settlers raised their houses, sank their wells, and built their barns.

3   Then a strange blight crept over the area and everything began to change. Some evil spell had settled on the community: mysterious maladies swept the flocks of chickens; the cattle and sheep sickened and died. Everywhere was a shadow of death. The farmers spoke of much illness among their families. In the town the doctors had become more and more puzzled by new kinds of sickness appearing among their patients. There had been several sudden and unexplained deaths, not only among adults but even among children, who would be stricken suddenly while at play and die within a few hours.

4   There was a strange stillness. The birds, for example—where had they gone? Many people spoke of them, puzzled and disturbed. The feeding stations in the backyards were deserted. The few birds seen anywhere were moribund; they trembled violently and could not fly. It was a spring without voices. On the mornings that had once throbbed with the dawn chorus of robins, catbirds, doves, jays, wrens, and scores of other bird voices there was now no sound; only silence lay over the fields and woods and marsh.

5   On the farms the hens brooded, but no chicks hatched. The farmers complained that they were unable to raise any pigs—the litters were small and the young survived only a few days. The apple trees were coming into bloom but no bees droned among the blossoms, so there was no pollination and there would be no fruit.

6   The roadsides, once so attractive, were now lined with browned and withered vegetation as though swept by fire. These, too, were silent, deserted by all living things. Even the streams were now lifeless. Anglers no longer visited them, for all the fish had died.

7   In the gutters under the eaves and between the shingles of the roofs, a white granular powder still showed a few patches; some weeks before it had fallen like snow upon the roofs and the lawns, the fields and streams.

8   No witchcraft, no enemy action had silenced the rebirth of new life in this stricken world. The people had done it themselves.

9   This town does not actually exist, but it might easily have a thousand counterparts in America or elsewhere in the world. I know of no community that has experienced all the misfortunes I describe. Yet every one of these disasters has actually happened somewhere, and many real communities have already suffered a substantial number of them. A grim specter has crept upon us almost unnoticed, and this imagined tragedy may easily become a stark reality.

Completing a Comparison-Contrast Chart

One technique for organizing information pertaining to similarities and differences is to create a comparison-contrast chart. Some material, such as that in "A Fable for Tomorrow," lends itself nicely to this type of chart. Following is a comparison-contrast chart to complete. It will help you identify the differences in the environment described by Rachel Carson "before the blight" and "after the blight." The first column (columns go up and down) lists the categories to be compared and contrasted. The second column is for the information before the blight, and the third column for the information after the blight. We have filled in the first two rows (rows go across) for you. Your assignment is to fill in the remaining rows. When you complete the chart, answer the questions that follow.

Category	Before Blight	After Blight
Birds	Abundance and variety, especially with flood of migrant birds in spring and fall	Gone or moribund; no voices or sound—silence
Farms	Prosperous	Cattle and sheep died, no chicks hatched, unable to raise pigs
Wildlife		
Trees		
Fishing		
People and families		
Roadsides		

Multiple Choice

Directions: For each item, write the letter corresponding to the best answer on the line provided.

_____ 1. The author has created a feeling that could best be described as
    a. loving.
    b. sorrowful.
    c. optimistic.
    d. admiring.

_____ 2. The author's primary purpose in writing this article is to
    a. tell a story about a particular town in a farming community.
    b. inform readers of the difficulties of living in a small town.
    c. entertain readers with a personal story.
    d. persuade readers of a serious environmental problem.

_____ 3. The blight described in the article was probably the result of
    a. a fire.
    b. a nuclear explosion.
    c. chemical pesticides.
    d. the population explosion.

_____ 4. From this article you could conclude that the author is
    a. a conservationist.
    b. CEO of a large corporation.
    c. a research assistant.
    d. a politician.

_____ 5. What is the relationship between paragraphs 1 and 2, taken together, and paragraph 3?
    a. cause/effect
    b. classification/division
    c. compare/contrast
    d. definition/example

_____ 6. "Then a strange blight crept over the area and everything began to change" is an example of a
    a. simile.
    b. metaphor.
    c. personification.
    d. symbol.

_____ 7. What is the meaning of the word *moribund* as used in paragraph 4?
    a. dying
    b. distressed
    c. confused
    d. frightened

_____ 8. Paragraph 7 contains a
    a. metaphor.
    b. simile.
    c. symbol.
    d. personification.

_____ 9. Paragraph 8 contains the following statement: "The people had done it
themselves." This is a statement of
   a. fact.
   b. opinion.

_____ 10. In the context of paragraph 9, the word *stark* means
   a. stiff or rigid.
   b. outlined or prominent.
   c. bleak or harsh.
   d. emptied or stripped.

True or False

Directions: Indicate whether each statement is true or false by writing **T** or **F** in the
space provided.

_____ 11. All of the people in the town died within 10 years of the incident
described.

_____ 12. The community described is urban.

_____ 13. After the blight, there were still plenty of apples available.

_____ 14. Before the blight, people came from long distances to view the birds.

_____ 15. The story probably takes place in the West.

In Your Own Words

1. Many Third World countries continue to apply DDT to control crop pests and
mosquitoes. Do you think the United Nations should impose a worldwide ban on
the use of this insecticide?

2. The use of DDT has been banned in the United States. Many farmers would still
like to be allowed to use DDT on a limited basis. Do you think this would be a
good idea? Why or why not?

3. Some scientists are working to increase crop yields by means of genetic engineering, which can make plants resistant to pest species and so reduce the need for
insecticide spraying. Do you think such genetic engineering is a good idea? Can
you think of any risks that could result from it?

4. List four words from the selection that show a positive bias and four words that
show a negative bias.

5. Why does Carson call her selection "A Fable for Tomorrow"? In the fable what
do the silent birds symbolize?

Written Assignment

Michael Pollan—a professor at the University of California at Berkeley, a best-selling
author, and an avid gardener—decided to plant a potato called "NewLeaf" that has
been genetically engineered to produce its own insecticide. The enemy of every potato is the potato beetle, a voracious insect. However, a potato beetle eating only a tiny
part of the NewLeaf plant is doomed by the toxin the potato plant manufactures. Do
you think genetically modified potatoes are a good idea? Should growers or sellers of
the new potato be required to warn the consumer? Currently, under existing regulations, warnings or labels are not required. In fact, Pollan speculates that most of us
have already consumed NewLeaf potatoes in either French fries or potato chips.

If everything in nature affects everything else, what are the possible consequences of genetically altered foods? How do you feel about eating genetically modified food?

Internet Activity

To find out more about Rachel Carson, visit the following Web site:

www.rachelcarson.org

For a more critical analysis, consult Rachel Carson in *Time* 100:

www.time.com/time/time100/scientist/profile/carson03.html

The author presents a mixed review of Carson's legacy.

Organizations such as Greenpeace are opposed to modifying food genetically. To find out why, key in "genetic engineering" at the following Web site:

www.greenpeace.org

Chapter Summary and Review

In Chapter 14, you learned how to scan material to locate specific pieces of information. You also learned how to skim a selection to gain an overview of the main points. Based on the material in Chapter 14, answer the following.

Short Answer

Directions: List some examples of written materials you might scan and the information you would be looking for. The first one is done for you as an example.

Written Material	**Information You Might Look For**
1. *Frommer's Guide to California*	attractions in San Diego
2. _____	_____
3. _____	_____
4. _____	_____

Vocabulary in Context

Directions: Choose one of the following words to complete the sentences below. Use each word only once.

headings	scan	skimming	substitute

5. If you had a limited amount of time to answer five specific questions on a chapter in a U.S. history textbook, you could _____ through the chapter to find the answers.

6. When _____ an article, you want to read the introduction and summary and the first and last sentence of each paragraph.

7. Noticing _____ and subheadings is a good idea when you are scanning.

8. Skimming is not a _____ for careful reading.

VOCABULARY   Unit 8: Word Parts and Review

Vocabulary Word Parts

Following is a list of the word parts we have studied.

Word Parts	Meaning	Examples
ad	toward	advance
ambi	both	ambiguous, ambidextrous
amphi	both	amphibian
ann, enn	year	annual, biennial
ante(i)	before	anteroom, anticipate
anti	against	antiperspirant
audio	hear	audience, auditory
auto	self	automobile, autograph
bi	two	bicycle, biathlon
biblio	book	Bible, bibliography
centi	hundred, 1/100	century, centimeter
circ	around, ring	circle, circumference
co, com, con	with	coordinate, compare, connect
contra	against	contradict, contrast
cycle	circle, wheel	bicycle
dec	ten	December, decade
demi	half	demitasse
di	two	dioxide
duo	two	duet, duel
equi	half	equator, equinox
extra	over, above	extraordinary, extraterrestrials
gam	marriage	polygamy
graph	write	polygraph
hemi	half	hemisphere
hetero	different	heterosexual, heterogeneous
homo	same	homogenized
hyper	over, above	hyperactive, hyperventilate
hypo	under, below	hypoactive, hypothermia
in	in, not	inside, invisible
infra	under	infrared, infrastructure
inter	between, among	intercollegiate, interstate
intra	within	intravenous, intrastate

Word Parts	Meaning	Examples
lat	side	lateral
macro	large	macroeconomics
magna	large	magnify, magnificent
mania	craving	pyromania
mega	large, 1,000,000	megabucks, megabyte
micro	small, 1/1,000,000	microwave, micrometer
milli	thousand, 1/1000	millennium, millimeter
mono	one	monologue, monoxide
multi	many	multicultural
nov, non	nine	November, nonagenarian
oct	eight	October, octopus
ology	study of	sociology, psychology
omni	all	omnipotent, omnivorous
pan	around	panorama, Panasonic
para	beside, partial, similar	parallel, paralegal, paraphrase
ped, pod	foot	pedal, pedestrian
pent	five	Pentagon, pentathlon
peri	around	periscope, perimeter
phobia	fear	claustrophobia, acrophobia
phono	sound	phonograph, phonics
poly	many	polygon
post	after	postscript, postnatal
pre	before	pre-test, prenatal
pro	for	pro-democracy
pseudo	false	pseudoscience, pseudonym
quad, quar	four	quartet, quadrangle
quint	five	quintuplets, quintet
retro	backward	retroactive
scope	instrument for seeing	microscope, telescope
scrib, script	write	inscribe, scripture
semi	half	semicircle
sept, hept	seven	September, septuplet, heptathlon
sex	six	sextuplet
sonar	sound	supersonic
spect	see	spectator, spectrum
sub	under, below	subtract, subscript
super	above, over	supersonic, superscript

Word Parts	Meaning	Examples
syn	same	synonym, symphony
tele	distance	television
tetra	four	tetrahedron
trans	across	transportation
tri	three	tricycle, triangle
ultra	over, more, beyond	ultraconservative, ultrasonic
uni	one	unicycle, unison
vis	see	vision, visionary

Vocabulary Review Exercise

Directions: Complete the following sentences with words from the vocabulary list on the preceding pages.

1. Your telephone bill may list _____ calls that you have made to other cities within your state.

2. If you eat a salad with your hamburger, you are eating both meat and plants, and so you are _____.

3. A jazz _____ would have five members.

4. The _____ occurs twice a year, once in March and once in September.

5. You now know that if you went to a nursery and bought some _____ flowers, they would not bloom again next year.

6. Most whole milk that you purchase at the store is called _____ because the milk and the cream are mixed together.

7. In Chapter 1, you learned about _____, visual, and kinesthetic learning styles.

8. *Panorama* is a(n) _____ for *vista*.

9. The chemical formula for water has a(n) _____ in it.

10. People who believe in unidentified flying objects are likely also to believe that _____ have visited us.

11. Many of us are _____ to some extent because we use both our hands.

12. The _____ in Washington, DC, houses the Defense Department.

13. Present-day jazz music is recorded on compact discs. Jazz used to be recorded on 78 rpm _____ records that could hold only three minutes on a side.

Vocabulary Review Puzzle

Directions: Complete the puzzle on the following page with words from vocabulary Units 1–7.

Vocabulary Unit 8: Crossword

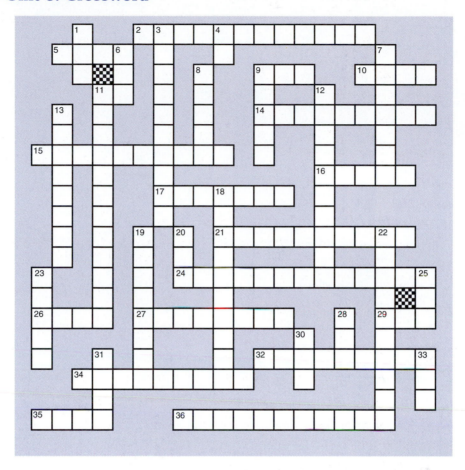

ACROSS CLUES

2. The ability to use both hands equally well.

5. A note written after the signature in a letter is a(n) _____ script.

9. A word part meaning "six."

10. A(n) _____ legal is a person trained to aid lawyers but not licensed to practice law.

11. A word part meaning "two."

14. A machine used on someone suspected of lying.

15. A one-sided decision.

16. A false name used by criminals to disguise their identity.

17. The time when day and night are of approximately equal length all over the earth.

21. "Seeing from a distance."

24. The measure of the distance around a circle.

26. A word part meaning "many."

27. Your listening skills; having to do with the sense of hearing.

29. A word part meaning "same; together."

32. A plant lasting more than two years.

34. An animal with four feet.

35. A word part meaning "same; equal; like."

36. A figure, letter, or symbol written above the line.

DOWN CLUES

1. Word part meaning "foot."

3. 1/1000 of a meter.

4. A word part meaning "two."

6. A word part meaning "three."

7. A cure-all; the act of going around the problem.

8. Pyro _____ is a compulsion to start fires.

9. The state of being overheated or too hot is _____ thermia.

11. Literally means "books written down."

12. A child with an energy level below normal could be called _____.

13. A five-sided building containing the U.S. military establishment.

18. Between or among states.

19. Light that is below red on the color spectrum.

20. Abbreviation for what was originally the 10th month.

22. "All-knowing."

23. A word part meaning "above or over."

25. A word part meaning "year."

28. A word part meaning "all; every; around."

30. A word part meaning "before."

31. A(n) _____ maton acts unthinkingly or automatically, like a robot.

33. A word part meaning "side."

15

Organizing Textbook Information

CHAPTER PREVIEW

In this chapter, you will

- Learn more about skimming and scanning.
- Learn more about annotating.
- Learn more about outlining.
- Learn more about mapping.
- Learn more about making a time line.
- Learn more about making a compare-and-contrast chart.

Organizing Textbook Material in Different Ways

Studying Textbook Chapters

This book has already introduced a variety of study techniques, and you have practiced many of them. In this chapter, we will review the techniques you are already familiar with and present some new ones. You will also have a chance to practice your skills with a chapter on jazz from a music textbook titled *The World of Music*.

Skimming

Chapter 14 discussed skimming, a technique for reading material very quickly to gain an overview of the key points. Skimming is very similar to the survey part of SQ3R, which was discussed in Chapter 1. As in SQ3R, you read the introduction to the chapter, the summary at the end of the chapter, section titles and subtitles, headings and subheadings, and the first and last sentences of many paragraphs. You also look at the illustrations and read the captions. Once you have skimmed a chapter, you should be able to state its main idea.

Skim through the textbook chapter on pages 579–585 and then answer the following questions.

Main Idea

State the overall main idea of the chapter _____

_____

True or False

Directions: Indicate whether the statement is true or false by writing **T** or **F** in the space provided.

_____ 1. Jazz has a broad historical and cultural base.

_____ 2. Jazz is complex and always changing.

_____ 3. Women have not played a role in the evolution of jazz.

_____ 4. Blues is synonymous with jazz.

_____ 5. Louis Armstrong was the most successful of the New Orleans musicians.

_____ 6. Modern jazz began in the 1960s.

_____ 7. Jazz is still mainly centered in New Orleans.

_____ 8. Jazz is based on a single style and technique.

_____ 9. Swing was the only style of jazz that became popular with the masses.

_____ 10. Jazz was a popular 19th-century music form.

Scanning

In Chapter 14, you learned about scanning, a technique for reviewing reading material to quickly find answers to specific questions. In that chapter, you scanned the telephone book, the *TV Guide,* and a reading selection.

Now scan through the textbook chapter on pages 579–585 to find answers to the following questions. Scan the headings and subheadings of the chapter to determine where the answers might be located.

1. In what section would you find a discussion of "sweet swing"? _____

   _____

2. Who is considered to be the "King of Swing"? _____

3. Name three men associated with bebop. _____

   _____

4. Jazz played a prominent role in what two cities? _____

5. Louis Armstrong's greatest contributions to the development of jazz were _____

   _____ and _____

6. One of the greatest blues singers of the 1920s was _____

7. Another name for funky jazz is _____

8. The pioneer of free jazz was _____

9. _____ is a respected jazz musician, a gifted trumpeter, and a recipient of the Pulitzer Prize.

10. _____, which originated in the 1990s, is featured today on many radio stations.

Annotating Your Textbook

To *annotate* means to make explanatory notes. Because you own your textbooks, you can annotate them by making "notes" on the pages as you read and study them. The common ways of annotating a textbook are underlining, highlighting, and writing in the margin. Annotating is something you may want to begin doing the first time you read a selection. It is the simplest organizational technique, and one you may want to use before employing any of the other techniques discussed here.

When annotating, keep in mind that less is often better. After skimming through the material, go back and carefully read it, underlining or highlighting key ideas or concepts, or ones that you have questions about or may want to refer to later. If you underline or highlight too much, you're defeating your purpose, because then the important material you've marked no longer stands out.

One reason for annotating is that it gets you involved right away in the material you are reading by requiring you to think about what is important or difficult.

While writing in the margins is useful for marking important or difficult material, it also lets you comment on what you're reading. Do you strongly agree or disagree with something you've read? Say so in the margin. Do you have a specific question about something? Put your question in the margin. In this way, you're beginning to develop your thoughts and feelings about the material.

We have annotated part of the "Jazz in America" chapter that follows. Examine what we've done (see pages 579–580), and then annotate the next section, titled "The Roots of Jazz."

Outlining

A more formal way to organize material is with an outline. An outline should reflect an orderly arrangement of ideas going from the general to the specific. Outlines vary depending on how detailed and complete the information contained in them is. We will introduce you to two kinds of outlines: the *topical outline,* which is easier to construct because it is made up of single words or phrases, and the *descriptive outline,* which is more detailed and requires more explanation.

The reason why outlining is called a *formal* way of organizing information is that it follows certain rules. These rules are described below.

Topical Outlines

The purpose of a topical outline is to organize material according to topics or subjects. It shows the topics covered, the relationships between the topics, and the importance of the ideas in the order in which they were covered in the original material.

One rule for making a topical outline concerns how the topics are enumerated. Each additional division in an outline must contain information that is more specific than the division before it. Main headings are enumerated with Roman numerals (I, II, III, IV, etc.), the next level of subheadings is enumerated with capital letters (A, B, C, D, etc.), the next level of subheadings is enumerated with Arabic numbers (1, 2, 3, 4, etc.), and the next level of subheadings is enumerated with lowercase letters (a, b, c, d, etc.).

Another rule for making a topical outline is that you cannot have just one subtopic; there must be at least two. So, if there is a subtopic A, there has to be a subtopic B; if there is a subtopic 1, there must be a subtopic 2. The reason for this is that if a topic is divided, there must be at least two parts, although there could be three or four or more parts depending on how many times the topic is divided.

Below is a topical outline for Chapter 6 of *The World of Music,* "Jazz in America."

    I. Introduction
   II. What is jazz?
  III. The jazz style
  IV. The roots of jazz

    V. Jazz styles
- A. New Orleans and Chicago jazz
- B. Stride
- C. Swing and big band jazz
- D. Bebop
- E. Cool, hard bop, soul jazz, and free jazz
- F. Modern jazz, fusion, and smooth jazz

   VI. Summary

Note that in constructing this outline, we generally used the author's headings and subheadings. There's nothing wrong with this. The idea is to organize the information presented; a well-organized essay, article, or book should help us do this. A good place to start in making a topical outline is often a book's table of contents.

Descriptive Outlines

A topical outline is good for obtaining an overview. But to fully organize your reading material, you need to place more information in your outline. When you take a topical outline and fill it in, making it more detailed and complete, what you end up with is a descriptive outline. Once you have put together a really good descriptive outline on your course material, that should be all you need to study for a test. Below is the start of a descriptive outline that takes the beginning of our topical outline and develops it.

Chapter 6, "Jazz in America."

    I. Introduction
- A. Began in the 20th century
  1. Originated in bars and nightclubs of poor urban areas
  2. Original music was a combination of songs from African and European cultures
- B. Today features widely divergent styles
  1. Jazz is international
  2. Jazz is heard everywhere
  3. Jazz is an accepted part of school music curriculums
  4. Women are involved in jazz

   II. What is jazz?
- A. Began in the early days of radio and recordings
- B. Today is part of a large entertainment industry
  1. Aspires to do more than entertain
  2. Is considered a form of art music

  III. The jazz style
- A. The music swings
- B. Musicians improvise
- C. The rhythm includes syncopation
- D. The music is played on certain key instruments

  IV. The roots of jazz
- A. Popular songs
- B. Blues songs
  1. Blues is not the same as jazz
  2. Came to be performed by women
  3. Bessie Smith was a noted blues singer
- C. Ragtime
  1. Originally for the piano
  2. Scott Joplin was a noted performer
- D. Brass band marches and dances
- E. Gospel songs

Now it's your turn. Starting with "Jazz styles" at Roman numeral V, continue making the topical outline on page 576 into a descriptive outline.

Mapping

Recall our discussion on left-brain and right-brain orientations in Chapter 1. If you had trouble making a formal outline, or you found it an unpleasant task, it may be that you have a right-brain orientation. What you may find more useful is an organizing technique that is more visual and free-form. Mapping is just such a technique.

Like a formal outline, mapping seeks to organize topics to show the relationships among the topics. But it organizes in a way that is less restricted by rules and has more visual significance.

To get a sense of what mapping is all about, look at our example on swing and the big band Jazz. To begin mapping, write down a short description of the main idea or thesis, and put a circle around it. Next, find the material that directly supports the main idea. Organize this material into categories, write down a short description for each category, and put circles around your descriptions. Now use lines to connect your category circles to the circle for the main topic or thesis. If you want, you can create subcategories for your categories, write brief descriptions, circle them, and use lines to connect these circles to your category circles. Of course, you can use boxes instead of circles. What you end up with is a logical, graphical summary of the material.

Now read the section on bebop. Using our map of the section of the chapter discussing swing and the big band Jazz as a model, prepare a map of the section discussing bebop.

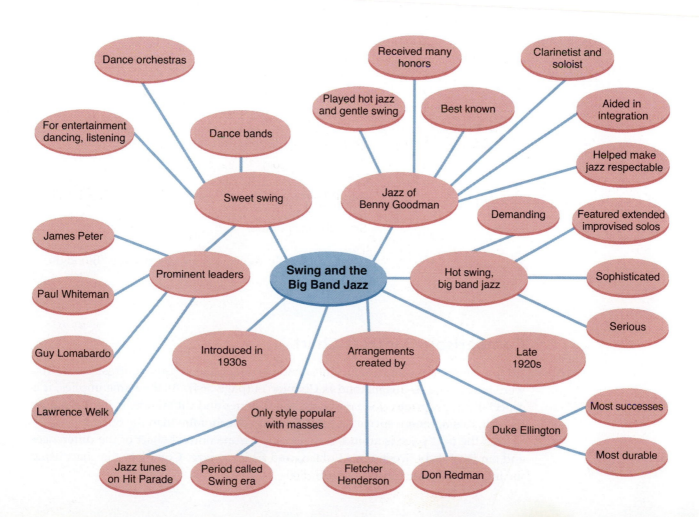

Time Lines

A time line is a specialized way of organizing information. Time lines are useful when material needs to be organized chronologically by dates, such as in a history class, though you could have a need to make one in almost any other class, too.

All that a time line does is list dates in chronological order along a line and then assign information to the dates. You can make a time line vertically (up and down) or horizontally (across). How specific you want to make a time line in terms of the number of dates and the amount of information you assign to each date depends on the reading material and your needs.

An incomplete time line of the chapter appears below. Complete the time line for the chapter using information from pages 579–585.

Late 1860s	End of Civil War, beginning of rural blues
1900	Ragtime, two-step, Latin dances popular
_____	Storyville closed down
_____	Very first jazz recording
_____	Blues and jazz inseparable
1912–1930	Urban blues popular
_____	Chicago jazz popular
_____	The Depression era
_____	Swing introduced
1940s	Bebop appears
_____	Free jazz, cool jazz, hard bop, and funky jazz are created
_____	Modern jazz with Miles Davis
_____	Smooth jazz popular
_____	Wynton Marsalis receives Pulitzer Prize for "Blood on the Fields"

Comparison-Contrast Chart

Another method of organizing information is the comparison-contrast chart. You were introduced to this method in Chapter 14 (page 564). As the name implies, it is especially appropriate when describing similarities and differences is important. As a result, this is a more specialized organizational technique than the others.

On the next page is an incomplete comparison-contrast chart of the differences and similarities between New Orleans and Chicago jazz. Complete the chart using the information found on pages 579–580.

NEW ORLEANS AND CHICAGO JAZZ	
Differences	**Similarities**
1. No recordings of New Orleans jazz were made in New Orleans.	1. Both have high energy and rhythmic vitality.
2. Chicago jazz was largely developed by transplanted New Orleans musicians.	2. Both styles have clarinet, trumpet or cornet, and trombone as solo instruments.
	3. Both styles use head arrangements.
	4. _____
	_____
	5. _____

Jazz in America

Introduction

Jazz—divergent styles, ever changing

Although Jazz is a relatively recent, twentieth-century American phenomenon, jazz artists and styles are recognized worldwide. Jazz includes widely divergent styles ranging from entertainment music to art music. It is ever changing and defies simple definition.

Jazz began in early part of 20th century

2 Jazz began in the early part of the twentieth century in the bars and night-clubs of poor urban neighborhoods, particularly in New Orleans. These bars and clubs were the places where musicians who aspired to a career playing jazz were able to find employment. The jazz they played emerged from combining the songs, dances, and musical instincts and preferences of people of African and European (particularly French and Spanish) heritage.

International in scope

3 Jazz has come a long way over the past hundred years. Today it is international in scope—performed and listened to nearly everywhere—and it has a strong following, especially in continental Europe, Scandinavia, Japan, Africa, South America, and Canada. It is heard not only in bars and nightclubs but also in the finest hotels, on college campuses, in concert halls, and even in churches.

Accepted in music curriculums

Jazz has become an accepted part of the music curriculum in schools and colleges. Courses are devoted to the study of jazz, and music students in many schools can pursue degrees in jazz. Students can play in jazz ensembles for academic credit in American colleges and universities, and most high schools have stage bands. The International Association of Jazz Educators was organized to further the study and performance of jazz in our educational system.

Women have been influential in jazz

4 Many women, such as Mary Lou Williams, Shirley Horn, Hazel Scott, Marian McPartland, and Toshiko Akiyoshi, have achieved distinction as jazz musicians, not to mention the large number of distinguished women jazz singers, such as Billie Holiday, Ella Fitzgerald, and Sarah Vaughn. In addition, many women have been influential as composers or arrangers, as leaders of jazz groups, or as writers and teachers.

What Is Jazz?

5 Jazz began in the early days of radio and recordings, and these media brought it to the attention of the public. Recordings, especially, brought the music of jazz musicians to their colleagues; they became an invaluable way to share, learn, grow, and influence other musicians and, indeed, the future course of jazz.

Jazz elements are in
other types of popular
music

6   Today, jazz is part of a large and lucrative entertainment industry. Jazz musicians make records to sell—to become popular—but not at the expense of the integrity of their art. Elements of jazz have become evident in many styles of popular music.

7   Jazz aspires to do more than entertain, and the great jazz musicians strive for better ways of expression, sometimes in very sophisticated forms and styles. Perhaps for these reasons, jazz has never achieved mass popularity except during the swing era. Most jazz today is not considered pop music, commercial music, or music created for the sole purpose of entertaining; rather, for many musicians, jazz is a genuine form of art music. The great jazz artists have a high level of musicianship, a sense of what jazz is and of its power to communicate feelings, and a desire to share their art with others.

Popular with masses in
swing era

The Jazz Style

8   Jazz includes many styles and techniques. This list describes the common characteristics of jazz:

- The music swings; this is the feel of jazz—the jazz rhythm.

Improvise means to
make something up as
you go along

- Musicians improvise, for **improvisation** is at the heart of jazz. To *improvise music is to make it up as you go along.* The concept does not imply total freedom; to improvise is not simply to play whatever you feel like playing. In all jazz styles, there is structure on which improvisation is based.

- The rhythm includes much syncopation—off-beat rhythms.

- The music is played on certain instruments, such as the saxophone, trumpet, trombone, drums, bass, and piano. These are jazz instruments only when they are played in a jazz style in a jazz context. Sometimes jazz is played on instruments that are not commonly used in jazz performance, such as the flute, tuba, organ, or harp.

The Roots of Jazz

9   Jazz—like American society—is the product of many cultures and influences. In some ways, it represents a merging of cultures and musical styles; in other ways, it retains distinct ethnic characteristics. In the late nineteenth and early twentieth centuries, Americans—both black and white, from both North and South—sang and danced to "jazzy" music. That music included several song types:

- *Popular songs.* These are the syncopated melodies and rhythms of minstrel songs, cakewalks, vaudeville songs and dances, and the dance music of New York City and other emerging centers of popular music. For the most part, these songs had considerable rhythmic vitality.

- *Blues songs. Blues* is not synonymous with *jazz.* Blues originally was part of the African American oral tradition. The feelings evoked by the music and the text may be mournful or melancholy. The original intent was to lift the spirits of people who were "feeling blue." After the blues culture shifted from rural communities to cities in the early decades of the twentieth century, blues songs came to be performed by women accompanied by a New Orleans–style jazz combo. By the 1920s, blues and jazz became inseparable, always influencing each other. One of the greatest blues singers of that time was Bessie Smith.

- *Rags.* **Ragtime** became a notated form of popular music, originally for solo piano. It developed in and around St. Louis, and its most popular creator and performer was Scott Joplin (1868–1917). Through performances by various traveling musicians and the sale of popular pieces, ragtime arrived in New Orleans and other southern cities. It was then arranged for instruments used in the popular black brass bands.

- *Brass band marches and dances.* Brass bands of New Orleans and other southern cities were associated with private black lodges, social clubs, and fraternal organizations that employed black musicians to play for dances, parties, parades, and especially funerals. A typical instrumentation included clarinets, trombones, cornets (similar to a trumpet), banjos, bass horns (tubas), and drums.
- *Gospel songs.* Early **gospel music,** particularly that of rural and nonliterate blacks, combined the shouts and moans of blues with exciting rhythms, high energy, religious fervor, theatrical presentations, and religious texts. This style developed through the nineteenth century and still exists today. It became popular among both blacks and whites.

Jazz Styles

10　The history of modern jazz begins with New Orleans jazz. Musicians increasingly found that the music they wanted to play and the public wanted to hear had jazzy characteristics. Jazz music became established in New Orleans when artists devoted to jazz began to emerge, particularly in the second decade of the twentieth century.

New Orleans and Chicago Jazz

11　New Orleans jazz, or traditional jazz, was performed mostly in the part of New Orleans known as Storyville, which contained bars, nightclubs, and brothels that hired jazz musicians to provide entertainment and dance music. In 1917, Storyville was closed down as part of "urban reform." With that closing, opportunities for aspiring jazz musicians were lost, so they left New Orleans. Some traveled on boats up the Mississippi River. Many went to Chicago. Others settled as far afield as New York and Los Angeles. By 1920, so many of the most accomplished musicians of New Orleans had moved elsewhere that no recordings of New Orleans jazz were ever made in New Orleans.

12　The most notable recording artists to come out of New Orleans were Jelly Roll Morton, piano; Kid Ory, trombone; King Oliver, cornet; Louis Armstrong, cornet; Sidney Bechet, clarinet; and Nick La Rocca, clarinet. La Rocca headed a jazz group from New Orleans that later became known as the Original Dixieland Jazz Band. While in New York City in 1917, this group made the very first jazz recording.

13　New Orleans jazz re-emerged in Chicago in the 1920s, largely through the music of transplanted New Orleans musicians. In its new location, it was called Chicago or Dixieland jazz, and it remains popular to this day.

14　New Orleans and Chicago jazz are actually quite similar:

- Both styles have high energy and rhythmic vitality.
- Both styles have clarinet, trumpet or cornet, and trombone as solo instruments. Both styles have a rhythm section of piano, bass—either string bass or tuba—and drums.
- Both styles use **"head" arrangements**—arrangements that are worked out in rehearsal [and] then performed from memory according to traditional jazz style (they are not notated).
- Both styles use group improvisation among the solo instruments.
- The role of the rhythm section is timekeeping. Sometimes the performers put equal emphasis on each beat. At other times they may stress the first and third beats or the second and fourth beats.
- The music has occasional **breaks** (stop time). All musicians stop except for a soloist who improvises for two bars.

15   The most successful and most famous of the New Orleans musicians unquestionably was Louis Armstrong. He had an illustrious career as a trumpet player, singer, and entertainer well into the 1960s. His primary influence was on jazz musicians through the recordings he made in Chicago in the 1920s with his combos, the Hot Five and the Hot Seven. They not only educated the public about New Orleans jazz but established a model for Armstrong's greatest contributions to the development of jazz: first, the possibility of innovative jazz improvisations extended for more than a two-bar break, and second, the possibility of solo, improvised jazz singing, a style known as **scat singing** (vocal improvising similar to instrumental improvising).

Stride

16   During the 1930s, the economic difficulties of the Depression meant that many clubs could no longer hire jazz groups, so people's craving for jazz was in large measure satisfied by the solo pianists that were hired instead. Ragtime evolved into the improvised, more energetic **stride** piano style. This style, like ragtime, featured a strongly rhythmic, walking or striding left hand and a syncopated right-hand melody, but it was typically improvised and more upbeat than ragtime. The stride style—the first pure jazz form to feature solo pianists—inspired the artistry of a series of great pianists: Fats Waller, Earl Hines, Art Tatum, Erroll Garner, and Oscar Peterson.

Swing and the Big Band Jazz

17   The 1930s introduced a big band form of jazz: swing, the only style of jazz to become popular with the masses. Thus, this period is commonly known as the "swing era." Swing was the most popular music of the day, and many of these jazz tunes were on the Hit Parade (the equivalent of the top-40 charts or current *Billboard* charts). As Americans rebounded from the Great Depression, they wanted to be entertained and to dance, and they were willing to pay for both. It was a great time for popular music, jazz, jazz musicians, radio, and the recording industry.

18   In the late 1920s, a number of musicians became interested in creating jazz arrangements for big bands. To perform these arrangements successfully, musicians had to read music, play precisely with others, and improvise in the context of notated music. The most important arrangers of early big band jazz pieces were Fletcher Henderson in New York; Don Redman, who played with Henderson's group and later became an influential jazz musician in Kansas City; and Duke Ellington, who became one of the most durable and successful of all jazz composers, arrangers, and big band leaders.

19   In the swing era, jazz took three different forms:

- *Sweet swing.* Sweet swing groups had existed since the early decades of the twentieth century; in the swing era, they took the form of dance bands, or syncopated dance orchestras. Sweet swing was, and is, intended for entertainment, dancing, and easy listening. Among the most prominent leaders of sweet swing dance bands were James Reese Europe in the late 1910s, Paul Whiteman in the 1920s, Guy Lombardo from the 1940s through the 70s, and Lawrence Welk as recently as the 1980s. Their bands, particularly Paul Whiteman's, frequently employed some of the best jazz musicians available.

- *The jazz of Benny Goodman, the "King of Swing."* Probably the best known of all jazz musicians, Benny Goodman (1909–1986) formed big bands and combos that played hot jazz and gentle swing. He received the highest honors from his peers and from governments. Books and articles have been written about Goodman, and a Hollywood movie about his life had wide exposure. He did more than any other jazz performer to make jazz respectable, and he did much to racially integrate jazz groups and jazz audiences. He also performed as a clarinet soloist with major symphony orchestras.

- *Hot swing or big band jazz.* This jazz served the more serious jazz composer, arranger, and performer. It included more musically sophisticated charts, featured more extended improvised solos, and was more demanding musically than sweet swing.

20   The most sophisticated big band charts were aimed at listeners rather than dancers. Among the best and most durable of the big bands were those of Duke Ellington and Count Basie. Other prominent bands included those of Glenn Miller, Woody Herman, and Tommy Dorsey.

Bebop

21   Three major economic and musical factors created **bebop.**

- Many jazz musicians wanted to find new ways of playing the same chords, improvising imaginative and unexpected chords, and creating new interpretations of melodies.

- Late-night jam sessions provided a venue for experimentation and creative exploration. People partied and danced at night; thus, jazz musicians worked at night. Too often, however, the style of jazz preferred by their paying audience—and thus required by their employer—did not allow room for creativity. So creative exploration took place in after-hours **jam sessions** frequently lasting all night. Bebop was born at these sessions.

- During World War II, people had less time and money for dancing and entertainment. Gasoline was rationed, restricting travel, and many men had gone to war, making it more difficult for band leaders to find the needed musicians. Consequently, in the 1940s, big band music declined in popularity. One response to these circumstances was a return to combo jazz and the creation of the bebop style.

22   The roots of bebop date to the 1930s, but it was not until the early 1940s in New York that Dizzy Gillespie, Thelonious Monk, Kenny Clark, and others gathered to explore new musical possibilities and to satisfy their own unfulfilled musical desires. Gillespie played the trumpet, Monk the piano, and Clark the drums. Their search for a new style, however, did not solidify until a saxophonist named Charlie Parker arrived in New York from Kansas City. Parker's skillful improvisation and musical instincts led to a clarification and synthesis of the bebop style.

23   Bebop is often complex, intense, and very fast. The emphasis is on unusual harmonic, melodic, and rhythmic treatments of a song and on the performer's virtuosity. The song itself was often a popular song of the day or a standard; but usually, all that remained of this song were its title and its underlying chords.

Cool, Hard Bop, Soul Jazz, and Free Jazz

24   Because the bop of the 1940s and 1950s was complex and sophisticated, it never achieved widespread popularity with the public or even among jazz musicians. Immediately, musicians began to explore alternatives. Many styles and influential artists emerged in the 1950s and the 1960s, a period of diversity in the history of jazz. Four important jazz styles from these years are cool jazz, hard bop, soul jazz—sometimes called funky jazz—and free jazz.

25   **Cool jazz** was personified by Miles Davis, a bebop trumpet player, in an album called *The Birth of the Cool.* It was an attempt to apply musically sophisticated ideas in a softer, more relaxed, more accessible manner than bebop. Cool jazz is typified by the early music of Miles Davis and by the music of the Modern Jazz Quartet, Dave Brubeck, Gerry Mulligan, Stan Getz, and Chet Baker.

26   **Hard bop** is perhaps a catchall name for the music of the next generation of bop musicians, who attempted to maintain the principles of bop in a way that would not alienate the listening public. Two of the most popular jazz musicians of

this period are Clifford Brown (trumpet) and Sonny Rollins (tenor sax). Other jazz musicians continued to experiment with new styles and techniques. One of the most outstanding was John Coltrane (tenor and soprano sax) whose tone quality and approach to improvisation have influenced countless other jazz musicians.

27   **Funky jazz** [and] *soul jazz* are the names sometimes used to describe the music of jazz performers who created a style that returned to the roots of jazz. These musicians explored a new style of jazz that capitalized on harmonic and rhythmic simplicity, a strong beat, and influences from gospel music, R&B, and, later, soul. Influential artists who represented funky jazz are Horace Silver, Art Blakely, Jimmy Smith, and Ramsey Lewis.

28   **Free jazz** was pioneered in the 1950s and 1960s by Ornette Coleman (alto sax and violin). He created a style that is almost pure improvisation with no adherence to predetermined chord structures, meter, or melodic motives. The idea is for the musicians to interact musically with each other, building on what others in the group are doing, but also being free to create according to their musical instincts. Like bebop, free jazz was not one of the more popular forms of jazz with the public or among many jazz musicians. Some people were averse to it because it lacked the structure on which jazz improvisation was traditionally based. It did, however, attract avid supporters who respected its level of creativity and its new sounds.

Modern Jazz, Fusion, and Smooth Jazz

29   Modern jazz began in the 1960s, with Miles Davis, again, as the driving force. It was not just Davis's music that was important, but the people he hired as sidemen. Many have become the biggest names in modern jazz.

30   A popular form of modern jazz is **fusion.** Fusion artists merge the jazz style with pop, classical, or rock styles to create *fusion jazz.* The most dramatic change involves instruments and techniques borrowed from rock; electronic keyboards, electric bass, and rock drumming. Synthesizers, computers, and other technological advancements have become widely used in contemporary ("modern") jazz. Some writers have argued that fusion has been the most popular form of jazz since the swing era. Perhaps the most successful fusion artists are Herbie Hancock (keyboards), Chick Corea (keyboards), and Pat Metheny (guitar).

31   Fusion, however, is a term more widely used in the 1970s and 1980s than in recent years. The styles of jazz today are extremely varied, ranging from the easy-listening jazz of many contemporary musicians to the extremely complex post-bop jazz of many others. Again, diversity is a major characteristics of this music. Without question, the impact of rock and electronic instruments is significant. But the term fusion may also signal a synthesis of jazz with other styles and traditions: jazz and classical music (third stream—Gunther Schuller, John Lewis), Caribbean and South American music (salsa and Latin jazz—Tito Puente and Stan Getz), country (bluegrass and jazz—David Grisman), and the blues (some B. B. King and some Van Morrison).

32   Among the artists who, in the early years, moved easily between traditional jazz, pop, and—in some cases—blues styles were singers such as Billie Holiday, Ella Fitzgerald, Tony Bennett, Frank Sinatra, and Mel Torme. In recent years, Diana Krall, Norah Jones, and Cassandra Wilson have also made this move.

33   Smooth jazz is the newest genre under the label "modern jazz," having emerged in the 1990s. Many well-known fusion and traditional jazz artists have adopted this less intense and more easy-listening style. The popularity of smooth jazz has increased as more and more radio stations have adopted a "smooth jazz" format. Tours and festivals have attracted huge followings, and hundreds of recordings of smooth jazz artists have become readily available in stores and online. Among the current popular artists are Boney James, David Sanborn, George Benson, and Grover Washington Jr.

34   In some styles of modern jazz, it is sometimes difficult to identify jazz in the traditional sense. The style of jazz—indeed, the definition of jazz—is changing.

But traditional jazz is not a thing of the past. The most prominent current jazz musician who builds directly on the past is the gifted trumpeter Wynton Marsalis. Marsalis, who is also an accomplished classical musician, received two Grammies in 1983, one for jazz and one for his recording of classical trumpet concertos. In 1997, he was awarded the prestigious Pulitzer Prize in music for *Blood on the Fields,* a three-hour work about slavery for solo singers and jazz band.

35   As in any art, some musicians are motivated artistically, others commercially. Some look backward and value history and traditions. Others look forward, valuing experimentation and new forms of expression. Future styles of jazz will almost certainly blend all these influences, for most artists respond to the challenges from various sources of inspiration and creativity.

Summary

36   This chapter on jazz is designed to help you know, appreciate, and respect the literature, heritage, people, and sounds of jazz.

37   Jazz is complex, always changing. The best jazz artists are driven to reach for new possibilities, to experiment, to resist permanent labels. For example, Miles Davis was at first a bebop musician, then an influential cool jazz artist, and later a leader in fusion and electronic jazz. Max Roach, one of the best bop drummers, has also performed on many cool jazz recordings. You can find cool jazz, bebop, and other styles all in the same piece. The big band jazz of Stan Kenton, for example, frequently has elements of bebop, cool, and swing in one arrangement. Many of the great artists defy classification because they continue to grow and change.

From David Willoughby, *The World of Music,* 6th Edition, pp. 107–34. Copyright © 2007 by The McGraw-Hill Companies, Inc. Reprinted with permission.

 COMPREHENSION CHECKUP

Multiple Choice

Directions: For each item, write the letter corresponding to the best answer on the line provided.

_____ 1. Jazz was influenced by all of the following *except*
   a. ragtime.
   b. gospel songs.
   c. brass bands.
   d. Motown.

_____ 2. All of the following is true about blues *except* for which of the following?
   a. Blues was originally part of the folk rock tradition.
   b. Blues was associated with sadness or melancholy.
   c. Blues singers came to be mostly women.
   d. Blues moved from rural areas to cities.

_____ 3. Stride is associated with
   a. the piano.
   b. Art Tatum.
   c. Fats Waller.
   d. all of the above.

_____ 4. A famous blues singer of the 1920s is
   a. Shirley Horn.
   b. Ethel Rosenberg.
   c. Bessie Smith.
   d. Toshiko Akiyoshi.

_____ 5. Big band jazz is associated with all of the following *except*
   a. Fletcher Henderson.
   b. arranging music.
   c. cakewalks.
   d. Duke Ellington.

_____ 6. The common characteristics of jazz include all of the following *except*
   a. rhythm.
   b. improvisation.
   c. big bands.
   d. syncopation.

_____ 7. Jazz has been known over the last century for its
   a. similarity to European classical music.
   b. greatly varied styles.
   c. singular style based on the blues.
   d. heavy emphasis on vocal music.

_____ 8. Jazz moved from New Orleans to Chicago
   a. after the development of scat singing.
   b. after World War II.
   c. after the death of Louis Armstrong.
   d. after the Storyville district was shut down.

_____ 9. New Orleans and Chicago jazz share all of the following characteristics *except*
   a. notated arrangements.
   b. group improvisations.
   c. a rhythm section for timekeeping.
   d. breaks for soloists.

_____ 10. All of the following musicians are associated with the trumpet or cornet *except*
   a. Louis Armstrong.
   b. Kid Ory.
   c. Wynton Marsalis.
   d. Dizzy Gillespie.

True or False

Directions: Indicate whether each statement is true or false by writing **T** or **F** in the space provided.

_____ 11. Jazz remains a vital feature of American music.

_____ 12. Free jazz became quite popular with the public at large.

_____ 13. Swing and big band jazz introduced "the art of the arranger."

_____ 14. Dave Brubeck is a practitioner of cool jazz.

_____ 15. Jazz has been influenced by both Black and White musicians.

Vocabulary in Context

Directions: Without looking in a dictionary, define the following words as they are used in the chapter "Jazz in America." The number in parentheses indicates the paragraph in which the word is located.

1. divergent (1) _____

2. phenomenon (1) _____

3. aspired to (2) _____

4. urban (2) _____

5. heritage (2) _____

6. scope (3) _____

7. distinction (4) _____

Directions: Choose one of the following words to complete each of the sentences below. Use each word only once.

notable	evolved	durable	averse
lucrative	improvisation	characteristic	prestigious

8. Harvard and Stanford are two of the most _____ universities in the United States.

9. As the year passed, her thinking on the subject of marriage _____.

10. Many players in Major League Baseball have signed _____ contracts worth millions.

11. In contrast to jazz, classical music does not emphasize _____ by musicians.

12. As a _____ actress, she received great acclaim for her performances.

13. After more than 40 years in business together, the brothers had to admit that their partnership had proved _____.

14. Even though she is a vegetarian, she is not _____ to eating turkey on occasion.

15. The ability to motivate oneself is a _____ needed for success in college.

Vocabulary Matching

Directions: Match the musician's name in Column B with the type of music the musician was known for in Column A. Place the correct letter in the space provided.

Column A	**Column B**
_____ 1. blues	a. Scott Joplin
_____ 2. stride	b. Louis Armstrong
_____ 3. ragtime	c. Paul Whiteman
_____ 4. cool jazz	d. Fats Waller
_____ 5. bebop	e. George Benson
_____ 6. sweet swing	f. Bessie Smith
_____ 7. New Orleans jazz	g. Charlie Parker
_____ 8. smooth jazz	h. Miles Davis
_____ 9. free jazz	i. Ornette Coleman
_____ 10. big band jazz	j. Duke Ellington

In Your Own Words

The Rock and Roll Hall of Fame opened in Cleveland, Ohio, in 1995. Where do you think would be a good place to locate a jazz hall of fame?

Written Assignment

Many jazz musicians have led difficult lives. Do you think there is something about being a jazz musician that leads to problems of this sort? Do you think that other sorts of artists, such as painters or writer or filmmakers, also endure unusually high levels of personal stress in their lives?

Internet Activity

A variety of jazz musicians have been discussed in this chapter. Select one whom you find interesting, search for an Internet article about this musician, and write a paragraph on what you learned.

Chapter Summary and Review

In Chapter 15, you practiced a variety of study skill techniques with actual textbook chapters. Based on the material in Chapter 15, answer the following.

Vocabulary in Context

Directions: Choose one of the following words to complete the sentences below. Use each word only once.

> annotating   comparison   mapping   scan   skimming

1. Writing notes in the margins and highlighting important information is called

   _____.

2. _____ is a study technique very similar to the surveying technique in SQ3R.

3. If you want to find a specific piece of information such as a date or a person's

   name, you can _____ the material.

4. A less formal and more visual way of outlining information is called

   _____.

5. You may want to make a _____ -contrast chart if the material you are studying discusses similarities and differences between two or more topics or points of view.

Appendices

We have chosen to include "Using the Dictionary," "Visual Aids," and "Test-Taking Techniques" in the Appendices. For these three sections, we include an explanation of the topic, as well as practice exercises. At the end of the Appendices, you will find summaries and copies of some of the forms that appear in the text.

As you learned in this book, you may need to use the dictionary to find a specific meaning for a word. For example, your textbook for a music appreciation class might contain the words "meter," "harmony," and "syncopation," and you would want to look up these words in the dictionary. This section will build your confidence in using dictionaries.

The section on visual aids will improve your skills in interpreting charts and graphs. Text is often supplemented by these materials, and the ability to work with them will help you understand what is being said. For example, a textbook for a music appreciation class might have a chart showing the percentage of CDs sold at mass-retail outlets such as Target versus those sold at smaller retail music shops.

Also included are some tips for improving your test-taking performance on both objective exams and essay exams. The key to doing well on a test is adequate preparation, but at the very least, these tips should help you keep your level of test anxiety under control.

Finally, we offer sample summaries.

Using the Dictionary

Introduction

The dictionary can be an invaluable tool for you, provided, of course, you have an appropriate one and know at least the fundamentals of how to use it. You now know that looking a word up in the dictionary is probably only useful if you already have a general idea what the unknown word means from the context of the sentence or article. The dictionary has tons of information, probably too much. You have to sort through it and find the information helpful to you.

Selecting a Dictionary

Rule 1

The dictionary needs to be up-to-date. Take a look at your dictionary. *Find the copyright date. If your dictionary is over 10 years old, you need a new one.* Our language changes. New words are added; other words take on new meanings. Let's take the word "gay" and see how its meaning pertaining to homosexuality evolved through three different editions of what is now called the *American Heritage College Dictionary*. The writers of the first edition, originally published in 1969, considered the term "slang." By 1982, the word "gay" had become commonly accepted, and so calling it "slang" was no longer necessary. The authors of the fourth edition, copyrighted in 2002, felt that the term was not only commonly used but needed further explanation. Therefore, they added a "usage note" to give readers further information.

1969 edition   **gay** (g̅) *adj.* **gayer, gayest.** **1.** Showing or characterized by exuberance or mirthful excitement. **2.** Bright or lively, especially in color. **3.** Full of or given to social or other pleasures. **4.** Dissolute; licentious. **5.** *Slang.* Homosexual. [Middle English *gay, gai,* from Old French *gai,* from Old Provençal, probably from Gothic *gaheis* (unattested), akin to Old High German *gāhit,* sudden, impetuous.] —**gay'ness** *n.*[1]

1982 edition   **gay** (g̅) *adj.* **-er, -est.** **1.** Showing or characterized by exuberance or happy excitement; merry. **2.** Bright or lively, esp. in color. **3.** Full of or given to social pleasures. **4.** Dissolute; licentious. **5.** Homosexual. —*n.* A homosexual. [ME *gai* < OFr., of Germanic orig.] —**gay** *adv.* —**gay'ness** *n.*[2]

2002 edition   **gay** (gă) *adj.* **gay•er, gay•est** **1.** Of, relating to, or having a sexual orientation to persons of the same sex.

2. Showing or characterized by cheerfulness and light-hearted excitement; merry.   **3.** Bright or lively, esp. in color.   **4.** Given to social pleasures.   **5.** Dissolute; licentious. ❖ *n.* **1.** A person whose sexual orientation is to persons of the same sex.   **2.** A man whose sexual orientation is to men. [ME *gai* < OFr., poss. of Gmc. orig.] —**gay'ness** *n.*

Usage Note: The word *gay* is now standard in its use to refer to homosexuals, in large part because it is the term that most gay people prefer in referring to themselves. *Gay* is distinguished from *homosexual* primarily by the emphasis it places on the cultural and social aspects of homosexuality as opposed to sexual practice. Many writers reserve *gay* for males, but the word is also used to refer to both sexes; when the intended meaning is not clear in the context, the phrase *gay and lesbian* may be used. *Gay* can sometimes be regarded as objectionable when used as a noun to refer to particular individuals, as in *There were two gays on the panel;* here phrasing such as *gay members* should be used instead. But there is no objection to the use of the noun in the plural to refer collectively either to gay men or to gay men and lesbians, so long as it is clear whether men alone or both men and women are being discussed. See Usage Note at **homosexual.**[3]

1. Copyright © 1969, 1981 by Houghton Mifflin Company. Reproduced by permission from *The American Heritage Dictionary of English Language.*

2. Copyright © 1982 by Houghton Mifflin Company. Reproduced by permission from *The American Heritage Dictionary, Second College Edition.*

3. Copyright © 2002 by Houghton Mifflin Company. Reproduced by permission from *The American Heritage College Dictionary, Fourth Edition.*

Note: Often discount department stores advertise dictionaries for a very cheap cost. Take off the cellophane wrapper and find the publication date. You may find it already a few years out-of-date. Remember that "you get what you pay for."

Rule 2

Have two dictionaries—one hardbound and one softbound. Preferably, the two dictionaries should be written by two different publishing companies.

Hardbound Dictionary

Hardbound dictionaries have hard covers. This dictionary should be kept at home on a shelf in your study area. Hardbound dictionaries include more words and information than their softbound editions. Contrast the two examples below, the first from the hardbound edition of the *Random House Webster's College Dictionary* and the second from its softbound counterpart, the *Random House Webster's School and Office Dictionary.* At first glance, the two dictionaries look the same, but you simply cannot cram 1,573 pages of the hardbound version into 630 pages, which is the length of the softbound book. The first example from the hardbound edition is, obviously, much more complete. The hardbound version of this dictionary has 207,000 entries while the softbound edition only has 75,000.

Hardbound Edition

jazz (jaz), *n.* **1.** music originating in New Orleans around the beginning of the 20th century and subsequently developing through various increasingly complex styles, generally marked by intricate, propulsive rhythms, polyphonic ensemble playing, improvisatory, virtuosic solos, melodic freedom, and a harmonic idiom ranging from simple diatonicism through chromaticism to

atonality.   **2.** a style of dance music marked by some of the features of jazz.
3. *Slang.* liveliness; spirit; excitement.   **4.** *Slang.* insincere or pretentious talk.
5. *Slang.* similar or related but unspecified things: *We like sightseeing, museums,
and all that jazz.* —*v.t.*   **6.** to play (music) in the manner of jazz.   **7.** *Slang.* **a.** to
excite or enliven. **b.** to accelerate. —*v.i.*   **8.** *Slang.* to act or proceed with great
energy or liveliness.   **9. jazz up,** *Slang.* **a.** to enliven. **b.** to embellish. [1910–15,
Amer.]

jazz•er•cise (jaz′ər sīz′), *n.*   vigorous dancing done to jazz dance music as an
exercise for physical fitness. [1985–90; JAZZ + (EX)ERCISE]

jazz•man (jaz′man′, -mən), *n., pl.*   **-men** (-men′, -mən). a musician who plays
jazz. [1925–30]

jazz′-rock′, *n.*   music that combines elements of both jazz and rock and is
usually performed on amplified electric instruments. [1965–70]

jazz•y (jaz′ē), *adj.,* **jazz•i•er, jazz•i•est.**   **1.** pertaining to or suggestive of jazz
music.   **2.** *Slang.* active or lively.   **3.** *Slang.* fancy or flashy: *a jazzy sweater.*
[1915–20, *Amer.*] —**jazz′i•ly,** *adv.* —**jazz′ i•ness,** *n.*

From *Random House Webster's College Dictionary,* Second Edition, copyright © 2001 by Random
House, Inc. Used by permission of Random House, Inc.

Softbound Edition

jazz (jaz), *n.*   **1.** music originating in New Orleans, marked by propulsive
rhythms, ensemble playing, and improvisation.   **2.** *Slang.* insincere or pretentious talk. —*v.t.*   **3. jazz up,** *Slang.* **a.** to enliven. **b.** to embellish.

jazz′y, *adj.,* **-i•er, -i•est**   **1.** of or suggestive of jazz music.   **2.** *Slang.* fancy
or flashy.

From *Random House School and Office Dictionary,* 2nd Edition. Copyright © 2002 by Random House,
Inc. Used by permission of Random House Reference and Information Publishing, a division of
Random House, Inc.

Softbound Dictionary

These dictionaries have soft covers, similar to the ones on the outside of this book.
Unless you're trying to build up your shoulder muscles, you probably don't need the
weight of that heavy hardbound dictionary in your backpack. We therefore suggest
that you buy a softbound dictionary for quick and easy reference while you are in
class or in the library.

Computer Dictionary

Dictionaries are now also published on CD-ROM. If you are going to be using a
computer to write your papers, you might also want to look into a good electronic
dictionary.

Unabridged Dictionary

You don't need to buy an unabridged dictionary, but such a dictionary can be very
useful. Unabridged dictionaries have all the words in our language. You can find
these dictionaries in your college library. Many students find them useful to locate obscure words.

Note: Why should you have a softbound dictionary written by one publishing
company and a hardbound version written by another? Having two dictionaries
gives you two different perspectives on a word. The definitions are written
slightly differently. When you are having problems understanding the definition
from one dictionary, then you can try the other one.

Organization

Now that we have found out about selecting an appropriate dictionary, let's see what's in this resource book. The discussion and examples below will often refer to the sample dictionary page found on the following page. We have taken an excerpt from the *Random House Webster's College Dictionary*, 2nd ed., 2001, enlarged the print, and adapted the pages for your use.

1. Entry words

Dictionaries are organized like telephone books, in alphabetical order. Each entry word is usually in **boldface** type. Often dictionaries will also give common two- or three-word phrases as entry words.

What boldface entry comes after "sawbones"? _____

2. Guide words

As in a telephone book, there are guide words at the top of each page that indicate the first and last entries on that page.

What are the guide words for this page? _____

3. Entry word division versus pronunciation—syllabication division

For each entry, the word division and the pronunciation and syllabication division are usually the same.

How many syllables are there in the word "saxophone"? _____

You should realize that some dictionaries divide their entry words as you would for printers and typesetting, so the entry word and pronunciation divisions may not be exactly the same. Take a look at the word "curious." Notice that the entry word is divided differently than its pronunciation.

cu•ri•ous (kyŏŏr′ē əs), *adj.*   **1.** eager to learn or know.   **2.** taking an undue interest in others' affairs; prying.   **3.** arousing attention or interest through being unusual or hard to explain; odd; strange; novel.   **4.** *Archaic.* **a.** made or done skillfully or painstakingly. **b.** careful; fastidious. **c.** marked by intricacy or subtlety. [1275–1325; ME < L *cūriōsus* careful, inquisitive, prob. back formation from *incūriōsus* careless, der. of *incūria* carelessness]—**cu′ri•ous•ly,** *adv.* —**cu′ri•ous•ness,** *n.*

From *Random House Webster's College Dictionary*, 2nd Edition, by Random House, Inc. Copyright © 2000 by Random House, Inc. Reprinted by permission of Random House Reference and Information Publishing, a division of Random House, Inc.

Look at the word "banana" and see how three different dictionaries divide the entry word.

American Heritage	ba•nan•a
Webster's New World	ba•nan∣a
Merriam Webster	ba•nana

4. Pronunciation

Notice how most entries are followed by their pronunciations, but the words are written quite differently. Dictionaries will use letters and symbols that represent sounds. Usually you will find a complete key to these sounds in the front part of the dictionary. On page A-7 is the Random House pronunciation key. Sometimes alternate pronunciations will also be given. For example, the word "sawyer" has two pronunciations (see next page).

savvy to sayyid

sav•vy (sav′ē), *n., adj.,* **-vi•er, -vi•est,** *.v.,* **-vied, -vy•ing.** —*n.* **1.** Also, **sav′vi•ness.** practical understanding; shrewdness or intelligence; common sense: *political savvy.* —*adj.* **2.** shrewdly informed; experienced and well-informed; canny. —*v.t., v.i.* **3.** to know; understand. [1775–85; prob. orig. < *sábi* "know" in E creoles (< Pg *sabe,* pres. 3rd sing. of *saber* to know < L *sapere* to be wise; see SAPIENT)] —**sav′vi•ly,** *adv.*

saw[1] (sô), *n., v.,* **sawed, sawed** or **sawn, saw•ing.** —*n.* **1.** a tool or device for cutting, typically a thin blade of metal with a series of sharp teeth. **2.** any similar tool or device, as a rotating disk, in which a sharp continuous edge replaces the teeth. —*v.t.* **3.** to cut or divide with a saw. **4.** to form by cutting with a saw. **5.** to make cutting motions as if using a saw: *to saw the air with one's hands.* **6.** to work (something) from side to side like a saw. —*v.i.* **7.** to use a saw. **8.** to cut with or as if with a saw. —*Idiom.* **9.** saw wood, to snore loudly while sleeping. [bef. 1000; ME *sawe,* OE *saga,* c. MLG, MD *sage* (D *zaag*), OHG *saga,* ON *sǫg;*] —**saw′er,** *n.*

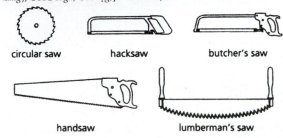

circular saw   hacksaw   butcher's saw

handsaw   lumberman's saw

saws (def. 1)

saw[2] (sô), *v.* pt. of SEE[1].
saw[3] (sô), *n.* a maxim; proverb; saying; *an old saw.* [bef. 950; ME; OE *sagu;* c. OFris *sege,* OHG, G *sage,* ON *saga* (cf. SAGA); akin to SAY]
Sa•watch (sə wäch′), *n.* a mountain range in central Colorado: part of the Rocky Mountains. Highest peak, Mt. Elbert, 14,431 ft. (4400 m).
saw•bones (sô′bōnz′), *n., pl.* **-bones, -bones•es.** (*used with a sing. v.*) *Slang.* a surgeon or physician. [1830–40]
saw•buck (sô′buk′), *n.* **1.** a sawhorse. **2.** *Slang.* a ten-dollar bill. [1860–65, *Amer.;* cf. D *zaagbok;* (def. 2) so called from the resemblance of the Roman numeral X to the crossbars of a sawhorse]
saw•dust (sô′dust′), *n.* fine particles of wood produced in sawing.
sawed′-off′, *adj.* **1.** cut off at the end, as a shotgun. **2.** *Slang.* smallish; of less than average size or stature. [1865–70, *Amer.*]
saw•fish (sô′fish′), *n., pl.* (*esp. collectively*) **-fish,** (*esp. for kinds or species*) **-fish•es.** any large, sharklike ray of the genus *Pristis,* living along tropical coasts and lowland rivers, with a bladelike snout edged with strong teeth. [1655–65]
saw•fly (sô′flī′), *n., pl.* **-flies.** any of numerous insects of the family Tenthredinidae, the female of which has a sawlike ovipositor for inserting the eggs in the tissues of a host plant. [1765–75]
saw•horse (sô′hôrs′), *n.* a movable frame or trestle for supporting wood while it is being sawed. [1770–80]
saw•mill (sô′mil′), *n.* a place or building in which timber is sawed into planks, boards, etc., by machinery. [1545–55]
sawn (sôn), *v.* a pp. of SAW[1].
saw-off (sô′ôf′, -of′), *n. Canadian.* **1.** an arrangement between political rivals by which each agrees not to run for the same office as another. **2.** any arrangement that involves concessions. [1905–10]
saw′palmet′to, *n.* a shrublike palmetto, *Serenoa repens,* native to the southern U.S., having green or blue leafstalks set with spiny teeth.
saw•tooth (sô′tooth′), *n., pl.* **-teeth** (-tēth′), *adj.* —*n.* **1.** one of the cutting teeth of a saw. —*adj.* **2.** having a zigzag profile, like that of the cutting edge of a saw; serrate. [1595–1605]
saw′-toothed′, *adj.* having teeth like a saw; serrate. [1580–90]
saw′-whet′owl′, *n.* a small North American owl, *Aegolius acadicus,* with a persistently repeated, mechanical sounding note. [1825–35, *Amer.;* from its cry being likened to a saw being whetted]
saw•yer (sô′yr, soi′ər), *n.* **1.** a person who saws wood, esp. as an occupation. **2.** any of several long-horned beetles, esp. one of the genus *Monochamus,* the larvae of which bore in the wood of coniferous trees. [1300–50; ME *sawier = sawe* saw[1] + *-ier* -IER[1]]
sax (saks), *n.* a saxophone. [by shortening]
Sax., **1.** Saxon. **2.** Saxony.
sax•a•tile (sak′sə til), *adj.* living or growing on or among rocks; saxicoline. [1645–55; < L *saxātilis* frequenting rocks, der. of *sax(um)* rock]
Saxe (sAks), *n.* French name of SAXONY.
Saxe-Co•burg-Go•tha (saks′kō′bûrg gō′thə), *n.* **1.** a member of the present British royal family, from the establishment of the house in 1901 until 1917 when the family name was changed to Windsor. **2. Albert Francis Charles Augustus Emanuel, Prince of,** ALBERT, Prince.

sax•horn (saks′hôrn′), *n.* any of a family of brass instruments close to the cornets and tubas. [1835–45; after A. *Sax* (1814–94), a Belgian who invented such instruments]
sax•ic•o•line (sak sik′ə lin, -līn′) also **sax•ic•o•lous** (-ləs), *adj.* living or growing among rocks. [1895–1900; < NL *saxicol(a)* (L *saxi-,* comb. form of *saxum* rock + -*cola* dweller; see -COLOUS) + -INE[1]]
sax•i•frage (sak′sə frij), *n.* any of numerous plants of the genus *Saxifraga,* certain species of which grow wild in the clefts of rocks, other species of which are cultivated for their flowers. [1400–50; late ME < L *saxifraga* (*herba*) stone-breaking (herb) = *saxi-,* comb. form of *saxum* stone + *-fraga,* fem. of *-fragus* breaking; see FRAGILE]
sax•i•tox•in (sak′si tok′sin), *n.* a neurotoxin produced by the dinoflagellate *Gonyaulax catenella,* the causative agent of red tide. [1960–65; < NL *Saxi(domus),* a clam genus infected by the dinoflagellates (L *sax(um)* stone + *-i- -i- + domus* house) + TOXIN]
Sax•o Gram•mat•i•cus (sak′sō grəmat′i kəs), *n.* c1150–1206?, Danish historian and poet.
Sax•on (sak′sən), *n.* **1.** a member of a Germanic people or confederation of peoples, occupying parts of the North Sea littoral and adjacent hinterlands in the 3rd–4th centuries A.D.: later notorious as sea raiders, groups of whom invaded and settled in S Britain in the 5th–6th centuries. **2.** a native or inhabitant of Saxony. **3.** a native of England, or person of English descent, esp. as opposed to an inhabitant of the British Isles of Celtic descent. —*adj.* **4.** of or pertaining to the early Saxons. **5.** of or pertaining to Saxony or its inhabitants. [1250–1300; ME, prob. < LL *Saxō, Saxonēs* (pl.) < Gmc; r. OE *Seaxan* (pl.)]
sax•o•ny (sak′sə nē), *n.* **1.** a fine, three-ply woolen yarn. **2.** a soft-finish, compact fabric for coats. [1825–35; from SAXONY]
Sax•o•ny (sak′sə nē), *n.* **1.** a state in E central Germany, 4,900,000; 6561 sq. mi. (16,990 sq. km). *Cap.:* Dresden. **2.** a former state of the Weimar Republic in E central Germany. 5788 sq. mi. (14,990 sq. km). *Cap.:* Dresden. **3.** a medieval division of N Germany with varying boundaries: extended at its height from the Rhine to E of the Elbe. German, **Sachsen;** French, **Saxe.** —**Sax•o′ni•an** (-sō′nēan), *n., adj.*
Sax′ony-An′halt, *n.* a state in central Germany. 3,000,000; 9515 sq. mi. (24,644 sq. km). *Cap.:* Magdeburg. German, **Sachsen-Anhalt.**
sax•o•phone (sak′sə fōn′), *n.* a musical wind instrument consisting of a conical, usu. brass tube with keys or valves and a mouthpiece with one reed. [1850–55; *Sax* (see SAXHORN) + -o- + -PHONE] —**sax′o•phon′ic** (-fon′ik), *adj.* —**sax′o•phon′ist,** *n.*

saxophone

say (sā), *v.,* **said, say•ing,** *adv., n., interj.* —*v.t.* **1.** to utter or pronounce; speak: *to say a word.* **2.** to express in words; state; declare. **3.** to state as an opinion or judgment: *I say we should wait here.* **4.** to recite or repeat. **5.** to report or allege; maintain. **6.** to express (a message, viewpoint, etc.), as through a literary or other artistic medium. **7.** to indicate or show: *What does your watch say?* —*v.i.* **8.** to speak; declare; express an opinion, idea, etc. —*adv.* **9.** approximately; about: *It's, say, 14 feet long.* **10.** for example. —*n.* **11.** what a person says or has to say. **12.** the right or opportunity to state an opinion or exercise influence: *to have one's say in a decision.* **13.** a turn to say something. —*interj.* **14.** (used to express surprise, get attention, etc.) —*Idiom.* **15. go without saying,** to be completely self-evident. [bef. 900; ME *seyen, seggen,* OE *secgan;* c. D *zeggen,* G *sagen,* ON *segja;* akin to SAW[3]] —**say′er,** *n.*
say•a•ble (sā′ə bəl), *adj.* **1.** of the sort that can be said or spoken. **2.** capable of being said or stated clearly, effectively, etc. [1855–60]
Sa•yan′Moun′tains (sä yän′), *n.pl.* a mountain range in the S Russian Federation in central Asia. Highest peak, 11,447 ft. (3490 m).
Say•ers (sā′ərz, sârz), *n.* **Dorothy L(eigh),** 1893–1957, English detective-story writer, dramatist, essayist, and translator.
say•est (sā′ist) also **sayst** (sāst), *v. Archaic.* 2nd pers. sing. of SAY.
say•ing (sā′ing), *n.* something said, esp. a proverb or maxim.
sa•yo•na•ra (sī′ə när′ə), *interj.* r. farewell. [1870–75; < Japn]
says (sez), *v.* 3rd pers. sing. pres. indic. of SAY.
say′-so′, *n., pl.* **say-sos. 1.** one's personal statement or assertion. **2.** right of final authority. **3.** an authoritative statement. [1630–40]
say•yid or **say•ed** or **say•id** (sā′yid, sä′id), *n.* **1.** a supposed descendant of Muhammad through his grandson Hussein. **2.** an Islamic title of respect, esp. for royal personages. [1780–90; < Ar: lord]

ENGLISH SOUNDS

a	act, bat, marry	l	low, mellow, bottle (bot'l)	th	that, either, smooth
ā	age, paid, say			u	up, sun
âr	air, Mary, dare	m	my, summer, him	ûr	urge, burn, cur
ä	ah, balm, star	n	now, sinner, button (but'n)	v	voice, river, live
b	back, cabin, cab			w	witch, away
ch	child, pitcher, beach	ng	sing, Washington	y	yes, onion
d	do, madder, bed	o	ox, bomb, wasp	z	zoo, lazy, those
e	edge, set, merry	ō	over, boat, no	zh	treasure, mirage
ē	equal, bee, pretty	ô	order, ball, raw	ə	used in unaccented syllables to indicate the sound of the reduced vowel in alone, system, easily, gallop, circus
ēr	earring, cheerful, appear	oi	oil, joint, joy		
f	fit, differ, puff	o͝o	oomph, book, tour		
g	give, trigger, beg	o͞o	ooze, fool, too		
h	hit, behave	ou	out, loud, cow	ᵊ	used between i and r and between ou and r to show triphthongal quality, as in fire (iᵊr), hour (ouᵊr)
hw	which, nowhere	p	pot, supper, stop		
i	if, big, mirror	r	read, hurry, near		
ī	ice, bite, deny	s	see, passing, miss		
j	just, tragic, fudge	sh	shoe, fashion, push		
k	keep, token, make	t	ten, matter, bit		
		th	thin, ether, path		

NON-ENGLISH SOUNDS

A	as in French **ami** (A mē')
KH	as in Scottish **loch** (lôKH)
N	as in French **bon** (bôN) [used to indicate that the preceding vowel is nasalized]
CE	as in French **feu** (FCE)
R	[a symbol for any non-English r sound, including a trill or flap in Italian and Spanish and a sound in French and German similar to KH but pronounced with voice]
Y	as in French **tu** (tY)
ᵊ	as in French **bastogne** (ba stôn'yᵊ)

What words show how "oi" is pronounced? _____

Write out the pronunciations for the following words:

sayable _____

sawyer (both pronunciations) _____

sawtooth _____

5. Parts of speech

Each word will also have its part or parts of speech listed: "n." is for a noun, "v." is for a verb, and so forth. Note that "v.t." is for a transitive verb and "v.i." is for an intransitive verb. A transitive verb takes a direct object while an intransitive does not.

Find the parts of speech for the words below. Write out the whole word, such as "adjective" for "adj."

Saxe   _____

sayable   _____

sayyid   _____

6. Etymology

We have been studying word etymologies, or word histories, in the vocabulary units throughout this book. We will not list all the abbreviations used for different languages, but "L" is the abbreviation for Latin and "Gk" stands for Greek.

Find out the Latin meaning for

savvy _____

saxicoline _____

Many words in English come from other languages. From what language does

the word "sayonara" come? _____

7. Words in phrases

Some dictionaries, such as the *Random House Webster's College Dictionary*, give some words in sample phrases. Take a look at the definitions for "say" and see how this word is used in sample phrases.

What are some of the phrases used for this word? _____

_____

_____

8. Geographical and biographical information

Most dictionaries place this information in with the regular entries. Other dictionaries, such as the Merriam Webster dictionaries, give this information at the end of the dictionary.

Where is Saxony and what is its capital city? _____

_____

Exercise 1: Dictionary Practice

Directions: Answer the following questions using any available dictionary.

1. How many definitions are there for the word **empty?** _____

2. From what language does **macho** originate? _____

3. What is the difference between **appeal** and **appease?** _____

   _____

   _____

4. What is a synonym for **loiter?** _____

5. After liver transplant surgery, a patient needs many weeks to recuperate. What does the word **recuperate** mean in this sentence?

   _____

   What is the part of speech? _____

Use your dictionary pronunciation guide to identify these movies. Write the titles on the lines below.

6. brāv härt _____

7. grāt ek spek tā shəns _____

8. pəlp fik-shən _____

9. Dī härd with a ven-jens _____

10. the brijiz əv mad-ə-sən kount-ē _____

_____

11. What is the plural of the word **family?** _____

12. What part of speech is **compulsiveness?** _____

13. What part of speech is **conventional?** _____

14. What language does **gaiety** come from? _____

Exercise 2: Dictionary Usage

Directions: Use the dictionary page provided to answer the following questions.

1. How many syllables does each of the following entry words have?

sawyer _____

saxicoline _____

sayable _____

2. Write the part(s) of speech for each of the following entry words:

saw _____

Saxon _____

3. Write the plural forms for the following words:

sawbones _____

sawfly _____

sayso _____

sawtooth _____

4. Find an entry word that is an example of each of the following:

a place _____

a person _____

_____

an animal _____

5. Name two entries that have pictures as aids to understand their meanings.

_____

_____

6. How many meanings are given for each of the following entry words?

saw¹ _____

sawyer _____

Saxon _____

7. What suffixes are used to change "savvy" to different parts of speech?

_____

8. What is the origin of the word "saxatile"? _____

_____

9. Pronounce the following words. Then write each word using correct spelling.

sak si tok sin _____

sā ing _____

sez _____

saks _____

Directions: Indicate whether the following statements are true or false by writing **T** or **F** in the space provided.

_____ 10. **Sawbones** is slang for a surgeon or physician.

_____ 11. To **saw wood** means to sing loudly.

_____ 12. A **savvy** person is dull-witted.

_____ 13. The British royal family no longer uses the name **Saxe-Coburg-Gotha.**

Exercise 3: Abbreviations

Directions: Most dictionaries use many abbreviations. Using the abbreviation key found on the next page, write what the following abbreviations and symbols mean.

1. ME _____   21. Gk. _____

2. pl. _____   22. sing. _____

3. n. _____   23. obs. _____

4. v.t. _____   24. orig. _____

5. v.i. _____   25. poss. _____

6. adj. _____   26. pres. _____

7. adv. _____   27. Russ _____

8. prep. _____   28. Sp. _____

9. conj. _____   29. Syn. _____

10. pron. _____   30. Heb. _____

11. fem. _____

12. masc. _____

13. OE _____

14. < _____

_____

15. E. _____

16. etym. _____

17. Fr. _____

18. Ger. _____

19. It. _____

20. L _____

ABBREVIATION KEY

•	unattested, reconstructed
<	descended from, borrowed from
<<	descended from, borrowed from through intermediate stages not shown
=	equivalent to
>	whence

ab.	about
Abbr., abbr.	abbreviation
abl.	ablative
acc.	accusative
adj.	adjective, adjectival
adv.	adverb, adverbial
AF	Anglo-French
Afr.	African
Afrik	Afrikaans
AL	Anglo-Latin
alter.	alteration
Amer	American
Amer.	Americanism
AmerSp	American Spanish
aph.	aphetic
appar.	apparently
Ar, Arab.	Arabic
assoc.	association
at. no.	atomic number
at. wt.	atomic weight
aug.	augmentative
b.	blend of, blended
bef.	before
Bot.	Botany
Brit.	British
Bulg.	Bulgarian
c	about (Latin *circa*)
c.	cognate with
CanF	Canadian French
Cap.	capital (of country or state)
cap., caps.	capital, capitals
cent.	century
Cf., cf.	compare (Latin *confer*)
Ch.	Church
Chin, Chin.	Chinese
cm.	centimeter(s)
Com.	Commerce
comb. form	combining form
comp., compar.	comparative
conj.	conjunction
contr.	contraction

Cor.	Corinthians
D	Dutch
d.	died
Dan, Dan.	Danish
Dan.	Daniel
dat.	dative
def., defs.	definition, definitions
der.	derivative
Deut.	Deuteronomy
diag.	diagram
Dial., dial.	dialect, dialectal
dim.	diminutive
disting.	distinguished
Du.	Dutch
E	English
e	east, eastern
EGmc	East Germanic
Eng.	England, English
esp.	especially
etym.	etymology, etymological
Ex.	Exodus
Ezek.	Ezekiel
F	French
fem.	feminine
fig.	figurative
Fin.	Finnish
fl.	flourished
fol.	followed
Fr.	French
freq.	frequentative
Fris	Frisian
ft.	foot, feet
fut.	future
G	German
Gal.	Galatians
Gallo-Rom	Gallo-Romance
Gen.	Genesis
gen.	genitive
Ger.	German
ger.	gerund, gerundive
Gk, Gk.	Greek
Gmc	Germanic
Go	Gothic
Heb, Heb.	Hebrew
Hos.	Hosea
Icel, Icel.	Icelandic
IE	Indo-European
illus.	illustration
imit.	imitative
imper.	imperative
impv.	imperative
in.	inch(es)
ind., indic.	indicative
inf.	infinitive
interj.	interjection
intransit.	intransitive
Ir	Irish
irreg.	irregular, irregularly
Isa.	Isaiah
It, It.	Italian
Japn, Japn.	Japanese
Jer.	Jeremiah
km	kilometer(s)
Kor.	Korean

L	Latin
LaF	Louisiana French
Lat.	Latin
l.c.	lowercase
Lev.	Leviticus
LG	Low German
LGk	Late Greek
Ling.	Linguistics
lit.	literally
Lith	Lithuanian
LL	Late Latin
m	meter(s)
Mach.	Machinery
masc.	masculine
Matt.	Matthew
MChin	Middle Chinese
MD	Middle Dutch
ME	Middle English
Mech.	Mechanics
MexSp	Mexican Spanish
MF	Middle French
MGk	Medieval Greek
MHG	Middle High German
mi.	mile(s)
MIr	Middle Irish
ML	Medieval Latin
MLG	Middle Low German
mm	millimeter(s)
mod.	modern
ModGk	Modern Greek
ModHeb	Modern Hebrew
MPers	Middle Persian
N	north, northern
n.	noun, nominal
Neh.	Nehemiah
neut.	neuter
NL	New Latin
nom.	nominative
Norw, Norw.	Norwegian
n.pl.	plural noun
Num.	Numbers
obj.	objective
obl.	oblique
Obs., obs.	obsolete
Oc	Occitan
OCS	Old Church Slavonic
OE	Old English
OF	Old French
OFris	Old Frisian
OHG	Old High German
OIr	Old Irish
OL	Old Latin
ON	Old Norse
ONF	Old North French
OPers	Old Persian
OPr	Old Provençal
OPruss	Old Prussian
orig.	origin, originally
ORuss	Old Russian
OS	Old Saxon
OSp	Old Spanish
PaG	Pennsylvania German
pass.	passive
past part.	past participle

perh.	perhaps
Pers, Pers.	Persian
pers.	person
Pg	Portuguese
pl.	plural
Pol, Pol.	Polish
Port.	Portuguese
poss.	possessive
pp.	past participle
prec.	preceded
prep.	preposition
pres.	present, present tense
pres. part.	present participle
prob.	probably
Pron., pron.	pronunciation, pronounced
pron.	pronoun
Pros.	Prosody
prp.	present participle
pt.	preterit (past tense)
ptp.	past participle
r.	replacing
redupl.	reduplication
repr.	representing
resp.	respelling, respelled
Rev.	Revelations
Rom	Romance
Rom.	Roman, Romanian
Russ	Russian
S	south, southern
s.	stem
Sam.	Samuel
Scand	Scandinavian
Scot.	Scottish
ScotGael	Scottish Gaelic
sing.	singular
Skt, Skt.	Sanskrit
Sp, Sp.	Spanish
sp.	spelling, spelled
SpAr	Spanish Arabic
sp. gr.	specific gravity
sq.	square
subj.	subjunctive
superl.	superlative
Sw, Sw.	Swedish
SwissF	Swiss French
syll.	syllable
Syn.	Synonym (Study)
trans.	translation
transit.	transitive
Turk.	Turkish
ult.	ultimately
uncert.	uncertain
usu.	usually
v.	verb, verbal
var.	variant
var. s.	variant stem
v.i.	intransitive verb
VL	Vulgar Latin
voc.	vocative
v.t.	transitive verb
W	west, western
WGmc	West Germanic
yd.	yard(s)

From *Random House Webster's College Dictionary*, 2nd Edition, p. xxv, by Random House, Inc. Copyright © 2000 by Random House, Inc. Reprinted by permission of Random House Reference and Information Publishing, a division of Random House, Inc.

Visual Aids

How to Use and Interpret Tables, Charts, Graphs, and Maps

Visual aids are useful tools that help us understand written material. Visual aids can be as simple as a street map or as complex as a statistical table. Because textbook authors frequently use visual aids to explain complicated information, it is very important to look closely at all illustrations and understand what they represent. Those of you who are strong in visual-spatial intelligence may find this section easier than those of you who have strengths in other areas. In this section, we will help you learn how to read and interpret the graphs and tables found in various books, magazines, and newspapers.

Here are some steps to follow when looking at a visual aid:

1. **Read the title and subtitle.** These will tell you what the table, chart, graph, or map is about.
2. **Read the key or legend.** These will explain how to interpret the visual aid.
3. **Determine the purpose of the visual aid.** Why did the author include it? Is it there to provide objective information? Or to support the author's bias?
4. **Determine the source of the information provided.** A table, chart, graph, or map published by a government agency may be more objective than one published by a special-interest group.
5. **Look at how the graph or chart is set up.** If there are horizontal or vertical scales, determine what they measure. If there is no scale, read the caption or look closely at the item to determine the scale. What is the unit of measurement? Thousands? Millions?
6. **Look for highs, lows, trends, and relationships.** What conclusions can you reach?

Exercise 1: Tables

Tables display information in rows (across) and columns (up and down). The table on the next page shows the 2007 earnings and 2006 unemployment figures for full-time wage and salaried workers age 25 and over by educational attainment. Refer to the table to answer the following questions.

1. What annual salary would you expect to make if you were a high school dropout? _____

2. If you earned a certificate at a two-year college but no degree, you would expect to earn how much per week? _____

3. What types of degrees are considered professional degrees? _____

   _____

4. How much more a year would you expect to earn with a bachelor's degree than with an associate's degree? _____

5. The unemployment rate is lowest for people who have _____ degrees.

EDUCATION PAYS

Education attained	Median weekly earnings ($)	Median annual earnings ($)	Unemployment rate (%)
Some high school, no diploma	$ 419	$21,788	6.8%
High school graduate	595	30,940	4.3
Some college, no degree	679	35,308	3.9
Associate's degree	721	37,492	3.0
Bachelor's degree	962	50,024	2.3
Master's degree	1,140	59,280	1.7
Professional degree*	1,474	76,648	1.1
Doctorate degree	1,441	74,932	1.9

*Professional degrees include such postbaccalaureate degrees as medical, dentistry, social work, and law.

Source: Unemployment rate, 2006 annual average: Bureau of Labor Statistics; earnings, March 2007: Bureau of the Census.

Exercise 2: Pie Charts

Pie charts are illustrations that show percentages or proportions as pie-shaped sections of a circle. The whole interior of the circle represents 100 percent. The pie graphs below illustrate the drinking habits of college-age students. For men, binge drinking is defined as consuming five or more drinks in one sitting; for women, the amount is four or more. The figures are based on a recent survey of 17,592 students at 140 four-year colleges and universities. The students were asked about their drinking behavior during the two weeks before the survey was taken. The study was published in the *Journal of the American Medical Association*. Refer to the two pie charts to answer the following questions.

1. Would a study published in the *Journal of the American Medical Association* be reasonably objective, or would it reflect a strong bias? _____

2. What percentage of men binge drink? _____ What percentage of women binge drink? _____

Drinking Habits of College Students

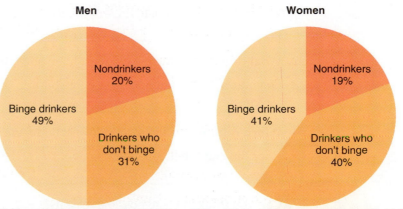

Men

Women

From Robert Feldman, *Understanding Psychology*, 8th Edition, 2008, p. 173. Reproduced with permission of the McGraw-Hill Companies.

3. Do a higher percentage of men or women engage in binge drinking?

_____

4. Is the percentage of nondrinkers about the same for men and women?

_____

Exercise 3: Bar Graphs

Bar graphs use vertical (top to bottom) or horizontal (left to right) bars to show how things compare. Usually, longer bars represent larger quantities. The bars in the graph below show firearm-related homicide rates for children. In this graph, the bars represent the number of firearm-related deaths per 100,000 juveniles under 15 years old. The bar graph below was published in *Juvenile Offenders and Victims: 1999 National Report*. Study the graph and answer the questions that follow.

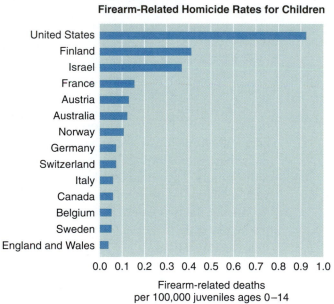

Firearm-Related Homicide Rates for Children

Firearm-related deaths
per 100,000 juveniles ages 0–14

From Freda Adler, Gerhard O. W. Mueller, and William Laufer, *Criminology*, 6th Edition, 2007, p. 246. Reproduced with permission of the McGraw-Hill Companies.

1. What is the approximate firearm-related homicide rate per 100,000 children in the United States? _____

2. What country has the next highest homicide rate for children? _____

3. How does France's homicide rate for children compare to the one for the United States? _____

4. Which country has the second-lowest homicide rate for children? _____

5. Does the graph tell you anything about why the United States has the highest rate? _____

   Can you think of some possible reasons? _____

As you can see, graphs give only a limited amount of data. Often, we need to look at written material that further explains the data given in the graph.

Exercise 4: Flow Charts

Flow charts are often used in textbooks to show cause-and-effect relationships and sequences of events. The action moves, or flows, in the direction of the arrows. The flow chart below, which appeared in an introductory college psychology textbook, shows possible cause-and-effect relationships among high energy levels, aggressive content on television, and aggressive behavior. Notice that the author uses the terms "possible cause" and "potential result."

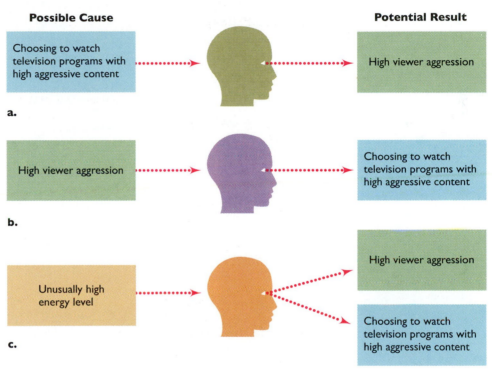

From Robert Feldman, *Understanding Psychology*, 8th Edition, 2008, p. 41. Reproduced with permission of the McGraw-Hill Companies.

1. The top flow chart proposes _____

   _____ as a possible cause of high viewer aggression.

2. The third flow chart proposes an _____ as a possible cause of choosing to watch shows with high aggressive content and high viewer aggression.

3. The first and second flow charts propose that _____ and

   _____ affect each other in a back-

   and-forth relationship.

Exercise 5: Tables and Maps

The following visual aids both relate to identity theft.

1. Which state had the highest number of victims of identity theft? _____

2. Which state had the lowest number of victims of identity theft? _____

IDENTITY THEFT VICTIMS BY STATE (PER 100,000 POPULATION),* JANUARY 1 THROUGH DECEMBER 31, 2006

Rank	Victim State	Victims per 100,000 Population	Number of Victims
1	Arizona	147.8	9,113
2	Nevada	120.0	2,994
3	California	113.5	41,396
4	Texas	10.6	26,006
5	Florida	98.3	17,780
6	Colorado	92.5	4,395
7	Georgia	86.3	8,084
8	New York	85.2	16,452
9	Washington	83.4	5,336
10	New Mexico	82.9	1,621
11	Maryland	82.9	4,656
12	Illinois	78.6	10,080
13	Oregon	76.1	2,815
14	New Jersey	73.3	6,394
15	Virginia	67.2	5,137
16	Michigan	67.2	6,784
17	Delaware	66.7	569
18	Connecticut	65.8	2,305
19	Pennsylvania	64.9	8,080
20	North Carolina	64.9	5,748
21	Missouri	64.2	3,753
22	Massachusetts	63.7	4,102
23	Oklahoma	63.0	2,254
24	Indiana	62.2	3,928
25	Utah	61.8	1,577
26	Tennessee	61.3	3,700
27	Alabama	60.3	2,774
28	Ohio	59.9	6,878
29	Kansas	58.8	1,626
30	Rhode Island	57.6	615
31	Alaska	57.3	384
32	South Carolina	55.7	2,408
33	Minnesota	55.6	2,872
34	Arkansas	54.7	1,537
35	Louisiana	52.6	2,256
36	Mississippi	51.3	1,494
37	Nebraska	49.1	868
38	Idaho	49.0	718
39	Hawaii	47.8	615
40	New Hampshire	46.1	606
41	Montana	45.9	434

		Victims per	Number of
Rank	Victim State	100,000 Population	Victims
42	Wisconsin	45.6	2,536
43	Wyoming	42.3	218
44	Kentucky	42.0	1,766
45	Maine	39.7	525
46	West Virginia	39.3	715
47	Iowa	34.9	1,041
48	South Dakota	30.2	236
49	North Dakota	29.7	189
50	Vermont	28.5	178

IDENTITY THEFT VICTIMS BY STATE (PER 100,000 POPULATION),*
JANUARY 1 THROUGH DECEMBER 31, 2006 (Continued)

Note: *Per 100,000 unit of population estimates are based on the 2006 U.S. Census population estimates (Table NST-EST2006-01–Annual Estimates of the Population for the U.S. states, and for Puerto Rico: April 1, 2000 to July 1, 2006). Numbers for the District of Columbia are 765 victims and 131.5 victims per 100,000 population.

Source: Federal Trade Commission, "Fighting Back against Identity Theft," at www.ftc.gov/bcp/edu/mirosites/idtheft/mediareference/writing.html (clearinghouse_2006.pdf).

3. What is the number of victims in the District of Columbia? _____

4. What is the identity theft victimization rate per 100,000 population for the following states? Maryland _____, California _____, and Florida _____.

5. Which state has the highest identity theft victimization rate per 100,000 population? _____

6. Which state has the second-highest identity theft victimization rate per 100,000 population? _____

7. What is the source of the data provided? _____

Maps are useful for presenting information visually.

Answer the following questions by reading the written material below the map on the next page and studying the map.

1. The information for the map was based on the _____ U.S. Census.

2. Which state has a higher rate of identity theft: New Mexico or Missouri?

_____

3. Which state has a lower rate of identity theft, Georgia or Ohio? _____

4. List three states that are least prone to identity theft. _____

_____

5. Do Hawaii and Alaska have low, medium, or high rates of identity theft? _____

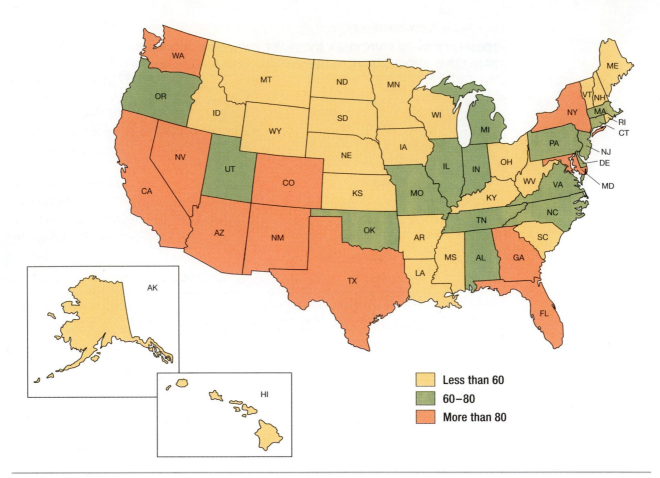

☐	Less than 60
☐	60–80
☐	More than 80

Identity Theft Victims by State (per 100,000 Population),* January 1 through December 31, 2006

Note: *Per 100,000 unit of population estimates are based on the 2006 U.S. Census population estimates (Table NST-EST2006-01–Annual Estimates of the Population for the U.S. states, and for Puerto Rico: April 1, 2000 to July 1, 2006). Numbers for the District of Columbia are 765 victims and 131.5 victims per 100,000 population.
Source: Federal Trade Commission, "Fighting Back against Identity Theft," at www.ftc.gov/bcp/edu/mirosites/idtheft/mediareference/writing.html (clearinghouse_2006.pdf).

U.S. Public Opinion and Number of Executions

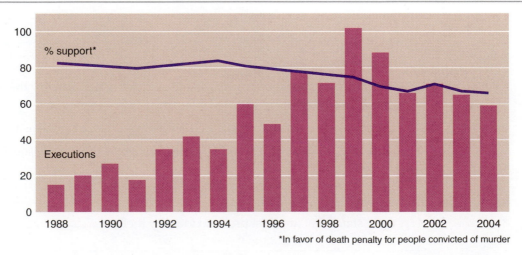

*In favor of death penalty for people convicted of murder

Data from Death Penalty Information Center, www.deathpenaltyinfo.org/article.php?scid=23&did=1266, and Gallup Organization, www.deathpenaltyinfo.org/FactSheet.pdf; retrieved 10/5/05.

Exercise 6: Combination Chart

The last visual aid combines a bar graph and a line graph. We already know what a bar graph is. A line graph, which takes the form of a line drawn in an L-shaped grid, shows the relationship between two variables. One of these variables will be defined along the bottom, horizontal (across) scale of the grid. The other variable will be defined along the side, vertical (up and down) scale of the grid. The line need not be straight and in fact is often jagged or curved. Often the bottom scale of the grid measures time (for example, minutes, years, or decades), and so the line graph shows changes over time.

The bar graph on the previous page gives the number of executions for particular years. The superimposed line graph shows public support for executions in various years. The horizontal scale gives the years, and the vertical scale gives the percentage of public support for executions. Look at the graph and then answer the following questions.

1. About how many executions were there in the United States in 2000? _____

   In 1995? _____

2. In what year was the percentage of public support for the death penalty the

   lowest? _____

3. Has there been a general trend in public support for the death penalty?

   _____

4. Has there been a general trend in number of executions? _____

   _____

5. How do these two trends appear to relate to each other? _____

   _____

   _____

Test-Taking Techniques
How to Improve Your Performance

The Multiple-Choice Test

As a college student, you are going to have to take many multiple-choice and true/false tests and quizzes. While nothing substitutes for thoroughly knowing the material and preparing well, the following are some basic test-taking tips that you should be familiar with:

1. Read directions carefully.

2. Pay attention to oral instructions.

3. Look through the entire test, and plan your time accordingly.

4. Do not dwell on any question too long. If you can't answer the question, move on and come back to the question if you have time at the end.

5. If in doubt between two answers, go with your first gut-level reaction. Don't change an answer unless you are positive you are making the correct choice. You may be changing a right answer to a wrong answer. Your time can probably be better spent elsewhere on the test.

6. Even if you think you have more knowledge about the material than the author of the material or you think the author is wrong, go with what the author says, not what you think.

7. Read through all the answers before picking one.

8. If one of your choices is a combination of two or more answers (such as "A and B"), remember that all parts of the answer must be correct (A must be a correct answer and B must also be a correct answer).

9. When in doubt, and one answer includes language from the question, go with that answer. Also look for clues in the question that may help give away the answer.

10. Look at long answers first, especially if one answer is much longer than the others. A longer answer is more likely to be correct than a shorter answer. Why? It usually takes more words to write a correct answer because it needs to be phrased carefully. Also, right answers may need qualifying phrases to make them correct. Wrong answers are wrong anyway, so it doesn't matter how they are written.

11. When the question asks you to pick a missing word, use grammar clues such as *a* and *an*. An *a* goes with words beginning with consonants, and an *an* goes with words beginning with vowels.

12. Eliminate answers with all-inclusive words like *all, everyone, none, always,* and *nobody.* Answers that include such words are quite likely wrong. Usually, the only time answers with such words are correct is when that is exactly what the author said. If there is one exception, the answer will be wrong.

13. When a question asks for the main idea of the selection or the best possible title, make sure your answer is broad enough to cover all parts of the selection.

14. Sometimes the last answer will be "All of the above." If you are fairly sure that two of the three answers are correct but are unsure about the third answer, go with "All of the above."

15. Two questions on the test may be similar. Use the correct answer for one question to help you find the correct answer for the other.

16. Allow at least a minute or two to check over your answer sheet. Is your name on it? Do you need to date it? Have you skipped any questions?

17. If you are putting your answers on a Scantron, make sure that you have completely erased any earlier answers. Scantrons will pick up incomplete erasures.

Now let's put this knowledge to work with the following test. Louise Scott from Upper Iowa University in Fayette tells students to examine multiple-choice questions carefully because they may contain clues to the correct answers. She gives them this "nonsense" test to demonstrate her point. You know nothing about what is being tested, but you can answer all the questions correctly by going back to the techniques just discussed. Don't get discouraged. If you are stumped by question 1, go on to question 2. After you complete the test, check the correct answers on page A-22.

The Fribbled What?

_____ 1. Trassig normally occurs when the
  a. dissels frull.
  b. lups chasses the vom.
  c. belgo lisks easily.
  d. viskal flans, if the viskal is zortil.

_____ 2. The fribbled breg will snicker best with an
  a. Mors.
  b. Ignu.
  c. Derst.
  d. Sortar.

_____ 3. What probable causes are indicated when tristal doss occurs in a compots?
  a. The sabs foped and the doths tinzed.
  b. The kredges roted with the rots.
  c. Rakogs were not accepted in the sluth.
  d. Polats were thonced in the sluth.

_____ 4. The primary purpose of the cluss in frumpaling is to
  a. remove cluss-prangs.
  b. patch tremalls.
  c. lossen cloughs.
  d. repair plumots.

_____ 5. Why does the sigla frequently overfesk the trelsum?
  a. All siglas are mellious.
  b. Siglas are always votial.
  c. The trelsum is usually tarious.
  d. No tresla are directly feskable.

_____ 6. The snickering function of the ignu is most effectively performed in connection with which one of the following snicker snacks?
  a. Arazma tol.
  b. Fribbled breg.

c. Groshed stantol.

d. Frallied stantol.

From "Here and Now," by Louise Scott, newsletter for *College Survival*. Copyright © 1993 Pearson Education. Reprinted with permission.

The Essay Test

Before the Test

There is no substitute for simply knowing all of the course material well. But that can be a big task, and realistically, some parts of the material are probably more important, and more likely to appear on an essay test, than other parts.

One way to give your preparation some focus is to try to think of questions that might appear on the test. Because your teacher will likely be the one who writes the test, ask yourself what questions you think your teacher might ask. Review your class notes and any handouts to determine what the teacher emphasized in the course. What topics did the teacher spend the most time on? What topics did the teacher seem to care the most about?

Keep in mind that an essay question may ask for information on a specific topic or it may be directed at a general understanding of the course material. You need to prepare yourself for both kinds of questions.

General or "big picture" essay questions often deal with relationships among topics or concepts. A good way to prepare for these questions is to make an outline or map of the course material. Look at your class notes, any handouts, and your textbook, and organize this material into an outline. If your teacher has closely followed a textbook, the book's table of contents should give you a good start on making your outline.

Once you have come up with a list of possible questions, use some of your study time preparing answers to these questions. You may even want to practice writing out answers.

During the Test

Carefully read the question; you can't expect to write a good answer to a question you don't understand. In fact, you might write a wonderful essay, but if it doesn't answer the question, it will not do you much good. What is the question asking you to do?

Fribbled Answers

1. *d.* The question uses the word "normally," and this is the only answer containing a qualifying phrase.

2. *b.* This is the only answer beginning with a vowel. The word "an" at the end of the query phrase is the tip-off.

3. *a.* The question asked for more than one cause.

4. *a.* This answer contains the word "cluss," which was used in the question.

5. *c.* The other answers are all absolutes.

6. *b.* Fribbled breg was linked with ignu in question 2.

Does the question use any of the keywords discussed on pages A-24–A-25? If so, think about what that keyword means.

Once you understand the question, begin thinking about how best to answer it. It's probably not a good idea to start writing immediately. Give yourself some time to think first. What material from the course will the answer involve? What do you remember about this material? At this point, you might want to start jotting some notes. If you prepared well for the test, the more you think about this material, the more of it you will remember.

Organizing Your Answer

Once you have recalled the material you need in order to answer the questions, you need to begin thinking about how to organize your answer. Knowing the information goes a long way toward writing a good essay, but how you organize the information also counts. This is especially true for a "big picture" essay question. Your organization will show the teacher how well you understand what is important and what the relationships are among ideas and concepts.

A traditional essay has an introduction, a conclusion, and three paragraphs of development. This does not mean that a good essay cannot have more or less than three paragraphs of development, but ordinarily an essay that is three paragraphs long will say what needs to be said without saying too much. Usually the three paragraphs of the traditional essay are developed in the same order in which their main ideas are mentioned in the introductory statement.

Here is an example of an introductory statement:

An increase in state financial aid for public education will raise student scores on standardized tests because (1) teacher salaries can be increased, which will attract more-talented people into teaching; (2) more teachers can be hired, which will reduce class size; and (3) school districts will have more money available for learning resources and activities.

So, the first paragraph of this essay would discuss the need for more-talented teachers and why the hiring of more-talented teachers should lead to an increase in the test scores. The second paragraph would discuss the need for smaller classes and how smaller classes should lead to increased scores. The third paragraph would discuss the need for more learning resources and activities and how improved resources and activities should boost test scores.

Often the secret to writing a good essay is constructing a good introductory statement, because once you have a good introductory statement, the rest of the essay follows from it. This is one reason it makes sense to do some thinking and organizing before you start to write.

To write a good introductory statement, it sometimes helps to take the question and rearrange it into an introductory statement. For example, assume that the question says the following:

Discuss whether an increase in state financial aid for public education will raise student scores on standardized tests.

Then you might use the following introductory statement:

An increase in state financial aid for public education will/will not raise student scores on standardized tests because . . .

Some Practical Pointers

1. Research shows that neatness counts, so write carefully and legibly. Try to avoid messy erasures, crossed-out words, and words written between lines and in the margins. You might want to consider using pens with erasable ink.

2. When a question has more than one part, make sure you answer all parts.

3. Remember that each paragraph should develop only one main idea.

4. Give specific examples to illustrate your points.

5. Answer in complete sentences.

6. Check to see if what you have written answers the questions *who, what, where, when, why,* and *how.*

7. Save some time to proofread your essay for spelling and other errors that are likely to produce a bad impression.

8. If you find you have no time to answer questions at the end of the test, write some notes in summary form. These will often earn you at least partial credit.

9. Make use of your returned test papers. You can learn a lot by reading the instructor's comments and correcting the answers.

Keywords That Often Appear in Essay Questions

Following is a list of keywords that often appear in essay questions. If you are going to write a good answer to an essay question that uses one of these terms, you need to know what the term means.

analyze to break down the subject into parts and discuss each part. You will want to discuss how the parts relate to each other.

comment on to discuss or explain.

compare to show differences and similarities, but with the emphasis on similarities.

contrast to show differences and similarities, but with the emphasis on differences.

criticize The narrow meaning of *criticize* is to examine something for its weaknesses, limitations, or failings. Does the theory, article, or opinion make sense? If not, why not? In a more general sense, *criticize* means to find both strengths and weaknesses. In this sense, the meaning of *criticize* is similar to that of *evaluate.*

define to state the meaning of a term, theory, or concept. You will want to place the subject in a category and explain what makes it different from other subjects in the category.

describe to explain what something is or how it appears. What you need to do is draw a picture with words.

diagram to make a chart, drawing, or graph. You also will want to label the categories or elements, and maybe give a brief explanation.

discuss to fully go over something. You will want to cover the main points, give different perspectives, and relate strengths and weaknesses.

enumerate	to make a list of main ideas by numbering them.
evaluate	to examine for strengths and weaknesses. You will need to give specific evidence and may wish to cite authorities to support your position.
explain	to make clear; to give reasons. An explanation often involves showing cause-and-effect relationships or steps.
illustrate	to use a diagram, chart, figure, or specific examples to further explain something.
interpret	to indicate what something means. A question that asks for an *interpretation* usually wants you to state what something means to you. What are your beliefs or feelings about the meaning of the material? Be sure to back up your position with specific examples and details.
justify	to give reasons in support of a conclusion, theory, or opinion.
list	to put down your points one by one. You may want to number each of the points in your list.
outline	to organize information into an outline, using headings and sub-headings. Your outline should reflect the main ideas and supporting details.
prove	to demonstrate that something is true by means of factual evidence or logical reasoning.
relate	to discuss how two or more conclusions, theories, or opinions affect each other. Explain how one causes, limits, or develops the other.
review	usually means to summarize, but a narrower meaning of it is to analyze critically.
summarize	to put down the main points; to state briefly the key principles, facts, or ideas while avoiding details and personal comments.
trace	to follow the course of development of something in a chronological or logical sequence. You will want to discuss each stage of development from the beginning to the end.

Exercise: Essay Exam Skills

Read the explanations below. In the blank, write a term that the instructor might use when posing the question to the students in the class.

1. In class, the instructor has discussed the contributions of Auguste Comte, Herbert Spencer, and Max Weber to the field of sociology. On the essay exam, he wants the students to briefly go over the contribution of each of these persons while avoiding their own personal comments. What term will he use for this question?

    _____

2. In a child development class, the instructor has discussed the development of language from birth to 36 months. She now wants the students to present the process of language acquisition in chronological sequence. What term should she use?

    _____

3. In an art history class, the instructor wants the students to show the difference between engraving, drypoint, and etching. Which term will she use in the question?

    _____

4. In an American history class, the professor has discussed the Manhattan Project, which developed the atomic bomb during World War II. He now wants the

students to examine the project for its weaknesses. What term will he use in the question?

_____

5. In a biology class, the professor has explained the term "cloning." On a quiz, she wants to make sure her students understand the meaning of the concept. What term will she use in her question?

_____

6. In an economics class, the professor wants the students to graph the 2000–2001 recession, showing the rise and fall of the unemployment rate and consumer spending. What term should she use on her exam?

_____

7. In a geography class, the teacher wants the students to make clear how pollution caused harm to the Costa Rican rain forest. What term will he use?

_____

8. In a psychology class, the instructor wants the students to describe the ways in which long-term memory and short-term memory are alike and the ways in which they are different. What term will she use?

_____

9. In a reading class, the teacher wants the students to write down the steps of SQ3R one by one, numbering each. What term will she use in her question?

_____

Sample Summaries

Who: high school and college students

What: are spending too little time studying and too much time working

Where: in the United States

When: the author compares attitudes in the 50s to attitudes in the late 80s

Why: students work to buy luxury items parents won't pay for

How: because of increased acceptance on the part of parents and teachers

Overall Main Idea

Student employment is a major cause of the decline in American education.

Other Main Ideas

1. Today student employment is widely accepted as normal for teens, but in the past going to school was a student's "job." (implied)
2. Working students have little time for homework. (directly stated)
3. Students work to buy luxury items and then feel they need to go out and have fun. (implied)
4. Thus, by the time they get to college, most students look upon studies as a spare-time activity. (directly stated)
5. The problem doesn't just affect the individual student, but the quality of education as a whole. (implied)

Student Summary

Walter S. Minot in his article "Students Who Push Burgers" feels that U.S. education has declined because students hold part-time jobs. Minot compares the educational system of the 1950s to that of the 1980s. In the past, kids only worked to help out their families financially. Today's students work to buy luxury items, fooling their parents into thinking that they are learning the value of a dollar. Because these students work so hard at their jobs, they feel they deserve to have a good time after work, and they don't have enough time or energy to do their homework. As a result, schools are finding it difficult to get quality work from their students, and have had to reduce their standards. Minot feels this problem doesn't just affect individual students or schools, but the quality of education as a whole.

Student Sample:
Summary of "Charley's Secret" (page 384)

This article is about a woman named Charley Parkhurst who, disguising herself as a man, became a well-known and respected stagecoach driver, living a life of independence unknown to women at the time.

Charley's early years in an orphanage probably shaped her outlook on life. She was born around 1812 and as a small child was abandoned at the orphanage. Her name is assumed to have been Charlotte. Orphanages at the time were harsh places. Both male and female children were dressed alike and given the same haircuts. Being in this type of environment could have encouraged Charley to "act like a man." In her teens, she ran away and became a worker in a livery stable. She was trained to drive coaches and one-horse buggies, and finally six-horse buggies.

As a top reinsman, Charley was persuaded to go to California to work for the largest stagecoach company in the world, the California Stage Company. There she was a well-respected driver earning a place in a group nicknamed "Kings of the Road." Many passengers considered it a great honor to be invited by Charley to ride up on the box next to him. In addition to being considered one of the fastest and safest drivers, Charley also earned the reputation of a hero.

At a time when women were not allowed to own property or vote, Charley managed to do both. In 1868, at the age of 55, Charley voted as a man, having lived that life for so long that no one thought to ask questions. This was 52 years before other females were given the right to vote. When Charley gave up driving, he owned a small place that became a stagecoach rest stop. In 1872, he sold off all his property and moved into a vacant house owned by a friend.

Charley, suffering from rheumatism and other symptoms of old age, complained of a sore throat, but refused to see a doctor. Eventually the sore throat was diagnosed as cancer. At no time during his illness did Charley confide his secret to any close friends. At his death, it was the undertaker who made the announcement that old Charley was in fact a woman. When the truth of Charley's deception was discovered, his friends were both shocked and angry. Tobacco-chewing Charley, who had handled a whip and a gun with the best of them, had become a legend in the Old West.

ASSIGNMENTS

MONDAY

TUESDAY

WEDNESDAY

THURSDAY

FRIDAY

OTHER ASSIGNMENTS, TESTS, ETC.

MONTH _____

SUNDAY	MONDAY	TUESDAY	WEDNESDAY	THURSDAY	FRIDAY	SATURDAY

ASSIGNMENT SHEET

Subject(s) _____

Date	Assignments	Due	Finished

STUDY SCHEDULES

	MONDAY	TUESDAY	WEDNESDAY	THURSDAY	FRIDAY	SATURDAY	SUNDAY
6:00–7:00 am							
7:00–8:00 am							
8:00–9:00 am							
9:00–10:00 am							
10:00–11:00 am							
11:00–12:00 pm							
12:00–1:00 pm							
1:00–2:00 pm							
2:00–3:00 pm							
3:00–4:00 pm							
4:00–5:00 pm							
5:00–6:00 pm							
6:00–7:00 pm							
7:00–8:00 pm							
8:00–9:00 pm							
9:00–10:00 pm							
10:00–11:00 pm							
11:00–12:00 am							
12:00–1:00 am							

Photo Credits

Introduction
Pages 1, 2: © Bettmann/Corbis; **p. 20:** © Jacques Pavlovsky/Sygma/Corbis.

Chapter 1
Page 29: © Bettmann/Corbis; **p. 46:** © Alex Gotfryd/Corbis; **p. 77:** © Porter Gifford/Getty Images.

Chapter 2
Pages 83, 84: Photo by Steve Granitz/WireImage; **p. 125:** © AP Photo/Lynne Sladky.

Chapter 3
Page 136: Photo by Steve Granitz/WireImage; **p. 141:** Paul Kalinian; **p. 146:** Roy Stevens/Time & Life Pictures; **p. 151:** © David Young-Wolff/PhotoEdit; **p. 159:** © Mark Alcarez; **p. 170:** © George Hall/Corbis; **p. 171:** © Hisham F. Ibrahim/RF Getty Images.

Chapter 4
Page 177: Photo by Steve Granitz/WireImage; **p. 204:** © Getty Images/Purestock.

Chapter 5
Pages 217, 218: © REUTERS/Ethan Miller/Landov; **p. 219:** © Courtesy of the authors; **p. 230:** © AP Photo/Douglas C. Pizac; **p. 239:** © USHMM. The views or opinions expressed in this book, and the context in which the image is used, does not necessarily reflect the views or policy of, nor imply approval or endorsement by, the United States Holocaust Memorial Museum; **p. 246:** © Scott Smith/Corbis; **p. 245:** © John-Marshall Mantel/Corbis; **p. 252:** © Tom McHugh/Photo Researchers, Inc.

Chapter 6
Page 254: © Stephen Saks/Photo Researchers, Inc.; **p. 259:** © REUTERS/Ethan Miller/Landov; **p. 274 top:** © AP Photo; **p. 274 bottom:** © 2003 Estate of Pablo Picasso/ Artists Rights Society (ARS), New York. Bridgeman-Giraudon/Art Resource, NY.; **p. 278:** © AP Photo/Gino Domenico; **p. 285:** © Historical Picture Archive/Corbis.

Chapter 7
Page 300: © REUTERS/Ethan Miller/Landov; **p. 305:** Reprinted by permission of the photographer Carin Clevidence; **p. 306:** © DVL/RF Getty Images; **p. 310:** © Royalty-Free Corbis; **p. 320:** Photo by Frank Capri/Hulton Archive/Getty Images; **p. 325:** © Andrew Ward/Life File/RF Getty Images.

Chapter 8
Pages 333, 334: © EMPICS/Landov; **p. 337:** Photo by Robert W. Kelley/Time Life Pictures/Getty Images; **p. 347:** © AP Photo/The Waterloo/Cedar Falls Courier, Dan Nierling; **p. 356:** Photo by Keith Philpott/Time Life Pictures/Getty Images.

Chapter 9
Page 373: © EMPICS/Landov; **p. 392:** John F. Kennedy Library, Boston.

Chapter 10
Pages 425, 426: © REUTERS/Dadang Tri/Landov; **p. 426:** © REUTERS/Dadang Tri/Landov; **p. 431:** © Photofest; **p. 435:** Library of Congress.

Chapter 11
Page 461: © REUTERS/Dadang Tri/Landov; **p. 479:** © Joseph Sohm; Visions of America/Corbis; **p. 484:** © Photo by Hulton Archive/Getty Images.

Chapter 12
Page 497: © REUTERS/Dadang Tri/Landov; **p. 498:** Photo by Newsmakers/Getty Images; **p. 503:** LOWE WORLDWIDE/America's Milk Processors; **p. 505:** Courtesy of The Advertising Archives.

Chapter 13
Page 523: © REUTERS/Dadang Tri/Landov; **p. 525:** Courtesy of PETA.org; **p. 549:** Office of National Drug Control Control Policy/Partnership for a Drug-Free America.

Chapter 14
Pages 553, 554: © AP Photo/Jeff Christensen; **p. 555:** © 2004 Dex Media, Inc. Used with permission.; **p. 556:** © Reprinted with permission from the May 14, 2005 edition by TV Guide Magazine Group, Inc. © 2005 TV Guide Magazine Group, Inc. TV GUIDE is a registered trademark of TV Guide Magazine Group, Inc.; **p. 562:** © Erich Hartmann/Magnum Photos.

Chapter 15
Page 573: © AP Photo/Jeff Christensen.

Appendix
Page A-6, A-7: From THE RANDOM HOUSE WEBSTER'S COLLEGE DICTIONARY by Random House, Inc., copyright © 1995, 1992, 1991 by Random House, Inc. Used by permission of Random House Reference and Information Publishing, a division of Random House, Inc.

Index